61st Yearbook of the Literacy Research Association

Edited by

Pamela J. Dunston
Susan King Fullerton
C. C. Bates
Kathy Headley
Pamela M. Stecker
Clemson University

With the editorial assistance of

Chris L. Massey, Lead Assistant Editor
Heather McCrea-Andrews, Lead Assistant Editor
Clemson University

Jenny Kasza, *Editor*
Technical Enterprises, Inc.

Michelle Majerus-Uelmen, *Graphic Designer*
Technical Enterprises, Inc.

Scott Sherer, *Executive Director*
Technical Enterprises, Inc.

Published by
Literacy Research Association, Inc.
Oak Creek, Wisconsin

2012

LRA Yearbook is published annually by the Literacy Research Association, 7044 South 13th Street, Oak Creek, WI 53154, Tel: (414) 908-4924.

POSTMASTER:
Send address changes to LRA Yearbook, 7044 South 13th Street, Oak Creek, WI 53154.

SUBSCRIPTIONS:
Institutions: $80 domestic or $90 foreign (surface), per year. Individuals who are LRA members in good standing as of October 1, 2012 will receive the *Yearbook* as part of their membership. Quantity discounts available for use in university or college courses. Write for information.

PERMISSION TO QUOTE OR REPRINT:
Quotations of 500 words or longer or reproductions of any portion of a table, figure, or graph, require written permission from the Literacy Research Association, and must include proper credit to the organization. A fee may be charged for use of the material, and permission of the first author will be secured.

PHOTOCOPIES:
Individuals may photocopy single articles without permission for nonprofit one-time classroom or library use. Other nonprofit educational copying, including repeated use of an individual article, must be registered with the Copyright Clearance Center, Academic Permission Service, 27 Congress Street, Salem, MA 01970, USA. *The fee is $1.25USD per article, or any portion, or any portion thereof, to be paid through the Center. The fee is waived for individual members of the Literacy Research Association.* Consent to photocopy does not extend to items identified as reprinted by permission of other publishers, nor to copying for general distribution, for advertising or promotion, or for resale unless written permission is obtained from the Literacy Research Association.

Microfiche copy is available from ERIC Reproduction Service, 3900 Wheeler Avenue, Alexandria, VA 22304. The YEARBOOK is indexed in *Psychological Abstracts, Index to Social Sciences & Humanities Proceedings and Educational Research Information Clearing House.* The LRA Yearbook is a refereed publication. Manuscripts must be original works that have been presented at the Annual Meeting of the Literacy Research Association, and that have not been published elsewhere.

ISSN
ISBN 1-893591-14-X
Printed in the United States of America

Editorial Advisory Review Board

61st Yearbook of the Literacy Research Association

Janis Harmon
The University of Texas at San Antonio

Rena M. Harris
Drexel University

Jessica L. Hoffman
Miami University

Teri Holbrook
Georgia State University

SuHua Huang
Midwestern State University

Elizabeth M. Hughes
Duquesne University

Amy Hutchison
Iowa State University

Chinwe H. Ikpeze
St. John Fisher College

Sabrina Peebles Izbrand
Texas Woman's University

Michelle Jordan
Arizona State University

Catherine M. Kelly
St. Catherine University

Ted Kesler
Queens College, CUNY

Amy Suzanne Johnson Lachuk
University of South Carolina

Jayne C. Lammers
University of Rochester

Barbara Laster
Towson University

Judson Laughter
The University of Tennessee, Knoxville

Kristin Lems
National-Louis University

Mellinee Lesley
Texas Tech University

Tisha Y. Lewis
Georgia State University

Xiaoming Liu
Towson University

Judith T. Lysaker
Purdue University

Sara Mackiewicz
Clemson University

Jacquelynn Malloy
Anderson University

Susan Marshall
Westminster College

Joyce E. Many
Georgia State University

Erin E. Margarella
University of South Florida

Barbara Marinak
Mount St. Mary's University

Pamela Mason
Harvard University

Prisca Martens
Towson University

Laura May
Georgia State University

Sarah McCarthey
University of Illinois at Urbana–Champaign

Dot McElhone
Portland State University

Gae Lynn McInroe
McMurry University

Jonda C. McNair
Clemson University

Denise N. Morgan
Kent State University

Carla K. Meyer
Appalachian State University

Charlotte Mundy
University of Alabama

William Ian O'Byrne
University of New Haven

Richard M. Oldrieve
Bowling Green State University

Mary Ellen Oslick
University of Central Arkansas

Barbara Martin Palmer
Mount St. Mary's University

Jeanne R. Paratore
Boston University

Seth Parsons
George Mason University

Julie L. Pennington
University of Nevada, Reno

Ellen Pesko
Appalachian State University

D. Ray Reutzel
Utah State University

Mary Roe
Arizona State University

Nancy L. Roser
The University of Texas at Austin

Diane Santori
West Chester University

Roya Qualls Scales
Western Carolina University

Diane L. Schallert
The University of Texas at Austin

Jenifer J. Schneider
University of South Florida, Tampa

Sarah E. Scott
University of Pittsburgh

Diane Carver Sekeres
University of Alabama

Peggy Semingson
The University of Texas at Arlington

Krishna Seunarinesingh
The University of the West Indies

Timothy Shanahan
University of Illinois at Chicago

Gerry Shiel
St. Patrick's College, Dublin

Sunita Singh
Le Moyne College

Kristine Lynn Still
Cleveland State University

Mary E. Styslinger
University of South Carolina

Pamela Sullivan
James Madison University

Jeanne Swafford
University of North Carolina, Wilmington

Sheelah Sweeny
Northeastern University

Nancy Walker
University of La Verne

Allison E. Ward
George Mason University

Patricia A. Watson
Texas Woman's University

Sarah Lohnes Watulak
Towson University

Sandra M. Webb
Georgia College & State University

Courtney West
Texas A&M University

Dana J. Wilber
Montclair State University

Nancy Williams
University of South Florida

Amy M. Williamson
Angelo State University

Angela M. Wiseman
North Carolina State University

Linda S. Wold
Loyola University Chicago

Jo Worthy
The University of Texas at Austin

Bogum Yoon
State University of New York, Binghamton

Debby Zambo
Arizona State University

Student Editorial Assistants

61st Yearbook of the Literacy Research Association

Heather McCrea-Andrews
Clemson University

Tyler S. Bennett
Clemson University

Elizabeth L. Cade
Clemson University

Katherine A. Jensen
Clemson University

Sangho Pang
Clemson University

Amy E. Rossi
Clemson University

Amy B. Terlitsky
Clemson University

Mary Elizabeth Weir
Clemson University

Julia Wilkins
Clemson University

61st Yearbook of the Literacy Research Association

Section II: Literacy Educators as Learners and Leaders

Section III: Researching How and Why We Use Technologies in Literacy Practices

Section IV: Discourse, Identity, and Social Practice

Section V: Research Methods

Preface

61st Yearbook of the Literacy Research Association

Widening the Circle for Literacy Research and Practice: Expanding Access, Knowledge, and Participation was the theme of the 2011 LRA Conference. The LRA circle encompasses many dedicated researchers and educators from around the world who think about, talk about, and study all aspects of literacy in its myriad forms. "Cutting-edge" research produced by our LRA colleagues is on the edge or boundary that forms the circle. Equally important is the research conducted at the center of the circle. Traditionally, a circle's center represents the gateway to the unknown. The strength of our professional circle is the continual movement from the center outward. In the words of T. S. Eliot, "We shall not cease from exploration. And the end of all our exploring will be to arrive where we started and know the place for the first time" (*Little Gidding*). Manuscripts presented in this year's *Yearbook* clearly reflect the conference theme.

This year's editor team included Pamela Dunston, Susan Fullerton, C. C. Bates, Pamela Stecker, and Kathy Headley. The team received 88 manuscripts for publication consideration. Each manuscript was reviewed critically by three to five Editorial Advisory Review Board and Student Editorial Advisory Review Board members. Twenty-one manuscripts were accepted for publication. Following procedures we developed last year, accepted manuscripts were grouped by topic and leading scholars in the literacy field were invited to write introductions for individual sections. Each luminary wrote an introduction based on the manuscripts contained within his/her respective area. This year, the following luminaries honored us by introducing sections of the *Yearbook*: Timothy Shanahan, Elfrieda Hiebert, Jamie Myers, Shirley Brice Heath, and Mark Sadoski. Their insights and comments assist *Yearbook* authors and readers in focusing on the gateway of literacy research.

The 61st *Yearbook* editors wish to thank our Dean, Dr. Lawrence Allen, and Director of the Eugene T. Moore School of Education, Dr. Michael Padilla, for financial and professional support that made this work possible. A simple "thank you" cannot convey our appreciation for the work our doctoral students, Chris Massey and Heather McCrea-Andrews, contributed to the *Yearbook*. They were responsible for retrieving, printing, organizing, and distributing manuscripts. Chris and Heather tracked and worked with manuscripts throughout the review and editing process. Chris Roper, Elisa Nelsen Oyervides, and Jenny Kasza at LRA Headquarters are without question our superheroes because we depended on them in numerous ways! They were always available to answer questions, assist with details, and encourage us when our energy flagged. We sincerely appreciate the Editorial Advisory Review Board and Student Editorial Advisory Review Board members' thoughtful reviews and constructive feedback throughout the manuscript-review process. Finally, a special word of thanks goes to our student editorial assistants for their close scrutiny of manuscripts—you are APA wizards!

Pamela J. Dunston
Susan King Fullerton
Lead Editors

A Summary of the 61st Annual Meeting of the Literacy Research Association

November 30-December 3, 2011

The Literacy Research Association met November 30 to December 3 for its annual conference in Jacksonville, Florida at the Hyatt Regency Hotel. The St. John's River, which flows directly in front of the hotel, provided a beautiful backdrop for each day of the meeting. The theme this last year was *Widening the Circle for Literacy Research and Practice: Expanding Access, Knowledge, and Participation.* It was gratifying to hear from so many LRA members who enjoyed the conference and felt that LRA was making good progress on being a more inclusive organization.

Our attendance was 1,125, exactly 100 shy of our numbers the previous year in Fort Worth but about typical for conferences held on the East Coast. LRA's leadership has expressed concern that the state of our national economy might negatively influence attendance, but to date, LRA is in excellent financial health thanks in part to continued strong attendance at our annual meetings. This last year, we received 660 proposals and we accepted 486. All accepted proposals were included in the conference program. Our size as an organization has allowed us to continue providing space to all presenters with accepted proposals. This is a nice benefit of LRA and one that the leadership is committed to continuing. Also, the thoughtful and conscientious work of the conference chairs and reviewers is greatly appreciated and their names are listed in the Annual Program.

LRA's vitality is particularly visible with respect to its award winners in the areas of scholarship and service. This year seven individuals received an award from LRA. Each award winner is determined by a chair and committee made up of LRA members who carefully review and consider all nominations. Again, we are fortunate that so many of our members are willing to do this work.

The 2012 recipient of the Oscar S. Causey Award is Linda Gambrell from Clemson University. She will present her address at the 2012 LRA Annual Meeting. The Oscar S. Causey Award is given each year for outstanding contributions to reading research. Also, Marla Mallette was this year's recipient of the Albert J. Kingston Award. She is a faculty member at the University of Southern Illinois. This award honors an LRA member for distinguished contributions of service.

In addition, Julie Coiro, of the University of Rhode Island, was the 2011 recipient of the Early Career Achievement Award. The Early Career Achievement Award is awarded annually to honor new members of the LRA community who have been actively involved in research, teaching, and service for approximately 3-7 years and have demonstrated outstanding commitment and accomplishment.

For work in the field of adult literacy, Laurie A. Henry received this year's J. Michael Parker Award. She is an Assistant Professor at the University of Kentucky. LRA awards the J. Michael Parker Award to new scholars—i.e., graduate students and those who completed their doctorates within the past six years—for papers they present at the conference that address adult literacy/language development and instruction. And, in 2011, there were two award-winning papers for the Student Outstanding Research Award. They were: "Disciplinary Literacy in New Literacies Environments: Expanding the Intersections of Literate Practice for Adolescents," authored by Michael Manderino at Northern Illinois University, and "Multimodality and Aurality: Sound Spaces in Student Digital Book Trailers," co-authored by Nathan Phillips and Blaine Smith at Vanderbilt University. The LRA Student Outstanding Research Award is given annually for an outstanding student conference paper. All forms of research, including conceptual papers, are welcomed and the winning paper is published in the *LRA Yearbook*.

As is typical at our annual meetings, the plenary speakers raised issues that stimulated thought and started conversations. Patty Anders got us off to a great start with her address, *Widening the Circle of Literacy Research: Sampling the Past and Envisioning Possibilities.* In her presentation, she brought to life our organization's history decade by decade from the 1970s to the present. She used her personal and insightful firsthand knowledge of many of our previous leaders to demonstrate where we have been, the changes we have gone through in terms of our understanding of literacy, and the challenges that currently face us. Also, her talk clarified the enormous contributions that past presidents have made to insuring that LRA continues to stand out as the premiere professional organization devoted to literacy research.

The other plenary speakers followed Patty's example with presentations that widened the circle for literacy research and practice. On Thursday morning, Lesley Mandel Morrow presented the Oscar S. Causey Address. She picked up on the changes that literacy theory, research, and instruction have gone through over time and how many of these changes have resulted, ironically, in better instruction but impoverished policies. On Thursday evening, Donaldo Macedo pointed out how injustice drives and defines the challenges that face those who want to distribute literacy more equitably. His recognition that poverty should never be viewed as natural or normal is a perspective that deserves more attention. Eve Gregory followed on Friday and she showed us how religious, cultural, and linguistic factors affect the literacy learning of immigrant children in London. Finally, Juan Guerra spoke to us at the Integrative Research Review about the need to recognize all of the linguistic and cultural understandings that young people bring into schools. He concluded that we need to better support students so that they can communicate effectively with all of the important people in their lives.

As you might guess, the plenary sessions were just the tip of the iceberg in terms of the really interesting and downright unforgettable presentations that occurred throughout the conference. I hope you enjoyed the conference as much as I did. Talk to the leadership if you have suggestions for how to improve the annual meeting. Your suggestions play an important role in the planning process. By the time you are reading this, we will either be in San Diego or we will be getting ready to leave for that city. It is sure to be a great meeting!

Robert T. Jiménez
President, Literacy Research Association
2011-2012

Marla Mallette

Albert J. Kingston Award

The annual Albert J. Kingston Service Award honors an LRA member for distinguished contribution of service to the Literacy Research Association. Established in 1985, the award was designed to honor the work of NRC/LRA's 1965-1966 president, Albert J. Kingston. Professor Kingston, an educational psychologist and reading specialist, played a major role in the development of the National Reading Conference.

Dr. Marla Mallette, Associate Professor in the Department of Curriculum and Instruction at Southern Illinois University Carbondale, is the recipient of the 2011 Albert J. Kingston Award of the Literacy Research Association.

After receiving a B.A. in Elementary Education from Southern Illinois University Carbondale, Marla moved to Las Vegas, Nevada where she taught first grade. She earned her M.Ed. in Literacy Education from the University of Nevada, Las Vegas in 1995 and, in 1999, completed her Ph.D. in Literacy with a specialization in Teacher Education from that same institution. While working on her doctorate, she served as an editorial assistant for the *Reading Research Quarterly*. Marla began her work in the professoriate at Southern Illinois University Carbondale before moving back to Las Vegas in 2006 to work as an Associate Professor at the University of Nevada, Las Vegas. She is currently an Associate Professor at Southern Illinois University Carbondale. Her most recent presentations and publications have focused on literacy research methodologies and on the use of new literacies in literacy education.

Professor Mallette attended her first NRC/LRA conference in 1994 and quickly began her extensive service to the organization. She has been the co-editor of the *NRC Newsletter* and a member of the Oscar S. Causey Award Committee. She has also served as a member and then as chair of the Student Outstanding Research Award Committee. In addition, Marla has demonstrated her service to the organization through her ongoing involvement with the annual conference. She served as the area co-chair for Inservice Teacher Education/Professional Development in Literacy and, in collaboration with Nell Duke, developed a special series of presentations that focused on research methodologies and issues. This series was an integral part of several conferences and led to the creation of a new permanent conference area—that of Research Theory, Methods, and Practices. Professor Mallette currently serves as the co-chair of this conference area.

We extend our thanks and congratulations to Dr. Marla Mallette, recipient of the 2011 Albert J. Kingston Award, in recognition of her service to LRA.

Susan L'Allier, Chair
Albert J. Kingston Award Committee
December 2011

Linda B. Gambrell

Oscar S. Causey Award

The Oscar S. Causey Award is presented each year at the annual conference to honor outstanding contributions to literacy research. Dr. Oscar S. Causey, the founder of the National Reading Conference (now the Literacy Research Association), was the chair of the Executive Committee for several years, and served as President from 1952 to 1959. Individuals who are honored with this prestigious award have conducted and published research that generates new knowledge and is deemed substantial, significant, and original. The individual is also recognized as a leader in the conduct and promotion of literacy research.

Dr. Linda B. Gambrell, the 2011 Oscar S. Causey Award honoree, is a Distinguished Professor of Education at Clemson University. She earned the B.S., M.Ed., and Ph.D. at the University of Maryland, College Park. She began her career as an elementary classroom teacher and reading specialist in Prince George's County, Maryland.

Prior to coming to Clemson University in 1999, she was Associate Dean for Research in the College of Education at the University of Maryland, College Park. From 1992-1997, she was a principal investigator at the National Reading Research Center at the University of Maryland, where she directed the Literacy Motivation Project. During this time she focused her research program on literacy motivation, which evolved into a distinguished research program and practice-based articles on the role of motivation in literacy development. Dr. Gambrell has also spent considerable time investigating visual imagery as a reading comprehension strategy and the role of discussion in teaching and learning. Currently, her research agenda focuses on the relationships among literacy achievement, motivation, and authentic literacy tasks.

Among her many services to the profession, Dr. Gambrell has served as President of the three leading professional organizations for reading—the International Reading Association, National Reading Conference/Literacy Research Association, and College Reading Association/Association of Literacy Educators and Researchers. Her research has been published in major scholarly journals, including *Reading Research Quarterly, Educational Psychologist, Elementary School Journal, Journal of Educational Research, Literacy Research and Instruction,* and practitioner journals, including *The Reading Teacher, Language Arts,* and *Social Studies for Young Children.* Most recently, she was appointed co-editor of *Reading Research Quarterly.*

Dr. Gambrell's honors and awards demonstrate the depth of her committment and her accomplishment in the field of literacy. In 2004, Linda was elected to the Reading Hall of Fame. She has received professional honors and awards, including the William S. Gray International Reading Association Award (2011), College Reading Association Laureate Award (2002), National Reading Conference Albert J. Kingston Award (2001), International Reading Association Outstanding Teacher Educator in Reading Award (1998), and the College Reading Association A. B. Herr Award for Outstanding Contributions to the Field of Reading (1994).

Linda Gambrell is an outstanding scholar, teacher, and leader. As her vita attests, she is an exemplary mentor who collaborates with colleagues as well as her current and past doctoral students. Over her impressive career she has made substantial and substantive contributions to our understanding of literacy theory, research, policy, and practice.

Lesley Mandel Morrow, Chair
Oscar S. Causey Award Committee
December 2011

Widening the Circle of Literacy Research: Sampling the Past and Envisioning Possibilities

Patricia L. Anders
University of Arizona

The Literacy Research Association members appeared to respond enthusiastically to the conference theme, *Widening the Circle for Literacy Research and Practice: Expanding Access, Knowledge, and Participation*. I was also impressed with the theme and, with a slight revision, reflected the theme in the title of this presidential address. This paper is structured in three parts: First, because our presidents are a reflection of the Literacy Research Association, formerly the National Reading Conference, I present an overview of the published presidential speeches. Following this overview, I offer an interlude, providing a context for the third part, a sample of my own recent work: "The Literacy Zones Project," a project providing a possible example of "widening the circle of literacy research."

My intention for this address was to call attention to the overarching impact of relationships for conceptualizing, doing, and sharing literacy research. Historically, the mark of a Ph.D. is the ability to do independent research. I have no quarrel with that criterion—we all need to be smart, independent, and capable—but it is a myth to assume that the independence criterion, especially in literacy research, is sufficient. Rather, relationships with those with whom we agree and disagree, both within and outside our scholarly circle, are needed to understand literacy processes, purposes, and practices. As described below, several past presidents echoed this perspective, challenging literacy scholars to view diversity of perspective and methods as strength; I push this theme further, asking literacy researchers to recognize diverse perspectives as a necessary criterion for the design and conduct of literacy research.

Another perspective, also encouraged by several past presidents and one I hope to underscore, asked literacy researchers to hold the answer to "why" they are in the field of literacy as a touch point for evaluating the meaningfulness of their work. They suggested that literacy work, including research, is the key to democracy. This point has been made by many, but one well-known reference is Louise Rosenblatt's (1995) classic *Literacy as Exploration*. She insists that democracy is a function of the quality of life and relationships earned from below, not a result of privileges imperially dispensed from above. A reader and writer is the best educational defense against the "true believer," and against the mechanically automated student. A person who reads and writes has faith in his/her own judgments, is a questioner of his or her own judgments and the judgments of others. Literacy scholarship is critical for creating readers and writers.

PART ONE: SAMPLING THE PAST

"Widening the circle," is poetic. But what does it mean? What circle? Widening from what to what? To explore possible dimensions of the circle, perspectives from the past as represented by published NRC/LRA presidential addresses are sampled. Previous commentaries of past presidents' addresses have been published—most notably, Hoffman, Duffy, Pearson, & Smith-Burke (1999), a compilation of past presidents' essays sharing their perceptions of NRC at the time of their presidency and since.

Methodology

I began by collecting and copying each of the published speeches and organized them chronologically. Copies of each address were scanned to produce Wordles (Feinberg, 2009), a software program that counts the times words are used in a text and displays them in a graphic organizer. The words used most often are in large print and the words used seldom are in small print. A Wordle was produced for each presidential address and then an additional Wordle was created using all ten presidential speeches for each decade. The decade Wordles are included in Figures 1-5 to allow for interpretation of each decade and comparison of decades.

Next, I conducted a content analysis (Rogers, 2004) reading each presidential speech, asking: What appears to be the purpose of each speech? I wrote memos about each speech and marked quotations that seemed relevant. I next read and re-read to ascertain themes and examples. In this paper I present each decade, first listing the presidents, then summarizing the presidential speeches for the decade along with displaying the wordles. At the end of the overview of each decade, I look back over the decades and draw some generalizations and conclusions.

The 1970s

Presidential speeches were not published before 1970; the first published presidential speeches were authored by Alton Raygor (1970, 1971), Earl Rankin (1972, 1974), Ed Fry (1976, 1977), and Jaap Tuinman (1979). Each was president for two years.

These founding fathers considered who reading researchers are and what NRC should be. They also described the potential value of methodological tools, including hardware and software that would influence the conduct of future research. Federal policy was addressed by a discussion of United States' President Johnson's "Right to Read" effort. The relationship of language and the reading process was presented. Hence, it seems that the literacy research circle of the 1970s included investigations of the reading process that were largely conceptualized as psychological, but

Figure 1. 1970s Wordle

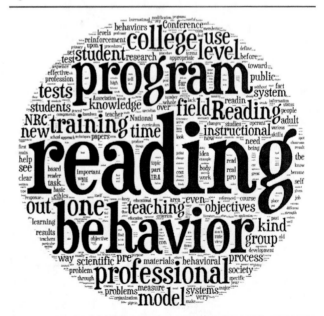

challenged by linguistic concepts; the potential for working at the federal policy level; and emerging methodological tools.

For example, President Raygor (1970, 1971), in both speeches, challenged the NRC membership to consider what they wanted NRC to be. He asked whether we should be a professional organization concerned with professional ethics and standards or a research society interested in explaining the process of reading. The next year, Fry's (1976) first address argued that NRC first and foremost is an organization dedicated to the support of and presentation of reading research.

Presidents Rankin (1974), Fry (1977), and Tuinman (1979) focused on methodological tools and research design considerations. Earl Rankin provided the Cloze procedure as a methodological tool and Ed Fry looked to the future by discussing hardware and software possibilities for future research; remember that in 1977, computers were big enough to fill a garage (Fry, 1977, p. 8).

The 1980s

The published presidential speeches of the 1980s were those presented by Harry Singer (1981), Frank Greene (1983), Irene Athey (1985), Lenore Ringler (1986), P. David Pearson (1987), Jerry Harste (1988), and Trika Smith-Burke (1989).

The decade of the 1980s widened the circle of literacy research in substantial ways. For the first time, the term literacy was used both in the title of the 35th Yearbook, *Solving Problems in Literacy: Learners, Teachers, and Researchers*. The term literacy, instead of reading, was used predominately from 1986 on and the speeches shifted in emphasis from questions dealing with the reading process and the purpose of NRC, to the introduction of topics like classroom process product research, instructionally valid assessment, the media, language, and the psychological, sociocultural, and sociolinguistic dimensions of literacy.

Figure 2. 1980s Wordle

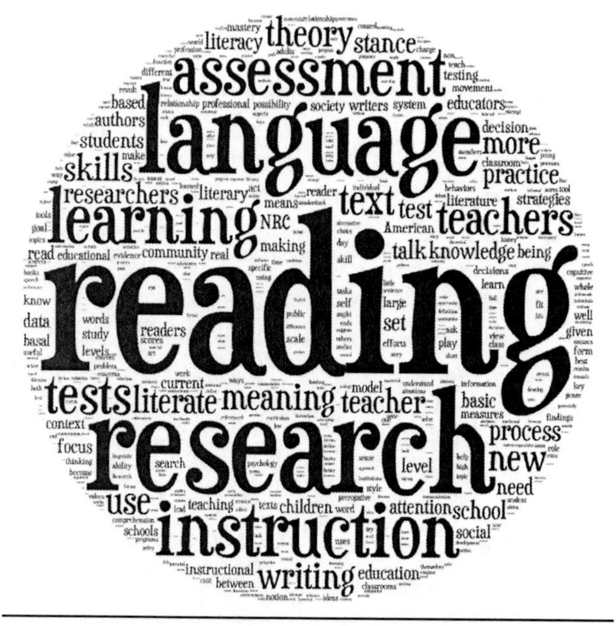

There was tension caused by this widening of the circle. During this decade, several of our founding members left the National Reading Conference and formed their own organization, the American Reading Forum. I recall two reasons: 1) members, at the business meeting, voted to NOT meet in states that had not ratified the Equal Rights Amendment. That meant NRC could not meet in Florida, where some members truly loved going;

and 2) the shift from reading research toward literacy research was huge; conference presentations and conversations abounded arguing about paradigms with discussions about "What is research?" "What are appropriate methods for doing research?" and "What is literacy?"

Many senior literacy researchers were involved in the process-product research during the 1980s; but our leaders, particularly Pearson and Valencia (1987), Harste (1988), and Smith-Burke (1989) challenged us to see the world of literacy research in a more complex and broader way. Pearson and Harste were particularly concerned with policies and practices that disenfranchised teachers limited their professionalism. Pearson and Harste each decried the increased influence of commercial materials and tests and the decreased influence of teachers on instructional and assessment decisions—a theme that continued into the 1990s. Smith Burke, in her talk, "Political and Economic Dimensions of Literacy: Challenges for the 1990s" powerfully called for "widening" the lens of literacy research by describing the sociocultural, sociolinguistic, and psycholinguistic dimensions of literacy and related research, suggesting that NRC moved into the postmodern age during this decade.

Harry Singer (1981) launched the process-product paradigm in literacy research. He argued that we should not be satisfied with studying the process of reading; rather, we needed to take our understandings to the classroom and conduct research to make a difference in classrooms for students not only in teaching students how to read, but also teaching students how to learn through reading in the content areas.

The importance of considering language when studying reading was discussed by Frank Greene (1983) and Jerry Harste (1988), building on Tuinman's plea from the last decade for researchers to pay more attention to language. Both Greene and Athey brought notions of communicative competence and speech acts to the discussion.

Also, this was the decade during which the Center for the Study of Reading was active and influential, as indicated by the publication of *Becoming a Nation of Readers* (*BNR*) (Anderson, Hiebert, Scott, & Wilkinson, 1985). In response to that book, and the only mention of policy influenced by the Federal government in the talks of this decade, Lenore Ringler (1986) presented an analysis of the media coverage of *BNR*. She found very little press coverage; for the most part newspapers and magazines took stories off the wire services and simply changed headlines to what editors thought would grab subscribers' attention. Ringler challenged NRC members to consider how we might better make our research available to the public.

Pearson and Valencia (1987), elaborated on constructs of assessment, extending the theme introduced in the 1970s by Rankin (1974) and Tuinman (1979). They argued for empowering teachers to be participants in the assessment and evaluation of children's reading achievement. They critiqued reading assessments for not representing the best we know about the reading process and the teaching of reading. They pleaded with NRC members to conduct assessment research; to take into account instructional systems and teacher judgment; and to better understand the accountability movement. They concluded that none of us can hide behind the "cloak of technology to explain errors in judgment." (p. 15).

Harste (1988) used the metaphor of learning to represent research; he called for teachers and researchers to collaborate so as to better understand the processes of teaching and learning. He said that research, theory, and practice are not unidirectional; rather they are circular: practice should inform research and theory and research and theory should inform practice; thus, teachers and academics both need to be teacher researchers.

The 1990s

The Presidential speeches of this decade extended the postmodern themes of the 1980s by taking on new topics and problematizing old topics. The Presidents during this decade were Jim Hoffman (1990), Gerry Duffy (1991), Rob Tierney (1992), Donna Alvermann (1993), Rebecca Barr (1994), Jim Flood (Flood & Lapp, 1995), Jane Hanson (1996), Richard Allington (1997), Kathy Au (1998), and Marty Ruddell (1999).

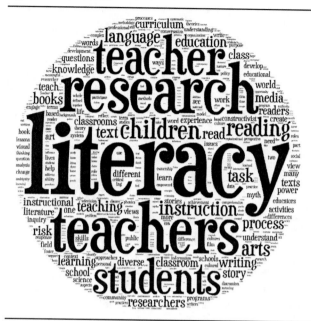

Figure 3. 1990s Wordle

The themes that rang through the presidential speeches of the 1990s encouraged NRC members to look deeply at the purposes of literacy research, especially in terms of teacher education research. Each of the presidents, in his/her own way, challenged positivist conceptions of teaching and learning, called for an increased consciousness of who we are as teacher educators and researchers, and asked us to look at our conceptions of literacy. These talks encouraged literacy researchers to study authentic literacy use. They continued the theme introduced in the 1980s describing the relationships between researchers and teachers as reciprocal, meaningful, and respectful.

Dissent also marked this decade as it did the 1980s. Researchers who proposed sessions representing a positivist and quantitative paradigm were not accepted on the program. Not surprisingly, in 1994 they left NRC, forming the Society for the Scientific Study of Reading (SSSR): They continue to meet and publish a journal.

I concluded reading these 10 talks with the sense that members of NRC had shifted paradigms; a few of the presidential speeches of the 1980s suggested as much, but in the 1990s, the sun had set on the day of reading process research and was replaced by the dawning of literacy teacher education research, considerations of language and literacy, acknowledgment of the value of social, historical, and comparative contexts, and an expanded definition of text, especially in terms of the visual arts and media.

In terms of teacher education, consider the talks by Jim Hoffman (1990) and Gerry Duffy (1991). Hoffman's talk was the first of all the Presidential speeches to seriously consider literacy teacher education research. He challenged the process-product paradigm of the 1980s, asking us to "become proactive in policy and programmatic initiatives" (p. 7) and encouraging us to be more involved in the world of practice stating that "the more involved researchers are in the world of practice; the more we will insure that practice and science are in tune with one another" (p. 7).

Duffy (1991) described a 5-year, school-situated professional development program. He said that university teacher educators needed to empower teachers and make teaching an intellectual and moral activity change our goal rather than teaching programs, materials, and procedures. In concert with Hoffman, he encouraged literacy researchers to embrace the complexities of teaching and learning in authentic contexts, reminding us that "once you embrace the complexities—that is, once you begin to understand that improved practice does not result from attempts to convert an inherently complex situation into an artificially simple one—everything else about how to improve practice is altered" (p. 16).

As Hoffman (1990) and Duffy (1991) folded teacher education into the circle of literacy research, Tierney (1992) struggled with subjectivities in the context of post-positivism. He sensed that the rhetoric of researchers for objectivity marginalized those doing qualitative research. He noted that the tendency to use terms such as traditional and mainstream as descriptors for intervention-based inferential studies reified the positivist paradigm. He called for cooperation rather than competition and the acceptance of diversity rather than attempting uniformity (p. 13).

Alvermann (1993) provided inspirational and provocative ruminations on the processes of research and the choices we make when reporting research. She challenged the construction of gender, race, and class within our field and described how our own voices are often muted in academic writing. Most importantly, she maintained that our research needs to be accessible to those outside our immediate academic circle; as such, we should write for a broader audience by relating our histories, beliefs, values, preferences, and cultural assumptions.

Barr (1994) pushed on the existing boundaries of literacy research by inviting us to consider cross-national comparisons of teaching reading. She used literacy instruction in Japan and France as her examples. She concluded with 3 implications: first, in U.S. elementary schools, instruction maximizes differences between children and does not provide a homogeneous experience for children, as it does in Japan and France. Second, assessment in the U.S. drives instruction with hidden consequences for curriculum, instruction, and student outcomes. And third, teacher education in Japan includes professional development that provides teachers with time to reflect and dialog about their teaching. This is in contrast to the U.S., which assumes good teachers are born and professional development tends to be top down.

President Jim Flood with colleague Diane Lapp (1995) considered the visual arts as text. Flood and Lapp pleaded with us to expand the concept of literacy to include the media/visual arts so as to motivate and engage students; to build bridges between school and community; to develop ESL/bilingual language and literacy; and to strengthen home school connections.

Jane Hansen (1996) called upon us to open up the "research club" to include teachers as researchers, thus expanding on Harste's (1988) address of the previous decade. She began her talk by relating her own development as a teacher researcher. She pointed out that as we investigate our own teaching, we become responsible for our own evaluation; that we adopt an inquiry stance in both our teaching and reflection; and that from that stance, new questions emerge.

Richard Allington (1997) linked research to social justice issues. He asked us "why does literacy research so often ignore what really matters?" He said that we do know a lot about teaching reading, but that our research seldom builds on this knowledge, rather we investigate topics that are on the periphery of what is important for teaching all children" (p. 7).

Kathy Au (1998) provided a primer on what is meant by constructivism in literacy theory and practice. She then demonstrated through her own research and the research of others what that means for practice. Of particular benefit is her compendium of 6 "understandings" that underlie literacy instructional practices.

Marty Ruddell (1999) closed out the decade by calling for literacy researchers to recognize and honor the diversity in literacy, an extension of many of the previous addresses, particularly Tierney's address. She used the metaphor of "stand-up comedians" to remind us that as we tell and retell stories, "we are seeing a reflection of ourselves and our lived worlds" (p. 2). She decried that literacy stories are being limited by funding mandates and that many forces are pushing for theoretical and conformity of questions and methods. She further illuminated the roots of our differences and proposed ways to address individual differences so as to keep the conversations going (p. 5).

The 2000s

Presidents were Linda Gambrel (2000), Taffy Raphael (2001), Peter Mosenthal (2002), Deborah Dillon (2003), Lee Guderson (2004), Lea McGee (2005), Don Leu (2006), Vickie Purcell Gates (2007) Patricia Edwards (2008), and Norm Stahl (2009).

A message of the 1990s was that honoring theoretical and methodological differences is critical to a thriving research agenda; the presidential speeches of the 2000s delivered on that message. The addresses of this decade are more different than they are alike. This decade brought to bear the influence and effects of federal legislation on both research and instructional practices. Three of the ten speeches addressed legislation and policy, more than any other decade. The theme of collaborating with teachers and promoting teacher voice, a concern of the 1980s and 1990s, was only discussed by two presidents in the 2000s. One possible commonality of these addresses is that the presidents encouraged NRC members to plan a research agenda; that change is not

Figure 4. 2000s Wordle

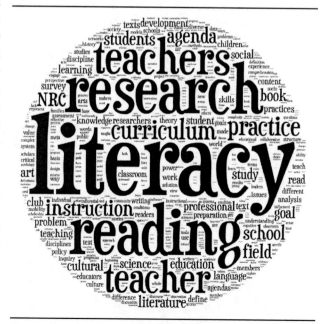

accomplished with one-shot studies; rather, literacy research should be planned to systematically accomplish change.

The question asked in the 1970s about what is reading research was revisited during this decade by Mosenthal (2002) and Stahl (2009). This seems natural as the experimental and quasi-experimental studies of the 1970s and 1980s are not sufficient for studying the evolving and multiple dimensions of literacy.

Two presidents (Dillon, 2003; McGee, 2005) made policy a focus of their talks; Lee Gunderson reminded us of the theme of language and literacy, emphasizing bilingual and ESL students and discussing the effects of the 'English Only' movement and Pat Edwards focused on the history of African American children's literature and the literacy instruction of African American children, calling for more research on family literacy.

Linda Gambrell (2000) launched the new millennium by surveying the NRC membership. Among several questions, she asked respondents: Who among literacy researchers had most influenced practice during the 1970s, 1980s, and 1990s? You need to read the paper for all the details, but in a nutshell she found the following: Durkin's comprehension work of the 1970s, Heath's socio-cultural ethnographic research of the 1980s, and Adam's synthesis of research on beginning reading in the 1990s. The work of Marie Clay was found influential across all three decades, and the work of Kenneth Goodman influential in the 1970s and 1980s.

Taffy Raphael (2001) asked us to think about teacher preparation: She continued the call of previous presidents for teacher educator's collaboration with teachers. She also advised that children's literature be integrated in teacher education curriculum. And further she proposed that Colleges of Education shift their focus from teacher preparation to the professional development of practicing teachers.

Peter Mosenthal (2002) took his listeners/readers to the mountaintops for considering the wrong-headedness of letting the disciplines dictate literacy research questions and methodology. He deconstructed the metaphor of "setting agendas" for research, suggesting that it guide each of our research plans.

In terms of federal legislation, *No Child Left Behind* was attended to by Deborah Dillon (2003). She called for the literacy community—researchers, teacher educators, classroom teachers—to advocate for children. Her talk links well with Allington's (1997) talk of the previous decade. *Early Reading First* was legislation discussed by Lea McGee (2005). She called for literacy researchers to be wise: highlighting the notion that research-based curriculum is not possible, let alone desirable.

Donald Leu (2006) revealed that: (1) the Internet is this generation's defining technology for literacy and learning; 2) the Internet is a literacy issue, not a technology issue; 3) new literacy skills, strategies, and dispositions are required to use the Internet effectively; 4) to fully understand the issue of new literacies, we must recognize that literacy is a deictic construct; and 5) only when each of us brings our special expertise to studying Internet literacy can we expect students to fully realize their potential as global citizens of the 21st century.

The purpose of literacy was explored by Vicki Purcell Gates' (2007) talk when she asked "What's it all about?" She reviewed literature in the popular press to demonstrate the need for critical literacy and challenged us to remember *why* we want people to be literate. Specifically, she asked that we each adopt a lifespan vision of literacy, expand the construct of literacy, and remember to ask: How does my study fit into the larger picture of developing thinking, critical citizens, the backbone of a democracy?

The 2010s

It is too early to note any trends in the present decade, but both Presidents Hinchman and Reinking, continued the exploration of the diversity inherent in literacy research. Hinchman (2010) told us the story of children identified as special education, especially those who are diagnosed with autism. She expressed concern that the professionals working with these children need our expertise.

Reinking (2011) took up the gauntlet to present models of research designed to address the complexities of literacy instruction. He told us the story of discovering and using the formative experiment to do design research that investigates meaningful questions.

Figure 5. 2010s Wordle

Themes Across Decades

Look at the decade wordles for the appearance of certain themes. The largest words in common across all decades are: "reading," and "research." Terms dealing with "Assessment/measurement/ tests" also span the decades, but appear smaller than might be expected, given the attention to accountability in the press; "learning;" and "students" was a very small entry in the 1970 wordle, bigger in 1980, and among the largest words in the 1990s and 2000s; a similar pattern is observed with the word "teachers," which barely appeared in the 1970s, was larger in the 1980s, huge in the 1990s, and smaller again in the 2000s; "teach" and "teaching" appeared in all 4 wordles, showing the most prominence in the 1990s; and "education" appeared in all the wordles, but was largest in 2000.

Next, the largest words common in 3 of 4 decades were: "literacy" in the 1980s, 1990s, and 2000s, but not in the 1970s; "language" in the 1970s, 1980s, and 1990s, but not the 2000s; "children" in the last three decades, but not youth or adults; and "writing" in the last 3 decades.

Largest words in 2 of 4 decades: "comprehension" in the 1970s and 1980s, but not in the 1990s, and very small in the 2000s; "program" in the 1970s and 2000s, but not in the 1980s and the 1990s; "instruction" appeared in the 1980s and 1990s, but not in the 1970s or 2000s; "school" appeared in the last two decades; and "books" or "literature" was visible in the 1990s and very small in 2000s.

Words found in 1 of the 4 decades included: "cloze" and "behavior" in the 1970s; in the 1980s the terms "text," "discourse," "cognitive," "strategies," "social," and "cultural;" in the 1990s, "phonics," and "constructivist;" and in the 2000s "parents" along with "social," "media," and the "internet."

Words, seldom if ever, appearing in the wordles include: community (appears very small in 1990s), critical (very small in the 2000s), and "theory," small in both the 1980s and 1990s. This last observation is particularly surprising.

What are the "take-away" points from this study of the presidential speeches? I propose six:

1. NRC/LRA presidents have invested a great deal to make NRC/LRA what it is today. We are all indebted to them for their leadership, intelligence, and dedicated service.

2. Several presidents challenged each of us to be reflexive, self-critical, and tolerant of differences among us; some encouraged us to use research to examine our own practices, and others argued that we must use our work to speak to many different audiences, not just academics.

3. Those of us in higher education are part of a larger system, including preschools, K-12 schools, other sorts of tertiary educational institutions and adult education. Literacy researchers are a part of an educational system, and each part is related to and serves the other parts, integral parts of a whole.

4. Although the field of psychology has been a dominant influence on our scholarship, other disciplines are important, too—one discipline does not possess a truth superior than another, they inform different questions. If one discipline is privileged over another, questions are limited.

5. Teachers, grade P-12 and tertiary educators, are our allies, partners, and collaborators.

6. Literacy researchers must renew a commitment to be the best critical thinkers possible; to incorporate the teaching of and use of critical inquiry intentionally and planfully. A democracy depends on it.

This review of presidential speeches sets the stage for what follows. Next, I provide an interlude of sorts, discussing some of the back story to my decision to embark on the community literacy project described in the last part of this talk.

What a Mess! Policies and Court Cases

Last year, a few of you told me that you couldn't wait for my presidential address because of all the "hot" political events going on in Arizona. You suggested that I would have a lot to say! I am not a whiner or complainer; I love the beauty of Arizona and the pioneer spirit and energy of Arizona people; but with regard to most things educational, Arizona is a discouraging place to work.

Table 1 summarizes relevant Arizona and United States demographic data. According to the 2010 census, 6,392,017 people live in Arizona; note that despite Arizona's reputation as a retirement state, less than 15% of the population is over age 65. Also, a relatively large percentage (27.9%) of Arizona's population speaks a language other than English in their home. Arizona is one of five

Table 1. Relevant Arizona and United States Demographics

Category	Arizona	USA
Persons under 18 years, 2010	25.5%	24.0%
Persons 65 years and over, 2012	13.8%	13.0%
Black persons, 2010	4.1%	12.6%
American Indian and Alaska Native persons, 2010	4.6%	0.9%
Persons of Hispanic or Latino origin, 2010	29.6%	16.3%
White persons not Hispanic, 2010	57.8%	63.7%
Language other than English spoken at home, age 5+, 2005-2009	27.9%	19.6%
English Language Learner, K-12 students	14%	
ELL's with Spanish as first language, K-12 students	81%	
High school graduates, persons 25+, 2005-2009	83.9%	84.6%
Median household income, 2009	$48,711	$50,221
Persons below poverty level, 2009	16.5%	14.3%

states in the United States with the highest concentration of English language learners. Within this demographic context, there are policies and judicial cases that affect the work of Arizona educators:

- From 1976 to 2011, the Tucson Unified School District was under a federal court order mandating desegregation. Although the order is lifted, schools remain highly segregated, despite a system of magnet and charter schools designed to offer choice.

- The State Superintendent of Schools and the Attorney General have declared the Tucson Unified School District's highly successful ethnic studies program to be illegal. The ethnic studies teachers and students are suing the state for violations of academic freedom. At the time of publication, the ethnic studies program has been eliminated by the district because of threats from the State to cut district funding.

- The voters of Arizona passed Proposition 203, declaring Arizona an *English Only* state.

- A class action suit continues, originally filed in 1992, claiming that Arizona does not provide adequate resources for English Language Learners. For the last 19 years a great deal of drama and a plethora of language-related legislative mandates have affected all educators. For example, a massive teacher education campaign was undertaken by the Arizona Department of Education (ADE) requiring that all preservice and inservice teachers be taught Structured English Immersion (SEI), a questionable method for teaching English to non-English speaking students.

- Test score achievement of Arizona's school children and youth is a very high priority. Arizona's criterion-referenced test is the Arizona's Instrument to Measure Standards (AIMS). It is given to every student each year. During the year, students are barraged with benchmark tests, in the hope that the more teachers focus on teaching discrete skills and the more often students are tested, the more likely students' scores will be high. District after district and school after school are reducing literacy instruction and narrowing the curriculum to the basic skills tested on the AIMS.

- Arizona ranks 50th among other states in the union in terms of per capita expense for schooling.

Given these and other realities, I have moved my research agenda outside of the school to the community. Am I contributing to the demise of public education? Recently when I asked this question, a colleague responded that I was being *cleverly devious*. That if communities were more literate and if citizens knew more about literacy education, our schools would improve. Several of our presidents, most especially Donna Alvermann (1993), made the same point, arguing that academic voices are mute and that we need ways to speak with a broad spectrum of society.

PART TWO: LITERACY CONNECTS! THE LITERACY ZONE PROJECT

"Literacy Connects! A Literacy Zone Project" grew out of The Literacy for Life Coalition, a coalition of civic leaders such as the Community Foundation *for* Southern Arizona, the Tucson Regional Economic Opportunities (TREO), Southern Arizona Leadership Council (SALC), and Tucson Metropolitan Chamber of Commerce, who sponsored a Tucson Regional Town Hall. At that Town Hall, improving literacy in Tucson was chosen as *the* top priority by 165 participants. During 2008 and most of 2009 a steering committee of more than 30 government, nonprofit, business, media, funding, and educational organizations worked to define literacy, agree on measures, and kick start three action teams: capacity building, advocacy, and awareness.

I was named the chair of the Capacity-Building Team. Through discussion, the steering committee agreed that the Capacity-Building Team should, among other projects, establish two literacy zones where we could "experiment" with ideas for promoting and enhancing a culture of literacy. We planned that each zone be targeted for about five years, that other literacy zones be developed over time, and that the process be studied so as to inform further development. We intended that the zone provide us with rich, nuanced, multifaceted information about what it means to promote, enhance, and sustain a culture of literacy.

What, specifically, is meant by a literacy zone? The idea is that if a community has coherent, comprehensive, and intensive literacy opportunities, a culture of literacy will be enhanced and the well-being of the entire neighborhood will improve. A literacy zone is established in a neighborhood that chooses to be a zone. Their first task is to create a Literacy Council, which is made up of community members, school administrators and teachers, students, business people, members of the faith community, law enforcement, healthcare providers, financial literacy providers—anyone from the neighborhood with a commitment to enhancing literacy in the neighborhood is welcome to join.

What are some examples of the Literacy Council's work?

- Provide families and child care providers knowledge about why and how language and literacy develops and offer access to literacy-related materials and practices so that more children are prepared for kindergarten;
- Promote working relationships between administrators, teachers, parents, and other members of the community around language and literacy;
- Establish youth language and literacy development opportunities in schools, the libraries, and the community so they will: be better able to understand themselves and their

world; learn across the disciplines; use multiple literacies; and engage in service to their community.

- Make available more opportunities for adults to acquire basic literacy, learn English, attend GED classes, and gain technology skills;

Our overall research question is "will a coherent, consistent, cohesive, and intensive literacy programming strengthen the culture of literacy in the Literacy Zone?" Possible sub-questions include: What is the relation of literacy opportunities to social opportunity in the literacy zone? Can a stronger culture of literacy within a neighborhood lead to changes within neighborhood schools? Is there a 'tipping point' for the identity of a rich literacy culture? How do changes in literacy practices diffuse throughout a community and what are the effects?

Related Literature

Our theoretical framework is based on the scholarship of Street (1984) and Moll (1988) and colleagues (González, Moll, & Amanti, 2005). Their theories maintain that: literacy is functional, a tool for getting information, for experiencing the aesthetic, for constructing knowledge and thinking critically and creatively. Literacy is not primarily technical, as in the acquisition of skills; rather, it is acquired within social contexts that are meaningful and purposeful. My colleagues and I theorize that literacy has the potential of being the social fabric of a community—a source; an expression; a networking tool, a means for the nurturing of relationships.

We are not, of course, the first to have had these ideas. Two particular projects include Chip Bruce's (2010) project in Chicago's Barrio *Paseo Boricua* and Linda Flower's (2008) Community Literacy Center in Pittsburgh. Bruce's project is a grass roots community development program with many literacy components. He describes the *Paseo Boricua* project like this:

> It is commonplace nowadays to think of the classroom or the school as a learning community, even if that is more often achieved in name than in fact. Some have argued for extending to the community beyond, bringing neighborhood experiences into the classroom, as with funds of knowledge approaches (Moll, Amanti, Neff, & González, 1992), or taking classroom learning out into the neighborhood, as with service learning, All of these ideas have merit, and may be considerably better than what we see in many schools oppressed by the No Child Left Behind regime today. But the *Paseo Boricua* learning goes a step further. Rather than seeing the community as simply a resource, or as an application area for learning, it puts community first. In this approach, *the community is the curriculum*. The mutual constitution of community life and education is thus evident in everything the community undertakes. And all of those activities build upon genuine conversation. (p. 110)

Linda Flower, (Higgins, Flower, & Peck, 1994) in a project she started during her days connected with the Center for the Study of Writing at Carnegie Melon, is based on the notion that the literate acts of ordinary community members can inspire innovative community action (p. 3). This project takes place in the Community Literacy Center where citizens receive writing instruction, encouragement, and support to use the power of literacy for change.

A couple years ago Dean Ron Marx was a plenary speaker at NRC. He suggested that the future of Colleges of Education lay in the connections that we make with the community, that our work as educators should not be isolated. Past President Raphael echoed this sentiment in her presidential address: "(C)ommunities form the context ... it's the context and the background of children and youth who come to school for instruction. They come to school but every night they return to the community. The school and the community are one system" (p. 14).

Setting and Participants

The Literacy Zone Project takes place in two neighborhoods—the Sunnyside Neighborhood and the South Park Neighborhood. The Capacity Team went through a process to select the neighborhoods invited to be a Literacy Zone. These two neighborhoods agreed. Each neighborhood formed a Literacy Council to develop the work of the Literacy Zone. The demographics of the neighborhoods are summarized in Table 2.

Table 2. Comparison of 2000 Census Data in Two Literacy Zone Project Neighborhoods

Demographics from 2000 Census Data	Sunnyside Neighborhood	South Park Neighborhood
Total Number of People	15,599	2,781
Total Number of Families	3,666	611
Poverty Count	25.5%	30.4%
Total Number of Adults	8,790 (56%)	1,388 (50%)
Total Number of Adults without High School/GED	3,968 (45%)	791 (57%)

Methodology

Our research plan utilizes mixed methods. Some of the data we collect is descriptive and responds to needs for project evaluation. The evaluative data and other descriptive data are used, when appropriate, to inform our research questions.

The research design utilizes Network theory. Social Network Analysis (SNA) (Wasserman & Faust, 1994) is a quantitative research and data analysis methodology being used increasingly in education. It measures qualities of individuals in relation to and dependent on others. SNA looks at the structure of the relations between actors in a network; the ties in the structures are the unit of analysis, rather than individuals. Nodes are typically people, but can also be any number of other things. Ties measure all kinds of connections, typically kinship or friendship, but also particular interactions or relations. They can also be varied by degree of connection, such as with strong ties (e.g., close friends) or weak ties (e.g., acquaintances). Measures of nodes are in relation to the rest of the network, such as betweenness and centrality, which can also be compared with individual measures. Standard statistical metrics (factor analysis, cluster analysis, correlation, regression, etc.) can be applied to network data itself or combined with other data.

SNA has been around for nearly half a century. It was first developed by anthropologists in the 1950s, but the tremendous increase in computing power has created a renaissance for SNA. Some studies have gained attention in recent times. The rise of social networks, Facebook and Twitter in particular, provide ideal sources of data, resulting in a whole sub-field based on them. For example, after 9-11, Krebs (2002) and others used SNA to map terrorist networks and draw conclusions about leadership roles. Fowler and Christakis (2008) used network data to tie the spread of obesity, smoking, and happiness to social ties in a community. Network theory is coming to be something of a zeitgeist as phenomena like globalization and the Internet make classic liberal views of individuality increasingly untenable.

Tentative/Projected Findings

We are in the midst of the SNA study; the following summary of four cases provides a taste of our findings at the project level.

Women's Literacy Network. The Women's Literacy Network (WLN) was created to respond to two issues in the neighborhoods: 1) few volunteer tutors live in the literacy zones. Most volunteers live north of the neighborhoods and they are not comfortable travelling to the neighborhoods where the zones are; and 2) people who live in the zone do not see themselves as tutors and are busy trying to support themselves and taking care of their families. In response to these two needs, the Women's Literacy Network was conceived. My students and I partnered with Literacy Volunteers of Tucson and with Pima Community College Adult Education. These two organizations helped us find 10 women with demonstrated leadership potential while studying for their GED. They received 20 hours of "training" based on Retrospective Miscue Analysis and Math instruction. They also role played being a tutor and learned principles of working with others. They were then assigned two women to tutor who are working on their GEDs. We provide ongoing mentoring for both tutors and students. For the tutors we provide a minimum hourly wage, a child care stipend, and transportation expenses; for the students we provided a stipend for child care and transportation costs.

Personal stories shared after the training and during the mentoring indicate that WLN participants think differently about literacy and learning. They report using their new skills to interact with their families in different ways. For example, both tutors and students report engaging their children in literature discussions and helping their spouses practice English. The women report improved communication with their children's teachers. The women use their increased confidence to fulfill personal goals: one woman obtained an adult education credential and now has a higher job classification and rate of pay; another is volunteering at the library; one woman applied for a national scholarship; four others are returning to school; and all report feeling a renewed sense of purpose through their work in the WLN. Four of the ten tutors, who were previously unemployed, obtained full-time employment after participation in the WLN. As of May 2011, all 20 students improved their Tests of Adult Basic Education (TABE) scores and 5 passed the GED, with 5 more in various stages of testing.

The Sunnyside Literacy Zone Outreach Project. Another project to help the literacy zones grow their own tutors is the Sunnyside Literacy Zone Outreach Project. A second rationale for this project is to improve relationships between Spanish-speaking parents and the elementary school their children attend. This project hired a Spanish-literate person from the neighborhood as an outreach coordinator to recruit and train volunteers and to recruit clients in need of adult education classes and English Language classes, which we offer at the school. Children get homework help and extra help with reading and writing while their parents attend classes. After one year, over 50 tutors are trained, and 100 adults receive adult education in either English or basic literacy. The second year of the project is underway, with more than 1,000 new and gently used books given to children in the schools, more volunteers being recruited and taught, and more adults receiving adult education in their children's school.

Stories of the Zone. This is a multi-generational, multi-modal celebration of literacy in the Literacy Zone. Stories that Soar, a local literacy provider, partners with a school and invites children to "feed" stories to a decorated "magic box." Stories are selected by Stories that Soar and, based on the children's story, a script is written and performed by actors and musicians. The performance is a community event, held either at the local library or at the school. Copies of all the stories are bound and a copy is given to the child and to the school library. This project is a huge motivator for children and teachers in participating schools. We have been through 3 cycles now, and each time the children's stories are longer and more complex. The performances are becoming huge community events.

The Peace Project. An asset of the Sunnyside Neighborhood is its Peace Garden. Several years ago, a neighborhood leader authored an alphabet book based on the neighborhood association-maintained "peace garden." Upon learning about this, one of our literacy providers, "Make Way For Books," (MWFB) assembled bilingual "text sets" on the theme of peace. They gave text sets to neighborhood preschools and childcare centers and provided workshops so teachers, caregivers, and parents could learn how to use them. Forty early childhood educators from five childcare centers, 10 home providers, and 3 kindergarten teachers—all the teachers in one of two schools in the neighborhood—participated. In addition to the workshops, MWFB partnered with the libraries to host family read-aloud nights both in the library and at the Peace Garden along with display materials and the text sets.

We have 20 on-going projects that are similar to these examples. I look forward to begin analyzing the social network data to see how close we are to a "tipping point"—to where the relations among all partners are so well developed that a culture of literacy is experienced by most and apparent to all.

CONCLUSION

The mess in my home state has driven me from literacy research bound by the walls of schools to the community. I am looking at the community as a unit. I am testing the theory that a systemic change in literacy opportunities and resources will enhance a culture of literacy that will benefit the quality of life in the neighborhood. This is an exciting venture and may be a direction others will find compelling.

In conclusion, we have explored possibilities and have sampled the presidential presentations of the past. We have found that throughout our history, our leaders have pushed us to "widen the circle of literacy research." You know, just a few professors met in the 1950s to study and to advance their scholarship and teaching. They brought their graduate students, their graduate students brought fresh ideas and their graduate students, and as they did so, the circle continued to widen. Those of us who are here today stand on their shoulders and is each making our own small contribution to the future of literacy research.

Over these years, if we have learned anything, it is that change is born from diversity; the circle is widened in a context that welcomes open, critical dialogue. Since the beginning of LRA, members have challenged the status quo, stretching ourselves to become more than we were. As Past President Dillon (2003) said:

> NRC/LRA gives us the power to re-arm ourselves, provide the sharing of knowledge and strategies to allow us to do our local work; the strength and

renewed resolve to remember for whom we do our work. When we look at those who matter most to us, we find the connection between our soul's desire for our lives and the meaning of our work. We make a difference through our actions. (p. 29)

The circle of literacy research will continue to widen. It will thrive as diversity is honored and relationships are valued.

AUTHOR'S NOTE

Patricia L. Anders, The University of Arizona, Department of Teaching, Learning, and Sociocultural Studies, University of Arizona. The author acknowledges the contributions of doctoral candidate Robert deRoock, doctoral student Charlene Mendoza, and her high school students for contributions to the preparation of this manuscript. Dr. Renée Clift and Dr. Kathy Hinchman offered suggestions when the manuscript was under development. I appreciate their efforts, insights, and contributions.

REFERENCES

Allington, R. L. (1997). Why does literacy research so often ignore what really matters? In C. K. Kinzer, K. A. Hinchman, & D. J. Leu (Eds.), *Inquiries in literacy theory and practice, 46th yearbook of the National Reading Conference* (pp. 1-8) Chicago, IL: National Reading Conference.

Alvermann, D. E. (1993). Researching the literal: Of muted voices, second texts, and cultural representations. In D. J. Leu & C. K. Kinzer (Eds.), *Examining central issues in literacy research, theory, and practice, 42nd yearbook of the National Reading Conference* (pp. 1-7). Chicago, IL: National Reading Conference.

Anderson, R. C., Hiebert, E., Scott, J. A., & Wilkinson, I. (1985). *Becoming a nation of readers.* University of Illinois: Champaign, IL.

Athey, I. (1985). Communicative competence: Cross-cultural perspectives. In J. A. Niles & L. A. Harris (Eds.). *Thirty-third yearbook of the National Reading Conference* (pp. 1-11). Rochester, NY: The National Reading Conference, Inc.

Au, K. (1998). Constructivist approaches, phonics, and the literacy learning of students of diverse backgrounds. In T. Shanahan & F. V. Rodriguez-Brown (Eds.), *47th yearbook of the National Reading Conference,* (pp. 1-12). Chicago, IL: National Reading Conference.

Barr, R. (1994). Comparative perspectives on literacy instruction, educational research, and knowledge of teaching. In C. K. Kinzer & D. J. Leu (Eds.), *Multidimensional aspects of literacy research, theory, and practice, forty-third yearbook of the National Reading Conference* (pp. 1-9). Chicago, IL: National Reading Conference.

Bruce, B. (2010). Coffee cups, frogs, and lived experience. In P. L. Anders (Ed.), *Defying convention, inventing the future: A tribute to Ken and Yetta Goodman,* (pp. 96-115). New York, NY: Taylor Francis.

Dillon, D. R. (2003). In leaving no child behind have we forsaken individual learners, teachers, schools, and communities? In C. M. Fairbanks, J. Worthy, B. Maloch, J. V. Hoffman, & D. L. Schallert (Eds.), *52nd yearbook of the National Reading Conference* (pp. 1-29). Oak Creek, WI: National Reading Conference, Inc.

Duffy, G. G. (1991). What counts in teacher education? Dilemmas in educating empowered teachers. In J. Zutell & S. McCormick (Eds.), *Learner factors/teacher factors: Issues in literacy research and instruction, 40th yearbook of the National Reading Conference,* (pp. 1-11). Chicago, IL: The National Reading Conference.

Edwards, P. A. (2008). The education of African-American students: Voicing the debates, controversies, and solutions. In Y. Kim, V. J. Risko, D. L. Compton, D. K. Dickinson, M. K. Hundley, R. T. Jiménez, K. M. Leander, & D. W. Rowe (Eds.), *57th yearbook of the National Reading Conference,* (pp. 1-30). Oak Creek, WI: National Reading Conference, Inc.

Feinberg, J. (2009). Retrieved from http://www.wordle.net

Flood, J., & Lapp, D. (1995). Broadening the lens: Toward an expanded conceptualization of literacy. In K. A. Hinchman, D. J. Leu, & C. K. Kinzer (Eds.), *Perspectives on literacy research and practice, 44th yearbook of the National Reading Conference* (pp. 1-10). Chicago, IL: The National Reading Conference.

Flower, L. (2008) *Community literacy and the rhetoric of public engagement.* Carbondale: Southern Illinois University Press.

Fowler, J. H., & Christakis, N. A. (2008). Dynamic spread of happiness in a large social network: Longitudinal analysis over 20 years in the Framingham Heart Study. *BMJ, 337.* a2338.

Fry, E. (1976). Presidential address: Who are NRC? In G. H. McNinch & W. D. Miller (Eds.), *25th yearbook of the National Reading Conference* (pp. 1-7). Milwaukee, WI: The National Reading Conference, Inc.

Fry, E. (1977). Tools for reading researchers. In P. D. Pearson (Ed.), *Reading: Research, theory and practice, 26th yearbook of the National Reading Conference* (pp. 1-10). Clemson, SC: The National Reading Conference. Inc.

Gambrell, L. (2000). Reflections on literacy research: The decades of the 1970s, 1980s, and 1990s. In T. Shanahan, & F. V. Rodriguez-Brown (Eds.), *49ᵗʰ yearbook of the National Reading Conference* (pp. 1-7). Chicago, IL: The National Reading Conference.

González, N., Moll, L. C., & Amati, C. (Eds.) (2005). *Funds of knowledge: Theorizing practices in households, communities, and classrooms.* Mahwah, NJ: Erlbaum.

Greene, F. (1983). Searches. In J. A. Niles & L. A. Harris (Eds.), *Searches for meaning in reading/language processing and instruction, 32nd yearbook of the National Reading Conference* (pp. 1-11). Rochester, NY: The National Reading Conference.

Gunderson, L. (2004). The language, literacy, achievement, and social consequences of English-only programs for immigrant students. In J. Worthy, B. Maloch, J. V. Hoffman, D. L. Schallert, & C. M. Fairbanks (Eds.), *53ʳᵈ yearbook of the National Reading Conference,* (pp. 1-15). Oak Creek, WI: National Reading Conference, Inc.

Hansen, J. (1996). Researchers in our own classrooms: What propels teacher research? In D. J. Leu, C. K. Kinzer, & K. A. Hinchman (Eds.), *Literacies for the 21ˢᵗ century: Research and practice, 45th yearbook of the National Reading Conference* (pp. 1-9). Chicago, IL: The National Reading Conference.

Harste, J. (1988). Tomorrow's readers today: Becoming a profession of collaborative learners. In J. E. Readence, & R. S. Baldwin (Eds.), *Dialogues in literacy research, 37th yearbook of the National Reading Conference,* (pp. 2-7). Chicago, IL: The National Reading Conference.

Higgins, L., Flower, L., & Peck, W. (1994). *Occasional Paper No. 34. Community literacy.* Berkeley, CA: National Center for the Study of Writing and Literacy.

Hinchman, K. A. (2010). Literacy identities of youth identified for special education: Who is responsible? In R. T. Jiménez, V. J. Risko, M. K. Hundley, & D. W. Rowe (Eds.), *59ᵗʰ yearbook of the National Reading Conference* (pp. 1-14). Oak Creek, WI: National Reading Conference, Inc.

Hoffman, J. V. (1990). The myth of teaching. In J. Zutell & S. McCormick (Eds.), *Literacy theory and research: analyses from multiple perspectives, 39th yearbook of the National Reading Conference.* (pp. 1-7). Chicago, IL: The National Reading Conference.

Hoffman, J., Duffy, G., Pearson, P. D., & Smith-Burke, T. (1999). The National Reading Conference: Presidential Retrospectives. *Journal of Literacy Research, 31*(1), 6-46.

Krebs, V. E. (2002). Mapping networks of terrorist cells. *Connections, 24*(3), 43-52.

Leu, D. J. (2006). New literacies, reading research, and the challenges of change: A Deictic perspective. In J. V. Hoffman, D. Schallert, C. M. Fairbanks, J. Worthy, & B. Maloch (Eds.), *55ᵗʰ yearbook of the National Reading Conference* (pp. 1-12). Oak Creek, WI: National Reading Conference, Inc.

McGee, L. M. (2005). The role of wisdom in evidence-based preschool literacy curricula. In B. Maloch, J. V. Hoffman, D. L. Schallert, C. M. Fairbanks, & J. Worthy (Eds.), *54th yearbook of the National Reading Conference* (pp. 1-12). Oak Creek, WI: National Reading Conference, Inc.

Moll, L. C. (1988). Some key issues in teaching Latino students. *Language Arts, 65*(5), 465-472.

Moll, L. C., Amanti, C., Neff, D., & González, N. (1992). Funds of knowledge for teaching: A qualitative approach to connect households and classrooms. *Theory into Practice, 31*(2), 132-141.

Mosenthal, P. (2002). Reading research as an agenda-setting enterprise: Bringing science to art, and art to science. In D. L. Schallert, C. M. Fairbanks, J. Worthy, B. Maloch, & J. V. Hoffman (Eds.), *51ˢᵗ yearbook of the National Reading Conference* (pp. 1-9). Chicago, IL: The National Reading Conference.

Pearson, P. D., & Valencia, S. (1987). Assessment, accountability, and professional prerogative. In J. E. Readence, & R. S. Baldwin (Eds.), *Research in literacy: Merging perspectives, 36th yearbook of the National Reading Conference* (pp. 1-9). Rochester, NY: The National Reading Conference, Inc.

Purcell-Gates, V. (2007). What's it all about? Literacy research and civic responsibility. In D. W. Rowe, R. T. Jiménez, D. L. Compton, D. K. Dickinson, Y. Kim, K. M. Leander, & V. J. Risko (Eds.), *56th yearbook of the National Reading Conference* (pp. 1-13). Oak Creek, WI: National Reading Conference, Inc.

Rankin, E. F. (1972). A simple model for the improvement of college-training programs for reading development. In P. L. Nacke (Ed.), *Diversity in mature reading: Theory and research, 22nd yearbook of the National Reading Conference* (pp. 1-10). Boone, NC: The National Reading Conference, Inc.

Rankin, E. F. (1974). The cloze procedure revisited. In G. H. McNinch (Ed.), *23rd volume of the National Reading Conference*, (pp. 1-8). Milwaukee, WI: The National Reading Conference, Inc.

Raphael, T. E. (2001). Literacy teaching, literacy learning: Lessons from the book club plus project. In J. V. Hoffman, D. L. Schallert, C. M. Fairbanks, J. Worthy, & B. Maloch (Eds.), *50th yearbook of the National Reading Conference* (pp. 1-12) Chicago, IL: The National Reading Conference, Inc.

Raygor, A. (1970). The problem of definition in a non-existing profession: Presidential address. In G. B. Schick & M. M. May (Eds.). *Reading process and pedagogy, the 19th yearbook of the National Reading Conference* (pp. 3-11). Milwaukee, WI: The National Reading Conference, Inc.

Raygor, A. (1971). Present and future trends in college reading and higher education. In F. P. Greene (Ed.), *Reading: The right to participate, 20th yearbook of the National Reading Conference* (pp. 3-10). Milwaukee, WI: The National Reading Conference, Inc.

Reinking, D. (2011). Beyond the laboratory and lens: New metaphors for literacy research. In P. J. Dunston, L. B. Gambrell, K. Headley, S. K. Fullerton, P. M. Stecker, V. R. Gillis, & C. C. Bates (Eds.), *60th yearbook of the Literacy Research Association*, (pp. 1-17). Oak Creek, WI: Literacy Research Association, Inc.

Ringler, L. (1986). *Becoming a Nation of Readers: Reactions from the media*. In J. A. Niles & R. V. Lalik (Eds.), *Solving problems in literacy: Learners, teachers, and researchers*. Rochester NY: The National Reading Conference, Inc.

Rogers, R. (Ed.) (2004). An introduction to critical discourse analysis in education. Mahwah, NJ: Lawrence Erlbaum Associates, Inc.

Rosenblatt, L. (1995). *Literature as exploration* (5th ed.).New York, NY: Modern Language Association.

Ruddell, M. (1999). Of stand-up comics, statisticians, storytellers, and small girls walking backward: A new look at discourses of literacy research. In T. Shanahan & F. V. Rodriguez-Brown (Eds.), *48th yearbook of the National Reading Conference*, (pp. 1-16). Chicago, IL: The National Reading Conference, Inc.

Singer, H. (1981). Hypothesis on research comprehension in search of classroom validation. In M. L Kamil (Ed.), *Directions in reading: Research and instruction, 30th yearbook of the national Reading Conference* (pp. 1-11). Washington DC: The National Reading Conference, Inc.

Smith-Burke, T. (1989). Political and economic dimensions of literacy: Challenges for the 1990s. In J. A. Niles & R. V. Lalik (Eds.), *Issues in literacy: A research perspective, 34th yearbook of the National Reading Conference* (pp. 1-13). Rochester, NY: The National Reading Conference, Inc.

Stahl, N. (2009). The doctorate as the framework and the future of literacy research and pedagogy. In K. M. Leander, D. W. Rowe, D. K. Dickinson, M. K. Hundley, R. T. Jiménez, & V. J. Risko (Eds.), *58th yearbook of the National Reading Conference*, (pp. 1-13). Oak Creek, WI: National Reading Conference, Inc.

Street, B. V. (1984). *Literacy in theory and practice*. New York, NY: Cambridge University Press.

Tierney, R. J. (1992). On matters of subjectivity, knowledge, claims, art, and ethics in literacy research. In C. K. Kinzer & D. J. Leu (Eds.), *Literacy research, theory, and practice: Views from many perspectives, 41st yearbook of the National Reading Conference*. (pp. 1-10). Chicago, IL: The National Reading Conference, Inc.

Tuinman, J. J. (1979). Beyond criterion-referenced measurement. In M. L. Kamil & A. J. Moe (Eds.), *Reading research: Studies and applications, 28th yearbook of the National Reading Conference*, (pp. 1-8). Milwaukee, WI: The National Reading Conference, Inc.

Wasserman, S., & Faust, K. (1994). *Social network analysis: Methods and applications*. New York, NY: Cambridge University Press.

'Invisible Teachers': Becoming Literate in a Wider Community

Eve Gregory
Goldsmiths, University of London, UK

First of all, I should like to express my thanks to Robert Jiménez, Chris Roper, and everyone here who has helped to organise my trip. Also thanks to my research team back at Goldsmiths, without whose help I could not be here talking today.

Like others who are here today, I find the title of our conference inspiring and have used part of it in the title of my paper. It can, of course, mean many different things to different people. To me, it relates well to those I refer to as 'invisible teachers' in children's lives. They are the families and communities I have worked with for over 2 decades in the poorer parts of London where I was, myself, born. By the end of my talk I hope to have unveiled some of the people I refer to as 'invisible teachers' in children's lives. But I'd like to start my talk with a story which, perhaps, epitomises the main points I'm trying to make tonight. The story centres around 2 items: the first is a Hungarian apple strudel and the second an English apple tart. Sorry, no American apple pie but certainly no insult meant! This story took place in England. You might think that both were equally delicious ways of using apples. It even looks likely that the strudel might be more complicated to make. But you might be wrong… Anyway, the story goes like this.

About 10 days ago I was teaching a master's course on multilingualism and multilingual literacy at my institution in central London. Of the 14 students, I have 7 Chinese, 1 Hungarian, 1 Moroccan Berber, 1 Colombian, 1 Peruvian, and 3 English students of all ages. We were discussing assumptions teachers make about the knowledge of the young children they teach and their families when our Hungarian student, mother of a nine-year-old boy, became highly agitated. She related her own story that had happened when her son came home from school last week: Coming from a Hungarian background, she is very keen and knowledgeable about cooking and is taking a pride in teaching her son to prepare all sorts of Hungarian dishes. She is particularly skilled at pastry-making. When her son's teacher told the class to go home and prepare an apple tart, she thought of her strudel and taught him how to prepare and spice the apples and how to make the pastry, which is complicated. You need to stretch the dough which contains eggs and sour cream as well as flour and margarine to make it paper thin before filling it with cooked apples, raisins, and nuts and pulling it carefully over the fruit mixture. Her son did all of this and proudly carried it all to school. To her surprise, her son returned later that day telling her that his strudel was 'rubbish.' His tart should have been a simple flour, margarine and water single layer pastry filled with apple puree from a pre-prepared jar. Now, most probably, the teacher hadn't meant to rubbish the attempts of my student's son, but it had severely humiliated the mother and shown her up before her child. Yet, as my student claimed, the strudel involved far superior and more complex skills than the simple tart the teacher wanted! But because his strudel was not a tart and these skills were outside the teacher's own experience, they remained simply invisible. The teacher hadn't realised what importance cooking might have as part of the community to which her student and his mother belonged. She may well have been so taken up with her targets and that things were either 'right' or 'wrong' that she had become blinkered in what counted as knowledge for children in her class.

You might be asking: What has all this to do with literacy?

My argument in this talk tonight will be that, like cake baking, literacy learning is about membership in a community. I'd like to show how literacy learning often takes place as much in families and communities as in schools and that these outside school literacies often involve as many or more direct **school** literacy skills but packaged in a different way. So I want to unpick how this intermeshing of becoming a community member and learning literacy skills takes place. Finally, I'd like to show how families in economically poor areas and whose roots are not in the UK do, indeed, have complex literacy skills through family and community literacies that often remain invisible to their schools and teachers.

I want, then, to ask: Who are the 'invisible teachers' in children's lives? Secondly: What types of family and community activities are we talking about and what skills and knowledge are young children learning within them? Finally, how does this learning actually take place?

Theoretically, I'm framing my interpretations using the established notion of ***prolepsis,*** but I want to both illustrate it and expand on our understanding of it in particular contexts.

So, what do I mean by prolepsis? By prolepsis, I mean a 'handing down' of knowledge and skills across generations and, crucially, what happens to both the knowledge and the people involved during this process. My interpretations draw particularly on the work of Gregory Bateson, who in his book 'Mind and Nature' (1979) says, 'We come to every situation with stories, patterns of events that are built into us. Our learning happens within the context of what important others did' as well as Michael Cole in 'Cultural Psychology: A Once and Future Discipline' (1996) who speaks of 'imagining the future from the past; the cultural mechanism that puts 'the end into the beginning.'

These authors sit within a wider sociocultural field of many who have contributed to the discipline: Vygotsky (1962, 1978), Rogoff (1990, 2003) Bakhtin (1986), Moll and his colleagues (1992), Cole (1996) and, of course, Shirley Brice-Heath (1983, 2012) to name just a few.

So my question tonight is: **What might prolepsis look like in 2011 as it takes place in multilingual and migrant urban communities?**

I want to begin to answer this question using 3 layers of data:

Layer One: Bringing the past to the present

Learning heritage literacies through community practices

Layer Two: Bringing the present to the past

Grandparents and young children exchanging literacy knowledge, skills, and practices

Layer Three: *Bringing the future to the present*

Siblings teaching school languages and literacy practices

My first layer then is: Bringing the past to the present: Learning heritage languages and literacies through faith communities. Faith is perhaps a very special part of community activities enabling newcomers to a country to gain a sense of belonging and one that not everyone feels able to participate in. Nevertheless, I use it here as an excellent example for all deeply felt community activities.

The examples I'm showing you are from a current 3-year project (we are now in our third year) on how children in 4 faith communities in London go about language and literacy learning, both in their faith settings, at worship and in faith classes; as well as with their families at home. 16 families from the Bangladeshi Muslim, Ghanaian Pentecostal, Polish Catholic, and Tamil Hindu faiths are participating in an in-depth ethnographic study. The children are aged between 3 and 12 and were either born in London or have lived there for most of their lives. So their English is good. The study is intergenerational, involving grandparents wherever possible (or older people over 50 who know the families). All 4 communities have large numbers in Britain and all have arrived in London since 1950.

So where are the communities? The communities are in the economically poorer parts of east and south-east of London (where migrants are literally in each area, not just the centres or outskirts). The map illustrates that the 2 groups closer to the centre (the Bangladeshi Muslim and the Tamil Hindu communities) came during the 1980s and 1990s, a little earlier than the Ghanaian Pentecostals and the Polish Catholics who came largely from the turn of the century.

Figure 1. Map of London and the Different Boroughs Showing the Four Research Sites

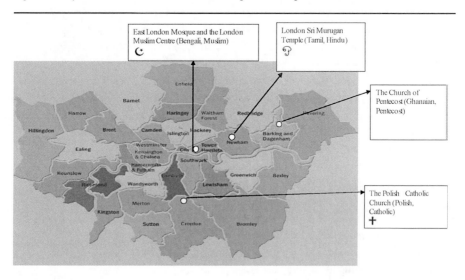

The families we are working with are representative of most others who are of the faith and you can see that the children spend considerable time either at church, temple, or mosque or at Sunday school or its equivalent, i.e., anything between 3 for the Pentecostal group and 9 or 10 hours per week for the Muslim children. (It was impossible to divide up actual worship and faith class for the Muslim children since they were really blended into one).

So, viewed within the frame of prolepsis, how are the children gaining a sense of membership, what **sense of values** and what **literacy skills** are they learning? I want to show how both aspects are passed down through one practice in each community.

I need to say that the photos and film clips you'll see were made by family members, parents or siblings, sometimes as young as 6, so you'll need to understand that they are not of professional quality.

Figure 2. Children's Attendance at Faith Settings (Classes and Services)

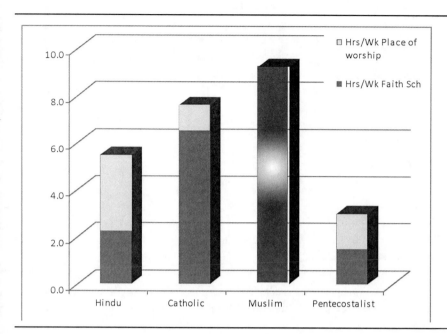

Below is 9-year-old Bema learning to read the Twi Bible. Although she understands and sometimes speaks Twi at home, this is the only written text in Twi that she knows. She reads Psalm 23, a very important text for Ghanaian Pentecostals:

The Holy Bible - English Psalm 23	Kyerɛw Kronkroŋ – Akuapem Twi Nnwom 23
1. The LORD is my shepherd, I shall not want.	Yehowa ne me hwɛfo, hwee renhia me.
2. He makes me to lie down in green pastures: he leads me beside the still waters.	☐ma meda wura fr☐mfr☐m adidibea, ogya me k☐ nsu a ɛho dwo ho.
3. He restores my soul: he leads me in the paths of righteousness for his name's sake.	Odwudwo me kra, ☐de me fa akwantrenee so, ne diŋ nti.
4. Yea, though I walk through the valley of the shadow of death, I will fear no evil: for you are with me; your rod and your staff, they comfort me.	Nso menam esum kabii boŋ no mu a, minsuro b☐ne bi: efisɛ wo ne me na ɛw☐ h☐, woabaa ne wo poma na ɛkyekye me werɛ.
5. You prepare a table before me in the presence of my enemies: you anoint my head with oil; my cup runs over.	Wotow me poŋ m'atamfo anim, wode ŋŋo f☐w me tirim, me kuruwa yɛ ma bu so.
6. Surely goodness and mercy shall follow me all the days of my life: and I will dwell in the house of the LORD for ever.	Yiye ne ad☐e nko na ebedi m'akyi me nkwa nna nyinaa, na mɛtena Yehowa fi daa.

Bema already knows the text in English, but she now learns to read and talk about it with her mother in Twi. Bema is learning a new language and script using very difficult lexis and grammatical structures. She also learns about symbolism and the notion of the Lord as a shepherd looking after his sheep. How does she do it? She partly memorises and imbibes the text after many readings. But at the same time, she is becoming a member of the faith community, performing and presenting the faith and discussing the meaning of the text for her everyday life and behaviour.

When Amoafi, researcher in this community, asked Bema about the meaning of this text for her life, she wrote down text as follows:

It means to me that my Lord is a living God

He always looks after me and my family

He's goodness and mercy shall follow us

And we will

Also follow he's word. (Bema, 2010)

The next excerpt you'll see in the video is 4-year-old Sumayah, who is learning to read the Quaida, the preparatory text before starting the Qur'an. What skills is she learning? Sumayah is learning the individual sounds of a new language (classical Arabic) and script, learning to blend them into words, learning careful intonation patterns, learning to pronounce words beautifully, learning one-to-one correspondence and right to left directionality. At the same time, she is becoming a valued member of a community, learning that she is reading to Allah, who listens to her efforts.

In the next video, we watch 9-year-old Adam, whose parents are Polish, from the Catholic faith community. Adam has memorised the Lord's prayer in Polish and recites it; he reads a very difficult text relating the Nativity in Polish, he performs it to his parents, he understands the text and its narrative as well as its significance. Watched over by his father and reciting with his mother, he is one of a large community of Polish Catholics in London. As well as being an altar boy and attending both church and Sunday school as well as other activities regularly, thus becoming a valued member of his community; he is a fluent bilingual and biliterate.

Finally, in this layer, we see how very young children, aged 3 or 4, learn to make their first letter, which is that of the name of the goddess Saraswati in Tamil. The letter is inscribed in rice. Symbolically, they learn the Tamil alphabet alongside the importance of literacy whilst being watched over by their family and the goddess.

So how does prolepsis take place through these faith communities? Both membership and knowledge are passed down through children imbibing texts through songs, dance, actions, use of artifacts, memorising, and learning the same practices over generations. They do, of course syncretise new faith practices such as using the computer, using English, etc. with the old, but these are rather grafted onto traditional practices rather than replacing them.

Layer Two of this lecture concerns *Bringing the present to the past: Grandparents and young children exchanging literacy knowledge, skills, and practices.*

What we are looking at here is an exchange of knowledge and skills; prolepsis as a two-way process whereby grandparents and young children teach and learn from each other. Of course, this happens in non-migrant communities, too—we are know that children are often more skilled in new technology than older people—but in migrant communities older people might be particularly vulnerable in terms of knowledge of the host language and cultural practices, etc.

In the video excerpt following, we see 4-year-old Anayah engaging in a computer game with her grandmother. Her grandmother has superior literacy skills and can read the text as well as count in English. Anayah, on the other hand, clearly has more colloquial English as well as confidence in handling the mouse on the computer. We typify this reciprocal or synergistic learning as a mutual vulnerability. The pair use a combination of English and Sylheti (a dialect of Bengali) to negotiate a counting up game and Anayah is anxious to show her gran how to use the mouse whilst giving her a little cuddle of reassurance as she hesitates.

Layer Three: Bringing the future to the present. A final part of the triangle as I describe it is the way in which siblings play what I think is a unique role in introducing and teaching school language and learning patterns to younger children.

In the next clip, Isha, aged 4, reads 'Dear Zoo' to her 4-month-old sister. She is being filmed by her 6-year-old brother. Isha can already read and understand some of the text, she turns pages appropriately, is aware of her audience, shows the illustrations, and can present and perform as her teacher does. She takes a 'teacher-like' approach and is able to say 'Stop making fun' (surely from her teacher). At the same time, she invents words she doesn't quite know: 'camelledon' for 'camel' using an Arabic intonation and accent, according to our researcher. Here is the text from the video:

1	Isha: He was too big
2	Isha: I sented him back
3	Isha: So the next
4	Isha: cc me
5	Isha: The next me
6	Husnara (Isha's mum): That says sent
7	Isha: They sent me (pauses)
-> 8	Isha: A giraffatoon!!
9	Isha: He was too tall
10	Isha: They sent him back
11	Isha: So they next me a...
12	Isha: He was too fierce!
13	Isha: His next
14	Isha: Him back
15	Isha: (self-corrects) Sent him back
16	Isha: So the next, they sent me
17	Isha: a (pauses)
-> 18	Isha: camelatoon!
19	Isha: (takes the book up to baby brother's face) Mwah!
20	Isha: He was too grumpy
21	Isha: He, I said
22	Isha: I sent him back
	[...]

(Isha, video-recording 15/09/2011)

The researcher, Halimun, goes on to say:

> 'It's fascinating how the baby just stares at Isha as she reads to him, it's almost like he wants to repeat after her. Isha really takes her role very seriously, she takes the book right up close to the baby's face so he can see and also learn at the same time.' (Halimun, researcher, 8/11/2011)

I'm now turning to an older 'teacher.' Eleven-year-old Wahida with her 8-year-old sibling Sayeeda. These are just two tiny snippets from her 'class' that went on for over one hour, covering maths, science, all types of literacy, including spelling and comprehension. The first snippet is from her choir. The children have already sung Alleleluyah and a Hindi song from a famous film. They now turn their attention to an English folk song 'There was a Tailor.' The lyrics are not too important, but note that the intonation, rhythm, and colloquialisms, 'Hi, diddle hum cum timi,' are all very Anglo Saxon, and the girls sing them as naturally as their Hindi song.

The second clip is much more serious business. The English curriculum now stresses quite structured teaching of English grammar including aspects such as 'homophones.' Wahida's lesson is an excellent example of Vygotsky's 'zone of proximal development' in that she knows exactly what her sister can do and stretches her just that little bit further. Siblings have always been important, but in migrant families they take on an extra role of introducing younger children to new languages and cultures in ways that their siblings often cannot. Their learning is synergistic in that both learn equally from each other—younger children from being taught and tested and older children from practising and explaining clearly in such ways that their younger siblings can understand. Clearly such familiarity with the host culture would be impossible for their parents, whose schooling was in Bangladesh.

Here is the text of the 'homophones' clip:

Wahida: Well done! Only two wrong. Now we're going to do homophones. Who knows what's a homophone is? No one? OK. I'll tell you one and then you're going to do some by yourselves. Like watch—one watch is your time watch, like what's the time, watch. And another watch is I'm watching you, I can see you. OK? So Sayeeda, you wrote some in your book, haven't you? Can you tell me some please. Sayeeda, can you only give me three please.

Sayeeda: Oh I have to give five.

Wahida: No, Sayeeda, we haven't got enough time. We've only another five minutes to assembly. And guess who's going to do assembly—Miss Kudija.

Sayeeda: OK.

Wahida: OK? So tell me one.

Sayeeda: Son is the opposite of daughter …

Wahida: Yeah

Sayeeda: and sun is … um … its shines on the sky so bright.

Wahida: Well done! That's one correct one. The next one?

Sayeeda: The cell means you go … to jail …in prison … you're going to prison and another sell means the selling money … they are giving money.

Wahida: The last one is ?

Sayeeda: Hear. Hear is you're hearing something… people are telling you something and here is come here, come.

Wahida: Well done! Now you can go to assembly. Sayeeda, line up in order. Otherwise you'll come back and do lines. So remember your order. OK? Well done, Sayeeda, you're in your correct order and Miss Kudija is going to take you down because I have to do some more things.

(Gregory, 2008: 90-91)

Finally, What direct literacy skills are being learned from all these families and communities?

To list just a few: bilingualism, oral, literacy and biliteracy skills, wide and difficult vocabulary, poetry, traditional songs from different cultures; phonics and grammar in 'spelling tests' and 'homophone practice' by siblings, memorisation, directionality, one-to-one correspondence, and fine motor control, etc.

I want to conclude by showing you a dance, performed by Bairavi, aged 4. I use Michael Cole's words to describe prolepsis as 'putting the end into the beginning' This dance is a mime to the lyrics of a song in Tamil to celebrate the life and character of Lord Krishna. It is filmed by Bairavi's brother and the audience is a group of 4-year-olds. It continues for at least 10 minutes. Bairavi learned to dance at 3. The dance shows the incipient literacy skills of a 4-year-old through membership in the faith practice of dance. We see fine motor control, multilingual understanding, narrative, symbolism, memory, close observation, listening, one-to-one correspondence, purpose, performance, and presentation to others. At the same time, woven through her skills is the culture of her community.

Thus we see how literacy practices are part of a thread holding generations of family members together, taught by a whole range of family and community members who impart a sense of values, membership, and belonging as strongly as direct literacy, and often multilingual literacy skills.

And so, what might distinguish the concept of prolepsis when occurring in the lives of migrant families? I suppose one important aspect is the importance of interaction or exchange (possibly we could refer to it as synergy) between generations rather than a more one-way process, as in families who have remained in the same country across generations. Another feature might be the conscious effort being made by the older generation to instil community knowledge, languages, and practices in the young. Overall, it is an area still ripe for research.

Finally, to return to the strudel and the tart: Of course, the English tart is just as important as the Hungarian strudel. But in order to teach about the tart as a teacher, one needs to recognise that strudels exist—and although one cannot be knowledgeable about everything, one needs to be interested in finding out. I hope to have shown in this talk that children often learn as many or even more complex language and literacy activities in family and community contexts as in school. I suppose it is up to us as researchers and ethnographers to uncover this knowledge and to work with teachers in recognising and valuing these skills.

Knowing how to make the tart is important, but just as important is the strudel and all the culture and history it represents.

REFERENCES

Bateson, G. (1979). *Mind and Nature.* London, England: Wildwood House.

Bakhtin, M. (1986). *Speech genres and other late essays.* Austin, TX: University of Texas Press.

Campbell, R. (1982). *Dear Zoo.* Middlesex: Puffin Books.

Cole, M. (1996). *Cultural psychology: A once and future discipline.* Cambridge, MA: Belknap Press of Harvard University.

Gregory, E. (2008). *Learning to read in a new language: Making sense of words and worlds.* London, England and New York, NY: Sage.

Gregory, E., & Williams, A. (2000). *City literacies: Learning to read across generations and cultures.* London, England: Routledge.

Gregory, E., Jessel, J., Kenner, C., Lytra, V., & Ruby, M. (2009-2013). *Becoming literate in faith settings: Language and literacy learning in the lives of new Londoners.* ESRC funded project RES - 062-23-1613

Heath, S. B. (1983). *Ways with Words: Language, life and work in communities and classrooms.* Cambridge, England: Cambridge University Press.

Heath, S. B. (2012). *Words at work and play. Three decades in family and community life.* Cambridge, England: Cambridge University Press.

Moll, L. C., Amanti, C., Neff, D., & Gonzalez, N. (1992) Funds of knowledge for teaching using a qualitative approach to connect homes and classrooms. *Theory into Practice. 31,* 132-141.

Rogoff, B. (1990). *Apprenticeship in Thinking. Cognitive development in social context.* New York, NY: Oxford University Press.

Rogoff, B. (2003). *The cultural nature of human development.* New York, NY: Oxford University Press.

Vygotsky, L. (1962). *Thought and Language.* Cambridge, MA: MIT Press.

Vygotsky, L. (1978). *Mind in society: The development of higher psychological processes.* Cambridge, MA: Harvard University Press.

From Code-Segregation to Code-Switching to Code-Meshing: Finding Deliverance from Deficit Thinking through Language Awareness and Performance

Juan C. Guerra

University of Washington at Seattle

BREAKING THE CHAINS: SWITCHIN' AND MESHIN' IN REAL TIME

Cuando empecé mi primer año de escuela en el sur de Tejas en 1956, todos los niños en mi clase eran mexicanos o mexicanos americanos. Ninguno de nosotros hablábamos ni siquiera una sola palabra de inglés. En esa época, la television estaba en su infancia y era algo desconocido entre personas pobres que apenas tenían dinero para mantenerse. Teníamos radios en nuestros hogares, pero como vivíamos por la frontera menos de treinta millas de la boca del Rio Grande, todas las estaciones que escuchaban nuestros padres tocaban música en español. En casa, en la comunidad, entre nosotros mismos, el español era el idioma que usábamos para comunicarnos y para interpreter el mundo conocido. En la escuela publica ubicada en nuestra comunidad, todo estaba al revés. El uso del español era completamente prohibido.

Para cuando llegamos a la junior high school, *bien conocíamos la realidad en cual existíamos. En casa hablabamos español* and at school we spoke English. *Y los dos idomas se mantenían segregados* just as we were kept segregated from *los gringos por una vía de ferro carril que dividía* the town in two. *Los gabachos* had their own communities and their own shopping establishments en *el* downtown *de la ciudad; nosotros vivíamos en nuestros barrios y teníamos nuestra plazita donde ibamos de compras.*

Para cuando llegamos a la high school, *la division linguistica entre el español y el inglés* collapsed *completamente y* we began to blend the two languages *en una forma desconocida*, in a way that surprised our parents y *a nuestros maestros*. Interestingly, *al mismo tiempo que nuestros padres aceptaron nuestra nueva forma de hablar*, albeit with some resistance, the public schools continued to prohibit *el uso del español y la combinación de los dos idiomas—el famoso espanglish. En casa y en la comunidad*, we artfully switched and meshed codes, borrowing from either language *lo que mejor nos servía para ser entendidos.*

But the situation was very different in school. Because we segregated ourselves from Anglo students in the public high school—or more to the point, were segregated from them by the racist system in place at the time—we thought we could speak our mother tongue among ourselves at school just as we did at home and in our community. But each time they caught us speaking Spanish, the teachers would take us to see the principal. His response to our so-called infraction? We would be paddled, kept for detention, or sent home with a note for our parents—that many of them couldn't read because it was in English—telling them we were not allowed to speak Spanish in school. And that is how they confused us, how they taught us that the clash between our languages and our cultures was going to create an identity problem that we would have to live with for the rest of our lives.

I wish I could tell you that the autoethnographic experience I just rendered bilingually is a relic of the past—a consequence of an unenlightened educational policy that long ago bit the dust here in the United States. Alas, I must confess, as every one of you already knows, that many children in this country today are still going through what I experienced more than 50 years ago as linguistic colonization. And matters are further complicated by the fact that children who speak or write a dialect other than Standard English face the same consequences. Why is that? And, what, if anything, can we do about it? That's the story I want to share with you this morning.

In my talk today, I want to examine three pedagogical approaches to language difference that we all have available to us as educators to teach language and literacy in our classrooms. Two of them—code-switching and code-meshing—are currently part of a hot debate in the field of composition studies about how we can best address the language and dialect differences that students bring with them to the classroom. The third—code-segregation—is one I'm introducing into the conversation in an effort to make sharper distinctions and overcome some of the confusion about whether or not, and if so, how all three of these approaches should be deployed.

My first task today is to unpack the three available approaches to the teaching of language and literacy—code-segregation, code-switching, and code-meshing—with the specific goal of demonstrating how they manifest themselves in our effort to address the educational needs of disenfranchised students. Because code-segregation is not now and has never been a tenable approach and because I don't believe that code-meshing in and of itself is better than code-switching, I conclude my talk by explaining why I believe our students should deploy both code-switching and code-meshing in the varied rhetorical and discursive circumstances they are likely to encounter in their personal, academic, civic, and professional lives. My ultimate goal is to propose an antidote to the deficit thinking that occurs whenever any one of these three approaches is presented as the singular answer to the challenges we face in the teaching and learning of language and literacy.

CODE-SEGREGATION: HOW THE PAST CONTINUES TO HAUNT US

What many of us living on the border between Texas and Mexico were put through as children in our public schools more than 50 years ago continues to be a problem. To this day, many of the children from my era and I carry the negative weight of our linguistic experiences in school with us—*una verguenza tremenda* that continues to color our perspective of the world-at-large. Despite the fact that we have all become proficient in English—some of us to the point of becoming professors of the language of power in the U.S.—and have figured out on our own why we were forbidden to speak our mother tongue in school, we still carry traces of the shame and self-doubt that our teachers—and especially the school systems that trained them to behave as they did—planted in us so many years ago. Today, because most children are no longer psychologically burdened by the pernicious ideology of code-segregation, that is, because they are no longer overtly told by their schools or their teachers that their first language or dialect is lacking in skill and grace, we consider ourselves enlightened. Many of us think we're avoiding the damage and harm that such a negative attitude among educators can visit on any child who speaks a language (or dialect) other than (Standard) English. But are we really?

Code-segregation, a term I coined in preparation for this talk because I didn't encounter it in the literature, is very familiar to any of us who grew up in pre-1960s America when racial segregation was the law of the land. As I noted in my opening remarks, we were not only constrained to live in different communities based on class, cultural, and linguistic differences; even when we all finally ended up sharing the same classrooms in middle school and high school, we were persuaded by the malevolent social, cultural, and political forces in play at the time to keep to ourselves and stay with our own kind. The personal narrative that began this talk describes the attitudes of a school system supported by a state mandate that utterly refused to acknowledge any value in the linguistic practices children in the housing project I grew up in directly across the street from our public elementary school brought to class. As the narrative makes clear, the ideology of code-segregation—founded on the basis of profound monolingual and monocultural values, beliefs, and practices—encourages total assimilation by children who speak a language other than English, as well as varieties of English that have little status in the broader society. It demands that children strictly and without deviation completely adapt to a hierarchical world that has been carefully construed to avoid dealing with difference.

At least until the pre-civil rights battles of the 1960s, most educators in the United States were generally persuaded to enforce nativist assumptions inherent in the widely accepted practice of code-segregation. Because Standard American English was (and continues to be) firmly ensconced in our educational system as the code of power—a way with words expected of all our students— most educators and the institutions that controlled their work had no qualms about disregarding the range of alternative codes children brought to school from their varied communities. In Texas, where I was born and raised, for example, the use of Spanish was banned from public schools for many years after I graduated. In his award-winning essay, "*Spanglish* as Literacy Tool: Toward an Understanding of the Potential Role of Spanish-English Code-Switching in the Development of Academic Literacy," Ramón Antonio Martínez (2010) informs us that English-Spanish code-switching is now "common in schools throughout the Los Angeles Unified School District . . . and [is] also becoming increasingly common in school districts nationwide, as demographic shifts and changing immigration patterns continue to significantly reshape the nation's linguistic landscape" (p. 125). I hope that's true, but I suspect that because of the on-going anti-immigrant hysteria and a deeply ingrained anti-Black racism in too many pockets of this country, immigrant children who code-switch between their native language and English, as well as African American children who code-switch between Ebonics and English, are still covertly and at times overtly discouraged from using both codes freely or simultaneously in the classroom.

The bilingual narrative with which I began my talk paints a bleak picture of what happens when schools forbid students from using all the linguistic and cultural resources at their beck and call. It is code-segregation at its worst. It is also a manifestation of what I refer to as *language-in-stasis*, language as an entity that has become fossilized over time into a standardized variant that everyone is expected to emulate. Whether it is patterned after an ideology that grows out of a belief that sharing one language contributes to patriotism and love of country, or out of a suspicion of what others may be saying in a language one doesn't understand, the end result is the same: a negation of any other means of communication that challenges the standard by which everyone in a community is supposed to be assessed. And despite the fact that code-segregation has never been and never will be a humane method for teaching language and literacy to disenfranchised students of all ages, it manages to persist in the insidious No-Child-Left-Behind tests and drills in our public schools which in turn reinforce the depressing realization that code-segregation will never be completely excised from our educational practices. Fortunately, continuing dissatisfaction with this language-in-stasis model has given birth to code-switching and code-meshing, two alternative models of what language is and how it works. To better understand how we can effectively combat code-segregation in our efforts to develop productive approaches to the teaching and learning of language and literacy, let's take a closer look at each of these two alternatives in turn.

CODE-SWITCHING: LINGUISTIC AND CULTURAL REPERTOIRES OF PRACTICE AS RESOURCES FOR TEACHING AND LEARNING

In a thought-provoking essay titled "Nah, We Straight": An Argument Against Code Switching," Vershawn Ashanti Young (2009) criticizes what he sees as "the prevailing definition of code-switching that language educators promote as the best practice for teaching speaking and writing to African American and other 'accent- and dialect-speakers' of English." In his view, it represents an approach that "advocates language substitution, the linguistic translation of Spanglish or AAE into standard English," and "characterizes the teaching of language conversion" (p. 50). To support his critique, he examines the work of Rebecca Wheeler and Rachel Swords who in a recent publication, *Code Switching: Teaching Standard English in Urban Classrooms*, promote a pedagogy based on the argument that Black English and standard English are equal, that is, that each is considered prestigious in its respective community, but then use the former only as transitional fodder for developing expertise in the latter. Young also criticizes prominent Black linguists John Russell Rickford and Geneva Smitherman, among others, for arguing that African American students must master both Black English and Standard English, then learn to deploy them appropriately. While his critique of Wheeler and Swords raises some valid concerns, I would argue that his critique of Rickford and Smitherman is misplaced because he conflates what I earlier described as code-segregation with code-switching, the latter of which, in contrast to his critique, can be construed as a powerful approach to addressing the weighty problems we all currently confront in our efforts to develop pedagogical support for the needs of disenfranchised students.

As far as I'm concerned, anyone who advocates dismissing the linguistic and cultural repertories of practice that students bring with them to the classroom as soon as they have served a transitional purpose is engaging in a modern day form of code-segregation. To dismiss the role of race, class, or gender as unimportant variables in the teaching and learning of language and literacy is to harken back to the day when Standard English was assumed to be the only code worth learning. I do, however, part ways with Young when he refuses to acknowledge the critical distinctions that progressive scholars make when they argue that we must expand the repertoires of practice students bring with them to the classroom and encourage them to deploy their full arsenal tactically, strategically, and appropriately as they navigate the multiplicity of linguistic and cultural contexts they encounter in the course of their lives. In so doing, these students are acknowledging their awareness of the role that hierarchical power plays in the choices they are called on to make. Moreover, I simply cannot ignore the critical contributions that some of the most highly acclaimed theorists, scholars, and researchers in the field have made to our understanding of how best to use the learning incomes disenfranchised students bring with them to the classroom to develop academic literacy, an indispensable tool in our society for anyone who wishes to successfully pursue a postsecondary education.

In K-12 settings, an authentic commitment to a form of code-switching that advances the cause of social justice has manifested itself in the development of an array of carefully researched pedagogical approaches that value and use the languages and dialects students bring with them to the classroom. Of the many researchers who have contributed to this work, I will focus on Carol Lee (2007) and Kris Gutiérrez (2008) this afternoon because their strategies are assiduously crafted and have been widely adopted by progressive scholars in the field. In her research, Lee has developed a *cultural modeling framework* that demonstrates how "powerful connections between African American students' everyday language practices and the skills required to interpret canonical literary texts . . . can be effectively leveraged in the service of academic learning" (Martínez, p. 127). Grounded in ethnographic research in an inner city high school setting, Lee has used her work on the African American rhetorical practice of signifying in particular to develop an alternative to theories informed by what she describes as structural differences, cultural deficits, and cultural mismatches that ignore the value inherent in the learning incomes students bring with them to school. Gutiérrez, on the other hand, has studied the linguistic and cultural repertoires that Latino and Latina students bring with them as Spanish and English bilinguals in the context of what she calls the Third Space, "a transformative space where the potential for an expanded form of learning and the development of new knowledge are heightened" (p. 152). In her work, Gutiérrez provides a well-travelled and thought-out map for how we can help what she calls nondominant and I call disenfranchised students acquire repertoires of practice, that is, "both vertical and horizontal forms of expertise . . . [that include] not only what students learn in formal learning environments such as schools, but also what they learn by participating in a range of practices outside of school" (p. 149). In her carefully construed ecological approach, learning is organized in such ways that conversation, dialogue, and examination of contradictions are privileged across learning activities with varied participation structures: tutorials, comprehension circles, writing conferences, *teatro*, minilectures, and whole-class discussions (p. 154).

Unfortunately, code-switching has manifested itself in more conservative terms in first-year writing programs and Writing Across the Curriculum (WAC) settings, primarily because its proponents have assumed that students in higher education need to be initiated into more rigorous and demanding English Only academic contexts. While proponents of this transitional approach have noted the importance of valuing the cultural and linguistic repertoires students bring to the classroom, until very recently, the inclination has been to focus on the demystification of academic language to make it easier for students to adapt to an array of academic discourses that grant little opportunity for the integration of the linguistic practices or the lived experiences students bring with them. This approach continues to be grounded in work that assumes disenfranchised students are being asked to learn a new dialect and new discourse conventions in the process of acquiring "a whole new world view" (Bizzell, 1986, p. 297). As David Bartholomae (1985) put it when this perspective first emerged: Any student entering the academy "has to learn to speak our languages, to speak as we do, to try on the peculiar ways of knowing, selecting, evaluating, reporting, concluding, and arguing that define . . . the discourses of our community" (p. 134). WAC's almost exclusive devotion to academic discourse at the expense of the linguistic and cultural repertoires students bring with them to the classroom has been no less stringent. In all these instances, it has been assumed that to be successful, students must learn how to code-switch from their home languages and dialects to academic discourse and in the process leave the linguistic and cultural repertoires they bring with them at the door.

Along a continuum with code-segregation at one end and code-switching at the other, there's no question that the pedagogical practices used in college and university settings are much closer to the former than the practices invoked in K-12 settings. I would argue that this occurs because of the different institutional contexts and time constraints that inform each set of practices. It is also true that like code-segregation, code-switching asks us to adapt to the world. There's no way around that. Educators who support code-switching certainly acknowledge the importance of having students develop a critical meta-awareness of how language works in varied contexts. But where the ideology that informs code-segregation is based on a profound fear of change to the point of paralyzing language, that is, freezing it in place as some idealized standard language performance, code-switching acknowledges that change is inevitable in this world and purports that the best option available to our students is for them to figure out how to use their "full quiver" of cultural, linguistic, and semiotic resources to address what Cynthia Selfe (2009) describes as the "wickedly complex communicative tasks" that we all face in an increasingly "challenging and difficult world" (p. 645). Unlike the code-switching promoted by such teachers and scholars as Wheeler and Swords, the brand of code-switching I advocate is a manifestation of what I call *individuals-in-motion* because it is a tool that our students can use nimbly, tactically, and self-reflectively rather than only intuitively to navigate and negotiate the provisional pedagogical spaces they inhabit in our schools, universities, and communities as they move *from* one space to another and *within* varied spaces as well.

CODE-MESHING: FROM A POLICY OF TOLERANCE TO A POLICY OF PROMOTION

In the back cover to their edited collection titled *Code-Meshing as World Englishes: Pedagogy, Policy and Performance*, Vershawn Ashanti Young and Aja Martínez (2011) posit what they see as the most striking difference between code-switching and code-meshing:

> Although linguists have traditionally viewed code-switching as the simultaneous use of two language varieties in a single context, scholars and teachers of English have appropriated the term to argue for teaching minority students to monitor their languages and dialects according to context. For advocates of code-switching, teaching students to distinguish between 'home language' and 'school language' offers a solution to the tug-of-war between standard and non-standard Englishes. . . . The original essays in this collection offer various perspectives on why code-meshing—blending minoritized dialects and world Englishes with Standard English—is a better pedagogical alternative than code-switching in the teaching of reading, writing, listening, speaking, and visually representing to diverse learners. (np)

In so describing them, Young and Martínez set up a discrete binary that renders invisible an even more important fact: The progressive proponents of code-switching whose work I described in the preceding section freely encourage disenfranchised students to engage in practices that involve the meshing of codes at the very same time that they make strategic use of the codes they bring with them to the classroom, along with the ones they learn in class, to gain access to the language of power.

According to Young (2009), the ideology behind code-meshing "holds that peoples' so-called 'nonstandard' dialects are already fully compatible with standard English. Code meshing secures their right to represent that meshing in all forms and venues where they communicate" (p. 62). Moreover, "while also acknowledging standard principles for communication," code-meshing "encourages speakers and writers to fuse the standard with native speech habits, to color their writing with what they bring from home" (pp. 64-65). A. Suresh Canagarajah (2006), who coined the term code-meshing, reinforces Young's position by arguing that advocates of code-switching stratify codes by limiting the use of dialect to literary texts, discoursal features, informal classroom interactions, speaking, the home, and local communication, while Standard English is exclusively permitted in "serious" texts, grammar, formal production, writing, school, and international communication (p. 594). Canagarajah further surmises that NCTE's Resolution on Students' Right to their Own Language—which code-meshing proponents believe has often been used as a rationale for code-switching—"is interpreted as a policy of tolerance (i.e., permitting nonvalorized codes to survive in less-prestigious contexts), not promotion (i.e., making active use of these vernaculars or developing them for serious purposes)" (p. 596). Despite his affinity for code-meshing, Canagarajah at times still sounds like an advocate for code-switching as progressive scholars conceptualize it: "Rather than developing mastery in a single 'target language,'" he contends, students should strive for competence in a repertoire of codes and discourses. Rather than simply *joining* a speech community, students should learn to *shuttle* between communities in contextually relevant ways" (pp. 595-596).

While Canagarajah (2006), along with Young and Martínez (2011), calls for multidialectalism rather than monodialectalism in the formal writing of all students, a number of scholars in composition studies have taken the matter a step further and are calling for multilingualism rather than monolingualism in the first-year writing classroom. This position is best exemplified by Bruce Horner, Min-Zhan Lu, Jacqueline Jones Royster, and John Trimbur's (2011) astute and paradigm-shifting essay titled "Language Difference in Writing: Toward a Translingual Approach." Building on a number of arguments raised in recent years by scholars in composition studies, Horner et al.'s call-to-action is grounded in a critique of a traditional approach to writing, what I earlier described as code-segregation, which takes as the norm "a linguistically homogeneous situation: one where writers, speakers, and readers are expected to use Standard English or Edited American English— imagined ideally as uniform—to the exclusion of other languages and language variations" (p. 303). In their view, the traditional approach attempts to "eradicate difference in the name of achieving correctness, defined as writers' conformity with a putatively uniform, universal set of notational and syntactic conventions" (p. 306). They are also critical of a second type of response, which Young and Canagarajah characterize as code-switching, that "has sought to distance itself from the eradicationist approach [by] acknowledging differences in language use; codifying these; and granting individuals a right to them" (p. 307). This response, they argue, has represented itself as more tolerant and accommodating than the first, but still proves itself inadequate "because it assumes that each codified set of language practices is appropriate only to a specific, discrete, assigned social sphere: 'home' language, 'street' language, 'academic' language, 'business' language, 'written' language (aka the "grapholect"), and so on" (p. 307). When all is said and done, the eradicationist and the accommodationist approaches they describe fall short because "these kinds of responses are aligned with the ideology of monolingualism by treating languages and language practices as discrete, uniform, and stable" (p. 307).

In their view, the only viable alternative to these failed responses to language difference is what they call a translingual approach, one that I consider representative of what I call *languages-in-motion* because it takes "the variety, fluidity, intermingling, and changeability of languages as statistically demonstrable norms around the globe" (p. 305). The translingual approach also confronts "the practice of invoking standards not to improve communication and assist language learners, but to exclude voices and perspectives at odds with those in power. It treats standardized rules as historical codifications of language that inevitably change through dynamic processes of use. [It] proclaims that writers can, do, and must negotiate standardized rules in light of the contexts of specific instances of writing" (p. 305). As someone who developed and taught what may well have been one of—if not the first—Spanish/English bilingual first-year writing course at a major research university in this country some 35 years ago, there is certainly nothing in their description of a translingual approach with which I would disagree. It is, as a matter of fact, one that the proponents of a progressive form of code-switching strongly endorse. Unfortunately, like Young and Martínez (2011), Horner et al. (2011) define code-switching in rigid and problematic terms that completely ignore the work of countless progressive scholars who refuse to dichotomize code-switching and code-meshing because their ultimate goal is to support the future-oriented desires of students who see value in academic, as well as in a range of other, literacies. For reasons that I will describe in the final section, I must respectfully disagree with my esteemed colleagues' conflation of code-segregation and code-switching. It is, as far as I am concerned, an untenable representation that emerges from an unwillingness to see the fluidity that many other scholars and I see between progressive representations of code-switching and code-meshing.

BEYOND FALSE DICHOTOMIES, OR, WHY STUDENTS NEED A FULL QUIVER OF LINGUISTIC AND SEMIOTIC RESOURCES

We have arrived, finally and inevitably, at the decisive moment when the genre I am working in requires that I take a stand and declare my allegiance to some set of truths. Over the course of my presentation, I have provided several hints about where I stand in this regard, so my closing remarks will not come as a complete surprise. Still, I am required by the socio-critical literacy context in which I find myself—a plenary address at a longstanding and well-respected conference—to state in clear and unambiguous terms why I have decided to take the stand that I have. In many ways, the easy way out for me would have been to lock myself into the "narrative of progress" (Harris, 1997, p. 55) that I have just described—the pristine movement from code-segregation to code-switching to code-meshing—and readily agree with the sizeable number of esteemed colleagues who have declared with an impressive degree of certainty and finality that code-meshing is the only game in town. As much as I want to make it easy on myself by nodding my head and saying yes, that code-meshing is the one and only viable approach to language difference, my own lived and linguistic experiences as someone who was born in a labor camp, grew up in a monolingual Spanish home in a housing project, and still managed to sneak into the ivory tower—along with my 38 years as a writing teacher, many of them spent in classrooms with some of the most underprepared students Chicago's inner-city communities produced in the 1970s and 1980s—have persuaded me that code-switching *and* code-meshing, rather than code-meshing alone, provide the best response at our disposal to make a difference in the lives of disenfranchised students. So why is it that my esteemed colleagues and I have what seem like diametrically opposed positions? In effect, I think it's because their discussion of the various responses to language difference frames it as a policy issue while I frame it as a matter of practice.

Let's take a look at my opening remarks—the bilingually rendered autoethnographic experience with which I began today's presentation—and use that narrative as a case study to explain what I see as the difference between policy and practice in this case. As you may recall, the first paragraph is written entirely in monolingual Spanish and represents my first language, the one that I spoke exclusively until I walked into my first grade classroom and our teacher Mrs. Rosales began to teach us English. The language of that first paragraph I speak today better than I write it because it's my mother tongue, but also because I never received any formal literacy training in it. The second and third paragraphs in the narrative illustrate the original definition of code-switching—what occurs when two languages are used simultaneously to communicate with an audience. In the context of the various responses to language difference that I outlined today, these paragraphs represent code-meshing at its best. You get to mesh codes in creative and productive ways that represent the broad range of linguistic resources available to you. The fourth and final paragraph illustrates the act of code-switching that I am still engaged in as I speak these words to you, at this very moment, right now, in real time. It's the response I felt compelled to call on to make sure I would have a good chance of communicating my ideas with the largest number of you.

Let's speculate for a moment. What if I had decided to speak in monolingual Spanish from the moment I begin my talk until its very end? While a handful of you might have praised me as the ultimate rebel for taking a definitive stance against the straight-jacketing constraints of the Standard and English Only academic discourse U.S. scholars still traffic in these days, a large number of you would have been disappointed because I would not have met your expectations. On the other hand, if I had kept code-meshing throughout my talk the way I did in the two middle paragraphs of my opening narrative, all of you would have managed to pick up at least half of what I said, but those of you with limited proficiency in Spanish would have had difficulty following the logic of my inquiry because large chunks of information would have been inaccessible. As a consequence, we would have suffered a different kind of communication breakdown. In the end, I obviously decided to use what I will call *academic conference English* for the rest of this talk because our ultimate goal as rhetoricians is always to communicate as effectively as possible with whatever audience we have elected to address. That choice, to me, is what code-switching is all about. We read our audience, and we perform in a way that reflects the dynamic tension between a clueless conformity and a relentless rebellion. It's never perfect, but it works. And, again, yes, I had other choices. As I said a moment ago, I could've given my whole presentation in monolingual Spanish or in meshed Spanish and English, but I felt compelled to code-switch to academic conference English because I wanted to make sure that the largest number of you would get as much as possible out of my talk. The policy that proponents of code-meshing describe is one I support wholeheartedly, but I chose to enact the response I did because in practice, I felt it was my best choice under the prevailing circumstances.

One thing I think we all have to keep in mind when we engage in debates about the terminology we use to represent our ideas is that the terms we use to discuss issues like language difference—code-segregation, code-switching, and code-meshing—are metaphors rather than transparent descriptors of reality. In keeping with feminist philosopher Rosi Braidotti (1994), I would take it one step further and argue that these terms are actually figurations—what she describes as politically informed accounts of alternative subjectivities designed to help us "learn to think differently about the subject, invent new frameworks, new images, new modes of thought" (p. 2). In short, we need different concepts to meet different needs. In that sense, for me, the key difference between code-switching and code-meshing is reflected in the vivid patterns one hears echoed in George Bernard Shaw's (1957) famous observation: "The reasonable man adapts to the world; the unreasonable one persists in trying to adapt the world to himself" (260). Putting aside its dated and problematic use of gendered language, what Shaw says certainly seems to ring true. We either accept the world as it is and do our best to self-consciously adapt to it by enacting code-switching in more productive ways than code-segregation would ever allow us to do, or we challenge it by embracing code-meshing and demand that the world adapt to us.

So, when all is said and done, what do code-switching and code-meshing, as I have described them, bring to the table? What do they allow our students to do as they confront a litany of social, cultural, linguistic and political challenges circulating out there in the world at large? I would argue that these two responses provide our students with a broader range of rhetorical choices that respond to their future-oriented goals and the array of contexts in which those goals will be enacted. Together, they do what Michelle Hall Kells (2007) argues the Writing Across Communities approach to the teaching of writing that she and her colleagues at the University of New Mexico instituted 7 years ago is designed to do: Invite students to consider how an understanding of cultural diversity enhances their ability to write *appropriately* (with an awareness of different discourse conventions), *productively* (to achieve their desired aims), *ethically* (to remain attuned to the communities they serve), *critically* (to learn to engage in inquiry and discovery, and *responsively* (to act responsibly as they negotiate the tensions caused by the exercise of authority) (p. 103). As I noted earlier, they also provide our students with what Selfe (2009) calls a full quiver of the cultural, linguistic, and semiotic resources they need to respond to the "wickedly complex communicative tasks" that we all face in an increasingly "challenging and difficult world" (p. 645).

As scholars and educators interested in creating conditions in our classrooms where our students can pick up the tools they need to navigate and negotiate the troubled waters of their lived and linguistic existence, we must first help our students develop a self-reflective and critical meta-awareness of how language works. While they should feel at home with their growing repertoire of linguistic and cultural practices, they also need to be able to enact them with some degree of dexterity. In Anis Bawarshi's (2003) words, we need "to teach our students how to become rhetorically astute and agile, how in other words, to . . . become more effective and critical 'readers' of the sites of action (i.e., rhetorical and social scenes)" (p. 165) within which—to borrow Young and Martínez's words—reading, writing, listening, speaking, and visually representing take place. Our students must also learn how to adapt themselves to each rhetorical or discursive situation they encounter by calling on whatever languages or varieties they deem most productive, knowing always that it is their responsibility to resist and respond to the constraining limitations imposed by each rhetorical or discursive situation to make themselves fully heard. In short, it is not up to us as educators to tell our students how they should deploy their linguistic and semiotic resources; it is up to each of them to decide which of those resources they wish to invoke based on the rhetorical or discursive circumstances they're facing. It is for this reason that I want to encourage us all to provide our students with the tools they need to make instantaneous decisions about how best to respond to any rhetorical or discursive situation they are likely to face. False dichotomies that cleave their options by framing them as either/or rather than both/and are more likely to impede them and grant the decision-making power to us rather than keeping it where it belongs—in our students' hands.

REFERENCES

Bartholmae, D. (1985). Inventing the university. In M. Rose (Ed.), *When a writer can't write: Studies in writer's block and other composing problems* (pp. 134-165). New York, NY: Guilford.

Bawarshi, A. (2003). *Genre and the invention of the writer: Reconsidering the place of invention in composition*. Logan, UT: Utah State University Press.

Bizzell, P. (1986). What happens when basic writers come to college? *College Composition and Communication, 37*, 294-301.

Braidotti, R. (1994). *Nomadic subjects*. New York, NY: Cambridge University Press.

Canagarajah, A. S. (2006). The place of world Englishes in composition: Pluralization continued. *College Composition and Communication, 57*, 586-619.

Gutiérrez, K. (2008). Developing a sociocritical literacy in the third space. *Reading Research Quarterly, 43*(2), 148-164.

Harris, J. (1997). *A teaching subject*. Upper Saddle River, NJ: Prentice Hall.

Horner, B., Lu, M. Z., Royster, J. J., & Trimbur, J. (2011). Language difference in writing: Toward a translingual approach. *College English, 73*, 303-321.

Kells, M. H. (2007). Writing across communities: Deliberation and the discursive possibilities of WAC. *Reflections, 11*(1), 87-108.

Lee, C. D. (2007). *Culture, literacy, and learning: Taking bloom in the midst of the whirlwind*. New York, NY: Teachers College Press.

Martínez, R. A. (2010). Spanglish as literacy tool: Toward an understanding of the potential role of Spanish-English code-switching in the development of academic literacy. *Research in the Teaching of English, 45*(2), 124-149.

Selfe, C. L. (2009). The movement of air, the breath of meaning: Aurality and multimodal composing. *College Composition and Communication, 60*, 616-663.

Shaw, G. B. (1957). *Man and superman: A comedy and a philosophy*. New York, NY: Penguin.

Wheeler, R. S., & Swords, R. (2006). *Code-switching: Teaching standard English in urban classrooms*. Urbana, IL: National Council of Teachers of English.

Young, V. A. (2009). Nah, we straight: An argument against code switching. *JAC, 29*(1-2), 49-76.

Young, V. A., & Martínez, A. Y.. (2011). *Code-meshing as world English: Pedagogy, policy and performance*. Urbana, IL: National Council of Teachers of English.

Becoming an Academic: Challenges, Guidance, Opportunities, Passion

Lesley Mandel Morrow
Rutgers University

Challenge calls for an individual to make a distinct determination or dedication to a cause. Impact, in reaction to the challenge, is producing change as a result of an event or an idea. For the purposes of this paper, an individual who desires to pursue the challenge of becoming an academic needs to have a passion to do so. When faced with a challenge one needs to seek guidance, look for opportunities, and be willing to take risks. Ultimately, an academic hopes to generate substantial, significant, and original knowledge as a result of their research. This new knowledge should have an impact when put into practice in a classroom.

In this paper I will describe the road I traveled as an academic, which included challenges, risks, opportunities, and those who helped along the way. To do this I will discuss:

- My early years as a classroom teacher,
- My move to academia.
- My research and how it evolved.
- My thoughts about the future.

My career was not planned, but opportunities arose and I always jumped on board to see what might happen. Along the way I worked hard and was passionate about what I was doing. I sought help when I needed it and I am grateful to those who provided guidance. I took some risks, but my strong desire to make early childhood instruction more relevant, meaningful, and explicit for young children made the risks worthwhile. Classroom teaching was the beginning of my life as a researcher. I researched the questions that continued to surface initially in the classroom, and later, from studies I conducted.

Careers evolve in many ways and my career has been the compass of where life was taking me. A prescription is not possible; however, viewing someone else's experience could be helpful to others. At the time I began my working life, it was very different for women than it is now. Our work was often thought of as temporary to support oneself until married, or to help one's husband build his career.

MY YEARS AS A CLASSROOM TEACHER

I began teaching in the primary grades after college and my initial goal was to help my husband through medical school. Teaching became my passion and I wanted to learn more about instruction, so I pursued a master's degree while teaching during the day. I realized that the master's taught me more, but I wanted to know specifically about reading instruction, so I furthered my education. Before I knew it I had a second master's that included both the reading specialist certification and a supervisor's certification. I took a few more courses to be certified as a principal.

After four years of teaching in one public school district, an opportunity arose where I secured a position at William Paterson University in a non-graded primary classroom at their elementary laboratory school on campus. In this setting, I taught children and also worked with college students in the teacher education program. This position allowed students to come to my room to observe or to watch me teach via closed circuit television. I was also invited to classes to give lectures. At the same time, I worked part time as a reading specialist with struggling readers at New York University's Reading Clinic.

When my husband was drafted to serve in Vietnam for a year, my career path was impacted. For his second year of service he was stationed in California, so I was able to join him. I needed to secure a position there. Subsequently I applied for several positions: a classroom teacher, a reading specialist, and a college instructor. Although I was offered all three, I decided to teach at Chapman College in Orange, California. It was an opportunity to try something new and I enjoyed my experience immensely. After my husband finished the year of duty, we moved back East so he could continue his medical residency. Upon my return I was offered a position at St. John's University in Queens, New York. I was told to achieve tenure, I would need a doctorate degree. I figured why not, and so I began a PhD program in Curriculum and Supervision at Fordham University at Lincoln Center. I taught at St. John's for three years while I worked on my doctorate at night. My life changed yet again once my husband completed his residency and was going into medical practice, and we were about to have a baby. We were moving to central New Jersey, which would make the commute to St. John's very difficult. Therefore, I resigned from my position at that university and decided to take care of our new little girl, and complete my dissertation since I was at this stage in the process. After completing the degree and a lot of job searching, I was able to secure a position at Rutgers University.

MOVING INTO ACADEMIA

There were new challenges to consider. Although I had a rigorous PhD experience, it had not prepared me for a Tier 1 Research University. My experience with higher education was in New Jersey's state colleges, and two small private universities. I was not aware of the rules for tenure at a Tier 1 research institution. I needed to publish about 12 research articles in the next five years where I was the first author or the only author. Most had to be published in top-tier-referred journals. I needed to secure a grant, present at conferences, and become known for an area of specialization that I would carve out for myself during this time.

There were many things I needed to learn about doing research and publishing that they did not teach in graduate school. They were:

- Be sure that there is a school district that will allow you to do the research you want to do. Many were not willing to deal with the interruptions that research can cause. If you are dealing with topics that will benefit their children, schools are more likely to allow you to do research.
- Be sure you can afford to carry out the research even if you have a grant. Research is expensive; you need materials, technology equipment, help with data analysis, etc.
- Will your research be sustainable after you leave, or will teachers just go back to what they did before you came?

- Can the research be scaled up? That is, did the school district find your work important enough to provide the resources to continue after you leave? Is it easy enough to put it into practice so that it will survive without you?
- Be aware of the many obstacles along the way such as:
  - o Teachers in control groups seem to find out the treatment. Even though you told them you would provide them with materials and training when the study was over, they still put the treatment into practice during the study since they wanted their children to look good.
  - o Students in the study are absent on testing days or move in the middle of the study.
  - o There is a snow storm on the posttest day in 20 schools which all end up being closed due to a snow day, therefore you must reschedule.
  - o There is a fire drill during pretesting

Once your research is done and before you begin to write for publication, read all the directions for authors provided, study the journals in your field, and note their writing style and the length of their articles. If your article is rejected, read the reviews and make changes you believe it needs, then send it immediately to another journal. Do not allow anything you think is good stay in the drawer. If you cannot publish on the national level, then try to publish what you have in a state journal. There are many outlets today such as online journals, newsletters, and websites that can be considered publications, as long as they are reputable. Make the most of the data you collect. If you have done a large study with many parts, divide it into multiple, smaller studies with only some of the data for different outlets. Then publish the entire study in the best journal you can find for your area of expertise. The same study you just published can be written for a journal of practice that is recognized as a quality outlet with a different purpose. A study can also be written in another style as a chapter in an edited book.

Be aware of the importance of presenting at local, state, and national conferences so people in your field get to know you and your work. It is also a way to connect with others and do collaborative investigations. Volunteer for committees in professional organizations on topics of your choice. Often as a result, a new partnership may emerge or you might receive an invitation to speak at another university about your research.

Prior to obtaining tenure, try for some small grants offered by a foundation or your university that will not take too much time. Since it is difficult to acquire a grant, don't spend an enormous amount of time preparing a proposal with only a minimal chance of reward or benefit. If, however, you can secure a small grant that wasn't too time consuming to write, it certainly can help with your research. Once you receive tenure you can work to pursue a large federal grant with a group of people working together with an idea that can really make a difference.

A RESEARCH AGENDA

Literacy-rich environments create an interest in reading and writing and increase independent reading and writing. It was not difficult for me to find an area of interest. From my background in teaching, I had become passionate about the importance of creating literacy-rich environments in classrooms to motivate young children's interest in reading and writing. I also had a strong concern about the organization and management of early childhood programs in which literacy strategies could be effectively learned. As a reading specialist and an early childhood educator, I combined the two areas into a program of research.

My research has been primarily field-based. Most of my studies can be classified as ecologically sound applied instructional research with strong implications for classroom practice. I used quantitative designs including descriptive analyses, correlational studies, and investigations with experimental and control groups. Models of early childhood education adapted from the theoretical and philosophical ideas of Froebel, Montessori, Dewey, Piaget, and Vygotsky have influenced my work by offering a rationale and heightened sense of significance for the areas I have pursued. My research is grounded in a theoretical base, which suggests children need to have new strategies modeled for them in an explicit manner and need to interact with more literate others who provide additional support by scaffolding and giving feedback for their thoughts. This helps the child to complete a task they couldn't do on their own. When the child begins to internalize the new information and is close to being able to do it alone—Vygotsky calls this the "Zone of Proximal Development"—it is important for the person who is doing the scaffolding to step back and allow the child to practice and perform the new skill independently.

My work has taken place in public schools from Prekindergarten through 4th grades in mostly urban districts with children from low socio-economic backgrounds who are considered "at risk." My early research was designed to create literacy-rich environments to motivate interest in reading and writing. The work describes:

- Creating literacy-rich environments to motivate reading and writing.
- Interventions into classroom practice to determine if children's interest in and voluntary participation in reading and writing could be increased.
- Types of literacy activities that occur when reading and writing materials are purposefully embedded into dramatic play settings.

Although there is widespread agreement about the importance and benefits of encouraging students to develop lifelong reading habits, substantial numbers of children apparently choose not to read either for pleasure or for information. Daniel Boorstin, who was Librarian of Congress, said that alliterates (individuals who can read but choose not to read) constitute as much of a threat as illiterates to a democratic tradition built on reading. "Voluntary reading or lack of it, will determine the extent of self-improvement and enlightenment, the ability to share wisdom and our capacity for self-government" (Boorstin, "Letters of Transmittal," in Books in our future: A report from the Librarian of Congress to the Congress. Washington, DC: Joint Committee on the Library, 1984.)

In the book, *Becoming a Nation of Readers*, Richard Anderson states, "America can become a nation of readers when the verified practices of the best teachers in the best schools can be enforced through the country." One of the major recommendations made in the report aimed toward reaching this goal was to allow children to independently read in settings where teachers maintain well-stocked libraries (National Institute of Education, Become a Nation of Readers, Washington, D.C., 1985).

Most of the professional literature in the area of creating literacy-rich environments to motivate interest in reading and writing, prior to my work, consisted primarily of anecdotal reports. My early research found that most early childhood classrooms did not include literacy centers, nor did they provide activities to motivate reading and writing. It has now become general practice to do so and can be seen in primary classrooms throughout the country. This is due, in part, to my publications in this area. I was fortunate to have my work accepted into top-tier research journals since little research was available at the time about this topic. I published in scholarly journals and interpreted the findings in practical journals that focused on classroom practice, in books and book chapters. Titles of some of these studies are:

- The effect of physical design changes and teachers' activities on children's use of literature. *Elementary School Journal* (1982);
- Relationships between literature programs, library corner designs, and children's use of literature. *Journal of Educational Research* (1982);
- Home and school correlates of early interest in literature in the *Journal of Educational Research* (1983);
- Encouraging voluntary reading: The impact of a literature program on children's use of library centers. *Reading Research Quarterly* (1986);
- Literature-Based Instruction, *Handbook on Reading Research Volume III*, (2000)
- Literature-Based Instruction in the Early Years, in *Handbook of Research in Early Literacy* (2002).

A completed study would give me the idea for the next one. A correlational study gave me the information to try a small experimental design, which then allowed me to try a more complex, larger endeavor in a similar area. The research seemed to gain strength the more I published about the same topic while adding new dimensions each time. Some work dealing with families became part of my investigations but with similar themes; for example: A family literacy program Connecting School and Home: Effects on Attitude, Motivation, and Literacy Achievement, in *Journal of Educational Psychology* (1997). This research combined much of what I had studied in previous work with the inclusion of a parent component.

In this study, parents were to work with their children at home to motivate them to want to read and write voluntarily for pleasure and for information. I also wanted children to look at literacy as a social activity to engage with family members as well as independently. The children in the classrooms were randomly assigned to control and treatment groups. The experimental group included the school and family literacy component and the control group used the school program only. There were a total of 56 children and their parents, with 28 in the experimental and 28 in the control randomly selected from two first, two second and two third-grade classrooms. The study took place in one urban public school where the population for the district was 62% Latino, 33% African American, and 5% Caucasian.

The School Program

The school-based program had been put into effect the year before the parent involvement was added. It included the creation of classroom literacy centers with a variety of literacy activities available for children. There were open-faced book shelves for featured books, and books categorized by topics. There were 5 to 8 books per child at three to four grade levels, representing multiple genres of children's literature that children could check out to take home from the classroom. Pillows, rugs, stuffed animals, and rocking chairs added comfort to the area. Manipulatives such as feltboards with story characters and taped stories with headsets were available for the children's use. There was an "Authors' Spot" equipped with varied types of paper, blank booklets, and writing utensils.

Teachers modeled activities to create interest in reading and writing by: (a) reading aloud to children, (b) telling stories, (c) telling stories using props such as felt figures, puppets, etc., (d) engaging in journal writing, (e) encouraging children to create their own stories, and (f) listening to stories read with headsets and CDs. Teachers used 4 selections from the magazine *Highlights for Children* and featured one selection a week. There was a literacy center time when children could participate in these literacy activities independently or with a friend.

The Family Highlights Program

I was interested in motivating children to want to read and write voluntarily for pleasure and for information. I wanted children to approach literacy as a social activity, by engaging in reading and writing with family members. Many of the activities and materials provided in the school program were provided for the parents as well. With this plan, the children were familiar with the home program because they had done similar tasks at school. If parents had limited literacy ability or did not speak English, children could help them. Parents received a feltboard and story characters, some puppets, two spiral notebooks for them to keep journals with their children, a few pieces of children's literature, and *Highlights for Children* magazine monthly.

Throughout the year parents came to meetings to learn to use new materials and activities so they could encourage reading and writing at home. For example, at the first session they learned good techniques for reading to children, and how to do partner journal writing. At the next meeting they practiced telling stories with or without props such as using felt figures or puppets. At another session, we talked about how to make a space a little literacy center at home which could simply be a place where books are stored. They were also taught to use the *Highlights for Children* magazines, which were sent home once a month. There were four activities for them to do with their children that had already been done in the classroom. The use of *Highlights* was a major activity in the program due to its function as a shared literacy activity with home and school. The teachers did the featured activities in school with the children which parents were to repeat at home. The sections of the magazine featured each week were written in Spanish and in English.

There were three meetings for the parents in the fall and three in the spring. When all strategies were modeled, they were reviewed at additional sessions. There was a handbook for the parents listing materials, and directions for using them. At meetings we had baby-sitting available for siblings, we had teachers to supervise children in the study when not working together with their parents, we gave parents materials to take home, we had children participate with parents, and we had refreshments (Morrow, 2003).

Assessments and results. On all quantitative measures using analysis of covariance with pretest scores as covariates and posttest scores as the dependent variables, children in the groups with the parent component tested significantly better than the children in the control group with no parent component. The quantitative measures were scores from a story retelling, story rewriting, and the California Test of Basic Skills reading section. A statistical analysis was also used on interview data collected to find out about after-school family activities in a multiple-choice measure and another one to find out if adults were reading and writing with their children at home, and participating in other literacy activities. Children in the family group reported that they read or looked at books more than children in the control group. The treatment group children also asked someone to read to them more often. The results of the second question found that parents in the family group did read and write more often with their children, and chose to do more literacy activities with them in general than parents in the control group.

My studies often included mixed methods to see why or why not treatments worked. Children in the family group were interviewed. The data were pooled with answers to all questions listed. When an answer occurred more than once, it was not repeated. The following are all the answers given by all the children interviewed.

What do you like about the family literacy program?

When I need help someone is there for me.

When I grow up I'll know how to help my kids.

It's nice to work with parents.

You may think your parents don't love you, but when they work with you, you know they do.

Many people help you, grandmas, aunts, sisters, moms, dads, mom's boyfriend, dad's girlfriend.

Parents were asked what they thought was the value of the family program. The following is pooled data:

What do you think the value of the family program was?

It is fun to work with your child.

I learned how to help my child and it is a wonderful feeling.

I learned about telling stories.

I learned to be more patient with my child.

I learned that doing fun things together helps my child learn.

When parents help, children will know that school is important.

When we work together my child teaches me, too.

When we work my child helps me with English (Morrow & Young, 1997).

The Family Fluency Program

The purpose of the Family Fluency Program was to heighten awareness of parents, children, and teachers concerning the important roles they play in the literacy development of children by helping with a fluency program initiated at school. The Family Fluency Program provided fluency strategies to do at home for those parents whose children were involved in the program. We wanted to find out if the parents involved in the fluency program did the following:

- Engaged in fluency-building activities at home.
- Had a heightened awareness about the importance of fluency training.
- Increased the level of literacy involvement at home with their children.

The Family Fluency Program was part of a larger investigation in school called the Fluency Oriented Reading Instruction (FORI).

The FORI school study. The purpose of the FORI study was to identify effective procedures for teaching fluency (Kuhn & Stahl, 2003). The study took place in two school districts in the southeast and one in the northeast. There were 24 second-grade classrooms involved in the large study with a total of 376 children. The study took place over a period of five years. I will discuss the northeast district and one year of the study.

Participants. There were six second-grade classrooms in the study from the Northeast region. Three of the six classrooms were in the FORI treatment group and the other three were in the control group. Participants in the study were 62 children, their families, and teachers. The treatment group was made up of 30 girls and 32 boys, and of those children 25% were African American, 25% were European-American, 41% were Latino American, and 8% were Asian American. The control group was made up of 53 children from a demographically similar school in the district (27 girls, 26 boys; 29% African American, 17% European American, 48% Latino American, and 6% Asian American. Although all of the children in the classrooms participated in the intervention, those receiving English language support services were not included in the assessments since they were not available in their language. The community consisted of working-class families with low-middle to low incomes and a 40% free and reduced-lunch rate. The assignment of school to the condition was random (Kuhn, Schwanenflugel, Morris, Morrow, Stahl, Woo, Meisinger, Bradley, Bradeley, & Smith, 2006)

The program in the treatment and control groups. The control group used the basal reading program and spent 90 minutes a day in reading instruction. The whole-group instruction consisted of a morning message lesson, which was followed by the teacher reading a trade book to the children, and a mini-skill lesson based on the basal reading anthology. Children took turns reading from the basal reader one at a time and there were a few minutes for independent silent reading. The teachers also had guided reading instruction after the morning whole-group activities.

The FORI treatment group also had 90 minutes of reading instruction that began with a morning message and a mini-skill lesson. The story that was read aloud was from the basal program and the FORI treatment to be described occurred at this time. Teachers also had small-guided reading groups similar to the control group, and ended their 90-minute period with a trade book read-aloud and some time for independent silent reading.

The major difference between the treatment and control groups was the manner in which the basal reader was used. The control classes had stories introduced to them and minimal discussion prior to reading the story. Next, the children completed oral reading one at a time and some silent reading. In the treatment group, the basal readings included strong support and guidance from the teacher before and after reading, and repeated readings of one selection in different formats on different days. The specifics of the program follow:

On Monday, the 30-minute lesson began with the teacher reading the basal story to the children as they followed along in their own books. Prior to reading, she introduced the vocabulary. The class also discussed major concepts and built background knowledge about the text they were about to hear. After reading, discussion about the story continued.

On Tuesday, the 20-minute lesson consisted of the class echo reading the same basal story. There was discussion about vocabulary, concepts, and relating the story to their life experiences before and after echo reading the story.

On Wednesday, the 20-minute lesson had the children choral-read the same story with discussion before and after reading. The discussion about the stories became more analytical and inferential with each day.

On Thursday, the 20-minute lesson was partner-reading of the same story. Students were instructed to discuss the story before and after reading. The guidelines for the partner reading were for one child to begin by reading one or two pages and his or her partner following by doing the same thing.

On Friday, teachers could do a 20-minute extension activity related to the story or read a trade book that engaged the children in reading and writing that book.

The family fluency program. In the Family Fluency Program the basal was sent home twice a week for parents to read with their children. They read the same story being read in school that week. Parents who could not read English listened to their children read. The children echo read the story and the parents then repeated what their children read. Parents filled out forms to document if they read with their child. There was a space for parents to comment.

We offered three evening workshops for parents in October, February, and April. The objectives of the workshops were to heighten awareness about the importance of fluency, to describe the school program, and to discuss activities that parents could do at home with their children to enhance fluency.

The parent meetings. The greatest challenge when creating a family program, especially in a low socio-economic community, is to get parents to attend. To help with attendance, we sent home several notes in advance of the meetings, and made phone calls to families on the day before the meetings. Teachers helped us by asking the children to remind their parents before and on the day of the meeting. Children were invited to the meeting to participate, which helped to get families to attend since the students encouraged their parents to take them. Parents are more likely to come to meetings when their children participate since they enjoy watching them involved in school activities.

The first parent workshop. The first training session was successful, with 35 parents and 50 children. The parents brought their second graders as well as some older and younger siblings. For parents who did not attend, we sent the packet of materials, which were given out at the training session, to their children to take home on the next day of school. We made phone calls to explain the program to parents.

The meeting began with refreshments then the children did a choral reading they had practiced where the boys read one part and the girls another. After this task, they went to another room with teachers to supervise them as they used center materials.

We worked with the parents alone and described the purpose of the school program and strategies being used. We demonstrated using a short reading selection similar to stories that the children were reading in school. We talked about building a background for the story before it is read, and how to connect the story to the lives of the children. We demonstrated echo-reading, choral-reading, and partner-reading. Using the same story, we engaged the parents in a discussion prior to reading and then asked the parents to try the fluency strategies with us. We echo-read the short story, then we choral-read the story together, and finally in pairs, the parents engaged in partner-reading. During partner-reading, we asked the partners to look at the pictures and discuss what they thought the story might be about. The readers rotated the reading of the story until the story was finished, at which time the partners talked about the parts they liked best and how the story connected to their lives.

We discussed the importance of oral reading and how oral reading as a group provides a sense of community so the teacher or parent can provide a good model for reading as the children follow along. The repetition helps with decoding, learning new vocabulary, understanding the text, and being able to use the correct pace and expression. We provided a handout for the parents, in both English and Spanish, which explained the strategies. We also had a Spanish interpreter for families which spoke Spanish. We explained to parents who could not read English how they could help by listening to their children read and letting their children echo-read to them. They could then repeat what was read. We encouraged them to choral-read as well. We made audiotapes of the stories for families who could not speak English to help them participate. We also told parents who could not read English that they could repeat-read familiar stories that they had at home in their language with their children. They could echo-read these stories, choral-read, and partner-read. Following is a handout they received:

Reading Activities to Do With the Books Your Child Brings Home from School

Echo-Reading: You read one line and the child reads the same line after you. Increase the number of lines you read at one time as the child's reading improves. To be sure the child is looking at the words, ask him/her to follow the print with a finger. Try to echo-read at least one story each week.

Choral-Reading: You and your child read the same text aloud at the same time. Choral reading should be done at least twice a week.

Partner-Reading: You and your child take turns reading. Start by reading one sentence and asking the child to read the next sentence. As the child's fluency improves, you read a page and he/she reads a page. Do partner-read about once a week.

Repeated Reading: Read the same book or story more than once in the same week.

Remember: Whenever you read with your child, use as much expression as you can so your reading sounds like speaking and the story comes alive.

We invited the children back into the room and this time we worked with another very short story. We talked about the story with the parents and children by looking at the pictures before we began. We talked about new vocabulary and concepts. Then the story was read to the group as a whole. Next, we echo-read the story with the parents and children. After echo-reading, we all choral-read the story. Finally, each parent and child partner-read the story together using the framework for partner-reading described earlier. Before the end of the meeting, we reminded parents to read the stories sent home twice a week. We asked them to do fluency strategies taught twice a week. When we finished with the workshop, we socialized while enjoying refreshments.

The second parent workshop. A second meeting was held mid-year to discuss what parents and children were doing at home. We taught the parents how they could assess or identify improvement in fluency. We played a tape of excellent fluent reading, good fluent reading, and reading that needed work. We used the same short story for each of these readings and the parents had the text to follow along. We evaluated the tape recordings by calling them **Excellent**, **Good**, and **Needs Work**. The **Excellent** fluent reading flowed smoothly and at a good pace. All words were decoded properly and expression demonstrated understanding of the text. We listened to good fluent reading and discussed the characteristics. **Good** fluent reading was done at a pace that was a little slow, but not choppy and words were pronounced properly with enough expression to show some understanding. Finally, we evaluated what we called reading that **Needs Work**. This reading was word-by-word, slow, choppy; lacking expression, and some words were read incorrectly.

The third parent meeting. At the third meeting we had 32 parents. Some of the parents had been to all three meetings, while others had attended two; none were there for the first time. We invited the children and the parents again. At this meeting the children performed an echo-reading, a choral-reading, and two children illustrated a partner-reading they had practiced with their teachers in school. Having the children participate in the parent meetings proved to be a way to get the parents to come and consequently participate at home. As always, we served refreshments. At the end of the meeting, parents received a VIP certificate for being *Very Involved Parents.*

Results of the fluency and family program. We wanted to find out if the parents involved in the fluency workshops:

- Increased their literacy involvement at home with their children.
- Engaged in fluency-building activities at home.
- Had a heightened awareness about the importance of fluency training in their child's literacy development

To determine parent participation in their children's schoolwork at home, we asked teachers to report how involved they thought the parents were. Teachers used a scale we provided to rank parents from 1 to 5, with 5 indicating a lot of home involvement and 1 indicating very little home involvement. The average for teachers ranking the extent of home involvement for families in the treatment group was 3, while the average for teachers ranking parent involvement in the control group was 2. Teacher's rankings were based on forms sent home to parents to report reading with their child. They were also based on teacher perceptions and on informal discussions with parents and children. We believed their responses suggested that our intervention had some positive effect.

Another measure of family involvement was a survey for parents we administered in both the treatment and control groups. The survey was sent home with the children; we made phone calls to the homes and teachers talked to the children daily to encourage the families to return the surveys. The surveys asked parents:

- How often they were able to help children with homework
- How often they were able to read to or with their children
- How they felt they could help their children to become fluent readers

We received 35 surveys back from the parents in the treatment groups, and 28 back from parents in the control group.

The nature of the family data is anecdotal and we also realize that we did not have large numbers of parents involved or responding. In spite of this, the information that was returned was promising.

Sixty-nine percent of the parents who completed surveys in the treatment group said they helped their child with homework 5 times a week compared to 45% in the control group.

In the treatment group 46% percent of the parents reported reading to or with their children 5 times a week, 12% read 4 times a week, and 21% read 3 times; this represents a total of 79% of the parents in the treatment group. In the control group 9% percent reported reading to or with their children 5 times a week, 21% read 4 times a week, and 28% reported reading 3 times a week; this represents a total of 58% of the parents in the control group. We are aware that this data is based on the parent self-report, but we believe the data is strong enough to suggest that there was a positive effect in the treatment group.

Parents were asked how they helped their children become more fluent readers. Many parents in the treatment group demonstrated an understanding of how to help children become fluent readers. They listed the strategies that they were taught at the parent sessions and the materials that were sent home with their children. They also used the vocabulary involved in fluency instruction. For example, they talked about repeated reading, echo-reading, choral-reading, partner-reading, pacing reading, and using expression. These are all activities for developing fluency. Some of these terms were used by control group parents, but with less consistency. The treatment group answers were more similar to each other while the answers in the control group were more varied (Morrow, Kuhn, & Schwanenflugel (2006-2007).

How to Help My Children to Become a Fluent Reader Treatment Group

Practice reading by repeating the same story over and over 17
Choral-read 15
Ask questions about the story. 15
Read to your child, read along with your child, partner-read 15
Sound out words 14
Help children to read at the right pace, not too fast, not too slow . . 10
Read with expression 7
Encourage and be patient with your child 7
Echo-read. 6
Use computer programs. 2

Control Group

Practice phonics. 18
Read to your child often/daily 17
Have your child read aloud 15
Work on increasing vocabulary 10
Read more difficult books 6
Help with writing. 6
Help with spelling 5
Provide parental support 5
Find books of interest to your child. 4
Use easy books. 4
Partner-read 3
Read with expression 2
Practice the same book over again 2
Set a good example. 2

Assessment and results of oral reading proficiency. To examine the effects of the home and school program the Gray Oral Reading Test, Fourth Edition (GORT-4) (Wiederholt & Bryant, 2001) was used as a standardized assessment of text reading fluency. It was administered as a pretest during the first month of school, and again during the final month of school. To assess the effectiveness of the FORI program for enhancing children's reading fluency, we carried out a repeated measures analysis of variance (ANOVA). The results showed a greater improvement in reading fluency among FORI children than children in the control group. An analysis of the progress of children in remedial programs indicated that struggling readers benefited from the program similarly to typical readers (Kuhn, et. al., 2006).

The BELLE project: Bellevue project for early literacy and language development. Another family literacy program I participated in was very different from the two previous programs. This is a community program initiated by pediatricians from New York University School of Medicine. This is a large randomized controlled study funded by the National Institute of Child Health and Human Development. The goal of this research was to determine the impact of mother-child relationship interventions on parenting, language, literacy, and child development. The intervention occurred during primary pediatric care appointments at an urban public hospital that serves ethnically diverse, low socioeconomic status (SES), at-risk families.

This study builds upon similar published research, for example, the Reach Out and Read (ROR) model. In this model, during primary care visits, volunteers read to the children while waiting for the doctor. During the visit the doctor makes an effort to find out about the language and literacy development of the baby, and what the mothers were doing to help at home. Suggestions for helping were made by the physician, and each parent-child pair received a book to take home. This part of the program was called Reach Out and Read (ROR), for which a large number of studies have documented a positive impact on a child's language development, based on parent-child shared read-alouds (Mendelsohn, 2002; Mendelsohn, Mogilner, Dreyer, Forman, Weinstein, Broderick, Cheng, Magliore, Moore, Napier, 2001; Needlman, Toker, Dreyer, Klass, & Mendelsohn, 2005). The BELLE project builds on varied interventions to assess what works best for families considered at-risk as a result of maternal education level. The program applies research results by Kubicek, 1996; Bernstein & McDonough, 1995; and Erickson, Endersbe, & Simon, 1999 from the field of child mental health, pediatric primary care setting, and literacy.

Research methodology. The inclusion criteria for the 450 mother and child participants were that the mother speak English or Spanish as a primary language, plans to have pediatric follow-up at the Belleview Hospital Clinic affiliated with New York University Medical School, has a consistent means of contact, and that the child has no significant medical complications. 85% of enrollees were Latino (from Mexico, Ecuador, and the Dominican Republic), 7.2% were Black/African American, and the rest South Asian or White/European American. About 40% of the mothers completed high school, 40% completed between 7th and 11th grade, and 20% completed 6th grade or less.

This empirical randomized experimental study took place during primary care pediatric visits. This part of the program used the ROR model described earlier. In these visits volunteers read to the children while waiting for the doctor. During the visit the doctor made an effort to find out about the language and literacy development of the baby and what the mothers did with the child to enhance language and literacy. Suggestions for helping were made, and each parent-child pair received a book to take home.

Enrolled families were randomized into one of two groups, including one intervention and one control group. The intervention, Video Interaction Project (VIP), applies work done in the field of infant mental health by Bernstein & McDonough, 1995; Erickson, Endersbe, & Simon, 1999; and Kubicek, 1996, to the pediatric primary care setting. In VIP, mother and child met with a Child Development Specialist (CDS) at each well-child visit for about 30-45 minutes. The first visit takes place within 1-2 weeks of discharge from the nursery, and subsequent visits were at 1–3 month intervals based on the recommendation of the American Academy of Pediatrics for well-child care. The CDS works with the mother to promote interactions and interactive play that facilitates language, literacy, and child development, as documented in research (Hart & Risley, 1995; Huttenlocher & Dabholkar, 1997; Tamis-LeMonda, Bornstein, & Baumwell, 2001; Morrow, 2009). The core component of VIP involves videotaping of mother and child for 5 to 7 minutes; the videotape is watched by the mother and the CDS to identify strengths and promote other positive interactions. The CDS gives each parent a toy, a children's book, and a booklet about early language, literacy, and child development activities. Research documents the efficacy of VIP with mothers who have limited education (Mendelsohn, Dreyer, Flynn, et al., 2005; Mendelsohn, Valdez, Flynn, Foley, Berkule, Tomopoulos, Fierman, Tineo, Dreyer, 2007).

The StimQ assessment utilized was an interview instrument developed by members of the project team, and validated in urban, low SES families. The gains were greatest for the VIP subjects. Mothers with 7th-11th grade education showed the most helpful language and literacy play interactions with their child that were significantly better than those in the control group. This was determined by using the StimQ assessment, an interview-based instrument.

Concluding remarks. Involving parents in the language and literacy development of their children is very important, yet it is one of the most frustrating aspects of the work because of the lack of attendance on the part of the parents. However, there are a myriad of factors that cause their absence: responsibilities of work and childcare, families consisting of only one parent, and families being raised by an elderly grandparent. These obstacles make it difficult for parents to take on more responsibilities, even though they are sincerely interested in their children. All family literacy programs share these common challenges, so in order to be successful, they institute the following supports:

- There was transportation if needed.
- The programs provided food for participants.
- There was supervision for children when the trainers wanted to work with the parents alone.
- To get the parents to participate, you must be persistent. Multiple contacts had to be made to encourage them to participate (letters were sent home; reminding phone calls were made).
- There were incentives for the parents. For example, they were given materials, books, and received stipends for attending.
- Tasks were done in school so that the children were familiar with them and could help parents who needed assistance at home.
- The information and community meetings were culturally sensitive.
- There were language interpreters at the meetings.

- The activities were easy to understand and initiate, could be done in a short period of time, and showed results quickly.

The programs heightened parents' awareness about literacy development based on their participation in the study. The activities enhanced parent involvement in literacy activities at home.

While providing professional development for teachers to learn new instructional strategies to enhance student performance is paramount, family programs both at school and in the community require just as much attention and effort. We must have parent coordinators to institute programs that include both home and school simultaneously. Without family literacy and the aid of the family in developing the literacy of children, we can never be completely successful in closing the achievement gap.

Changing ideas about early literacy require research. During the time that I was carrying out much of this research, attitudes about early childhood were being questioned; that is, can we be more explicit in our instruction? Should we be teaching with more intention literacy in prekindergarten and kindergarten? There were many differences in attitudes ranging from a hands-off policy concerning explicit instruction to those who wanted an emphasis on early literacy but from an emergent literacy perspective. Instruction should be developmentally appropriate and not look as if prekindergarten and kindergarten was first grade. I felt the need to address the topic in some way and believed in the necessity for a playful environment in prekindergarten and kindergarten and studied the Preparing the Classroom Environment to Promoting Literacy During Play. *Early Childhood Research Quarterly,* 1990. The purpose of this study was to determine if the voluntary literacy behavior of children could be increased in type and quantity through design changes by including reading and writing materials in dramatic play areas. Thirteen preschool classes were distributed into one control group and three different experimental groups: one in which thematic play with literacy materials was guided by teachers; one in which thematic play with literacy materials was *not* guided by teachers; and one in which books, pencils, and papers were supplied in dramatic play areas without a theme or teacher guidance. The type and quantity of literacy behavior in each of the experimental settings were determined by direct observation prior to intervention, during intervention, and after a delayed period of time. Literacy behaviors increased significantly in the experimental groups over the control group. Thematic play with teacher guidance yielded the greatest gains. The provision of books, pencils, and paper with teacher guidance had the next greatest gains, and thematic play without teacher guidance yielded the third greatest gains. The effect of the treatments continued after a delayed period of time.

Strategy instruction for early literacy development. A position statement by the International Reading Association, entitled *Using Multiple Methods of Beginning Reading Instruction* (1999), suggests there is no single method or combination of methods that can successfully teach all children to read. "Therefore, teachers must have a strong knowledge of multiple methods for teaching reading and a strong knowledge of the children in their care, so they can create the appropriate balance of methods needed for the children they teach." A balanced perspective for literacy instruction includes careful selection of the best theories available and the use of learning strategies from those theories to match the learning styles of individual children to help them learn to read. This might mean the use of skill-based explicit instruction or some more constructivist methods that include problem-solving strategies (Morrow & Tracey 1997). According to Pressley (1998), explicit teaching of skills is a good start for constructivist problem-solving activities, and constructivist activities permit consolidation and elaboration of skills. One method does not preclude or exclude the other.

The National Reading Panel Report (2000) presents findings about the most effective strategies for teaching children to read. The panel reviewed more than 100,000 studies to inform their results. The panel found that the following elements: phonemic awareness, phonics, vocabulary, comprehension, and fluency were crucial to reading success in early literacy.

Children need to be fluent readers on grade level by the end of third grade. If they aren't, they are not likely to get to grade level and fall further and further behind. It has been documented that young children need instruction early in decoding skills, vocabulary development, and strategies to comprehend. This motivated my research dealing with development of strategies involving children as active participants in literacy experiences to develop comprehension skills. I also researched exemplary practice, including the organization and management of language arts programs.

The research I carried out on strategy instruction that has had the most substantial impact in early literacy is the work dealing with the development and assessment of comprehension through story retelling. I created a method of assessment and instruction that is cited in most current college textbooks and professional development books. Retelling is used in many programs created for teaching reading in the United States. The work originally appeared in the article, "Retelling Stories: A Strategy for Improving Young Children's Comprehension, Concept Of Story Structure, and Oral Language Complexity," *Elementary School Journal*, 1985.

Although story retelling seemed like a tool to serve many purposes in enhancing reading, little research had been done on the topic. The first of three studies was to find out whether retelling stories that had been read to kindergarten children would improve their comprehension of stories. The sample consisted of 82 children randomly selected from 17 different public kindergarten classes. Pretests and posttests were devised for comprehension. The comprehension tests included five questions about story structure, and five questions that asked for literal, inferential, and critical responses. The same stories were read to the treatment and control groups. The children were read eight stories over a period of 8 weeks. The children in the treatment groups were given guidance in retelling after each story, concentrating on the structural elements: the beginning, middle, and end. The children in the control group were asked to draw a picture about the story. Both groups were allowed to use the story book to draw about it or to retell. An analysis of co-variance demonstrated significantly better comprehension scores $p<.05$ in retelling for the experiment over the control on the comprehension scores. Retelling stories functions as both an assessment tool, and an aid in helping students to comprehend. It is an active procedure which involves children in the reconstruction of literature; this strategy improves concept of story, oral language, and literal and inferential comprehension.

Other work that gained attention was the work done with interactive behavior during storybook reading and the importance of read-alouds for young children in whole-group, small-group and one-on-one settings. Some of the titles from this research include: "Young Children's Responses to One-to-One Story Reading in School Settings," published in *Reading Research Quarterly*, (1988), " The Effect of Group Size During Story Book Reading and Verbal Participation and Story Comprehension," also published in *Reading Research Quarterly* (1990), and "The Effects of a Storybook Reading Program on the Literacy Development of At Risk Kindergarten

Children," *Literacy Research Journal* (1990), formerly *Journal of Literacy Behavior*. This last study investigated the effects of storybook reading programs as one means for literacy development with at-risk children in eight Title 1, extended-day, and urban kindergartens. It combined all of the strategies I had studied separately. Children in four experimental classes followed a daily program of literature experience that included being read to, retelling stories, looking at books with partners, and repeated storybook readings. It also had well-designed literacy centers with multiple genres of children's literature and manipulatives for retelling stories such as puppets, felt figures with a felt board, and props. At the same time students in four control groups followed the prescribed reading program used in the district that emphasized letter recognition and letter-sound correspondence. Based on the results of pretests in September and posttests in May, the experimental groups scored significantly better than the control groups on story retellings, attempted reading of favorite stories, comprehension tests, and other measures. There are no significant differences between the groups on standardized measures.

Fortunate Experiences

With a bulk of research on early literacy, I was asked to speak about my work, invited to write chapters in others' books about my work, and published in more practical journals related to my research to disseminate the information to teachers. I also wrote some professional development books and texts on early literacy, and I was fortunate to find that many of the strategies are still being used in classrooms today.

My work was recognized by different literacy centers and I was invited by Richard Anderson, one of the Directors of the Center for Study of Reading, to share my work at the University of Illinois in Urbana/Champaign. John Guthrie and Linda Gambrell asked me to carry out research on behalf of the National Reading Research Center since my work shared similarities with their work on motivation. I was invited to complete, in New Jersey, a portion of a national study that Michael Pressley at SUNY's Center for English Language Arts and Assessment was doing with Richard Allington and Peter Johnston on Exemplary Teachers. Steven Stahl and Melanie Kuhn asked me to add a home component to their national study on fluency, which I described earlier.

Presently, I am working in collaboration with pediatricians at New York University Medical School on enhancing school readiness and literacy of "at-risk" children by involving them in an interactive storybook reading and playing project, a program discussed earlier in this paper.

Professional Organization

Aside from my work, I was introduced to professional organizations in literacy such as the Literacy Research Association (LRA), the International Reading Association (IRA), and the National Association for the Education of Young Children (NAEYC), and the American Educational Research Association (AERA). When serving on committees, I met many people and became more deeply involved in the work in two of the organizations, IRA and LRA. However, I still attended and presented my work at conferences of other related groups. The more involved I became, the more projects I participated in. Some of the projects consisted of edited books, position statements, editing themed issues of journals, work on editorial advisory boards, the family literacy committee, and the early literacy committees for IRA. I was initially elected member of the Board of Directors of IRA and eventually President of IRA, which was an excellent learning experience.

I was able to testify before Congress, which enabled me to learn a great deal about the workings of our government. As IRA President, I traveled all throughout the United States and abroad to speak with members and attend important meetings about educational funding, new legislature, etc. For the Literacy Research Association, I chaired the publication's committee, was a co-editor of the *Journal of Literacy Research* (formerly the *Journal of Reading Behavior*), was elected to the Board of Directors, and served as a section chair for evaluating proposals, among other responsibilities. I was honored to receive an invitation to attend a symposium titled Early Reading First, which was led by Laura Bush, that provided me with the privilege of meeting President George W. Bush. These experiences not only furthered my knowledge about policy issues around literacy, but they also placed me at the forefront of the literacy audience: teachers, supervisor, college professors, publishers, and professional organizations.

I mentioned the use of *Highlights for Children* magazine in the family programs I put into place. The magazine donated old copies which we gave to the children with a newsletter we created for parents, and a newsletter we created for teachers as well. Teachers would feature parts of the magazine with the newsletter and then the parent newsletter went home explaining what had been done in school and directions about how to continue. Highlights eventually made this into a *Parent Involvement Program*, and instead of me having to make the newsletters and the ideas, their editors did it all. The program was used for about 8 years, and was extremely successful. Parents said it helped them to understand more about learning to read, as well as helping them with their own acquisition of English. Children talked about feeling important since their parents were spending more time with them. I marvel at the number of opportunities that have arisen from my work.

I was contacted by the Public Broadcasting System to work with the program *Reading Rainbow*, since their work was closely related to mine. They had read some of my articles and wanted me to develop a literacy program for them that would include the creation of a handbook and provision for professional development. The program was designed for 200 after-school and summer day care centers for "at-risk" 6-to-8-year-olds. The handbook was called *Reading Rainbow Recreational Reading Program*. The book included materials that needed to be purchased, including book titles. The goal of the program was to create literacy centers that contained 5 to 8 pieces of children's literature per child, a rocking chair, rug, throw pillows, stuffed animals, open-faced shelving for easy selection of books, book check-out systems, and multiple genres of children's literature. There were manipulatives used to tell stories such as chalk talks, stories with puppets, props, music, sound effects, head sets with taped stories, and literacy embedded in play. There were sample floor plans for literacy centers to guide facilitators in creating their room design. A series of lesson plans for story reading, story telling, telling stories with manipulatives, and rules for using the center were provided as well. All of the elements of my research went into the program design. As a result of this work I wrote a book titled, *The Literacy Center: Contexts for Reading and Writing, Stenhouse, 2003,* which made the program well known to many who used all or parts of it in school programs. The work with Corporation for Public Broadcasting and with schools was most rewarding, since I was able to see my research being used to promote both voluntary and independent reading, and to enhance the joy of reading. Another important thing was happening; I was being identified as a person who specializes in early literacy, with a focus on independent reading, the classroom environment, family literacy, and literacy in play.

My work was a reflection of the times in which it existed, and times have definitely changed with standards for literacy development: No Child Left Behind legislation, the National Literacy Panel and the Early Literacy Panel Reports, and now the Common Core State Standards. There are greater expectations for preschool and kindergarten, yet I haven't change my theoretical ideas about how young children learn and the best teaching methods for teaching this age span, but I have looked more closely at the content they are being offered, the quality of teaching they are receiving, and the organization and management of classroom activities.

Michael Pressley was a professor at the Center for English Language Arts and Assessment, and along with Richard Allington and Peter Johnston, he began work on a study on Exemplary Teaching Practices in grades first through fourth. The first year Michael asked me if I would be the coordinator New Jersey sites for the exemplary teacher studies he was about to begin. There would also be sites in California, Texas, New York, and Michigan. This would be a quality investigation in which 8 classrooms in each state would be selected to be observed for specific characteristics. These characteristics would be documented on a coding sheet and in addition to other characteristics that were observed and recorded. Teachers were selected as exemplary based on recommendation of their principal, a literacy supervisor, and children's test scores over the past 5 years, and by children and parents. Each teacher was observed 6 times over the course of the year during their language arts block. The list that evolved as exemplary practice from observations found the behavior on the part of this group of teachers to be very similar. They used varied strategies: they grouped children based on achievement to meet individual needs, they had high expectations for children, and teachers genuinely cared about their students. Teachers used a lot of constructive feedback; they were never punitive. Their children were always productively engaged, either by teaching, or time on task, completing independent and collaborative activities. The teachers used standards, explicit instruction, and problem-solving techniques when children could work on their own to build independence and self-direction. The rooms were very well organized and managed. Children were taught in whole-group, small-group, and one-on-one settings. Children in the exemplary classrooms were on task and engaged 96% of the school day; in classrooms with less effective teachers, children were on task 63% of the time. Although this was not a criterion for selection, we found that all of our effective teachers sought professional development and the majority of the teachers had master's degrees. They went to conferences, belonged to professional organizations, and read about improving their teaching. The original work for this was published in book by Michael Pressley, Richard Allington, Ruth Wharton-McDonald, Cathy Collins Block & Lesley Mandel Morrow (2002) entitled *Learning to Read: Lessons from Exemplary First Grade Classrooms*. The group published another article that appeared in the *Scientific Study of Reading* (2001) entitled "A Study of 1st Grade Literacy Instruction." I wrote an article for *Reading Teacher* titled, "Characteristics of Exemplary 1st Grade Literacy Instruction" (1999) and received several invitations to write book chapters. I was also invited to write a chapter for the *Handbook of Organization and Management* about this work. The study suggested to me that more professional development was necessary to create excellent teachers. The purpose of this following study was about improving teacher practice.

What are the Benefits of a Multi-faceted Professional Development Program? This research focused on a multi-faceted professional development initiative to enhance literacy instruction with specific emphasis on small-group guided reading instruction and the creation of excellent center activities. The program included weekly study groups, peer observation, workshops, individual coaching sessions, and an on-site university course in literacy instruction.

The setting was a low-SES northeast community with 75% African American and 25% Hispanic children. The project was initiated by a principal in one elementary school in the district and designed with the administration, reading coaches, teachers, three professors, and one PhD student. The school serves 250 children in grades Prekindergarten through five.

Research Questions:

- What are the components of the study groups, coaching sessions, classroom visits, and workshops?
- What response do the teachers, reading teachers, and administrators have to the different types of professional development activities?
- What change has occurred in school and in the individual classrooms?

Data/Sources. Data sources include capturing the components of the project with anecdotal records, surveys, observation forms, interviews, photographs, and children's work. State evaluation of the school and children's progress were a major source of data.

The data were examined through a constant comparative method (Strauss & Corbin, 1988) to determine evidence of information integration from multiple sources. Findings supported by triangulated data will be presented.

Description of the Development Program

Demographics. The school district where the study took place is one of the most "at-risk" in its state. The children come from economically disadvantaged homes and the scores on standards-based tests are amongst the lowest in the state.

I was contacted by the school principal, who asked me to devise a professional development program that would enhance literacy instruction, assessment-guided reading instruction, use of small-group instruction based on achievement, and to motivate children in science and social studies with interesting hands-on activities that embedded the teaching of literacy as well. She wanted her teachers to become a Professional Learning Community, who collaborated, shared materials, and were interested in improving their craft.

Teachers were frustrated from multiple plans for professional development in the district in which they had no input and often workshops with no follow-up sessions. They were not particularly interested in another plan for the school. The school had a strong union presence. The only time teachers would stay after school is if they were paid extra. Teachers also said that there was a lack of administrative support when it came to change.

Effective professional development must be job-embedded, relevant to the teachers and their students, and perceived as needed. The models that motivate sustained change are multi-faceted (Guskey, 2000; Roe, 2004; Yoon, Duncan, Lee, Scarloss, & Shapley, 2007). Successful programs must have momentum from internal sources such as coaches, teachers, the principal, and administrators (Ferrance, 2000; Deussen, Coskie, Robinson, & Autio, 2007; National Staff Development Council [NSDC] policy, 2001; Knapp, 2004). Everyone must participate in the professional development if the school culture is to become a community of learners (Stotnik & Smith, 2008; Talbert & McLaughlin, 2002).

The elementary school was located in an old residential section 4 blocks from the ocean. The school building was new, clean, very attractive, and well equipped. There were 26 classroom teachers in the prekindergarten to 5 building, which also had special education classrooms. The average number of children in the classroom was 16 and most rooms had two teachers. There were two reading specialists in the building who helped with materials for teachers, assessing children's progress, coaching through modeling strategies, and working with students who needed intervention beyond the whole-group and small-group instruction. There were 4 reading teachers who came into specified classrooms during the small-group reading instruction to teach struggling students.

The collaborative professional development (PD) plan: We met first with the building principal to discuss a plan. We then met with the reading teachers and reading specialists. They helped us to organize in a manner that the school could handle. We then met with the entire staff to discuss the plan and received input from them as well. I recruited four colleagues and assigned each of us a different job in the PD plan. With the input from my colleagues, I led the group in discussion of the plan. The following professional development pieces are what we put into practice.

There were mixed grade level study groups for prekindergarten to grade 2 and grades 3 to 5. They met every week for 40 minutes. We supervised the 250 children in the school by having prekindergarten through grade 2 children meet in the gym and watch videos about current topics of study. Grades 3 to 5 met in the all-purpose room and also viewed DVDs that matched their curriculum. The children were supervised by parents, custodians, art and music teachers, aides, and security personnel in the building. The success of the study groups had to do with the leadership of students taking the Reading Course and their assignment to run the study groups, record findings, and share ideas from the course.

Teachers met and selected a teacher leader to run the group. The original plan was a list of topics coupled with readings we believed the teachers wanted to talk about, but because of union rules, the teachers would not read the materials from the book chosen for the different grade levels after school hours, therefore the plan had to change. The leader of each group gathered very short 2-page pieces around topics of interests from a journal such as *Reading Teacher.* The article was read the minute the teachers entered the room and discussion took place after reading about the topic. The teachers then were placed in study groups where rich, in-depth discussion occurred. Unfortunately, the study groups were rushed due to lack of time. Topics that were popular in prekindergarten to grade 2 were reading and writing strategies, both phonics and comprehension. The teachers wanted to learn more about embedding literacy into content areas and so that this part of the school day would be a motivational experience, and they also wanted to learn more about teaching writing. In Grades 3 to 5, preparing for the state standards test was high on the list of concerns along with classroom management, writers' workshop, the writing process, motivating students, and how to do literature circles as a form of small-group instruction.

For workshops, classroom visits with reflective conversations required the principal to get substitutes. There were short workshops upon request, done for prekindergarten through 2 and for 3 to 5 separately. The workshops were specific to teachers' needs. For example, I performed one on teaching short vowels, another on embedding literacy into content area teaching, and motivating children with hands-on interesting activities, for example. There was an on-site course for 3 credits for the teachers who chose to take it. They became the leaders in the building for the professional development

Towards the end of October, we introduced classroom visits to observe peers in the building and to engage in reflective conversations. Initially, it was difficult to get teachers to volunteer for observations, but after the first day of observing four different teachers, it was no longer difficult to get volunteers. The visits were about 20 minutes and we observed guided reading and center time. Some teachers were reluctant to see this as valuable, as one said, "I could be teaching my children instead of doing this." As time went on, the attitudes changed. In the reflective conversations, teachers asked questions of those who had allowed us to observe their rooms such as, "How did they get the management of your program together with the center activities and children working independently. They asked, "How often do you meet with groups?", "How do you assess children's growth to decide what they needed to learn?" We often heard comments to each other such as,"I would like to talk to you more about your centers and come back and see how you organize them." The visits with debriefing became quite popular, which definitely caused change to occur in classrooms. We met regularly with study group leaders, reading teachers, reading specialists, the principal, and individual teachers.

Slowly a change began to happen in the school. We were treated warmly and told it was the best PD they had ever had since we met their needs and included them on decision making. They were anxious to show off their rooms and the changes they had made, they volunteered to be observed by peers, and in the teachers' room or hallways you heard teachers talking about trying new strategies they had learned from the PD course, study groups, workshops, or classroom visits. The principal remarked she had never heard talk about teaching between teachers in the teachers' room or in the hallways.

At about the same time classroom visits began we also began providing in-class coaching for teachers. This was often by the recommendation of the reading specialist or principal. It included teaching strategies taught by the coach. It followed with the teacher discussing what was done, followed by the teacher trying the strategies, concluding with a discussion after the teacher tried the strategy.

The wonderful part of the experience was to see reluctant teachers embrace the ideas, look at us as partners, and value our collaboration and ideas. There was change in every room we worked in. The school was moving toward becoming a community of learners who sought out new information and shared ideas with others. In failing schools in NJ, the state evaluates the building a few times a year, looking at teacher strategies, and the environmental design of the classroom, small-group instruction, and innovative motivating activities for children. On this evaluation the school went from a 3.3 rating in the fall to an 8.3 in the spring. In the spring of the next year, the school made their annual yearly progress, which they hadn't done for the last 10 years. In April, the governor announced the tax cuts that would affect schools. The result was many of the teachers in our study were eliminated. The sad part of the experience is that we didn't have time to enjoy, reflect upon, or celebrate our success with the teachers.

What skills did teachers believe most important to teach literacy, and what type of professional development was ranked most valuable in helping to teach those skills?

This paper takes a general look at the different parts of professional development. There were surveys given to teachers at the beginning, middle, and end of the year asking about the different parts of the PD. The questions asked of the teachers were:

- What did teachers believe were the most important strategies for teachers to teach children in reading and writing?
- What professional development components were liked best by teachers at the beginning, middle, and end of the project?
- Which if the strategies seemed to cause the most change?

Data collection includes surveys, interviews, anecdotal records, photographs, observations, and artifacts collected to describe and document the effectiveness of this part of the professional development and data from the state (Marshall & Rossman, 2006; Seidman, 2006).

Results reveal that teachers were reluctant to allow peer visits, but are now open to having their classrooms observed. During classroom visits teachers began taking notes, talking to the children about what they were doing, and in the reflective conversations asking each other about particular practices. This data suggest the teachers were learning from each other and internalizing new ideas. The workshops, based on their requests, were well received since ideas were presented to support practice with which they felt they needed help. Changes in practice are being observed in the classrooms (Schuck, Abusson, & Buchanan, 2008). The classroom physical environments improved with the organization of materials, creation of excellent centers with work that challenged children, teachers were talking more about strategies that work or asking for support from others. The atmosphere in the school changed from pessimistic to optimistic, from a building of teachers who did not collaborate, to one that was caring and respectful, interested in learning, and wanting to improve. We had a true professional learning community. When the state came to evaluate the physical environment of the school and teacher behavior, one of the questionnaires revealed that the school had truly become partners in learning, and their evaluation score went from 3.3 to 8.5 on a scale of 0 to 10. In academic behavior, the school achieved annual yearly progress for achievement, which hadn't happened in 10 years.

Thoughts about the future. In this paper I have discussed my early years as a classroom teacher, moving into academia, and research accomplishments. My career was not planned, but opportunities arose, and I took a leap to see what might happen. Along the way was hard work, a passion to achieve, guidance from others, risks, and a desire to help to make early childhood instruction more explicit, relevant, and meaningful. I researched what I knew from being a classroom teacher, and one study would raise a question for another. I was and still am passionate about my work. I was fortunate to have colleagues who were interested in working with me. In addition, it was a time when research on early literacy that took place in schools was a new trend and there was not much classroom-based research available. Hopefully, I have generated new, substantive, significant work that has caused some positive change in early literacy practice.

What about the future? I think we know a lot about early literacy development. Instead of jumping in and reinventing the wheel and looking for the next silver bullet, I hope that we will refine what we have learned. There are still many questions to be answered, such as how to achieve the new Common Core State Standards in our classrooms so our children become creative thinkers, critical problem solvers, good communicators, and are able to collaborate with others. We need to create after-school programs for many purposes. It could be to do homework, get extra help, meet recreational needs, but schools need to be open to much later in the day. This would lengthen the school day, which is necessary, and I believe we should think about lengthening the school year. Although not researched, it seems like there are more 4-day weeks at school than 5-day weeks during the course of the school year. We know that a quality preschool and all-day kindergarten are an advantage for all children but especially for those who are economically "at risk." We know that parent involvement is critical for children to reach their potential. We know that it is an excellent teacher and not a program that helps children do well, therefore we need to spend time and money for professional development. We also know that the mentoring during the induction year will help to retain teachers and create quality teachers. Work in early childhood is crucial. If children aren't reading fluently on level at the end of third grade, only 10% of these students will reach grade level. If a person does not learn to be functionally literate, they are not likely to finish high school. Without a high school diploma, it will be difficult to get a good job, which creates poverty and increased potential for issues with the law; they will tend to become chronically ill, and have children who grow up not able to read either.

What will I do now? I will continue with the work that I am still passionate about. I will select projects that are exciting to me. The small studies in the past, carried out by one individual about little topics, are not going to be useful now. I will try and work on the big picture in collaboration with others throughout the country.

Earlier I mentioned that we know how important parent involvement is. I can think back to my childhood and remember how important literacy was to my family. We talked at dinner and almost always ate together. My parents included us in multiple experiences to broaden our background knowledge. There was never a question about whether you would go to college, it was which college you would go to. The message also was you need to learn to be independent and take care of yourself, so select something to learn in school that will help you to do that.

Although the road was long with curves along the way, I was fortunate to be born into the family in which I was raised. When in school, there was guidance and support, and always an emphasis on succeeding. I was also fortunate meeting the people I met and the opportunities that arose in a time when doing research in the field of education was a new adventure. I have had a wonderful career for which I am grateful, and grateful for the fact that I can still participate.

REFERENCES

Anderson, R. (1985). *Becoming a Nation of Readers*. Washington, D.C.: National Institute of Education.

Bernstein, V. J., & McDonough, S. (1995). Using video to identify family strengths. Zero to Three 10th Annual Training Institute, Pre-Institute Seminar, Atlanta, GA.

Boorstin, D. (1984). Letters of transmittal. *A report for the librarian of Congress to the Congress*. In books in our future, Washington, D.C.: Joint Committee on the Library.

Deussen, T., Coskie, T., Robinson, L., & Autio, E. (2007). *"Coach" can mean five things: five categories of literacy coaches in Reading First* (Issues & Answers Report, 2007-#005). Washington, D.C.: U.S. Department of Education, Institute of Education Sciences, National Center for Education Evaluation and Regional Assistance, Regional Education Laboratory Northwest. Retrieved from http://ies.ed.gov/ncee/edlabs.

Erickson, M., Endersbe, J., & Simon, J. (1999). Seeing is believing: Videotaping families and using guided self-observation to build parent skills. Minneapolis, MN: Regents of the University of Minnesota.

Ferrance, E. (2000). Action Research. Office of Educational Research and Improvement. U.S. Department of Education.

Gee, J. P. (2004). Reading as a situated language: A socio-cognitive perspective. In Ruddell, R.B., & Unrau, N. J. (Eds). *Theoretical Models and Processes of Reading* (5th ed. pp. 33-68). Newark, DE: International Reading Association.

Guskey, T. R. (2000). *Evaluating Professional Development*. Thousand Oaks, CA: Corwin Press.

Hart, B., & Risley, T. R. (1995). *Meaningful differences in the everyday experience of young American children.* Baltimore, MD: Brookes Publishing.

Huttenlocher, P. R., & Dabholkar, A. S. (1997). Regional differences in synaptogenesis in human cerebral cortex. *The Journal of Comparative Neurology, 387*(2): 167-178.

International Reading Association. (1999). Using multiple methods of beginning reading instruction. Newark, DE: International Reading Association.

Knapp, M. S. (2004). "Professional Development as a Policy Pathway." *Review of Research in Education, 27,* 109-157.

Kubicek, L. F. (1996). Helping young children become competent communicators: The role of relationships. *Zero to Three, 17,* 25-30.

Kuhn, M. R. & Stahl, S. (2003). Fluency: A review of developmental and remedial strategies. *Journal of Educational Psychology, (95-1),* 3-21.

Kuhn, M. R. Schwanenflugel, P. J., Morris, R. D., Morrow, L. M., Stahl, S. A., Woo, D., Meisinger, B., Bradley, B., & Bradeley, B. & Smith, C. H. (2006). Teaching children to become fluent and automatic readers. *Journal of Literacy Research, 38*(4), 357-387.

Marshall, C. & Rossman, G. (2006). *Designing qualitative research.* Thousand Oaks, CA: Sage Publications.

Mendelsohn, A. L., Dreyer, B. P., Flynn, V., Tomopoulos, S., Rovira, I., Tineo, W., Pebenito, C., Torres, C., Torres, H., & Nixon, A. F. (2005). Use of videotaped interactions during pediatric well-child care to promote child development: A randomized, controlled trial. *Journal of Developmental and Behavioral Pediatrics, 26*(1), 34-41.

Mendelsohn, A. L., Mogilner, L. N., Dreyer, B. P., Forman, J. A., Weinstein, S. C., Broderick, M., Cheng, K. J., Magliore, T., Moore, T., & Napier, C. (2001). The impact of a clinic-based literacy intervention on language development in inner-city preschool children. *Pediatrics, 107,* 130-134.

Mendelsohn, A. L. (2002). Promoting language and literacy through reading aloud: The role of pediatrician. *Current Problems in Pediatric and Adolescent Health Care, 32*(6), 183-210.

Mendelsohn, A. L., Valdez, P., Flynn, V., Foley, G., Berkule, S., Tomopoulos, S., Fierman, A. H., Tineo, W., & Dreyer, B. P. (2007). Use of videotaped interactions during pediatric well-child care: Impact at 33 months on parenting and child development. *Journal of Developmental and Behavioral Pediatrics, 28*(3), 206-212.

Morrow, L. M., & Weinstein, C.S. (1982) Increasing children's use of literature through program and physical design changes. *Elementary School Journal, 83*(2), 131-137.

Morrow, L. M. (1982). Relationships between literature programs, library corner designs and children's use of literature. *Journal of Educational Research, 75,* 339-344.

Morrow, L .M. (1983). Home and school correlates of early interest in literature. *Journal of Educational Research, 76,* 221-230.

Morrow, L. M. (1985). Retelling stories: A strategy for improving young children's comprehension, concept of story structure, and oral language complexity. *Elementary School Journal.*

Morrow, L. M. (1986). Encouraging voluntary reading: The impact of a literature program on children's use of library centers. *Reading Research Quarterly, 21,* 330-346.

Morrow, L. M. (1988). Young children's responses to one-to-one story reading in school settings. *Reading Research Quarterly, 23,* 89-107.

Morrow, L. M. (1990). The impact of a literature-based program with parent involvement on literacy achievement, use of literature and attitudes of children from minority backgrounds. *Reading Research Quarterly, 27,* 250-275.

Morrow, L. M. (1990). Preparing the classroom environment to promoting literacy during play. *Early Childhood Research, 5,* 537-554.

Morrow, L. M., & Smith, J. K. (1990). The effect of group size on interactive storybook reading. *Reading Research Quarterly, 25*(3), 213-231.

Morrow, L. M. (1990). The effect of a storybook reading program on the literacy development of at-risk kindergarten children. *Literacy Research Journal.*

Morrow, L. M., & Tracey, D. (1997). Strategies for phonics instruction in early childhood classrooms. *Reading Teacher, 50*(8), 2-9.

Morrow, L. M. (2000). Literature-based instruction. *Handbook on reading research.* (Vols. 1-3).

Morrow, L. M. (2002). Literature-based instruction in the early years. *Handbook of Research in Early Literacy.*

Morrow, L. M. (2003). *The literacy center: Contexts for reading and writing.* Portland, ME: Stenhouse.

Morrow, L. M. (2003). *Organizing and managing the language arts block*. New York: NY: Guilford Press.

Morrow, L. M. (2004) Organizing and managing the language arts block. In *Hanbook of Organization and Management*. (C. Weinstein, Ed.) New York, NY: Erlbaum.

Morrow, L. M. (2011). *Best Practices in Literacy Instruction*. New York, NY: Guilford Press.

Morrow, L. M., (2012). *Literacy development in the early year: Helping children read and write* (7th Ed.). Boston, MA: Pearson.

Morrow, L. M., Kuhn, M., & Schwanenflugel, P. (2006-2007). The family fluency program. *The Reading Teacher, 60*(4), 322-333.

Morrow, L. M., & Young, J. U. (1997). A family literacy program connecting school and home: Effects on attitude, motivation, and literacy achievement. *Journal of Education Psychology, 89,* 736-742.

Morrow, L. M., Tracey, D., Woo, D., & Pressley, M. (1999). Characteristics of exemplary 1st grade literacy instruction. *Reading Teacher, 52,* 462-476.

National Governors Association Center for Best Practices, Council of Chief State School Officers. (2010). Common core state standards: English language arts. Washington, D.C.: National Governors Association Center for Best Practices, Council of Chief State School Officers.

National Reading Panel. (2000). Teaching children to read: An evidence-based assessment of the scientific research literature on reading and its implications for reading instruction. Reports of the subgroups. Bethesda, MD: National institutes of Health [Online] Available: http://www.nichd.nih.gov/publications/nrp.

National Staff Development Council (NSDC) Standards. Retrieved June 2, 2009 from http://www.nsdc.org/standards.

Needlman, R., Toker, K. H., Dreyer, B. P., Klass, P., Mendelsohn, A. L. (2005). Effectiveness of a primary care intervention to support reading aloud: A multicenter evaluation. *Ambulatory Pediatrics, 5*(4), 209-215.

No Child Left Behind (NCLB) Act of 2001, Pub. L. No. 107-110, 115, Stat. 1425 (2002).

Pressely, M. (2002). *Learning to read: Lessons from exemplary first grade classrooms*. New York, NY: Guilford Press.

Pressely, M., Wharton-McDonald, R., Allington, R. L., Block, C. C., Morrow, L. M., Tracey, D., Baker, K., Brooks, G., Cronin, J., Nelson, E., & Woo, D. (2001). A study of effective 1st grade literacy instruction. *Scientific Studies of Reading, 5,* 35-58.

Richardson, V. (2001). Alexis De Tocquville and the Dilemmas of Professional Development. (CIERA Pub. 01-12). Retrieved October 10, 2008 from http://www.ciera.org/library/archive/2001-12/22OCT01.

Roe, M. F. (2004). Professional Learning Catalysts: Unveiling the Influences on One Teacher's Literacy Practices. *Reading Research and Instruction, 44*(1), 32-61.

Schuck, S., Abusson, P., & Buchanan, J. (2008). Enhancing teacher education practice through professional learning conversations. *European Journal of Teacher Education, 31,* 215-227.

Seidman, I. (2006). *Interviewing as qualitative research: A guide for researchers in education and the social sciences*. New York, NY: Teachers College Press.

Stotnik, W. J., & Smith, M. D. (2008). *Focus on literacy: Professional development audit*. Boston, MA: Community Training Assistance Center (CTAC).

Talbert, J. E. & McLaughlin, M. W. (2002). Profession communities and the artisan model of teaching. *Teachers and Teaching: Theory and Practice, 3/4,* 325-343.

Tamis-LeMonda, C. S., Bornstein, M. H., Baumwell, L. (2001). Maternal responsiveness and children's achievement of language milestones. *Child Development, 72*(3), 748-767.

Vygotsky, L. S. (1978) *Mind in society: The development of higher psychological processes*. Cambridge: MA: Harvard University Press.

Wiederholt, J. L. & Bryant, B. R. (2001). *Gray oral reading tests* (4th Ed.) Austin, TX: Pro-Ed.

Yoon, K. S., Duncan, T., Lee, S. W. Y., Scarloss, B., & Shapley, K. (2007). *Reviewing the evidence on how teacher professional development affects student achievement* (Issues & Answers Report, REL 2007-No. 033). Washington, D.C.: U.S. Department of Education, Institute of Education Sciences, National Center for Education Evaluation and Regional Assistance, Regional Education Laboratory Southwest. Retrieved from http://ies.ed.gov/ncee/edlabs.

Collaborative Writing: Is There Any Other Kind?

Janet Emig
Professor Emerita
Rutgers University

No. But perhaps I should elaborate.

My theme here is not about the open and classic modes of collaboration most of us have been a part of: co-writing or co-editing research projects and reports, articles, and books. Nor, in another genre like popular fiction, where, say, a crime writer like James Patterson explicitly acknowledges his co-author on the title page, albeit in a paler color and smaller font! Nor even about those illegitimate and underground modes we as teachers and administrators know all too well: the parental essay on, say, mollusks submitted by that desperate middle-schooler, or that freshman comp essay cloned from Google. Rather, my focus is on the more subtle, pervasive, but often unacknowledged modes of collaboration, unacknowledged because they are as encompassing as air for those of—that is, almost all of the world—who live in a literate culture.

A few observations first, however, on the markers of collaboration we as scholars and researchers readily observe: acknowledgments, footnotes, and bibliographies—often, the origins of footnotes. To take each of these in turn: There has been a growing spate of acknowledgments recently beyond the familiar sets of the over-effusive without-whoms from first-timers cataloguing everyone from kindergarten teachers to great aunts; and the de rigeur bows from the experienced to the obviously long-suffering spouses, partners, friends, editors, and agents. More and more, there are acknowledgments to another set, those who seem to form the author's writing group, a phenomenon more marked, I believe, since the advent of writing projects, the women's movement, and our more informed ways of teaching writing.

Acknowledgments also provide us with a trio of the three Rs. Let's call them re-assurance, remorse, and revenge. An example of each. Re-assurance: No living politicians were maimed or killed in the writing of this book. Remorse: I apologize to my grandmother for quoting some of her ill-advised remarks about her husband, my grandfather, because she didn't realize that she was being taped. Revenge: Every word I have written about this lying, scheming twit has been checked and vetted by my research assistant and the publisher's counsel.

The dedication is a privileged species of acknowledgment usually highlighted by claiming a page of its own. It differs from direct collaboration by usually signifying a lifelong influence rather than a specific interaction with the current text.

Despite our own scrupulosity, footnotes in this age of technology may now be an endangered species. In her end-page essay in the October 9, 2011 *New York Sunday Times* Book Review (you won't catch me not acknowledging!), Alexandra Horowitz describes how even scholarly e-books are now appearing without their footnotes. Such truncation is a loss of one of our major acknowledgments of collaboration. There is enough actual plagiarism around without giving the impression that we are engaged in intellectual stealing when we are not.

Where acknowledgments are usually directed to persons, bibliographies and other forms of sources denote texts. A characteristic, some say particularly of American biographers and historians, is the sheer heft of their research. Two recent publications could serve as confirmation—the fourth volume of Robert Caro's magisterial biography of LBJ, *The Passage of Power*, and Wade Davis's moving account of the climbing of Everest by World War I veterans, *Into the Silence*.

At the beginning I noted that many of us are often unaware of the two major phenomena with which we must collaborate when we write. These are, of course, our culture and our language. Why? Because we must inevitably live inside both. We have no alternative. They are as inevitable and inescapable as air. Indeed, if we are post-modernists, we regard both as formidable, if not total, determinants of how and what we write.

Language and culture are tightly intertwined; but I would like to tease them apart and treat them separately. First, language. I was at Harvard during the beginning of the reign of Noam Chomsky. We all cross-registered at MIT and took classes on the evolving theory of transformational-generative grammar. The times were very heady and exciting, with professors rushing into our classrooms trailing trains of scotch-taped legal paper and announcing that they had just formed a new hypothesis about "an" or "the."

I am, however, a Pinkerian rather than a Chomskyan. That is because Steven Pinker espouses an evolutionary biological hypothesis of language that I find more persuasive than Chomsky's theory. At the beginning of *The Language Instinct: How the Mind Creates Language*, he presents it succinctly:

> Language is not a cultural artifact that we learn the way we learn to tell time or how the federal government works. instead, it is a distinct piece of the biological makeup of our brains. Language is a complex, specialized skill which develops in the child spontaneously, without conscious effort or formal instruction, is deployed without awareness of its underlying logic, is qualitatively the same in every individual, and is distinct from more general abilities to process information or to behave intelligently (p. 18).

Can one be both a Pinkerian and a post-modernist? Although I am not, I think that it is possible even though, at first, and then, at ever-deepening scrutiny, the two theories seem at odds, if not openly irreconcilable. To reconcile them, consider a continuum with a theory of what language is preceding the concerns of how language forms and shapes culture, here—notably—writing. So far as I can ascertain, the post-modernists seem not to ask themselves about how language came to be; rather, they treat it as an all-powerful given. A fused definition of writing that would then emerge is: "Writing is a cultural construct created by language, which is a biological instinct."

Can our relation with language accurately be described as collaboration?

For post-modernists the effect of language upon writing is chiefly uni-directional. If the user affects the language, it is in relatively trivial, not substantive, ways. Other schools of literary critics might claim, for example, that James Joyce in *Finnegan's Wake* affects the language; but the post-modernists and the evolutionary biologists like Pinker would undoubtedly say that the additions are lexical; the basic syntactic constraints hold.

As for culture, when we write, we collaborate with our entire reading histories, as well as with the vast canon that informs it. T.S. Eliot describes it as the interplay between the tradition and the individual talent. Some of us are more susceptible than others to what we have just read, becoming baby Hemingways or very junior Faulknera. Some seek out a deliberate influence. Willa Cather once said that she read the King James version of the Bible every morning before she started writing; the sonorous rhythms are evident in *Song of the Lark* or *My Antonia*.

For me, reading good writing almost impels me to start writing myself: lately, David McCullough, Julian Barnes, and William Trevor incite. And, curiously, the effect that I believe still qualifies as collaborative can cross genres: Reading a Barnes' essay might turn me to writing a poem; or a Trevor short story, a talk/essay like this one.

In all this, there are, of course, implications for teaching.

In almost every current critique of what is most needed in educational reform, teaching collaboration is invariably highlighted. The reason is evident: Collaboration, simply, is how much of the world actually works.

Here, then, are a few curricular possibilities:

1. Provide a model. If you are currently engaged in a collaborative project with colleagues, hold your meetings and share your drafts with your students.

2. Design assignments that sponsor—indeed, require—collaboration. Have as part of the process their analysis of how their collaboration did or did not work, and why.

3. Invite teams involved in other genres of collaborative writing like film or TV writers to discuss their ways of working together.

4. Compile a reading list accompanying all of the above.

Even quite young writers are aware that that they are drawing or borrowing from literary and other cultural sources. The second-grader who begins her story "Once upon a time" and closes with a flourish ("The End") has already internalized conventions of the canon.

My claim is that making explicit to ourselves and to our students the power and inevitability of collaboration strengthens their poise and even their validity as assured and sophisticated writers.

Disciplinary Literacy in New Literacies Environments: Expanding the Intersections of Literate Practice for Adolescents

Michael Manderino
Northern Illinois University

Adolescent literacy has received considerable attention in recent years as reports about the lack of achievement exhibited on national standardized tests like the National Assessment of Educational Progress (NAEP) and the American College Testing (ACT) (ACT, 2006; Grigg, Donahue, & Dion, 2007) proliferate. Reports like *Time to Act: An Agenda for Advancing Adolescent Literacy for College and Career Success* argue that it is crucial to focus on improving adolescent literacy achievement by focusing on reading in the disciplines (Carnegie, 2010). History, like science, math, and English/ Language Arts, is one of the core disciplines in any middle or high school curriculum. And yet, the performance of students on measures of historical knowledge has also been historically lamented throughout the 20th century (Wineburg, 2001). But attention to content alone will not ameliorate the lack of literacy or content achievement as measured by tests like the ACT or NAEP. As a result, a focus on disciplinary literacy has been suggested as a way to improve both content area learning and literacy achievement (Moje, 2008).

The 2010 Carnegie Report, *Reading in the Disciplines: The Challenges of Adolescent Literacy,* suggests that adolescent literacy possesses its own set of challenges because middle and high school students read more complex expository texts that are situated in subject areas than students in earlier grades (Lee & Spratley, 2010). This shift from the emphasis on narrative to expository texts has been described as a shift from "learning to read" to "reading to learn" (Chall, 1983). Many students have difficulty "reading to learn" and fall behind their peers in terms of reading achievement. One approach to improve literacy achievement across school subject areas has been to instruct students in the use of content-area reading strategies. In the quest to remediate the gaps in reading achievement, literacy research has focused on strategy instruction designed for use in all subject areas. Researchers have developed and studied the impact of strategies that are rooted in literacy theory to apply to the study of expository texts in any subject area. These strategies include, but are not limited to, reciprocal teaching (Palinscar & Brown, 1984), KWL (Ogle, 1989), Question-Answer Relationships (Raphael, 1982), Inquiry Charts (Hoffman, 1992), Concept Oriented Reading Instruction (Guthrie, McGough, Bennett, & Rice, 1996), and Questioning the Author (McKeown, & Beck, 1993). These reading strategies are well-researched and grounded in literacy practices and theory and they are often applied by teachers as general strategies to be used by students across subject areas without taking into account the specific literacy demands of the subject or discipline (Conley, 2008). However, the application of generic reading strategies does not appear to help students read complex disciplinary texts. As recent National Assessment of Educational Progress (NAEP) data suggests, high school students have not improved in reading over the past 15 years (Grigg, Donahue, & Dion, 2007), nor are they very prepared to tackle the rigorous demands of disciplinary texts in college (ACT, 2006).

In 2010, 46 states adopted the Common Core Standards for English Language Arts and Mathematics that increase the rigor of texts students should encounter in school. The English Language Arts standards also include specific guidelines for literacy in History/Social Studies. Standards for upper high school include the "ability to integrate and evaluate multiple sources of information presented in diverse formats and media" and "integrate information from diverse sources, both primary and secondary, into a coherent understanding of an idea or event, noting discrepancies among sources" (CCSO, 2010). Teaching historical thinking, for example, is now an integral part of a common core curriculum that is rooted in the use of multiple multimodal texts.

In this study, I argue that considerations of the range of texts that are prevalent within a discipline like history must be examined in order to better understand how disciplinary learning transpires in a high school classroom. The purpose was to describe the reading processes of students who read multiple, multimodal texts in an online environment to create historical meaning about an inquiry question. Next, this study aimed to investigate how different types of multimodal texts influenced students' historical understandings of a controversial historical topic. Lastly, because historical thinking involves the creation of interpretations of history with evidence from multiple sources, this study sought to learn how students come to synthesize various texts when they have the task of creating a historical argument in response to a historical inquiry question. The study was needed because the study of multiple texts has not focused on academic understanding of multimodal texts and how they contribute to historical thinking despite the fact that students engage with multiple media sources on a daily basis.

THEORETICAL FRAMEWORK

Theorists in the 20th century recognized the importance of the linguistic turn (Rorty, 1967). That is, they acknowledged the primacy of language in understanding phenomena. In the 21st century, some have argued that we are at the dawn of the visual or pictorial turn (Mitchell, 1994). This turn acknowledges that multiple modes of meaning cannot necessarily be separated. This line of literacy research, that addresses the intersection of words—spoken and written—and images—static and moving—in the construction of meaning, highlights the need for an examination of the role of these texts in specific disciplines.

Reading comprehension has a long line of research, but the role text plays in comprehension in a specific discipline has not been deeply studied (Moje, Stockdill, Kim, & Kim, 2010). And since text can be broadly construed to include any representations that create meaning (Bloome & Egan-Robertson, 1993), it is important to expand research on the role of non-traditional texts in particular disciplinary contexts. That is, how do readers comprehend a range of texts in discipline-specific contexts and how do those texts impact a reader's comprehension? Moje et al. (2011) suggest also, that a careful study of the role of non-traditional printed texts in the study of history "seems long overdue" (p. 465).

Both cognitive science and sociocultural research perspectives have aimed to expand understandings of the processes by which students come to make meaning from different kinds of texts. Cognitive science has studied students' text processing primarily through think-aloud protocols. These studies have illuminated the reading processes that students exhibit during the reading of either single or multiple texts. Studies that take a sociocultural perspective have provided insights into how the role of the activity and context of learning impact student reading. Whether the focus is on individual student processes associated with meaning-making or social processes that influence meaning-making, the changing nature of literacy and its impact on adolescent learning demands that multimodal sources be considered. This study drew on both cognitive and sociocultural perspectives in order to inform the design of the task and the analysis of the data. The two intersecting theoretical frameworks that guided this study were domain learning (Alexander, 1998, 2003) and multiliteracies (New London Group, 1996).

Literacy scholars have argued that particular literacy practices are unique to each domain or discipline (Alexander, 1998; Moje, 2008; Shanahan & Shanahan, 2008). The comprehension of the texts in a discipline is situated within these contexts. So, rather than solely advocating the teaching of strategies for reading texts that can be applied across content areas, researchers advocate the teaching of discipline-specific strategies (Lee, 2006; Lee & Spratley, 2010; Moje, 2008; Shanahan & Shanahan, 2008). To develop discipline-specific strategies, the language and literacy practices that govern a discipline need to be understood (Shanahan & Shanahan, 2008).

Content knowledge is often the primary focus of subject area classes like history. The study of history is considered an academic domain. Domain knowledge refers to the scope of an individual's knowledge, including content knowledge, in a given field of study (Alexander, Shcallert, & Hare, 1991). Alexander (1992) claims that domain knowledge consists of declarative, procedural, and conditional knowledge that are not equal across domains of learning. Domain knowledge is a specialized field of content knowledge. And, domain knowledge in history is different than domain knowledge in chemistry and both possess a broader scope of knowledge than non-academic domains. Subordinate to the more broadly construed construct of domain knowledge is the more formalized subset of disciplinary knowledge (Alexander, et al., 1991). Shanahan (2009) distinguishes disciplinary knowledge to include knowledge of how information is created, what information is valued, how knowledge is communicated, and who controls knowledge dissemination in a domain. The focus of disciplinary knowledge is not on content itself but on how readers come to make sense of content based on their knowledge of how the domain functions.

In his seminal study of historians' reading processes, Wineburg (1991) compared the reading processes of students and expert historians. The historians' high level of disciplinary knowledge allowed them to easily make sense of historical sources they found unfamiliar. Based on the ways that the historians approached new content within the domain of history, Wineburg (1991) proposed that historians utilize three heuristics, *contextualization, corroboration, and sourcing*, when reading a text. These heuristics entail a level of disciplinary thinking in the domain of history that allows them to construct interpretations in areas where they may possess little prior experience or knowledge.

Disciplinary literacy, therefore, is an approach to building the requisite disciplinary knowledge required by a given domain. Disciplinary literacy then is comprised of the cognitive literacy processes used to make meaning, the cultural tools—including language and texts that mediate thinking—and the epistemic beliefs about knowledge and knowledge production that constitute the discipline (Moje, 2007; Shanahan & Shanahan, 2008).

Experts within various disciplines do not make sense of single texts; rather, their interpretations of a text involve complex intertextual integrations. Whereas much research has focused on single text comprehension (Anderson & Pearson, 1984; Kintsch, 1994; RAND, 2002), it is evident that in order to engage in a discipline, readers must make meaning across multiple texts that vary in mode, genre, and structure. It follows that students, in mirroring discipline-based practices, must learn to interpret multiple texts as well.

Multiple-text comprehension, in contrast to single-text comprehension, is the reading of multiple texts simultaneously (within a given task or activity) and interdependently (Boyd & Ikpeze, 2007). While single-text comprehension has predominated reading research, researchers argue that even single-text comprehension elicits intertextual processes for the reader (Goldman, 2004). From both cognitive and sociocultural perspectives, texts do not stand alone either in one's constructed mental representations (Kintsch, 1994) or through one's previous textual experiences (Smagorinsky, 2001). Issues of text structure (Goldman & Rakestraw, 2000), considerateness of text (Beck, McKeown, & Worthy, 1995), authorial voice (Paxton, 1999), genre (Bazerman, 2000), and text type (Boyd & Ikpeze, 2007) all impact how meaning is made from texts and how that meaning is used to deepen thinking within the practices of the discipline.

Reading multiple texts differs from reading single texts largely because the purpose for reading varies. Students often read multiple texts for the purpose of coming to an overarching understanding of a particular topic that can only be achieved by reading multiple texts interdependently. A bulk of research on student reading of multiple texts has also been conducted in the cognitive sciences (Rouet, Favart, Britt, Mason, & Perfetti, 1996; Rouet, Favart, Britt, & Perfetti, 1997; Wiley & Voss, 1996, 1999; Wolfe & Goldman, 2005). These studies used the discipline of history as a context for the ways in which students process multiple texts. Perfetti, Rouet, & Britt (1999) posit that proficient readers marshal a situation model that re-presents meaning across all of the texts as a whole. In addition to the situation model, readers also create an *intertext model* that positions the various texts in the text set in relation to one another. Together these create an integrated *documents model* that creates a mental representation of the entire set of texts being read (Perfetti, et al., 1999).

Studies of multiple-text comprehension situated in classrooms demonstrate that students rarely create a cohesive intertext or documents model, however (Hynd-Shanahan, Holschuh, & Hubbard, 2004; Stahl, Hynd, Britton, McNish, & Bosquet, 1996; VanSledright & Kelly, 1998). In the various studies of students reading multiple texts during classroom tasks, students lacked the cognitive and social processes to engage in the type of disciplinary thinking that experts in the field engage in (Leinhardt & Young, 1996; Wineburg, 1991, 1998). Even the most capable students struggle to create meaning across multiple texts (Hartman, 1995; Stahl, et al., 1996; Wineburg, 1991).

The Internet has afforded access to an exponential number of sources, including ones that are multimodal, and the nature of historical inquiry draws on resources that contain multiple semiotic potentials. History in particular makes use of these multiliteracies in order to construct historical meaning. Students' successful negotiation of these sources is essential to build strong disciplinary knowledge. In the study of history, one goal for students is to be able to understand how historical knowledge is constructed and begin to think like a historian. Since historians use multiple sources of information to make sense of history and write their interpretations of history based on those texts, students should have the opportunity to understand how those narratives are constructed.

Information and communication technologies are a medium in which students negotiate meaning-making through the reading of multiple multimodal texts that are disciplinary based.

Multimodal texts make use of multiple semiotic tools such as words and images together to create meaning that is more textured than that created by mono-modal texts. Multiple semiotic signs are not read as individual signs but as an integrated sign (Kress & Van Leeuwen, 1996). Multimodality, then, has implications for new constructions of meaning in and across texts (Kress, 1998). Print text can evoke one meaning while visual text evokes another, and the two together can act synergistically to evoke even other meanings (Kress & Van Leeuwen, 1996). A visual image may elicit meanings that contradict the text or elaborate on it and vice versa. The combination of various textual modes provides a multitude of potential configurations and integrated forms of representation (Lemke, 2002). These potential configurations are multiplicative as the student works with an increasing number of texts. The ways in which text, image, sound, etc. come together have the potential to expand meaning-making opportunities for students engaged in historical inquiry. And, because there are so many possibilities for the interpretation of multimodal texts, it is important to understand the role of multimodality in disciplinary learning rather than just assume that multimodal texts will simply improve learning. Multimodality is not a new phenomenon, but with the advent of the Internet and other technologies, multimodal texts constitute a large amount of texts that are utilized by students.

CONTEXT AND METHODOLOGY

The study was conducted towards the end of the spring semester in the large metropolitan high school in which I taught. The students were majority Latino/a, comprising 65% of the student body. More than one-half of all students self-reported speaking Spanish at home. The school had a low-income rate of 13.4% and a dropout rate of 6.1%. The average ACT reading score for the school was 19.2 and the state average was 21.9. Eight students with a range of reading ability as measured by the ACT reading test were selected from two intact American history classes taught by the same teacher who was in his second year. Think-aloud protocols (Ericsson & Simon, 1980; Pressley & Afflerbach, 1995) and semi-structured student interviews were employed with all eight students. All think-aloud and interview data were video/audio-recorded and transcribed in full.

A bounded Internet-based task was designed to investigate a central historical question about American involvement in the Vietnam War. The central historical question posed follows. *"Was President Johnson justified in asking Congress for a resolution for war after the Gulf of Tonkin Incident?"* To provide information for students to formulate a response to this question, a website was created using *Google Sites* that included eight multimodal sources about the United States' involvement in the Vietnam War surrounding the Gulf of Tonkin Incident in 1964. The website contained an introduction text and introduction video, two audio files, two embedded videos, and two images that provided information addressing justification for U.S. involvement in the war circa the Gulf of Tonkin Incident. Each source was embedded into its own page and listed the author, the source, and the date of publication at the top of the source. Students could navigate the site in any manner they chose after reading the introduction text and watching the three-minute introduction video.

After reading each source, students were asked to provide usefulness and trustworthiness ratings on a five-point Likert scale. Students also provided an open-ended response to explain their usefulness and trustworthiness ratings. Lastly, students provided an open-ended response to the question, "Has your opinion changed? Why or why not?"

At the end of the task, students were also asked to rate all of the documents cumulatively for usefulness and trustworthiness. In addition to ranking all eight sources, students selected the most and least useful sources and the most and least trustworthy sources. Finally, students participated in a semi-structured interview about their experience with the task.

To guide the uncovering of conscious processes of reading multiple multimodal sources, previous research that utilized think-aloud protocols guided the coding structure (Hartman, 1995; Hynd, 2003; Pressley & Cho, 2009; Wineburg, 1991, 1998; Wolfe & Goldman, 2005). Each of the previous studies employed think-aloud codes for students reading multiple texts about a historical topic. These studies drew on think-aloud protocols as students or experts read across multiple texts that consisted of traditionally written primary and secondary sources. Whether tracing intertextual connections (Hartman, 1995), historical thinking processes (Wineburg, 1991, 1998), or cognitive reading processes (Wolfe & Goldman, 2005), all four studies used an idea unit or an utterance as the unit of analysis. That is, individual statements were parsed based on their reference to a single idea or type of processing. The unit of analysis for the think-aloud protocols, in this study, was most consistent with Wolfe and Goldman's (2005) comments and events. A comment was defined as the entire burst of speech that followed student reading. An event was defined as a unit of speech that represented a distinct type of reading process. Following transcription, the think-aloud data was parsed into comments and events. Across over 200 pages of transcripts, 1,006 events were parsed. Once parsed, the event units were coded by utilizing constant comparative analysis (Glaser & Strauss, 1967). That is, codes for the types of decisions students used when reading the sources and the ways students integrated multiple texts were created and refined based on reading and re-reading all transcripts. What emerged, as a result of this process, was that several layers of historical thinking were demonstrated. Consequently, think-aloud interviews were coded at 3 levels. The first level of coding addressed the depth of historical thinking (Reisman, 2010; Wineburg, 1991). The coding scheme utilized a progression of historical thinking from value-based statements and generic sense-making statements to historical analysis that draws on student use of Wineburg's heuristics (1991) of contextualization, corroboration, and sourcing. The final level of historical thinking was coded as historical analysis. If a student employed one or more of the historical thinking heuristics and made a direct follow-up statement or evaluation, the code of historical analysis could be applied.

The second level of coding marked the specific literacy processes that occurred within the level of historical thinking (Afflerbach & Cho, 2009; Pressley & Afflerbach, 1995). These codes were mapped to provide insight into the generic literacy processes that students exhibited while engaged in the task. They were nested within each of the 6 historical thinking codes. The purpose of these codes was to provide insight into the types of literacy processes employed by students during their historical reading/thinking. Codes included agreeing or disagreeing with the author, historical actors, or situations, asking clarifying questions, paraphrasing, evaluation, elaboration, making predictions, and summarizing.

Finally, think-aloud comments were mapped for the textual location: local, intratextual, intertextual, and global. The site and reference of the utterance determined the textual location. For example, when a student made a think-aloud utterance, it was mapped to be *local* if the utterance referred to what was previously read only. An utterance was mapped as *intratextual* if the utterance referred to the current text being read but prior to the most previous think-aloud utterance. The *intertextual* code was used for a think-aloud utterance that referred to a previous source or prior knowledge and the *global* code was used for an utterance that referred to the entire text set or the task as a whole.

The purpose for using a nested coding scheme was to be able to identify the types of literacy processes that occur within levels of historical thinking and map the textual locations of those thinking and reading processes. This coding system provided a layered picture of the reading processes students exhibited as they read different types of multimodal texts. The codes provided clues to the ways students think historically by using sets of literacy practices. In addition to the codes, student usefulness and trustworthiness ratings of each source both during and after the task and the semi-structured interviews were utilized to triangulate the think-aloud data.

FINDINGS

Analysis of historical thinking codes revealed that students predominately engaged in more generic sense-making (62%) during their reading instead of employing discipline-specific reading behaviors. All eight students did exhibit unprompted use of historical thinking heuristics, however. They did demonstrate varying degrees of disciplinary thinking as they read both primary and secondary sources. Analysis of the reading processes that were nested within the levels of historical thinking revealed that students engaged in more complex reading processes like questioning, evaluating, and elaborating rather than less complex processes like quoting text, paraphrasing, and summarizing. The division of the codes based on complexity of mental representations resulted in 31.8% of events not adding to a complex mental representation, whereas 65.5% of think-aloud events were coded as contributing to a complex mental representation. Students were able to engage deeply with multiple multimodal texts. Finally, students were able to construct intertextual mental representations that depended on the reading of multiple sources.

The analysis of the eight think-aloud interviews revealed important ways that students of varying reading ability used multimodal texts to mediate their understandings of the Gulf of Tonkin Incident. First, students were able to utilize multiple texts to build their representations of the Gulf of Tonkin Incident regardless of their reading ability as measured by the ACT. Second, the eight students indicated their preference for multiple sources in multimodal format as contributing to their ability to reason across the sources. Finally, while the eight students demonstrated their ability to construct complex mental representations, they were not critical about the authorship of the sources, nor did they often question the veracity of the production of the sources, suggesting that while multimodal sources provide opportunities for students to access rigorous disciplinary texts, they cannot be added indiscriminately into the curriculum.

Making Text Accessible

Reading across multimodal texts appeared to have the effect of helping students, who were identified as less proficient readers as measured by the ACT, to create complex historical interpretations that were similar to students who were considered more proficient readers. The bridging of differences in interpretations was apparent as less proficient readers moved through the task. While the most proficient readers exhibited some disciplinary thinking and complex reading processes early in the task, less proficient readers began to exhibit similar disciplinary thinking and processing towards the end of the task. For example, two contrasting students in terms of ACT reading performance demonstrated how both exhibited sophisticated interpretations of the Gulf of Tonkin Incident. Both students made the same percentages of historical thinking categories and number of think-aloud statements. Initially, each student started by asking several clarifying questions but by the end of the task assembled a nuanced mental representation of the event.

Michele (pseudonym), a highly proficient reader based on an ACT reading score of 31, demonstrated the historical thinking skill of corroboration while she watched the source, *The Fog of War,* and contrasted it with Johnson's *Midnight Address* speech to the American people.

> Michele: Um, he's kinda just saying that like um, that there was attacks on it but like really from the other videos I know that like they, he didn't even know for sure if the attacks had been made do it wasn't just something that was like wrong with their sonar or something so I doesn't seem like he is actually telling the truth really. He kinda just seems like he's just relaying like information, kinda like he's just saying what somebody else has already told him. Like it doesn't seem like he really knows much about it which makes me think like he actually doesn't know much about it and that he's just kinda saying it because that's what somebody had like told him.

Michele questioned the veracity of Johnson's claims based on the evidence from *The Fog of War* clip that asserts that the attack never happened. She not only comprehended the text but also created her own historical analysis by corroborating multiple videos.

Jovany (pseudonym), a less proficient reader based on the ACT with a score of 18, corroborated sources during the task as well. This following excerpt, while he listened to a phone call between President Johnson and National Security Advisor McGeorge Bundy, highlighted Jovany's use of multiple heuristics to create his own historical analysis.

> Jovany: Um, the introduction is saying that um, this conversation was I believe before the Gulf of Tonkin Incident. Ok. (rewinds tape) At the time, the war in Vietnam was only a small dark cloud on the very distant horizon. Here is an excerpt from that conversation. Ok that brings me back to the one diagram of the cartoon, where he has a scar on his belly and that kinda tells me like um, he did, he doesn't know what he's doing. He did regret what happened. That's what that scar was.

Jovany contextualized the phone call by stating that he believed it took place before the Gulf of Tonkin Incident. After fixing up his comprehension by rewinding to listen again, Jovany made a corroboration back to *Vietscar,* a political cartoon, and asserted that the Tonkin Gulf Resolution was a mistake that Johnson would later regret. These comments reflect Jovany's ability to create global, historical reasoning about the topic. Despite vastly different reading abilities as measured by traditional constructs of comprehension, Jovany was able to engage in the construction of historical knowledge through complex historical sources in ways that a very proficient reader like Michele might.

Multiple Multimodal Texts Matter

Think-aloud data consistently demonstrated the necessity of multiple texts to build complex mental representations. As students worked through the task, they created historically accepted interpretations by evaluating single sources and as multiple sources to be contrasted and compared. Students also continually cited the presence of multiple sources to create their own representations. In the transcript below, Annika (pseudonym), who was considered a less proficient reader with a score of 16 on the ACT reading test, stated that she valued the different opinions that were presented in the various videos.

> Annika: Cause on, cause if you just have one video it's just one person's opinion but if you have other videos it's gonna be different opinions what like just different stuff. So instead of just being oh you know, that guy's true he so true but here it's like oh yeah he's so true but then you get more information and then you just like hold on, hold on is it really like that? And then you just start thinking and you change your perspective on the stuff other than just like a video, you are going to keep it up.

In this example, Annika stated the affordances of using multiple video sources in order to engage in disciplinary thinking like sourcing and corroboration even though she didn't explicitly use those terms. She was aware of the potential of reading multiple sources, particularly in video format, and why that motivated her to read several authentic disciplinary texts.

Student understandings were mediated by the visual nature of the texts, especially when coupled with textual information either embedded in the source or explaining the source. One video contained embedded transcripts that could be read. One of the phone calls also contained an embedded transcript. One of the visuals contained textual information to accompany the image. Students most often evidenced these sources in building their mental representations. Bianca (pseudonym), a less proficient reader with a 19 on the ACT, discussed why she preferred videos over other sources of text.

> Bianca: For history I think videos. I'd look for videos more because I think for history because it's easier cause once you have a visual image of what's happening instead of just reading it, reading it, sometimes you know they try to just paint a picture for you but it doesn't always seem to work that way. Having video makes it easier to understand.

The multimodal nature of the texts mediated student understandings by aiding the comprehension of complex primary and secondary sources. All of the students were drawn more to video in their comments during the semi-structured interviews. They consistently stated that video helped them to create an overarching understanding of the topic.

Complex but not Critical

While the multimodal texts afforded the ability of students to build mental representations around multiple texts that are highly valued in the discipline, they did not elicit a critical stance towards the production of those texts. Students were critical of the content contained within sources but were less likely to question why a source was produced or who constructed the source and what the motivations were for doing so. The only source that drew question about its authorship or production was the political cartoon, *Vietscar*. The other sources, especially the videos, were not questioned as to their authorship. For example, students rated *The Fog of War* clip, from the Academy Award-winning documentary, as the most trustworthy source but never questioned why it was made in 2003 or who made the film. Below is an example of Bianca (pseudonym) addressing the trustworthiness of *The Fog of War*.

Michael: Ok, how trustworthy was that video?
Bianca: I think it seems pretty trustworthy, because of like all the stuff you can see, the visualization of it, and how they can back up their information.

Bianca based her trustworthiness rating on the content contained in the video but not on the authorship of the video.

One of the hallmarks of historical thinking is not only analyzing the content of text but also the sources of their production. The author's bias and perspective are paramount to critically understanding the historical source and how it corroborates with other sources. The findings from this study suggest that students need explicit scaffolding with multimodal sources much like they do with traditional printed texts.

DISCUSSION

Based on the analysis of the eight think-aloud interviews, I argue that all of the students exhibited complex reading behaviors using multimodal historical sources, created complex mental representations about the historical topic, and made evaluations of the content contained in the sources indicating the ability to comprehend and synthesize primary and secondary historical sources. Despite demonstrating complex reading behaviors, students did not consistently engage in discipline-specific reading throughout the task. While this finding may be expected, it demonstrates the need for scaffolds in history instruction even when using multimodal texts.

For the most part, students did not spontaneously engage in the use of historical thinking heuristics, much like high school students in other multiple text studies in history (Stahl, et al., 1996; Wineburg, 1991). These students did not receive explicit instruction in how to source, contextualize, or corroborate historical sources; yet, when prompted, they were able to source a document. When unprompted, they used historical thinking heuristics 20% of the time. It is insightful to look at the ways that students utilized historical thinking to answer the inquiry question. For example, students noted that multiple perspectives on the Gulf of Tonkin Incident helped them determine if Johnson was justified in asking Congress for a resolution for war. It is evident that students viewed historical sources as contested and the ability to create an argument as central to historical inquiry.

The demonstration of complex reading across multiple texts indicates that high school students can engage in a complex task that includes multiple sources. It also demonstrates that students want to engage with multiple sources. The presentation of multimodal sources provided an element of motivation for the students as they indicated a high preference for the task. It appears that teachers would be able to engage students in an inquiry task by including the use of audio, video, and images instead of only printed texts. The addition of multimodal texts will not automatically lead students to engage in historical thinking without instruction, however.

As expected, a bulk of student reading occurred at the sense-making level, however the analysis revealed that students engaged in complex reading behaviors like making inferences, evaluations, and elaborations more so than quoting, paraphrasing and summarizing. Sixty-five percent of the sense-making events recorded from the think-aloud data were representative of complex reading behavior. Students demonstrated the ability to make sense of complex texts and exhibit complex reading processes while doing so. Students' ability to make evaluative and elaborative explanations indicated they were building an integrated documents model (Perfetti, et al., 1999). Their intertextual connections between texts are evidence for use of an intertext model, which is necessary to build a more integrated documents model (Perfetti, et al., 1999). The example of Jovany exemplifies the way he came to a complex mental representation of the Tonkin Gulf Incident as he continued to read across all of the texts like his peers who were more proficient readers. Jovany's construction of a complex interpretation over the course of the task also indicates that single sources may not elicit complex reading behaviors in the same way that multiple sources do. Typical classroom instruction around a single text may not have evoked Jovany's ability to develop a rich historical interpretation about the Gulf of Tonkin incident.

Several students demonstrated that they were able to build an increasingly complex mental representation of the Gulf of Tonkin Incident as the read across the documents provided. Students updated their documents models by forming updated situations and intertext models (Perfetti, et. al, 1999) throughout the task. Evidence of changing opinion throughout the task and evaluating the veracity of the content as well as the source of the content reflect these complex mental representations from students who possessed low background knowledge on the topic.

The adolescents in this study were able to process and reason across multiple multimodal sources that were both primary and secondary in nature. These are the types of texts a historian would analyze to investigate the Gulf of Tonkin Incident. The majority of the sources were primary sources and all of the sources contained elements of a primary source. Students in the think-aloud condition and whole class task consistently commented on the primary source elements within a secondary source as being useful and trustworthy. Students pointed to the authenticity of the primary sources like the phone calls or the footage from the deck of the *USS Maddox* as helping them to form their opinion. It is clear that primary sources impacted their understandings, but it also seemed that the presentation of primary sources in a multimodal format contributed to students' understanding and creation of complex mental representations.

Like Bain's (2006) study on the use of primary sources demonstrated, students can comprehend complex primary sources in historical inquiry. Teachers should not eschew primary source documents because they are too difficult. Additionally, students were able to develop a complex understanding of the event without being directly taught the event first. They were able to read multiple multimodal primary sources to create a historical interpretation. It is also evident, however, that students need additional supports when reading primary sources. While multimodal features may aid student comprehension of primary sources, it does not ensure comprehension. Teacher scaffolding is necessary.

The implications for classroom practice extend that called for by previous research on reading multiple texts in history. Students can read across multiple multimodal texts and can engage in complex reasoning around those texts. If a teacher is to take a disciplinary literacy focus, then it is important to investigate central topical knowledge but also how that knowledge is constructed and disseminated. Typically, research on students reading multiple texts has been conducted with more proficient readers in high school or with college-aged readers (Braåten, I., Strømsø, & Britt, 2009; Stahl, et al., 1996; Wiley & Voss, 1996; Wineburg, 1991). These high school students represented a range of reading ability from well below average to well above average, who also possessed limited prior knowledge on the topic and limited exposure to thinking like a historian. The students in this study demonstrated complex reading of the event across multiple sources. Teachers can teach historical thinking skills that are germane to the discipline through the use of multiple multimodal sources.

Because it appears that multimodal sources may help to bridge gaps in prior knowledge, teachers may consider adding multimodal sources into their text sets to make disciplinary texts more accessible to less proficient readers. This does not suggest that teachers should eschew written text for video, audio, or image sources only. These multimodal texts can be leveraged because of high student interest, so that students will be more likely to engage in rigorous examination of historical phenomena and perhaps be used as scaffolds to more dense and complex written primary and secondary sources.

Teacher preparation in content area or disciplinary literacy needs to focus on how to select quality multimodal texts for students to read. Text selection is crucial for engaging students with multiple complex texts. For example, in this study, students were unable to see the *Vietcsar* cartoon as a possible reflection of public opinion in 1966. Perhaps some additional text may have helped students better comprehend the cartoon.

As Internet usage grows in classroom settings, the promises and possibilities of accessing quality historical sources will be realized. An important caution needs to be stated, however. Simply giving kids multimodal texts will not lead them to be better readers or writers. That being said, the introduction of multimodal sources may help students build content knowledge and provide students with opportunities to learn and think about the past. This study did not identify all of the modal affordances (Jewitt, 2003) of multimodal texts, and more research is needed.

The results of this study are significant for three reasons. First, the study demonstrates that a wide range of readers who were not in the top of their class could reason across multiple multimodal primary and secondary historical sources in a complex manner, engaging in complex and discipline-specific inquiry. Multimodal texts appeared to facilitate the reading of multiple texts in history. Students still needed appropriate scaffolds for accessing the texts, however. For example, they were stymied in their attempts to understand the political cartoon because of their lack of contextual knowledge. Students also neglected to consider all aspects of disciplinary literacy, including how sources are produced and disseminated when engaged in historical inquiry.

Second, the study is significant because of its applicability to urban public high school contexts. The study population also reflects the nature of many of these schools: A majority of the students came from a linguistically diverse background, and more than 50% of the students spoke a language other than English (primarily Spanish) at home. Thus, the study's findings are useful for high schools exhibiting these characteristics. Traditionally underperforming students showed evidence of performing on par with their higher-achieving peers. These findings suggest that multimodal text may help students with limited disciplinary vocabulary and background knowledge. Multimodal texts can be leveraged not just for motivational purposes but also to help remediate larger gaps in background knowledge that allows for more complex disciplinary reading.

Finally, the study provided a needed empirical analysis of how students engage with multimodal texts in a discipline-specific context. Much more research is needed in this area because it is clear that demands for multiple text comprehension in a digitized world are not going away. While the central focus of this study was on how students read multiple multimodal texts for a school- and discipline-specific task, the ability to navigate a multitude of texts will impact their lives both in and out of school. We need to further conceptualize how to provide instruction with multimodal texts and continue to increase the complexity of texts for students.

REFERENCES

Afflerbach, P., & Cho, B. (2009). Responsive comprehension strategies in new and traditional forms of reading. In S. E. Israel & G. G. Duffy (Eds.), *Handbook of research on reading comprehension* (pp. 69-90). New York, NY: Routledge.

Alexander, P. A. (1992). Domain knowledge: Evolving themes and emerging concerns. *Educational Psychologist, 27*(1), 33.

Alexander, P. A. (1998). The nature of disciplinary and domain learning: The knowledge, interest, and strategic dimensions of learning from subject matter text. In C. R. Hynd (Ed). *Learning from text across conceptual domains.* Mahwah, NJ: Erlbaum.

Alexander, P. A. (2003). The development of expertise: The journey from acclimation to proficiency. *Educational Researcher, 32*(8), 10-14.

Alexander, P. A., Schallert, D. L., & Hare, V. C. (1991). Coming to terms: How researchers in learning and literacy talk about knowledge. *Review of Educational Research, 61*(3), 315-343.

American College Testing (2006). *Reading between the lines: What the ACT reveals about college readiness for reading.* Retrieved from http://act.org/path/policy/reports/reading.html

Anderson, R. C., & Pearson, P. D. (1984). A schema-theoretic view of basic processes in reading comprehension. In P. D. Pearson, R. Barr, M. L. Kamil, & P. Mosenthal (Eds.), *Handbook of reading research.* White Plains, NY: Longman.

Bain, R. (2006). Rounding up unusual suspects: Facing the authority hidden in the history classroom. *Teachers College Record, 108*(10), 2080–2114.

Bazerman, C. (2000). *Shaping Written Knowledge: The Genre and Activity of the Experimental Article in Science.* Madison: University of Wisconsin Press.

Boyd, F. B., & Ikpeze, C. H. (2007). Navigating a literacy landscape: Teaching conceptual understanding with multiple text types. *Journal of Literacy Research. 39*(2), 217-248.

Bloome, D., & Egan-Robertson, A. (1993). The social construction of intertextuality and classroom reading and writing. *Reading Research Quarterly, 28*(4), 303-333.

Bråten, I., Strømsø, H. I., & Britt, M. A. (2008). Trust matters: Examining the role of source evaluation in students' construction of meaning within and across multiple texts. *Reading Research Quarterly. 44*, 6–28.

Britt, M. A., & Aglinskas, C. (2002). Improving students' ability to identify and use source information. *Cognition and Instruction, 20*(4), 485-522.

Chall, J. S. (1983). *Stages of reading development.* New York, NY: McGraw-Hill.

Conley, M. W. (2008). Cognitive strategy instruction for adolescents: What we know about the promise, what we don't know about the potential. *Harvard Educational Review, 78*(1), 84-108.

Ericsson, K. A., & Simon, H. A. (1980). Verbal reports as data. *Psychological Review, 87*, 215-251.

Glaser, B., & Strauss, A. (1967). *The discovery of grounded theory: Strategies of qualitative research.* London, England: Wledenfeld and Nicholson.

Goldman, S. (2004). Cognitive aspects of constructing meaning through and across multiple texts. In N. Shuart-Faris & D. Bloome (Eds.), *Uses of intertextuality in classroom and educational research* (pp. 313-348). Charlotte, NC: Information Age Publishing.

Grigg, W., Donahue, P., & Dion, G. (2007). The nation's report card: 12th-grade reading and mathematics 2005 (NCES 2007-468). U.S. Department of Education, National Center for Education Statistics. Washington, D. C.: U.S. Government Printing Office.

Guthrie, J. T., McGough, K., Bennett, L., & Rice, M. E. (1996). Concept-oriented reading instruction: An integrated curriculum to develop motivations and strategies for reading. In L. Baker, P. Afflerbach, & D. Reinking (Eds.), *Developing engaged readers in school and home communities* (pp. 165-190). Mahwah, NJ: Erlbaum.

Hartman, D., K. (1995). Eight readers reading: The intertextual links of proficient readers reading multiple passages. *Reading Research Quarterly, 30*(3), 520-561.

Hoffman, J. (1992). Critical reading/thinking across the curriculum: Using I-charts to support learning. *Language Arts, 69*, 121–127.

Hynd, C. (1999). Teaching students to think critically using multiple texts in history. *Journal of Adolescent and Adult Literacy, 42*(6), 428-436.

Hynd-Shanahan, C., Holschuh, J. P., & Hubbard, B. P. (2004). Thinking like a historian: College students' reading of multiple historical documents. *Journal of Literacy.*

Jewitt, C., & Kress, G. (2003). *Multimodal Literacy.* New York, NY: Peter Lang.

Kintsch, W. (1994). Text comprehension, memory, and learning. *American Psychologist, 49*, 294-303.

Kintsch, W., & van Dijk, T. A. (1978). Toward a model of text comprehension and production. *Psychological Review, 85*, 363-394.

Kress, G. (1998). Visual and verbal modes of representation in electronically mediated communication: The potentials of new forms of text. In *Page to screen: Taking literacy into the electronic era*, ed. I. Snyder, (pp. 53–79). London, England: Routledge.

Kress, G., & Van Leeuwen, T. (1996). *Reading images: The grammar of visual design.* New York, NY: Routledge.

Kress, G. & Van Leeuwen, T. (2001). *Multimodal discourse: The modes of media of contemporary communication.* New York, NY: Edward Arnold.

Lee, C. D., Spratley, A. (2010). *Reading in the disciplines: The challenges of adolescent literacy.* New York, NY: Carnegie Corporation of New York.

Leinhardt, G., & Young, K. M. C. (1996). Two texts, three readers: Distance and expertise in reading history. *Cognition and Instruction, 14*(4), 441–486.

Lemke, J. L. (1998). Multiplying meaning: Visual and verbal semiotics in scientific text. In J. R. Martin & R. Veel, Eds., *Reading Science.* London, England: Routledge. (pp. 87-113).

Lemke, J. L. (2002). "Travels in hypermodality." *Visual Communication, 1*(3).

McKeown, M. G., & Beck, I. L. (1993). Grappling with text ideas: Questioning the author. *The Reading Teacher, 46*(7).

Mitchell, W. J. T. (1994). *Picture theory: Essays on verbal and visual representation.* Chicago, IL: University of Chicago Press.

Moje, E. B. (2007). Developing socially just subject-matter instruction: A review of the literature on disciplinary literacy teaching. *Review of Research in Education 2007, 31*, 1-44.

Moje, E. (2008). Foregrounding the disciplines in secondary literacy teaching and learning: A call for change. *Journal of Adolescent & Adult Literacy, 52*(2), 96-107.

Moje, E. B. (2009). A call for new research on new and multi-literacies. *Research in the Teaching of English, 43*(4), 348-362.

Moje, E. B., Stockdill, D., Kim, K., & Kim, H. (2011). The role of text in disciplinary learning. In M. Kamil, P. D. Pearson, P. A. Afflerbach, & E. B. Moje (Eds.), *Handbook of reading research (Vol. IV)*. New York, NY: Taylor & Francis.

National Governors Association Center for Best Practices & the Council of Chief State School Officers (2010). *Reaching higher. The Common Core State Standards* Validation Committee. Retrieved from http://www.corestandards.org/assets/CommonCoreReport_6.10.pdf

Ogle, D. (1989). KWL: A teaching model that develops active reading of expository text. *Reading Teacher, 39*, 546-570.

Palincsar, A. S., & Brown, A. L. (1984). Reciprocal teaching of comprehension fostering and monitoring activities. *Cognition and Instruction, 1*, 117-175.

Perfetti, C. A., Britt, M. A., Rouet, J. F., Georgi, M. C., & Mason, R. A. (1994). How students use texts to learn and reason about historical uncertainty. In M. Carretero & J. F. Voss (Eds.), *Cognitive and instructional processes in history and the social sciences* (pp. 257-283). Hillsdale, NJ: Lawrence Erlbaum Associates.

Perfetti, C. A., Rouet, J. F., Britt, M.A. (1999). Toward a theory of document representation. In H. Van Oostendorp & S. R. Goldman (Eds.). *The construction of mental representations during reading* (pp. 99-122). Mahwah, NJ: Erlbaum.

Pressley, M., & Afflerbach, P. (1995). *Verbal protocols of reading: The nature of constructively responsive reading.* Hillsdale, NJ: Erlbaum.

RAND Reading Study Group. (2002). *Reading for understanding: Toward a research and development program in reading comprehension.* DRU-2453. Santa Monica, CA: RAND Corporation.

Raphael, T. E. (1982). Question-answering strategies for children. *Reading Teacher, 36,* 186-190.

Reisman, A. (2010). Reading like a historian: a document-based history curriculum intervention with adolescent struggling readers. In Proceedings of the 9th International Conference of the Learning Sciences- olume 2 (ICLS '10), Kimberly Gomez, Leilah Lyons, and Joshua Radinsky (Eds.), Vol. 2. International Society of the Learning Sciences 24-24.

Rorty, R. (1967). *The Linguistic Turn.* Chicago, IL: University of Chicago Press.

Rouet, J. F., Favart, M., Britt, M. A., Mason, R., & Perfetti, C. A. (1996). Using multiple sources of evidence to reason about history. *Journal of Educational Psychology* 88(3), 478-493.

Rouet, J. F., Favart, M., Britt, M. A., & Perfetti, C.A. (1997). Studying and using multiple documents in history: effects of discipline expertise. *Cognition and Instruction, 15*(1), 85-106.

Shanahan, C. (2009). Disciplinary comprehension. In S. E. Israel & G. G. Duffy (Eds.), *Handbook of research on reading comprehension* (pp. 240-260). New York, NY: Routledge.

Shanahan, T., & Shanahan, C. (2008). Teaching disciplinary literacy to adolescents: Rethinking content-area literacy. *Harvard Education Review, 78*(1), 40-61.

Smagorinsky, P. (2001). If meaning is constructed, what's it made from? Toward a cultural theory of reading. *Review of Educational Research, 71*(1), 133–169.

Stahl, S., A., Hynd, C., Britton, B., McNish, M., & Bosquet, D. (1996). What happens when students read multiple source documents in history? *Reading Research Quarterly, 31*(4), 430-456.

Stahl, S. A., Hynd, C., Montgomery, T., & McClain, V. (1997). In Fourteen hundred and ninety two, Columbus sailed the ocean blue: The effects of multiple document readings on student attitudes and misconceptions. National Reading Research Center. Athens, University of Georgia, 9-21.

The New London Group (1996). A pedagogy of multiliteracies: Designing social futures. *Harvard Educational Review, 66*(1), 60-92.

van Dijk, T., & Kintsch, W. (1983). *Strategies of discourse comprehension.* New York, NY: Academic Press.

VanSledright, B. A., & Kelly, C. (1998). Reading American history: The influence of multiple sources on six fifth graders. *Elementary School Journal, 98,* 239–265.

Wiley, J., & Voss, J. (1996). The effects of 'playing historian' on learning in history. *Applied Cognitive Psychology, 10,* S63-S72.

Wineburg, S. S. (1991). Historical problem solving: A study of the cognitive processes used in evaluation of documentary and pictorial evidence. *Journal of Educational Psychology, 83*(1), 73-87.

Wineburg, S. S. (1998). Reading Abraham Lincoln: An expert/expert study in the interpretation of historical texts. *Cognitive Science, 22,* 319-346.

Wineburg, S. S. (2001). *Historical thinking and other unnatural acts: Charting the future of teaching the past.* Philadelphia: Temple University Press.

Wolfe, M. B., & Goldman, S. (2005). Relations between adolescents' text processing and reasoning. *Cognition and Instruction, 23*(4), 467–502.

Multimodality and Aurality:
Sound Spaces in Student Digital Book Trailers

Nathan C. Phillips
Blaine E. Smith
Vanderbilt University

In the U.S., a growing majority of young people, 64% of those ages 12-17 who use the Internet, create and share content online (e.g., posting photos or videos, writing blogs; Lenhart, Madden, Smith, & Macgill, 2007). While a smaller percentage of youth online post video content (19% of boys and 10% of girls; Lenhart et al., 2007), young people are increasingly taking advantage of the now relatively low cost of production and distribution of video content in order to share in an online "participatory culture" (Jenkins, 2008) of new media consumption and production (Ito, et al., 2010; Smith, 2010). Media production (including but not limited to video and audio production) has been integrated into media education curricula in schools, where formerly such instruction focused more on critical assessments of media products (see, e.g., Buckingham, 2003; Hobbs, 2007), and educators have argued for the necessity of young people developing media production skills and competencies in order to participate fully in civic dialogue and literacy practices in the 21st century (Alvey, et al., 2011; Jewitt, 2008; Kafai & Peppler, 2011; Kress, 2003).

The global, fluid, and networked nature of contemporary societies (Jewitt, 2008; Leander, Phillips, & Taylor, 2010) that has made it possible for broad media production distributions and circulations by and for young people has, as Jewitt (2008) has argued, also altered the nature of those productions: "a key aspect of this is the reconfiguration of the representational and communicative resources of image, action, sound, and so on in new multimodal ensembles" (p. 241). Researchers have studied the emergence of these ensembles from the perspective of theories of multimodality that assume that meaning is created and interpreted in and through multiple representational and communicative modes (Jewitt, 2009; Kress & van Leeuwen, 2001). These modes, or "organized sets of semiotic resources for meaning making" (Jewitt, 2008, p. 246), include image, sound, gesture, gaze, body posture, music, and written text. Despite this broad conception of modes for meaning-making, what Kress (2003) has called "the new dominance of the image" (p. 1; replacing the old dominance of writing) has overshadowed investigations of other modes (see, e.g., Kress & van Leeuwen, 2006). While other modes have not been ignored in studies of multimodal composition (see, e.g., furniture in Björkvall, 2009; gesture and movement in Jaworski & Thurlow, 2009; language in Scollon & Scollon, 2009; sound in Dalton, Smith, & Alvey, 2010; van Leeuwen, 1999; and music and sound in West, 2009), far less attention has been paid to modes outside of the image in studies of multimodal composition.

In this study, we investigate a set of youth-produced multimodal ensembles from the perspective of theories of multimodality, focusing specifically on one mode, sound, in an effort to extend and expand our understanding of the meaning-making potentials of such multimodal compositions. Why sound? Initially, we were drawn to sound as we first viewed our data set, which consisted of 50 digital book trailers (2-minute long videos advertising books in the style of movie trailers) produced by young people ages 5-18. These trailers, award-winning entries in a contest sponsored by several book publishers and public libraries, were posted online at the contest website (www.storytubes.info). Because the contest is called StoryTubes (after YouTube), we refer to the trailers themselves as StoryTubes. When we saw our first StoryTubes, we were struck by the sounds young people incorporated in their videos—driving guitar music to open an energetic romp through New York City, a young man singing and accompanying himself on the piano to introduce a favorite holiday story, sword-fighting sound effects to evoke an ancient battle, and the shriek of a child acting like a zombie to show the fear and fun of a tale of terror.

Our interest in sound is also theoretical. Scholars of cinema sound have argued that "we do not *see* and *hear* a film, we *hear/see* it" (Murch, 1994, p. xxi; emphasis original). That is, sound influences everything audiences see in a film. The importance of and historical lack of attention to sound in multimodal composition has also been recognized in art education (Duncum, 2004) and rhetoric and composition (Ball & Hawk, 2006; Selfe, 2009). The presence of sound in multimodal compositions—both those compositions generally present in the media ecologies that surround us and specifically present in the set of student-produced compositions we analyze for this paper—coupled with the importance of sound in viewers' meaning-making processes and the relative lack of attention on sound in multimodality led us to focus on sound.

Studies of the semiotics of sound have longer histories in music (Copland, 1939/2009; Leonard, 2001) and film studies (e.g., Altman, 1992; Bordwell & Thompson, 2010; Chion, 1994, 2009; Kerins, 2011; Lastra, 2000; Sider, Freeman, & Sider, 2003) and we are particularly indebted to analyses in film studies that have identified and codified systems of meaning-making for sound in film. Bordwell and Thompson (2010) have identified perceptual properties of sound in film (loudness, pitch, timbre); selecting, altering, and combining sounds for particular functions; and the dimensions of film sound that arise from interactions among sound and visuals (rhythm, fidelity, space, time). These properties, functions, and dimensions of film sound informed our analysis of student-produced StoryTubes by alerting us to possible systems of meaning-making. Specifically, we found the spatial dimension of sound in film—its source within the visual, conceptual, and story space of the StoryTubes and its role in producing visual, conceptual, and story spaces—carried significant meaning. We describe our conception of sound spaces within larger soundscapes in the Findings section of the paper.

Within multimodality, studies of sound have also worked to inventory semiotic modal resources. Van Leeuwen (1999) identified the materiality of sound resources including pitch, volume, breathiness, and rhythm. He further refined some sound systems to classify them as parametric rather than taxonomic systems. That is, unlike some visual domains, which Kress and van Leeuwen (2006) have described as having multiple semiotic choices arranged in structural taxonomies, van Leeuwen (1999) has come to see vocal quality, for example, as having a set of parameters that are all always included but to different degrees (e.g., tense/lax, loud/soft, high/low, rough/smooth, breathy/non-breathy, vibrato/plain, nasal/non-nasal).

METHODS

In order to describe and understand meaning-making with sound in StoryTubes, we asked the following questions:

- How is sound (music, sound effects, speech) and silence used in StoryTubes to construct and enhance a multimodal message?
- What are the semiotic resources for making meaning with and through sound in the multimodal composition of StoryTubes?

Data Sources

The StoryTubes videos analyzed for this study include all 50 of the winning videos posted on the StoryTubes website (www.storytubes.info) from 2008 to 2011 (for a complete list of all StoryTubes cited in this paper organized by year of submission, see Appendix A; for other analyses of StoryTubes, see Hollett & Ehret, 2011; Jocius & Wood, 2011). The contest is open to "English-speaking kids anywhere" between the ages of 5 and 18. Along with individual submissions, students are able to make videos with groups of five or fewer individuals. The "top prizes" for Judge's Choice Award Winner and Judge's Choice Honorable Mention are awarded by a panel that "consider[s] performance, script, creativity, and other factors" when making their decisions. The public can also vote online for the Online Voting prize (StoryTubes, 2011).

We chose this set of multimodal compositions because it is representative of the kinds of compositions young people create for their own purposes. In this case, the ostensible purpose for creating these compositions is to enter a contest. However, there are likely other purposes for creating and submitting StoryTubes (e.g., to fulfill a school assignment, to appease the requests of a parent, to do something fun with friends, to share a favorite book with a broad audience online). We see these as authentic compositions that afford us the potential to investigate sound in multimodal compositions across one corpus.

Regarding authentic compositions: We make no claims that these are entirely student-produced. The rules for participation in the StoryTubes contest (StoryTubes, 2011) list no requirements regarding the involvement or non-involvement of parents, siblings, teachers, or other adult collaborators in the production of the StoryTube. The rules state that "parents, teachers, and other adults may also appear in a video with a student or by themselves, but to qualify for prizes a video must have at least one entrant who is a student between the ages of five and eighteen years" (StoryTubes, 2011). For younger children, in particular, it is likely that there is extensive adult participation and collaboration in the making of the videos. For older students, it is possible that there is no adult involvement. But in either case, we know there is collaboration—even if only in operating a camera. It might be that some videos are scripted in advance and child actors are directed by adults or that adults simply operate the camera while children improvise. Some young children's videos include significant editing (e.g., with the addition of pre-produced sound effects and music, cuts between shots, and digital special effects and animation), pointing to the involvement of adults, while others do not appear to have been post-produced at all.

We make no claims, then, about the relative roles of adults and young people in creating the soundscapes we analyze or about the composers' rhetorical purposes. Rather, we take these videos as they have been distributed, as representing, in some way, the work of young people in composing multimodally and consider the rhetorical effects of these compositions on audiences. For these reasons, when we talk about the producers of these compositions, we interchangeably refer to them as composers, students, and young people. These compositions involve sound and silence in complex interplays with images to do work that affords meaning-making by audiences in particular ways. Those meaning-making processes with sound, rather than the processes of production, are the focus of this paper.

Data Analysis

Data analysis involved qualitative coding procedures informed by Grounded Theory (Corbin & Strauss, 2008). The process of developing a coding system began by first examining a subset of 10 videos. Each video was watched numerous times—sometimes by only listening to the sound without any visuals. Through open coding, codes for types of sounds and their rhetorical effects were developed. For example, we coded how sound related to the surrounding modes (e.g., visuals, gesture, text) occurring simultaneously in the video and the purposes we perceived the sound having for viewers. In the axial-coding stage, the entire sample of videos was examined for the final set of codes developed in the first phase—noting patterns and differences. These refinements included noticing that composers used sound to construct three distinct *sound spaces*, social productions of space (e.g., story spaces, spaces for arguments related to advertising a book), that overlapped and interacted in various ways to build complex soundscapes. Throughout analysis, codes and emergent findings were reviewed, refined, and discussed by both researchers. Twenty percent (10 of the 50 videos) of the entire sample were coded by both researchers and an inter-rater reliability of 95% was achieved.

In addition to coding for overall themes of sound use, all 50 of the videos were also coded *a priori* for the type of sound employed including music, narration, and sound effects. We also noted if the sounds appeared to be student-created or prefabricated (e.g., a song by a professional musician or a digital audio file of an audience clapping) and whether narration was said in front of the camera while it was rolling or layered on top of the video through voiceover technology. Within these codes, we examined the sound qualities of voices and if students impersonated the voices of characters within their on-camera narration, voiceover, or role-play. Along with coding sound effects, music, narration, and silence, we also noted the placement of sound within the narrative, frequency, and duration of sounds, and use of any sounds derived from popular culture.

Lastly, examples of the various uses of sound were identified and an illustrative case was developed. The case demonstrates the different ways composers employed sound in their StoryTubes, including to create sophisticated and layered sound spaces. Sound was also used to emphasize elements within videos and to organize the videos.

FINDINGS

Overall Sound Usage

Sound was integral to all 50 StoryTubes (see Table 1)—composers layered and combined sounds for a variety of rhetorical effects (see Chion, 2009). Each video included speech, whether by a student using his or her natural voice in front of the camera (76%), voiceover technology to electronically lay student voices over footage (12%), or both on-camera speech and voiceover (12%). Music was also central for conveying information, telling a story, or setting a mood, with a majority of StoryTubes (64%) including some form of music. Many students (48%) integrated pre-fabricated music—both instrumental and songs with lyrics. Some (10%) created their own music either by singing, rapping, or playing an instrument, and 6% of submissions included both prefabricated and student-created music. Sound effects were also present in exactly half of all StoryTubes, with some incorporating prefabricated sound effects (22%), others, student-created sound effects (e.g., hitting a gavel; 22%), and a few (6%) using both sources for sound effects. Often, if a video included sound effects, many would be included.

A key difference in sound usage between age groups was that students 10 years of age and younger were more likely (85%) than those 11 and older (59%) to only use on-camera speech in their StoryTubes. Composers 11 to 18 years old were more likely to only use voiceover (29%) compared to the submissions of younger students (3%).

Table 1. Sound Usage in StoryTubes

Sound	Age group				Total	
	10 yrs. and below (n=33)		11 yrs. and above (n=17)			
	#	%	#	%	#	%
Speech (n=50)						
Voiceover only	1	3	5	29	6	12
On-camera only	28	85	10	59	38	76
Both voiceover & on-camera	4	12	2	12	6	12
Music (n=32)						
Pre-fabricated only	16	48	8	47	24	48
Student-created only	4	12	1	6	5	10
Pre-fabricated & student-created	2	6	1	6	3	6
Sound Effects (n=25)						
Pre-fabricated only	8	24	3	18	11	22
Student-created only	6	18	5	29	11	22
Pre-fabricated & student-created	1	3	2	12	3	6

Along with finding that young people included a broad range of sounds, our analysis of StoryTubes revealed that videos also incorporated a depth of sophisticated layers of sound, which worked together to support or change meaning. Three distinct *sound spaces* emerged across the corpus of videos that would many times interact to construct hybrid *soundscapes*. In addition, composers used sound for multiple purposes, including to accent and help structure StoryTubes. These sound spaces and uses of sound were not discrete. Many times one use of sound achieved multiple rhetorical purposes and hybridized more than one sound space. Each of these patterns will be discussed in the following section, along with an illustrative example. In addition to sound spaces, sound was used in StoryTubes for *notation*, that is, to organize and emphasize parts of the videos—much as textual features such as bullets, bolded words, and highlighting serve to organize and emphasize text. After discussing sound spaces, we will briefly describe the features of sound notation in the StoryTubes.

Sound Spaces

In our repeated viewings and listenings of the 50 StoryTubes we study here, we came to see sounds operating to produce social spaces. We call these productions *sound spaces* (this term is used by Lastra, 2000, and others in film theory). We see sound spaces as interacting and layering together to form a soundscape. We say sound spaces are social because the construction of these spaces always occurs in the interactions among video producers, elements of the video, and audiences. Among the spaces produced by sound are narrative or story spaces, conceptual spaces of arguments for why a particular book should be read, spaces of affect and emotion connected to music and sound effects, and spaces of fun inhabited by young people enjoying the process of multimodal composition. Our views of spatial production align with theorists of space (e.g., Massey, 2005), who see it as produced through interrelations and interactions and with film sound theorists who argue that narrative cinematic space-times are constituted in interrelations among sounds and images (e.g., Chion, 2009). Considering sound in multimodal compositions from the perspective of sound spaces affords us the opportunity to consider sounds as assemblages for meaning-making and to identify the roles that such assemblages play in the formulation of meaning.

StoryTube sound spaces are constructed for particular effects (Lastra, 2000, p. 182). We identified three specific sound spaces evident in StoryTubes: *book sound space, report sound space,* and *kid sound space.* Student composers produced these sound spaces, which are each assemblages of speech, sound effects, and music, in StoryTubes to achieve rhetorical purposes. Next we describe each of these sound spaces, their rhetorical purposes, and examples of each from the corpus of StoryTube videos.

Book sound space. In StoryTubes, the book sound space evoked the narrative world of the book being advertised. In this space, music, sound effects, and voice were used to represent elements of the book world—including characters, setting, and plot. Instead of just telling about these features, sound served as a conduit for the viewer to experience the book through aural senses and gain insight into the events of the book and emotions of characters. Book sound space was created in a variety of ways. Many times, actors would take on the persona of different characters as indicated in a shift in their voices—often using different pitches of voice intonation, embodying the emotions of these characters, or utilizing a distinct accent. Across the corpus, there were numerous instances of students using accents to evoke a book's narrative world, including an Australian accent for *Diary of a Wombat* (#10), British accents for *Harry Potter and the Sorcerer's Stone* (#11), moaning noises of a zombie for *Zombies* (#7), or animal noises to represent non-human main characters. (Note that all examples will be cited with StoryTube number (e.g., #1), which corresponds to the list of StoryTubes in Appendix A.)

The physical setting was also represented through music on numerous occasions—including twangy banjo music to indicate life along the Mississippi River in *The Adventures of Huckleberry Finn* (#8) or steel drum music to evoke Calypso's Island in the *Odyssey* (#12). Lastly, sound effects represented actions one would hear if experiencing the book firsthand, including the sound of screeching tires while on a wild taxi ride, splashing water from the ocean, or a New York Yankees cheer while at Yankee Stadium *(New York, New York: The Big Apple from A to Z;* #2). Sound used in these ways moved beyond the student telling about the book from an outsider perspective to enacting the sounds of characters and indicating important plot elements to the viewer without explicitly having to state them.

Report sound space. The report sound space identified in many StoryTubes was indicative of schooled ways to talk (or write) about a book, usually taking the form of book reports, summaries, or book talks. These examples of report sound space portrayed the students in the videos as studious, practiced, and detached from the narrative world of the StoryTube, with the main objective being to convey information to the viewer. For example, in Zachary's (#2) StoryTube, he began by holding up the book and saying, "Hi my name is Zachary and I'm in first grade. Today we're talking about *New York, New York: The Big Apple from A-Z* by Laura Krauss Melmed. This book tells you about a different place in New York City for every letter in the alphabet." Many students began their StoryTubes in a similar fashion—by clearly introducing the book and giving a summary of key elements from the plot and their favorite parts. Students held a copy of the book while describing it and then concluded with a pitch as to why the viewer should also read it. The schooled, formal tone of the book sound space was also apparent in the tone of their voices, which seemed indicative of a school presentation as opposed to informally speaking to friends or dramatically reenacting a character.

Another way the report space was organized was through the use of sound to create a framework of an information-seeking television show (e.g., a talk show or news report). Some videos (16%) included narration, music, and sound effects to construct the world of a news report. This format—with the composer embodying the role of a reporter—served as a way to structure the StoryTube and access characters from the book. In these StoryTubes, reporters interviewed different characters from books in order to understand how they felt about their experiences. For example, in the StoryTube for *Stone Fox* (#3), the interviewer asked a main character, "How did it feel to compete against the world champion Stone Fox?" Questioning in the report sound space was utilized as a way to organize and extract information from the narrative world.

Six other StoryTubes (12%) also used sound in a way that indirectly accessed the book's content through the structure of a TV show, including a cooking show, trivia competition, and book show (e.g., "Must Read Theater"). For example, Hannah's StoryTube for *Chrissa* (#9) began with the serious, staccato beats of a news show and an introduction, "Hello, I'm Hannah with Beyond W Book Review Weekly." Next, a boy wearing a headset with an attached microphone held up a sign that said, "Cheer!" followed by the sound effect of a cheering audience.

Kid sound space. This third sound space involved auditory elements outside the realms of the book or book trailer. Instead, kid sound space was a mixture of noises from the composer's lifeworld, including popular music, affective reactions, cultural tropes, and ambient background noise. The music from these instances did not position the students in the videos as characters, students, or reporters, but rather as themselves. Often, composers included upbeat music—usually at the beginning or end of their StoryTubes—that had no relation to the book but worked to create a distinct impression of the composers. For example, in a StoryTube for *Your Chickens: A Kid's Guide to Raising and Showing* (#1), Stacey's submission began with her standing in a backyard (presumably her own), holding the book with a chicken standing on each shoulder. Van Morrison's soulful song, "Caravan," played for a few seconds until the chickens startled and jumped off her shoulders, causing Stacey to laugh out loud. The concluding 25 seconds of her StoryTube also incorporated the same Van Morrison song—while Stacey danced and twirled free-spiritedly—not acknowledging the camera—with a baby chick balanced on her head. Morrison's song from 1969 about gypsies had nothing to do with a nonfiction book on chickens, but worked to portray Stacey as a laid-back, earthy, and fun person. Her spontaneous laughter was an element of kid sound space identified in other StoryTubes. Similar to Goffman's (1974) description of *flooding out*, some composers would spontaneously break frame from the roles they were enacting or their narratives to laugh or giggle.

Cultural sound tropes were also seen in a variety of StoryTubes across the corpus. Along with inserting popular music, students also interjected language in their narratives that served as a bridge to language in popular culture. For example, in the StoryTube for the *Odyssey* (#12), Odysseus landed on Calypso's island and when he discovered that he was trapped, exclaimed, "Oh crap!" Later on in the StoryTube, the teens acted out a sword fight from a part in the book when Odysseus came home to find other men vying for his wife's hand in marriage. The boy who played Odysseus drew his sword (a plastic light saber) and said, "Brah, get out of my house." The other actor responded by saying, "No, brah," and they began fighting over Penelope. The teens interjected a colloquial expletive and the surfer-slang word for "bro" or "brother" into Homer's epic poem from the Eighth Century BCE.

Lastly, ambient sounds from the actual shooting of the StoryTube were included in this category. These real-life sounds, many of which students did not control, included the rustling of equipment, sounds from using props, the audible "OK" at the beginning of a StoryTube to indicate the camera should begin filming, or spontaneous laughter not edited out of the final production.

Layered and Hybrid Soundscapes

Sounds were layered in a manner that supported, enhanced, or transformed meaning. Similar to the work on intermodal relationships constructed between visuals and language in social semiotics (Unsworth, 2006), multimodality (Kress & van Leeuwen, 2001, 2006), and comic books (McCloud, 1993, 2006), sounds were layered to create new meanings that one sound could not express on its own. In film sound theory, Chion (1994, 2009) has referred to this layering as *added value* when new meaning is made from layers of sounds and images. Kerins (2011) focuses specifically on the possibilities for new meanings in multi-channel or layered soundtracks, in which multiple sounds, even competing sounds, combine to create meaning with images. Many StoryTube videos simultaneously played more than one sound (e.g., sound effects over music or speech over music) for different rhetorical effects. Often, sounds would be played in tandem to support an idea, what Unsworth (2006) referred to as *concurrence* in visual design. An example of sound concurrence can be heard in Zachary's video for *New York, New York: The Big Apple from A-Z* (#2), where he described the 26 locations in the book he also visited in his video. For the letter 'h' he says, "The Harlem Market where you can play instruments"—he then proceeded to hit on a bongo and strum a ukulele—providing the sounds for his spoken narrative. An example of sound enhancement, where sounds work together and share new information that could not be achieved by the individual sounds, included a StoryTube about the *Odyssey* (#12)—voiceover narration explained that Odysseus killed the Cyclops along with a student making the sound "ahhh!" indicative of the Cyclops's pain when a sword kills him. Through the teen's voiceover, the viewer gains an understanding from the Cyclops's perspective and pain along with the omniscient narrative. Lastly, sound was also layered to create new meaning. In these instances, the interaction between sounds created a message that one sound source could not achieve solely. An example of this rich layering is heard in the StoryTube for *Eighth Grade Bites (Chronicles of Vladimir Tod, Vol. 1)* (#4) where church bells and dramatic music in a foreign language were juxtaposed with the narrator explaining that Vladimir lived a double life as a junior high student and vampire, thus a *divergence* (Unsworth, 2006) of sounds created the feeling of urgency and heightened drama through the driving bells that makes the story seem to be of epic scale. In film sound theory, this effect is called counterpoint or anempathetic effect (see, e.g., Chion, 2009, pp. 208-209).

Notation: Sound for Structuring

Organization. Sound was used to structure the narrative of the video in various ways, including segmenting different parts of the video and creating a unifying organization. Many students employed music to establish an overarching arrangement for their videos, by which all other modes were organized. In these instances, music unified the video and created a rhythmic structure for the StoryTube that aligned with the action, text, and narration. For example, in the StoryTube for *Th1rteen Rea3ons Why* (#5), the Marilyn Manson song "White Coma" played throughout to give the video coherence. The actions of characters in the StoryTube were organized according to the song's beat and content. The beat of the song was started at the exact moment the first character appeared; the lyrics of the song began at a pivotal point in the plot (he picked up a box of tapes sent from a student), and the chorus began at the climax of the StoryTube (when a character overdosed on pills). Along with pre-fabricated music, some composers chose to sing songs to create this undergirding structure. One student sang the content of his StoryTube to the beat of Queen's "We Will Rock You." Sounds also established organization by indicating the introduction or conclusion of a video, including bells chiming in the beginning of a video or a jarring surge of sound at the end.

Accent. Very short clips of sound accented significant aspects of the StoryTube narratives and created dramatic contrast. Frequently, accent, what Chion (2009) called *punctuation*, also imposed an organizational structure within the video; however, accenting was different because it emphasized brief sound effects, speech phrases, or clips of music. For example, some students used sound effects when a new character was introduced in the narrative or if someone had traveled to a different location or time period in the StoryTube. Another common use of accent occurred when a group of students would say the same phrase simultaneously to underscore its importance.

In some StoryTubes, silence or the absence of music was as rhetorically powerful as sound. Silence achieved similar effects by accenting action or indicating the introduction or conclusion. In Zachary's StoryTube described earlier, the majority of his video included upbeat rock music, yet he did not use any background music at a few times, which accented humorous speech and provided the feeling that the speaker was giving an aside directly to the viewer. In addition, many composers chose to have their videos quickly become silent in the last seconds to accentuate a closing image or to create a dramatic contrast.

AN ILLUSTRATION: STORYTUBE FOR *SUMMER OF THE MONKEYS*

To illustrate the complexities of sound space constructions in StoryTubes, we focus on one StoryTube for detailed analysis, "Summer of the Monkeys" (#6), a trailer for *Summer of the Monkeys* by Wilson Rawls. The book follows 14-year-old Jay Berry Lee as he tries to catch some escaped circus monkeys near his home in the Oklahoma Ozarks in the late 1800s. This StoryTube was the Judges' Choice Award winner for group entries from grades K-5 in 2010. We chose this StoryTube for its representative and complex use of sounds in the construction of sound spaces. It does not include all uses of sound seen across the corpus (for example, there is no voice over in this StoryTube), but does include many uses of sound. We are aware of the difficulty of describing sound in our paper and urge readers to view the StoryTube for themselves at http://storytubes.info/drupal/node/40.

The "Summer of the Monkeys" StoryTube opens with an image of a book cover. The book is titled, *Summer of the Monkeys*, and beneath the title is an image of a boy wearing a wig with wild brown hair, wearing eyeglasses, holding a book, and sitting in a high-backed wicker chair next to a table. On the table is a stuffed animal wearing a monkey mask and some books. As the StoryTube starts, this image comes to life as an embedded video, and the boy says "OK," very quietly, then takes off his glasses and introduces himself: "Welcome to Mr. Read-A-Lot's reading corner. Today let's talk about one my favorite books, *Summer of the Monkeys* by Wilson Rawls." We can also hear some American Southern-style instrumental music with a prominent fiddle sound. The volume is low on this music and plays behind the opening sequence. The camera zooms in to the video so that it occupies the full screen. The narrator continues, "It's 1910 in the Ozarks. But rather than me telling you about the book, let's go into it and meet some of the characters." Next, the camera pulls out to reveal multiple images pasted into a book and then pans to another picture of the narrator in another location (standing in front of a whiteboard). This image will come alive as an embedded video in following scenes.

These opening 15 seconds exhibit the kinds of sophisticated and complex layering of sound spaces in the creation of the StoryTube's opening soundscape. These opening seconds include sound assemblages that create book space, report space, and kid space. These spaces also interact and combine together to form hybridized spaces that make meaning possible beyond any of the individual spaces. Further, individual sounds are contained in multiple assemblages (i.e., one sound can serve to construct book space and kid space).

As examples of the sounds that assemble to form book space, the opening Southern-style instrumentals texturize the soundscape of the time and place of the book when layered with the narrator's description: "1910 in the Ozarks." Sounds that assemble to form report space include the narrator's vocal quality, his even tone and calm, relaxed manner, suggesting seriousness and professionalism as he informs the audience of his role as a reporter: "Welcome to Mr. Read-A-Lot's reading corner. Today let's talk about one of my favorite books." Assemblages that construct kid space include the opening, "OK," spoken by the narrator, which is clearly intended to be inaudible and is a signal to the camera person to begin filming. Kid space is also filled out by the instrumental music, which designates the children participating in this project as fun, relaxed, and upbeat.

Together with visual images, these sound spaces interact to form hybridized kid-book-report space as the StoryTube opens. For example, the visual of the monkey mask on a stuffed animal laminates kid space (fun), book space (the monkey is a character in the book), and report space (it is part of the show set) in interaction with sound spaces that include the multiple possible meanings of the opening music (book-kid space), the spoken title of the show—"Mr. Read-A-Lot"—with its allusions to popular culture (e.g., Sir Mix-A-Lot; kid space), and the narrator's calmly spoken suggestion, "let's go into [the book] and meet some of the characters" (report-book space).

As one more example of sound spatial production in "Summer of the Monkeys," we focus analysis on the final 40 seconds of the StoryTube. A detailed transcription of this section of the StoryTube is included in Appendix B. For analysis of "Summer of the Monkeys," we created a multimodal transcript of the entire StoryTube that included music, sound effects, transcript of spoken or uttered dialogue, vocal qualities, description of the visual field (including camera movements), a representative visual frame image, and sound spaces. The segment included in Appendix B is representative of the rest of the multimodal transcript. At the start of this section of the StoryTube (1:17), the narrator says, ">If I could just _help_ c- Jay Barry catch one of these _mon_keys.<" (transcription conventions note rapid speech (><), emphasis (__), and a word cut off (-); note also that the main character's name is misspelled at the beginning of the StoryTube and that we maintain the composers' spelling). The vocal quality of the narrator is distinct from most of the rest of his spoken lines. He is hurried—so much so that he stutters and starts to say, "catch" too quickly.

His words also point to a laminated report-book-kid space. Whereas he has previously only interviewed the characters from the book, he now inserts himself into book space by offering to participate in catching monkeys. The shift is also noted visually, with the narrator holding a green net as he says these lines. Kid space is identified by his hurried speech, his stuttering, and his excitement at the prospect of the monkey chase to come. The subsequent scenes make it clear that the action is fun to participate in (pelting someone with balls or being pelted by balls). In fact, the next scene, in which the narrator creeps up behind a monkey, seems pure kid space—there is no reason for this scene to take place in the book world nor for it to be an example of reporting; it is young people having fun. And the music makes this clear: fast-paced instrumental music with drums and horns.

One final example of a hybridizing of sound spaces in this closing section of the StoryTube begins at 1:38, when the narrator says, "Now, if you want to see if Jay Barry had better luck than me catching those _darn_ monkeys-". These words are spoken in the calm, relaxed, subdued tones of the reporting from the beginning of the StoryTube except for the word "darn," which the narrator says with emphasis, connecting in sound back to when Jay Barry said this same word with the same emphasis when introducing himself (at :37). Here, book space and report space are laminated to create new meaning typical of kid space—that readers of the book will feel some of the sense of adventure and fun that characters of the book feel.

DISCUSSION

Our descriptive analysis of the 2008-2011 StoryTubes contest winners, as well as a detailed analysis of one StoryTube, makes clear that youth composers of StoryTubes used sound in sophisticated and varied ways that created laminated narrative and conceptual spaces that conveyed multiple and layered meanings for audiences. We found that StoryTubes exhibited sound assemblages to construct book sound space (evoking the narrative world of the book being advertised), report space (exhibiting schooled and formal ways of reporting and talking about books), kid space (displaying the lived world of the young people making the videos, often flooding out from book and report sound spaces), and hybridized versions of these spaces that all work to produce meaning in viewings. Further, StoryTubes included sounds used for structuring the video—that is, to organize and accent (or punctuate) elements of the StoryTube.

What accounts for the obvious sophistication of sound usage by young people composing StoryTubes? Without knowledge of the process composers used (e.g., the tools children used for recording and editing, the adult support and involvement they had, their previous expertise with shooting and editing video, the expertise of any adult help, the interactions with other kids during the process of composition), we cannot identify influences and interactions that shape the uses of sound by these young people. No doubt, some of them were influenced by the genre of movie trailers they have seen their entire lives; however, we are unable to know sources of intertextuality in content and modal use from these videos alone, although they do signal cultural connections in many places. Future studies should take up the question of intentionality and purpose in composition practices in order to investigate the social structures that surround completing video projects like these. More needs to be known about how students choose, create, find, and edit sound. In addition, research needs to investigate how students think about and produce sound in connection to other modes (e.g., visuals, text, bodies, etc.).

This study is located at the intersection of film studies and studies of multimodal compositions, attending to sound in youth-produced compositions in a way that has not previously been done and offering a new way of theorizing young peoples' productions of sound in multimodal compositions. For teachers of literacy at all levels, who increasingly recognize the importance of students' need to be able to produce multimodal compositions in order to engage in 21st century literacy practices, we offer first, a focused attention to the nuanced sophistication of sound productions within multimodality; second, a way of thinking about these productions—as assemblages of sounds into sound spaces with layered rhetorical effects on audiences; and third, an analytic framework for investigating sound spaces utilizing a multimodal transcript, a framework and method that we believe could be constructively applied to analyses of other kinds of composition. In this way, youth composers, teachers, and researchers can help young people be heard and not just seen.

AUTHORS' NOTE

We are grateful to Bridget Dalton and Deborah Wells Rowe for their support and guidance of this research as well as to our colleagues in the Multimodal Composition Research Group at Vanderbilt University.

REFERENCES

Altman, R. (Ed.). (1992). *Sound theory sound practice*. New York, NY: Routledge.

Alvey, T. L., Phillips, N. C., Bigelow, E. C., Smith, B. E., Pfaff, E., Colt, W., . . . Ma, J. Y. (2011). From I-search to iSearch 2.0. *English Teaching: Practice and Critique, 10*(4), 139-148.

Ball, C. E., & Hawk, B. (Eds.). (2006). Sound in/as compositional space: A next step in multiliteracies [Special issue]. *Computers & Composition, 23*(3), 263-398.

Björkvall, A. (2009). Practical function and meaning: A case study of IKEA tables. In C. Jewitt (Ed.) *The Routledge Handbook of Multimodal Analysis* (pp. 242-252). New York, NY: Routledge.

Bordwell, D., & Thompson, K. (2010). *Film art: An introduction* (9th ed.). New York, NY: McGraw-Hill.

Buckingham, D. (2003). *Media education: Literacy, learning and contemporary culture*. Cambridge, UK: Polity Press.

Chion, M. (1994). *Audio-vision: Sound on screen*. (C. Gorbman, Trans., Ed.). New York, NY: Columbia University Press. (Original work published in 1990).

Chion, M. (2009). *Film, a sound art.* (C. Gorbman, Trans.). New York, NY: Columbia University Press. (Original work published 2003.)

Copland, A. (1939/2009). *What to listen for in music* (Rev. ed.). New York, NY: New American Library.

Corbin, J., & Strauss, A. (2008). *Basics of qualitative research: Techniques and procedures for developing grounded theory* (3rd ed.). Thousand Oaks, CA: Sage.

Dalton, B., Smith, B. E., & Alvey, T. L. (2010, December). *Fifth grade students compose and reflect on their multimodal stories.* Paper presented at the annual conference of the National Reading Conference/ Literacy Research Association, Fort Worth, TX.

Duncum, P. (2004). Visual culture isn't just visual: Multiliteracy, multimodality and meaning. *Studies in Art Education, 45*(3), 252-264.

Goffman, E. (1974). *Frame analysis: An essay on the organization of experience*: Harvard University Press.

Hobbs, R. (2007). *Reading the media: Media literacy in high school English.* New York, NY: Teachers College Press.

Hollett, T., & Ehret, C. (2011, November). Exploring the potential of a Deleuzian analysis of digital book trailers. In B. Dwyer (Chair), *A multimodal analysis of narrative worlds: Digital book trailers as sites of persuasion and identity construction.* Symposium conducted at the annual conference of the Literacy Research Association, Jacksonville, FL.

Ito, M., Baumer, S., Bittanti, M., boyd, d., Cody, R., Herr-Stephenson, B., . . . Tripp, L. (with Antin, J., Finn, M., Law, A., Manion, A., Mitnick, S., Scholssberg, D., & Yardi, S.). (2010) *Hanging out, messing around, and geeking out: Kids living and learning with new media.* Cambridge, MA: MIT Press.

Jaworski, A., & Thurlow, C. (2009). Gesture and movement in tourist spaces. In C. Jewitt (Ed.) *The Routledge Handbook of Multimodal Analysis* (pp. 253-262). New York, NY: Routledge.

Jenkins, H. (2008). *Convergence culture: Where old and new media collide* (Updated ed.). New York, NY: New York University Press.

Jewitt, C. (2008). Multimodality and literacy in school classrooms. *Review of Research in Education, 32,* 241-267. doi:10.3102/0091732X07310586

Jewitt, C. (Ed.). (2009). *The Routledge Handbook of Multimodal Analysis.* London, UK: Routledge.

Jocius, R., & Wood, S. (2011, November). Narrative worlds: Connections between text and constructed identities. In B. Dwyer (Chair), *A multimodal analysis of narrative worlds: Digital book trailers as sites of persuasion and identity construction.* Symposium conducted at the annual conference of the Literacy Research Association, Jacksonville, FL.

Kafai, Y. B., & Peppler, K. A. (2011). Youth, technology, and DIY: Developing participatory competencies in creative media production. *Review of Research in Education, 35,* 89-119. doi:10.3102/0091732X10383211

Kerins, M. (2011). *Beyond Dolby (stereo): Cinema in the digital sound age.* Bloomington, IN: Indiana University Press.

Kress, G. (2003). *Literacy in the new media age.* London, UK: Routledge.

Kress, G., & van Leeuwen, T. (2001). *Multimodal discourse: The modes and media for contemporary communication.* London, UK: Edward Arnold.

Kress, G., & van Leeuwen, T. (2006). *Reading images: The grammar of visual design* (2nd ed.). London, UK: Routledge.

Lastra, J. (2000). *Sound technology and the American cinema: Perception, representation, modernity.* New York, NY: Columbia University Press.

Leander, K. M., Phillips, N. C., & Taylor, K. H. (2010). The changing social spaces of learning: Mapping new mobilities. *Review of Research in Education, 34,* 329-394.

Lenhart, A., Madden, M., Smith, A., & Macgill, A. (2007). *Teens and social media.* Retrieved September 27, 2011, from http://www.pewinternet.org/Reports/2007/Teens-and-Social-Media.aspx

Leonard, John A. (2001). *Theatre sound.* New York, NY: Routledge.

Massey, D. (2005). *For space.* London, UK: Sage.

McCloud, S. (1993). *Understanding comics.* New York, NY: HarperCollins.

McCloud, S. (2006). *Making comics: Storytelling secrets of comics, manga and graphic novels.* New York, NY: HarperCollins.

Murch, W. (1994). Foreword. In M. Chion, *Audio-vision: Sound on screen.* (C. Gorbman, Trans., Ed.) (pp. vii-xxiv). New York, NY: Columbia University Press. (Original work published in 1990.)

Scollon, R., & Scollon, S. W. (2009). Multimodality and language: A retrospective and prospective view. In C. Jewitt (Ed.), *The Routledge Handbook of Multimodal Analysis* (pp. 170-180). New York, NY: Routledge.

Selfe, C. L. (2009). The movement of air, the breath of meaning: Aurality and multimodal composing. *College Composition and Communication, 60*(4), 616-663.

Sider, L., Freeman, D., & Sider, J. (Eds.). (2003). *Soundscape: The school of sound lectures 1998-2001*. London, UK: Wallflower Press.

Smith, B. E. (2010, December). Multimodal persuasion: An examination of media, gender, and self-presentation in adolescents' videos. In B. Dalton (Chair), *Media for and by adolescents: Emerging social, modal, and spatial practices of production and interpretation*. Symposium conducted at the annual conference of the National Reading Conference/Literacy Research Association, Fort Worth, TX.

StoryTubes. (2011). StoryTubes contest [Web site]. Retrieved from http://storytubes.info

Unsworth, L. (2006). Towards a metalanguage for multiliteracies education: Describing the meaning-making resources of language-image interaction. *English Teaching: Practice and Critique, 5*(1), 55-76.

van Leeuwen, T. (1999). *Speech, music, sound*. London, UK: Macmillan.

West, T. (2009). Music and designed sound. In C. Jewitt (Ed.), *The Routledge Handbook of Multimodal Analysis* (pp. 284-292). New York, NY: Routledge.

APPENDIX A

StoryTubes Videos Cited as Examples

#	Year	Book Title	Author	Grade/Age[a]	Award
1	2008	*Your Chickens: A Kid's Guide to Raising and Showing*	Gail Damerow	N/A	Online Voting Winner
2	2009	*New York, New York: The Big Apple from A to Z*	Laura Krauss Melmed	K-4	Judges' Choice Winner
3	2009	*Stone Fox*	John Reynolds Gardiner	K-6	Online Voting Winner
4	2009	*The Chronicles of Vladimir Tod: Eighth Grade Bites*	Heather Brewer	7-up	Judges' Choice Winner
5	2010	*Th1rteen Rea3ons Why*	Jay Asher	6-up	Honorable Mention
6	2010	*Summer of the Monkeys*	Wilson Rawls	K-5	Judges' Choice Winner
7	2010	*Zombies*	Krensky	K-5	Honorable Mention
8	2011	*The Adventures of Huckleberry Finn*	Mark Twain	14-18	Judges' Choice Winner
9	2011	*Chrissa*	Mary Cassanova	8-10	Honorable Mention
10	2011	*Diary of a Wombat*	Jackie French	8-10	Judges' Choice Winner
11	2011	*Harry Potter and the Sorcerer's Stone*	J.K. Rowling	8-10	Runner-up
12	2011	*The Odyssey*	Homer	14-18	Runner-up

Note. Contest categories and titles for awards have changed over the course of the contest. The information in this table matches what is shown on the StoryTubes website (www.storytubes.info).

[a]For contests held in 2009 and 2010, awards were divided by grades (e.g., K-4, 6-up). In the 2011 contest, awards were divided by ages (e.g., 8-10, 14-18).

APPENDIX B

Multimodal transcript of one section of StoryTube for *Summer of the Monkeys*

Transcription conventions are as follows:

- word cutoff; either interrupted or left hanging by the speaker

stress

(( )) non-linguistic sounds

>rapidly<

. sentence-final falling intonation

	Music	Sound effects	Transcript of spoken or uttered dialogue	Vocal qualities	Description of visual field (including camera movements)	Representative visual frame	Book Sound Space	Report Sound Space	Kid Sound Space
1:17	No music		Nar: >If I could just _ help_ c- Jay Barry catch one of these _mon_keys.<	Narrator's voice is more urgent than at other times in the video. Typically unflappable in saying his memorized lines, he stutters saying this line.	Close up of narrator holding a green net.				
1:20	Fast-paced instru-mental music with drums and horns				The narrator slowly creeps up behind the monkey with a net.				
1:33		Slow motion sound effect so that monkey makes a low-pitched roaring sound.	Monkey: ((High-pitched monkey shriek)) Nar: ((Grunts as he gets hit by balls))		The monkey turns around, in slow motion for a second, and then in fast motion and pelts the narrator with red balls.				

	Music	Sound effects	Transcript of spoken or uttered dialogue	Vocal qualities	Description of visual field (including camera movements)	Representative visual frame	Book Sound Space	Report Sound Space	Kid Sound Space
1:38			N: Now, if you want to see if Jay Barry had better luck than me catching those _darn_ monkeys-	Narrator's voice returns to even and relaxed tone except on the word "darn," which he says with emphasis.					
1:42	Opening measures of "Chariots of Fire"				Slow motion replay of monkey hitting narrator with red balls				
1:48	Upbeat music with leading guitar begins to play softly		go to your local library and check out *Summer of the Monkeys* by Wilson Rawls.		Narrator speaks to the camera with net over his face				
1:53	Volume increases				White text on screen: "Summer of the Monkeys: Wilson Rawls"				
1:57	Music resolves into a final cord that is repeated as volume fades.								

Timothy Shanahan
Professor of Urban Education
University of Illinois at Chicago

Section I:
Writing Research

Research on any topic ebbs and flows. The curiosity of researchers is piqued by a perplexing problem or by some intriguing new theory, but this interest eventually flags as understanding increases or the demands for methodological rigor become more formidable (initial forays into a topic are usually not as methodologically sophisticated as later explorations must become to satisfy journal reviewers and doctoral advisors, whose understanding is increased by the burgeoning body of research). Once a topic is well explored, researchers move on to greener pastures, where the collective ignorance is more obvious.

Writing research fits that mold. There were few studies of writing during the 1940s and 1950s. The first truly concerted efforts to understand writing behavior appeared in the 1960s—with *each year's* productivity accounting for more studies than had appeared in the previous two decades combined. Composition study ramped up aggressively during the 1970s, by more than 400% over the previous decade. But, despite the formation of a national research center devoted to writing and the appearance of new journals on the topic, writing research began to tail off, with less research appearing during the subsequent two decades (a 20% decline in the 1980s, and another 10% drop during the 1990s). This trend line appears to have stabilized now, with a very slight upturn in amount of writing research from 2000-2009—growth that appears to still be accelerating.

What are the major writing topics that are attracting this renewed research interest? One major area of writing inquiry now deals with text genre. Of particular interest in this regard are studies on the writing of arguments, but other genres and subgenres are gaining attention, too. Much past research on how to teach students to write emphasized the use of particular structural elements or text features. Now such research is likely to contextualize these features within a genre—the idea being that genre mediate communications between writers and readers, and that students must understand not just how to use such elements, but why one would employ them.

A second major emphasis in current research deals with writing in the academic disciplines and how students develop an academic identity through their writing choices (two studies in this collection deal with identity, but neither addresses the formation of academic identity per se). Studies on how to write math or science are burgeoning, mirroring the current interest in disciplinary literacy generally. One might classify these studies as being just more examples of the previously cited genre research. However, "science literacy" and other forms of disciplinary reading and writing are just too diverse to constitute a single genre, and, thus, deserve to be considered as a separate topic.

A third popular topic explores how writing develops in second-language students or across cultural boundaries. The extensive immigration taking place in wealthy countries has resulted in large numbers of second-language learners and how best to understand and address their literacy learning needs are a growing concern among writing researchers. Two studies in this collection are good examples of such investigation: "Spanish Speakers Writing in English Language Pre-Kindergarten" by Lucy K. Spence, and "Writing Across Lifeworlds" by Allison Skerrett, Michelle Fowler-Amato, Katharine Chamberlain, and Caron Sharp.

Text evaluation represents a fourth major thrust in current writing studies. Researchers who engage in such research analyze text, particularly text features like cohesive links or the relationship between objectively measured features and writing quality. The growing use of academic assessment (e.g., No Child Left Behind, Common Core State Standards) is likely stimulating this interest.

What about instructional issues in writing? Such studies are not rare by any means, but they definitely lag other topics (and this has been noted over several decades in various reviews of writing research). Studies of teaching are complex and difficult to implement and they often depend upon constructs developed in the more prolific topic areas. For an example of a pedagogical study in this collection, this one exploring the development of writing teachers, see "Exploring Poetry Writing in a Methods Course: Changes in Preservice Teachers' Identities as Teachers of Writing" by Belinda S. Zimmerman, Denise N. Morgan, Melanie K. Kidder-Brown, and Katherine E. Batchelor. Another example is the study by Angela M. Wiseman and Kelly Wissman, "'People Suffer More Than You Think': Witnessing Trauma in Children's Poetry," which both examines students' trauma experiences through writing, but also considers how teachers must respond to such revelations if students are to benefit.

The results of these five strands of research taken together will, over time, form the modern garment of writing education, as they deal with what to teach, how to teach, and how to assess student composition. Continued explorations into curriculum, instruction, and assessment, one hopes, will allow us greater purchase on how to open the world of writing to students, no matter what their language backgrounds or how harrowing their past experiences may have been.

Spanish Speakers Writing in an English Language Pre-Kindergarten

Lucy K. Spence
Diane DeFord
Hope Reardon
University of South Carolina

As researchers, we have explored children's writing development and the influence of language and classroom environments on young writers (DeFord, 1980, 1994; Spence, 2010, 2011). Most recently, we wanted to examine how Spanish-speaking children learn and grow as writers in an English language environment. One pre-kindergarten classroom teacher was also interested in pursuing this same question. Our research in Hope Reardon's preschool classroom focused on the five children who speak mostly Spanish at home. We will refer to these children as emergent bilinguals since they are in the process of learning English while continuing to develop as Spanish speakers. In Hope's room, the four-year-olds follow their interests and interact with learning materials in centers based on a variety of theme units as they talk, work, and play together. The children are encouraged to express themselves through media and talk in the classroom. This context provides an active, language-rich environment. Yet, Hope does not speak Spanish and the classroom assistant is a beginning Spanish speaker.

The school is in the southeastern United States, a region with a growing Latino population. The school has few resources for developing biliteracy, but otherwise, Hope's classroom exhibits optimal conditions for literacy learning, and she attempts to make her classroom culturally relevant (Ladson-Billings, 1995). Hope reads aloud throughout the day and encourages the children to voice their observations and reactions as she reads. Occasionally her assistant or a visitor reads a Spanish or bilingual book to the class. The children sing and dance along with music and text projected on a large screen. Some Spanish songs are included in the weekly musical repertoire. Each week, a new poem or story is presented to the children for shared reading. These texts are read and reread until the children join in the reading with confidence. Each day after shared reading, the children are encouraged to write in their journals about topics of their choice. Given this rich, literate environment, we explored how five Spanish-dominant children learned to write in an English-dominant classroom.

THEORY

We draw upon three theoretical assumptions in our approach to analyzing children's writing. Briefly, we assume that writing is a social act, that writing can contain multiple modes of expression, and also writing is the result of children's purposeful intentions.

From a sociocultural perspective, children are seen to acquire literacy in a process of meaning-making through social interaction within a particular context. They draw upon their social worlds in learning literacy. In classrooms that encourage talk, children negotiate meaning with one another as they talk and write (Dyson, 2008). As children sit side by side at a table with crayons, pencils, and journals in front of them, they draw upon their conversations and the writing of other children as inspiration for their work. They also bring previous experiences and knowledge to these literacy engagements. All children have seen family members engage with literacy in some way, and have interacted with literacy in their communities well before starting school (Dyson, 2008; Heath, 1983; Moll, Amanti, Neff, & Gonzalez, 2001). They bring this knowledge to their understanding of what it means to read and write in various contexts. When they enter preschool programs, they must draw upon these "outside of school" practices and learn new practices situated in the current context. They will rely upon each other, their teacher, and their experiences with storybooks, songs, and other media in their pre-k classroom.

Writing involves multiple modes of expression. Literacy is now understood to encompass more than printed letters on a page (The New London Group, 1996; Kress, 2010; Narey, 2009). A multimodal perspective includes oral, visual, spatial, and gestural modes of sign-making. Children use what is at hand (Kress, 1997), be it building blocks, pillows, toys, crayons, or paint in their transformative work and expression of meaning.

Children's sign-making is intentional. They choose from a broad array of literacy practices, and experiment with new practices according to their needs, interests, and perceptions (Harste, Woodward, & Burke, 1984). Children's sign-making is constructed within a social context with the expectation that the signs will have meaning based on shared culture. Yet the creation of the sign depends upon the materials at hand and the interests of the child. Children have different styles, supported by different social contexts and sign systems (Dyson, 2003a).

Given that children learn language and literacy through social practices in their homes, use multiple modalities to represent meaning, and are intentional in their use of symbols, it is clear that children should have the means for negotiating preschool.

This study adds to on-going research toward understanding the literacy development of emergent bilinguals entering preschool in the United States. A review of relevant studies follows.

YOUNG EMERGENT BILINGUALS' WRITING

Research has clearly demonstrated that children are able to create meaning through writing in English while they are still learning the language (Campano, 2007; Hudelson, 1989; Parker & Pardini, 2006; Samway, 2006). Research with preschool children has shown that even very young children use what they know about English as well as their home language as they learn to write.

Ferierro and Teberosky's (1982) Argentinian study of Spanish-speaking children described children's writing through a developmental perspective. A later study of four-year-olds in the U.S. by Yaden and Tardibuono (2004) concurred with their findings and also stressed the complexity of written language development. Current research teaches us that children's writing should not be interpreted as an inflexible developmental trajectory (see Gentry, 1992, 2000; Ferriero & Teberosky, 1982, for descriptions of developmental levels in English and Spanish). We are a long way from clearly describing how a second language develops over time. Valdez, Capitelli, and Alvarez's (2011) study makes progress toward such a description, although their research focused on oral language acquisition and did not address writing.

From the current research on preschool emergent bilinguals' writing, we know that young children use writing to express meaning. Moll, Sáez, and Dworin (2001) demonstrated kindergarten children knew their marks on paper represented meaning and engaged in incipient bilingualism using Spanish and English in their writing. The children used drawings, letters, and letter-like marks to express their ideas. Rubin and Carlan's (2005) study of bilingual children also concluded that children used both English and Spanish toward the goal of expressing ideas. Reyes and Azuara (2008) found that four- and five- year old emergent bilinguals develop knowledge about print concurrently in the languages to which they are exposed. This study of home and school environments demonstrated children's bilingual print concepts were situated and mediated by peer and family interactions. Several recent studies have explored how children use multiple scripts in their writing, (Genishi, Stires, & Yung-Chan, 2001; Kabuto, 2010; Kenner & Kress, 2003). These studies draw attention to written scripts as one of many modes of communication young children use for communicative purposes. As emergent biliteracy research grows, the view of writing has shifted to seeing writing as one of multiple ways of signifying meaning. Multiple languages, scripts, and other sign systems interplay with writing as children share their thoughts and ideas in purposeful communication.

PARTICIPANTS AND SETTING

This research study was conducted in a public Title I elementary school serving 359 pre-kindergarten to fifth-grade children located in a working-class residential neighborhood in a mid-sized southeastern city. Four-year-old children in this school were assessed with the Developmental Indicators for the Assessment of Learning (DIAL-3; Mardell & Goldenberg, 1998) at the beginning of the school year to screen for learning delays as part of district progress monitoring. The DIAL-3 is a normed assessment measuring motor ability, concepts, and language. It was used to determine eligibility for the 4K program. The 17 children (12 boys and 5 girls) assigned to this classroom were a young group of four-year-olds. All children qualified for free and reduced lunch and qualified via the DIAL-3, for the 4K program. There were six Latinos, one European American child, and 10 African American children in the class. One of the Latino children was a fluent English speaker. Of the five children who spoke primarily Spanish, three children knew some English and two started the year knowing only Spanish. Although data were collected from all children in the class, this paper focuses only on the five Spanish-speaking children.

The classroom teacher followed a constructivist and sociocultural approach to teaching and working with young children (Vygotsky, 1986). She incorporated play centers and initiated instruction following the children's lead. Environmental print was a very important part of the classroom. To begin the school year, Hope began a word wall with the children's names, pictures, and print from snack container labels. Soon the children started bringing print from home, including Spanish product labels, which they discussed and added to the wall. Seasonal word cards were included in the writing center. A pocket chart was set aside for the children's pictures and names to use when writing and another pocket chart held illustrated word cards. The teacher sometimes demonstrated using word cards to support her own writing, talking about the letters as she wrote. This promoted interest in using the cards during journal writing.

A typical day in the classroom began with the children unpacking their book bags, picking a new book to take home, and signing their name in the sign-in book. When the children finished their morning routines, they chose from their individualized bags of books for independent reading. During this time, their teacher moved about the room, conferring with the children as they engaged with the books. After all the children arrived and had breakfast, they gathered for a morning meeting of language play, music, movement, and read-aloud. Then the children were given a large uninterrupted block of time to work in learning centers of their choice. These centers included dramatic play, blocks, writing, art, listening, computers, music, puzzles and games, math manipulatives, sand and water, discovery, and play dough. All centers were equipped with books, pencils, pens, and paper to support literacy during play.

As the year progressed, the children began to look forward to the time set aside each day for writing workshop (Calkins, 1986; Graves, 1983). Workshop began with a teacher think-aloud on the interactive white board. After this demonstration, the children moved to two large rectangular tables where a journal was placed at each child's place. While the children wrote, the teacher and her assistant moved from child to child, talking about their writing, sometimes writing notes on the back of the child's writing. Writing workshop ended with two children sharing their writing on the interactive white board to highlight a skill or strategy Hope had observed. Hope scanned the child's journal entry into a document and then scribed the child's words on the projected digital document as the child dictated details. The sharing session ended with questions and comments from the other children.

Each school day ended with free choice reading. As the children waited for the bus or parent pick-up, they reread the weekly shared reading, books the teacher had previously read aloud, or books (mostly informational) the children chose from the school's library.

DATA COLLECTION AND ANALYSIS

Hope invited Lucy, a university researcher, to visit her classroom and offer suggestions regarding teaching methods for emergent bilinguals. Lucy has an extensive background teaching emergent bilinguals and is a developing Spanish speaker. Lucy suggested engaging in a research study to gain insight into how the Spanish-speaking students were learning literacy. Diane was invited to contribute because of her extensive background studying young children's emergent writing. Three classroom routines offered opportunities to study children's writing: (a) a daily sign-in attendance sheet, (b) writing journals, and (c) the daily Author's Chair sharing period. Data collection began in September with Hope collecting the children's written names on the daily sign-in sheet. The children began writing in their journals in October. From January through June, Lucy and Diane observed once each month for a full day. The Oral Language Acquisition Inventory (OLAI; Gentile, 2003), which has both Spanish and English versions, was administered in January and again in March to document children's oral language, reading, and writing development.

The university researchers, Diane and Lucy, collected data during monthly visits from January through May. They administered the OLAI, took field notes, and interacted with the children. A bilingual psychology student helped administer the OLAI. Lucy demonstrated methods for teaching emergent bilinguals several times during the semester.

Hope collected the children's writing samples and provided three video-recorded sharing sessions for analysis. They were recorded between October and May. In addition, she provided information captured from the sharing sessions using the document camera, interactive white board, and computer. These sharing sessions involved two children each session, who took turns sitting on a small chair in front of a circle of their peers. They described their journal entries, using a pointer to draw attention to certain aspects of the entry projected on the interactive white board. The child's peers, seated on the floor in front of the white board, asked questions and made comments related to the journal entry. Hope wrote the child's exact words on the interactive white board. These sharing sessions were captured several times each week from October through June.

The first level of analysis dealt with devising a coding scheme. The codes were based on the work of prior research on emergent writing (DeFord, 1994; Ferreiro & Teberoski, 1982; Gentry, 1992; Harste, Woodward & Burke, 1984). Lucy, Diane, and Hope coded the daily sign-in sheets for a subsample of each child's written names to finalize the coding system and to establish reliability. Then Lucy coded the remaining samples for the five children to provide insights into how a particular child represented his or her name from September through May. With this background information, Lucy then coded the journals for types of marks made and she counted the number of letters, words, and numbers children wrote in their journals across the school year. Table 1 shows the coding system used for the sign-in sheets and journals. The description of the children's writing is listed on the left and the abbreviated code is listed on the right.

Table 1. Type of Mark and Code used for Journal Analysis

Type of Mark	Code
Linear	Lr
Lines	Ln
Up and Down Strokes	UD
Linear Up and Down Strokes	Lr UD
Vertical	V
Horizontal	H
Right to Left Letters	RL L
Loops	Lp
Linear Loops	Lr Lp
Linear waves	Lr W
Uniform Size and Shape	Us
Linear Letters	Lr L
Pseudo Numbers	PN
Pseudo Letters	PL
Pseudo Words	PW
Circles	C
Mini Pictures	MP
Picture	Pc
Coloring	Cl
People	Pl
Dots	D
Symbol	S
Decoration	Dc

The journals were a particularly rich source of information that included drawings as well as written representations and numbers. If a letter-like mark seemed very similar to a letter or number, it was counted as a letter or number and this was listed in addition to the codes for the other written marks. If a group of letters seemed very similar to a particular word, then the letter grouping was counted as a word. If a number grouping seemed like a multi-digit number, then it was counted as that number. For instance, one child wrote the year, 2010. This was counted as one number: two thousand ten. It was also counted as 2, 0, and 1.

Lucy coded all five Spanish-speaking children's journals. This process facilitated a micro-analysis of the children's writing using well-known aspects of emergent writing such as up-and-down strokes, circles, and letter-like shapes. Patterns such as extensive circle drawing were noted. This micro-analysis engendered insights into individual students' preferences and abilities with making meaning through multiple modes including drawing pictures and referencing video games. Memos were written as patterns began to emerge or as significant shifts were noticed while coding journals. An example of a memo for Lorenzo follows:

Memo: Theme Unit

>Jan. 13 he drew several people surrounded by green colored-in circles. This might be the pumpkin patch.
>Feb. 2 he drew a bear and wrote an O. In Spanish, bear begins with O, Oso.
>Feb. 4 the journal entries show his representation of the pumpkin patch using the letter P, then four days later, on Feb 8., a representation of the pumpkin patch with pictures
>The pumpkin patch was a continuing theme throughout his journal.

This memo was compared with other data such as classroom observations and sharing session transcripts. These categories that emerged in the data were then verified with Hope to confirm, for example, that Lorenzo was writing about the classroom theme unit on pumpkins and using various symbol systems for expressing meaning within his writing. After coding was complete, Lucy, Hope, and Diane reviewed the data and memos to consolidate perspectives.

Because Spanish was not used for classroom instruction, we used the OLAI to help us understand the children's Spanish writing concepts. We asked the children if they preferred to have the OLAI administered in English or Spanish. If the children chose Spanish, Lucy or the Spanish-speaking graduate student asked the children to complete the language tasks. Four of the five children chose the Spanish language. Section three of the OLAI provided information on Spanish print awareness. The children drew a picture and the proctor scribed the child's statement about the picture. The proctor then read the child's statement slowly as the child wrote it. For our purposes, this was the most useful aspect of the OLAI and was used to triangulate findings from the memos regarding how Spanish or English was used in emergent writing from September through May. For example, if a child seemed to be writing a letter to represent Spanish in a journal entry, Lucy checked the OLAI writing sample to see if the child used that letter in a designated Spanish writing task. Lucy compared each child's memos with information from the sharing sessions (transcribed video and digitally captured) and field notes. If a finding based on the data was confirmed by multiple data sources, the finding was considered trustworthy. If the tentative finding was disconfirmed by any data source, we abandoned it. Together, the data analysis allowed us to see how Spanish-speaking children used writing to communicate meaning in an English classroom.

FINDINGS

Moving from Spanish Oral Language to English Literacy

The five children in this study are represented using pseudonyms. There were four boys and one girl: Gilberto, Lorenzo, Raul, Ivan, and Dulce. The journals, transcripts, and field notes yielded codes derived from memos made while coding the journals. These codes were: (a) telling stories, (b) friends' names, (c) media, and (d) classroom theme units. After compiling the coded data, two themes were found to be consistent across the five children: The children drew upon a variety of

Figure 1. Lorenzo's Journal Entries Representing a Pumpkin Patch

resources for their writing and they focused on a self-determined program of work which carried them throughout the year. We found that the children drew upon their knowledge of Spanish and English as they wrote, and also language from their homes and classroom. They also drew upon other resources such as field trips and video games. They followed their own interests, such as drawing stories, or experimenting with letters. A constructivist classroom based on a Vygotskian theory of learning afforded the children opportunities to expand on rich classroom experiences and bring their home experiences into their class work.

The children drew upon classroom units of study, particularly a field trip to a pumpkin patch in the fall. Later, they wrote about their pumpkin patch experience using drawings of pumpkins. In some drawings, a large pumpkin dominated the page. In other drawings, many small pumpkins filled the page, representing the pumpkin patch. Some children made the leap from picture-as-symbol, to letter-as-symbol. Lorenzo wrote the letter "P" all over the page, representing a pumpkin patch. He also drew a human figure in the middle of all the *P*s. Lorenzo clearly understood that letters could represent objects and words (Figure 1).

The children also used video games and other "child culture" media such as the *Super Mario Bros.* video game (1985), and comic book heroes, Spiderman (Lee and Ditko, 1962), and Batman (Kane, 1939). Gilberto used letters as symbolic markers to represent Luigi and Mario, two video game characters. He wrote "L" and "M" on the characters' hats and included other symbolic markers which represented levels and other aspects of the game. These drawings early in the school year showed that Gilberto understood that letters can be used to represent names. By the end of the school year he used his understanding of letter as symbolic marker to write 24 different letters (upper or lower case), and 6 different words. Gilberto used his knowledge of video games as a resource in using letters and words to communicate meaning.

All five children wrote according to their interests, yet individual children seemed to have a particular focus that carried them throughout the year of journal writing. The children used many symbol systems in order to follow a work program of their own design and purposes. These purposes included creating adventures for familiar videogame characters; experimenting with letters and other marks; imitating writing; exploring numbers; and using pictures and letters to recreate experiences. We refer to these individual foci or themes as individual work goals.

Individual Work Goals

Each student's individual work goals were intrinsically motivated as a result of the classroom teachers' stance of allowing children to choose their own writing topics. Hope intentionally implemented writing workshop pedagogy with an emphasis on choice and this afforded the children the time and space for following their own work goals.

Some children drew intricate pictures, which were embellished as the story unfolded. They used pictures and symbols to tell stories and represent their experiences. Raul drew a picture of a house and two figures, telling his teacher, "The bear is going into Dulce's house." He used his knowledge from stories read in class and his relationship with a classmate in this instance. Lorenzo was also interested in drawing intricate pictures. He moved from unrecognizable colored shapes in October, to drawings which included many small details such as eyes and legs on tiny creatures set upon a tree's many branches. Lorenzo's interest in using marks to represent details began with colored shapes, concentric circles, and sets of perpendicular lines, dots, and people. He used his journal to experiment with these and other shapes and combinations until he became quite skilled with fine motor coordination. He used his knowledge of insects and animals from the many informational books shared in the classroom.

The children also used a variety of symbolic markers such as letter-like and number-like marks and recognizable letters, numbers, and word-like groups. The journals contained a mixture of pictures and letters with an increasing amount of recognizable letters as the year progressed. This was especially evident for Dulce, who seemed to have taken on a work goal dealing with writing letters and words. Dulce focused on letter-like shapes and eventually many letters and some words. This focus on letters began at the onset of the school year and was consistent throughout. The continual practice of letter and number writing for her own purposes resulted in having written 23 different letters (upper or lower case), and 8 different words by the end of the school year. In April she wrote words using invented spellings. She told her teacher the words said, "A dog, a bird, and a fish." Dulce used word cards, experimentation with lines and circles, picture drawing, whole-group lessons, and other children at her table as resources for writing. As an example of drawing upon other children as resources, one day Dulce drew and colored a picture which was very similar to Lorenzo's. Both children's pictures included many horizontal lines emanating from a large central figure. Freedom to use their journals for exploration resulted in these emergent bilingual children using many different resources and individual interests to tell stories through drawing and writing, and enabled them to develop fine-motor skills and practice letters, numbers, and words.

Figure 2. Instances of Drawings, Letter-Like Marks, and Letters Across the School Year

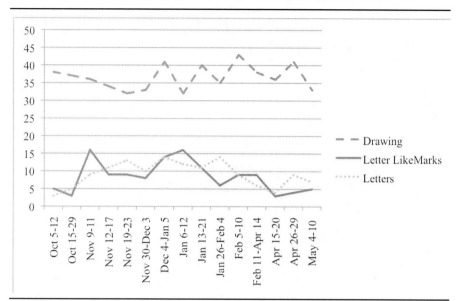

Spanish Writing Concepts

Although Hope honored the children's home language, she was not able to draw upon this strength as much as she would have liked. Hope was monolingual English and her assistant was a beginning Spanish speaker. For our research purposes, the OLAI prompts given in Spanish by a Spanish-speaking researcher and graduate student provided some insight into the children's understandings of Spanish writing. In May, for example, Lorenzo drew a picture and dictated the word "casa" (house). Without prompting, he wrote the letters, "Cs Cs xcii." At age 5 years, 3 months, Lorenzo was drawing and writing to communicate meaning in his home language, Spanish. The children wrote letters in their journals that could possibly connect with pictures they drew, such as P for "perro" and O for "oso" however, we were not able to confirm this in all cases. These data revealed that emerging bilinguals were developing a pool of language resources across both languages such that emerging biliteracy was a strong possibility.

Writing Across the School Year

Lucy analyzed the children's writing over the nine-month school year by grouping the codes from journal analysis into "marks conveying meaning through picture" such as drawings of people and circles, "writing-like marks" such as waves and loops, and "alphabetic marks" such as names and letters. She segmented the year by month and graphed the progression of marks the children used over time (Figure 2). The results show the children used far more marks that conveyed meaning through picture than any other type of mark. The use of these picture-like marks decreased slightly from October through November, the beginning of the school year. At this same time, there was an upswing in letter-like marks and alphabetic marks. Perhaps the children were focusing their attention on these aspects of print, which lessened their focus on picture-making. During this time, the children were introduced to the letters in their names as they signed their name in the sign-in sheet each day. The use of letter-like and alphabetic marks peaked in mid-January and tapered off by mid-February, when pictures and other symbols became more dominant. These five-year-old children expressed meaning through pictures and other modes of representation besides alphabetic modes (Kress, 2010). They moved between modes, purposefully choosing the mode that suited their communicative needs across the school year.

Diane and Lucy observed the children as they worked in the classroom, at times engaging them in conversations about writing. These observations revealed how the children were developing concepts of pictures, letters, and words. By April the children were differentiating between pictures and letters, and were equating pictures with words. At that time, Gilberto was sitting on the floor by the chick, which had just hatched from an egg in the classroom incubator.

Lucy: Look at all these Os (pointing to a journal).

Gilberto: They're circles, not Os.

Lucy: Is an O a circle?

Gilberto: No, just circles.

Lucy: Can you write the word, "egg?"
             (Gilberto draws a circle and colors it in).

Dulce: Egg.

This conversation showed how Gilberto differentiated between the letter, "O" and "just circles." He also associated writing the word, "egg" with drawing an egg. Following our conversation, Dulce read "egg" based on his picture. Journal writing about classroom theme units provided a way for the children to explore concepts of letter, picture, and word. They constructed their meanings based on resources including social interactions as they worked side by side.

Toward the end of the school year, the teacher gave the children paper for writing and drawing. Each paper had a large square for the picture, a line at the top for the child's name, and lines at the bottom for writing. This was meant to scaffold the children toward a conventional format for writing and drawing. The teacher demonstrated this new medium for the children, who then used the paper according to their individual purposes. Ivan wrote his name in the space provided, then wrote some of the letters in his name below that space. He drew a picture in the square and wrote letter-like shapes on the lines provided for writing. These marks were of uniform shape and size, just like alphabetic letters. Ivan, at 4.5-years-old, differentiated between writing and drawing when given a format for both modes of communication and demonstrations by the teacher.

In April, we recorded Ivan as he shared a journal entry with his classmates. In response to their questions, his teacher labeled elements of the journal entry.

Ivan: This is Katie the caterpillar. This is a bunny rabbit, a monkey, and a
             mouse. This is Katie flying Charlie.

Child 1:   What is this?

Ivan: My name.

Child 1:   Your name?

Ivan: Uh huh. That one?

Child 2: What is that, me?

Ivan: That's a circle.

In response to further questioning, Ivan repeated, "A monkey, and a mouse, and a rabbit." And "circles." He also told the children, "They're trying to be Charlie's friend." "And this is the catifillar." This and other sharing sessions further exemplified how the children drew from social interactions to create stories. Ivan used the names of his classmates, names of pets, theme units, and personal experiences in telling his story to the teacher and an audience of his peers. Ivan used what he knew about symbols, pictures, letters, and his name to represent meaning through writing.

DISCUSSION

Genishi, Stires, and Yung-Chan (2001) describe a classroom of emergent bilinguals in which preschool children explored symbols in an integrated curriculum. The symbols took on a variety of meanings such as sounds, objects, or people that overlapped as the children moved among the symbols. The children moved from experiences with symbols of the Chinese language to knowing about multiple symbolic systems including English. Using language to signify meaning undergirded both languages. Spanish-speaking children in the present study used symbols and resources to signify meaning in similar ways.

The children in this study had many authentic experiences, and in response, used pictures and letters as symbolic representations of experiences in and out of the classroom, such as visiting the pumpkin patch, watching a chick hatch, and playing video games. They also made up stories about their friends and pets. The teacher realized the limitations of her own Spanish language, and sought the help of other people and resources to augment the rich literacy experiences in her classroom with Spanish and Spanish/English language texts, songs, poems, and dual-language labels. She also invited Spanish-speaking guests into her classroom. Consequently, the children learned to express themselves in a variety of modes: with crayons and paper, English and Spanish oral language, costumes and props from the dramatic play center, and other modes available to them. The children wrote about field trips, daily play, storybooks, oral storytelling, and their home lives. Rich experiences and opportunities for expressing meaning resulted in drawing and writing that reflected these experiences. The opportunity to draw and write with crayons in their journals resulted in experimentation with pictures, letters, numbers, and words. The children communicated meaning using multiple sign systems and developed their skills through a work goal of their own devising.

Both Spanish and English languages filtered into the children's written and oral language interactions. However, demonstrations of how to read and write in Spanish were not consistently available. Opportunities to use a full range of signs and modes of communication would be greatly enhanced by more consistent opportunities to read Spanish storybooks, count in Spanish, and learn about content using Spanish vocabulary. In classrooms where Spanish models are not available for four-year-old children, opportunities to expand their language repertoires through oral and written language contexts in both English and Spanish are lost.

Limitations

This study presents a portrait of one classroom context with a small sample of emergent bilinguals. The analysis of journal writing focused on a limited amount of features, with other features left out. We focused on letters, letter-like marks, and on pictures in a general sense. Aspects of pictures such as color, size, and placement, for example, were not analyzed. Our focus on journal writing, rather than recording children's talk during writing or interviews with children about their writing resulted in a product, rather than a process-oriented analysis. Future studies on the topic of four-year-old emergent bilinguals could address these limitations by including more participants and including recordings of student talk and student interviews in the data collection.

Delineations

The present study was bounded by an existing classroom in a geographical area and historical time in which emergent bilinguals are increasingly found in prekindergarten classrooms, yet are not numerous in many such classrooms. Because of this situation, some teachers have not learned how to work with emergent bilinguals. The data for this study focused on the product of journal writing rather than the process. Although much can be learned by studying children's talk during the writing process, this work has been explored by other researchers (Dyson, 2003b; Laman & Van Sluys, 2008), yet the writing product of four-year-old emergent bilinguals has not been fully explored. This study adds to our knowledge of young emergent bilingual writers.

CONCLUSIONS

Emergent bilingual children in English-only classrooms bring many resources to their literacy development, yet these resources can be underutilized. In English-only classrooms, teachers must make efforts commensurate with their knowledge and resources in regard to students' home languages. Teachers must provide explicit links to the home language through the use of bilingual materials and bilingual talk. The capacity for biliteracy should be capitalized upon by linking the child's home language with classroom literacy in the form of bilingual story book readings with discussion, and bilingual children's songs with corresponding movements. Word cards and labels in the child's home language should be present in the classroom and explicitly referred to during journal writing time, so that children can experiment with writing such words. Four-year-old children use their available resources to make meaning through literacy practices. The home language is a valuable resource that should be included to the greatest degree possible from the very beginning of school to encourage the child's biliterate development.

Oral language is developed through social interactions within a variety of contexts. When children are developing bilingually, they must be given opportunities to hear and speak both languages in order for both languages to develop appropriately for their age. In order to move past early stages of oral language development in the home language, they must be exposed to their language within an academic context. In 4K, teachers can read bilingual stories and informational books aloud so children will internalize the organizational patterns. By hearing examples of oral language in a variety of academic contexts such as mathematics, science, and literature, children will have models of complex sentence structures as well as vocabulary. Bilingual informational books are an excellent resource for teachers who do not have enough proficiency in the child's home language to produce extended oral language, yet have enough knowledge of the language to read aloud. When the teacher does not have the ability to read in the child's native language, family and community members can be invited into the classroom to read, commercial recordings can be used, or websites with reading and singing may be found. Children should be encouraged to speak to one another in their home language in the classroom context. Parents and community members should be invited into the classroom to talk with children in their home language about academic content. And the classroom teacher should explicitly value the home language even if he or she cannot speak it. It is the responsibility of the classroom teacher to provide early literacy experiences, which make explicit links between oral and written language, including non-English oral languages.

REFERENCES

Calkins, L. M. (1986). *The art of teaching writing*. Portsmouth, NH: Heinemann.

Campano, G. (2007). *Immigrant students and literacy: Reading, writing, and remembering*. New York, NY: Teachers College Press.

DeFord, D. E. (1980). Young children and their writing. *Theory Into Practice, 19*, 157-162.

DeFord, D. E. (1994). Early writing: Teachers and children in Reading Recovery. *Literacy, Teaching and Learning: An International Journal of Early Literacy, 1*, 31-57.

Dyson, A. H. (2003a). *The brothers and sisters learn to write*. New York, NY: Teachers College Press.

Dyson, A. H. (2003b). Writing and children's symbolic repertoires: Development unhinged. In S. Neuman, & D. Dickerson (Eds.), *Handbook of early literacy research*, Vol. 1. (pp. 126-141). New York, NY: Guilford Press.

Dyson, A. H. (2008). Staying in the (curricular) lines: Practice constraints and possibilities in childhood writing. *Written Communication, 25,* 199-159.

Ferreiro, E., & Teberosky, A. (1982). *Literacy before schooling*. Portsmouth, NH: Heinemann.

Genishi, C., Stires, S. E., & Yung-Chan, D. (2001). Writing in an integrated curriculum: Prekindergarten English language learners as symbol makers. *The Elementary School Journal, 101*, 399-416.

Gentile, L. (2003). *Oral language acquisition inventory: Linking research and theory to assessment and instruction*. Carlsbad, CA: Dominie Press.

Gentry, J. R. (1992). An analysis of developmental spelling in GYNS AT WRK. *The Reading Teacher, 36,* 192-200.

Gentry, J. R. (2000). A retrospective on invented spelling and a look forward. *The Reading Teacher, 54,* 318.

Graves, D. (1983). *Writing: Teachers and children at work*. Portsmouth, NH: Heinemann.

Harste, J., Woodward, V., & Burke, C. (1984). *Language stories and literacy lessons*. Portsmouth, NH: Heinemann.

Heath, S. (1983). *Ways with words: Language, life, and work in communities and classrooms*. New York, NY: Cambridge University Press.

Hudelson, S. (1989). *Write on: Children writing in ESL*. Englewood Cliffs, NJ: Prentice Hall.

Kabuto, B. (2010). Bilingual writing as an act of identity: Sign-making in multiple scripts. *Bilingual Research Journal, 33,* 130-149.

Kane, B. (1939). The legend of Batman. *Detective Comics*. New York, NY: National Periodical Publications.

Kenner, C., & Kress, G. (2003). The multisemiotic resources of biliterate children. *Journal of Early Childhood Literacy, 3,* 179-202.

Kress, G. (1997). *Before writing: Rethinking the paths to literacy*. New York, NY: Routledge.

Kress, G. (2010). *Multimodality: A social semiotic approach to contemporary communication*. New York, NY: Routledge.

Ladson-Billings, G. (1995). Toward a theory of culturally relevant pedagogy. *American Educational Research Journal, 32*, 465-491.

Laman, T. T., & Van Sluys, K. (2008). Being and becoming: Multilingual writers' practices. *Language Arts, 85,* 265-275.

Lee, S., & Ditko, S. (1962). Introducing Spider-man. *Amazing fantasy.* New York, NY: Marvel Comics.

Mardell, C., & Goldenberg, D. (1998). *Developmental indicators for the assessment of learning,* (3ʳᵈ ed.). San Antonio, TX: Pearson Clinical Assessments.

Mario Bros. [Computer software]. (1985). Kyoto, Japan: Nintendo.

Moll, L., Amanti, C., Neff, D., & Gonzalez, N. (2001). Funds of knowledge for teaching: Using a qualitative approach to connect homes and classrooms. *Theory Into Practice, 31,* 132-141.

Moll, L., Saez, R., & Dworin, J. (2001). Exploring biliteracy: Two student case examples of writing as a social practice. *Elementary School Journal,* 101, 435-449.

Narey, M. (Ed.). (2009). *Learning through arts-based early childhood education.* New York, NY: Springer Publishing Company.

Parker, E., & Pardini, T. (2006). *"The words came down!" English language learners read, write, and talk across the curriculum.* New York, NY: Stenhouse.

Reyes, I., & Azuara, P. (2008). Emergent biliteracy in young Mexican immigrant children. *Reading Research Quarterly, 43,* 374-498.

Rubin, R., & Carlan, V. G. (2005). Using writing to understand bilingual children's literacy development. *The Reading Teacher, 59,* 728-739.

Samway, K. D. (Ed.). (2006). *When English language learners write: Connecting research to practice.* New York, NY: Heinemann.

Spence, L. K., & Cardenas-Cortez, K. (2011). To me, writing means having a voice: Learning to write and teaching writing from a multilingual perspective. *TESOL Journal, 2,* 1-23.

Spence, L. K. (2010). Discerning writing assessment: Insights into an analytical rubric. *Language Arts, 87,* 337-347.

The New London Group (1996). A pedagogy of multiliteracies: Designing social futures. *Harvard Educational Review, 66,* 60-92.

Valdés, G., Capitelli, S., & Alvarez, L. (2011). *Latino children learning English: Steps in a journey.* New York, NY: Teachers College Press.

Vygotsky, L. (1986). *Thought and language.* Cambridge, MA: The MIT Press.

Yaden, D. B., Jr., & Tardibuono, J. M. (2004). The emergent writing development of urban Latino preschoolers: Developmental perspectives and instructional environments for second language learners. *Reading & Writing Quarterly, 20,* 29–61.

"People Suffer More Than You Think": Witnessing Trauma in Children's Poetry

Angela M. Wiseman
North Carolina State University

Kelly Wissman
University of Albany-SUNY

It is Thursday morning, which means it is time for Theo Jones (all names of students and teachers are pseudonyms) to teach his weekly poetry lesson in Pamela Martin's eighth-grade classroom. Theo is an artist and poet who works at a local non-profit community center. Carrying a portable CD player, Theo walks into the classroom wearing jeans and a football jersey and exchanges greetings with students as he makes his way to the front of the room.

To introduce the idea of striving for goals in the face of adversity, Theo bases his lesson for today on the song "The World's Greatest" by R. Kelly (2001). The lyrics describe Muhammad Ali and how he had to struggle in order to fulfill his dreams:

…used to be locked doors

Now I can just walk on through

Hey, uh, hey, hey, hey

It's the greatest

I'm that star up in the sky (Kelly, 2001)

After playing the song, Theo invites the students to think about hurdles and difficult times in their lives. The students begin writing and conferring, many moving around the room. Near the end of the session, Theo asks for volunteers to read their writing. Jasmine comes to the front of the room and reads from her poem entitled "God Created Me," including these lines:

God created me

Mommy loved me

Grandma sheltered me

Teachers tried for me.

I believe in me.

Daddy no comment

Daddy, where are you?

I wish you were here.

As Jasmine reads, it is clear that this poem is difficult for her to share and that it brings up painful memories about her father and his lack of involvement in her life. When she finishes reading, several classmates clap for her and give her high fives. Suddenly, the bell rings and she is off to her next class.

Across the contexts in which we have taught and conducted research, students have composed and shared autobiographical writing reflecting what Dutro (2011) calls the "hard stuff of life"

119

(p. 193), including: sexual abuse, poverty, racial discrimination, divorce, domestic violence, and homelessness (Wissman & Wiseman, 2011). Despite the widespread invitations for students to write from personal experience in English Language Arts curricula, however, there is little discussion among educators and researchers about how students are affected when they compose and share difficult or sad stories in school. There is also little consideration of how teachers respond to the stories (with notable exceptions in the work of Dutro, 2008, 2010; Jones, 2004; McCarthey, 1994). As a result, when children attest to difficult experiences that challenge middle-class notions of childhood as a time of innocence and security, refer to illegal or violent activity, or call attention to social inequalities or injustices, their stories may be met with uncomfortable silence (Jones, 2004).

The purpose of this article is to present case studies illustrative of the difficult stories children compose in the writing classroom and to consider the implications of sharing those stories for the students themselves and the broader classroom community. Aligned with scholars who work with young people in schools and communities to inspire writing from lived experience, e.g., Appelsies & Fairbanks, 1997; Jocson, 2006; and Kinloch, 2005, we contend that autobiographical writing can nurture a "stronger sense of self" (Tatum & Gue, 2010, p. 92); however, we also seek a deeper and richer understanding of what happens when difficult stories of loss or trauma are shared within educational contexts. In order to explore the pedagogical significance and emotional implications of the emergence and sharing of difficult personal experiences in classrooms, we first consider perspectives from the literature on trauma studies. Using a trauma studies lens, we then present case studies of two students, providing insight into features of their poems about difficult experiences and how responses to the students' poems affected their understanding of those experiences. We pay attention not only to the students' writing, but also to how relationships were built among teachers, students, and their parents both in and out of school. We conclude with considerations and implications for literacy research and practice. The following research question guides our inquiry in this article: What happens when students write and share stories from personal experience within writing classrooms, especially stories that may attest to trauma, injustice, poverty, or loss?

TRAUMA STUDIES

Drawing from psychological frameworks developed to understand how victims of trauma testify to traumatic experiences and how others witness those testimonies, work within trauma studies (Caruth, 1996; Felman & Laub, 1992) helps to illuminate how writing based on personal reflection can reveal conflicting emotions, painful experiences, and unhappy events in the classroom. Goggin and Goggin (2005) delineate trauma in three categories: national, natural, and personal. Studies of trauma have typically focused on historic events that have extensive impact on large numbers of people such as the Holocaust (Rogers & Leydesdorff, 2004) or Hurricane Katrina (Bedford & Brenner, 2010), but trauma can also be felt on an individual level in response to sexual abuse or a familial death. bell hooks (1995) also argues that structural and internalized racism can inflect "psychic wounds" (p. 137) that result in "psychic trauma" (p. 138), necessitating acknowledgement and healing. For children, trauma can be defined as any situation where they feel powerless and are rendered helpless by overwhelming forces (Sitler, 2008). In this regard, trauma can also include situations that are chronic or long term that result in feelings of helplessness or lack of control, such as poverty or racism (Masko, 2005). Coping with trauma can prevent students from reaching their full academic potential and can affect their day-to-day social interactions. In the classroom, trauma can be masked in negative behaviors, such as passivity with little concern about the future, trouble concentrating, acting out verbally or physically, frequent absences, or general actions that reflect turmoil (Nader, 2008). Anderson and MacCurdy (2000) capture the all-encompassing, disorienting, and disempowering nature of trauma, writing, "As trauma survivors, we share one very important characteristic: We feel powerless, taken over by alien experiences we could not anticipate and did not choose. Healing depends upon gaining control over that which has engulfed us" (p. 5).

In trauma studies literature, the act of sharing is one aspect of healing and is referred to as "testifying." The survivor's testimony is an important aspect of identifying and understanding trauma. As Laub (1992) writes, "The testimony is, therefore, the process by which the narrator (the survivor) reclaims his position as a witness" (p. 85). While this testimony allows the narrator to reclaim the experience, a significant aspect of the healing process is also how others receive this testimony or, in trauma studies terms, "witnessed." If the testimony is rejected, it can cause one to re-experience the situation, feeling the same painful emotions that occurred during the traumatic event itself (Felman & Laub, 1992). If the testimony is witnessed, however, the act of testifying can be restorative and healing (Laub, 1992). MacCurdy (2000) writes:

> ...personal and cultural recovery from trauma requires a conversation between the victim and a witness, that indeed the witness is an utter necessity to complete the cycle of truth telling. If we shy away from offering our students the opportunity to tell their truths, we may be preventing them from learning what control they can have over their own lives. (p. 197)

Similarly emphasizing the role of a teacher as a witness to the stories children tell, Dutro (2011) writes, "...if a student chooses to take the risk of testifying to trauma, it is the very least we can do to risk the role of witness, to refrain from steering response to safer ground, and to allow another's testimony to speak to our own wounds" (p. 208).

TRAUMA STUDIES AND DIFFICULT STORIES IN THE WRITING CLASSROOM

We see promise in drawing from trauma studies (Felman & Laub, 1992) to understand the writing and sharing of difficult stories within writing classrooms, especially stories that may attest to trauma, injustice, poverty, or loss. This body of literature provides important conceptual tools and language, e.g., testimony, witnessing, for analysis of how those stories are both shared and received in the classroom. Below, we provide a description of the research context from which we selected two case study students who used poetry to testify to difficult experiences in their lives and then use perspectives from trauma studies to analyze their writing and the responses to their poetry.

Research Context

The two case study students are drawn from a research study that took place in an eighth-grade English classroom in an urban public middle school where 97% of the students qualified for free or reduced lunch. Of the 22 students in the classroom, 17 were African American, 1 was Asian, and 4 were Hispanic; 9 were male and 13 were female. The poetry program began because Pamela, the English teacher who was in her third year of teaching, was looking for a way to connect students' learning in the classroom to the community. Pamela was a White female who left her career in journalism because she wanted to work with adolescents. English instruction in Pamela's classroom was a balance of skills instruction and what she described as "service-based projects," where students would engage in projects in the community that foster learning while also developing awareness and understanding to improve the neighborhood. By working with a local nonprofit educational organization called Urban Voices in Education, Pamela was introduced to Theo, an African American youth coordinator at a nearby neighborhood center. Theo agreed to teach a weekly poetry workshop and then emcee bimonthly evening poetry coffeehouses. Theo worked in different contexts to promote poetry for youth in the area and also read and recorded his own poetry and lyrics for performances. Theo had relationships with many students in the classroom from his community work. In addition, his involvement in this school fostered new relationships with other students who began to attend programs at the nonprofit agency.

Theo's poetry workshops lasted approximately 45 minutes and took place once a week. Music was often the catalyst for introducing a theme or lesson and provided a model for writing; Theo selected songs or poems from a variety of genres that he felt conveyed an important message. Within the poetry workshop, students were encouraged to draw upon their own experiences to come up with writing topics, to use creative language to express their thoughts and ideas, and to write and revise their work to be precise and concise using minimal language for the maximum potential. Lessons introduced various styles, themes, and language forms by using a model piece that was featured as a springboard for ideas and could serve as a way for students to organize their own poetry. Students were encouraged to analyze the writing presented. They could then either choose to use the example and craft a poem with a similar format or theme or elect to write about a different topic or format. Using brief minilessons and individual conferences, Theo further encouraged students to focus on metaphorical language and create strong visual images. At the end of each poetry workshop, students had time to share their poetry with the class and students provided feedback and encouragement to each other.

An evening poetry coffeehouse was scheduled bimonthly at the school where students, parents, and community members wrote and performed poetry together. The end product from the workshops and coffeehouses was an anthology that was bound at a local print shop with contributions from students, teachers, parents, and community members.

Research Methods

This study employed qualitative research methods that involved data collection and analysis focusing on many aspects of the poetry program, including family participation and collaboration with community members. While Angela collected and analyzed the data, both authors of this article (Angela and Kelly) re-analyzed the data informed by perspectives from trauma studies and narrative inquiry and then crafted the case studies. Data were generated from three sources: (1) classroom observations and interactions recorded through fieldnotes and audio recordings; (2) student writing that was collected and copied each week; and (3) interviews and focus groups with students, family members, and Theo and Pamela. Classroom lessons, focus groups, and interviews were audiotaped and transcribed.

Angela employed ethnographic methods of participant-observation (Miles & Huberman, 1994) as data were gathered from October through May. Angela observed 12 classroom English lessons and 18 poetry workshops during the school year in their entirety (90-minute class sessions). In addition, data were collected during three evening poetry coffeehouses and four after-school poetry events. In addition to observing poetry workshops and regular English class sessions, Angela also attended field trips and met participants for interviews and member checks in the community.

Additional data were gathered through five focus groups, two teacher interviews, and eight informal conversations. In the five focus groups sessions (Krueger & Casey, 2009), Angela met with a group of five students who were identified by Pamela as representative of students in this classroom based on race, ethnicity, academic success, and interest in poetry. Angela used primarily open-ended questions such as, "Tell me about your family participation at the poetry coffeehouses," or "Tell me about the poetry that you wrote today," and from there, Angela moderated the focus groups while students discussed their ideas and thoughts (Seidman, 2006). At times, Pamela and Theo would suggest topics for her to discuss with the groups based on their own observations and interactions with the students. The focus group also helped Angela write descriptive profiles of students which included details of their participation in school and the poetry program, self-selected writing topics, and interests and hobbies outside of school. In addition, the focus group provided member checks as she wrote about the context of the classroom and shared preliminary findings from her data analysis. Both of the students profiled in this article participated in the focus groups.

Data Analysis

Our (Angela's and Kelly's) joint data analysis began with purposeful sampling (Maxwell, 2005) to identify students in Angela's study who used poetry to testify to the traumas in their lives. Most of the students in this classroom wrote about "difficult" stories during the poetry workshops. The traumas and difficulties written about in their poems included sexual abuse, isolation from friends, deaths of relatives, physical violence at school and home, and poverty in their community, among other topics. In Goggin and Goggin's (2005) framework, we saw the children writing about "personal" traumas (as opposed to national or natural ones). In our initial analysis, we engaged in repeated reading and inductive analysis of their poetry, interviews, and field notes of classroom observations (Merriam, 2009). We chose two students, Jasmine and Hector, because they were especially illustrative of how witnessing opened up new possibilities in and out of school given how teachers, students, and family members responded to their poems. We present our research in the form of case studies, an approach to qualitative data collection, analysis, and representation that provides multi-dimensional consideration of phenomena by drawing on multiple data sources (Dyson & Genishi, 2005; Stake, 2005).

Our analyses and writing of the cases were further informed by narrative inquiry (Clandinin & Connelly, 2000) which prompted us, especially when considering the students' poetry, to "listen to the narrator's voices—to the subject positions, interpretive practices, ambiguities, and complexities —within each narrator's story" (Chase, 2005, p. 663). Narrative inquiry provided us with a lens to address issues of complexity that emerged in the classroom and coffeehouse performances, to focus on students' opportunities to express their feelings about an event, and to consider how students' stories reflected their experiences with the world (Webster & Metrova, 2007). After identifying our cases, we engaged in narrative analysis by searching through the data to understand *how* these students told stories of their trauma in the classroom. We then looked again through fieldnotes, student writing, focus group interviews, and classroom interactions to consider their stories and how their experiences were expressed across contexts (Clandinin, Murphy, Juber, & Orr, 2010). We reviewed data to determine: the nature of the students' poetry, how members in the classroom and broader community "witnessed" the students' poems, and how the cases informed our understanding of the research question (Stake, 2005). Analysis revealed three important themes related to the research question: (1) the students used poetry to understand and represent trauma in various ways in response to personal topics; (2) the classroom context was an important factor in supporting trauma narratives; and (3) relationships among teachers, students, and family were reflected and/or affected by the sharing of traumatic events. In the next section, we present our two case studies of students who provide complementary and contrastive insight about sharing difficult stories in the classroom.

Jasmine

Jasmine, a 13-year-old African American girl, described herself as "loud, outgoing, high in self-esteem, aggressive, and upfront." Her thoughts flowed quickly, often faster than her hand could write. She explained, "...whatever comes to my mind, as soon as I get it, that's what you get." When she recited her poetry in class and at coffeehouses, she spoke with a strong voice and always from memory. Jasmine's grandmother, who was a clinical social worker, described Jasmine's ability to express herself through poetry as a "legacy" that many men and women in the family shared. She noted, "[Jasmine's] very much like her grandfather. He wrote and could memorize poetry as well." Jasmine also referred to the familial roots of her poetry, noting, "I come from a group of women who provide a lot of support." Members of Jasmine's extended family joined her at every coffeehouse, including her aunts, grandmother, mother, and cousins. At one coffeehouse, Jasmine's grandmother told Angela:

> Jasmine came home and someone had been murdered next door. I worry about Jasmine taking it the wrong way and going the wrong direction with it…We're a loving family. I'm watching to make sure that Jasmine, who is aggressive – and when I say that, I don't mean in a bad or violent way, but in a way of being assertive and independent – doesn't take it in the wrong way and come out going in the wrong direction.

Jasmine wrote about a range of topics in her poetry, from neighborhood violence to losses within her family. Theo described Jasmine's writing as "very courageous...her anger is used as power" and encouraged her to tap that anger to write poetry. Jasmine was very expressive and responded well to the opportunity to write about her own experiences. In one poem, Jasmine chose to write poetry about the violence in her neighborhood, writing, "A loud sound broke the silence/and now it's all violence/because he didn't have any tolerance..." Throughout her poems, she asserted an awareness of the challenges in her neighborhood and her own self-confidence to craft her own path. In one poem she wrote, "I don't need clothes to succeed, but/I do need self-determination, self-control, and strong will."

While Jasmine's poems included allusions to violence in her neighborhood, her poems also reflected her inner turmoil and pain resulting from her father's departure. As we described above, Jasmine felt sadness about her relationship with her father and recalled, "I was angry that my dad left and I would tell my mom, but she didn't want to talk about it." Jasmine's plea, "Daddy, where are you?" in her poem in response to Theo's invitation to write about a hurdle in her life, suggests her confusion and pain about her father's lack of involvement in her life. She wrote several poems about her father and showed them to her mother. Her mother "broke down" when she heard Jasmine's poems and crafted her own poem in response, "A Mother's Cry," which she read at a poetry coffeehouse. An excerpt from her poem to Jasmine reads:

Last night my dear child

I cried for you

I cried for I could not stand

to see the pain you're in

Then, I prayed to God

to take your pain away

and let you see you can ask.

I ask you my child

to take a look at me

and remember.

Remember the pain, the confusion,

the loss of hope.

So I ran.

I did not know.

Jasmine's mother provided a layered "witnessing" to Jasmine's testimony, including listening to Jasmine's poems, crying in response, writing her own poem, and performing it publicly at the coffeehouse. Jasmine was affected by responses she received to her poetry, both from her peers in class who applauded her work and encouraged her to keep writing, as well as from her mother in the coffeehouse.

In addition to these public shows of support, Pamela also witnessed privately Jasmine's testimony about a family loss. In April of the school year, Jasmine's grandmother passed away. Jasmine's strength and resilience was reflected as she recited a poem at her funeral about the support and love her grandmother had provided for her. While she did not share the poem with the class and was very quiet about her loss, her poetry provided an opportunity for Jasmine to acknowledge the loss. She confided in and shared her poem with Pamela, a poem that Pamela described as a powerful tribute to her beloved grandmother.

Jasmine's poetry that explored a range of difficult experiences and losses was well-received in both private and public settings and by both her family and her classmates. She was able to use poetry to testify to her own personal trauma as well as to show concern for her community. Furthermore, writing provided a way for mother and daughter to communicate about Jasmine's feelings regarding a traumatic experience in her life. The exchange between them provided an opportunity for them to seek understanding in a way that acknowledged her feelings and provided insight into her relationship with her father. Rather than seeking to diffuse Jasmine's anger or sadness, Theo and Pamela both encouraged her to channel these feelings into her poetry, while her family members and classmates also provided support as they witnessed her poems.

Hector

The first time Hector, a 13-year-old Latino student, volunteered to read his poetry at the beginning of the school year, he surprised many of his classmates with his passion and emotion. Hector at times struggled with his engagement and attitude towards school. He also had little interest in poetry before participating in the poetry workshop. As the year progressed, his classmates commented on his ability to articulate his feelings in complex ways and to create and perform lyrics that flowed with rhythm. At a focus group, Hector told Angela, "I never thought about writing poetry until last year when I started writing poetry for this class. And now I like it. I like to write lyrics."

Hector's poetry addressed a range of traumatic events, including a death within his family, community violence, and racism. As he was composing during one workshop where students had listened to and read lyrics from *The Miseducation of Lauryn Hill* (Hill, 1998), Angela asked him what he was writing about and he said, "I am writing about stereotypes of Hispanic males and how I've been made to feel like I can't succeed." After revising and editing his piece, he offered to read his own poem, entitled "The Miseducation" to the class, which included these lines:

> All I was taught is that I would suffer more
>
> Grow up to be a bad person angry and poor
>
> Day by day told that I would never make it
>
> But little did they know that I always take it
>
> …All I heard is that my race would do nothing
>
> But I guarantee momma raised me as something

Unlike Jasmine, Hector did not have the support of his family in attendance at poetry coffeehouses, but Theo, Pamela, and his fellow students were important witnesses to his poems. Theo was very intentional in encouraging Hector to write poems in order to make sense of his school struggles. As Hector was able to reflect on his experiences and to consider how he was receiving negative messages about being Latino, he also received feedback on the power and importance of his words. Hector's poem, "The Miseducation," was received with resounding cheers and applause from the class. Later in a focus group, several students responded to his poem by discussing times they had dealt with racism. When asked how and why he crafted poetry that testified to difficult life experiences, he told the focus group, "Being able to write about what I want is important. Some kids write about being angry or mad, but that's just how they are feeling. They have to get it out." Hector speaks to the importance of naming difficult issues and emotions, of testifying to their presence and significance, within school.

Hector enjoyed Theo's poetry workshop not only because of the opportunity to write about what was important to him, but also because it enabled him to discover and work toward his future goals of becoming a writer or lyricist. Theo spent one Saturday afternoon with Hector to record his lyrics at a studio. As Theo came to know Hector through spending more time with him at the studio, in school, in an after-school program, and through his poetry, Theo learned that Hector was very close to his mother, was very hurt due to estrangement from his father, and often took responsibilities for helping with his nephew. Theo also learned that Hector still had family in El Salvador and his cousin had recently been shot and killed. Hector tried writing about his cousin, but found it was too soon to talk specifically about him. He found he could express himself more abstractly about violence, writing:

Never take anything for granted...

You should never underestimate the preciousness of life

People's lives are lost, but we bless the rest with life...

Some people shoot others while others run for their lives

So whenever you get the feelings inside that you are less

People suffer more than you think

Your life is precious.

Poetry provided a space for Hector to express anger related to his experiences with racism and sadness at the loss of his cousin. His writing also resulted in stronger relationships with his classroom English teacher as well as with Theo.

After Hector had improved both his attendance and grades during this school year, many were optimistic about the progress he had made in eighth grade. In his poetry, though, Hector reflected on how his life often teetered between dichotomies that might lead to success or failure. In one poem he read aloud to the class, he asked:

...will I end up a fighter of freedom or the racism

Will I end up the fighter that's leading where my place is

Die a bloody death full of blades like blenders and the hurt

Or will I go quiet and peaceful be remembered on the earth?

While Hector had made much progress in school, an incident in April showed the delicate "teetering" in his life that could result in his own success or failure. Hector was expelled from school when he was accused of marking walls with graffiti. He maintained his innocence and Pamela was devastated that, after making good grades and showing improvement, this incident could possibly affect his school engagement or alienate him further from educational opportunities. Hector's poetry had tapped his strengths, opening up possibilities for him in the classroom providing and mentoring from Theo. However, it was clear he would continue to struggle with how to fit the pieces of his life together—his emotional pain, school experiences, and outside influences.

DISCUSSION AND IMPLICATIONS

In reflecting on some of the most destabilizing and often silenced experiences of death, violence, racism, and abandonment, we see how Jasmine and Hector embraced poetry as an opportunity to reflect on and explore complex emotions. Perhaps even more powerfully, their difficult stories were witnessed by members of their classroom community who provided inspiration and support. Jasmine's writing extended her literacy development both in and out of school and gave her a place to channel her power and emotions. In Hector's case, opening up these topics through a poetry workshop supported his understanding of personal experiences, provided an outlet for social analysis, and affected his school engagement. Despite the difficult topics addressed in their poetry, their teachers did not shy away with uncomfortable silences (Jones, 2004), nor did they approach their writing from a deficit paradigm (Dutro, 2009a). Rather than alienating students by responding to their stories with silence or disapproval, Pamela and Theo responded in ways that showed students they were valued and supported in school. Not only did sharing difficult poems bring Jasmine and Hector closer to their teachers, their poetry also opened up conversations among their fellow students and family members. The opportunities for students to express themselves in the classroom carried over to out-of-school contexts, affected relationships with family, and provided opportunities for mentorship from caring adults.

As we consider the emotionally rich and linguistically powerful poems created by Jasmine and Hector, we see how a poetry workshop opened up many opportunities for students to embrace literacy as a form of truth-telling, demonstrating the power of providing opportunities for students to share their own experiences (Dutro, 2011). At the same time, though, Theo also stated he wished students had not experienced such things at such young ages, noting:

> You shouldn't be able to write about abuse and violence and all these things you can write at thirteen. Because you should not have had to have such intimate encounters with them. So the writing shouldn't be as therapeutic as it is. It should be fun. It should be a landscape to a dream. It should be something to challenge yourself and have fun with it...you shouldn't have had that level of scars...

Acknowledging that those experiences and those scars are all too present for many young people, however, Theo also contended the poetry workshop he facilitated in the school was an ideal way to "...create space where we can support each other."

From both a pedagogical and psychological standpoint, we feel it is important to understand how the difficult stories children tell in these kinds of school spaces work to support their meaning-making related to difficult and traumatic events in their lives. As teachers and researchers, creating a space for these stories and witnessing them is undeniably difficult, not only in considering the impact they may have on our own psyches, but also how they challenge us to respond in ways that support students. We recognize that methods that work in counseling contexts do not translate directly to classroom environments, given issues such as large class sizes, teachers' lack of formal psychological training, competing individual needs of students, and curricular/testing demands. We believe, however, that Pamela's classroom, Theo's poetry workshop, and the monthly coffeehouses explored in this manuscript provide many important insights for consideration of how teachers might respond responsively and responsibly to the difficult stories children share.

Across these contexts, poetry was envisioned and enacted as having the potential to be personally meaningful to students and to connect purposefully with their lives. By positioning everyone as a poet and by considering every story as valuable and welcome, poetry was not reduced to "exercises" to be completed or lessons to be delivered. The atmosphere created in these contexts was unique in that they each allowed for differently situated adults, including community poets, parents, grandparents, and researchers to work with and listen to young people. As a result, many valuable opportunities for testimony and witnessing were created. In addition to Pamela's openness to inviting Theo into her classroom and her own efforts to reach out to parents, we also see Theo's presence and pedagogy as reflecting so much of what would be considered "culturally relevant pedagogy" (Ladson-Billings, 1994). Theo skillfully built on the knowledge and experiences students brought with them to the classroom in ways that enhanced their academic engagement and achievement; he participated in the students' lives outside the classroom; and he developed open and trusting relationships with the students' parents. What stands out as well in this classroom was not only how a context for students to write and share poetry was created, but also that Pamela and Theo both listened actively when difficult stories emerged and both followed up with students and families when these stories were shared.

Given the ways in which students may make themselves vulnerable in testifying to their difficult stories, careful, non-judgmental, and compassionate listening is necessary. Research on trauma narratives demonstrates how important response is when a story of trauma is shared. Often, when difficult topics such as this arise in the classroom, the initial response is to steer the conversation to "safer ground" (Dutro, 2011). However, rather than responding passively or silencing difficult topics, research on trauma demonstrates how important it is to listen carefully and reflexively, to *witness* the pain and trauma that have been experienced. When stories emerge in the classroom that describe conflicting emotions, painful experiences, and unhappy events, it is important to understand the significance of witnessing a child's trauma narratives, listening carefully, and responding in ways that offer support.

CONCLUSION

As we consider the ways in which Jasmine and Hector wrote about difficult experiences in their lives and communities, we see the value in trauma studies perspectives for illuminating how writing enabled them to grapple with complex emotions and to share those experiences within a community that heard, witnessed, and responded to them. The students' poetry suggests the power to name experiences of trauma, loss, and inequities that are often silenced within schools and in the broader society. While the poems written by Hector and Jasmine were based on their own personal experiences, their topics reflected larger social issues of neighborhood violence, racism, and loss, issues faced by many children. As students engaged with the process of naming their experiences, they were able to transform their understanding in ways that were simultaneously emotionally and personally powerful, while also speaking to their own power to use literacy in critical and transformative ways.

Turner (2011) suggests that public schools are "one of the few remaining social safety nets for families and children in marginalized communities" (p. 454) and yet their ability to serve liberatory or social justice ends is increasingly imperiled with the rise of commercialized and scripted literacy programs and high-stakes testing (Dutro, 2009b). As a result, we see the particular significance of attending to students' desires to write from personal experience and how the stories that emerge can support students' efforts to name difficult experiences and realities. As the cases of Jasmine and Hector suggest, the way teachers and other members of the classroom community respond to students' stories of trauma can offer both solace and inspiration, despite the unfair, painful, and violent events in children's lives (Cowhey, 2006). It is our hope that children in schools can continue to envision poetry as a "landscape to a dream," as Theo contends, and also as a possible pathway to healing and change-making within a difficult world.

REFERENCES

Anderson, C. M., & MacCurdy, M. M. (Eds.). *Writing and healing: Toward an informed practice*. Urbana, IL: National Council of Teachers of English.

Appelsies, A. & Fairbanks, C. M. (1997). Write for your life. *Educational Leadership, 54*, 70-72.

Bedford, A. W., & Brenner, D. (2010). Making contact in times of crisis: Literacy practices in a Post-Katrina world. In L. MacGillivray (Ed.), *Literacy in times of crisis: Practices and perspectives* (pp. 15-31). New York, NY: Taylor & Francis.

Caruth, C. (1996). *Unclaimed experience: Trauma, narrative, and history*. Baltimore, MD: Johns Hopkins University Press.

Chase, S. E. (2005). Narrative inquiry: Multiple lenses, approaches, voices. In N. K. Denzin & Y. S. Lincoln (Eds.), *The Sage handbook of qualitative research, 3rd ed.*, pp. 651-680. Thousand Oaks, CA: Sage.

Clandinin, D. J. & Connelly, F. M. (2000). *Narrative inquiry: Experience and story in qualitative research*. San Francisco, CA: Jossey-Bass.

Clandinin, D. J., Murphy, M. S., Juber, J., & Orr, A. M. (2010). Negotiating narrative inquiries: Living in a tension-filled midst. *Journal of Educational Research, 103*, 81-90.

Cowhey, M. (2006). *Black ants and Buddhists: Thinking critically and teaching differently in the primary grades*. Portland, ME: Stenhouse.

Dutro, E. (2008). "That's why I was crying on that book": Trauma as testimony in responses to literature. *Changing English, 15*, 423-434.

Dutro, E. (2009a). Children's testimony and the necessity of critical witness in urban classrooms. *Theory Into Practice, 48*, 231-238.

Dutro, E. (2009b). Children writing "hard times": Lived experiences of poverty and the class-privileged assumptions of a mandated curriculum. *Language Arts, 87*, 89-98.

Dutro, E. (2010). What 'hard times' means: Mandated curricula, middle-class assumptions, and the lives of poor children. *Research in the Teaching of English, 44*, 255-291.

Dutro, E. (2011). Writing wounded: Trauma, testimony, and critical witness in literacy classrooms. *English Education, 43*, 193-210.

Dyson, A. H., & Genishi, C. (2005). *On the case: Approaches to language and literacy research*. New York, NY: Teachers College Press.

Felman, S., & Laub. D. (1992). *Testimony: Crises of witnessing in literature, psychoanalysis, and history*. New York, NY: Routledge.

Goggin, P. N., & Goggin, M. D. (2005). Presence in absence: Discourses and teaching (in, on, and about) trauma. In S. Borrowman (Ed.), *Trauma and the teaching of writing* (pp. 29-52). Albany, NY: State University of New York Press.

Hill, L. (1998). The miseducation of Lauryn Hill. On *The miseducation of Lauryn Hill* [CD]. New York, NY: Columbia Records.

hooks, b. (1995). *Killing rage: Ending racism*. New York, NY: Henry Holt & Company.

Jocson, K. M. (2006). There's a better word: Urban youth rewriting their social worlds through poetry. *Journal of Adolescent & Adult Literacy, 49*, 700-708.

Jones, S. (2004). Living poverty and literacy learning: Sanctioning the topics of students' lives. *Language Arts, 81*, 461-469.

Kelly, R. S. (2001). The world's greatest. On *Chocolate factory* [CD]. New York, NY: Jive Records.

Kinloch, V. F. (2005). Poetry, literacy, and creativity: Fostering effective learning strategies in an urban classroom. *English Education, 37*, 96-114.

Krueger, R. A., & Casey, M. A. (2009). *Focus groups: A practical guide for applied research.* Thousand Oaks, CA: Sage.

Ladson-Billings, G. J. (1994). *The dreamkeepers: Successful teachers of African-American children.* San Francisco, CA: Jossey-Bass.

Laub, D. (1992). An event without a witness: Truth, testimony and survival. In S. Felman & D. Laub (Eds.). *Testimony: Crises of witnessing in literature, psychoanalysis, and history* (pp. 75-92). New York, NY: Routledge.

MacCurdy, M. M. (2000). From trauma to writing: A theoretical model for practical use. In C. M Anderson & M. M. MacCurdy (Eds.), *Writing and healing: Toward an informed practice* (pp. 158-200). Urbana, IL: National Council of Teachers of English.

Masko, A. L. (2005). "I think about it all the time": A 12-year-old girl's internal crisis with racism and the effects on her mental health. *Urban Review, 37*, 329-350.

Maxwell, J. (2005). *Qualitative research design: An interactive approach.* Thousand Oaks, CA: Sage.

McCarthey, S. J. (1994). Opportunities and risks of writing from personal experience. *Language Arts, 71*, 182-191.

Merriam, S. B. (2009). *Qualitative research: A guide to design and implementation.* San Francisco, CA: Jossey-Bass.

Miles, M. B., & Huberman, A. M. (1994). Qualitative data analysis (2nd ed.). Thousand Oaks, CA: Sage

Nader, K. (2008). *Understanding and assessing trauma in children and adolescents: Measures, methods, and youth in context.* New York, NY: Routledge.

Rogers, K. L., & Leydesdorff, S. (Eds.). (2004). *Trauma: Life stories of survivors.* New Brunswick, NJ: Transaction Publishers.

Seidman, I. (2006). *Interviewing as qualitative research: A guide for researchers in education and the social sciences.* New York, NY: Teachers College Press.

Sitler, H. C. (2008). Teaching with awareness: The hidden effects of trauma on learning. *The Clearing House, 82*, 119-123.

Stake, R. E. (2005). Qualitative case studies. In N. K. Denzin & Y. S. Lincoln (Eds.), *The Sage handbook of qualitative research* (3rd ed., pp. 443-466). Thousand Oaks, CA: Sage.

Tatum, A. W., & Gue, V. (2010). Adolescents and texts: Raw writing – A critical support for adolescents. *English Journal, 99*, 90-93.

Turner, K. C. N. (2011). Socially engaged scholarship: Linking youth popular literacy practices and social justice. *Language Arts, 88*, 454-458.

Webster, L., & Metrova, P. (2007). *Using narrative inquiry as a research method: An introduction to using critical event narrative analysis in research on learning and teaching.* New York, NY: Routledge.

Wissman, K. K., & Wiseman, A. M. (2011). "That's my worst nightmare": Poetry and trauma in the middle school classroom. *Pedagogies: An International Journal, 6*, 234-249.

Writing Across Lifeworlds

Allison Skerrett
Michelle Fowler-Amato
Katharine Chamberlain
Caron Sharp
The University of Texas at Austin

In this article, we report a Latina urban youth's narratives of her identity and practices as a writer. We portray how this adolescent responded to her teacher's invitations to cocreate a hybrid learning space that recruited and enhanced her multiple literacies, languages, subjectivities, and interests drawn from many lifeworlds. We bring into relief the student's writing life because it provides a rebuttal to reports that can create a feeling of crisis that today's youth, especially those of color, do not read and write enough, or well enough (ACT, 2006; National Center for Education Statistics, 2002). Our analysis argues that literacy education is most productive and fulfilling when it both draws from and builds up the multiple languages, literacies, interests, and subjectivities students engage within and across lifeworlds.

THEORETICAL FRAMEWORK

We view all language and literacy as social practice situated in nested cultural, sociopolitical, and spatiotemporal contexts (New London Group, 1996; Scribner & Cole, 1981). However, people do not live or engage in language and literacy practices within neatly divided contexts. The language and literacy practices that youth develop, independent of and in concert with adults, are likewise produced within and across multiple geographic, sociocultural, and historical contexts (Barton, Hamilton, & Ivanic, 2000) or lifeworlds (New London Group, 1996). The New London Group (1996) challenged the concept of "mere literacy" (p. 64) that was centered only on language, and often, a stable form of one language. In place of this notion they proposed "multiliteracies" (p. 64) that acknowledged other modes of representation that were culture- and context-specific and broader than language alone. Their imperative for replacing mere literacy with multiliteracies arose from mounting cultural and linguistic diversity in societies, an increasingly globalized world, rapidly advancing technologies, and proliferating subcultural diversity in which people create subcommunities according to shared interests and world views.

In his discussion of literacy and identity, Gee (1990, 1994) posited that identity is coconstructed and socially situated. Young people develop understandings of who they are as they engage with others in literate activity within and across lifeworlds. Furthermore, each individual claims multiple identities using the tools of Discourse (language, values, social interactions, etc.) to enact different social roles or identities to meet changing needs or circumstances (Gee, 1990, 1994). Hence, though physical or ideological boundaries are frequently inscribed or perceived among lifeworlds, the borderzones, or places where these contexts intersect, are potentially generative sites for learning (Gutiérrez, 2008; Martínez, 2010; Orellana & Reynolds, 2008; Skerrett, 2010, 2011; Skerrett & Bomer, 2011; Kalantzis & Cope, 2005; New London Group, 1996).

The New London Group (1996) initially theorized a pedagogy of multiliteracies in which teachers recruit the multiple literacy skills that students develop in various lifeworlds for literacy education. The authors detailed four components to multiliteracies pedagogy: Situated-Practice, Overt Instruction, Critical Framing, and Transformed Practice. Situated Practice draws on students' meaning-making experiences in their numerous lifeworlds. Overt Instruction facilitates students' development of a metalanguage of Design that allows them to identify and analyze the tools and processes they are using to design meaning and the contexts for which these tools and processes are effective. The goal of Overt Instruction is for students to develop conscious awareness and control over what they are learning. Critical Framing introduces the social, cultural, political, historical, and ideological dimensions of Design. Students should not only be able to access the variety of Available Designs for meaning, they should also be able to engage critically with their forms, functions, and interrelations and discern how these influence their Redesigns of meaning. Finally, Transformed Practice allows students to imbue their Redesigned meanings with their own goals and values and transfer their literacy learning across contexts. These theoretical concepts help us consider how a teacher designed a literacy curriculum that encouraged interconnections among her students' languages, literacy practices, and identities across lifeworlds.

REVIEW OF THE LITERATURE

Recent research has explored the connections among adolescents' language and literacy practices across lifeworlds (Gutiérrez, 2008; Martínez, 2010; Orellana & Reynolds, 2008; Skerrett, 2012; Skerrett & Bomer, 2011; Weinstein, 2007). Embedded in this research is the salience of identity. Young people may see themselves and be positioned by others as highly literate in some lifeworlds, but may struggle to claim academic identities (Skerrett, 2012; Skerrett & Bomer, 2011). Often, these struggles stem from students' rejection of or discouragement from literacy work that is disconnected from their affinity groups, cultural and linguistic identities, and their goals as users of literacy (Skerrett & Bomer, 2011). Consequently, there is increasing theoretical and research activity into how students' language and literacy practices and identities, within and across lifeworlds, may productively inform each other.

For example, Martínez (2010) explored the potential of Spanish-English codeswitching, or Spanglish, as an academic resource. In an educational program for the children of Mexican migrant farm workers, Gutiérrez (2008) recognized that the youth traversed daily multiple contexts—their local neighborhoods, their transnational communities, and the educational program that was housed at a prestigious university—each bearing distinct spatial, ideological, and cultural dimensions. She theorized the educational program as a Third Space that merged and addressed the academic and social concerns of students and their communities and facilitated students' development of a range of language and literacy skills. And Weinstein (2007) stopped fighting her African American students' writing and performance of rap lyrics in her English classroom and turned it into official curriculum study. In this vein, our study inquired into what happened when a teacher purposefully designed a curriculum that encouraged interconnections among students' languages, literacy practices, and identities across multiple lifeworlds, to enhance literacy learning.

METHODS

The article draws from a study that explored the literate lives of adolescents and how knowledge about those lives might inform the teaching and learning of literacy (Skerrett & Bomer, 2011). Data were collected over a period of 1 year in a diverse high school and the surrounding community in a southwestern state. Participants included an English/reading teacher, 13 of the 16 students in one of her ninth grade reading classes, and, within the student group, seven focal students who agreed to undertake a deeper exploration of their literacy practices. Students came from Latina/o and African American middle- and working-class backgrounds. The teacher, Molly (all names are pseudonyms), was a White middle-class woman. Molly was selected for this study because she was knowledgeable about adolescent literacy research, having recently completed her master's degree in language and literacy studies. She and the researchers enjoyed a strong professional relationship and were mutually interested in exploring ways in which the teacher could apply knowledge of adolescent literacy in her classroom to support students' literacy development.

Case study methods (Dyson & Genishi, 2007) were used for this project, including semistructured in-depth interviews of the teacher and focal students (an average of three 1-hour long interviews per participant). Interviews with the teacher focused on the ways in which she was drawing on her growing knowledge and understanding of her students' literate lives in designing her curriculum. Students were asked to discuss their experiences with language and literacy within and across the contexts of their lives and how they were experiencing the curriculum in Molly's classroom. Additionally, we observed Molly's classroom one to two times each week and these visits were audio-taped and accompanied by detailed observational notes. Documents and artifacts related to curriculum, instruction, and assessment produced by the teacher and students were also collected. Data also include audio- and video-recordings as well as field notes of outside-school observations of focal students (an average of two per participant). They were observed in theater, dance, soccer, and online social networking activities and interviewed about these literacy practices. We also paid a home visit to each focal student. Furthermore, focal students, serving as ethnographic partners (Farrell, 1990), collected data on their literacy practices using cameras. They also shared literacy artifacts they produced, such as videos, scrapbooks, and artwork, and they described these literacy artifacts to us.

Analysis involved iterative reading of data and a process of progressive focusing (Glaser & Strauss, 2006) to reduce the data to portions related to the adolescents' discussions of their writing lives and identities and how these were taken up within the official curriculum in Molly's class. A process of open coding resulted in the identification of emerging themes (Dyson & Genishi, 2007). Recurrent themes constituted broad categories such as writing identity and Molly's class. More focused coding resulted in subcategories. For instance, under the category of writing practices, focused codes included journaling and "when I write." Writing analytic memos provided opportunities to think through the data, first to develop case bound propositions about how these students and their teacher recruited their writing identities and practices across lifeworlds for literacy learning, and then more general assertions about, and implications of, this phenomenon for language and literacy education.

Limitations

Although we learned much from the seven focal students we worked with, due to limitations in human resources and the reticence of some students in the class, we were not able to study in-depth the literate lives of all the students in Molly's class that year. The students who declined to be focal students are possibly the ones who have been most damaged by educational environments that have been unappreciative or dismissive of their language and literacy practices. We recognize that their voices urgently need to be heard. In our work with the focal students, we relied heavily on their reports of their literate lives and augmented that with a year of classroom observations of their reading class and some out-of-school observations. We believe our data set is strong but admit that it cannot fully capture these students' literate histories and the spectrum of their literacy experiences during that year of data collection. Admitting these limitations, we nonetheless see our study as an important contribution to the growing knowledge base about the literate lives of culturally and linguistically diverse youth and how knowledge about those lives can be productively recruited for literacy education.

FINDINGS

We offer the case of one focal student, Nina, whose story exemplifies how Molly's pedagogy enabled students to draw upon, and also strengthen, their writing identities and practices within and across lifeworlds. First, we provide a description of Nina's lifeworlds and language and literacy practices. We then explore the development of her writing identity and practices, from early significant memories of writing to her year spent in Molly's classroom. Thereafter, we detail Molly's pedagogy of multiliteracies, sharing from our observations of Molly's classroom. These observations helped us better understand how Molly encouraged cross-lifeworld interactions and connections that enabled students like Nina to strengthen their writing abilities and identities. In our final section of findings, we discuss two examples of Nina's writing for this class that portray how Molly's pedagogy encouraged Nina to draw upon her multiple languages, literacies, and experiences across lifeworlds for written composition.

Nina's Lifeworlds, Languages, and Literacy Practices

A 15-year-old Mexican American youth, Nina was born in a U.S. border town to a Mexican American father and Honduran mother. Although she now lived on the outskirts of the city in which our study took place, Nina and her family regularly drove to her hometown straddling the two nations, and across the border to Mexico, to spend time with her mother's family. With her parents now divorced, Nina lived with her mother and younger brother in the community surrounding Southwest High. Nina also had an older sister who had recently moved out of the home. This sister had a young son and Nina explained that "I take care of him a lot, and I don't mind cuz my sister works a lot." Family was very important to Nina, and these relationships were prominent in the literary texts she crafted. Nina claimed Spanish as her first language but by her ninth grade year, she lamented:

> I'm losing my Spanish….Spanish was my first language and I started learning
> English when I was in first grade, so almost my whole life now and I'm losing

my Spanish. Every once in a while I tell my mom, "Mom, how do you say this?' I hate it!"

For this bilingual youth, who made intentional efforts to hold on to her home language, schooling had, in her experience, often been linguistically subtractive (Valenzuela, 1999). She reported:

> I used to be in native Spanish class. You know native is like the highest. You have to write Spanish. You have to read Spanish…And I couldn't do it….And it was so hard for me. I went back to easy Spanish. And I was like, "this sucks! That class is too easy for me and the native, it's too hard for me."

Likewise, Nina was placed in an ESL English class. "It's English…for immigrants. … I don't even know why I'm in that class because I know perfect English as you can tell…" We shall show how Nina used writing in Molly's classroom to tell a counterstory (Matsuda, 1995) about the significant role of Spanish in and across her lifeworlds.

Although this article focuses on Nina's writing life, she was passionate about a number of literate activities. One context for textual practice for Nina was her spiritual life, a space that was hybrid because of its frequent overlap with the secular world of school and other lifeworlds. She spoke frequently about "trying to get closer to God," and described how she used literacy to pursue this relationship. For instance, Nina prayed before she read her Bible. "I pray before I read it…'tell me what you need to tell me.' I pray for like 5 minutes and then I go…to the Bible and whatever I land on bam! And then later on He'll talk to me." Throughout the year, she made references to being more or less active in church depending on whether or not she felt she was living on "God's path."

Nina was also passionate about dance. In another multimodal literacy practice, she and some girlfriends had created a hip hop dance group, and for part of the school year, they composed their own choreographies and practiced regularly after school. Nina eventually quit the dance group because her girlfriends were selecting songs whose lyrics she "didn't think God was happy with" and since "I wanted to move back with God, I stopped."

Nina's Development of Writing Identity and Practices

Nina was confident in her identity of writer. She attested, "I write a lot. Honestly, that's like my thing…I just have to write. I'll write anything, how I feel… like when I write how I feel it's just awesome." Nina's writing identity had been fostered over time, within and across several lifeworlds, by her own actions and those of her teachers and other significant others. In discussing her earliest memories of writing, Nina asserted that she had no early or current models of writers at home: "No one writes." Yet when probed, Nina volunteered information about her mother's Instant Messaging, a practice in which she also engaged. Nina also remembered that, while she was in the third grade, her uncle was incarcerated at a facility in her hometown, and she remembered her mother writing letters to him. "We would always write letters to my uncle. Like we were just so close to him." Reflecting on her early memories of writing in school, Nina recalled how, as early as the fourth grade, she had developed confidence that she was a writer, an identity that her literacy teacher affirmed.

In fourth grade I was like the top one out of everyone in my writing because we would have to write little essays…and I remember the teacher would say like, "Oh, Nina, she's the top one. She's the best at this." And she even put it up and everything. It made me feel like I'm a writer. It made me feel that I can really write then. I remember I was just so good at it. I was so proud! Like it wasn't even funny. I was like, "Man, I want to be writing now!"

During fifth grade, Nina had kept a diary, although she only used it to document daily events. "I used to have a diary. And I would always write about just how my day went and that's basically it." Now, Nina's personal purposes for writing were primarily to process emotion, "just for the heck of it when I would write how I feel." She explained how "If I'm down I would write so much… But if I'm in a good mood I wouldn't write." Instead of writing in a diary, she used sheets of paper to write at any point she felt an emotional need. She used to keep these papers that contained her private thoughts on her desk or elsewhere in her bedroom but had stopped doing so as "one time I kept it in my desk [and] the next thing I know, I left it there and my mom read it." Consequently, to ensure her privacy, she would now "write it anywhere [but then] get rid of it."

Nina contrasted her personal writing with formal writing for school that "has to have a specific thing in there." Nonetheless, she regularly transgressed these boundaries. Her writing for school was a form of transformed practice (New London Group, 1996) in which she used writing to contemplate personal issues related to family, religion, and romantic relationships. For example, Nina often wrote about her relationship with her dad. As early as elementary school, "I wrote about my dad a lot since I don't live with him and I don't see him or talk with him." Some of her teachers also supported the practice of writing across borders. In third grade, her teacher connected their class with children in other countries as pen pals. "I remember I had a pen pal in third grade and they were in fifth grade…they were like from another country…And we would write to each other and we would send pictures too. I thought it was pretty cool."

Nina could not identify any other memories of substantive formal writing until her ninth grade year in Molly's class. However, she had continued writing for personal purposes, and she pointed to this as evidence of her deep affinity for writing.

> I really do like writing because I used to just write. After fourth grade I used to just write for the heck of it. And then I get to Miss Molly's class and I'm like, "Wow! I actually like writing." I really started noticing that I like writing this year in Miss Molly's class.

As such, Nina credited Molly's pedagogy with strengthening her identity as a writer. We describe this pedagogy in the section below.

Molly's Pedagogy of Multiliteracies

Administrators placed students like Nina in Molly's class because they had failed, or were judged to be at risk of failing (e.g, as English language learners) the state reading test required for graduation. Molly's reading curriculum made available for students texts that reflected their lifeworlds and the languages and literacies used within and across these spaces. The classroom library offered graphic novels and cartoons reflective of the TV shows students watched and low-rider and sports magazines. Texts were written in English and Spanish and often contained African American English (AAE) and Spanglish. Transnational students like Nina often encountered tales about border crossing that resonated with them. From our field notes, "Vanesa is reading her journal to Nina. Nina is listening. She is reading something about border crossing, a woman thinking about getting work, she doesn't know what her real job is [will be]" [field notes, March 3, 2010.] These reading materials, and conversations surrounding them, legitimized all lifeworlds as official curriculum and so served as boundary objects (Bowker & Star, 1999), located at the borders of divergent activity systems and sociopolitical valuing systems, brokering the practices and discourses of different lifeworlds into and across each other.

Writing pedagogy. Writing was a significant component of Molly's curriculum. The texts students read served as models for their own writing and thus were taken up in extending the impact of converging lifeworlds. Moreover, students' reading materials were usually accompanied by sticky notes, journals, composition notebooks, sheets of paper for sketching, or some other composition surface. In keeping with Overt Instruction, in which students develop a metalanguage of Design and control over what and how they were learning (New London Group, 1996), Molly taught students to write in varied formats and for different purposes and audiences. Sticky notes contained noticings of themselves as readers and writers—how they felt about reading or writing on that particular day and why they thought that might be; places where they got engaged, disinterested, or confused in the text; the strategies they used to keep going; and evaluations of the successes of these efforts. Folders archived loose sheets of paper where students had scribbled or sketched informal thoughts or responded to formal writing prompts. Composition notebooks were a place to try out more extended writings on a variety of topics, self-selected and teacher-suggested.

Journals expressed personal connections students had made between the texts and their lives or strong reactions to the themes or events in their books. They were also a tool for processing emotional states that affected students' academic work. In alignment with situated practice (New London Group, 1996) that privileges students' lifeworlds as official curriculum, Molly challenged every student to write and asserted that their emotional states were acceptable topics for academic writing. In Nina's words, "Miss Molly always tells me when you're down it really helps to write." Nina also explained how in Molly's class, for at least 15 minutes "every morning we have to write what we did on the weekend or it doesn't even matter, like just whatever is on your mind."

One substantial writing event was the class magazine. This was an intensive process entailing weeks of writing and revision. In keeping with research on effective writing instruction and the situated practice of multiliteracies pedaogogy (Bomer, 2011; New London Group, 1996), Molly conferred individually with students to help them decide on a topic that was personally fulfilling as well as rich enough for an extended composition. Students also combed through their earlier writings for inspiration. They further brainstormed lists, attempted opening paragraphs on several possible topics, and dialogued with their peers to ascertain which topic was most emotionally satisfying and intellectually promising. For example, Nina and Allison (first author) brainstormed with another focal student, Lydia, who had changed her mind about finishing her first story but was having difficulty finding a new topic. She had been talking with Nina about how she had cut school the day before and hung out with her older brother, and she showed us a picture of the two of them, taken then, on her cell phone. Knowing her original story was about this brother, and the two of them shared a special relationship, "I say, 'do you want to write just about yesterday, taking the picture with him?'" She says, "but how do I start?" I say, "you can just write about what you all were doing and then taking the picture together." [field notes, December 1, 2009.] Michelle (second author) discovered in her home visit to Lydia that she transported this text into her home life as a treasured literacy artifact. It was one of only two examples of print literacy Michelle saw in her house.

After many mini-lessons on topics such as word choice, audience, dialogue, imagery, punctuation, and characterization, students engaged in multiple revisions of their text. Acknowledging "this is the hard part," Molly mimicked students' protests, "aah, I don't want to punctuate my story; aah, I don't want to put dialogue." She stressed their stories were "already fantastic. It's like taking a piece of jewelry and polishing it up" [field notes, May 5, 2010.] In drawing on students' literate lives, Molly accepted their linguistic diversity, and this receptivity was prominent in her lessons. While teaching students how to use dialogue,

> She asks Kandace for permission to use her story again. She starts reading Kandace's story. "Where's your momma at?" What did I just say? When a new person talks, new paragraph....Nina repeats, "where your momma at?" and giggles a bit, presumably to hear Molly speaking AAE without the full intonation of an AAE speaker. [field notes, December 1, 2009]

Because Molly invited and legitimized students' entire linguistic repertoires in the academic and social life of the classroom, students drew upon all their linguistic tools for composing academic texts. Lydia, after the brainstorming session described in part earlier,

> ...starts writing in the texting language...I wonder whether Molly would rather she use the standard language that she was using for her previous story....After class I ask Molly and she says it's fine, especially since she has nothing. She's writing, and for the first class magazine she has kids writing in there in all sorts of ways....it's just celebrate, celebrate, celebrate, look at your story, look how good your story is. [field notes, December 1, 2009]

In another lesson on revision we observed, Molly drew on students' literacies with their cell phones to teach the writerly skill of zooming in.

> She says to the class, "I want you to zoom in on a moment in your story. Some of you have cameras on your phone, you can zoom in...raindrops on the petals... writers do that." She puts up a story of a student in another class on the overhead. She says, "This is Yaris' [story]....see if you can find the moment in her story, "The day my grandpa died." Kandace: "Miss, she writes like she's texting." Molly reads from Yaris' story. There is a line about blue veins in Yaris' Grandpa's hands. Kandace: "I can picture that, his hands." Nina rubs her fingers together and looks over to Lydia. Lydia says, "I can smell the cigarettes." She and Nina laugh. [field notes, November 20, 2009]

Above, in alignment with situated practice (New London Group, 1996), Molly connected the writerly skill of "zooming in" to students' knowledge and uses of their cell phones, a tool with which they text and compose multimodal stories. She again used an example of student work to impress upon them that they are capable of mastering this academic skill. The model of student work she selected contained the unofficial language students used for texting, and this is noticed by Kandace. Through the overt instruction (New London Group) of this mini lesson, Kandace, Lydia, and Nina seem to get a strong sense of what it means to "zoom in."

After several weeks of mini-lessons and revisions like these, students completed their compositions. Molly compiled their pieces; students like Vanesa and Shawn, who were admired by their peers for their drawing abilities, designed the magazine cover; and the class held a party that Molly called a "campfire reading"—she placed a lamp in the center of the room, and she and students sat around it. There, each student and the teacher shared a story from his or her life. Students' personal investments in their compositions sustained them through developing mastery of these challenging academic processes. As Nina expressed, "I love it. I feel like I love writing when I'm in her class. When it's in another class, it just doesn't feel like I'm in Miss Molly's." We saw this entire process as an architecture for crossing borders between personal, civic, social, and spiritual concerns, interests, and literate abilities the students valued and engaged with within and across lifeworlds. Two examples of Nina's writing in Molly's class portray how students, immersed in this pedagogy, created hybrid texts that integrated lifeworlds and attendant language and literacy practices.

Nina's Writing in Molly's Class

In keeping with how she used writing as a tool for exploring her emotional states, Nina used writing in Molly's classroom for this kind of reflection. One day, Nina had had an argument with her boyfriend, and she wrote in her class journal to process her emotions around this incident. Although Molly read students' journals as part of her assessment system, students knew they could indicate which journal entries they did not want her to read and that she honored their requests. In this case, however, Nina wrote this entry during a class period when the academic task was for students to continue developing their stories for the first-semester class magazine. Nina had not yet begun this work that she understood to be an academic task, "an essay" for "a project grade." In circulating the room to check on students' progress, Molly arrived at Nina's desk, assumed that this piece of writing was Nina's "story," and read it. Nina recollected how:

> That wasn't even supposed to be my project but I do that a lot. I write when I'm
> sad and I express how I feel and like it's just so crazy. I get into it like really deep
> like that. And one time we had to do like an essay. It was a project grade and
> she thought that was my project, how I felt. And I was like, "Oh, my God, you
> weren't supposed to read that!"

As we shared from our fieldnotes above, Molly's goals for the first semester's class magazine were to encourage, celebrate, and eventually strengthen her students' already existing identities and abilities as writers. Seeing that Nina already had written a poignant and lengthy journal entry, Molly encouraged her to work with this text for her contribution to the class magazine. Accordingly, Nina reported how Molly responded to what she had written with enthusiasm and encouragement "[Miss Molly's] like, 'This is perfect! You could use this.'" Nina initially expressed surprise and hesitation at Molly's assurance that this text was suitable for undertaking what to her was an academic task. "I was like, 'Oh really?' She's like, 'Yeah.' And then I was…'Okay, I'll do it.'" Nina highlighted the hybrid personal-academic nature of this process and resultant text.

> We [had] to write our own stories and me and my boyfriend…we broke up…
> And I was really sad [and] we had to write about something. I mean anything we
> want but yet it has to have a specific thing in there. And I didn't even feel like
> writing. I even wrote on the paper, 'I can't even write right now because I'm so
> hurt. Like it sucks that I have to write but okay, I'm doing it for my project. And

I wrote how I felt…like there's this one part where I said, "I feel for him, it's just more than just feelings. It's like…way too much." I really like writing when I'm like am sad, I can write a lot. I can write like a five-page thing if I want.

Reflective of the situated practice of multiliteracies pedagogy (New London Group, 1996), Molly legitimized Nina's romantic lifeworld as an appropriate tool with which to conduct academic work. Portraying the transformed practice that the New London Group argued was the outcome of this pedagogy, Nina transferred her romantic lifeworld into the classroom and infused her own literacy goals into the academic context.

Nina's composition for the second-semester class magazine further demonstrated how she recruited from her lifeworlds and language and literacy repertoires for writing.

As tools, Nina's lifeworlds and language and literacy repertoires served a dual purpose—to signal her linguistic and social identities and a more academic purpose of composing a literary work. The topic of the text made evident the centrality of family in Nina's life, then and now—the narrative was about the life and death of the bedrock of her family, her great grandmother, who Nina interchangeably called grandma. Furthermore, the story took place in the border town in which Nina was born. Recruiting from her border-crossing experiences, the characters in Nina's story crossed spatial, ideological, and metaphysical boundaries over the many years her story spans. Further drawing in her identity, the importance of her relationship with God was also a key feature of this text. Nina employed linguistic tools to privilege this relationship: Her purposeful capitalization of the word GOD emphasized the importance of her great grandmother's, and subsequently her own, relationship with God. The references to music and dancing in church also suggested an early affinity for dance. Although at 15 years old, she experienced conflicts between her identities and literacy practices as a Christ follower and dancer, in an earlier time and sociocultural context, Nina comfortably integrated these identities and literate activities by dancing to music in church. Finally, and of great importance, Nina, whose schooling experiences had denied her opportunities to build upon her home language, reclaimed a significant role for Spanish in this text. The Latina/o characters in her story speak confidently and interchangeably in Spanish and English, and Nina fully controlled the language of the first-person narrator—herself—and the characters she created. The hybridity of identities, literacies, and languages in Nina's text reflected Molly's pedagogy that encouraged students to integrate lifeworlds, languages, and literacy practices.

DISCUSSION

With the window we provided into Nina's lifeworlds of writing, including that of Molly's classroom, we portrayed how a pedagogy of multiliteracies (New London Group, 1996) may be lived by a teacher and her students. We demonstrated how Molly invited and accepted her students' lifeworlds and attendant language and literacy practices, and, without disrespecting or co-opting them (Gustavson, 2007), created an authentic use for them within the official curriculum. Students developed and demonstrated the academic writing skills she sought to teach while composing stories that served meaningful purposes in their lives.

A pedagogy of multiliteracies can raise alarm in teachers who envision students tagging, tattooing, and rapping their way through the official curriculum (Skerrett, 2011). Molly's pedagogy was anchored in none of those things. Yet her instruction was decidedly relevant and transformative. Yes, students' cell phones, with their cinematic capabilities and texting language, were often discussed in class. But these conversations served Molly's curricular goals of teaching students to "zoom in" on poignant moments in their texts and create authentic dialogue for the characters in their stories. Yes, students showed off and admired each other's tattoos, tags on their notebooks, and rap beats in sometimes spontaneous and other times more deliberate responses to Molly's authentic questions about, and invitations of, their literacies. But she asked because she wanted them to consider how they were already skilled at writing and interpreting multimodal stories, which made students more amenable to her insistence that they already knew and did lots of things that could help them be better at school. With this situated practice, she hoped to strengthen students' identities and skills as writers. Nina's self-affirmation and strengthening of her writing identity and language and literacy practices after engaging with Molly's curriculum provided evidence of such transformed practice.

REFERENCES

ACT. (2006). *Aligning postsecondary expectations and high school practice: The gap defined: Policy implications of the ACT national curriculum survey results 2005-2006.* Iowa City, IA.

Barton, D., Hamilton, M., & Ivanic, R. (Eds.). (2000). *Situated literacies: Reading and writing in context.* London, England: Routledge.

Bomer, R. (2011). *Building adolescent literacy in today's English classrooms.* Portsmouth, NH: Heinemann.

Bowker, G. C., & Star, S. L. (1999). *Sorting things out: Classification and its consequences.* Cambridge, MA: MIT Press.

Dyson, A. H., & Genishi, C. (2007). *On the case. Approaches to language and literacy research.* New York, NY: Teachers College Press.

Farrell, E. (1990). *Hanging in and dropping out: Voices of at-risk high school students.* New York, NY: Teachers College Press.

Gee, J. P. (1990). *Social linguistics and literacies. Ideology in discourses.* London, England: Falmer Press.

Gee, J. P. (1994). Discourses. Reflections on M. A. K. Halliday's "Toward a language-based theory of learning." *Linguistics and Education, 6*(1), 33-40.

Glaser, B. G., & Strauss, A. L. (2006). *The discovery of grounded theory: Strategies for qualitative research.* Chicago, IL: Aldine Publishing Co.

Gustavson, L. (2007). *Youth learning on their own terms: Creative practices and classroom teaching.* New York, NY: Routledge.

Gutiérrez, K. D. (2008). Developing a sociocritical literacy in the third space. *Reading Research Quarterly, 43*(2), 148-164.

Kalantzis, M., Cope, B., & the Learning by Design Project Group (Eds.). (2005). *Learning by design.* Alton, VIC: Common Ground.

Martínez, R. A. (2010). Spanglish as literacy tool: Toward an understanding of the potential role of Spanish-English codeswitching in the development of academic literacy. *Research in the Teaching of English, 45*(2), 124-149.

Matsuda, M. (1995). Looking to the bottom: Critical legal studies and reparations. In K. Crenshaw, N. Gotanda, G. Peller, & K. Thomas (Eds.), *Critical race theory: The key writings that formed the movement* (pp. 63–79). New York, NY: The New Press.

National Center for Education Statistics. (2002). *National assessment of educational progress (NAEP). Reading results: Executive summary for grades 4 and 8.*

New London Group. (1996). A pedagogy of multiliteracies: Designing social futures. *Harvard Educational Review, 66,* 60-92.

Orellana, M. F., & Reynolds, J. F. (2008). Cultural modeling: Leveraging bilingual skills for school paraphrasing tasks. *Reading Research Quarterly, 43*(1), 48-65.

Scribner, S., & Cole, M. (1981). *The psychology of literacy.* Cambridge, MA: Harvard University Press.

Skerrett, A. (2010). Lolita, facebook, and the third space of literacy teacher education. *Educational Studies, 46*(1), 67-84.

Skerrett, A. (2011). "Wide open to rap, tagging, and real life": Preparing teachers for multiliteracies pedagogy. *Pedagogies: An International Journal, 6*(3), 185-199.

Skerrett, A. (2012). "We hatched in this class": Repositioning of identity in and beyond a reading classroom. *The High School Journal, 95*(3), 62-75.

Skerrett, A., & Bomer, R. (2011). Borderzones in adolescents' literacy practices: Connecting out-of-school literacies to the reading curriculum. *Urban Education, 46*(6), 1256-1279.

Valenzuela, A. (1999). *Subtractive schooling: US-Mexican youth and the politics of caring.* Albany, NY: State University of New York Press.

Weinstein, S. (2007). A love for the thing: The pleasures of rap as a literate practice. *Journal of Adolescent & Adult Literacy, 50*(4), 270–281.

APPENDIX A: NINA'S COMPOSITION, GUELA GALLINAS

I was the only one that called her "Guela Gallinas". The reason for it, is because at he r house she had a lot of roosters. Always running around the yard. My cousins and I would always chase them in circles where her garden was. We were in our 4-6, My younger cousin   was 4, I was 5, and my cousin   was 6 or 7. Since our roosters had long feathered tails my cousins would always try to grab them by their tails, and the chickens would always cackle and jump up a little.

She was really into GOD, and that would make me look up to her. That's the most important thing about her, she was in GODs hands. As I grew up I would go to church with my aunt, she's also named was named after her. Me, my sister, my mom, my aunt, and her kids would go to church together. I loved going because the music was beautiful everybody would dance and me and my cousins would hold hands and start dancing all together. My great grandma was the reason for me being in church up to today. Sometimes "Guela Gallinas" would read the bible to me when I was a little girl. I remember when she would tell me in spanish "Hay un senor que se llama Jesucristo que te quiere mucho y el es muy bueno". Man, that made me think maybe I can be happy as well with me being in GODs path.

Everything went well; years past by. Our family would visit my grandma in the Valley everytime we had a chance. Until one day we heard that my grandma was in the hospital. I'm not sure where I was when my mom had told me that "Guela Gallinas" was in the hospital. I think that I was in school. Well that weekend we went to the hospital. Our whole family was there. Me, my mom, and my sister walked fast through the white walls of the hospital going up to the 3rd floor, doctors walking all over the place back and forth.

My mom had asked the nurse "What room is   " the nurse responded and pointed at the room. We walked in there and just looked at her. My mom started crying, and me and my sister just started crying as well. Guela looked like if she was in pain with all those machine around her and including oxygen machine on her. She didn't look to comfortable. And she couldn't move a single muscle in her body. She couldn't talk, move, or even open her eyes. All we got from her was breathing in and out.

Next thing my grandpa walks in really quiet and is very speechless. I remember him talking to her telling her in Spanish "Ama' estoy aqui. Me escuchas? Levantate porfavor" He gave her a kiss on her forehead and he decided to step out the room. Me and my older sister walked up to her bed again and we were holding her hands. My sister had tears running down her cheeks as she sees my grandma's nails. She grins a little at my mom and tells her "Mira todavia tiene sus unas rositas pintadas cuando se las ise." She kisses her hand and she puts her hand back down by her side. When I was holding her hand, her hand was so warm like if she had a fever. It was a long night, we didn't go home till later.

She was already dead. We found out that it was a machine that kept her breathing. Well I would talk about the funeral but sadly I didn't get to go to my own grandmother's funeral. My mom had told me that I had to go to school. Mainly because it happened back where I was born in

Guela Maria was a loving person, she means so much to me. What I really loved about her was that she was always in GOD's path and now that she's up there with him. Man she lived a good life with our family. She loved us very much she never showed us bad examples. That's probably why I miss her so much, but not just me our whole family. Up to this day I feel like she's still here sometimes. Sometimes I can feel her watching over me and my family. She'll always be in my heart and memories.

Exploring Poetry Writing in a Methods Course: Changes in Preservice Teachers' Identities as Teachers of Writing

Belinda S. Zimmerman
Denise N. Morgan
Melanie K. Kidder-Brown
Katherine E. Batchelor
Kent State University

Being able to write well allows one to fully participate in a democratic society (Bomer, 2011). Writing allows people to express themselves to others, clarify and communicate inner thoughts and issues, and influence a wider populace. The classroom is the first place most people are introduced to writing for an audience beyond themselves. Central to the literacy process, teachers have a professional obligation to their students to help them become confident, capable writers (Applebee & Langer, 2009). As the National Council of Teachers of English (NCTE; 2004) asserts, teaching future teachers how to teach writing must be of vital concern to teacher educators and should be an important part of teacher education.

There is a paucity of research related to how preservice teachers (PSTs) are taught to teach writing. Researchers have found PSTs receive limited, if any, instruction about teaching writing in their preparation programs (Grisham & Wolsey, 2011). In a recent review spanning 20 years of the writing research literature in the United States, only 31 peer-reviewed studies were identified that focused on PSTs' preparation to teach writing and of those studies, only three focused exclusively on preparing early childhood educators to teach writing (Zimmerman, Morgan, Kidder-Brown, and Batchelor, 2011). Poetry is one such genre that PSTs should be prepared to teach young children to write as the genre is a mainstay of early childhood education (Parr & Campbell, 2006; Rasinski, Rupley, & Nichols, 2008). Yet studies investigating how preservice teachers come to teach poetry are scant (Dymoke & Hughes, 2009; Mathis, 2002; Parr & Campbell, 2006).

As teacher educators concerned with these issues, we wanted to study the teaching of writing, particularly poetry writing, within a writing methods course. We were especially interested in what past educational experiences shaped PSTs' identities and experiences as writers. To study these issues we draw from the concepts of *figured worlds* and *positional identities* (Holland, Lachicotte, Skinner, & Cain, 1998). We examined PSTs' situated learning experiences (Lave & Wenger, 1991) within a methods course devoted to the teaching of writing to better understand the opportunities PSTs had for ongoing, social, and collaborative interaction with the potential to alter their sense of themselves as writers and future teachers of writing. We posed the following overarching question for our study: How do poetry-centric writing experiences within a writing methods course shape PSTs' writing and identities as future teachers?

REVIEW OF LITERATURE

Unavoidably, a person's perspective is bounded by individual knowledge and experience. Teachers are no exception. How teachers approach their students, content, and pedagogy is shaped by previous educational experiences, circumstances, and contexts (Grossman, Valencia, Evans, Thompson, Martin, & Place, 2000; Mahurt, 1998). Prior experience provides a foundation for the assumptions and beliefs that underscore teachers' thinking, instructional choices, and the ways content is presented. It bounds the manner in which teachers envision possibilities. This bounded experience perpetuates itself, as teachers cannot learn or apply things in their classrooms in which they have never had the opportunity to partake.

Bounded understandings may result in educational inadequacies (Bourdieu, 1977). Bourdieu (1977) suggests teacher knowledge is limited by historical, social, and cultural forces. These socio-cultural influences shape the ways teachers present literacy instruction to their students, as teachers are guided by their own belief systems. This can become problematic since many PSTs have had negative or limited writing experiences in schools (Bomer, Bogard, Lawrence, & Steen, 2007; Mahurt, 1998; Norman & Spencer, 2005; Street, 2003). PSTs need to develop deep understandings about teaching writing, since "what teachers do makes a difference in how much students are capable of achieving as writers" (NCTE, 2004, p. 1). Due to the complexity of teaching writing, methods courses must cultivate PSTs' knowledge and abilities to address the difficulties of teaching writing. Therefore, university coursework must attend to these pedagogical issues (Moore-Hart & Carpenter, 2008; Street & Stang, 2008).

PSTs arrive at schools of education with their own writing histories and conceptualizations. They enter methods courses with individually preconceived notions about the nature of teaching and what content should be taught (Brookfield, 1995). In turn, PSTs' identities are based on their previous experiences and resulting belief systems. These beliefs are foundational to their understandings about how and what to teach. These understandings provide the foundation for the development of the figured world, an envisioned self within a realm of action that each PST inhabits (Holland, Lachicotte, Skinner, & Cain, 1998).

Figured Worlds and Positional Identities

Figured worlds originate in past experiences (Holland et al., 1998; Rubin, 2006; Urrieta, 2007). As Holland et al. (1998) explain, a figured world may be defined as "a socially and culturally constructed realm of interpretation in which particular characters and actors are recognized, significance is assigned to certain acts, and particular outcomes are valued over others" (p. 52). Holland et al. (1998) suggest an account of identity in practice in which individuals "are composites of many, often contradictory, self-understandings and identities" (p. 8). Theories of identity formation begin with the premise that identities are lived in and through activity and develop in social practice. Accordingly, individuals' figured worlds provide a context where identities are produced, socially constructed roles and culturally comprised activities are enacted, and individuals come together to cultivate new understandings (Urrieta, 2007). As a site of identity development and a space to acquire new learning, figured worlds are also "sites of possibility" (Urrieta, 2007, p. 109). These "as if" realms shift from the imagined to the real through work and activity with others (Holland et al., 1998, p. 55).

In application, these constructs help us to understand the ways PSTs experience their coursework interactions with other prospective teachers. When methods courses are structured so that dialogue and interaction are central to the pedagogical approach, PSTs become members of a shared classroom community. Although the university classroom lacks some of the hallmarks of true communities of practice, we argue that if structured to support new learning within "sites of possibility," the communities of practice framework can help explain how PSTs experience new forms of writing pedagogy.

Communities of Practice and Situated Learning

In communities of practice (CoPs), Lave and Wenger (1991) contend that learning is situated. That is, learning is authentically embedded within activity, context, and culture. As Wenger (1998) notes, "Engagement in social practice is the fundamental process by which we learn and so become who we are" (p. 1). This sustained pursuit of a shared enterprise brings individuals together for collective learning experiences. Individuals learn, grow, and change through sustained practice and situated activity within communities (Lave, 1996; Niesz, 2010; Wenger, 1998).

The CoP literature clearly positions learning in four "deeply interconnected and mutually defining components" (Wenger, 1998, p. 5): (a) learning as belonging (community), (b) learning as becoming (identity), (c) learning as doing (practice), and (d) learning as experience (meaning). In each case, learning is central to human activity. When individuals come together to form an emergent CoP, they must find ways to uncover shared understandings about the ideas and activities in which they engage. As such, meaning-making is a communal process where members simultaneously challenge old beliefs and construct new understandings. It is the belonging to the group and learning by doing that ultimately influences a new way of thinking, feeling, and questioning (Niesz, 2007).

Thus, figured worlds are historically based, socially situated, and evidenced by the ways members interact, the values to which they ascribe, and the ways they engage in learning. Similarly, CoPs have been proposed as a vehicle for establishing a social context where collaborative learning, innovative or novel approaches, and problem-solving flourish. Both theories focus on the ways individuals change or hone their identities in the face of new knowledge, practices, and attitudes. They can be considered mutually informing. From figured world theory, perspective is gained by looking backward to older thoughts and practices as new stimuli are encountered. New ideas, constructs, and strategies are developed and refined in CoPs. In turn, new identities can be created as older memories and postitionings are modified in the context of newer, more robust understandings and conceptual interpretations.

METHODS

Context of the Methods Course

Early childhood (Pre K-3) PSTs take four literacy courses before student teaching. Instead of diluting the teaching of writing across four courses, faculty and administration decided to devote one entire course to the teaching of writing. This writing class was designed to provide opportunities for PSTs to live the writing process, to engage in the practice of writing regularly, and ultimately enable them to mirror what they could do with their own students. We believed providing them with a unit of study approach (Ray, 2004) within a workshop experience (Graves, 1983; Atwell, 1998) could serve as the foundation for their future teaching.

Within the writing workshop, we focused on writing strategies (Graham & Perin, 2007) interweaving a "number of writing instructional activities in a workshop environment that stresses extended writing opportunities, writing for authentic audiences, personalized instruction and cycles of writing" (p. 4). PSTs were taught to make intentional decisions concerning voice, word choice, and written conventions. By merging the intensity of the writing workshop with a focus on strategies for planning, revising and editing their compositions, PSTs were able to experience as genuine a writing experience as possible in a coursework setting.

PSTs engaged in several units of study throughout the semester (Ray, 2004). Employing a unit of study format in teaching writing offered PSTs a predictable structure to follow as they engaged in their writing work. Within this format, several key understandings are considered to be true: (a) students benefit from writing texts that resemble writing found in the world beyond the classroom, (b) studying strong examples (i.e., mentor texts) of what students will eventually write will help them develop a vision for what they can do as writers, and (c) helping students learn to read like writers gives them a way to study writing in terms of structure and craft and provides them with strategies they can apply to any new writing situation. Texts read in the course were *About the Authors* (Ray, 2006) and *On Writing Well* (Zinsser, 2006).

Design

In this interpretative qualitative study, we gathered data over a 16-week semester as part of a larger study. Participants included all students (*N* = 35) from two cohorts and included 3 males and 32 females. One student was Latina and the remaining students Caucasian. All PSTs were 22-25 years of age, except one male nontraditional returning student. For the purpose of this paper, we examined data collected during the poetry unit of study, a five-week focused experience. From our experiences teaching this course collectively over 18 times, we found that this genre generates the most angst, but often yields the most surprising changes for PSTs as writers and future teachers of writing. We wanted to better understand the changes that occurred in PSTs' identities during this unit.

Data Collection

Data collected for this study included responses to open-ended questions, poems, and reflections. Prior to the start of the unit, PSTs wrote an initial essay that asked them to answer questions about their past experiences with poetry. In addition, PSTs responded to eight open-ended questions (e.g., Poetry is ..., What does it take to be a poet?).

At the end of the unit of study, PSTs wrote a final essay and responded to the same eight open-ended questions. In addition to the pre-post data, each PST wrote at least three poems during the study, contributing 145 poems for our analysis. PSTs wrote a reflection for each poem highlighting their intentional decisions and experiences writing and sharing their poems. In addition, the instructor kept observation and reflection notes as she conferred with PSTs about their writing.

Data Analysis

Data were analyzed inductively, coded using a constant comparative method (Strauss & Corbin, 1990) and occurred in multiple phases. During Phase One, the before- and after-course experiences of each PST were examined. To increase consistency in coding, one set of essays and poems was coded by the research team, and through a process of collegial challenge and consensus, a code-book and anchor profile was developed. This process was completed for each of the PSTs' open-ended question responses and poetry analysis. Codes included items such as: (a) prior experiences with writing, (b) prior experiences with poetry, (c) definitions of what writing and poetry entailed, and (d) specific course experiences credited with changed understandings and attitudes.

During Phase Two, we examined our data within and across individual PSTs. We explored individual PST data and then group data to examine common and unique experiences during this unit. Memos were written highlighting patterns for the research question. Charts and tables were created throughout the data analysis process to aid in our understanding of patterns across the data. We discussed the individual PST's experiences during this unit and also examined the group's experience. During Phase Three, we examined the findings in light of four constructs germane to learning within a CoP—belonging, becoming, doing, and experience.

We adopted the CoP framework to provide a conceptual learning theory perspective and to serve as a lens through which PSTs' growth could be examined. Within this framework, we were able to privilege "learning as social participation" (Wenger, 1998, p. 4) and call attention to how PSTs were able to become active participants in the classroom community and form identities in relation to content and pedagogical practice. We use the CoP as Wenger (1998) does as "a point of entry into a broader conceptual framework of which it is a constitutive element" (p. 5). In doing so, we were able to integrate the components of classroom pedagogy within a social theory of learning and underscore PSTs' growth.

Several limitations of this study should be mentioned. First, this study's findings focus on a five-week window of time involving PSTs writing and studying poetry and how to teach it. It does not portray their learning throughout the entire semester, but highlights their experiences within a specific genre; one, as instructors, we have noted PSTs view with apprehension. Second, this study focuses on PSTs' in-class learning. While PSTs identify the ways in which they hope to teach poetry to their future students, it does not examine exactly how PSTs will translate these ideas into classroom practice. Furthermore, we are aware of the limited community the university methods course setting provides. For example, if the setting was a CoP in its purest form, PSTs might have had opportunities to apprentice with a professor of poetry or even a published poet. Additionally, we acknowledge that the methods course is required and social desirability bias (i.e., PSTs' final essay responses may have been skewed to reflect the expectations of the instructors) may have been present (Fisher, 1993).

FINDINGS

PSTs' past writing experiences were focused on writing mechanics and formulaic writing. PSTs overwhelmingly reported that writing, no matter the genre, was a solo venture. Furthermore, they saw writing poetry as unattainable and beyond them. These experiences formed the basis of their figured worlds. Our course positioned PSTs as learners and as future teachers of poetry in a "new-to-them" model of writing instruction. The course emphasized principles such as peer collaboration, choice in topic selection, discussion, reflection, and a process orientation to assignments. As PSTs adopted these principles as a means of shaping themselves, engaging in learning, and negotiating an identity, they began to transform from novices to practitioners of teaching writing. We present our findings in light of learning as belonging, becoming, doing, and experiencing.

Community: Learning as Belonging

To belong to a community of practice requires more than passive membership or tangential affiliation to an agenda of work. Instead, belonging—as PSTs experienced in the methods course—requires that community members be actively engaged with the values, activities, and social relationships of the community (Lave & Wenger, 1991). Broadly, this means that PSTs shared common understandings of how to act and interact, and how to engage in joint enterprise and were invested in each other so that commonly held outcomes were achieved. As the community grew, values concerning professional and pedagogical practice were shared and reinforced. A common agenda of activities within the course set forth the intellectual work that belonging required and defined the ways PSTs socially interacted. As community was developed, belonging became personal, interpersonal, and interactive. Trust and respect bound the PSTs together and provided the foundation for risk-taking and meaningful learning.

The idea of learning as belonging refers to groups that "foster the commitment of time, energy, and perhaps something of ourselves" (Niesz, 2007, p. 606). We contend that PSTs were more than just attending class. As they learned and changed throughout the course, social and cognitive connections were strengthened. They began to rely on one another for ideas and feedback. There was an "in the know" communication developed across PSTs that represented new understandings of the writing process. PSTs lived learning as belonging when they shared their poems with others and looked to mentor texts to shape their own writing.

Vulnerability and sharing poetry. The PSTs experienced trust and respect for one another as they shared personal poetry writing. Usually, when students write for a course, the only other person who reads their writing is the instructor. Sharing writing was new to most of the PSTs. As Daniel stated, "What I am most proud of is … that I was able to be vulnerable and show more of my soul than I am accustomed to doing." Tonya was surprised by her willingness to share, "I usually *never* want to share my writing with others. I believe this poetry experience will impact my future writing and hopefully help me teach passionately about writing and writing poems." As PSTs shared their writing, many learned that their poetry affected others. Their fellow students' laughter and tears in response to the poems shared provided PSTs with feedback about the power of their writing. They expressed appreciation for peer feedback and developed increased confidence in writing, even though it was "nerve racking" or they felt "apprehensive" about sharing their emergent identities as teachers of writing.

Studying the work of other poets. In order to understand how to teach poetry, PSTs needed to understand how poetry was crafted. The PSTs began to look to other poets to study how they constructed their writing. Emma tried something her professor did in her own poem. She shared, "She [the instructor] repeated the same first line in all of her stanzas. I think it brings the reader back to the point of the poem and I wanted to try that in my own." As Emma and the course professor worked together on iterative drafts of several poems, a sense of belonging grew as writing became a joint enterprise and both collaborated to create a successful product.

PSTs' sense of belonging was enhanced as they closely studied a variety of mentor texts. These "close reads" introduced PSTs to the variety of structures and forms (Linaberger, 2004) that poetry can take. The CoP approach, with its emphasis on belonging and joint enterprise, stands in stark contrast to the example provided by Kerry who, like many students, remembered how her teachers required her to write about specific topics with a "certain type of poem." She reflected, "It was more of a puzzle than a creative process." Breanne echoed Kerry's experience, stating, "I dreaded writing poetry because there were so many rules and regulations we had to follow … it made me feel anxious."

Most PSTs entered the methods class belonging to a world where poetry followed tight structures of form and presentation. As they grew as writers and teachers of writing in the course, their figured worlds were altered. Through this process they gained new insights from the instructor and the mentor texts. By building a CoP where social and intellectual connections were fostered, PSTs had a chance to examine their prior figured worlds and shift orientations.

Identity: Learning as Becoming

Learning as becoming suggests that as CoPs evolve, members become connected in personal and professional ways. This is contrary to traditional notions of methods coursework where learning is considered an individual enterprise. When learning is regarded as resulting in only an individual good, students do not necessarily need to be connected in any meaningful way. However, when the methods course CoP was developed, learning was communal and students became part of a connected community to which they had a responsibility for contribution. In the case of early learning, as was present in the methods course, these contributions included the development of and engagement in new experiences, language of the discipline, and use of resources. As the individual contributions of community members grew, the ways members were able to interact, assist each other in understanding challenging content and activity, and construct new knowledge grew as well. The growth process actively engaged PSTs, contributing to the richness of the learning experience.

As the CoP grew, PSTs gained new experiences, language, and resources. As PSTs became more versed in the multiple forms poetry can take, they developed a joint vision of themselves as teachers of poetry. Reading and writing poetry in the course allowed PSTs to discover that others outside of their CoP may not share their same enthusiasm and appreciation for their newfound understandings. Erica witnessed this firsthand, "I first showed my boyfriend the poems, but due to the fact that he isn't really into poetry, he just said 'they're fine.' I wanted more, so I asked my classmates." This suggests that when students participate in a CoP, group members develop a shared awareness of professional language and pedagogical approaches.

When outsiders fail to interpret events as members of the community do, conversations do not unfold as expected. As PSTs confronted who they were becoming, they realized that their prior forms of interaction were less meaningful. In turn, they preferred more substantive professional dialogue. When PSTs experienced learning as becoming, they recognized both writing and teaching challenges and realized the instructional potential of poetry.

Challenges PSTs faced. Research acknowledges that PSTs gain confidence in their ability to write poetry by living the experience (Dymoke & Hughes, 2009; Parr & Campbell, 2006). PSTs have opportunities to become more active learners by writing poetry. Through immersion in the difficult process of writing poetry, PSTs were able to gain "professional awareness and pedagogical empathy" (Reid, 2009, p.198). The assignments enabled them to directly engage in experiences similar to other poetry writers such as the struggle to begin the poem, the search for the right word, the starts and stops along the way, and the negotiation of multiple ideas. Additionally, as PSTs worked through each poetry assignment, they faced frustration, challenge, and success much like their future students will experience.

Many PSTs noted that they felt challenged by "getting started," "choosing a meaningful topic," and "finding the right words" to express themselves clearly. Additionally, they struggled with conventions such as "punctuation usage," the overall "format" of the poem, and the use of "white space." More substantive considerations included confronting past experiences and understandings related to their inner trials and difficulties. By "rehashing" their own personal struggles and attempting to capture their feelings and memories, they experienced a shift in their understanding of poetry and teaching. Expressing themselves in poetry allowed them to see themselves as teachers of writing poetry, enabling them to empathize with their students' new learning. Thus, the course provided a supportive environment, the CoP, which allowed new professional identities to emerge.

Seeing the potential of poetry. When PSTs were immersed in poetry writing and supportive collaborations with "groups of people who share a concern or passion for something they do" (Wenger, 2006, p. 1), their vision for teaching poetry changed. For instance, PSTs in the course shifted from viewing poetry as a "workhorse" for teaching phonics skills to a meaningful, creative, and expressive experience that they can recreate in their own classrooms. When PSTs have positive experiences with poetry, it can make them "eager to invite their students into rich experiences with poetry, language, and expressions of life" (Mathis, 2002, p. 18). Immersion in poetry can help change a student's sense of self (Feder, 2000; Linaberger, 2004). Micala described her transformation from a reticent, even resistant student, to becoming a willing learner and eager teacher. She linked her methods course experiences to her future teaching by stating, "I connected [the writing of poetry] to my [future] students because if they enjoy what they are writing, they may want to write more. I want my students to write." Thus, Micala decided to change her views concerning writing "in order to become a better teacher."

These experiences allowed PSTs to build "poetitude," or "the value and belief in the power of poetry as a teaching and learning tool for all students" (Parr & Campbell, 2006, p. 36). In order for PSTs to passionately teach poetry, they must have positive experiences with poetry (Hughes & Dymoke, 2011; Mathis, 2002). PSTs reflected on specific course experiences that allowed their disposition toward and identity of themselves as teachers of poetry to evolve. By composing poems, sharing their poetry, and experiencing peer and instructor feedback, poetry became a teachable genre rather than one they preferred to avoid.

Practice: Learning as Doing

Undoubtedly, the tandem notions of learning as belonging and learning as becoming bound PSTs to the educational process in social and intellectual ways. However, belonging and becoming cannot provide the necessary foundation for a CoP to advance, nor do they guarantee that members will transfer the experiences beyond their current setting. For communities to advance and for PSTs to transfer their new learning, they must be actively engaged in practice. By doing new things and doing older things differently, PSTs made public their own nascent intellectual knowledge. The CoP provided PSTs a safe space where new ideas could be tested and performed and formative feedback could be provided. As new learning(s) became solidified, PSTs developed an increasingly clear sense of purpose and efficacy in their work. PSTs experienced learning as doing by creating their own poetry books comprised of at least three original poems.

Creating a poetry book. The PSTs credited the creation of a poetry book as a pivotal experience that helped shape their identities as teachers of poetry. The assignment required them to compose at least three nonrhyming free-verse poems to be shared with one another (although many PSTs wrote far more). Class time was provided for the PSTs to discuss, design, and develop their poetry book projects.

Sabrina recognized the importance community plays in a classroom, "This will be a great process for the students to work with one another, share their thoughts and ideas, as well as build close relationships with their classmates." Lena agreed, "I will teach my students to allow other classmates' work to inspire them and guide their own thinking." As Nikki stated, "I appreciate poetry more. Now that I've had [this] opportunity, I do see the value in it, and hope to give my students [similar] opportunities and experiences with poetry." Immersing PSTs in writing poetry enabled them to recognize the power in combining writing, sharing, reflecting, and making connections between life and curriculum.

Poetry does not have to rhyme. A transformative realization PSTs reported was their new understanding that poems do not have to rhyme. Tessa remembered, "In elementary school, I was taught that poems needed to rhyme. By doing this project, it has helped me to realize that poems don't have to rhyme and they can be about anything the poet wants." The assignment to write at least three nonrhyming poems was met by disbelief and resistance by many. Halle captured this sentiment well by throwing her hands up and exclaiming, "I can't believe I have to write poems, especially nonrhyming ones. This seems like an impossible assignment. I'm just not good at this!"

As PSTs "did poetry" they were exposed to a variety of new-to-them ideas. As part of the process of writing as doing, they developed an increased awareness of the diverse forms poetry can take. Even more impressive PSTs learned they could inhabit these worlds themselves.

Meaning: Learning as Experience

An intended purpose of teacher education coursework is to provide PSTs new knowledge and skills that can be employed when they enter the profession. Methods coursework was designed to provide experiences for PSTs that required them to reflectively consider their long-standing assumptions of teaching and learning and to acquire new orientations and understandings. When a CoP supports PSTs through learning experiences designed to promote reflection and new learning, those ideas became personal and meaningful. When meaning-making is at the core of learning, PSTs were better able to take away messages and practices that could sustain them in their future work. Through their personal experiences with poetry, PSTs found themselves embracing poetry, recognizing how healing and emotionally powerful poetry can be, and envisioning transferring these new understandings to their future students.

Embracing poetry. Rather than avoiding or fearing poetry, PSTs came to believe that poetry is an exciting, meaningful form of self-expression. Nadine reflected on her experiences:

Today I feel writing poetry is a process and is magic...sometimes poetry just comes to you, other times it takes work, just like any other piece of writing... writing poetry isn't something to be afraid of, it should be embraced.

At the beginning of the course Marcus suggested, "Poetry is something that I do not think should take a whole lot of time because I feel the best poetry is inspired by a moment and the ideas should be as fresh as possible." In the end, Marcus spent hours writing his poems and showed the instructor and other PSTs multiple drafts before he was satisfied with the completed product. He was proud of his final pieces indicating that he had gained an understanding that writing quality poems is a longer process than originally anticipated.

Like many undergraduates, PSTs often believed they could start and finish a writing assignment in one night, typically the night before it was due and still receive a "good grade." This meant their writing was "fine." The course challenged this thinking. Course experiences created a space for them to draft, revise, and rewrite many times before submitting completed work. When PSTs shared their poems with others and realized that it was difficult to find the exact word or phrase to convey the appropriate feeling, the importance of multiple drafts was reinforced. The recognition that writing poetry is challenging and takes multiple attempts was unexpected. PSTs identified this as an important idea for their future teaching.

Poetry is healing and powerful. Poetry writing can be an empowering, influential, and liberating form of self-expression. PSTs enjoyed discovering how they could express ideas, solve problems, and share experiences. In their role as poet, PSTs were able to rethink, relive, and reframe past experiences and ideas in ways that reconciled their feelings and understandings of important, even traumatic, events in their lives. Corey described poetry writing as a "therapeutic tool" to assist her in navigating personal difficulties. Figure 1 provides an excerpt from one of Corey's poems demonstrating her utilization of poetry as a restorative device.

PSTs' experiences of poetry and poetry writing allowed them to understand this genre in new and often startling ways. By engaging in the practice of writing poems that required them to attend to the process and the content of their life experiences, PSTs shifted their understandings of what poetry can be and what it offers them as future teachers. Because learning was positioned as dynamic rather than static, PSTs became active and interactive learners as they engaged in course activities and began to envision using these activities in their forthcoming student teaching placements and beyond.

Developing instructional identities for teaching poetry in the classroom. PSTs initially viewed poetry as an entree into teaching early literacy skills in context. After the course, all PSTs said they would teach poetry as a genre study rather than only as a means to develop early reading proficiencies. Shannon stated, "I will encourage [students] to explore and write in all forms of

Figure 1. Excerpt from Corey's Poem "Free of You"

I will not be your companion in this darkness.

I refuse to be your wintertime, your sad movie line, your reason to cry.

You have tried over and over to break me.

But I am not glass; not fragile nor weak.

I will NOT shatter and I do NOT need you to pick up my pieces.

poetry. Expressing themselves individually through poetry is something that I want to establish in my classroom and encourage my students to embrace." Marcus planned to:

> … expose my students to different forms of poetry. I want them to see that poems do not have to rhyme and be silly, but that they can send a powerful message. I want them to see as many styles at an early age and allow them to develop a strong liking toward poetry.

In this expanded view of teaching poetry, PSTs envisioned: (a) allowing their future students choice of topics, (b) providing ample time to write poetry, (c) offering encouragement as students wrote, and (d) building students' confidence to write poetry. Furthermore, they intended to communicate to their future students that there is not a right or wrong way to write poetry and no specific format is needed to write meaningful poems. Instead, their students would write about self-selected topics that reflect their lives, interests, and passions. Clearly, the PSTs were picturing themselves in their future teacher roles, informed by their identity of themselves as writing teachers. CoPs are best experienced when shared norms and values are present. At the conclusion of the poetry unit of study, PSTs discovered poetry to be a distinct and important genre in and of itself. This signified a change about teaching poetry and its purposes in their figured worlds. This shift in understanding was a shared value emerging out of their work in the CoP.

DISCUSSION

The research base examining how to teach PSTs to teach writing is limited (Morgan, Zimmerman, Kidder-Brown, & Dunn, 2011). This may be, in part, because few universities offer specific methods classes in the teaching of writing. Yet, teaching writing is complicated and nuanced. Many teachers enter classrooms without a strong pedagogical foundation for the teaching of writing and in particular, writing poetry.

This study suggests that carefully crafted poetry experiences in methods courses can foster greater understanding of poetry writing and teaching poetry writing. The course offered opportunities for PSTs to confront their prior figured worlds and invited them to reflect on and modify their identity as teachers of writing. PSTs acquired new understandings; new methods of instruction; and changed attitudes toward poetry; and found poetry to be an inspiring, significant, and cathartic form of self-expression, one worth teaching to their future students.

Additional key findings suggest that PSTs' level of familiarity and expertise with poetry matters; meaningful and intentional teaching within methods coursework can reposition prior negative or limited experiences. Our experience suggests that methods courses can provide a venue in which PSTs can assimilate the ideas, practices, and learning outcomes they will be required to provide for their future students.

The study of poetry writing provided PSTs with a powerful context for learning the genre and how to teach it. This study highlights the importance of immersion in learning opportunities, such as those found within CoPs, that offer PSTs new ways of seeing content and themselves in relation to content. The poems PSTs wrote were critical in mediating new understandings as well as subsequent shifts in their figured worlds. The CoP provided opportunities for PSTs to see possibilities for new identities as writers and future teachers of writing.

As members of an emergent CoP, PSTs were able to reframe their prior orientations, the figured worlds within which they entered the course concerning teaching writing. PSTs' framing of their sense of self as teacher of writing expanded to include their individual voices. In turn, PSTs' sense of agency increased as they grappled with instructional problems and practices as their future students might and considered their learning as future teachers of writing. By creating collaborative learning environments, teacher educators can prioritize instruction that deepens the process of participation, builds on PSTs' interests and choices, allows them to reframe prior dispositions, enables their reformed identities to emerge, and ultimately brokers a different dynamic for writing instruction.

REFERENCES

Applebee, A. N., & Langer, J. A. (2009). *What is happening in the teaching of writing? English Journal, 98*(5), 18-28.

Atwell, N. (1998). *In the middle: New understandings about writing, reading, and learning.* Portsmouth, NH: Boynton/Cook.

Bomer, R. (2011). *Building adolescent literacy in today's English classroom.* Portsmouth, NH: Heinemann.

Bomer, R., Bogard, T., Lawrence, B., & Steen, S. (2007). *The writing life-histories of pre-service teachers.* NRC Conference, Austin, TX.

Bourdieu, P. (1977). *Outline of a theory of practice.* Cambridge, MA: Cambridge University Press.

Brookfield, S.D. (1995). *Becoming a critically reflective teacher.* San Francisco, CA: Jossey-Bass.

Dymoke, S., & Hughes, J. (2009). Using a poetry wiki: How can the medium support pre-service teachers of English in their professional learning about writing poetry and teaching poetry writing in a digital age? *English Teaching: Practice and Critique, 8*(3), 91-106.

Feder, L. G. (2000). Using poetry in adult literacy classes. *Journal of Adolescent & Adult Literacy, 43*(8), 746.

Fisher, R. J. (1993). Social desirability bias and the validity of indirect questioning. *Journal of Consumer Research, 20*(2), 303-315.

Graham, S., & Perin, D. (2007). *Writing next: Effective strategies to improve writing of adolescents in middle and high schools—A report to the Carnegie Corporation of New York.* Washington, DC: Alliance for Excellence in Education.

Graves, D. (1983). *Writing: Teachers and children at work.* Exeter, NH: Heinemann.

Grisham, D. L., & Wolsey, T. D. (2011). Writing instruction for teacher candidates: Strengthening a weak curricular area. *Literacy Research and Instruction, 50*, 348-364. doi: 10.1080/19388071.2010.532581

Grossman, P., Valencia, S., Evans, K., Thompson, C., Martin, S., & Place, N. (2000). Transitions into teaching: Learning to teach writing in teacher education and beyond. *Journal of Literacy Research, 32*(4), 631-662.

Holland, D., Lachicotte, W. Jr., Skinner, D., & Cain, C. (1998). *Identity and agency in cultural worlds.* Cambridge, MA: Harvard University Press.

Hughes, J., & Dymoke, S. (2011). "Wiki-Ed poetry": Transforming preservice teachers' preconceptions about poetry and poetry teaching. *Journal of Adolescent & Adult Literacy, 55*(1), 46-56.

Lave, J. (1996). Teaching, as learning, in practice. *Mind, Culture, and Activity, 3*(3), 149-164.

Lave, J., & Wenger, E. (1991). *Situated learning: Legitimate peripheral participation.* Cambridge, MA: Cambridge University Press.

Linaberger, M. (2004). Poetry top 10: A foolproof formula for teaching poetry. *Reading Teacher, 58*(4), 366-372.

Mahurt, S. F. (1998). Writing instruction: University learning to first-year teaching. In T. Shanahan, F. V. Rodriguez-Brown, C. Worthman, J. C. Burnison, & A. Cheung (Eds.), *47th yearbook of the National Reading Conference* (pp. 542-554). Chicago, IL: National Reading Conference.

Mathis, J. B. (2002). Poetry and preservice teachers: Perceptions and possibilities. *The Dragon Lode, 20*(2), 12-19.

Morgan, D. N., & Pytash, K. E. (2011, December). A research synthesis of preservice teachers and writing. Paper presented at the 61st Annual Conference of the Literacy Research Association, Jacksonville, FL.

Morgan, D. N., Zimmerman, B. S., Kidder-Brown, M., & Dunn, K. J. (2011). From writing methods to student teaching: Vision development and the implementation of conceptual and practical tools by preservice teachers. In P. Dunston, L. B. Gambrell, S. K. Fullerton, V. R. Gillis, K. Headly, P. M. Stecker (Eds.), 60th Literacy Research Association Yearbook (pp. 100-112). Oak Creek, WI: Literacy Research Association.

Moore-Hart, M. A., & Carpenter, R. (2008, December). *Improving preservice teachers' attitudes toward writing: An avenue to enhanced instructional practices.* Paper presented at the presented at the National Reading Conference, Orlando, FL.

National Council of Teachers of English. (2004). *NCTE beliefs about the teaching of writing.* Retrieved from www.ncte.org/positions/statements/writingbeliefs

Niesz, T. (2007). Why teacher networks (can) work. *Phi Delta Kappan, 88*(8), 605-610.

Niesz, T. (2010). Chasms and bridges: Generativity in the space between educators' communities of practice. *Teaching and Teacher Education, 26,* 37-44.

Norman, K. A., & Spencer, B. H. (2005). Our lives as writers: Examining preservice teachers' experiences and beliefs about the nature of writing and writing instruction. *Teacher Education Quarterly, 32*(1), 25-40.

Parr, M., & Campbell, T. (2006). Poets in practice. *The Reading Teacher, 60*(1), 36-46.

Rasinski, T., Rupley, W. H., & Nichols, W. D. (2008). Two essential ingredients: Phonics and fluency getting to know each other. *The Reading Teacher, 62*(3), 257-260.

Ray, K. W. (2004). *About the authors: Writing workshop with our youngest writers.* Portsmouth, NH: Heinemann.

Ray, K. W. (2006). *Study driven: A framework for planning units of study in the writing workshop.* Portsmouth, NH: Heinemann.

Reid, E. S. (2009). Teaching writing teachers writing: Difficulty, exploration, and critical reflection. *College Composition and Communication, 61*(2), 197-221. Retrieved from http://www.ncte.org/library/NCTEFiles/Resources/Journals/CCC/0612-dec09/CCC0612Teaching.pdf

Rubin, B. C. (2006). Learner identity amid figured worlds: Constructing (in)competence at an urban high school. *The Urban Review, 39*(2), 217-249. doi: 10.1007/s11256-007-0044-z

Strauss, A., & Corbin, J. (1990). *Basics of qualitative research: Grounded theory procedures and techniques.* Newbury Park, CA: Sage Publications, Inc.

Street, C. (2003). Pre-service teachers' attitudes about writing and learning to teach writing: Implications for teacher educators. *Teacher Education Quarterly, 30*(3), 33-50.

Street, C., & Stang, K. (2008). Improving the teaching of writing across the curriculum: A model for teaching in-service secondary teachers to write. *Action in Teacher Education, 30*(1), 37-49.

Urietta, Jr., L. (2007). Figured worlds and education: An introduction to the special issue. *The Urban Review, 39*(2), 107-116.

Wenger, E. (1998). *Communities of practice: Learning, meaning, and identity.* Cambridge, MA: Cambridge University Press.

Wenger, E. (2006). *Communities of practice. A brief introduction.* Retrieved from http://www.ewenger.com/theory/

Zinsser, W. (2006). *On writing well: The classic guide to writing nonfiction.* New York, NY: Harper Collins.

Elfrieda Hiebert
President and CEO
Text Project, Inc.

Section II: Literacy Educators as Learners and Leaders

For adult learners—the focus of this section—literacy can be a means for knowing, seeing, and feeling in new ways. Literacy for adults can increase in depth as life's experiences are brought to interactions with texts. But breaking from business as usual is no stroll along a garden path. Whether one is challenging one's own literacies or challenging others to grow their literacies, the path is fraught with tensions and risks. At the same time, opportunities for learning are rich when we choose this path for teaching and learning.

The perspectives on adults' literacy learning of the contributors to this section are especially germane in the present policy context with its emphasis on college and career readiness. As Appatova and Hiebert (2012) have argued, the construct of college and career readiness—at least in the Common Core State Standards—represents a static view of literacy across the lifespan. Being able to read a text with a particular Lexile may be sufficient to pass a college board exam or a qualifying test for licensure in a trade. Such accomplishments, however, are no guarantee that literacy demands will remain at that level for decades to come.

The perspective that literacy across the lifespan is a dynamic process that adapts to personal, technological, cultural, and political shifts is not a new one (see, e.g., Chall, 1983). But it is a perspective that urgently needs elaboration in light of rapid societal changes and the expectations of policy-makers. The contributors to this section provide precisely such a needed perspective. Three themes in these papers illustrate their contributions to views of literacy across the lifespan.

- *A dynamic view of literacy and literacy learning is not only theoretically sound—it is of practical necessity.*

The static view of literacy that now typifies the college and career readiness view can have disastrous effects—not just in lost human potential but in real life-and-death situations. In a ground-breaking study, Waibel, Rice, Kelley, and Anders examine the nature of literacy in the mining industry, where misunderstood or disregarded texts can engender accidents and loss of life. Waibel et al. direct literacy educators' attention to new domains that could benefit from our knowledge and focus. In a similar vein, Draper raises cautions about simplistic interpretations of disciplinary literacies that are implicit within the Common Core State Standards. Draper underscores the necessity of understanding disciplinary literacies if practices are to be created that support the proficiencies individuals need in the 21st century and beyond.

- *Literacy learning has an emotional component that teachers/facilitators recognize and, indeed, attend to directly in their teaching.*

Individuals' beliefs and emotions about literacy are a critical component of the social constructive perspective, as is poignantly illustrated by Albers, Holbrook, and Harste in their autoethnographical study. There are new epiphanies for learners when this history is recognized and, indeed, cultivated within a social context.

Hathaway's case study of a literacy coach shows that our beliefs and emotions in our capacity as teachers and teachers of teachers influence our efficacy. The case study coach's need to maintain relations meant that she often avoided conversations where teachers' beliefs were challenged. As a result, deep learning and change often did not occur.

In their study of a video study group, Shanahan and Tochelli raise a similar point about the vulnerability and fears of teachers as they share videos of their instruction. The emotions that learners bring to the task require attention, if they are to develop new proficiencies.

- *A social constructivist perspective of literacy offers much more to the teacher of literacy than simply supporting proficient literacies in their students.*

Wetzel, Martínez, Zoch, Chamberlain, and Laudenheimer illustrate this point well in their study of preservice teachers tutoring low-income parents who are English learners. The tutees' literacy increased but, additionally, the preservice teachers grew in their knowledge of culture, community, and literacy instruction.

The contributors to this section offer useful perspectives and possibilities for practice, theory building, and research. In the spirit of the work, I offer ways in which these papers have fostered my thinking as a literacy educator. In so doing, I hope to illustrate ways in which findings of these studies can be applied and extended to support lifelong literacy learning.

Waibel et al.'s study of literacies and literacy instruction in the mining industry is one that I have shared with a family member who works in healthcare. He has described a crisis in "health literacy" where, for example, the elderly can misinterpret the cryptic and often inscrutable text on prescription bottles (with often disastrous results). Hopefully, LRA soon will be the context for sharing new work in new industries such as health.

Reading the Albers's study left me with an insatiable urge to return to an art project that has lain dormant for the past year while I have concentrated on implications of the Common Core State Standards. For the first time ever, I am reflecting on how my work as a literacy educator is linked to my involvement in art and music. The active learning that Wetzel et al. describe among their preservice teachers has led me to think of ways of learning more about teachers' needs and concerns before I interact with them in professional development venues. As a result, my most recent conference proposal included ways of interacting with participants before (using social media), not just during and after the session.

Becoming Responsive Literacy Teachers in an Adult Literacy Tutoring Practicum

Melissa Mosley Wetzel
Ramón Antonio Martínez
Melody Zoch
Katharine Chamberlain
Kelly Laudenheimer
The University of Texas at Austin

In 2007, Leah, a participant in a study we conducted of our own teacher education program, told us that she was not prepared to connect with communities and families when she left our program to begin a career in teaching. Leah explained:

> I didn't fully understand the community aspect of it [teaching] as deeply as I do now, or just like the family connection that you make during a parent conference. It is so hard, but now it is like, "how did I not get this?" because it is so core to the teaching experience, so core to the child.

Through our research, we identified that although Leah's program included multiple practicum experiences focused on student-centered, culturally responsive literacy pedagogy, these experiences did not necessarily prepare teachers to draw on students' families or communities as resources when they began teaching. In response to comments such as these, which were pervasive in the review that we conducted of our program, we created an innovative practicum called *El Puente* to connect preservice elementary school teachers with adult English learners through an English as a Second Language (ESL) tutoring program. Our purpose for creating this practicum was for teachers like Leah to learn to effectively draw on community and family resources as literacy teachers in multilingual and multicultural settings. Building on perspectives from culturally responsive teaching (e.g. Villegas & Lucas, 2002) and generative teaching (Freire, 1995), preservice teachers were guided in literacy and language teaching across linguistic and cultural borders, as well as provided with practical experience forming relationships linked to teaching and learning.

REVIEW OF LITERATURE

Practicum Settings

Our review of the literature on practicum experiences for preservice elementary school teachers (1990-2010) revealed variation in the settings in which they are typically engaged (Mosley, Cary, & Zoch, 2010). Experiences included visiting students' homes (e.g., Bollin, 2007; Rymes, 2002), tutoring students after school (e.g., Matusov & Smith, 2007), and working in a community on a multicultural project related to a historic part of town (Boyle-Baise, 2005). In each study, preservice teachers became aware of the work and preparation necessary to be a successful teacher of students whose backgrounds differ from their own.

While most practicum experiences involve working with children, some research also documents preservice teachers working with adults or families in preparation for their career as elementary educators (e.g., Burant & Kirby, 2002; Gallego, 2001). One example is Burant and Kirby's (2002) study of what preservice teachers learned in a practicum experience that included community-based inquiries around issues like bilingual education, interacting with parents informally within a school setting, taking care of young children during school events, and participating in school-community events like a Turkey Trot running race. Preservice teachers, through conversations with families and communities, were able to better discuss issues in class and developed clear commitments to political activism and inquiry in their work as teachers. The experience allowed them to begin "to see different futures for themselves as beginning teachers" (p. 567). In other studies, researchers found that preservice teachers gained confidence by working with families as well as an understanding of the importance of parent-teacher relationships. The authors noted that although these practicum experiences are invaluable for people who are learning to teach, there are constraints on the impact of the programs. Burant and Kirby (2002) found evidence that some students maintained misconceptions of families and communities or only participated peripherally in the experience. They concluded that for preservice teachers with inclinations towards teaching in socially just ways, the incorporation of community-based field experiences prompted seeing students' community as a resource.

There are only a few studies of projects that provide preservice teachers structured opportunities to work directly with Latino families. These studies showed that participants developed confidence, found commonalities with families, and that both parents and teachers came to appreciate each other's contributions and gain a better understanding of how best to support the child's literacy development (Riojas-Corteza & Bustos-Flores, 2009). Preservice teachers felt empowered through the progress they saw in tutoring and mentoring settings, and the proximity to students contributed to an understanding that interaction with others was essential in learning how to teach (Abrego, Rubin, & Sutterby, 2006; Hale, 2008; Reyes, 2009; Rymes, 2002). They also gained an awareness of what English language learners contend with in today's complex schools (Burant & Kirby, 2002; Cooper, 2007; Gallego, 2001; Reyes, 2009) and discovered that drawing on students' home language was invaluable in teaching (Rymes, 2002).

Work in this area highlights the significance of practicum experiences for preservice teachers: Teachers learn about the work necessary to prepare to teach in culturally and linguistically diverse settings; understand disconnects between the structure of schools (e.g., high-stakes testing practices) and the needs of linguistically diverse student populations; and build confidence as teachers in diverse contexts. However, we are not sure how preservice teachers develop literacy and language teaching practices in these settings. Our research bridges earlier work with a close focus on the ways in which teachers plan, implement, and reflect on instruction while also connecting with communities and families.

Reflective Teaching

Along with our understandings of how practicum experiences support developing teachers' practice, we also drew on literature on reflective teaching in teacher education programs as a support for preservice teachers' developing teaching practices (Howard, 2003; Mosley, Hoffman, Roach, & Russell, 2010; Pedro, 2005; Tomlinson, 1999; Ward & McCotter, 2004). Dewey (1933) defined reflection as a persistent act in which the individual considers his or her assumptions and beliefs, bases their decisions on evidence, and looks at everything with a critical eye. According to Schön (1983), when teachers are confronted with an unfamiliar situation, they must think critically, experiment with the approach in that particular moment, and reflect later on how their approach worked within the lesson. Pedro (2005) found in her study of five preservice teachers that they understood the concept of reflection, and that the use of reflective writing activities seemed to advance their critical reflection skills (c.f. Ottesen, 2007; Pultorak & Barnes, 2009).

With respect to becoming reflective practitioners, Fairbanks et al. (2010) highlight the importance of opportunities for preservice teachers to gain greater self-consciousness about their vision of themselves. Visions are closely related to beliefs about teaching, students, and one's role as a teacher and the moral, political, and social reasons that a person is drawn to teach. To construct visions, those beliefs must be uncovered and interrogated (Friedman & Shoen, 2009). Duffy's (1998) argument is this: Teachers are always trying to enact their visions for practice within contexts that do not necessarily reflect or support those visions. Strong visions lead to teachers being able to sustain such practices, even in the face of challenges.

THEORETICAL FRAMEWORKS

Theories of culturally responsive pedagogy (e.g., Ladson-Billings, 1994; Villegas & Lucas, 2002) informed our creation of spaces for preservice teachers to think about teaching and learning. We worked from the assumption that adults learn to read and write when they are able to draw on print literacy for meaningful purposes and when teachers draw on communities' cultural resources to support learners (Freire, 1983, 1995; Rogers & Kramer, 2007).

In the Community Literacy course that houses this practicum, one of the key assigned texts is *The Importance of the Act of Reading* (Freire, 1983). This text framed our use of generative themes in the adult literacy teaching context. Generative themes come from Freire's work with adults in times of revolution—they are codifications of complex ideas that generate dialogue about critical social issues. Because of the structure of English orthography, we could not use Freire's work in the exact ways it has been used in Spanish and Portuguese-speaking countries. Rather than using just a word as a codification of a theme, we asked adults to compose short texts based on themes that were important to them, and those texts became the basis of vocabulary, phonology, and grammar work within the tutoring sessions.

Using many resources, our preservice teachers worked with parents who were learning English to encourage literacy development using students' own words and ideas as texts (Cramer, 2004). We encouraged teachers to draw from what they were learning about literacy teaching with all learners (e.g., ways to promote fluency and build vocabulary during reading instruction), but we also had to prepare our preservice teachers with a sociocritical perspective to work with adults who come from different racial, ethnic, linguistic, and socioeconomic backgrounds than they do (Villegas & Lucas, 2002). Most preservice teachers have not worked with adults who speak Spanish, are new to the U.S., or who live in working-class communities, regardless of their race or ethnicity (Zeichner, 2005). Therefore, we talked about societal discourses about the early literacy experiences of children who live in Spanish-dominant communities that often lead to teachers' misconceptions about families' involvement or the literacies of children and families (Compton-Lilly, 2007; Rogers, 2002). For example, we often asked questions during debriefing sessions such as, "In what ways do parents support their children's literacy development, and in which contexts are those ways recognized or overlooked?"

In the next sections, we briefly describe the context of our work and our research methods. We then describe what we learned about how this practicum supported preservice teachers' emergent ideas about teaching students in ways that are responsive to communities.

RESEARCH METHODS

Context

Our classroom was located in a portable building behind Hernandez Elementary School in a large southwestern city in Texas. Nestled within small ranch-style homes, and in close proximity to an interstate highway, the school serves a predominantly Latino community. Families generally find work in the service industry, factory work, and construction.

Reading specialization cohort. Reading specialization teacher candidates in our program are undergraduates and postbaccalaureates who follow a three-semester program with intensive field experiences: one semester of observation in an early grades classroom (prek-1), one semester of adult ESL tutoring (*El Puente*), three semesters of one-on-one or small group tutoring (grades 1-6), and two semesters of student teaching (grades 1-6). They complete four literacy courses during their program of study, as well as courses in language acquisition. The research occurred during semester one, when they were enrolled in Early Childhood Education, Reading Assessment and Development, and Community Literacy courses.

Community literacy. The course associated with *El Puente* is focused on literacy as a set of social practices that occur in communities, as well as on the literacy learning of English learners. Our objectives are to: (a) explore literacy as a social and cultural practice, (b) identify resources present in communities, (c) challenge assumptions about predominantly low-income communities that are culturally and linguistically diverse, (d) attend to stories that people tell about their lives and use those stories as the basis of literacy instruction, and (e) build relationships and a shared responsibility for teaching with those responsible for children's early literacy experiences (parents and other family members). In addition, we taught methods and strategies for teaching English as an additional language. The course was designed for students who aspire to teach in the elementary grades and pursue an endorsement in teaching English as a Second Language (ESL), but are not pursuing a career as bilingual or dual-language teachers.

El Puente. The researchers designed *El Puente* with the cooperation of the elementary school staff. Parents were matched one-to-one with preservice teachers for a 12-week tutoring program. We designed a pedagogical approach called *Mundos de Palabras* (Worlds of Words), in which adults combined text and images to compose their own narratives in a multimodal format. The adult students brought in family photos to include in the *Mundos de Palabras*. Figure 1: *Apples Story: A Student Writing Sample* is an example of a page from a book that illustrates this process. Each preservice teacher elicited oral language that became written text in support of students' print literacy (Allen, 1976; Dyson & Genishi, 1994). Although traditional ESL classrooms center

Figure 1. Apples Story: A Student Writing Sample

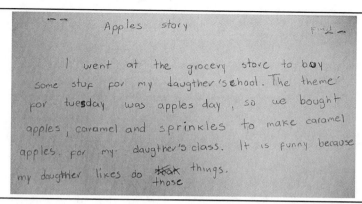

instruction on grammar, pronunciation, and rote vocabulary memorization, *El Puente* valued what students already knew and wanted to learn (Rogers & Kramer, 2007). Using a funds of knowledge approach, the preservice teachers were guided to identify students' goals, strengths, and interests as the basis of instruction (González, Moll, & Amanti, 2005).

Participants

Nineteen preservice teachers worked one-on-one with adults learning English at a local elementary school. Demographically, 12 of our participants were White women (our designation), 5 were bilingual and from Asian backgrounds (Vietnamese, Chinese, Japanese, Indian, and Korean), 2 were Latina, and all but 2 teacher candidates were from Texas and planned on teaching in Texas after graduation. Twice a week, parents and grandparents of children attending the school came for an hour-and-a-half of whole-group and one-on-one instruction in English from these students.

Table 1. Participant Characteristics

Teacher's Name	Teacher's Characteristics	Adult Student's Name(s)	Adult Student's Characteristics
Deanna	• Filipino • Framed herself as a learner • Valued *El Puente* for the opportunity to learn that taking risks engendered trust and strengthened the relationship with her adult students	Emilia	• Moved to the U.S. from Mexico in 1993 • Attended alone or with her three children • Interested in expanding her knowledge of English in order to help her children and to help her mother pass her Citizenship Test in the future
Gail	• White (Ethnicity not reported) • Continually tried to make the time spent with Yolanda beneficial to both her and her family	Yolanda	• Wrote with comfort in English • Speaking abilities in English were especially strong • Attended *El Puente* in order to help her children and her husband in their learning of English

Teacher's Name	Teacher's Characteristics	Adult Student's Name(s)	Adult Student's Characteristics
Hillary	• One Cuban parent, one White parent • Emerging proficiency in Spanish • Valued *El Puente* because it showed her that teaching is an interaction between people and being flexible is important	Jorge & Imelda	• Husband and wife • Attended with kindergarten-age daughter, Carmela • Worked well together • Imelda was more proficient in English than Jorge • Imelda focused on how to support her daughter in school • Jorge focused on English to help him in his construction job
Jennifer	• White (Ethnicity not reported) • Knew Spanish, but was not confident • Valued *El Puente* for the opportunity to build her own confidence as a teacher of adults, while helping to build her student's confidence as a learner	Eduardo	• Working knowledge of English • Attended alone • Initially reluctant to speak English • Interested in acquiring the appropriate English vocabulary for his bricklaying job
Kaci	• White (Ethnicity not reported) • Confident in her Spanish language proficiency • Valued *El Puente* for the interconnection of relationships, teaching, learning, and motivation	Jorge & Imelda	• See above
Kristen	• Polish ethnicity • Did not have a consistent *El Puente* partner • Valued *El Puente* for teaching her to be flexible and how to negotiate her role with her peers	Lupita	• Attended for a few weeks, then returned at the end of the semester • Interested in practicing dialogue to be used at her hotel job
Lily	• Parents emigrated from China • Felt connections to Sergio because of her experience with her parents learning English • Valued the experience of building on what the student knew	Sergio	• Moderate-to-advanced English proficiency • Attended *El Puente* alone • Interested in expanding his written communication in English for work
Rubina	• Parents emigrated from India • Speaks Guajarati and English • Valued *El Puente* for the opportunity to understand how important learning another person's story is in teaching	Dalia	• Grew up in Mexico • 60 years old • First language is Spanish • Attended *El Puente* alone • Interested in learning English so that she could become more independent

Most adult learners knew English vocabulary because they lived in bilingual spaces, but most were not comfortable speaking English.

In this paper, we draw on data from eight complete cases. Table 1 is a list of those eight participants, their students' names, and each of their backgrounds. Our selection criteria were the following: (a) we included participants who worked with a range of partners or just one partner, (b) completed their lesson logs and papers, and (c) agreed to a follow-up interview.

The researchers participated in the teaching and learning, as well as data collection. We reviewed lesson plans before each tutoring session, observed and provided assistance during tutoring, and provided specific feedback on preservice teachers' written reflections. We also facilitated a debriefing session after each session. Melissa, the primary instructor, is a White woman and monolingual English speaker. She brings a background and stance of teacher-as-researcher and discourse analyst to her work with preservice teachers in this setting. Ramón is a Chicano male who is bilingual in English and Spanish. He brings expertise in the ethnographic study of linguistic variation, and his research focuses on the social, cultural, and spatial dimensions of language teaching and learning. He collected data but did not teach. Our co-authors are doctoral students who supported the research and were teaching assistants. Each of us has teaching experience in culturally and linguistically diverse settings, including English as a Second Language classes, adult literacy, and K-12 classroom contexts.

Data Sources

Our data sources included video recordings, field notes, and student work. Each night, our research assistants collected video recordings of participants' work together. We used small, unobtrusive iPod cameras to collect video recordings of one-on-one work. Field notes (Carspecken, 1996; Emerson, Fretz, & Shaw, 1995) were recorded in the form of reflective memos about the school community, the process of setting up and running the *El Puente* program, and the experience of teaching in the Community Literacy course and at *El Puente*. Field notes were also generated from videos.

We also collected data from the students. Preservice teachers kept a weekly planning and reflection log that documented their work with their adult students and were used to plan future lessons that directly catered to students' individual needs. They also wrote a final case study that described: (a) the program, including activities, lessons, goals, ESL tutoring principles implemented, and assessments; (b) the adult student (i.e., background, work, educational experiences, family); and (c) the strengths of their student and the how they built on those strengths. In the case study, participants reflected upon their practices and connected their work to articles from their coursework. We also collected the *Mundos de Palabras* (for a fuller description of the theoretical and practical use of these books, see Hoffman & Roser, 2012).

Final group oral interview and individual follow-up. A final interview was conducted at the end of the Community Literacy course (30 minutes in length). Preservice teachers responded orally to structured questions. We conducted a preliminary analysis in order to extend, clarify, and probe in the areas of interest to the research project. From those analyses, we agreed on eight cases that warranted closer inspection (see selection criteria under Participants.) We conducted follow-up interviews (20 minutes) in an unstructured format, inviting preservice teachers to "talk us through" the *Mundos de Palabras* and address questions from our preliminary analysis.

Data Analysis

Our procedures included: (a) transcription of interviews, constructing analytical notes, and reconstructive analysis of field notes and video field notes; (b) constant comparative analysis of themes that emerged across data sources; (c) discourse analysis of key selections of texts (e.g., sessions of teaching and learning, narratives told in interviews); and (d) a thematic analysis of the *Mundos de Palabras*. Analytical notes were written during our reading of all data sources. By looking across the *Mundos de Palabras* books next to a lesson described in a log, alongside a reflection written in a case study, we identified patterns, explored disconfirming evidence, and tested emergent hypotheses. We compiled charts that helped move us towards themes that would characterize the participants' work with the students.

From those final interview transcriptions, we repeated our analytic process, reading the interview and noting themes across our analytic notes. Then, we compared those themes to the themes that came up in data collected before the interview, noticing similarities, differences, and extensions of the themes. We wrote about those themes in a case study analytic summary and member-checked those case studies. We then conducted a cross-case analysis of those case study analytic summaries, comparing the types of themes that came up in each. We located three cross-cutting themes that were present in each of the cases.

FINDINGS

Our preservice teachers: (1) described themselves as learning collectively along with their adult students, (2) worked to make instruction relevant to their students, and (3) made "on-the-spot" language teaching decisions in order to meet their students' instructional needs. Below we discuss these three findings, drawing examples from the eight cases we analyzed to illustrate each finding.

We then look more deeply at each finding through the exemplary case of one preservice teacher, Hillary, whose experience illustrates how the preservice teachers developed responsive teaching practices in this context. Hillary's case reveals how working beside adult learners facilitated this process of becoming a responsive literacy teacher. Hillary reflected:

> At first, I was so anti-*El Puente*, I don't know how to do this. Uggh. What I got out of it was really this idea that I'm not the teacher. I'm a person who has maybe some way of thinking but I'm not doing the learning for the person, you know? Here's an idea, either you click with it or not. My point is as a teacher to make as many ways for you to connect with it. I need to be flexible enough to change perspective and put this in front of you instead. And that's what I learned a lot, in terms of being more flexible. (Final Interview)

This quote captures important aspects of Hillary's work with her students, Imelda and Jorge, two adults who were married to one another and had a young daughter, Asella, who was in prekindergarten at Hernandez Elementary. First, Hillary questioned her new role as the teacher when working with adult learners. Hillary realized that teaching is a collective activity—an interaction between people whose ideas about how to learn may differ. She also emphasized the importance of a teacher's flexibility to "change perspective"—what we might call reflection—in order to respond to her students' interests and needs. In her work with Imelda and Jorge, Hillary constructed a vision of how a teacher acts in response to the differences between learners.

Collective Learning

Overview. On the first evening of *El Puente*, adult learners and preservice teachers alike were nervous. The preservice teachers expressed their concerns in reflective logs: They worried they would not meet the expectations of their adult partners because of their inexperience with teaching and their young age. Kristen, for example, reflected after teaching the second week:

> I was more confident this week when working with my adult. Last week I was definitely more intimidated about the situation. I still feel a lot of pressure though because I know that these adults are taking valuable time out of their day to come and I hope the program will help them. (Log, February 2, 2010)

However, as relationships grew between tutors and adult learners, preservice teachers began to take on the position of a co-learner with their partner, recognizing they were "learning a lot about each

Table 2. Collective Learning and Growth

We learned that preservice teachers...	Example
Related personal experiences to students' struggles as language learners	Kristen applied an observation she had at a post office to a whole group lesson at *El Puente*: "I thought it [focusing on the post office] was a great idea. I think places like the post office or doctor's office can be intimidating for everyone. The last time I went to a post office, I saw some people trying to get their passports renewed. The postal worker was raising her voice and getting frustrated saying things like, 'It's not my fault if you don't know how to fill out the form correctly.' Trying to get simple errands done can be a real hassle for someone who happens to get an impatient worker. I was terrified and I wasn't even getting my passport renewed!" (Log, March 11, 2010).
Envisioned what parent-teacher relationships should look like based on this experience	Deanna reflected, "It's truly amazing how close I have become to Emilia and her family. Positive relationships between teacher and families [...] will be extremely important when I have a classroom of my own. (Log, April 27, 2010) [...] I also hope that we have set a good example of the relationship parents and teachers should have together. (Log, April 20, 2010)
Articulated how trust and relationships led to adult students' confidence	Deanna reflected back on her experiences: "I was not confident working in such a novel experience. As the weeks progressed, Emilia and I both gained confidence working with one another because we created a 'safe environment' where everyone understood that they would not be judged. With the relationship that was created between the two of us, we were able to teach and learn from one another, which helped create such a trusting relationship." (Case Study, May 2010)
Shared their stories as ways to be a co-learner at *El Puente*	Rubina brought pictures of herself in traditional Indian clothes to share with Dalia as Dalia brought pictures representing her life: "This past weeks reading dealt with different cultures, and I like that Dalia is so immersed in her culture, and still goes back to Mexico. I feel a deep connection with my roots, and I liked to tell her about India." (Log, March 1, 2010)

other, constantly learning from one another" (Deanna, Log, March 2, 2010). In all eight cases, we heard evidence of this process of collective learning and growth.

The preservice teachers' reflections across data sources allowed us to gain insight about this process of collective growth and learning. Table 2 provides an overview of what we learned with illustrations from reflections. Each insight refers to the interpretation the teacher made of her work with her partner(s) and was common across cases. There were also counterexamples to each insight. For example, Jennifer found it easy to be a learner in her work with one student, but reflected on her work with a different partner, who "rarely speaks about his personal life or the problems that he's encountering" (Log, March 24, 2010). We have highlighted these counterexamples in our overview of each theme.

We found that the preservice teachers positioned themselves as learners in relation to the knowledge their partners brought related to their work lives, their families, and cultural practices. In turn, preservice teachers shared personal stories, experiences, and their culture with their adult partners. For example, Kristen carried photos of her family with her into tutoring, and wrote side-by-side with Emilia, her partner, as Emilia wrote about her own photograph. We closely analyzed the discourse that preservice teachers used in their reflections and learned when they talked about their teaching, they used the collective "us," "we," and "our" in their descriptions.

Also, the preservice teachers—with the exception of Jennifer, who did not use the Spanish she knew to teach her adult students (Interview, July 22, 2010)—saw themselves as learners of their students' language. We did not pose this as a potential benefit of working with adults, but as the adults practiced and learned English, the preservice teachers practiced and learned Spanish. In their interactions with their Spanish-speaking instructors and peers, the preservice teachers often asked questions about Spanish vocabulary and grammar. They also focused on connections between English and Spanish in their teaching.

The preservice teachers focused on the different ways a teacher can collectively learn with a student and in turn, constructed a vision of teaching that included these practices. This vision of teaching as collective learning and growth was a confident vision. Preservice teachers could take risks as learners in their work, draw on the knowledge of others around them, and try out difficult strategies of culturally responsive instruction within this vision.

Hillary's case. This emphasis on collective learning and growth was reflected in Hillary's work with Imelda and Jorge. In her reflections on her tutoring, Hillary rarely distinguished between *their* learning and *her own* learning. When asked to reflect on what her students had learned, she often used the words "we" and "our." For example, she observed in one log, "When I think of interpreting all the learning that went on this semester, my head gets overwhelmed and starts racing with all the ways we all grew" (April 27, 2010). Hillary also explicitly framed herself as a learner in this context, invoking comparisons between her students' experiences as English learners and her own experience as both a preservice teacher and a Spanish learner. Describing her interactions with Imelda and Jorge, she commented: "We all are learning and teaching each other. I made it very clear that I am a student-teacher learning to be a better teacher" (Case Study). With respect to her status as a Spanish learner, Hillary observed: "Together we worked towards the goal of improving their English and, as a result, I improved my Spanish" (Case Study). Hillary's view of learning as a collective endeavor is perhaps best reflected in her comments after a particularly successful night of tutoring, when she and Imelda together searched for an alphabet book that Imelda could read with her daughter: "Overall, it was a good night, with learning happening from all of us" (Log, February 25, 2010).

Making Instruction Relevant

Overview. The preservice teachers taught based on what the adults knew and wanted to learn. The more they learned about their students, the more relevant the lessons became. We based our model of instruction on the language experience model (Allen, 1976; Stauffer, 1980), in which print language emerges from talk. As their relationships developed, the preservice teachers initiated and sustained productive dialogue around their partners' personal goals for literacy, strengths for learning language, funds of knowledge (González et al., 2005), and goals in terms of family literacy. The *Mundos de Palabras* book was a valuable tool in this regard, assisting preservice teachers in the generation of themes for teaching.

Preservice teachers taught based on students' personal goals for literacy. Toward the end of the semester, Emilia shared with Deanna her goal to help her mother pass a citizenship exam, and Deanna tailored her teaching to that goal. Lily found ways to build on what Sergio needed most in his work life—to respond in English to text messages related to his work in construction. In these cases, the students' goals for literacy led teachers to focus on generative themes (e.g., citizenship) and the associated vocabulary of those themes.

Centering work on family and the adult partner's children was another way that preservice teachers made instruction relevant. The photographs that went into the *Mundos de Palabras* books gave them insight into their students' families and helped them to create and sustain dialogue. For Kaci, she found that when there was a lull in the lesson, all she had to do was take the conversation back to her student's daughter, because she always had a story to tell about her. Imelda often brought photographs of her daughter and composed texts that became the basis for instruction on grammar, vocabulary, and pronunciation.

Table 3 represents more fully the richness of how preservice teachers made instruction relevant. Because of our interest in preparing preservice teachers to teach in settings where they may not share background experiences or language with their students, it was significant that we saw evidence of visions for teaching built around relevant instruction (Fairbanks et al., 2010). We also see collective learning and growth as closely tied to making instruction relevant. In both areas, it was clear that preservice teachers understood the deep importance of building a relationship with students, and more importantly, the ways that a relationship supports learning. Beyond trust or affinity between teacher and student, preservice teachers learned how what they know about students can be drawn upon in creating lessons.

Hillary's case. Hillary made instruction relevant by adjusting her teaching to meet her students' individual instructional needs and by drawing on generative themes that emerged from her conversations with them. As Hillary got to know Imelda and Jorge better, she developed an understanding of their respective educational histories that helped inform her instruction. She learned, for example, that Imelda had more traditional experiences than Jorge, and therefore, acted more like a conventional student—she worked diligently and independently, asked for Hillary to "check" her answers, and so forth. In contrast, Hillary noted that, although Jorge was "very intelligent," he "hadn't had the opportunities that she had. He had confidence in a different way" (Final Interview). Hillary adjusted her teaching to account for her students' histories of learning,

Table 3. Making Instruction Relevant

We learned that preservice teachers...	Example
Tailored instruction to their students' personal goals for literacy	Deanna connected Emilia's goal to help her mother pass the citizenship test to a reading for class (Clark, 1990): "Similar to the Civil Rights Movement, there are many people in America who are working towards gaining the rights they deserve and to gain this power they seek others to help them get to whatever goal they seek (e.g., right to vote, become a citizen.)" (Log, April 13, 2010).
Interpreted lessons that drew on students' expertise as successful	Lily helped Sergio with grammar in his text messages, "However, one useful and 'real' tool we used was Sergio's cell phone, and the texts he'd sent with them the week before. The first time we explored this medium of instruction, it was actually on Sergio's suggestion. I'd been asking him about work-related text and how he was required to read and write in his job. I was thinking he had forms to fill out or something along those lines, when he pulled out his cell phone and started looking at past text messages. After finding one, he showed it to me and told me about the story behind the text, asking me if his response 'made sense.' After that, we made it a routine during individual time to look at his texts and talk about the grammar, vocabulary, spelling, and any other aspects that he had questions about. An example of when it worked really well was when we worked on sentence order. Sergio had sent out a text that said, 'send out an order for 45 sf (square feet) tiles. 16x16 no cost for now.' Although all the information is presented well in this sentence, we worked on how we could get all of the information into one sentence and ended up with, 'send out an order for 45 16x16 sf tiles at no cost for now, please.' When we had experiences like these, I felt that Sergio was getting the most out of our time together, because it directly pertained to his work, which was one of his primary goals for signing up for *El Puente* in the first place." (Case Study, May 2010)

working directly with Jorge to model English vocabulary, syntax, and conversational practices while Imelda tried to independently use new aspects of English she was learning.

As she drew on the generative themes that emerged from her conversations with Imelda and Jorge, Hillary also began to appreciate how important their daughter's academic success was to them. As she commented in one of her reflections, "I see that they really care about their daughter's success and...it is worth working here for their daughter to have a good education. I really admire them as parents and as individuals" (Log, March 25, 2010). As a parent herself, Hillary felt motivated to focus on themes related to Asella's schooling. For example, she spent the bulk of one session exploring parent-teacher communications. Imelda told Hillary that Asella was getting in trouble at school, and the conversation led to questions about whether the curriculum challenged her intellectually. Hillary saw this session as particularly successful because the conversation led Imelda to recognize her parental power within the school context. Hillary reflected in her lesson plan: "When I asked if they had talked to the principal she said that the teacher told them that they should not talk to her....When I told them that they could and that they did not even need the teacher with them, they were surprised" (Log, March 25, 2010).

At this point, Hillary began to see that her "lessons" might extend beyond choosing relevant topics to choosing ways of interacting around those topics that might be empowering for her students. In this sense, Hillary distinguished herself from some of the other preservice teachers by using relevant instruction as a starting point for a problem-posing approach to teaching. Just like the other preservice teachers, Hillary's positive relationship with her students enabled her to better identify relevant themes and issues to focus on in her instruction.

On-the-Spot Reflection and Teaching

Overview. Making instruction relevant meant that the preservice teachers often found themselves addressing content they felt unprepared to teach. Because many of them had not previously examined the structure of the English language for pedagogical purposes, they did not always have ready answers for the questions their adult students posed about English language. The preservice teachers were often uncomfortable in these moments, and called on an instructor or another person to help them explain a convention. Lily wrote, "I think I should plan ahead a little more and figure out how I'm going to explain certain concepts so they don't catch me off guard when someone asks me a question or something" (Log, February 16, 2010). These were not always the best moments in their teaching. However, over time, each preservice teacher became more adept at making on-the-spot instructional decisions. Table 4 is a summary of what we learned with illustrative quotes from data sources.

Because their goal was to follow their students' interests, each preservice teacher began with compositions or dialogue (e.g., Figure 1) and encoded text on paper or on a white board. Then, in most cases, they used sentence strips or the markers on the white board to convert a sentence to a more conventional form, to teach new vocabulary towards specificity, or to change a sentence's tense. Because another goal was to use Spanish to support English learning, the preservice teachers often used translation first and then proceeded with their teaching. In some cases, preservice teachers used materials created by instructors (e.g., a chart of English irregular verbs) to teach a mini-lesson.

Although there were often sticky moments in teaching, preservice teachers thought they were valuable moments and reflected at length in their logs. As preservice teachers learned to read their students' nonverbal cues and anticipate questions, they were less likely to be caught off-guard. Their reflections suggest that they began to see themselves as more successful teachers of language and literacy as they learned to address students' questions with quick mini-lessons. Further, in moments of uncertainty, they began taking an inquiry stance towards language conventions, finding answers with their students using the resources around them.

Hillary's case. Hillary engaged in on-the-spot reflection and teaching in many of her interactions with Jorge and Imelda. For example, although she encouraged Jorge to draw on his knowledge of Spanish as he learned to spell words in English, Jorge regularly challenged her to extend what she knew about English orthography. This dimension of their instructional interactions compelled Hillary to learn more about English spelling conventions.

Hillary drew on her emerging knowledge of Spanish vocabulary, a Spanish-English dictionary, the Internet, and other tools in order to help Jorge and Imelda compose sentences, translate texts created in Spanish, and to teach about language on-the-spot. The following is a reflection from her log:

Table 4. On-the-Spot Language Teaching

We learned that preservice teachers…	Example
Focused closely on students' English grammar	Lily reflected: "So Sergio and I were able to work a little on sentence structure and grammar because when we wrote sentences using the new vocabulary, instances popped up where a grammar lesson would be convenient. For example, Sergio wrote as a question he would ask a teacher, 'What's my child behavior in the class?" So we were able to work on different possibilities of forming that sentence." (Log, March 23, 2010)
Noticed how much they needed to know about language to accomplish on-the-spot teaching	Kaci struggled when confronted with questions about different grammar points: "I am noticing that although I feel like I know a lot about grammar, there are some things that I will be stumped on, and it takes running into those situations sometimes to learn from them. Next time I hope to think about the grammar that we will be using for our activities in order to maybe prepare myself for explanations so that I am not on the spot." (Log, February 8, 2010)
Learned how to make on-the-spot teaching decisions based on their close observations over time	Deanna reflected: "I am noticing that I am utilizing more teaching moments than I was in the past. I think this is in part because Emilia is the only student I have been working with so it is easier to observe and notice patterns in her use of English." (Log, March 30, 2010)
Drew on materials we provided to teach aspects of English	Kaci commented: "It was great that we had the conversion sheet for the irregular verbs, because in the one instance Imelda was helping Jorge to translate his sentences about his food mart into English, and she asked me if 'goed' was correct, when talking about a time where they 'went' to the food mart. I showed them how to use the table on the back and they were able to correct themselves." (Log, February 15, 2012)

[Imelda] was really excited to look up words on her own in their Spanish-English dictionary. This did offer up a nice conversation about the meanings given in a dictionary versus what we really use in conversation. One example was she translated in her homework *pan dulce*, which the dictionary said was Mexican bread. We then talked how most people translate it into the English order of sweet bread. (March 4, 2010)

In this example, Hillary valued the conversation about vocabulary that emerged from a critical use of the tools for translation that a student might use when learning a language. She located learning in conversation that occurred around the use of this tool. Another example occurred on the last day of *El Puente*. Imelda and Jorge asked for information on English classes where they could continue to learn together after the close of *El Puente*. Although she knew little about these programs, Hillary searched online with them to locate other ESL courses. As these examples illustrate, Hillary, like the other preservice teachers, was often called upon to reflect on her teaching and make on-the-spot decisions about how best to spend her instructional time.

CONCLUSION

At *El Puente*, the preservice teachers and their adult students generated important discoveries about culturally responsive literacy teaching. First, they discovered that learning alongside students can become part of the day-to-day life of the classroom, and that such learning is an essential component of teaching. Unexpectedly, they learned more Spanish, important to their teaching in Texas. Secondly, they learned to generate relevant instruction directly from their adult students' stories, and they witnessed the power of drawing on relevant themes to teach literacy. Finally, they learned many important things about English orthography, grammar, and vocabulary as they made pivotal teaching decisions in real time. These were all aspects of their developing visions of how to teach culturally and linguistically diverse students. Because this practicum was focused on literacy and language teaching, we saw how these recognizable theories of culturally responsive teaching translated into teaching practices.

Across cases, we also saw that preservice teachers and adult learners took on the most difficult aspects of teaching and learning: (a) perceived barriers related to language and cultural differences, (b) materials and curriculum disconnected from authentic purposes for literacy, and (c) gaps in knowledge about language. Why would they take these on, beyond the goals of doing well in a class or implementing pedagogy from their class readings? We conclude that it was the relationship with the person sitting beside them that led them to want to take on such challenges.

These adult learners played a pivotal role in our preservice teachers' learning, which adds a new dimension to our understanding of how teachers are prepared in practicum experiences. The adult learners garnered our preservice teachers' respect and admiration, based on their commitment to family, literacy, and learning English. Preservice teachers did not focus on perceived deficits, but instead saw their students' literacy practices through a lens of appreciation. In a child-centered practicum, we may have seen this appreciation, but in the adult tutoring setting, the family and community literacy practices of the school community were more evident. The adult students articulated their goals for literacy and goals for their family in ways more informative to the preservice teacher. Preservice teachers learned about a system of connections—including family, community, and school—that supports literacy learning. Parents were provided the opportunity to show how they supported their children's literacy learning, which in turn contributed to the preparation of culturally responsive literacy teachers.

From 5:00 to 7:00 p.m. each Tuesday and Thursday, we were moved by the hard work, learning, and growth in this practicum. We end with a quote from Hillary's Log: "Overall, it was a good night, with learning happening from all of us" (Log, February 25, 2010).

REFERENCES

Abrego, M. H., Rubin, R., & Sutterby, J. A. (2006). They call me "Maestra": Preservice teachers' interactions with parents in a reading tutoring program. *Action in Teacher Education, 28*(1), 3-12.

Allen, R. V. (1976). *Language experience in communication.* Boston, MA: Houghton-Mifflin.

Bollin, G. G. (2007). Preparing teachers for Hispanic immigrant children: A service learning approach. *Journal of Latinos & Education, 6*(2), 177-189.

Boyle-Baise, M. (2005). Preparing community-oriented teachers: Reflections from a multicultural service-learning project. *Journal of Teacher Education, 56*(5), 446-458.

Burant, T. J., & Kirby, D. (2002). Beyond classroom-based early field experiences: Understanding an "educative practicum" in an urban school and community. *Teaching and Teacher Education, 18*(5), 561-575.

Carspecken, P. F. (1996). *Critical ethnography in educational research: A theoretical and practical guide*. New York, NY: Routledge.

Clark, S. (1990). *Ready from within: Septima Clark and the civil rights movement*. African World Press.

Compton-Lilly, C. (2007). The complexities of reading capital in two Puerto Rican families. *Reading Research Quarterly, 42*(1), 72-98.

Cooper, J. (2007). Strengthening the case for community-based learning in teacher education. *Journal of Teacher Education, 58*, 245-255.

Cramer, R. L. (2004). *The language arts: A balanced approach to teaching reading, writing, listening, talking, and thinking*. Boston, MA: Allyn & Bacon.

Dewey, J. (1933). *How we think*. Chicago, IL: Regnery.

Duffy, G. (1998). Teaching and the balancing of round stones. *Phi Delta Kappan, 79*(10), 777-780.

Dyson, A. H., & Genishi, C. (1994). Introduction: The need for story. In A. H. Dyson & C. Genishi (Eds.), *The need for story: Cultural diversity in classroom and community* (pp. 1-10). Urbana, IL: National Council of Teachers of English.

Emerson, R., Fretz, R., & Shaw, L. (1995). *Writing ethnographic fieldnotes*. Chicago, IL: University of Chicago Press.

Fairbanks, C. M., Duffy, G., Faircloth, B. S., He, Y., Levin, B., Rohr, J., & Stein, C. (2010). Beyond knowledge: Exploring why some teachers are more thoughtfully adaptive than others. *Journal of Teacher Education, 61*(1), 161-171.

Freire, P. (1983). The importance of the act of reading. *Journal of Education, 165*(1), 5-11.

Freire, P. (1995). *Pedagogy of the oppressed* (new rev. 20th-Anniversary ed.). New York, NY: Continuum.

Friedman, A., & Shoen, L. (2009). Reflective practice interventions: Raising levels of reflective judgment. *Action in Teacher Education, 31*(2), 61-73.

Gallego, M. A. (2001). Is experience the best teacher? The potential of coupling classroom and community-based field experiences. *Journal of Teacher Education, 52*(4), 312-325.

González, N., Moll, L. C., & Amanti, C. (Eds.). (2005). *Funds of knowledge: Theorizing practices in households and classrooms*. Malwah, NJ: Lawrence Erlbaum.

Hale, A. (2008). Service learning with Latino communities: Effects on preservice teachers. *Journal of Hispanic Higher Education, 7*(1), 54-69.

Hoffman, J. V., & Roser, N. (2012). Reading and writing the world using Beautiful Books: Language Experience re-envisioned. *Language Arts, 89*(5), 293-304.

Howard, T. C. (2003). Culturally relevant pedagogy: Ingredients for critical teacher reflection. *Theory into Practice, 42*(3), 195-202.

Ladson-Billings, G. (1994). *The dreamkeepers: Successful teachers of African American children* (1st ed.). San Francisco, CA: Jossey-Bass Publishers.

Matusov, E., & Smith, M. P. (2007). Teaching imaginary children: University students' narratives about their Latino practicum children. *Teaching and Teacher Education, 23*(5), 705-729.

Mosley, M., Cary, L. J., & Zoch, M. (2010). Becoming culturally responsive: A review of learning in field experiences for prospective literacy educators. In D. Wyse, R. Andrews & J. Hoffman (Eds.), *The Routledge international handbook of English, language and literacy teaching* (pp. 282-293). New York, NY: Routledge.

Mosley, M., Hoffman, J. V., Roach, A. K., & Russell, K. (2010). The Nature of Reflection: Experience, Reflection and Action in a Preservice Teacher Literacy Practicum. In E. G. Pultorak (Ed.), *The purposes, practices, and professionalism of teacher reflectivity: Insights for 21st century teachers and students* (pp. 73-96). Lanham, MD: Rowman & Littlefield Education.

Ottesen, E. (2007). Reflection in teacher education. *Reflective Practice, 81*(1), 31-46.

Pedro, J. (2005). Reflection in teacher education: Exploring pre-service teachers' meanings of reflective practice. *Reflective Practice, 6*(1), 49-66.

Pultorak, E. G., & Barnes, D. (2009). Reflectivity and teaching performance of novice teachers: Three years of investigation. *Action in Teacher Education, 31*(2), 33-46.

Reyes, R. (2009). Frustrated, but hopeful and empowered: Early field experiences shaping the thinking and pedagogy of future educators of English language learners. *Texas Association For Bilingual Education Journal, 11*(1), 130-161.

Riojas-Corteza, M., & Bustos-Flores, B. (2009). Sin olvidar a los padres: Families collaborating within school and university partnerships. *Journal of Latinos and Education, 8*(3), 231-239.

Rogers, R. (2002). Between contexts: A critical discourse analysis of family literacy, discursive practices, and literate subjectivities. *Reading Research Quarterly, 37*(3), 248-277.

Rogers, R., & Kramer, M. A. (2007). *Adult education teachers: Designing critical literacy practices.* Malwah, NJ: Lawrence Erlbaum Associates Inc.

Rymes, B. R. (2002). Language in development in the United States: Supervising adult ESOL pre-service teachers in an immigrant community. *TESOL Quarterly, 36*(3).

Schön, D. A. (1983). *The reflective practitioner: How professionals think in action.* London, England: Temple Smith.

Stauffer, R. G. (1980). *The language-experience approach to the teaching of reading* (2nd ed.). New York, NY: Harper & Row.

Tomlinson, P. (1999). Conscious reflection and implicit learning in teacher preparation. Part 1: Recent light on an old issue. *Oxford Review of Education, 25*(3), 406-424.

Villegas, A. M., & Lucas, T. (2002). Preparing culturally responsive teachers: Rethinking the curriculum. *Journal of Teacher Education, 53*(1), 20-32.

Ward, J. R., & McCotter, S. S. (2004). Reflection as a visible outcome for preservice teachers. *Teaching and Teacher Education, 20*(3), 243-257.

Zeichner, K. (2005). A research agenda for teacher education. In M. Cochran-Smith & K. M. Zeichner (Eds.), *Studying teacher education: A report of the AERA panel on research and teacher education* (pp. 737-759). Malwah, NJ: Lawrence Erlbaum.

Speaking With/in the Lines: An Autoethnographical Study of Three Literacy Researchers-Artists

Peggy Albers
Teri Holbrook
Georgia State University

Jerome C. Harste
Indiana University

Figure 1. Poetic Analysis of Jerry's Collage, Watercolor and Paper

	Goats tumble Metaphors settle Signs of literacy Metaphors of inscription—Peggy	**Goats and Metaphors** I'd say they evolved in our words if it weren't for trails of tenacity (unless you want to argue that evolution is bullheaded)—Teri	Let's look At literacy From the other side As inscribed goats—Jerry

Several years ago, we engaged in a series of conversations about ourselves, our art, and how art informed our writing as literacy scholars. These initial conversations prompted us to pursue a systematic, longitudinal study of ourselves both as artists and literacy researchers, now in its second year. We were preoccupied with a quest to understand internal dialogues regarding our inquiry in the arts and external dialogues regarding our work as literacy researchers. All three of us have a deep personal passion for the arts and over the course of our lives have participated in them in some form or another, starting in childhood and continuing into our professions as teachers and teacher educators. All three of us have fused this passion with literacy research and, in so doing, continue to investigate how our interest in the arts interlocks with our academic scholarship. In essence, we study our embodied selves both as literacy scholars and artists to understand how our scholarship in literacy has shaped us as artists and how our being artists has shaped our literacy scholarship.

As researchers and writers, in our scholarly and artistic lives we had adopted rhythms of practice that seemed as natural to us as breaths. The fine grit of clay between fingers, the close observation of children in classrooms, the translucence of pigment swept on paper—these were well-honed facets of our collective lives. Similarly, we were well-practiced in conventional qualitative research methods and the authoring of conventional research texts. For this study to produce insights, we knew we needed to take our inquiry into what for us were uncommon textual spaces; we would need to think and speak with and in language that "allowed ourselves to be startled" (Neilsen, 2004, p. 54). To that end, we invoked autoethnography as a method through which to study ourselves, literacy, literacy teaching, and literacy research, and we drew upon poetic analysis to expand and disrupt our commonplace notions of how to analyze research. Our aim was to respond to Neilsen Glenn's (in press) conceptualization of poetry as "philosophy" through which we are "learning to pay attention, to listen, to be awake…[and] to ask bigger questions, to take down the name of ghosts" (http://learningthreshold.blogspot.com/2011/02/excerpt-from-homing-chapter-on-poetic.html). While in this work we call ourselves artists, we do not call ourselves poets. Instead, we frame ourselves as writers pulling upon what we conceive as poetic impulses in our voiced language to look at our lives newly and with "beginner's eyes" (Neilsen, 2004, p. 54).

The multi-vocal study presented here—one point in an ongoing autoethnographic inquiry—attempts to highlight our "out-of-school" experiences as artists with our "in-school" experiences as literacy scholars. In so doing, we seek to thread together our discourse communities as artists and literacy researchers, to make visible and tangible the recognition that our scholarship is borne out of our experiences as artists as much as our work as artists draws from our experiences as scholars. Art is not a "hobby" that we engage in on the weekends, but deliberate study that engages us in deep thought about literacy and social semiotics, and their significance to meaning-making, whether in academic journals, trade journals, or on our Etsy sites. We situate the arts and ourselves as artists directly in our work as scholars, not only expanding our definition of literacy, but also articulating how our scholarship in literacy has evolved as a result of our work as artists. Our research questions are situated in embodied experience, or what Spry (2001) calls the "body as site from which the story is generated" (p. 708). We asked: (a) How does working in the arts enable us to understand how we are becoming different from what we have been as literacy researchers?; (b) What is the role of embodied knowledge in our work as artists and as researchers?; and (c) What does autoethnography allow us to understand about stories as sites for producing knowledge?

Education has only recently acknowledged embodied knowledge as significant to literacy scholarship. From a philosophical standpoint, Lakoff and Johnson (1999) argue that the mind is inherently embodied. According to an interview with Lakoff (1999):

> Anything we can think or understand is shaped by, made possible by, and limited by our bodies, brains, and our embodied interactions in the world. This is what we have to theorize with....Our brains take their input from the rest of our bodies. What our bodies are like and how they function in the world thus structures the very concepts we can use to think. We cannot think just anything - only what our embodied brains permit" (http://www.edge.org/3rd_culture/lakoff/lakoff_p1.html).

Scholarship in embodied knowledge is limited; however, we highlight several studies of note. In 2011, a series of papers at the 2011 Literacy Research Association conference addressed the relationship between body and mind in preservice education (Jones, 2011), struggling readers (Enriquez, 2011), and high school students (Johnson, 2011). Collectively, these researchers found tangible evidence that described body responses and literacy engagements, and suggested the importance of continued study in embodied knowledge to inform practice and research. Davies, Dormer, Gannon, Laws, Rocco, Taguchi, & McCann (2001), through collective biography, closely examine the process of subjectification, specifically locating how their bodies were subjected within available discourses of what it meant to be school girls. Through discussion of their memories, they recognized when and how they took up and/or contested these discourses. In a self-study, Lussier-Ley (2010) describes her embodied experiences and the role of the body in her consulting work with athletes and dancers, finding that an embodied perspective is an important part of a relational pedagogy. Cryle (2000) argues that "'the body'…is shaped by, and made available through, discourse . . . [T]he only body we can ever talk about, the only body we can think, is shaped and indeed disciplined by the language in which it is known and recognized" (p. 18).

Alongside these scholars and others, we argue for the importance of examining embodied experiences in literacy research and practice. Our embodied experiences are shaped by and disciplined by languages—art and written/oral language. In turn, our embodied selves shape and discipline these languages. We use "experiences" not simply to define events in which we participate as artists and researchers, but to understand that we are *experiencing* artists and researchers in which experience is not the "the origin of our explanation, not the authoritative (because seen or felt) evidence that grounds what is known, but rather that which we seek to explain, that about which knowledge is produced" (Scott, 1992, pp. 25–26).

To engage in such inquiry is to participate in what Greene (1988) calls the dialectic of freedom, or the open spaces that provide opportunity for articulation of multiple perspectives. Figure 1 that opens this writing reflects the shift in our scholarship to employ autoethnographical and poetic methods to study ourselves, to investigate within our experiences the significance of the arts to our lives as literacy researchers, and the tensions and possibilities that emerge from such practices. Understanding ourselves as texts, a "discursive template" (Kaufmann, 2005, p. 577) on which we write our world as well as being written by it, this research is riveted in methods of ethnography and theories of aesthetics and critical literacy. This dialectal process between theory and method enables us to acknowledge how embodied knowledge has shaped our thinking, our making, and our reflecting on our work, as well as allows us to shape the very methods with which we take on this inquiry.

Informed by the multi-vocal, multi-faceted textual format of published autoethnographies, throughout the remainder of this article we interrupt our descriptions of the study's design with our data—artworks, poems, and dialogues that we had with each other—at times without written explanation, situating meaning in the image or the way in which written and visual language is captured. These data function as illustrations or counterpoints to our understanding of ourselves as artist/literacy researchers. Our own thoughts are off-set by text boxes at times, and recorded as dialogue in others. Our findings reflect the themes that we saw operating within our conversations, artworks, and analyses, again, illustrated by data. Because we are artists, we re-story our experiences through a multi-voiced dialogue between our various "bodies" at play.

DOING CRITICAL AUTOETHNOGRAPHY

We are now into our second year of systematic study. This work reflects our desire to explore the best we know how to be in talking about the significance of the arts in our lives as researchers, to "do" ethnography, a practice located "in an interpretive search of meaning" (Geertz, 1973, p. 5), in a move to push our thinking forward. By theoretically invoking Greene's (1988) concept of the dialectic of freedom, we open spaces around which we, as artists and researchers, have creatively played in for years but now do so freshly. In exploring the issue of freedom, Greene (1988) wrote,

> … for those authentically concerned about the 'birth of meaning,' about breaking through the surfaces, about teaching others to 'read' their own worlds, art forms must be conceived of as an ever-present possibility. They ought not to be treated as decorative, as frivolous. They ought to be, if transformative teaching is our concern, a central part of the curriculum (p. 131).

Greene's (1988) words situate precisely our many years of work within the arts; transformation does not result from a one-year study of one's processes and thinking, but occurs through many experiences as artists, literacy teachers who are artists, and now researchers as artists. By naming ourselves as artists, we locate our identities as both scholars and artists, and in this writing, pay clear attention to what the arts have done and continue to do for us. Greene (2000) positions the arts as a path towards defamiliarization, the freedom to think otherwise, to say it strange, and to release the imagination. Such a critical perspective fits our own. We have written about the importance of engaging multiple perspectives in considering ideas, disrupting the commonplace assumptions of what constitutes literacy, and promoted and enacted social justice through our work and writings. Alongside this critical perspective, we have continued to advocate for the arts, primarily as literacy scholars, but now as artists-researchers-scholars. For us, the arts give permission for people to become different than they might otherwise be, to open up dialogue with others, and to engage the intellect through multiple symbol systems. They engage us in metaphorical, theoretical, and pragmatic thinking about social issues, and offer us spaces to share these perspectives through our art. In this vision, the arts require an aesthetic staying power to explore imaginative possibilities and aesthetic daring to take interpretive risks to explore these possibilities.

To do autoethnography is, as Kaufmann (2005) writes, "to recognize that in a dialectical process, every text [we] read is interpreted and rewritten through [our] own biography and [our] autobiography is rewritten as [we] read it through alternate texts, a reciprocal writing and rewriting" (p. 577). The context of this study began with conversations about our biographies, our early and ongoing experiences with the arts. We are three literacy researchers who have studied in community arts programs over many years. Peggy has been involved in the arts, first as an actress in school and community plays, and then as a director of high school plays. As a result of her dissertation work with an art teacher and her first encounter with clay, she shifted her interest towards pottery, studying at a local community arts center for 15 years, all the while showing and selling her work at local venues. Her work focuses closely on arts-based literacy practices and critical analyses of visual information in student- and professionally-generated texts. Teri's childhood endeavors in creative writing led to a career as a published novelist. Her more recent interest to "beat back language" and to interrogate its disciplining function engaged her in the study of photography and collage at a notable school of art and design. She currently explores the role of the arts to speak to and against issues surrounding discourses of disability/ability as they involve texts. Jerry has studied drawing nearly all his life, developed interest in sand sculpting during his family vacations to the beach, and is currently studying watercolor. His work initiated discussions in the significance of semiotics to literacy, and what can be learned about children's literacy when multiple sign systems are an essential part of literacy practices. In essence, the three of us have been artists since childhood and have engaged continuously in the study of an art form, continue today to study art forms, participate as artists in art venues, and have made the arts a significant part of our current scholarship.

Figure 2. Found Poems of Jerry's Watercolor, "Baby Crow"

| **Signing the Crow**
Do you think now about the
name on the front?
I wish I hadn't put it there. I
could have reprinted
And signed the original
Artists do that.
When they reprint, they
double signature |  | Is it a crow or a
blackbird?
It's a crow, a little baby
crow.
It's meant to capture
the essence of black
of grouchiness of
limiting your palette
but getting your voice
heard. |

Data Collection and Analysis

As autoethnographic researchers, we claim ourselves as primary social actors in the research. We are fully immersed both in the collection and reporting of the data. For this study, data were comprised of 10 self-selected pieces of artwork by each artist (N = 30 pieces), four Skype digitally recorded conversations, and four face-to-face recorded conversations that totaled 12 hours of recorded talk. To prepare, each of us looked over our years of artwork and chose 10 pieces that signified a meaning for us that other examples of our work did not. We then presented these 10 artworks to each other. The selection and discussion of these 10 pieces as we presented them to each other constituted our first layer of analysis. The second layer of analysis occurred as we interviewed each other about these pieces, with focused attention on questions such as: What were you trying to say with this piece? Do you feel you were successful? What did you learn about the discipline by doing this piece? Our conversations were not linear. That is, although we had focused questions, in our talk we moved between and among what we were saying about our art, who we were becoming as artists, and the significance the arts had for us as scholars. Subsequent conversations focused on understanding how we had become different as artists and literacy scholars, what we had learned about the process of making art, and how this contributed to our knowledge of an expanded notion of literacy. All conversations were transcribed, coded, and analyzed to elicit analytic insights (Anderson, 2006) about our art and its relationship to our work as literacy scholars.

Data analysis was multi-faceted, particularly drawing upon visual discourse analysis and poetic transcription and analysis to study our data, which we believed were apt methods that captured specific aspects of our scholarship and art. Visual discourse analysis (Albers, 2007) enabled us to study the artworks as texts. We discussed organizational structures, the content, colors, design, layout, and studied how these elements in combinatorial relationship made discourses visible within each other's pieces. Each of us has had experience reading and analyzing student-generated visual texts as well as professionally generated art, and Peggy and Jerry have written elsewhere about the procedures in detail (Albers, Harste, Vander Zanden, & Felderman, 2008; Albers, Frederick, & Cowan, 2010). Simultaneously, as informed researchers, we studied the written transcripts, open coded for key points, and collapsed these codes into idea units, or key concepts we saw emerging in our conversations (Table 1).

We found this method of coding artistically and theoretically unsatisfying; it did not offer us the level of insight we sought in our research questions. We decided to explore our transcribed

Table 1. Initial Analysis of Transcripts, Open Coding

Project: Literacy Artists
Method: Poetic Analysis
Transcript: 4-49-2010
Lines: 1-260
Date: 4.17.11
Brief: Identify idea units; create 4-line found poems; analyze for semantics, idea unit overlaps, effective of poetry to capture both.
R

Open Codes	Transcript Line #	Collapsed codes	Transcript Line #	Idea Units	Transcript Line #
Talking to/ Talking back	1-15; 151	Talking to/Talking Back Political/Intentions/Envisioning	1-15; 151; 125; 149; 149	Talking to Talking Back	1-15
Impetus & interest	16-22; 86-89	Traces/personal history/impetus & interest/ Emotion/passion/ significance	16-22; 24-30; 86-89; 80-90; 106-108; 167-168	Impetus & Interest	16-22
Emotion/passion	24-30	Echoes	96-100; 105-109; 193-194; 245	Emotion/Passion	24-30
Ugly writing/ugly art	31-55	Kinds of thinking Affordances In the round thinking	57-61; 224-245	In the round thinking	224-245
Kinds of thinking Affordances In the round thinking	57-61; 224-245	Surveillance/Surveyed Watching-Being Watched	103-104; 122-124; 134-141; 145-146; 148	Metaphor	71-76
Metaphor	71-76	Embodied/Disembodied Making/Process/Noticing/ Doing/Reflect/ Readings of art/Read around/Caught/Envisioning/ Playful work/Reflect	125-132; 230-237; 146-147; 147-148; 149; 153-154; 157-159; 161-165; 168; 201-208; 212; 160-224; 170-172; 188	Traces	80-90
Traces/personal history	80-90; 106-108	Collaboration	154-159	Echoes	96-100
Color	91-94; 162	Materials Canvas/fragments /photos architecture	110-117; 118-121; 120; 124-125; 144-145	Watching/Being Watched	134-141
Line	162; 180	Elements Color/Line/Metap	71-76; 91-94; 162; 162; 180	Canvas	110-117

conversations by way of found poems, a process that entailed reading across transcripts to locate key phrasing and recurring motifs. Distilling our words into found poems enabled us to tap into both our literacy and artistic imaginations and to study our embodied experiences in unfamiliar ways. Maynard and Cahnmann-Taylor (2010) write, "Poetic drafts may push forward how we remember or think about our experience, or, ultimately, how we want to present and explain our materials . . . may help build toward a more rigorous analysis and theoretical understanding of what we observe" (p. 4). We note here that we indeed conceptualized these texts as "poetic drafts"; they were not intended to be polished poems or final drafts but rather poetically informed and analyzed research units that opened spaces to engage with our data differently than we might otherwise. In this article, we use the term *found poems* to describe the short forms we made of our data during analysis. Specifically, we returned to our transcriptions, independently generated "poem-like compositions" (Glesne, 1997, p. 202) from the language in the transcripts (first level), and shared these found poems with each other. We found that we captured similar words, phrases, and ideas from which we then generated another set of conversations about the power of poetry "to sum up" (Friedrich, 1996), and succinctly capture ideas about the relationship between art and scholarship. We delved deeper into our Level 1 found poems and distilled each poem to four lines (Level 2) with the purpose of "remov[ing] excess, highlighting emotions and attitudes … as well as ideas" (Maynard & Cahnmann-Taylor, p. 8). We came together yet again to study how each of us further distilled our analysis in short four-line found poems. Table 2 represents a sample of the analysis of our data:

Table 2. Deeper Level of Analysis, Distilled Poems

Visual discourse analysis	Transcript (excerpted)	Level 1 found poem	Level 2 found poem (distilled)
	Jerry: *I did this painting and realized I needed to make this a lot darker to get the contrast of the face to stand out. I wanted the eye to go in... this was a real study in how to get the eye to move into a picture and to be where you wanted it to be.* **Peggy:** *And I see also that she has a little cleavage in there too.* **Jerry:** *… I like the dark here. [Indicates the upper background] Because it forces the eye back in here.*	**Eye Sockets** I took color out of her cheek, her arm. Put a little cleavage there. I wanted the eye to go there… To force the eye back in.	**Eye Sockets** color out cleavage in the artist forces the eye to move

This analysis led to three key findings which we present in the next section.

WORKING WITH/IN THE LINES

Dialogue about our work was essential in helping us understand how our previous experiences in literacy really had informed our artistic practices, creating echoes that reverberated across our selected artworks. For Peggy, it was a focus on satire and parody, pushing the edges of what she thought was safe art, purposefully making art that would stop viewers, for good or bad, and force them to take a closer look. For Teri, surveillance emerged as a recurring mark, whether it was in her use of cameras, images of windows, or transparent velum that overlay other images and objects to create the effect of a lens. For Jerry, it was a focus on mastering technique, whether it was a poppy, a cornflower, or the subtle use of gradation to stimulate the senses, especially sight and smell, in a piece he simply called "The Fireman." Significance in three areas related to meaning—the aesthetic, transmediation, and signature—continually rose to the surface, breaking through in our art, our talk, and our analyses.

Meaning-making began with the aesthetic and stimulations of the senses, including pleasure and discomfort.

> I think one has to be
> A damn optimist
> To see peeling paint
> As hopeful.

For us, discussions around our meaning-making were situated initially in the aesthetic, evoking a stimulation of the senses, the first avenue to consciousness. Aesthetics is in a triadic relationship to our skills (flexible use of technique) and the art object that signals our intent in the making of the object (transmediation). Each of us had many experiences with galleries, museums, and readings about art. However, as apprentices to the art form that we study, we found that our art forms engaged us in imagining and discovering, opening up spaces to speak visually.

Figure 3. Found Poems

Poppies
That ephemeral red
A good breeze would make them fall apart
A subtle sense of essence.—Jerry

Our meaning-making began with our desire to know the art form; we wanted to know skills associated with the art form, how the media within the art form worked, and how art objects provoked sensations of joy, desire, intrigue, inquiry—even discomfort or confusion. We noticed our desire to play with media and its affordances, as Teri stated about a photograph she took of a historic prison: "I like the pattern in here and the level of depth through here. That you have to look through this window and through the grid and down into the prison yard behind it." Lana Wilson (personal communication, January, 2011), a potter from California, stated in a workshop, "It's not helpful having rules with art. The most fun you have is discovering for yourself by following possibilities, not rules. Use rules to get acquainted with art." Peggy discovered the value of using rules and following possibilities through a workshop she took with a noted potter who:

…throws very loose. He throws a quick cylinder, does a trim here, pulls it off the wheel, sets it aside for an hour, comes back and trims the foot, and then he paints it. So my painting and my technique of throwing loose came as a result of that. That was extraordinarily huge for me. It reminded me of Tom Romano's idea that once you know the rules you can break the rules. So I knew the rules of how to make a tight cylinder, to make a perfect cup, but now choose to break them.

At the same time that we learned about art, we learned through art. We learned to perceive, to notice closely and with an informed artistic eye perspective, beauty, line, and design. As we talked about our art-making and what drew us to it, we discovered that our art was informed by our past experiences, and that those experiences were tied to particular sensations. In other words, we drew from what called to us.

Aesthetics also elicited pleasure and desire in us and pushed us to continue our artistic inquiry. Each of us takes classes at various studios in our cities; these classes drive our interest and provide spaces for us to study others' work and to listen to others' remarks about our own work. Jerry imagined a still life, and in so doing, discovered the relationship between ink and color. This learning demystified techniques in doing pen and ink paintings, and his immediate and sensory newfound learning prompted him to do "about 50 more."

Working in the arts fostered transmediation that enabled us to see ourselves and the world differently.

> I got interested in capturing essence
> And then how the eye would travel
> And now I accidently got thinking about things
> like line
> and design

For all of us, the arts fostered transmediation, a rearticulation of content, ideas, thoughts, from one sign system to another that enabled us to see ourselves and the world differently. As artists, we understood meaning-making as a dynamic process, a way to reposition ourselves as new in the world that allows us to think metaphorically and symbolically and to try on new perspectives. That new-ness arose in our work through the development of series—pieces of our art related by subject matter, technique, or statement. We entered into new series because of some breakthrough or pivotal piece, which caused us to look differently at our mediums. Through a series of work, we were able to rearticulate—sometimes over and over again—a concept that we ourselves had not yet worked through.

Transmediation also provided space to study technique, to understand its affordances, and to work it and work it, often in dialogue with others, especially instructors. A found poem unit, followed by transcript data, depicts Teri's inquiry into how she thinks about collage construction in the context of instructor feedback and studio critiques:

> Six collages!!
> They say it doesn't work.
> Why do I not feel discouraged
> Rather, I want to figure out why.

Teri: The first level is just a paper layer. I start with torn paper either tissue paper, frequently it's tissue paper, but it can be butcher paper that I've colored. Then after that, I just start playing with image and other papers and color elements like crayons, pastels, paints, and go back and forth, layering paper, color elements and images back and forth on top of each other.

Peggy: So these are photos and you apply other media on top of them. So how do you make the choices that you do?

Teri: I have a big box—I have all my photos in different sizes. Some of them have been manipulated and colored in different ways. I typically turn them—this is what my instructor told me—I typically turn them upside down so I'm not reading the image. I start looking at color and line, and not context and not the whole piece, and start ripping and start putting them together.

Jerry: Art for us is a playground. It allowed me to step away from being a professor. The art teacher I'm working with says things like, "Okay, we're going to start with a line today." Now that is no direction whatsoever from my vantage point. What's a line? A curved line, a straight line, a jagged line? What do you mean? She never did tell us.

Take a pen
(It wasn't watercolor?)
Do a quick line drawing
(A gestural drawing?)
Add watercolor
(And your life changed after that, didn't it?)
Presto!! Art.

Transmediation centered our attention on making critical statements through our art, and displaying pieces in public spaces by entering them in shows, galleries, or trade journals. Across conversations, we noted the significance of art as a subversive language, a way to communicate social issues through metaphor. Peggy's interest in such speaking-back surfaced in her anthropomorphized animals, animals that took on issues of gay marriage, artificiality of reality shows like *The Real Housewives of….*, or classical literary and art texts. (Figure 4)

Figure 4. Parody and Found Poems in Clay

Rabbits, no less,
With buck teeth
As if they haven't been maligned enough
Now fornicating on my cup
Questioning marriage
Making trouble

Moving beyond the notion of visual art as the merely pretty, we see how art can chafe and bother the taken-for-granted. In schools, the arts are often used as rewards or positioned as entry points to content areas. Our work as both artists and literacy researchers has led us to see the deep transformative value of the arts as sociocultural critique (Albers, Holbrook, & Harste, 2010). **Our identities were signaled throughout our work by the signatures that could be traced across our pieces.**

My doodles
I never saw them as art
I never made the connection
Who knew
they were an early
Signature

Where the hell am I going to sign this piece?
I don't want to screw up where the eye goes.
Is "signing your name on the front" a requirement?
What's that you're asking?!?

One of our most interesting discoveries about ourselves was our unconscious marking of signature, not the signing of our names on the front, back or bottom of our pieces, but rather signature as inscription. From the tools we used, to the way in which we marked our surfaces, our processes of inscription signaled our identities, our interests, our beliefs. They appeared time and time again, collectively voicing a signature that was particularly ours. These (re)marks (Albers & Frederick, 2009) made visible how we inscribed ourselves in our art through tools, technique, color, design, and subject matter. Only when we presented our 10 pieces as a collection to each other did we discover, and delightfully so, our signatures. Jerry reflected, "If you look at my work, every now and then, there's a poppy picture because I have something still about poppies. I guess because I was successful once, I think maybe I could do something good with poppies." For him, poppies became one of the signature marks in his work. In Teri's photographic and collage images, references to surveillance and eluded escape dominate. In a description of a 19th century prison surveillance system that relied on mirrors inset into fancy wooden casings, she noted, "In the early photographs, I was not thinking about the panopticon because I didn't know about it. By the time I took this one, I knew about the panopticon, which is why I have other pictures of this [pointing to the mirror surveillance system]. I thought this was interesting, not just the cabinetry around them, but the idea that they reflect off each other to create the surveillance system." Signature windows, light, and open spaces cut across her artworks. (Figure 5)

Signature surfaced not only in our images but in our discussions. Jerry remarked, "One of the other things I haven't thought about yet is that all of us are playing with highly cultured symbols. [Peggy is] taking the American Gothic to task, sort of [through her parody of classic art], and Teri is taking on surveillance. I'm taking very traditional watercolor things. It's highly cultured. In a way we're all speaking back to what we see as some sort of omnipresence that the rest of the world sees as invisible."

Figure 5. Surveillance as Signature in Collages

Windows come up in all three collages because, again, windows dominate the photographs. I also tried to do a series of collages with doors that I didn't pick as (one of my ten images) because they're not as interesting to me as the windows are.

DISCUSSION

Transgression as Technique
Technique as Aesthetics
Aesthetics as Abduction
Abduction as Transgression

Autoethnography encourages a discussion of how researchers make sense of studying themselves. For us, poetic and visual analyses encourage us to find what is strange and to work with/in spaces and lines that open up our concepts of literacy, research, and meaning-making. Embodied knowledge offers insights into who we are becoming as individuals who do not just have experiences with the arts, but who constituted ourselves and are constituted as experiencing subjects (Davies et. al., 2001).

Autoethnography as a method enabled us to articulate through an understanding of ourselves the larger issue of "why the arts" in literacy. First, we recognize how the arts have made us different from what we were before. The format of this article—a fusion of exposition, found poems, image, and conversations—released us from interpreting through the known and dared us to think about the arts otherwise. From this investigation, we acknowledge that art stimulates our senses and heightens in us an awareness in *how* we look. By studying the marks we inscribe and how we see, we come to an understanding of how the marks signal meaning for us and for others. As artists, we are comfortable with uncertainty and ambiguity; we cannot always know the direction of our thinking, and a single experience can make way for new series of thought to emerge. Art also makes us vulnerable and opens us up to criticism and critique. Through the on-going learning of technique in art classes and workshops, we transgress; we increase the flexibility in how we use art as a language, what we can say through art, and what we can say about art.

As our study suggests, poetic and visual analyses encourage us to find what is strange. Deep and thorough analysis of our talk and our work led us to notice that ideas and concepts can be distilled poetically and more importantly, capture that part of ourselves which we call *artist*. This method of inquiry disrupts and transforms how data is analyzed and calls for researchers to consider new spaces of possible analysis. It calls for different "research/scholarly practices and oftentimes requires a dismantling of normal ways of thinking about and doing and representing research" (O'Donoghue, 2007, cited in Prendergast, Gouzouasis, Leggo, & Irwin, 2009, p. 2). While our artworks, conversations, and transcriptions provided data, our found poems also became data when we studied to what extent they reflected key ideas presented in the transcripts. In this way, found poems served a dual purpose: to present the data as well as a way to interpret the results of the data. Poetic analysis enabled us to take "the risk of seeking insight, not just information," (Maynard & Cahnmann-Taylor, p.9). Further, poetic analysis for us was about breaking through the surfaces of adopted rhythms of practice and teaching others to 'read' our worlds in new ways (Greene, 1988). As an art form, found poems offered "an ever-present possibility" to re-present data and interpretation of findings (Greene, p. 131).

Embodied knowledge offers insights into who we are becoming not as literacy researchers or artists, but as experiencing subjects (Davies et al., 2001) or the "body as site from which the story is generated" (Spry, 2003, p. 708). We cannot but help fuse our work as artists with our work as literacy researchers. Our study of art and the critical talk around it allows us to see literacy newly. Our heightened awareness of social issues is brought to the surface of our physical art, art that embodies our emotional, intellectual, social, and political responses. Our stories are situated directly within the social and discursive processes in which we participate as artists and literacy researchers. Our participation in gallery shows, art fairs, and art communities position us to recognize that in these spaces/places/discourses new embodied knowledge is produced. This knowledge signals that threads of both art and oral/written language are inextricably woven in our embodied selves.

Intrinsic to embodied knowledge is perception, a noticing and becoming aware of the many facets of a work, such as medium, textures, light, color and so on; an example is when Jerry noticed how he could apply color on simple pen and ink drawings to create beautiful poppies. With such noticing comes informed and critical talk about art objects, not just as naïve interacters with such objects, but as attentive perceivers whose talk is more precise, imaginative, and articulate, and which elucidates a deeper apprehension of particular works of art. How Teri discusses her techniques for collage helps us understand that art is a language. Much like a linguist studies written language, the design choices she makes (tearing, layering, placement) contribute to the significance of its reading and viewing. Developing our imagination enables us to explore new possibilities and frees us from the literal and mundane, allowing us to experience life vicariously that we have not yet experienced directly. Peggy's clay baskets move into parody and satire, communicating not only function but echoes of literary conventions. These are examples of how embodied knowledge allows us to particularize, to see, hear, and experience things in their concreteness and within our own contexts. This is what we have to theorize with, and our how our bodies respond and interact in the world structure the very concepts that we use to think (Lakoff, 1999).

Aesthetics, transmediation as critical expression and public signification, and signature allow us to imagine freshly the sensitivity that comes with studying the arts. When studied as a discipline as well as a way to communicate our thoughts and values, art brings to the surface the signature in our voices, the visible marks that position us uniquely, and the subtle marks that gesture to the discourse communities we inhabit. We do not believe we would have understood the importance of this shift in perspective had we not become practicing artists ourselves.

By enacting an embodied autoethnography, we recognize the importance of reflexivity, a self-conscious introspection in which we, the researchers, are both investigators and the investigated, and as such, a visible part of the story we are telling. According to Willig (2001), there are two types of reflexivity, personal and epistemological. Personal reflexivity situates reflection in the researcher's experiences, values, cultural and political beliefs, and so on, and how the research itself has changed the researcher. As individuals who constituted ourselves and are constituted as experiencing subjects, we acknowledge the significance of our past experiences—the daughter of an artist, a former actress and English teacher, and a drawer who liked to doodle—and recognize these influences in the work we do as meaning-makers and producers. As researchers, we notice how inscription is (re)marked and then becomes signature, leaving traces through which the textmaker cannot hide her or his identity, beliefs, values, or convictions. We notice how signatures emerge across time in data we collect in a range of spaces (e.g., classrooms, communities, families). When studied across time, educators and researchers will notice elements that recur among the many visual texts they create; reflexivity allows them to notice how these elements direct attention to the situated stories that learners bring into various spaces.

Epistemological reflexivity engages the researcher in considering questions of design, such as how the research questions defined and limited the findings and how the design of the study constructed the data and findings. From this study, we suggest that the level of our analysis allowed us to capture and record research strangely, using poetic forms to succinctly, holistically, and critically identify significant ideas we saw operating in our art and in our talk about art and literacy. A poetically informed analysis enabled us to see how poetry may present (Cahnmann-Taylor, 2003) as empirical evidence. By writing it we commit to our desire to defamiliarize and disrupt commonplace ways of analyzing data, and inform our thinking about teaching, research, and the work we do as artists. To do such analysis is to understand design, findings, and theoretical contributions in new light. Poetic, visual and written analyses allowed us to speak to and between the lines, to "know" in unique ways (Cahnmann-Taylor, 2003), and to commit to our desire to say something freshly. From its inception, this study was energized with passion, commitment, and a dare to think and say that things could be otherwise. We could embrace the imaginative spaces all three of us inhabited—on the weekends in studios, in community art classes, and with like-minded others—as well as to open spaces where we practiced the freedom to speak about it.

Most importantly, we suggest that this study situates lingering in language—visual, linguistic, dramatic, musical—as key in developing an appreciation for the affordances that languages offer in not only what is said, but how something is said. As artists, we recognize the significance of lingering in the art itself, in the spaces where we make it, and in the conversations around which we create our work. We value the collective thought that emerges from such spaces. It is just this talking about our work that propels us into continued and motivated inquiry and makes us active listeners to each other's stories. As artists, we also linger in our studio spaces, reluctant to leave. While we're in our studios, long stretches of time seem like minutes; we are lost in the world of making. Even when we are forced to leave, we linger in the thoughts of how to work with our art when we return.

CONCLUSION

The way to turn fifty
Is to kill off the light
And begin over
In slow motion

—David Allan Evans, 1976

This study arose from our conversations with each other about our passion and commitment to the arts as part of our own scholarship and as part of our understandings of literacy as a semiotic process of meaning-making. The above short excerpt from a longer poem by Evans provides us with a final metaphor that defines the future of our work as researchers and artists. Now that we have begun to identify the significance of the arts to our personal and professional lives and named ourselves as artists, we can begin over in slow motion, through continued and longitudinal study, to look closely at ourselves as artists and literacy researchers. Greene (2001) argued that "'education'... is the process of enabling persons to become different" and that it is through the arts that we may come to see the world anew. To participate in fresh perspectives, she wrote, "the learner must break with the taken-for-granted...and look through the lenses of various ways of knowing, seeing, and feeling in a conscious endeavor to impose different orders upon experience" (p. 5). As literacy researchers and artists, we argue that significance resides in our own willingness to accept inquiry-as-risk, to forego the comfort of our privilege, and to trust that knowledge can be made in unknown spaces and through tentative practices. In this way, we situate this analytical autoethnography as an ethical project in which we engage vulnerabilities in order to perceive freshly—or, as St. Pierre (1997) said, "to produce different knowledge and to produce knowledge differently" (p. 175).

REFERENCES

Albers, P. (2007). Visual discourse analysis: An introduction to the analysis of school-generated visual texts. In D. W. Rowe, R. T. Jiménez, D. L. Compton, D. K. Dickinson, Y. Kim, K. M. Leander, & V. J. Risko (Eds.), *56th Yearbook of the National Reading Conference* (pp. 81-95). Oak Creek, WI: NRC.

Albers, P., & Frederick, T. (2009). Literacy (re)marks: A study of seven teachers' visual texts across time. In V. J. Risko, D. L. Compton, D. K. Dickinson, M. Hundley, R. T. Jiménez, K. M. Leander, D. W. Rowe, & Y. Kim (Eds.), *58th Yearbook of the National Reading Conference* (pp. 112-128). Oak Creek, WI: NRC.

Albers, P., Frederick, T., & Cowan, K. (2010). Visual conversations: A study of the visual texts of elementary grade students. In D. L. Compton, D. K. Dickinson, M. Hundley, R. T. Jiménez, K. M. Leander, D. W. Rowe, Y. Kim, & V. J. Risko, (Eds.), *59th Yearbook of the National Reading Conference* (pp. 234-260). Oak Creek, WI: NRC.

Albers, P., Harste, J. C., Vander Zanden, S., & Felderman, C. (2008). Using popular culture to promote critical literacy practices. In Y. Kim, V. J. Risko, D. L. Compton, D. K. Dickinson, M. Hundley, R. T. Jiménez, K. M. Leander, & D. W. Rowe (Eds.), *57th Yearbook of the National Reading Conference* (pp. 70-83). Oak Creek, WI: NRC.

Albers, P., Holbrook, T., & Harste, J. C. (2010). Talking trade: Literacy researchers as practicing artists. *Journal of Adolescent & Adult Literacy, 54*(3), 164-171.

Anderson, L. (2006). Analytic autoethnography. *Journal of Contemporary Ethnography, 35*(4), 373-395.

Cahnmann, M. (2003). The craft, practice, and possibility of poetry in educational research. *Educational Researcher, 32*(3), 29-36.

Cryle, P. (2000) The Kama Sutra as curriculum. In C. O'Farrell, D. Meadmore, E. McWilliam, & C. Symes (Eds.), *Taught Bodies* (pp. 7-25). New York, NY: Peter Lang.

Davies, B., Dormer, S., Gannon, S., Laws, C., Rocco, S., Taguchi, H. L., & McCann, H. (2001). Becoming schoolgirls: The ambivalent project of subjectification. *Gender and Education, 13*(2), 167–182.

Enriquez, G. (2011, November). Embodiments of struggle: Examining the melancholy, loss, and interactions with print of two Adolescent struggling readers. Paper presented at the Literacy Research Association Annual Conference, Jacksonville, FL.

Evans, D. (1976). *Train windows*. Athens, OH: Ohio University Press.

Friedrich, P. (1996). The culture in poetry and the poetry in culture. In E. V. Daniel and J. M. Peck (Eds.). *Culture/Contexture: Explorations in anthropology and literary studies* (pp. 37–57). Berkeley, CA: University of California Press.

Geertz, C. (1973). *The interpretation of cultures*. New York, NY: Basic Books.

Glesne, C. (1997). That rare feeling: Re-presenting research through poetic transcription. *Qualitative Inquiry, 3*(2), 202-221.

Greene, M. (1988). *The dialectic of freedom*. New York, NY: Teachers College Press.

Greene, M. (2000). *Releasing the imagination: Essays on education, the arts, and social change*. San Francisco, CA: Jossey-Bass.

Greene, M. (2001). *Variations on a blue guitar: The Lincoln Center Institute lectures on aesthetic education*. New York, NY: Teachers College Press.

Johnson, E. (2011, November). *"I'm not sure if you'll like it": Embodying and confounding canonical text connections in high school English*. Paper presented at the Literacy Research Association Annual Conference, Jacksonville, FL.

Jones, S. R. (2011, November). *Round robin reading: The embodiment of print reading pedagogies*. Paper presented at the Literacy Research Association Annual Conference, Jacksonville, FL.

Kaufmann, J. (2005). Autotheory: An ethnographic reading of Foucault. *Qualitative Inquiry, 11*(4), 576-587.

Lakoff, G. (1999). *Philosophy in the flesh: A talk with George Lakoff*. Retrieved from http://www.edge.org/3rd_culture/lakoff/lakoff_p1.html

Lakoff, G. & Johnson, M. (1999). *Philosophy in the flesh: The embodied mind and its challenge to western thought*. New York, NY: Basic Books.

Lussier-Ley, C. (2010). Dialoguing with body: A self study in relational pedagogy through embodiment and the therapeutic relationship. *Qualitative Report, 15*(1), 197-214.

Maynard, K., & Cahnmann-Taylor, M. (2010). Anthropology at the edge of words: Where poetry and ethnography meet. *Anthropology and Humanism, 35*(1), 2–19.

Neilsen, L. (2004). Provoked by astonishment: Seeing and understanding in inquiry. In A. L. Cole, L. Neilsen, J. G. Knowles, & T. C. Luciani (Eds.), *Provoked by art: Theorizing arts-informed research* (pp. 52-61). Halifax, Nova Scotia: Backalong Books.

Neilsen Glenn, L. (in press). *Homing*. In S. Thomas, A. Cole, & G. Knowles (Eds.). *The art of poetic inquiry*. Retrieved from http://learningthreshold.blogspot.com/2011/02/excerpt-from-homing-chapter-on-poetic.html

Prendergast, M. Gouzouasis, P., Leggo, C., & Irwin, R. L. (2009). A haiku suite: The importance of music making in the lives of secondary school students. *Music Education Research, 11*(3), 303-317.

Scott, J. (1992) Experience. In J. Butler & J. Scott (Eds.), *Feminists theorize the political* (pp. 22–40). New York, NY: Routledge.

Spry, T. (2001). Performing autoethnography: An embodied methodological praxis. *Qualitative Inquiry, 7*(6), 706-732.

St. Pierre, E. A. (1997). Methodology in the fold and the irruption of transgressive data. *International Journal of Qualitative Studies in Education, 10*(2), 175-189.

Willig, C. (2001). *Introducing qualitative research in psychology: Adventures in theory and methods*. Maidenhead, England: Open University Press.

Video-Study Group: A Context to Cultivate Professional Relationships

Lynn E. Shanahan
Andrea L. Tochelli
University at Buffalo/SUNY

Research indicates that effective professional development (PD) is intensive, sustained over long periods of time (e.g., Darling-Hammond & McLaughlin, 1996; Horn & Little, 2010), and incorporates modeling, opportunities for collegial inquiry, and feedback (Joyce & Showers, 1995). Furthermore, effective PD entails teachers working together as an inquiry community to generate knowledge (Cochran-Smith & Lytle, 1999) around a specific literacy practice. Collaborative learning based on the active participation of teachers is more likely to lead to teacher change in the classroom (Sherin & van Es, 2009).

Relationships and collegial support within learning communities are often the main determinants of change, retention, increased professionalism, and engagement levels (Daly, 2010). Strong professional relationships "support the transfer of tacit, non-routine, and complex knowledge; joint problem solving; and the development of coordinated approaches" (Daly, 2010, p. 4). However, work within learning communities can also be problematic (Fernandex, Cannon, & Chokski, 2003; Grossman, Wineburg, & Woolworth, 2001) if teachers engage in *contrived collegiality*, which is a type of collaboration that maintains the status quo, instead of the construction of new learning (Hargreaves, 1994).

In recent decades, video-study groups (VSGs) have become a collaborative inquiry space used in PD. Video can serve as a PD tool to view one's own teaching or student learning as part of a knowledge-building activity (Pea & Lindgren, 2008). Video analysis has been shown to promote reflection and dialogue about teaching practice with both preservice and inservice teachers (Harford & MacRuairc, 2008; Harford, MacRuairc, & McCartan, 2010; Rosaen, Degnan, VanStratt & Zietlow, 2004) as well as changes in instructional practice (Rich & Hannafin, 2008, 2009; Sherin & van Es, 2009; van Es, 2009). Collaborative intellectual communities, such as VSGs, can be a fertile context for teachers' construction of knowledge and we have much to learn about how to foster the professional relationships within these communities to maximize teacher learning of complex concepts.

Knowing that social interactions and the development of professional relationships are instrumental in teachers' construction of knowledge, we asked the following research question: In what ways, if any, did teachers' analysis of their own and their colleagues' implementation of explicit strategy instruction facilitate the development of professional relationships in a VSG?

This study stems from a larger qualitative study where the goal was to analyze, interpret, and theorize about the use of VSGs for teacher development when teachers independently analyzed their own video prior to attending the PD. In the larger study we asked: What impact would this structure of VSGs have on teachers' learning and their development of professional relationships? Due to space restrictions, we present only the findings related to how teachers developed professional relationships in the VSG.

REVIEW OF LITERATURE

Socially Situated Learning

Our work is situated in several theoretical perspectives. First, we draw on Vygotsky's (1978) assertion that higher psychological processes are socially contextualized and internalized through social interaction. We hold that the social interactions and instructional contexts are instrumental in the teachers' construction of new knowledge, development of metacognitive acts of thinking, and relationships with one another. Furthermore, we draw from Lave and Wenger's (1991) *communities of practice*, which is defined as "a set of relations among persons, activity, and world, over time and in relation with other tangential and overlapping communities of practice" (p. 98).

In this PD model, learners are engaged in a community of practice to learn from one another and a mentor. In our case, the mentor, as well as members of the VSG, work within a community of practice in order to engage in a social practice centered on strategy instruction. This model is based around apprenticeship. However, Lave and Wenger (1991) expand the idea of a more traditional thought of mentor-mentee relationship to include multiple apprentices working with a mentor. Within this article, our focus is on the interactions among multiple apprentices and not their interactions with their mentor who facilitated the PD.

Social coparticipation in the community is focused on the relationship between learning and the social situation where it occurs. Learning with others in an apprenticeship relationship therefore occurs in Lave and Wenger's (1991) model through *legitimate peripheral participation*. Apprentices learn, through varying types of participation, the skills necessary to allow them to fully participate in the practice. Particularly important is the identity of the individual in bringing their personal diversity into the community, especially with the other communities of practice he/she is involved in as well as the changing identity developed as this individual becomes a member of the new community of practice (Wenger, 1998).

Critical Components of Explicit Strategy Instruction

The teachers and administrators involved in designing the PD chose to focus on the development of strategic readers. For this study, teachers used Almasi and Fullerton's (2012) Critical Elements of Strategy Instruction (CESI), which draws on the work of Pearson and colleagues (e.g., Fielding & Pearson, 1994; Pearson & Dole, 1987; Pearson & Gallagher, 1983), as the instructional framework. The components of the CESI include: (a) creating a safe and risk-free environment, (b) providing explicit instruction, (c) reducing cognitive processing demands, and (d) creating opportunities for students to verbalize strategy use.

METHODS

The larger study was conducted over a 2-year period from 2008–2010 in Sunnyside School District. The district is approximately 15-square miles, and borders a mid-sized northeastern city. Sunnyside District is comprised of two elementary schools, one middle school, and one high school: each elementary school is composed of grades K–5; the middle school consists of grades 6–8 and the high school is home for grades 9–12. Together, the four schools serve approximately 3,000 students.

Participants

Participants in this case study (Merriam, 2009) were one male and eight female inservice teachers, who ranged in experience from 6–18 years, and all had master's degrees. The participants were employed by the same school district, but worked in two different elementary schools. Five teachers taught in Oak School. Oak School qualified for Title I funding and serviced a culturally and economically diverse population. In contrast, four teachers taught at Cedar School, which was repeatedly recognized as one of the top-ranked elementary schools.

Table 1. Study Participants

Participants	School	Gender	Certifications	Years Teaching	Current Grade Position
Group 1					
Stephanie	Oak	Female	Elementary Education Reading Specialist	8	Reading Specialist-2-5
Dan	Cedar	Male	Elementary Education English Literature	11	Grade 5
Robin	Cedar	Female	Elementary Education Special Education Concentration in Reading	6	Looping 3-4
Group 2					
Donna	Oak	Female	Elementary Education Special Education	18	3, 4, 5 special education
Nancy	Oak	Female	Elementary Education Special Education Gifted Education	10	Gifted-all grades
Liz	Oak	Female	Elementary Education	10	Grade 3
Group 3					
Kelly	Cedar	Female	Elementary Education English 7-12 Reading Specialist	11	Looping grades 1-2
Sarah	Cedar	Female	Elementary Education	13	K, 1, 2 multiage
Caroline	Oak	Female	Elementary Education	6	1-2 multiage

Figure 1. Partner Analysis Example of Caroline Time-Stamping Sarah's Video

Explicit Teaching Element	Explanation	
	Time Observed	Statement Made
What: What is the <u>content</u> being taught?	•	use schema & pictures to give us clues
	•	use context clues
What is the <u>strategy</u> being taught?	4:04 →	Today we will learn a reading strategy called "inferencing"
Goals of lesson	21:52 →	What was the name of the strategy called? Share the name of the strategy. Inferencing.
	23:14 →	When we use our brains & clues from the story. We are making an inference.
How: How is the content being taught in the lesson? For example: modeled, talk-aloud, working in pairs/trios.	• →	think aloud
	→	modeling by charting info
	8:41 →	modeling - I'm going to stop right now and let you know what I'm thinking
How is the strategy being taught in the lesson?	10:07 →	models plugging in thinking to the inference formula anchor chart
	10:49 →	think aloud - what is going on in my head right now
	12:07 →	I'm going to share with you what I'm thinking
	15:23 →	Think aloud... "I'm thinking"
When: State when to use the strategy.	5:30 →	Sometimes authors do this in a book & you have to make an inference
	6:30 →	As I read
	7:00 →	When I read, I don't just say the words. I have to think
Where: State where to use the strategy.		
Why: State why to use the strategy.	7:16 • →	There's no point in reading a book if I just say da. da. da. I need to learn by understanding.
	24:16 →	An inference helps us better understand the story.
Verbalization: Time used to verbalize about strategy use.	end of lesson	pair talk aloud
Reduce Processing Demands: Make the abstract concept concrete.		→ Pictionary game
		→ Anchor chart of inference formula

Teachers worked in groups of three for the VSGs. Table 1 outlines the composition of the three groups, including the specific information about the participants' certifications, years of teaching, school where employed, and grade levels taught.

Video-Study Group Preparation and Context

Prior to attending the meeting, teachers learned the CESI, analyzed their own baseline video using CESI, set goals, and collaboratively planned their next lesson. With goals set from the first two PD meetings, all nine teachers signed up for a time to record their strategy lessons, which were video- and audio-recorded by a research assistant. Two weeks prior to attending the VSG, each participant received a partner analysis packet that contained three: (a) DVDs (i.e., one lesson per group member), (b) partner analysis forms (see Figure 1), (c) Gradual Release charts (Pearson & Gallagher, 1983), (d) Scaffolded Instructional Support for Strategic Processing charts (Almasi, 2003, p. 63), and (e) directions for playing their DVDs. The school district paid the teachers for 3 hours of video analysis outside of the school day.

Because previous research on the use of video for learning indicated that viewers who did not have a task when viewing typically focused on the teacher's personality (Miller & Zhou, 2007; Tochon, 2007) or were overwhelmed with the amount of information available through video (Newell & Walter, 1981), we asked teachers to view the video and independently time-stamp (see Figure 1) when they observed themselves or their colleagues using a component of CESI. Additionally, both the Gradual Release and the Scaffolded Instructional Support charts were used to self-identify where their lesson fell within both constructs.

In the VSG context, the teachers, who were all novices in implementing CESI and apprentices in the community of practice, sat together in groups of three with one laptop per group, their partner analysis packets, and were given the following directions: "Now what I would like you to do is get back into your original groups of three. Then I'd like you to look at that partner analysis and start to give each other feedback as to the implementation of the model." Teachers were also encouraged to replay and discuss time-stamped moments of video.

Researchers' Roles

Up to this point in our paper, we have presented as one voice. In order to effectively communicate our roles as researchers, however, we briefly switch to third person. The first author, Lynn, assumed two roles in the study, that of researcher and mentor. Because Lynn was a former elementary teacher, she was interested in examining ways video could serve as a PD tool with experienced teachers to gain insight into their own pedagogical practices. With the help of a research assistant, Lynn collected, cataloged, and coded all data. With the goal of scrutinizing researcher subjectivity, she maintained a journal with initial impressions of data collection, and emerging patterns. In addition, to ensure trustworthiness, Lynn engaged Andrea as second author. Together they: (a) conducted data analysis using dual coding, (b) triangulated findings with multiple data sources from multiple participants, and (c) member-checked findings.

Data Collection and Analysis

This smaller case study occurred 5 weeks into the PD on March 20, 2009. The VSG session ranged from 38-41 minutes in duration. The videos analyzed were the teachers' first strategy lessons after learning the CESI. The primary data sources consisted of: (a) written descriptive field notes of strategy lessons and the VSG session; (b) audio data and transcripts of the VSG session and strategy lessons; (c) video data and transcripts of strategy lessons; and (d) artifacts such as teacher lesson plans, photographs from strategy lessons, partner analysis sheets, and gradual release sheets. Post interviews were used as secondary data sources.

Using inductive analysis (Strauss & Corbin, 1990), data were analyzed in a recursive manner. Throughout the coding process, double-coding (Miles & Huberman, 1984) was used to establish reliability. Two coders independently analyzed and coded the data. Then the coders compared results and discussed each observation until agreement was reached.

The analysis began at a microlevel and concluded with macrocodes that led to our themes. We began our first level of analysis by individually labeling and defining the concepts within the transcripts (e.g., specific attainment, specific improvements). At this microanalysis level we identified 42 labels as our initial codes. In the second level of analysis we moved to more interpretative levels of analyses, where we classified the previously labeled concepts. We identified three categories: (a) cultivating professional relationships, (b) constructing knowledge through peripheral participation, and (c) developing a shared purpose. For the purposes of this paper we discuss the category of cultivating professional relationships.

Once these categories were established, we returned to the transcripts and recoded them by collapsing the codes into the three categories. The teachers' topics of discussions became the unit of analysis within each category because this allowed us to see the depth of conversation and understand the ways in which teachers developed social relationships and group identity in VSG. A unit of analysis began when a teacher started the discussion around a topic and ended when there was a shift in topic. Drawing on conversation analysis (Sacks, Schegloff, & Jefferson, 1974), we extended our analysis and counted: (a) the number of conversations, (b) the turns-of-talk, and (c) who started each topic of conversation. Utilizing conversation analysis afforded us the opportunity to better understand the group interaction and structure.

FINDINGS

Risk and Vulnerability

When using video as a mediational tool, it was evident that the presence of video did influence the relationship and interactions among participants. Most teachers described their initial feelings about recording and viewing videos as involving a sense of risk as sharing made them feel vulnerable, even within this group of well-respected teachers within the district. Stephanie explained:

> I think that all of us were sensitive to the fact that the video made us feel vulnerable. In the beginning we were all a little more careful about our comments and looked for positives. I think that this became a lot more natural and honest as we built trust with each other. Ultimately, I think the video really helped us to deepen our collaborative relationships because we were inviting each other into our lessons and we began to rely on each other to nurture our growth. It was exciting to see our colleagues teach and experiment. I think it challenged us to push ourselves.

Capturing teachers' lessons as they were learning a new instructional method situated them in a risky position. As Dan said, "watching someone teach is—dare I say it—intimate. Like most forms of intimacy, though, you need to exert a certain amount of energy to keep the system going." He expanded by saying that the "person has made a sacrifice which has to be honored by giving them something back; specific praise...honest appraisal...looking for the good but always being curiously mindful of what could be better." We specifically focus our discussion on the findings related to

Figure 2. Video-Study Group Community of Practice Model

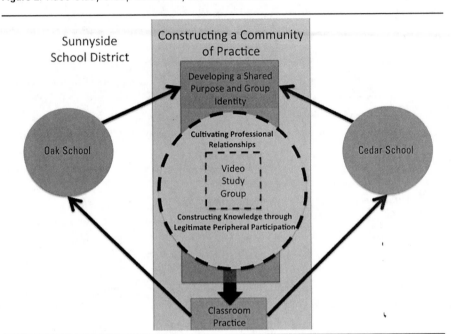

cultivating these professional relationships within the VSG Community of Practice Model (see Figure 2).

Cultivating Professional Relationships

Teachers' conversations cultivated relationships with one another by: (a) sharing information to provide both the context for their video-recorded lesson as well as for their classrooms, students, schools, and the district; (b) providing positive feedback (i.e., specific attainments and approvals) more so than stating areas of improvements; and (c) sharing feedback in collective terms. First, we describe how teachers exchanged information that was specific to their lessons, classrooms, or schools to develop relationships with one another. Then we discuss how this sharing was not consistent across all groups.

Information exchange. Information exchange (IE) was defined as a time when the teachers shared information to provide the context for the lesson that was video-recorded (Wenger, White, & Smith, 2009). Five different types of IE based on inquires from other group members were identified. Information was shared about the: (a) lesson, (b) classroom, (c) students, (d) school, and (e) school district. For instance, in one conversation coded as an IE, Stephanie inquired about whether or not the students had seen the graphic organizer Dan used. He responded with "actually no. The graphic organizer they hadn't seen before." This provided the group members with background knowledge about Dan's students' familiarity with materials used in his lesson and allowed the group to contextualize his pedagogical decisions.

Next, we provide several examples of student and classroom IEs. Those that focused on students typically led to discussions of student achievement.

Caroline:	But I think you did a great job.
Kelly:	I think so too. Absolutely.
Caroline:	I did not know those were kindergarteners.
Sarah:	Yeah mostly kindergarteners.

Prior to this part of the discussion, Caroline had remarked on how well Sarah did in her think-aloud with her students. When Sarah shared that her group in that lesson was mostly kindergarteners, Caroline was shocked at how she was able to conduct a think-aloud about inferring with this age group and how attentive they were during the lesson.

Another example of an IE was when teachers asked one another about their classrooms. Group 3 took turns explaining the format of their classrooms, including number of students and classroom set-ups. Below is an excerpt of an IE focused on classroom information where it is revealed that the children are "loopers." Looping is a structure where one teacher follows the same cohort of children for 2 years.

Caroline:	They're all loopers?
Kelly:	Mm hmm. Absolutely.
Caroline:	Now how many do you have?
Kelly:	25.
Caroline:	That's a lot!
Kelly:	Yeah. Pretty big group.

Each of these teachers was in a different teaching situation within the two elementary schools. By sharing the format of their classrooms, including the number of students, their co-teaching situations, and the grade levels, it allowed group members to understand each other's classroom context. Being familiar with one another's classroom helped them build relationships through understanding their similarities and differences (Wenger, 1998; Wenger et al., 2009). In sharing information about the schools they worked in, group members explained aspects of the school's culture as well as administrative practices and expectations. Given that all of the teachers were members of the same school district but from different schools, IEs raised their awareness about district expectations and current practices at the two schools. All of these discussions where information was exchanged assisted in the development of relationships.

In order to further understand the function of IEs within the VSG, we analyzed the talk further by calculating frequency counts for each of the five types of IEs. Figure 3 depicts the total number of IEs by each VSG. Notice the difference in IEs across groups, with Groups 1 and 3 having the most IEs and Group 2 the least. When we saw the difference in how teachers in the different groups spent time contextualizing their teaching (e.g., lessons, students, and classroom), we decided it was necessary to explore why two groups of teachers spent more time engaged in these types of conversations. Upon reviewing the data and earlier research, we found that previous research indicated that proximity and the perception that others are similar to you impacted interactions within communities (Borgatti & Cross, 2003). First, we already knew that the teachers from Oak and Cedar Schools taught very different populations of students, thus, sharing information about their students and classroom became important in exploring similarities between the teachers from different schools.

Second, when revisiting VSG membership, we identified a difference between Group 2, and Groups 1 and 3. The members of Groups 1 and 3 were not all from the same elementary school. Consequently, there were two different school communities of practice, Cedar and Oak, within the groups that engaged in more IEs. Conversely, in Group 2: (a) all members taught at Oak Elementary School, (b) they had closer proximity with one another because their classrooms were near one another on the second floor, and (c) in the first week of PD, these three teachers worked together on video analysis of their baseline lessons. As a result of group membership, Groups 1 and 3 held more conversations that familiarized and contextualized all of the group members to each teaching context and pedagogical practices, with the ultimate goal being to build trusting relationships (Daly, 2010; Lave & Wenger, 1991; Moolenaar & Sleegers, 2010; Wenger, 1998). Because Group 2 worked together in the same school and in close proximity to one another, group members had already developed relationships where they were familiar with the type of information the other groups exchanged. Therefore, Group 2 spent more time in the VSG discussing issues related to changing their school's literacy instruction based on the CESI.

Feedback: A way to value one another. Teachers provided one another with feedback stating specific attainment, approval, or specific improvement. Specific attainments provided descriptive remarks about successful implementation of CESI, while approvals were positive expressions of support. Specific attainment and approvals were considered positive verbal feedback that functioned to reinforce a particular teaching practice or indicate mutual cooperation and support (Murray, Ma, & Mazur, 2009). On the other hand, specific improvements provided information about areas for growth for a group member. First, we describe the constructs of specific attainments and approvals, and then specific improvements.

Approval and specific attainments. Statements of approval tended to be approximately a sentence long, and contained a positive statement of support. The following statements serve as examples: "It was a great lesson" (said by Stephanie to Dan) and "I was super-impressed with both of your lessons" (said by Caroline to both Sarah and Kelly). In contrast, the specific attainment statements provided an example from the lesson. We defined specific attainment statements as points in the

Figure 3. Number of Total Information Exchange Conversations Held by Each Group during the VSG Meeting

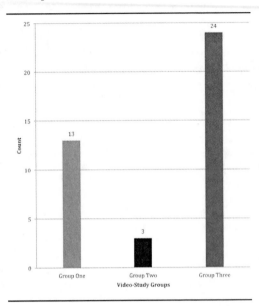

VSG discussions when teachers specifically told their partners about components of the CESI they had effectively included in the lesson. The following is an example of Robin providing Stephanie with a specific attainment regarding her visualizing lesson:

Robin: And you also showed them the difference. Like in something like using your schema like you said, "This is where I had a lot of schema on one of the articles I read." And then you said, "Then this one I really didn't know much." So I couldn't really picture it. And I like when you related it to a movie.

Stephanie: Mm hmm. Like it is a movie.

Robin: Yeah. Like a movie in our head.

Robin used a specific example from Stephanie's video that was helpful to her students learning the strategy. This specific attainment statement told Stephanie what she was doing well in relation to learning the CESI and allowed her to further engage in the community of practice, moving towards full participation (Lave & Wenger, 1991).

Specific attainment statements were also used as an opportunity to share both a precise statement and a different opinion. In the following example, Caroline provided Sarah feedback regarding her use of a wordless picture book to teach kindergarteners inferring:

Caroline: I don't know if I would have used a picture book without words to do that kind of lesson.

Sarah: Mm hmm.

Caroline: For kids so young.

Sarah: Mm hmm.

Caroline: But it was great! ["it" meaning the use of a picture book to teach the strategy]

While Caroline stated that she would not use that material in her classroom, she recognized the positive practice of one of her fellow teachers, which served to create a positive relationship with her as well as to recognize the differences between them and the legitimacy of each of their participation in the community (Lave & Wenger, 1991; Wenger, 1998).

Specific improvements. Statements surrounding specific improvements made by group members were couched in a positive manner. Members of Group 3 did not make any specific improvement statements. However, the statements made by members of Group 1 showed that they attempted to make these comments in the least harmful way possible. For example:

Dan: Alright, I thought your lesson was very interesting (pause) to me.

Robin: Uh oh.

Dan: I was puzzled by it.

In the excerpt just mentioned, Dan carefully pointed to the lack of clarity in Robin's lesson as an area in need of specific improvement by using words like "interesting" and "puzzled." Below in Dan's first and second turns of talk, he continued his specific improvement statement by questioning his own understanding. He concludes in his fourth turn of talk by providing Robin with an approval statement regarding her use of why her students would use the strategy:

Dan: Why is it important for you to understand the elements, what makes up a folktale? Yes. That was the question. Right. That kind of stuff. Um, but I was, the section where I was confused was here. Or, or this part.

Robin: OK.

Dan: What I wasn't sure, what the strategy was versus the content.

Robin: Well it was text structure.

Dan: Text structure.

Stephanie: Mm hmm.

Dan: OK. When, when she [mentor] came up with, when she came up with the um, graphic before on your lesson, on your, on the celebration, I was like, oh okay. I kind of see it now.

Dan did not come straight out and say that he felt that Robin was unclear in her teaching of the strategy of text structure. He began by saying he was puzzled by her lesson. In his follow-up explanation he was hesitant in his wording. When Robin confirmed that her lesson was on the text structure, he referred back to a portion of the video the mentor showed earlier in the PD. He stated "I kind of see it now," backing off from his original claim that he was puzzled. When member-checking the interpretations, Dan acknowledged the specific improvement statement:

> This is only my attempt to take others seriously and respect what they do by understanding it. The truth is I was trying to do two things, trying to understand the whole skill/content/strategy concept better and be a help to her. It was way too early in the process for me to come out 'swinging' like I know everything, but by the same token, I don't believe anything is gained by just saying good job over and over.

Because this VSG occurred 5 weeks into the PD and Dan and Robin work in the same school building in close proximity (Borgatti & Cross, 2003) to one another, he was trying to both build and preserve his relationship with Robin. Dan explained that he knew Robin "socially but had near zero experience with her professionally" and it was his "goal to build a relationship with Robin." In addition, as Dan and Robin were grouped with another teacher from a different school building, they were beginning to form a relationship within the VSG community of practice and Dan did not want to outwardly critique his colleague, wanting instead to promote a trusting and positive community (e.g., Daly, 2010; Lave & Wenger, 1991; Moolenaar & Sleegers, 2010).

Group 2: Providing feedback differently. While Group 2 members' approvals functioned in similar ways to those of Groups 1 and 3, in being short statements of positive support, their statements of specific attainments and specific improvements were quite different (see Figure 2). In five of the conversations, the specific attainment was constructed around the collective "we." For example (italics indicates words emphasized):

Donna: And I think we were all really good at modeling [the how], I mean.

Liz: And watch me do it.

Later in the VSG they also discussed their success with other parts of the CESI with a group, not individual focus.

Liz:	I think *we* all, I think it's funny because *all three of us* were good at: the how and the what. *We* all had the visuals. *We* all had the concrete.
Donna:	Concrete.
Liz:	*We* all modeled, *we* read aloud.

Unlike the other two groups, this group of teachers—all from the same school—recognized the positives in what they collectively did well. Along the same lines, when the group discussed specific improvements, these were all phrased in the collective "we."

Nancy:	And maybe that's something that *we* need to work on—is to get them to verbalize it throughout.
Liz:	Throughout the lesson, not just in your closure.

All five of Group 2's specific improvement comments were phrased as "we" statements. This collective use of "we" is pointing out that all group members needed to improve in the same area and they all had the same strengths. The collective perspective positioned them as members of a community of practice working together to improve instruction (e.g., Wenger et al., 2009).

Summarizing feedback. Figure 4 depicts the specific attainment, approval, and specific improvement conversations held by all three groups. These numbers indicated that Groups 1 and 3 shared more positive forms of feedback and less specific improvements than Group 2. As indicated earlier, although Group 2 shared more specific improvements, they were all couched in the collective "we," as an aspect of the instruction they all needed to improve.

Conversations such as these functioned to develop a trusting and positive relationship with one another through the sharing of specific attainment and approvals, and collectively stating areas of improvement (Daly, 2010; Moolenaar & Sleegers, 2010). As creating an environment of mutual respect is an integral part of developing a community of practice (Lave & Wenger, 1991; Wenger et al., 2009), it was necessary for these teachers to participate in these conversations. The use of "we" in a number of Group 2 members' specific attainment statements as well as all of their specific

Figure 4. Number of Feedback Conversations Held by Each Group during the VSG Meeting

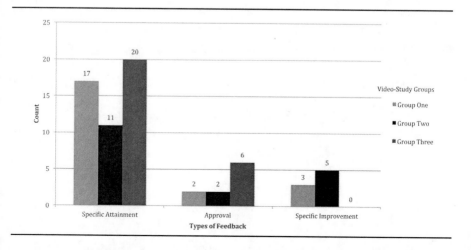

improvement statements indicates that they built a community of practice with one another and were setting collective goals for each of them to work towards for the next video-recorded lessons. All of the three VSGs verified what Murray et al. (2009) found, regarding teachers' unwillingness to provide feedback that critiques their colleagues' practices, as the specific improvements that were brought up were very few (i.e., 8) and were either couched in a less harmful manner (i.e., Group 1) or phrased as a "we" statement (i.e., Group 3).

More evidence of the teachers' unwillingness to critique specific areas of growth in one another's teaching and their desire to have the mentor take on that role were evident in the post interviews. Liz expressed that the feedback was "more general comments about the process" and that she "hadn't gotten a lot of constructive criticism from VSG members." Nancy, who was a mentor to new teachers, commented on providing constructive criticism:

> It's a hard role to take on. And I had asked people, "Do you want me to be a critical friend?" And they're like "yes." Just in my, you know, in my mentoring role I have said to new teachers, "I'm your mentor. Do you want me to be critical, do you want me to be nice or do you want me to be a critical friend?" And I've been a critical friend to improve their lessons.

Teachers commented that in most cases they did not feel comfortable entering the role of providing critical feedback, thus, had not received a lot of constructive criticism from their peers. They preferred that the mentor provided the critical feedback so that they could remain a "group of learners that were all on the same level."

DISCUSSION

The teachers who participated in the VSGs developed a community of practice in which they cultivated professional relationships with other group members. Numerous prominent learning theorists maintain that learning is a fundamentally social process (e.g., Lave & Wenger, 1991; Piaget, 1932; Vygotsky, 1978). However, PD does not often plan for ways to cultivate these professional relationships. Research points to the importance of strong professional relationships to support the transfer of complex knowledge within a school system so that coordinated teaching approaches can be developed (Daly, 2010). Further, relationships and collegial support are vital for change and engagement (Daly, 2010). In our VSG community of practice model, we acknowledge that these teachers were participants in multiple communities: (a) district, (b) elementary building, and (c) strategy instruction PD.

In the community of practice model, (Figure 2), notice the two different elementary schools from one district are placed outside the rectangular "developing a community of practice" for the VSG. This was an intentional placement in that although these schools were in the same district, they functioned very differently and serviced dissimilar populations of students. Prior to this PD, the participants had relatively little time to learn about one another. Consequently, in order to cultivate a professional community of practice, they worked on understanding one another within the VSG. It was evident that those groups of teachers who came into the VSG from different schools spent more time learning about one another so that they might build a trusting relationship within this community where they could support one another. Conversely, the other group of teachers who came from the same building did not have to do this type of work.

The desire to develop trust by being cooperative and supportive of one another, through: (a) positive feedback, (b) specific attainment statements, (c) lack of feedback on specific improvement statements, and (d) couching improvement statements in a "we" format, led to collegial conversations or conversations that were positive in nature. This finding is similar to Wilson and Berne's findings (1999) that teachers have limited practice providing constructive feedback to one another, so they tend to be positive. Although collegial conversations are a strength in developing communities of practice because there is minimal competition (Dufour, Dufour, & Eaker, 2008), it can also be a limitation in that these teachers may not push each other's thinking and understandings. Not providing constructive feedback could impede progress toward the shared vision or goal for the group. Hence, having a mentor within the group who attends to misunderstandings, aspects of practice, and challenges teachers to think differently about their current practices may be instrumental in moving participants towards higher levels of learning.

Knowing the importance of having time to cultivate relationships led us to reflect on job-embedded PD. In other words, PD that facilitates "teacher learning that is grounded in day-to-day teaching practice and is designed to enhance teachers' content-specific instructional practices with the intent of improving students learning" (Croft, Coggshall, Dolan, Powers, & Killion, 2010, p. 9). Moreover, this view of PD supports the idea that PD is social, situated, and distributed among colleagues (Croft et al., 2010). If this important view is taken up in schools and teachers are unwilling to be critical, then the role of the mentor is extremely important to advance the learning process.

Our research indicates that how a mediational tool like video is used will shape what is learned and will influence the interactions within the VSG. Thus, the influence of the structure of the VSG needs to be considered when analyzing how these teachers' cultivated professional relationships. One purpose of using the partner-analysis sheet that asked teachers to view video and time-stamp components of the CESI prior to attending the VSG was to align the structure of VSG with previous research that indicates that having a focus when viewing video is essential (Miller, & Zhou, 2007; Newell & Walter, 1981; Tochon, 2007). Because teachers engaged in time-stamping analysis of CESI prior to attending the VSG, they had already begun to reflect on their practice as well as their colleagues. Developing a better understanding about how different formats of VSG influences teacher learning is essential in understanding how to structure VSG.

Several questions mentors may want to ask are: (1) How can PD be structured to provide time to foster relationships across those communities?, and (2) How can relationships be built so teachers are comfortable functioning as critical friends? Facilitating strong networks within communities is essential for increased professionalism, sustained learning, and change (Daly, 2010; Cochran-Smith & Lytle, 1999), thus, we argue that these are questions to consider.

We would be remiss if we did not point to several limitations of this study. Because this analysis was only one of three VSG sessions within our larger PD model, we do not know yet if teachers became more critical as they developed relationships over time. This particular VSG occurred 5 weeks into the PD process, thus, maybe participants were not yet comfortable providing critical feedback. Further, an important point to remember when interpreting these findings is that these teachers were all experienced and volunteered to participate; they willingly put themselves in a vulnerable learning situation. Participants who are not experienced teachers or who are unwillingly required to engage in a VSG may not develop professional relationships at the level that the teachers in our study formed with one another.

<h1 style="text-align:center">REFERENCES</h1>

Almasi, J. (2003). *Teaching strategic processes in reading.* New York, NY: Guilford Press.

Almasi, J., & Fullerton, S. K. (2012). *Teaching strategic processes in reading* (2nd ed.). New York, NY: Guilford Press.

Borgatti, S. P., & Cross, R. (2003). A relational view of information seeking and learning in social networks. *Management Science, 49,* 432-445.

Cochran-Smith, M., & Lytle, S. L. (1999). Relationships of knowledge and practice: Teacher learning in communities. *Review of Research in Education, 24,* 249-305.

Croft, A., Coggshall, J. G., Dolan, M., Powers, E., & Killion, J. (2010). *Job-embedded professional development: What is it, who is responsible, and how to get it done well.* Retrieved from: www.tqsource.org/publications/ JEPD%20Issue%20Brief.pdf.

Daly, A. J. (2010). Mapping the terrain: Social network theory and educational change. In A. J. Daly (Ed.), *Social network theory and educational change* (pp. 1-16). Cambridge, MA: Harvard Education Press.

Darling-Hammond, L., & McLaughlin, M. W. (1996). Policies that support professional development in an era of reform. *Phi Delta Kappan, 76,* 597-604.

Dufour, R., Dufour, R., & Eaker, R. (2008). *Revisiting professional learning communities at work: New insights for improving schools.* Bloomington, IN: Solution Tree.

Fernandez, C., Cannon, J., & Chokski, S. (2003). A US-Japan lesson study collaboration reveals critical lenses for examining practice. *Teaching and Teacher Education, 19,* 171-185.

Fielding, L. G., & Pearson, P. D. (1994). Reading comprehension: What works. *Educational Leadership, 51*(5), 62-67.

Grossman, P., Wineburg, S., & Woolworth, S. (2001). Toward a theory of teacher community. *Teachers College Record, 103*(6), 942-1012.

Harford, J., & MacRuairc, G. (2008). Engaging student teachers in meaningful reflective practice. *Teaching and Teacher Education, 24,* 1884-1892.

Harford, J., MacRuairc, G., & McCartan, D. (2010). 'Lights, camera, reflection': Using peer video to promote reflective dialogue among student teachers. *Teacher Development, 14,* 57-68.

Hargreaves, A. (1994). *Changing teachers, changing times: Teachers' work and culture in the postmodern age.* New York, NY: Teachers College Press.

Horn, I. S., & Little, J. W. (2010). Attending to problems of practice: Routines and resources for professional learning in teachers' workplace interactions. *American Educational Research Journal, 47,* 181-217.

Joyce, B., & Showers, B. (1995). *Student achievement through staff development* (2nd ed.). New York, NY: Longman.

Lave, J., & Wenger, E. (1991). *Situated learning: Legitimate peripheral participation.* New York, NY: Cambridge University Press.

Merriam, S. B. (2009). *Qualitative research: A guide to design and implementation.* San Francisco, CA: John Wiley and Sons.

Miles, M. B., & Huberman, A. M. (1984). *Qualitative data analysis: A sourcebook of new methods.* Thousand Oaks, CA: Sage Publications.

Miller, K., & Zhou, X. (2007). Learning from classroom video: What makes it compelling and what makes it hard. In R. Goldmann, R. Pea, B. Barron, & S. J. Derry (Eds.), *Video research in the learning sciences* (pp. 321-334). Mahwah, NJ: Lawrence Erlbaum.

Moolenaar, N. M., & Sleegers, P. J. C. (2010). Social networks, trust, and innovation: The role of relationships in supporting an innovative climate in Dutch schools. In A. J. Daly (Ed.), *Social network theory and educational change* (pp. 97-114). Cambridge, MA: Harvard Education Press.

Murray, S., Ma, X., & Mazur, J. (2009). Effects of peer coaching on teachers' collaborative interactions and students' mathematic achievement. *Journal of Educational Research, 102,* 203-212.

Newell, K. M., & Walter, C. B. (1981). Kinematic and kinetic parameters in information feedback in motor skill acquisition. *Journal of Human Movement Studies, 7,* 235-254.

Pea, R., & Lindgren, R. (2008). Video collaboratories for research and education: An analysis of collaboration design patterns. *IEEE Transactions on Learning Technologies, 1,* 235-247.

Pearson, P. D., & Dole, J. A. (1987). Explicit comprehension instruction: A review of research and a new conceptualization of instruction. *The Elementary School Journal, 88,* 151-165.

Pearson, P. D., & Gallagher, M. C. (1983). The instruction of reading comprehension. *Contemporary Educational Psychology, 8,* 317-344.

Piaget, J. (1932). *The moral judgment of the child.* London, England: Routledge & Kegan Paul.

Rich, P. J., & Hannafin, M. J. (2008). Decisions and reasons: Examining preservice teacher decision-making through video self-analysis. *Journal of Computing in Higher Education, 20,* 62-94.

Rich, P. J., & Hannafin, M. J. (2009). Scaffolded video self-analysis: Discrepancies between preservice teachers' perceived and actual instructional decisions. *Journal of Computing in Higher Education, 21*(2), 128-145.

Rosaen, C. L., Degnan, C., VanStratt, T., & Zietlow, K. (2004). Designing a virtual K-2 classroom literacy tour: Learning together as teachers explore "best practice." In J. Brophy (Ed.), *Using video in teacher education* (Vol. 10, pp. 169-199). Amsterdam, Holland: Elsevier.

Sacks, H., Schegloff, E. A., & Jefferson, G. (1974). A simplest systematics for the organization of turn-taking for conversation. *Language, 50,* 696-735.

Sherin, M. G., & van Es, E. A. (2009). Effects of video club participation on teachers' professional vision. *Journal of Teacher Education, 60*(1), 20-37.

Strauss, A., & Corbin, J. M. (1990). *Basics of qualitative research: Grounded theory procedures and techniques.* Thousand Oaks, CA: Sage Publications.

Tochon, F. V. (2007). From video cases to video pedagogy: Video feedback in an educational culture sharing differences. In R. Goldman, R. D. Pea, B. Barron, & S. Derry, (2007). (Eds.), *Video research in the learning sciences* (pp. 53-66). Mahwah, NJ: Lawrence Erlbaum Associates.

van Es, E. A. (2009). Participants' roles in the context of a video club. *The Journal of the Learning Sciences, 18,* 100-137.

Vygotsky, L. S. (1978). *Mind in society: The development of higher psychological processes.* Cambridge, MA: Harvard University Press.

Wenger, E. (1998). *Communities of practice: Learning, meaning, and identity.* Cambridge, England: Cambridge University Press.

Wenger, E., White, N., and Smith, J. D. (2009). *Digital habits: Stewarding technology for communities.* Portland, OR: CPsquare.

Wilson, S. M., & Berne, J. (1999). Teacher learning and the acquisition of professional knowledge: An examination of research on contemporary professional development. *Review of Research in Education, 24,* 173-209.

Digging Deeper: Literacy, Language, and Learning in the Mine Safety Industry

Aly Waibel
Susan Rice
J.J. Kelley
Patricia L. Anders
University of Arizona

Literacy Research Association members are challenged to widen the circle of literacy research. In this study, we take up this challenge by exploring language and literacy practices in the mining industry in the western U.S. Workplace literacy is fundamental to training and successful participation in any industry; in the high-risk industry of mining, miners must critically assess the conditions of the work site continuously in order to respond promptly and efficiently to potentially hazardous situations (Vaught & Mallett, 2008). Literacy is required, for example, to read signs and posters, electric breaker panels, labels on hazardous chemicals and safety equipment, and maps (Rose, 2003). The mining industry acknowledges that accidents occur as a result of misunderstandings around text, mine-specific language and vocabulary, and that safety trainers lack understanding of literacy and language processes required to address these concerns in trainings (Cole, 1994; Peters, 1991; U.S. Department of Health and Human Services, 2010). However, "there has been little investigation of the relationship between how trainers train, and what learners learn in the workplace" (Somerville & Abrahamsson, 2003, p.19). Here we describe our entry to the mining industry: We explore workplace literacy demands and theorize literacy, language, teaching, and learning in mine safety training.

This report is the first step in an investigation of language and literacy in the mining industry conducted by researchers in the Mining Workplace Language and Literacy (MWLL) Project. The MWLL Project is part of a larger partnership, the Western Mining Safety and Health Resource Center, at a large southwestern research university. The partnership, funded by the National Institute for Occupational Safety and Health (NIOSH), seeks to improve safety and health in the mining industry and is comprised of research teams from the Colleges of Public Health, Education, and Mining and Engineering. The MWLL Project supports the work of the partnership by providing current research-based information on literacy, language, and learning in adulthood.

The following questions are the focus of the larger project: How do trainers perceive language and literacy practices? How is safety training accomplished in the mining industry? How do miners with low literacy cope with text-dominated safety training? And, how do English language learners negotiate the English-speaking workplace?

THEORETICAL PERSPECTIVES AND RELATED LITERATURE

Our investigation is grounded in constructivist and sociocultural teaching and learning theories (Merriam & Caffarella, 1999), where meaning is constructed by individuals using language, space, actions, emotions, and objects in a social context for specific purposes (Heath, 1983; Street,

1984; Street, Rogers, & Baker, 2006). New Literacy Studies, consistent with a constructivist theoretical framework, recognizes the multimodal nature of workplaces (Billett, Fenwick, & Somerville, 2006; Rose, 2003, 2004). The role of prior knowledge and experiences, perceptions of literacy and language, and beliefs about teaching and learning are critical and are assumed to influence how trainers both receive instruction and transform the instruction to fit his or her style, sense of responsibility, and identity (Billett et al., 2006; Hull, Jury, & Zacher, 2007). Instruction for adults must respond to characteristics of adult learners such as age, ethnicity, and culture (Kowalski & Vaught, 2002; Street et al., 2006). Thinking develops through the mediation of others, where the novice learns through contact with a more knowledgeable other (Moll, 2001); this type of mediation happens naturally on a mine site (Somerville & Abrahamsson, 2003) and enables the new miner to move toward full participation in the community of practice (Lave & Wenger, 1991).

Critical thinking and reflection on practice (Schön, 1983) are also elements of sociocultural and constructivist perspectives, essential to safe practice in mining. Workers negotiate many discourses in their daily routine and need to move from reading or hearing a safety concept to application, that is, safe practice on site (Rose, 2004). It is necessary for workers to know when they do not understand a safety regulation or concept (Peters, 1991). For safety trainers, reflection on practice is critical because trainers' beliefs about language, literacy, teaching, learning, and their trainees impacts how they teach (Somerville & Abrahamsson, 2003).

Within this framework, what is literacy on the mine site? To operationalize the term, we define literacy as the practice of using symbol systems (e.g., print, signs, maps, gestures) to function safely and productively on the job and in society, to achieve goals, and to develop one's knowledge and potential (Kirsch, Jungeblut, Jenkins, & Klstad, 1993). Miners are skilled in a profession which is physically rigorous and requires a high degree of mechanical and technical literacy. Much nonverbal communication takes place on-site using sound, gesture, and symbol systems (Gee, 2001). For example, miners listen for audible signs that a vehicle or piece of machinery is in need of repair. Therefore, in the mining workplace, literacy means safe and fluent use of machines, tools, physical space, social interaction, and symbol systems (Rose, 2004). We hypothesize that appreciation for the many discourses (Gee, 2001) that are used to communicate in the workplace leads to safer practices and better trainings.

Two questions guided this study: How is safety training accomplished in the mining industry? And, how do trainers perceive language and literacy practices on mine sites and in safety trainings?

METHODS

This report is a case study of the mining industry in the western U.S. and includes characteristics of the industry and trainings, and a description of safety trainers' beliefs and practices (Merriam, 2009). Data sources included belief surveys, interviews, and a focus group. Interpreting this data, we constructed a preliminary understanding of language and literacy in the workplace and of the classes safety trainers teach.

In order to meet potential participants, we attended Mine Safety and Health Administration (MSHA) new miner and annual safety refresher courses. We also attended Mine Safety Conferences and met with industry stakeholders and mine safety professionals at the College of Mining and

Engineering training facility. Through these activities, we built a network of safety trainer contacts who we invited to complete surveys, engage in interviews, and participate in a focus group. Snowball sampling techniques were used to select participants for the focus group.

Participants

Participants in this study are members of the mine safety training community. Eight participants responded to a survey, two were interviewed, and six participated in a focus group. All participants worked many years in mining, attended mandatory MSHA trainings at least once per year, or taught the courses on a regular basis. Focus group participants ranged in age from 45 to 65 and represented the following roles in the mining industry: owners of a private safety training company, a mining engineer, and safety trainers; one participant is bilingual (Spanish/English) and the rest are monolingual English speakers.

Researchers are language and literacy specialists: one university professor of literacy education, and three graduate students. Three have little background knowledge of the mining industry; one is from a mining town in the western U.S. and is familiar with the culture, language, and literacy practices of miners and their families. Two speak and write Spanish and English, and two are monolingual English speakers.

Data Collection

The survey was collected online and asked the trainers to give short answers to the questions "What is teaching?" and "What is learning?" We conducted interviews with two highly respected and experienced safety trainers, one from the State Mine Inspector's Office, and one manager of a safety department at a gold mine. The purpose of the interviews was to discover how trainings are organized and how language and literacy impacts safety.

The focus group met at the College of Education. Each meeting was approximately 2 hours of lively and often humorous discussion. We took observational notes, audio-recorded the meetings, and transcribed the recordings. The focus group met once per month for 3 months: first, we focused on teaching methods that currently work for safety trainers; second, we discussed challenges trainers face in working with miners in the western U.S., and third, we brainstormed about the overall picture of language and literacy in mine safety training.

Data Analysis

We transcribed surveys (S), interviews (I), and focus group (FG) data, coded each data source using constant comparative analysis (Glaser & Strauss, 1967), and triangulated our findings. Two core categories emerged: *characteristics of the industry* and *trainers' practices and beliefs.*

FINDINGS

Characteristics of the industry, organized into five properties, are described next. The trainers' practices and beliefs were sorted into three properties, which are also described.

Characteristics of the Industry

The five salient properties of the industry included literacy, language, mining culture, trainers' tensions, and playing school.

Literacy. Mine safety trainers in the western U.S. work with "people from every educational level, cultural level, ethnic level—we've got a real smorgasbord" (FG2). Participants acknowledged their shortcomings in understanding the literacy processes of such a diverse group and spoke at length on the topic, sharing examples of how literacy impacts their safety trainings. One focus group participant coined the phrase "selective literacy loss" during a discussion about signage: "After a while, a sign gets really jaded. You know how children get what's called selective hearing loss? [laughter] you get selective literacy loss" (FG3). One long-time miner, who recently became a safety trainer, shared his uncertainty about handling cases of low literacy:

> So I'm tryin' to do the best I can. I had a PowerPoint presentation, so I was asking each person to read that slide, and the gentleman says, "I'm not reading that slide. We all can read." So I said, "Okay." So I went ahead and read it. You know what I mean? And when I got done reading, another gentleman took over and read his part. But I [thought], "Okay, now I know where I'm at with this guy." And he's a good friend of mine. I've known him for 3 years in the office now. But, whether he couldn't read, I don't know. Whether he didn't wanna read because he reads poorly, I have no idea. I didn't ask him. I guess I should've asked him. (FG2)

The above reveals the trainer's lack of preparation in identifying and working with individuals with low text literacy. He recognizes that reading PowerPoint slides is not effective but does not have other strategies for teaching the content. A more experienced, highly regarded trainer in the focus group described how he approaches trainees who may have low literacy:

> I don't go directly and ask, "Well, can you read or write?" I try to have a conversation, try and get to know that individual. I said…"What do you think of the course? I'm noticing that we're askin' you guys to do something, and you're not doin' anything"…I do this during the breaks, during lunch, or after class. Or a lotta times I'll give 'em my business card, [and say] "I'm here to assist you at any time. If you have any questions when you go – you're at the mine-site, you're at home, give me a call." At that point I make it personal with that individual. And I get calls all the time. (FG1)

The above comments and the statement "I get calls all the time" indicate that illiteracy is an issue in the industry. One interview participant shares a personal example:

> You know it boils down to, you don't wanna hurt the guy's feelin's so you help him this one time. Then you help him again. Next thing you know you're ten years into it. The guy can't read, he can't write, he's doin' things he *shouldn't* be doin', everybody on the property knows he has a problem. (ID)

Later in the interview, he elaborates:

> There're some people out there that can't read, period. There's a guy that cannot read. But yet he does a lot of the electrical out at the property. How does he read breaker panels? Unless he can open up a shop manual to order his parts and there's an exploded view of the motor or whatever he's working on, he has no idea. He can't write out a purchase order. He's been with this mine 12 years. How it happened, how he got here I have no idea. (ID)

In a focus group meeting, we asked, "How do workers know how to read the MSDS (Material Safety Data Sheet)?" and one participant explained:

> They don't. So we train them in the process of learning how to read one, and then they have to come back and demonstrate how to find the information. So it's a learning process...And after that they say, "You know I've been using this chemical for 20 years, and I had no clue about the potential hazards. Now, I'll be more careful." (FG1)

The MSDS is notoriously confusing to read; the majority of workers cannot read it, and most trainers do not address this issue.

Language. In addition to literacy challenges, participants expressed concerns about language: "I don't think illiteracy is much of a problem as in the past. It's language that is the issue" (FG3). Because of the proximity of the U.S.-Mexico border, western U.S. mines are likely to employ a large number of English language learners. Language impacts safety in critical ways; it is potentially life-threatening for a worker and his colleagues if an instruction is not understood on the mine site. The following comment alludes to the danger involved when a truck driver needs instructions translated over the radio:

> We had a couple truck drivers that really only spoke Spanish. I think they could understand some English, so in the line-up in the morning or at the beginning of shift, you'd notice they would sit with someone who would translate very quietly to 'em. But when you're in a truck and your only communication is a radio... (FG1)

Attitudes about language difference influence how workers interact and how trainers approach English language learners in the classroom. One participant explained:

> There's a lot of bad feelings. A lotta people say, "You know what, they're in our country, they need to learn our language...they're makin' more money than me." Well, it's not me to sit back and judge and say, "Hey, this guy makes more than me." You know, there's two, three guys that I've trained over there that speak very little English that are makin' 10 dollars [an hour] more than I am. Does it bother me? No. They're great workers. They're great guys. Tryin' to do what's right. You know, they came over here legal. They just don't speak really good English. (ID-161)

One focus group participant revealed an underlying deficit belief about language difference (Burt, Peyton, & Adams, 2003; Tse, 2001), saying that when it comes to training, "Spanish is our biggest problem" (FG3). This statement was absorbed into the group discussion without notice and without further comment, suggesting that trainers who are monolingual English speakers are influenced by and reproduce myths and misconceptions about students who are not proficient in speaking, reading, or writing English (Burt et al., 2003).

Much of the data reveals that trainers believe it is the responsibility of the company either to not hire workers who are not fluent English speakers or to not send them to English-only trainings. One participant explained, if there is a "language issue...we deal with that out of the classroom and we have sent people home" (FG2). Focus group participants agreed that separate trainings benefit Spanish speakers even though they work on English-speaking mine sites. One participant commented, "We really try not to do what some people call Spanglish class because it's not great for anybody" (FG1). The burden of responsibility is not on the trainer to incorporate effective teaching techniques that will assist the English language learner.

The following comment illustrates how monolingual English speaking trainers struggle to address language difficulties in safety trainings:

> I do a lot of looking around, it's easy to spot someone that may not understand what you're talking about. Gosh, a lot of the stuff that we put out is so important, if you miss something, you've really *missed* something. I don't know how to get around that. (IR)

These comments about language variation among miners in the western U.S. reveal safety trainers' need for new information and techniques for working with English language learners.

Mining culture. Mining is a high-risk profession. Among miners, there is a strong sense of camaraderie and a morbid sense of humor, similar to what might be observed among other professionals working together in high-risk situations. The following illustrates this trait:

> There are not too many new ways to kill yourself in a mine. They've all been done before [laughing with others]. I could put 10 videos on the table tomorrow of incidents of trucks bein' run over by one of the big haul trucks. It's unfortunately a very common occurrence and almost always fatal for the people involved. (FG2)

And, "usually every accident in the mine, you don't come out. Not too many of 'em come out. They're always either serious or fatalities" (FG2). One focus group member spoke of "hooking" trainees into the importance of safety by stressing that safety is about trainees' ability to go "home to their family at night with all their hands and toes, or not squashed under a [haul truck], you know, that's your ultimate hook" (FG2). The mining industry is also largely male-dominated and "somewhat of a macho culture" (FG2). One female focus group member explained:

> Year after year after year, I was about the only female in the class out there. And it's a male-dominated field. They got to know me. I don't cuss. I don't participate in the jokes. But I don't make a big stink about it either…Even when I worked in the tank house I could do the job as well as anybody out there. Then you build your own environment around you. And, I mean, you're in a male-dominated field, a very rough field. It's a very coarse business. And you choose to be there. If nothing else, it makes you work harder because you do have to prove yourself all the time. (FG2)

In addition to being very dangerous and a "very coarse business," everyone seems to know everyone; most safety trainers have been in the industry for decades. One interviewee explains that the mining industry is "a large family, and really, kind of small. If you get into mining, no matter where you go, you'll almost always know someone who knows someone that you knew" (IR). In the mining "family," new workers are tutored on-site by older miners, as one focus group participant explains:

> The experienced individual is always the one, even more so in a mining environment, if you were to work in a manufacturing plant tomorrow, you wouldn't find anywhere near the degree of this kind of older guy consciously taking the new guy under his wing [as in mining]. It's kinda his job to explain the whole breadth of what the hell goes on here, not just the safety aspect of things. (FG3)

This comment indicates that mentoring assists the new worker to move toward full participation (Lave & Wenger, 1991; Moll, 2001) into the mining culture and miner identity.

Trainers' tensions. Mine safety trainers are passionate about their work. However, most trainers have no background in adult education and have little understanding of language and literacy processes. Typically, trainers are older "master miners" who have earned the position of safety trainer because of extensive experience and safe practice in the field. When asked "What kind of training do trainers receive in order to teach other people?," focus group responses were: "[simultaneously] Zero. Zip. Nada. Nothing." One person elaborated, "I just sent my resume in to Denver and they said 'Okay, be a trainer for MSHA'" (FG2-832). Perhaps because of their lack of theoretical background and information about effective adult teaching strategies, trainers struggle to "maintain control" and "earn respect" in the classroom:

> Miners are also a somewhat unusual, or at least a distinctly separate subspecies of adult learner...one of the challenges that our instructors face is to establish their bona fides, their credibility. You can recite credentials until you're blue in the face and that doesn't impress these guys. You need to... relate your own anecdotes, establish the fact that you've been there, done that, you know what you're talking about. (FG2)

Focus group participants strongly emphasized the general sense of dread workers feel about mandatory trainings:

> More often than not, you have a benignly indifferent group of people in front of you. Not a one of them would be in that room if they didn't have to be. And many of them have a very dim view of what's about to happen. (FG2)

Some trainers are known to rush through material and dismiss class early because everyone, trainer included, is "bored to death." One trainer explained that "at the end of the day [trainees] don't hardly take time to sign their certificates before they're wanting to bolt out the door" (IR). The following exchange further explains that the average miner or contractor "dreads" attending trainings, reports not learning much, endures it, and looks forward to getting back to work:

Frank: You have to go to refresher training every year. And if it's not different, you're just sittin' there...just bored to death [others laugh and affirm].... You're just bored to tears. So if the guy doesn't come up with somethin' different, and you've known him for 20, 25 years, it's the same guy gonna give the course...

Sally: Oh man, you dread going in there for that day. [laughing]

Frank: Even though they're paid to go, they don't wanna go. They'd rather be at work.

Debbie: It's more active.

Frank: They'd rather be at work than sit in a class and listen to some guy talk. (FG2)

Safety trainings are conducted in the banking model (Freire, 1970), where trainees passively receive information from the instructor, who often talks or shows videos for several hours while trainees "zone out." Trainers feel tension when attempting to cover the required information and make it interesting for the "benignly indifferent" group of trainees sitting in front of him or her.

Playing school. The mine site is a highly social workplace, where nonverbal, mechanical, physical, and technical literacies inform safe practice. In safety trainings, however, very little physical movement or interaction occurs and content is primarily conveyed through text. Trainees sit at tables in rows while trainers stand in front of the room and use teaching strategies which do not fit with the industry's culture or personality:

> Most safety training is woefully presented. Safety training to most people in the industry is something that must be endured. It's really tedious. And frequently… the same guy's been giving it for the last 20 years…and he wasn't a teacher to begin with, and he hasn't had a bright idea since. I mean, we've had people who've shown the same old video for the last 20 years, and you think that's safety training. And then sign here. Go forth, you've been blessed now. And we'll suffer through this together next year. (FG2)

Participants describe trainers standing in front of the room, at times struggling for control and order, while trainees whisper amongst themselves or attempt to stay awake. One participant commented, "You have to be an extremely good facilitator to keep it under control" (FG1). The following exchange reveals thoughts on the need for discipline:

Jim: The animosities that were there yesterday in that workplace come right in along with it. That's been one of the reasons we've had to exert discipline. These are adults who are not used to being in a learning environment. They've got this predisposition to: "I'm going to be bored out of my skull today. This whole thing is gonna be a waste of time. They're gonna put some turkey who just drones on all day long in front of me, and this altogether is going to be a disagreeable experience." If you can't shake 'em out of that right from the get-go, you're fighting it all day long no matter how good you are.

Ben: Yeah, they've got a preconceived notion that's set. You know, when their supervisor comes up and says, "Joe, next Monday you're going to annual refresher," they could have a terrible, miserable week, just anticipating having to go to it. (FG2-809)

In the above, Jim equates "learning environment" with "classroom," revealing a limited view of how, where, and when learning takes place.

Focus group participants provided several suggestions for countering the tendency of trainers to "play school" in a banking model; however, several comments revealed fear about allowing trainees to talk in class. For example:

> You gotta be careful, because these guys love to talk too. You create your own monster if you cast a guy the role of surrogate teacher [in class]. The next thing you know, he's got something to say about every darn thing that comes up. (FG3)

Another participant suggests that learning happens when the instructor speaks and the students listen, suggesting that trainees "talking amongst themselves" is equivalent to not paying attention or sleeping (FG2). Another participant spoke of the perceived danger of letting students talk in class, saying, "you have to continually rope them in" (FG3). While acknowledging the value of on-site mentoring, the comments above demonstrate trainers' fear of bringing the mentoring model into the training classroom.

Trainers' Beliefs and Practices

The following properties describe trainers' practices and how their affiliation with a transmission notion of teaching and learning, reminiscent of the behaviorist theoretical orientation, and uninformed understanding of literacy and language processes affects their teaching.

Beliefs. Trainers' beliefs about teaching and learning were revealed throughout the data. The survey gave us an opportunity to examine trainers' beliefs. Responses to the survey question, "What is learning?" included: "Learning is the knowledge you try to gain through some type of schooling" and "Learning is where the concept or the message becomes internalized to help someone understand or change behavior" (S1, S3). Responses to "What is teaching?" included: "Teaching is the giving of instruction or information to a trainee or class so they can improve their performance and achieve a certain level of skill and knowledge" and "Teaching is presentation of materials in a way that the information is transferred from the teacher to the student" (S1, S3). Survey responses indicated a behaviorist view of the purpose of learning: skill development and behavioral change (Merriam & Caffarella, 1999). Participants in this study spoke of literacy only in terms of reading and writing text; they did not identify alternative ways of being literate, and they did not discuss learning the physical, mechanical, and technical literacies of mining.

PowerPoint. PowerPoint is used frequently in mine safety trainings. Because of the pressure trainers feel to cover all of the MSHA material in limited time, PowerPoint presentations often include all of the required information. In focus group meetings, participants revealed an orientation to teach the content, rather than the student: "Some of it's repetitive. You do have to cover a certain amount of information" (FG1). When asked, "Do you find some instructors that are afraid to ask questions?" Participants responded: "It's a completely foreign concept" (FG2). Heavy reliance on presentation of content through PowerPoint creates a lack of connection with students. Although trainers recognize that, "These guys relate better to the stories than they do me readin' off the slide" (ID), many trainers spend the majority of class time reading directly from the PowerPoint slides to trainees.

Videos. Trainers use videos frequently, but participants spoke about the ineffective use of videos in trainings: "If you show them all the time you're gonna have people just fallin' asleep in your class" (FG1). One participant explains, "I got lotsa videos 'cause it's 32 hours. I like to talk a lot. I got a lotta good stories, but, basically you gotta train 'em" (FG1). This comment indicates that personal stories do not count as training. Often, safety videos are outdated and unrealistic. Some of the generic, "plastic" videos are simply laughable and tedious, "like the old Walt Disney safety or health films" (FG1). Rarely, companies will make videos in-house, which are highly entertaining and informative. One interviewee explained that when he worked at a company as a safety engineer:

> We made all our safety videos that we observed. And that takes a lot of work, but it's very fulfilling, because if you see yourself in a video and we're talking about something safety, you have more of a tendency to listen, or if I see you and I know you, I have more of a tendency to listen to what's being said. (IR)

Focus group participants shared anecdotes about safety classes in which trainers show only videos for the duration of the class. Trainers who do this are "covering the material" according to MSHA guidelines and trainees receive their certification to safely enter the mine site after watching 8 hours of generic safety videos (FG1). This practice further highlights the tendency to transmit content rather than connect with the trainee.

Reflection on safety. In order to be safe, miners need to be able to reflect on safety in a dynamic, continuously changing worksite (Vaught & Mallett, 2008). The ability to identify potential safety violations and hazards is critical for every worker on the mine site. In order to teach reflection on safe practice in trainings, trainers guide trainees through a review of fatalities and accidents, all called "incidents," by tracing the event backward to examine what went wrong, when and how it happened, and who was involved. They show pictures of damaged equipment and tell first-hand stories to impact trainees and help them think critically about how accidents happen (FG1). Through this type of reflection activity, trainees learn to recognize why a specific regulation is important and when they do not understand how an accident was caused.

However, many trainers assume and teach that safety on-site is "common sense." Participants said the following:

Ben: I realized that in these classes you have people that are absolutely new and have completely no knowledge. It's like sending 'em to the planet Mars. For those who have lived on Mars for a while, it's just fine.

Lee: And it's "common sense"…[laughter]

Jim: That old song.

Ben: Yeah. But you have…a *language*, there's a language all its own. (FG3)

This was the only instance of a participant speaking directly about workplace-specific language and literacy; this comment suggests that a new miner's inability to understand the language of the industry could be a safety hazard. During the focus group, we asked, "What do learners do in these classes when a term is used that some student doesn't know?" One participant responded, "Generally, the young pups will not ask" (FG2). Trainers often do not realize they are using unfamiliar terms and do not define terms during classes unless the new trainee asks a question.

Reflection on teaching. While reflection on workplace safety is a standard element of training classes, data reveal trainers' mixed abilities to reflect on their teaching practices (Anders & Richardson, 1991; Schön, 1983). Study participants expressed sensitivity and concern for their trainees, coupled with frustration over not knowing how to meet their needs. One participant explained, "It is tough when everybody in my office has 30-plus years of experience so how do you keep their attention without them sittin' there, [thinking] 'Oh god, another 8 hours'?"(FG1). Several comments revealed intuitive understanding of learning principles, for example, "You have people from different areas that, depending on their culture, depending on their education, they will learn a little bit different. Not everybody learns the same way" (FG1). The idea that learning can be collaborative and "fun" is expressed here: "When I hear the students participating and laughing…as an outsider I'm thinking, 'That's a terrific class. They're havin' a good time in their learning'" (FG1). Drawing on trainees' experiences is a novel concept in safety training. One participant describes a colleague's unconventional techniques:

To utilize the experience of the people in his class, he has 'em pick out a hazard or chemical that they have been exposed to in the mine-site. And that's their chemical, and it's their job to take 5 minutes and tell the rest of the class about it. They have to do mini-research projects in the class. (FG1)

Participants in this study revealed an ability to reflect on practice and recognize effective strategies within a limited framework of understanding of language, literacy, and learning.

DISCUSSION AND IMPLICATIONS

Discovering the language and literacy practices in mine safety training led us to theorize about the teaching challenges trainers face. Mine safety trainers in the western U.S. typically have little understanding of workplace literacy and language acquisition, and they lack strategies to teach safety concepts using non-text-based methods. Our observations and experiences as outsiders placed us in a unique position to bring awareness to language and literacy issues in existing mine safety training pedagogy. In trainings we attended, unfamiliar terms were used without explanation (e.g., names of equipment parts and locations on the mine site: berm, lockout-tagout, front loader), and the safety concept or regulation was completely lost on us. In fact, it became clear that, especially for new miners, teaching safety is a matter of teaching language and literacy.

Finding One, *characteristics of the mining industry*, includes five properties which help paint the picture of mining in the western U.S. The properties are: *literacy, language, mining culture, trainers' tension*, and *playing school*. Data reveal that trainings are often "woefully presented" (FG2), boring, and in great need of improvement. Participants in this case study easily and enthusiastically described the mining industry's culture and expressed their desire to see workers become passionate about safety for the sake of their families and communities (FG3).

Finding Two, *trainers' practices and beliefs*, illuminates commonly held beliefs about literacy and language that limit trainers' abilities to reflect on their practice and make improvements (Anders & Richardson, 1991; Tse, 2001). Data reveal that trainers often lack awareness of teaching and learning principles required to justify changing their teaching practice. Trainers need to further develop their reflexivity to better evaluate teaching practices in trainings (Rose, 2004; Schön, 1983). Tension exists when trainers are required to "cover" specific material in the classroom in order to meet industry requirements; they default to a banking model (Freire, 1970) of teaching in which they stand and read or speak information to trainees who are seated in front of them.

Trainers do not usually think about safety training in terms of teaching the language of mining and do not explicitly teach workplace-specific vocabulary. While experiential and self-directed learning based on prior knowledge and contact with more experienced colleagues takes place naturally on the mine-site, trainers lack strategies for creating learning opportunities through discussion and relationship-building in the classroom.

The results of this study were used to develop a course called *Teaching Strategies for the Mine Safety Trainer*. Through several iterations of reflection and changes to the curriculum, we discovered alternative ways to bridge the gap between our academic understanding of language, literacy, teaching, and learning, and the understanding of mining industry professionals (Cochran-Smith

& Lytle, 1993; Merriam & Caffarella, 1999). We are analyzing the success of this course and are currently investigating the language and literacy demands of the mining worksite.

CONCLUSION

This study widens the circle of literacy research by exploring language and literacy practices and pedagogies in the mine safety industry. The results of this research are intended to improve the education of mine safety instructors training in high-risk environments. As we continue investigating language and literacy in mining, we encourage literacy researchers to explore language and literacy practices and beliefs in other industries. In addition, we hope that literacy researchers might find our study design and methods of value as they consider investigating diverse settings and industries. Workplace research provides space and opportunity to investigate our understanding of literacy theory and practices. This work contributes to the revitalization of workplace and adult literacy research.

AUTHORS' NOTE

This article was supported by grant number 1U60OH010014-01 from the Center for Disease Control (CDC), National Institute of Occupational Safety and Health (NIOSH). Its contents are solely the responsibility of the authors and do not necessarily represent the official views of NIOSH.

REFERENCES

Anders, P., & Richardson, V. (1991). The relationship between teachers' beliefs and practices in reading comprehension instruction. *American Educational Research Journal, 28*(3), 559-586.

Billett, S., Fenwick, T., & Somerville, M. (2006). *Work, subjectivity, and learning: Understanding learning through working life.* Dordrecht, The Netherlands: Springer.

Burt, M., Peyton, J. K., & Adams, R. (2003). *Reading and adult English language learners: A review of the research.* Washington, DC: National Center for ESL Literacy Education & Center for Applied Linguistics.

Cochran-Smith, M., & Lytle, S. (1993). *Inside/Outside: Teacher research and knowledge.* New York, NY: Columbia Teacher's College.

Cole, L. T. (1994). Mining sector basic needs assessment. *Workplace Education Manitoba, CE 068 690,* 1-30.

Freire, P. (1970). *Pedagogy of the oppressed.* New York, NY: Continuum.

Gee, J. (2001). Reading as situated language: A sociocognitive perspective. *Journal of Adolescent and Adult Literacy, 44*(8), 714-724.

Glaser, B., & Strauss, A. (1967). *The discovery of grounded theory: Strategies for qualitative research.* Chicago, IL: Aldine.

Heath, S. B. (1983). *Ways with words: Language, life and work in communities and classrooms.* New York, NY: Cambridge.

Hull, G., Jury, M., & Zacher, J. (2007). Possible selves: Literacy, identity, and development in work, school, and community. In A. Belzer (Ed.), *Toward defining and improving quality in adult basic education* (pp. 200-219). Mahwah, NJ: Lawrence Erlbaum.

Kirsch, I. S., Jungeblut, A., Jenkins, L., & Klstad, A. (1993). *Adult literacy in America: A first look at the results of the National Adult Literacy Survey* (Report prepared by the Educational Testing Service under contract with the National Center for Education Statistics, Office of Educational Research and Improvement). Washington, DC: U.S. Department of Education.

Kowalski, K. M., & Vaught, C. (2002). *Principles of adult learning: Application for mine trainers* (pp. 3-8). Washington, DC: NIOSH Information Circular 9463.

Lave, J., & Wenger, E. (1991). *Situated learning: Legitimate peripheral participation*. Cambridge, UK: Cambridge University Press.

Merriam, S. B., & Caffarella, R. S. (1999). *Learning in adulthood*. San Francisco, CA: Jossey-Bass.

Merriam, S. B. (2009). *Qualitative Research*: A Guide to Design and Implementation. San Francisco, CA: Jossey-Bass.

Moll, L. (2001). Through the mediation of others: Vygotskian research on teaching. In V. Richardson (Ed.), *Handbook of research on teaching*. Washington, DC: AERA.

Peters, R. (1991). The challenge of enforcing safety rules in remote hazardous work areas. *NIOSH Professional Safety, 1*, 27-31.

Rose, M. (2003). Words in action: Rethinking workplace literacy. *Research in the Teaching of English, 38*, 125-128.

Rose, M. (2004). *The mind at work: Valuing the intelligence of the American worker*. New York, NY: Viking.

Schön, D. A. (1983). *The reflective practitioner*. New York, NY: Basic Books.

Street, B. V. (1984). *Literacy in theory and practice*. New York, NY: Cambridge.

Street, B. V., Rogers, A., & Baker, D. (2006). Adult teachers as researchers: Ethnographic approaches to numeracy and literacy as social practices in south Asia. *Convergence, XXXXIX*(1), 31-44.

Somerville, M., & Abrahamsson, L. (2003). Trainers and learners constructing a community of practice: Masculine work cultures and learning safety in the mining industry. *Studies in the Education of Adults, 35*(1), 19-34.

Tse, L. (2001). *Why don't they learn English?: Separating fact from fallacy in the U.S. language debate*. New York, NY: Teacher's College Press.

U.S. Department of Health and Human Services, Centers for Disease Control and Prevention, National Institute for Occupational Safety and Health. (2010). *Funding Opportunity Announcement* (FOA No. FRA-OH-10-001). Retrieved from http://grants.nih.gov/grants/guide/rfa-files/RFA-OH-10-001.html

Vaught, C., & Mallett, L. (2008). *Guidelines for the development of a new miner training curriculum* (Department of Health and Human Services Publication No. 2008-105).

The Influence of a Literacy Coach's Beliefs about Her Work

Jennifer I. Hathaway
University of North Carolina at Charlotte

In today's high-stakes world of education, school districts and administrators are searching for ways to improve student learning and achievement. Often, they find themselves relying on professional development to exact change (Rodgers & Pinnell, 2002). Within the field of literacy, coaching as a model of professional development is believed to be a powerful intervention (International Reading Association [IRA], 2004). In their *Standards for Reading Professionals – Revised 2010*, the International Reading Association describes a literacy coach as a reading specialist who provides professional development for teachers by supplying the additional support needed to implement a variety of instructional practices and programs. This notion of the provision of support for teachers, often leading to increased student learning, is a common theme across definitions of coaching (e.g., Rodgers & Rodgers, 2007; Toll, 2005). However, coaches' beliefs about the purpose of their work can ultimately influence their ability to bring about teacher change (Killion, 2009) and ultimately student learning. This paper describes the beliefs of one literacy coach and how they influenced her work.

RESEARCH PERSPECTIVES

Traditional models of professional development including one-size-fits-all presentations to teacher audiences in one-shot workshops with no follow-up support (Robb, 2000) have been shown to be ineffective (Guskey, 2000). Therefore, new models of professional development, such as literacy coaching, have emerged to take their place.

Coaching as Professional Development

Literacy coaching is viewed as a promising practice (IRA, 2004) in part because of its adherence to principles of effective professional development. To bring about change, professional development must be systematic (Rodgers & Rodgers, 2007), provide a clear focus on learning and learners (Guskey, 2000), and be ongoing and embedded in the practice of teaching (Guskey 2000; Lyons & Pinnell, 2001). Effective professional development also needs to provide intensive and extensive support to teachers, to provide space for teacher reflection, purposeful conversations, collaboration, and should assist teachers in assimilating new information into their pre-existing beliefs (Hughes, Cash, Ahwee, & Klingner, 2002). A final characteristic of effective professional development is it allows for interactions between teachers and a more experienced other (Joyce & Showers, 2002; Lyons & Pinnell, 2001; Rodgers & Rodgers, 2007)—in other words, coaching.

The actual work of coaching is quite varied. There are many understandings regarding coaching (IRA, 2004; Rodgers & Rodgers, 2007), as it is a situated, complex activity. Even within school districts, the role of coach may be actualized very differently from school to school (Hathaway & Risko, 2007). However, Bean (2004) describes three levels of intensity in coaching activity. Level 1 includes informal activities that serve to build relationships between coaches and teachers.

These may include providing resources and materials, participating in curriculum development, helping with student assessment, and teaching students. Level 2 activities allow coaches to begin to identify areas of need on which to base future coaching interactions. These activities may include co-planning lessons, analyzing student work, interpreting assessment data, or providing formal professional development presentations. The third and final level of activity is characterized by formal, intense interactions. Included within this level are common in-class supports, which may include modeling new techniques, teaching side-by-side in teachers' classrooms, and observations of teachers' instruction followed by feedback sessions. These forms of in-class support are the distinguishing feature of literacy coaching (IRA, 2004). Regardless of the specific activities in which coaches engage, Lyons and Pinnell (2001) argue the purpose of coaching sessions is to provide teachers with needed feedback in order to allow them to refine their instructional practices.

A final critical component of a successful coaching relationship is trust (IRA, 2004; Lyons & Pinnell, 2001). While coaches often do play the role of the more knowledgeable other in a coaching relationship, it is crucial that they not always position themselves as experts. Instead, coaches should work to establish a co-learner role with teachers. This allows coaches to be seen as peers and helps them move away from the more threatening role of an evaluator (Rodgers & Rodgers, 2007). As Rainville and Jones (2008) found, the way coaches position themselves will ultimately impact their work as a coach.

The Impact of Coaching

Though literacy coaching is a widespread phenomenon, it is as Rodgers and Rodgers (2007) note, "an example of an idea that seems to hold so much promise that it has gotten ahead of the very necessary research that needs to be done to help answer a number of questions" (p. xviii). However, in recent years researchers have begun to fill in the gap in the empirical research base regarding the impact of coaching. In a review of literature from 1990 to 2010 addressing instructional coaching, Rosemary, et al. (2012) identified 49 articles meeting standards of high-quality research, 21 of which were published between 2007 and 2010. These studies indicate that while the effects of coaching are variable, coaching can have an impact on teachers' beliefs and perceptions (e.g., Vanderburg & Stephens, 2010; Veenman, Denessen, Gerrits, & Kenter, 2001) as well as their practice (e.g., Batt, 2010; Rudd, Lambert, Satterwhite, & Smith, 2009). Coaching has also been found to have a positive impact on student learning (e.g., Biancarosa, Bryk, & Dexter, 2010; Elish-Piper & L'Allier, 2010).

Since literacy coaching is based on social constructivist theories of learning that hold that "our past experiences and beliefs influence how we interact with others, learn new ideas, and discard or refine old ones" (Lyons & Pinnell, 2001, p. 4), one important component of coaching is considering and building upon teachers' perspectives, or beliefs, which are the personal truths they hold about the world around them (Pajares, 1992). Teachers' beliefs influence classroom practices (e.g., Korth, Sharp, & Culatta, 2010; Richardson, Anders, Tidwell, & Lloyd, 1991) and ultimately student learning (e.g., Reutzel & Sabey, 1996; Sacks & Mergendoller, 1997).

In order to foster collaboration as they work with teachers toward change, coaches need to understand why and how teachers make their instructional decisions. This understanding allows coaches to provide teachers with rationales for trying new instructional possibilities (Rodgers & Rodgers, 2007) and changing their beliefs. Kise (2006) argues the key to professional development is helping teachers understand where their beliefs bind them and keep them locked into practices that limit their ability to help students succeed. If coaches are unable to successfully address teachers' beliefs and theoretical understandings, they may find that teachers develop repertoires of practices they perform in mechanical ways rather than developing deep understandings of teaching (Rodgers & Rodgers, 2007).

Not only do coaches need to be aware of teachers' beliefs, they also need to be aware of their own so they can clearly communicate those beliefs (Casey, 2006). Killion (2009) also argues that coaches' beliefs about their work will influence the impact they are able to have on teachers' beliefs and practices. She describes two different approaches to coaching—coaching light and coaching heavy—that are distinguished by coaches' intention for and beliefs about their role rather than the activity in which they engage as coaches. Coaches who coach light provide support without the expectation that teachers will put what they learn to use in their classrooms. Coaches engaged in coaching heavy, on the other hand, enter coaching activities with the belief that teachers must improve their teaching and ultimately student learning. Teacher change is not just desired, it is required. These ideas are also recognized by McKenna and Walpole (2008) in their metaphor of soft coaching versus hard coaching. The work shared here supports the theories put forward by these authors as it examines the impact of one coach's beliefs about her role as a coach on her work.

RESEARCH METHODOLOGY

The data reported here were collected as part of a larger study focusing on teachers' beliefs and how they influenced the ways the teachers chose to participate in literacy coaching as professional development. While a variety of research questions were addressed in that study, this paper examines the literacy coach rather than the teachers and answers two questions: What beliefs did a reading specialist hold about coaching? How did those beliefs influence her work as a coach?

Setting and Participants

The study was conducted at Blue Mountain Elementary (pseudonyms are used for the school and all participants), a K-4 school serving approximately 500 diverse students in a metropolitan school district located in the Southern United States. Following a collective case study design (Stake, 2005), three individual cases were developed, each focusing on the coaching relationship between a reading specialist, Sarah, and a classroom teacher. The job responsibilities of a reading specialist, as indentified by the district, included serving as a reading instructional coach to all classroom teachers and providing reading instruction to at-risk students. Reading specialists also provided on-going, job-embedded professional development and coordinated the balanced literacy program within schools. While reading specialists in this district were called upon to wear many hats, this paper focuses solely on Sarah's work as a literacy coach.

Sarah was in her eighth year as an educator, 5 of which had been completed at Blue Mountain Elementary. She had been a first grade teacher for 2 years at the school before transitioning into her role as the reading specialist. At the time of the study, Sarah was in her third year as a reading specialist. Upon assuming the position of reading specialist, she received 2 days of training involving an introduction to the responsibilities and procedures associated with the position, but no specific preparation for coaching. There was no formal coaching program or model being implemented in the district, therefore Sarah was free to determine her own style as a coach. Much of what she knew about coaching was self-taught; she sought out professional readings and attended conference sessions focusing on coaching when feasible.

Data Sources

Data collection occurred over a 7-month period. Primary data sources included survey measures, written statements of the participants' instructional visions, and semi-structured interviews. Additional sources of data included observations of the participants' teaching as well as the coaching interactions between Sarah and the participating teachers.

Surveys. In order to uncover preexisting orientations to teaching and literacy instruction, 2 survey instruments were administered at the beginning of the study. The first instrument, the Literacy Orientation Survey (LOS) (Lenski, Wham, & Griffey, 1998), is designed to examine the consistency of teachers' beliefs and practices with constructivist theory. The LOS contains 30 items—15 statements of beliefs and 15 statements of practice—used to determine a beliefs score, a practice score, and a total score. Each score is related to one of three orientations to literacy learning. Traditional teachers believe in a transmissive approach to learning and rely on traditional reading methods and direct instruction. Constructivist teachers use an inquiry approach to teaching and view students as meaning-makers. Finally, teachers with an eclectic orientation demonstrate a combination of traditional and constructivist approaches and views on student learning.

The second instrument, the Educational Beliefs Questionnaire (EBQ) (Silvernail, 1992), assesses teachers' educational philosophical orientations by examining their beliefs regarding five different concepts including the role of schools in society, the curriculum content, instructional methods, and the roles of the teacher and student. The EBQ contains 21 belief statements organized into three subscales that measure the orientations of traditionalism, progressivism, and romanticism. Traditional teachers view schools as a vehicle for transmitting cultural heritage, value drill and practice in learning, support strong authority roles, and view students as passive receivers of knowledge. Progressive teachers recognize schools as places for inquiry and building socially conscious adults, value a facilitative role, and view students as active participants in their own learning. Finally, romantic teachers see schools as child-centered organizations charged with building new social ideas and individual awareness, in which teachers guide students in their natural development.

Teacher visioning. The teacher visioning protocol (Hammerness, 1999, 2006) uses five open-ended questions to prompt respondents to describe an ideal day in their classroom, specifically addressing elements such as the role of the teacher and students, instructional materials, and the larger purposes of schooling. This measure helps reveal unconsciously held beliefs (Squires & Bliss, 2004) and can help teachers develop a greater awareness of their own beliefs (Hammerness, 2003). It also addresses many of the concepts included in the EBQ, thus allowing for a triangulation of data from these two sources.

Interviews. Seven semi-structured interviews were conducted with each participant. Each interview lasted approximately 1 hour and was audio-recorded and transcribed. Initial interviews were held to learn more about participants' teaching backgrounds and their perceptions of reading instruction. Guiding questions for these interviews were adapted from a Teacher Belief Interview (see Appendix A) from Richardson, Anders, Tidwell, & Lloyd (1991). In subsequent interviews, participants were asked to reflect on their responses on the LOS and EBQ to discuss how well they felt the orientations identified by their scores matched their perception of their beliefs. A modified version of Hammerness's (1999) interview protocol was also used to investigate themes emerging from their written vision statements (see Appendix B). Additionally, participants discussed their perceptions of their own teaching and their coaching interactions with Sarah. A final interview technique used was a stimulated recall procedure (Calderhead, 1996). Participants viewed short video segments (typically lasting 5 to 10 minutes) of their own practice and reflected on their personal thought processes at the time of the interactions they viewed and considered how they saw their beliefs being represented. Sarah participated in four stimulated recall events as she responded to interactions she had with each of the three teachers and the faculty as a whole.

Observations. Throughout the study, a variety of videotaped observations were conducted in order to examine the participants' beliefs in action. For Sarah, these observations included her planned individual coaching interactions with the other study participants. I was physically present for all but two of the planned coaching interactions, however, because of the nature of coaching, there were on-the-fly interactions I was not able to capture. I also observed many of Sarah's group coaching sessions as well as professional development she led for the school's faculty. During all observations, field notes were recorded and relevant written documents were collected.

Data Analysis

Analyses presented in this paper draw mainly on interview data as well as observations of Sarah's coaching. Qualitative data analysis was ongoing using a constant comparative method (Strauss & Corbin, 1998). Throughout the data collection period, I read and reread my field notes from observations, reviewed the video recordings of these observations, and read transcripts of and listened to audio recordings of interviews. As I reviewed the data, I looked for emerging patterns and categories of beliefs, actions, and interactions. I used these emerging patterns to help shape the direction of future data collection, such as the selection of specific questions to be asked during subsequent interviews. For example, I noticed that Sarah often used the phrase "meeting teachers where they are" when describing her ideas about coaching. After recognizing the recurring theme and noticing through my observations of her coaching interactions that she provided different kinds of support for different teachers, I chose to pursue this idea directly during her later interviews.

After data collection concluded, I assigned descriptive category labels to data units of varying size. The data units most often consisted of questions and their answers, though at times smaller units such as sentences or phrases were identified. Field notes from observations of coaching interactions were coded by hand following similar procedures. Within the data collected during coaching interactions, data units tended to consist of several exchanges of action or conversation that comprised critical incidents. Throughout the data analysis, I returned to observational data and artifacts to ensure a triangulation of the data.

During axial coding, five categories emerged: content of beliefs, basis for beliefs, thinking and talking about personal practice, teachers' interactions with coaching, and role as coach. These categories, each containing a number of themes within them, were developed both from a priori hypotheses and also patterns emerging in the data. For example, because of the research questions guiding the larger study, I knew I needed to identify specific beliefs the participants held about teaching and learning. Thus, the notion of coding for the literal content of their beliefs was a priori.

I also made the decision to examine Sarah's role as a coach and the beliefs that were involved with her coaching separately from her other beliefs about the nature of literacy and instruction examined in the larger study. As such, this paper focuses solely on the "role as coach" category and four of the relevant themes within it (see Figure 1). However, within the predetermined "role as coach" category, several themes emerged from the data. For example, as I reviewed Sarah's data, I realized that she often talked about the importance of building a relationship with her teachers and the ways she worked to do this. She felt strong relationships allowed her to carry out all of her duties as a reading specialist effectively, including her role as a coach. This attention to relationships was visible in the observational data as well. For example, Sarah often provided treats for teachers in professional development sessions she led and engaged in friendly conversations with the teachers about events going on in their personal lives before and after these sessions.

Figure 1. Relevant Coding Themes from the "Role as Coach" Category

Theme	Description
purposes of coaching	Sarah's beliefs about the nature of coaching and how they impacted her work
positioning	ways Sarah positioned herself with her teachers or was positioned by others
relationships	beliefs about the importance of knowing teachers and building relationships; impact on coaching
meeting teachers where they are	importance of providing individualized coaching support; ways she worked differently with different teachers; differentiation based on teachers' needs

RESULTS

Over the course of the study, many of Sarah's beliefs about her role as a coach became clear, both through her statements and her actions. In this section, I first describe Sarah's coaching interactions with two of her teachers. I then explore Sarah's stated beliefs about her role as a coach and how she enacted them.

Sarah's Coaching Interactions

Sarah engaged in a variety of coaching activities with individual teachers. Though the focus of the coaching interactions varied from teacher to teacher, the nature of support resembled patterns of support Bean (2004) refers to as a coaching cycle. Sarah began with a conversation to address teachers' concerns and plan more targeted support for a future time. Then Sarah spent time supporting teachers in their classrooms. Finally, she followed up with a conversation she referred to as debriefing in order to determine teachers' reaction to her support and lingering questions. Below I provide a general description of the coaching cycles she engaged in with two of the study participants, Rachel and Lauren.

Coaching interactions with Rachel. Rachel was a third grade teacher in her fifth year of teaching. She and Sarah had five planned and observed coaching contacts. They first met to discuss plans for support. Having moved down to third grade from fourth, Rachel had questions about how to meet the needs of her students who were still struggling with decoding during guided reading. Sarah offered to share a set of materials used to teach specific word-solving strategies and to model a lesson using these materials with Rachel's lowest reading group. During their next coaching interaction, Sarah modeled a guided reading lesson in Rachel's classroom using the instructional materials she had suggested. Sarah and Rachel met at the end of the day to debrief and discussed keeping a tight focus for instruction during a guided reading lesson by including only one teaching point. Sarah shared her written plan for the lesson and Rachel asked questions regarding the strategy materials and how to best use them in her instruction. They decided Sarah would next come and observe Rachel as she led a guided reading lesson. After Sarah's observation, they met again to debrief. Rachel acknowledged that she had difficulty sticking to one strategy in the lesson. Sarah prompted her to think about the strategies she had seen her students spontaneously using in order to determine which strategies she still needed to reinforce or teach. Rachel was still struggling with using the strategy materials that Sarah had provided, so Sarah walked her through the next lesson in the series, showing her how to use the teacher's guide and posters. As the study drew to an end, Rachel acknowledged that her guided reading instruction had not really changed as a result of these interactions, and I also saw little evidence of change during my observations in her classroom.

Coaching interactions with Lauren. Lauren was a first grade teacher in her third year of teaching. She and Sarah had seven planned coaching interactions after Lauren approached Sarah to learn about word study and how to implement it in her classroom. When they first met, Lauren shared the types of word study activities she had tried so far. Sarah explained how the district's assessment tool could be used to differentiate word study instruction. However, Lauren indicated she wanted to continue word study as a whole-group activity and Sarah agreed she could do so. Sarah then offered to model a typical 5-day word study routine using the materials provided by the district. Their next five interactions took place in Lauren's classroom as Sarah modeled different word study activities (e.g., word hunt). Occasionally as the students worked, Sarah would speak to Lauren privately and explain the decisions she made for the lesson (i.e., how many words to use), why she chose certain instructional approaches, how she modified the materials, or suggestions for how Lauren might organize the word study time in her classroom. After the final session of modeling, Sarah met with Lauren to debrief. Lauren liked the idea of word study the way Sarah had modeled it and planned to incorporate it into her daily schedule. Sarah encouraged Lauren not to forget that the activities needed to be accompanied by instruction and not just assigned as individual activities. Sarah agreed to follow up with Lauren after she had a chance to try the activities to see if she had additional questions or would like to learn other activities for her students to complete. As the study came to a close, Lauren was still using the word study ideas Sarah shared with her and did not feel she needed additional support.

Sarah's Beliefs about Her Role as a Coach and Their Impact

As noted earlier, not all of the teachers chose to take up the ideas Sarah presented to them during their coaching interactions. In other work (Hathaway, 2012) I explore how the teachers' personal beliefs about literacy and teaching impacted their decisions about whether or not to adopt new practices. However, here I argue that though there were different outcomes with these two teachers, in each case Sarah's beliefs led her to coach light. In the following sections, I describe

Sarah's beliefs, both stated and in action, about the purpose of coaching, how she was positioned as a coach, the importance of strong teacher relationships in coaching, and finally about the need to meet teachers' unique needs while coaching.

Beliefs about the purposes of coaching. Sarah did not believe there was one correct way to teach reading. Thus, she was hesitant to require all of her teachers to teach the same way and had no expectation that instruction would be the same across classrooms and/or grade levels. She explained:

> The framework that [the district has] that teachers are supposed to be doing is very broad and I feel like as long as they've got those pieces that within those pieces [of guided reading, shared reading, read-aloud, independent reading, word study, and writing] there's a lot of room for individuality and letting teachers figure out how it works for them. (Interview 1)

Sarah's belief that there is no one correct way of teaching reading allowed her to remain flexible about the types of practices her teachers worked to adopt. She argued, "This isn't Sarah's reading program. It's not, everyone has to do Sarah's model" (Interview 1). This flexibility led her to value learning from her teachers as she sought their input and was open to ideas they shared. For example, during one of the grade-level meetings she led, when the teachers shared their concerns about students that she also taught in her intervention groups, Sarah asked the teachers to provide advice to her as well, saying, for example, "What can we do more with John?" or "What are some other ideas for [the teacher] and me?" (Grade 1 Meeting).

However, while Sarah believed teachers should have flexibility in their instruction, this belief was at odds with what she knew the district expected of her. The district's expectation was that she would facilitate teachers' close implementation of a balanced literacy framework. She described situations in which she was forced to go to teachers who were not following the framework and clearly state the district's requirements. She always followed the reminder with offers of support for the teacher. However, she admitted if those teachers chose not to take up the district's ideas, she did not believe it was her job to enforce the implementation of the framework. She ultimately believed teachers needed to take personal responsibility for their choices regarding instruction in their classrooms.

Sarah believed her role as a coach was to act as a guide for teachers and to help them discover what worked for them in their classrooms rather than provide them with all of the answers. To facilitate this, she felt she needed to provide her teachers with choices. She said, "I always give [teachers] choices. I always give 'em choices….'cause I feel like if I don't give 'em choice, then it's more I'm telling them what to do—which is not my job" (Interview 1).

This belief in the need for choices was evident during her coaching interactions with Rachel and Lauren. For example, when Sarah met with Rachel, she provided a choice over the types of support Rachel might receive. This is seen in the exchange below that took place between Sarah and Rachel at the end of their planning meeting as they decided on a plan of action for supporting Rachel's guided reading instruction.

Sarah: Do you want to see just the whole group or do you want to just see how the *Reading With Strategies* works? Or do you want to see how it all gets put together? You tell me what you want.

Rachel: I want to see how I need to teach it. (Planning Meeting)

Sarah placed the power in Rachel's hands to name the type of support that would be most beneficial for her as they ultimately decided that Sarah would model an entire guided reading lesson.

Finally, Sarah felt providing teachers with choices about the type of support she provided or the topics addressed in coaching also fostered greater teacher ownership over their learning. She did not want to encourage teachers to take on new practices without understanding the importance and reasoning behind them. She explained,

> I think [buy in is] absolutely crucial. Because if it's something that [teachers] don't understand or something that they feel like they couldn't do, or don't get it, then they're not gonna' follow through with it. They're not gonna' keep up with it. They're not gonna' be comfortable with it....And so even though you go in and show them this is what it is, they still may not understand the purpose behind it. So, you've gotta' get them to understand and see it as being valuable so that they will make it a priority. (Interview 2)

To support teachers' understanding, Sarah provided rationales for the ideas and practices she offered. For example, as part of their debriefing, Lauren asked how word study would support her students' spelling. Sarah explained that focusing on the patterns of the words would reinforce their spelling development. In a final interview, Lauren shared this explanation with me as a reason why she was continuing to use word study.

Beliefs about how a coach should be positioned. Sarah had clear beliefs about what the role of the coach should be. Because of this, she was very concerned about how she was positioned as a coach at Blue Mountain. Coaches are often cast into the role of expert (Gibson, 2006) and while Sarah acknowledged that some of her teachers saw her this way, it was not how she wanted to be perceived. As noted earlier, Sarah wanted to be seen as a guide on teachers' paths of self-discovery.

Along with not positioning herself as an expert, Sarah was also adamant that she not be positioned as an administrator. Unfortunately, the direct line of communication she had to the school's principal and the messages she was often required to deliver to teachers from the district sometimes made it hard for her to avoid the appearance of an administrative role. However, she was clear that she was not an administrator, she was not an evaluator, and she was not an enforcer. She said,

> We've been told in our reading specialists meetings we are not administrators. It is not our job to make teachers do guided reading. It is not our job to make them do read-alouds. We can't make them do anything. You know we just give 'em tools. (Initial Interview)

Sarah worked to overcome perceptions of her as an expert and administrator by positioning herself as a co-learner or equal with her teachers. She encouraged her teachers to share ideas with each other and would often refer teachers with questions to other teachers in the building who had experience with a certain practice. For instance, she suggested that one teacher talk with Rachel about writer's workshop. Sarah and Rachel had worked together in previous years to establish the practice in Rachel's classroom. Sarah explained, "I try to emphasize to [the teachers] you know, I'm learning too. I don't pretend to know everything. So I say I'm a resource, not an expert" (Vision Interview).

Sarah's efforts seemed to work, as the teachers in the study did not perceive her as an administrator. One study participant, Lauren, described her as "another teacher in the school" (Interview 2 Continued) and thought this positioning was an asset. She respected that Sarah worked with students on a daily basis and felt it gave Sarah greater credibility than previous coaches with whom she had worked. Similarly, Kathryn, another participant, clearly described her understanding of Sarah's role:

> The way I understand Sarah's role is that she's not an administrator. And she doesn't have the law to say, "You do this or else." And she doesn't have, it's not her job to go back and tattletale to [the principal] that we're not doing this. Her job is to work with us and help us….She's not gonna' go where she's not welcome. She will do what she's supposed to as far as her job is concerned, but she's not gonna' go make you come to her. (Interview 3)

Beliefs about relationships with teachers. Sarah also believed having a strong relationship with her teachers was a critical element of successful coaching. It was one of the reasons she fought against being positioned as an expert or administrator. She counted the relationships she had built working side-by-side with teachers before assuming the role of reading specialist as an asset for her coaching. In describing the type of relationship she hoped to build with teachers she explained, "I want to foster the relationship where they would come to me wanting some ideas or bouncing ideas off of me" (Vision Interview).

Sarah counted the growing of a relationship as a sign of success in her coaching. When asked to evaluate whether or not her coaching had been effective with Lauren, Sarah believed that having established a relationship with her was a positive outcome of their interactions. As a new teacher in the building, Sarah was pleased that Lauren had come to see her as a support and felt free to approach her when she had questions or needed assistance.

Because Sarah believed her relationships with teachers were key, their concerns were important to her. She wanted to provide support for them as they took on the process of change. She was aware that change is uncomfortable and can be overwhelming for teachers and worked to anticipate and address teachers' concerns in proactive ways. One way Sarah did this was by offering to share her own practice with teachers first as she did with Rachel and Lauren. By offering to model instruction in their classrooms rather than asking to come and observe, she in her own words "put myself out there first" (Interview 1). She believed this helped her teachers grow more comfortable with her and to see her as a support rather than an evaluator. Sarah was also vigilant about following up with teachers after their initial interactions to check on their progress or need for additional support.

Sarah also used choice as a tool for building and maintaining strong relationships with teachers, as teachers were able to choose whether or not they worked with her. Sarah did not push her way into classrooms where she was not invited. Her principal did not require her to work with teachers against their will and Sarah noted she would be quite uncomfortable in a job where she was required to do so. Because she respected the teachers' autonomy in their classrooms, she did not want to be perceived as someone who could come in uninvited and disrupt their classrooms.

While Sarah chose not to force her way into classrooms, she also did not ignore teachers who were less than eager to work with her. Instead, she established a repertoire of strategies for gaining access to teachers' classrooms in non-threatening ways. These included surveying teachers at the beginning of the school year to learn about their specific needs and concerns, using assessment data to open conversations with teachers, and asking general questions about how things were going in classrooms. I asked Sarah if there were times she offered teachers choices about the types of support she could provide and they chose not to accept her help. She explained,

> Yeah. And they're like, "No, I got it." And I always follow up with, "Okay but, we'll check in a week or two and just see how it's going." And I try to be really good about the checking in. "How's it going?" And then if I need to, offer the options again. But I don't push myself into classrooms….And again, it's one reason I do those surveys is because that's kind of my foot in the door so I don't feel like I'm pushing. Or being too pushy. (Interview 1)

Once she was able to establish relationships with teachers, Sarah believed she was then able to approach the teachers in non-confrontational ways. She explained, "I've been with these teachers… and have those relationships. I can go up to a teacher and say, 'So, how's word study going?' And that just starts the conversation" (Interview 1).

Beliefs about differentiating coaching support. Relationships were also crucial because Sarah felt they were what allowed her to *know* her teachers. This intimate knowledge of the teachers allowed her to differentiate her coaching to meet her teachers "where they were." Sarah's goal was to build on teachers' strengths as she continued to help them grow and develop. She noted:

> I try to always start with where [teachers] are.…I do have teacher[s] that come to me and they'll just say, "This just isn't working." And so I try to figure out where they are before I know where they need to go. I don't want to be the person that runs in and puts out the fire because that's not gonna' be sustainable. (Interview 3)

As Sarah worked to determine what her teachers were ready for, she learned to pay attention to the clues teachers provided through their conversations and actions. She gathered these clues together to help her paint a picture of each of her teachers and then matched her support to their needs. For example, Sarah described Rachel as a teacher who was eager to try new things in her classroom and willing to take risks. She based this on Rachel's willingness to take on writer's workshop during the previous year, and indeed this matched Rachel's description of herself during our conversations. Sarah felt that Rachel struggled with her confidence in being able to meet students' learning needs. Therefore, Sarah's approach to their coaching interactions was to help Rachel build confidence with her instruction. Rachel often sought clear-cut, black and white answers to her questions when interacting with Sarah. For example, during their planning meeting, Rachel asked Sarah to help her group her students for guided reading. Once the students were in groups, Sarah asked Rachel what level text she would use with one of the groups to which Rachel responded, "That's why you're here" (Planning Meeting). Rachel did eventually suggest a text level of 18 and Sarah tried to explain to her why that would be an appropriate selection. However, rather than engaging in the cognitive work Sarah invited her to do, Rachel twice more asked, "So level 18?" until Sarah eventually agreed with her selection.

During her final interview, I asked Sarah to reflect on this interaction with Rachel. She explained why she had persisted in not answering.

I want her to understand the thinking behind it. Because I could've said, "Start this group at a level 18 on word attack strategies." And the next time it came up, she wouldn't know, she wouldn't know what to do....So I try to do a lot of thinking aloud so hopefully they can take on some of that. (Interview 4)

Sarah was very much aware that Rachel often saw her as a person with all of the answers and therefore was willing to push Rachel to think for herself, even if she eventually knew she would give in and provide the answer Rachel wanted.

DISCUSSION/IMPLICATIONS

Many of the beliefs Sarah held about her role as a coach focused on the affective aspects of coaching. These beliefs impacted her work as a coach as she worked to respect teachers' autonomy and professionalism and to build collegial relationships. She recognized their uniqueness as learners while her willingness to consider many different approaches to literacy instruction allowed her to act as a guide for her teachers as they found the approaches that worked best in their own classrooms. In addition, Sarah's beliefs led her to struggle against attempts to cast her in the role of the expert. She recognized, as Toll (2005) argued, that placing herself in the role of the expert hindered her ability to build trusting relationships with her teachers. Sarah's focus on the affective aspects of coaching fostered the establishment of a trusting environment, which has been identified as one key to effective literacy coaching (Lyons, 2002). Indeed, Rainville and Jones (2008) studied how coaches' verbal and nonverbal language can be used to position themselves, both consciously and unconsciously, in ways that are supportive or detrimental to their work as a coach. They found that power struggles between teachers and coaches were less likely to occur when coaches were able to develop some type of relationship with their teachers.

While Sarah successfully built strong relationships with teachers, the impact of her coaching on their classroom practice was mixed. As described in the previous section, not all teachers chose to take up the practices demonstrated during coaching. While their personal beliefs may have hindered their adoption of new practices (Hathaway, 2012), it is also possible that Sarah's vision of herself as a coach may have had an impact. Sarah was interested in having teachers understand "the why" and therefore offered explanations and rationales for the practices she shared. However, there was no real expectation the teachers had to act on these ideas, either in her eyes or in the eyes of the teachers. They saw what she offered as suggestions they were free to use or not use. For example, Lauren described her thoughts on whether or not she had to try out the word study practices Sarah offered to her during their coaching interactions. She said,

> I know I've heard [Sarah] say to other teachers, "You could try it this way." And I think she spins it the right way where if she, like for instance with word study. I wasn't using word study and she basically said, "You should give it a go. If it doesn't work for you, fine. We'll try something else." (Interview 2 Continued)

Indeed, as described earlier, while Lauren did implement word study, she chose to do so in a whole-class setting rather than the small-group setting preferred by the district and Sarah did not challenge her decision. Thus, while Lauren appropriated the practices Sarah shared during coaching, that outcome may have been more a result of Lauren's interest than Sarah's expectation that she would do so.

Because Sarah did not have strong expectations that teachers had to act on the ideas she shared, she was engaged in what Killion (2009) describes as coaching light. From this perspective, coaches are more interested in establishing relationships with teachers than improving teaching and students' learning. Coaches who coach light do not hold expectations that what teachers learn during coaching will be put to use in their classrooms. They also may avoid the types of challenging conversations in which teachers' beliefs are challenged and deep change occurs. Thus, by coaching light, Sarah was able to maintain strong personal relationships with her teachers; however, her coaching efforts did not necessarily promote changes in the teachers' beliefs or practices.

While coaching light leads to positive relationships with teachers, it does not encourage changes in teachers' beliefs or practices, which is often the ultimate goal of professional development. Successful professional development provides opportunities to create what Lyons & Pinnell (2001) refer to as "good dissonance" (p. 140), allowing teachers to modify their beliefs and practices. However, as Freedman and Ball (2004) explained, "the social interactions that are most effective in promoting learning are those that are filled with tension and conflict" (p. 6). As described earlier, a coaching light approach leads coaches to avoid such conflict. For Sarah, while she was willing to address teachers' conflicting beliefs, she did so in ways that preserved the coaching relationship more than spurred new thinking in her teachers. For example, when addressing Rachel's lack of focus in her guided reading lessons, Sarah suggested Rachel create written plans and notes for future guided reading sessions, a practice Rachel was not currently doing. But, that suggestion was not followed with a concrete plan to hold Rachel accountable for a shift in her practice.

The alternative to coaching light is coaching heavy, which occurs when coaches engage in what Killion (2009) calls "high-stakes interactions" (p. 23), such as those in which personal and professional beliefs are considered as well as the influence they have on practice. "Coaching heavy occurs when coaches ask thought-provoking questions, uncover assumptions, have fierce or difficult conversations, and engage teachers in dialogue about their beliefs and goals rather than their knowledge and skills" (Killion, 2009, p. 24). She argues that while these interactions will prompt teachers to question their practice, it also provides them with an increased sense of professionalism, stronger feelings of efficacy, and greater satisfaction with teaching. Coaches are willing to risk not being liked in order to improve teaching and learning.

Even though Sarah appeared to be coaching light, she was poised to ignite more consistent change in teachers' beliefs and practice by coaching heavy. She differentiated her support based on what she knew about her teachers. These understandings were, in part, a result of her close observation of the teachers. Thus, for Sarah, a shift may have to occur in her own beliefs about her role as a coach and the purpose of coaching in order to engage teachers more purposefully in a consideration of their beliefs. Instead of simply inviting teachers to consider using new practices, she needs to expect teachers to try them out in their classrooms.

The findings from this study hold implications for understanding and addressing teachers' growth and professional development. For coaching to be a successful setting for addressing teachers' beliefs and practice, coaches may have to shift the approach they take to coaching. However, Killion's (2009) notion of coaching heavy may require coaches to approach their teachers in flexible ways. Coaches may also need to first examine their own beliefs about the role they play as a coach and their goals for coaching interactions if they desire to bring about more pronounced changes in teachers' beliefs and practice.

AUTHOR'S NOTE

Jennifer I. Hathaway is at Department of Reading and Elementary Education, University of North Carolina at Charlotte. Correspondence concerning this article should be addressed to Jennifer I. Hathaway, Department of Reading and Elementary Education, University of North Carolina at Charlotte, 9201 University City Boulevard, Charlotte, NC 28223. Email: jhathaway@uncc.edu

REFERENCES

Batt, E. G. (2010). Cognitive coaching: A critical phase in professional development to implement sheltered instruction. *Teaching and Teacher Education, 26*, 997-1005.

Bean, R. M. (2004). Promoting effective literacy instruction: The challenge for literacy coaches. *The California Reader, 37*(3), 58-63.

Biancarosa, G., Bryk, A. S., & Dexter, E. R. (2010). Assessing the value-added effects of literacy collaborative professional development on student learning. *Elementary School Journal, 111*(1), 7-34.

Calderhead, J. (1996). Teachers: Beliefs and knowledge. In D. C. Berliner & R. C. Calfee (Eds.), *Handbook of educational psychology* (pp. 709-725). New York, NY: Macmillan.

Casey, K. (2006). *Literacy coaching: The essentials.* Portsmouth, NH: Heinemann.

Elish-Piper, L., & L'Allier, S. K. (2010). Exploring the relationship between literacy coaching and student reading achievement in grades K-1. *Literacy Research and Instruction, 49*(2), 162-174.

Freedman, S. W., & Ball, A. F. (2004). Ideological becoming: Bakhtinian concepts to guide the study of language, literacy, and learning. In A. F. Ball & S. W. Freedman (Eds.), *Bakhtinian perspectives on language, literacy, and learning* (pp. 3-33). Cambridge, UK: Cambridge University Press.

Gibson, S. A. (2006). Lesson observation and feedback: The practice of an expert reading coach. *Reading Research and Instruction, 45*(4), 295-318.

Guskey, T. R. (2000). *Evaluating professional development.* Thousand Oaks, CA: Corwin Press.

Hammerness, K. (1999). *Seeing through teachers' eyes: An exploration of the content, character and role of teachers' vision.* Unpublished doctoral dissertation, Stanford University, CA.

Hammerness, K. (2003). Learning to hope, or hoping to learn? The role of vision in the early professional lives of teachers. *Journal of Teacher Education, 54*(1), 43-56.

Hammerness, K. (2006). *Seeing through teachers' eyes: Professional ideals and classroom practices.* New York, NY: Teachers College Press.

Hathaway, J. I., & Risko, V. J. (2007, April). *Reading specialists as professional development leaders: Contextualizing school change.* Paper presented at the annual meeting of the American Educational Research Association, Chicago, IL.

Hathaway, J. I. (2012). *Considering how teachers believe: Expanding understandings of beliefs within professional development.* Manuscript in preparation.

Hughes, M. T., Cash, M. M., Ahwee, S., & Klingner, J. (2002). A national overview of professional development programs in reading. In E. M. Rodgers & G. S. Pinnell (Eds.), *Learning from teaching in literacy education: New perspectives on professional development* (pp. 9-28). Portsmouth, NH: Heinemann.

International Reading Association. (2004). *The role and qualifications of the reading coach in the United States.* Newark, DE: International Reading Association.

International Reading Association. (2010). *Standards for reading professionals—Revised 2010.* Retrieved November 18, 2011 from http://reading.org/General/CurrentResearch/Standards/ProfessionalStandards2010.aspx

Joyce, B., & Showers, B. (2002). *Student achievement through staff development* (3rd ed.). Alexandria, VA: Association for Supervision and Curriculum Development.

Killion, J. (2009). Coaches' roles, responsibilities, and reach. In J. Knight (Ed.), *Coaching: Approaches and perspectives* (pp. 7-28). Thousand Oaks, CA: Corwin Press.

Kise, J. A. G. (2006). *Differentiated coaching: A framework for helping teachers change.* Thousand Oaks, CA: Corwin Press.

Korth, B. B., Sharp, A. C., & Culatta, B. (2010). Classroom modeling of supplemental literacy instruction: Influencing the beliefs and practices of classroom teachers. *Communication Disorders Quarterly, 31*(2), 113-127.

Lenski, S. D., Wham, M. A., & Griffey, D. C. (1998). Literacy orientation survey: A survey to clarify teachers' beliefs and practices. *Reading Research and Instruction, 37*(3), 217-236.

Lyons, C. A. (2002). Becoming an effective literacy coach: What does it take? In E. M. Rodgers & G. S. Pinnell (Eds.), *Learning from teaching in literacy education: New perspectives on professional development* (pp. 93-118). Portsmouth, NH: Heinemann.

Lyons, C. A., & Pinnell, G. S. (2001). *Systems for change in literacy education: A guide to professional development.* Portsmouth, NH: Heinemann.

McKenna, M. C., & Walpole, S. (2008). *The literacy coaching challenge: Models and methods for grades K-8.* New York, NY: Guilford.

Pajares, M. F. (1992). Teachers' beliefs and educational research: Cleaning up a messy construct. *Review of Educational Research, 62*(3), 307-332.

Rainville, K. N., & Jones, S. (2008). Situated identities: Power and positioning in the work of a literacy coach. *The Reading Teacher, 61*(6), 440-448.

Reutzel, D. R., & Sabey, B. (1996). Teacher beliefs and children's concepts about reading: Are they related? *Reading Research and Instruction, 35*(4), 323-42.

Richardson, V., Anders, P., Tidwell, D., & Lloyd, C. (1991). The relationship between teachers' beliefs and practices in reading comprehension instruction. *American Educational Research Journal, 28*(3), 559-586.

Robb, L. (2000). *Redefining staff development: A collaborative model for teachers and administrators.* Portsmouth, NH: Heinemann.

Rodgers, E. M., & Pinnell, G. S. (2002). Professional development scenarios: What is and might be. In E. M. Rodgers & G. S. Pinnell (Eds.), *Learning from teaching in literacy education: New perspectives on professional development* (pp. 1-8). Portsmouth, NH: Heinemann.

Rodgers, A., & Rodgers, E. M. (2007). *The effective literacy coach: Using inquiry to support teaching and learning.* New York, NY: Teachers College Press.

Rosemary, C., Bean, R. M., Belcastro, B., Hathaway, J. I., Risko, V. J., & Roskos, K. (2012). *Synthesis of research on instructional coaching: Over two decades, what have we learned?* Manuscript in preparation.

Rudd, L. C., Lambert, M. C., Satterwhite, M., & Smith, C. H. (2009). Professional development + coaching = enhanced teaching: Increasing usage of math mediated language in preschool classrooms. *Early Childhood Education Journal, 37*(1), 63-69.

Sacks, C. H., & Mergendoller, J. R. (1997). The relationship between teachers' theoretical orientations toward reading and student outcomes in kindergarten children with different initial reading abilities. *American Educational Research Journal, 34*(4), 721-739.

Silvernail, D. L. (1992). The educational philosophies of secondary school teachers. *The High School Journal, 76,* 162-167.

Squires, D., & Bliss, T. (2004). Teacher visions: Navigating beliefs about literacy learning. *The Reading Teacher, 57*(8), 756-763.

Stake, R. E. (2005). Qualitative case studies. In N. K. Denzin & Y. S. Lincoln (Eds.), *The sage handbook of qualitative research* (3rd ed.) (pp. 443-466). Thousand Oaks, CA: Sage.

Strauss, A., & Corbin, J. (1998). *Basics of qualitative research. Techniques and procedures for developing grounded theory* (2nd ed.). Thousand Oaks, CA: Sage.

Toll, C. A. (2005). *The literacy coach's survival guide: Essential questions and practical answers.* Newark, DE: International Reading Association.

Vanderburg, M., & Stephens, D. (2010). The impact of literacy coaches: What teachers value and how teachers change. *Elementary School Journal, 111*(1), 141-163.

Veenman, S., Denessen, E., Gerrits, J., & Kenter, J. (2001). Evaluation of a coaching programme for cooperating teachers. *Educational Studies, 27,* 317-340.

APPENDIX A

Guiding Questions for Initial Interviews

Teacher Background

1. How long have you been teaching? What grades have you taught? Where?

2. How did you come to your current position?

3. Why did you decide to become a teacher?

4. Before you obtained a job, what did you expect teaching to be?

5. How has your experience differed from or been similar to those early expectations?

6. What do you find to be the most challenging part of your job? the least challenging?

7. Where do you see yourself in 10 years?

   1. Do you plan to continue in this field? If so, in what capacity (e.g., teacher, administrator, specialist)? If not, when do you plan to leave, why, and what other fields/jobs do you intend to pursue?

Reading and Learning to Read

1. When a student enters _____ grade, what should he/she be able to do in terms of reading?
   - On what are those expectations based? personal convictions? district standards?

2. When that student leaves this grade level, what can he/she do?
   - On what are those expectations based? personal convictions? district standards?

3. What can a really good reader do?
   - Is the difference in good and struggling readers quantitative or qualitative?

4. What accounts for the differences between a good and struggling reader?

5. Is it possible to help a struggling reader become a good reader?

The Students

1. Describe the students in your class.
   - Is this a typical group of students for this grade level?

2. Describe a student who is having great difficulty in reading.
   - What do you think is the cause of this difficulty?
   - What are you doing about it?
   - (repeat probes for each question below)

3. Describe a student who is just slightly behind in reading.

4. Describe a student who is doing really well.

The School

1. Do you feel there is a characteristic way of teaching reading in this school?
   - If so, how did this way of teaching come to be? On what is it based?
   - If not, do you know of other teachers who have similar styles to you?

2. Do you know what the other teachers are doing?

- If so, how? Do you observe in other classrooms? Do you exchange materials, ideas, methods? Do you talk with other teachers?

3. Describe any professional development you have addressing reading in the school?

- Have you found this professional development to be useful? If so, how?
- If not, what type of professional development would you find useful?

APPENDIX B

Guiding Questions for Visioning Interview

1. Before we start, do you want to elaborate on what you wrote in any way? Do you want to add/revise anything you said?

2. How did this become your vision of the ideal classroom?

3. Why do you believe this is the ideal classroom?

4. How does your vision compare to what you are currently doing in your classroom? Does your vision match your actual teaching experiences? Why/why not?

5. What is the relationship between your ability to carry out your vision and the school where you currently teach?

- Does the school have a vision?
- What is the relationship between your vision and the vision of the school?
- Is your vision school specific, or would this be your vision regardless of where you teach?

6. What is the relationship between the kinds of students you teach and your ability to carry out your vision?

- Do you think your vision would be different/the same if you had different students?

7. Has your vision of the ideal classroom changed since you began teaching? If so, how has it changed? If not, why do you believe it has remained the same?

8. If your vision matches your reality, how did you make that happen? Do you think you will be able to maintain this ideal classroom in the future? If your vision does not match your reality, do you anticipate in the future that you will be able to reach this ideal you hold? Will you/How will you work to do this? What aspects are you trying to achieve right now in your classroom?

9. How often do you think about your vision?

10. On what is your vision based?

- Did any of it come from your own background as a student or teacher?
- Have you ever seen/been part of/read about a classroom like this?
- Does it come from your experiences in your undergraduate work?
- Does it come from your professional development experiences?
- Is there anything else about your vision that's come up today that you'd want to add or clarify?

Issues in Supporting Disciplinary Literacies with the Common Core State Standards

Roni Jo Draper
Brigham Young University

The Common Core State Standards (CCSS) is the result of an effort by the National Governors Association Center for Best Practices and the Council of Chief State School Officers to create a common framework for curriculum and instruction across the 45 of the U.S. states and territories that have adopted them (Common Core State Standards, 2010). The CCSS outline curricular standards in English Language Arts and mathematics for elementary and secondary grades. For grades six through twelve, the CCSS specify literacy standards for content-areas including history, social studies, science, and technological subjects. While not specifying literacy standards for all subjects, the CCSS do promote literacy across the curriculum by suggesting that teachers in all content areas support students' abilities to use and create complex print text "to facilitate a comprehensive, schoolwide literacy program" (p. 6). On the surface, the attention to literacy in the content areas promoted by the CCSS seems a long time coming and a welcomed change from the assumption that literacy instruction is solely the purview of English Language Arts teachers. However, a closer examination of the messages about content-area literacy found in the CCSS calls into question the value placed on disciplinary participation, and, thus, the commitment to support students' acquisition and learning of content knowledge and disciplinary skills.

Like other educational and curricular standards, the CCSS offer a view of the kind of people that their framers seek to create (Popkewitz, 2004). As for the CCSS, they seek to create individuals who are "career and college ready" (p. 6). To this end, the CCSS for English and Language Arts posit that, "[a]s students advance through the grades and master the standards in reading, writing, speaking, listening, and language, they [will be] able to exhibit with increasing fullness and regularity [the] capacities of the literate individual" (p. 6). The inclusion of standards for literacy in history/social studies, science, and technical subjects is predicated on the understanding that, "[c]ollege and career ready reading in these fields requires an appreciation of the norms and conventions of each discipline" (CCSS, 2010, p. 60).

For literacy educators, this vision of content-area classrooms serving as spaces in which students acquire and use literacies is one they have advocated for nearly a century (Moore, Readence, & Rickelman, 1983). As such, many literacy educators may view the CCSS as the policy they have been waiting for to make literacy across the curriculum a reality in secondary schools. However, educators must be clear on the purpose of literacy instruction for the disciplines promoted by the CCSS: Is the purpose of literacy-across-the-curriculum to promote disciplinary participation or to promote general literacy?

Historically, "school subjects have little relation to the intellectual fields that bear their names" (Popkewitz, 2004, p. 249). Instead, school subjects—mathematics, history, science, music, and so on—represent a kind of alchemy between the disciplines and the technologies of learning and schooling. Educational and curricular standards, including the CCSS, play into this alchemy and serve both to construe and constrain possibilities for children (Popkewitz, 2004). For example, some literacy educators have argued for content-area instruction that introduces students to disciplinary discourses and norms (Draper, Broomhead, Jensen, Nokes, & Siebert, 2010; Langer, 2011) and it may be that the CCSS seek to promote this view. Certainly the CCSS recommend practices like inquiry and argumentation, which are central to disciplines like history and science. For example, the writing standard for science and technical subjects, which states that for grades 11-12 students should be able to conduct "research projects to answer a question (including a self-generated question) to solve a problem" (CCSS, 2010, p. 66). Meanwhile, a possible constraint to the aim of disciplinary literacy promoted by the CCSS is their description of what counts as texts and the literacies for science and technical subjects. For example, the CCSS state that students should be able to "read and comprehend science/technical texts…" (p. 62), but the description of texts offered by the CCSS for science and technical classrooms constrains what and how students read in these classrooms, thus, constraining the possibility that disciplinary literacies can be acquired and practiced.

However, the CCSS may not intend to promote disciplinary participation. Rather, the discussion of content-area literacy promoted in the CCSS may serve simply to use content-area classrooms as contexts in which students can practice their literacy skills and a way for students simply to use literacy as a tool for learning content. Statements in the CCSS, such as the following, seem to give some credence to this possibility: "[b]y reading texts in history/social studies, science, and other disciplines, students build a foundation of knowledge in these fields that will also give them the background to be better readers in all content areas" (CCSS, 2010, p. 10). Similarly, returning to the reading standards for science and technical subjects, the statement that students should be able to "read and comprehend science/technical texts in the grades 11-CCR [College and Career Readiness] text complexity band independently and proficiently" (p. 62) can be viewed as a promotion of text and general literacy as much as a promotion of the discipline.

The purpose of this paper is to share my close reading of the CCSS. The caveat for this reading is the understanding that the implementation of the CCSS relies both on how the CCSS describe literacy for content-area classrooms and how teachers and literacy educators read and respond to those descriptions. I recognize that my reading of the CCSS, as represented in this paper, is quite narrow. Indeed, I offer here one particular reading of the CCSS based on my view of the disciplines, texts, and literacy. I recognize that alternative, broader, and more generous readings of the CCSS are possible. Alternative readings of the CCSS, and the ensuing discussions, will shape a shared understanding of the possibilities and limitations presented in the CCSS and will ultimately shape how content-area teachers implement the CCSS. To this end, my hope is that my critique of the CCSS sheds light on the weaknesses of the CCSS that will allow teachers (and individuals charged to assist teachers) to implement the CCSS in their classrooms in ways that promote disciplinary participation.

Disciplinary Participation

As a literacy teacher educator and researcher, my understanding of the disciplines has been shaped by my background as a mathematics and science teacher and my continued participation with a group of content-area teacher educators over the past 5 years (see Draper, 2008; Draper, et al., 2011). Our collaboration around disciplinary literacy and teacher education has forced me to consider the aims of literacy instruction from a disciplinary point of view. I have come to view disciplinary participation—as opposed to knowledge—as the ultimate aim of content-area instruction.

I view the disciplines as communities of practice as opposed to bodies of knowledge. This view is based largely on the work of Wenger (1998). Viewing disciplines as communities of practice acknowledges that people and associated activity are at the center of the disciplines. As such, I view a discipline such as science as made up of people who interact together to address particular problems in particular ways. Certainly these people must possess funds of knowledge (facts about how the natural world works); however, they must also have the requisite social skills (literacies) to use that knowledge to work together to negotiate and create new knowledge. This view of the disciplines values both the cognitive and the social aspects of disciplinary participation.

Viewing disciplines as social practice means that I also realize that these societies (societies of historians, mathematicians, scientists, engineers, or artists) must create and use objects to mediate their interactions (see Blumer, 1969). These objects, or signs or texts, not only provide the means for people to represent and communicate their understanding of and in the world, they also mediate the understandings people have in the world (Sebeok, 2001). Thus, meanings and the use of the symbols used to represent those meanings construct each other (Sebeok, 2001; Sfard, 2000). These objects, which I refer to as texts, are not limited to alphabetic symbols. In science, for example, texts include graphs, charts, diagrams, mathematical symbols, and other signs used to represent meaning. Therefore, to be literate in science settings requires the ability to use texts to represent meaning and to participate successfully with the objects and people in those settings. This kind of literacy requires both content knowledge and knowledge of how to use texts in appropriate ways. As such, the definition of literacy that I espouse consists of the ability to use texts in discipline-appropriate ways or in ways that disciplinary experts would recognize as correct (Draper & Siebert, 2010), which necessarily requires both funds of knowledge related to a discipline as well as knowledge of text use and creation.

My view of literacy for the disciplines goes beyond conveying information and includes perspective taking and scaffolding action (Gee, 2001). Looking again at science, in addition to conveying information about the natural world to scientists, scientists work to critique the theories and ideas presented by others. These activities require more than mere understanding of representations. They also require scientists to question motives, biases, and perspectives of both the author and themselves as readers (Luke, 1995). Additionally, the activities carried out by scientists from designing inquiries to collecting and analyzing data require the use of texts that scaffold their inquiry (e.g., note-taking, calculation-making, sketching conclusions).

Finally, my approach to literacy instruction is shaped by my views of disciplinary participation and literacy. I contend that the purpose of literacy instruction for content-area classrooms is to prepare students with all the cognitive and social knowledge and skills necessary to participate fully in disciplinary activities (Langer, 2011; Siebert & Draper, 2012). Note that this stance is quite different than one that suggests that the purpose of literacy instruction beyond the primary grades is to be a tool for learning in content-area classrooms. To promote disciplinary participation and the literacies that accompany it, instruction in content-area classrooms should allow students to engage in disciplinary practices as much as is possible. This focus on disciplinary activity is not merely to engage students or to promote motivation. Rather, engaging students in disciplinary activities (e.g., problem-solving, inquiry) allows students to approximate disciplinary activities in a way that allows them to learn and acquire identities associated with disciplinary participation (Airey & Linder, 2008; Wenger, 1998).

With these views of disciplinary participation and literacy in mind, I read the CCSS to determine the extent to which they support students' acquisition of disciplinary literacies. I brought to my reading of the CCSS questions about how the CCSS describe texts and literacy for content-area classrooms. My close reading of the CCSS reveals a view of texts and literacy that is too narrow to promote full disciplinary participation. This occurs due to two related issues. The first is the promotion by the CCSS of texts that consist primarily of alphabetic print at the exclusion of the other texts necessary for reasoning and participating in the full range of disciplinary activities. The second is the promotion of literacies associated with learning (getting and conveying information) at the exclusion of other disciplinary activities such as those associated with problem-solving or inquiry. The remainder of this paper contains my review of the CCSS to support these claims. I have organized this review around the descriptions of texts and literacy standards provided in the CCSS. I counter those descriptions with examples from various disciplines to demonstrate the limitations of the position taken by the CCSS.

Describing Complex Text

The CCSS encourage instruction around increasingly complex text. However, it is clear that they promote alphabetic texts (either print or electronic) and only acknowledge other objects (e.g., graphs, diagrams, pictures, mathematical symbols) as representations that augment texts. This position is made clear in the description of the reading standard for grades 9-10 in science and technical subjects. The standard states that students should be able to:

> Translate quantitative or technical information expressed in words in a text into visual form (e.g., a table or chart) and translate information expressed visually or mathematically (e.g., in an equation) into words. (CCSS, 2010, p. 62)

Thus, while the CCSS do not explicitly define text, it is clear from this statement that according to the CCSS, texts consist of words. Other forms of representation, it follows, are just that, other forms of representation.

Elsewhere, in describing the anchor standards for reading, the CCSS explain that students should be able to "integrate and evaluate content presented in diverse formats and media, including visually and quantitatively, as well as in word" (CCSS, 2010, p. 60). Thus, one may argue that the definition of text espoused by the CCSS is inconsequential as long as the CCSS value and promote multiple forms of representation. However, given the examples of texts described throughout the CCSS, including the appendices, it is clear that the CCSS neither recognizes nor promotes non-print texts as the focus of literacy instruction—despite the centrality of such texts in many of the disciplines. The narrow definition of text espoused by the CCSS has at least three possible negative consequences for content-area classrooms: (a) the full range of texts used to participate in the disciplines will not be used in content-area classrooms, (b) texts will be introduced in content-area classrooms that do not conform to disciplinary norms, and (c) the texts central to the discipline may be underused or slighted all together in content-area classrooms. Any of these consequences has the potential to affect what is taught and how it is taught in content-area classrooms, ultimately affecting content and literacy learning. For the remainder of this section, I explore each of these consequences.

The narrow view of text promoted in the CCSS as print material means that the texts suggested for content-area classrooms does not include all the texts used to participate in the disciplines. In science, scientists create and use many non-print texts to complete scientific inquiries (e.g., charts, diagrams, apparatuses, and natural phenomenon) (Airey & Linder, 2008; Draper & Adair, 2010). Among the non-print texts used in science settings are those created to model phenomena and/or processes—texts that consist of multiple modes of representation. Thus, the privileging of print texts in science classrooms would exclude two- and three-dimensional models of molecules and single-celled organisms as the focus of literacy instruction. For example, I recently observed a middle-school science classroom in which the science teacher, espousing a broad notion of text that includes images and models, supported students as they worked to create diagrams to model the changes of the forms of energy (potential to kinetic) in a swinging pendulum. Students worked to create a diagram that represented the motion of the pendulum and the locations of the pendulum at which the energy transformed from potential to kinetic energy. While the CCSS would recognize the diagrams created by the members of this class of eighth graders as appropriate scientific activity, it is not clear if the CCSS would make the use or creation of this text a focus of literacy instruction. Instead, it appears that the CCSS privilege written descriptions that consist primarily of words and sentences as target texts around which to focus literacy instruction.

The CCSS do not include an exhaustive list of text recommendations for content-area classrooms. Instead, they recommend that students have opportunities and instruction around texts of increasing sophistication and complexity. When the CCSS do recommend particular texts for content-area classrooms (as they do in appendices B and C), those texts do not always conform to disciplinary norms. For example, of the six texts suggested as exemplar mathematics texts, all are primarily traditional alphabetic texts consisting of words and paragraphs rather than mathematics texts that consist primarily of symbols, equations, diagrams, and graphs. Only one of the exemplar mathematics texts, the *Elements* by Euclid (2005/300 BC), would be considered an authentic mathematics text or a text that was created and/or used in conjunction with authentic mathematical activity. The other texts, such as John Allen Paulos' (1988) *Innumeracy*, are popular texts reflecting philosophical or popular topics related to or about mathematics. This distinction is important

Figure 1. Classification of the Texts Described in the CCSS

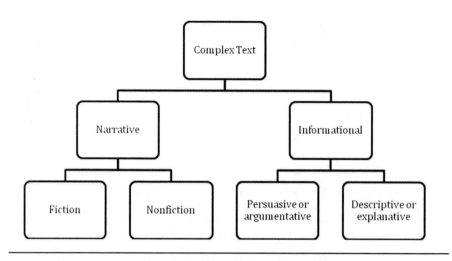

because while learning to read a book like *Innumeracy* may be a noble pursuit, it does not represent the texts central to *doing* mathematics (Lemke, 2004; Siebert & Draper, 2008).

This focus on print texts and texts only tangentially related to the disciplines is also evident in the description of exemplar writing texts. For example, the CCSS include an example of an informative/explanatory text that they suggest is appropriate in a technical class. The text is an essay about wood joinery. However, the three-page essay does not include one image of a wood joint, calling into question the usefulness of such a piece to an individual truly interested in knowing more about wood joinery. In contrast, a similar descriptive piece found in Douglass and Roberts' (1967) book on building wood furniture includes 16 drawings to accompany their description of wood joints. Arguably, the latter text is more appropriate and useful to carpenters interested in designing and building wood furniture. It would be impossible and imprudent for the CCSS to create an exhaustive list of texts appropriate for the various disciplines. Nevertheless, the guidance provided by the exemplars constrains what readers may determine is appropriate for content classrooms.

Supporting Literacies

The texts described and recommended for use in content-area classrooms have implications for the literacies promoted by the CCSS. In this section I focus my critique of the CCSS on the two following issues: (a) the CCSS promote literacies focused primarily on conveying and extracting information, and (b) the CCSS do not acknowledge the need for individuals to learn how to coordinate multiple texts and literacies in order to function effectively in disciplinary activities.

Figure 1 provides a classification of the texts described in the CCSS. The narrative texts represent those texts most appropriate for English Language Arts classrooms while the informational texts are those described in the CCSS as most appropriate for content-area classrooms. Using Gee's (2001) description of the three functions of language (conveying information, perspective-taking, and scaffolding action), it seems that the CCSS provide provisions to assist students in acquiring the literacies necessary to consider multiple perspectives and convey information. However, they do not list texts used to scaffold action. For example, consider the texts a mathematician creates and reads to support reasoning during problem-solving. These texts are likely not created for an audience and are not meant to be read later by the creator except to review in case of error or to check work. Instead, these texts are created and read to aid mathematical reasoning. The absence of the full range of texts used in the disciplines—including multimodal texts, non-print texts, and those used to scaffold action—means a neglect of the literacies necessary to create and use these texts and hinders the possibility that students will acquire all the literacies needed to engage in disciplinary activities.

Notwithstanding the exclusion of many texts and literacies, the bulk of the CCSS is devoted to describing benchmarks and standards for the literacies that adolescents should develop. For example, the CCSS, as part of their description of students who meet the standard for career and college readiness, offer the following:

> Students can, without significant scaffolding, comprehend and evaluate complex texts across a range of types and disciplines, and they can construct effective arguments and convey intricate or multifaceted information. Likewise, students are able independently to discern a speaker's key points, request clarification, and ask relevant questions. (CCSS, 2010, p. 7)

While information-gathering and sharing are certainly central to communication and learning, many of the texts used in the disciplines require literacies beyond those needed for gaining and conveying information. Indeed, summarizing is of limited use in disciplinary activities. For example, consider plans for making a birdhouse from a 1" x 6" x 4'4" piece of lumber. A builder may certainly use the text to get information, but the builder likely will not create a summary of the text. Instead, the builder will use the text to build a birdhouse. It is equally likely that the reader or user of the text will use the schematics and building directions as simply a starting-off point and make modifications to personalize the birdhouse or to create the birdhouse from material that differed in size and kind from that specified on the plans. In this way, the builder is involved in a complex combination of reading and rewriting the building plans. Moreover, the evidence of successful reading of the plans is not found in a proper retelling of the text, but in the creation of a birdhouse.

Similarly, the recommendation in the CCSS (2010) that students should, "…determine the central ideas or information of a primary or secondary source" (p. 61) and "provide an accurate summary that makes clear the relationships among the key details and ideas" (p. 61) does not take into account how a historian might read a primary or secondary source document. For example, consider a photograph of a sign with an arrow containing the words "colored waiting room." On the surface, the central idea is that there is a waiting room for African Americans in a particular direction—that is the information. However, there is much more to this document, and the purposes held by an historian for reading this text do not include gaining summarizable information. Rather, it is to consider the veracity of this text as a source of historical evidence as part of a project that includes creating an account of an historical event or era (see Nokes & Nielson, 2011; Wineburg, 1991). Likewise, chemists rarely seek to paraphrase the periodic table of elements. As such, the privileging of summarizing literacies may obfuscate many important disciplinary literacies.

Similar issues arise with other texts and literacies advocated by the CCSS. For example, when creating a descriptive text, the CCSS (2010) explain that students should "…introduce a topic and organize complex ideas, concepts, and information so that each new element builds on that which precedes it to create a unified whole; include formatting (e.g., headings), graphics (e.g., figures, tables), and multimedia when useful to aiding comprehension" (p. 65). Because the CCSS do not recognize the centrality of hybrid (Lemke, 2004) or multimodal (Kress, 2000) texts, they do not promote literacies that require the coordination of print and non-print elements. For instance, consider again the task of diagraming a swinging pendulum and labeling it to indicate points of energy transfer. The creation of the still diagram requires the creation of images to represent the three-dimensional pendulum that is in motion. While this description does not conform in form or structure to the literacies associated with creating an exemplar description as portrayed in the CCSS for science classrooms, it certainly is a valued form of description or scientific modeling in a science setting (Airey & Linder, 2008).

Moreover, the CCSS do not discuss the complex coordination that must take place as individuals work to negotiate and create several complex texts, virtually simultaneously, as they participate in disciplinary activities. For example, engineering frequently culminates in the creation of a report or text that uses a variety of evidence to make a case or argue for particular solutions to real, human problems (Shumway & Wright, 2010). However, texts and literacies are used throughout the problem-solving process and not exclusively during the culmination of the process. Consider the following engineering text. It represents the kind of summative text described by the CCSS as a complex text. The text is from an actual technical memorandum from a mining engineering firm describing two possible solutions to storing mine waste (the names of the firm and the client have been changed to maintain anonymity).

> This technical memorandum summarises the results of a trade-off study carried out by Mining Engineering Team Pty Ltd (MET) for the Big Mine Project (BMP)…This trade-off study evaluates the "In-Pit On-Site" tailings management concept with, and without the use of a flocculant. Both options have been evaluated taking the following into consideration:
> • Cost
> • Technical Risk
> • Potential Environmental Impacts. (Minard, 2011, p. 1)

This engineering text includes both descriptive and persuasive elements. It also includes both traditional print and non-print elements (e.g., maps, diagrams, spec tables, graphs). By focusing on the literacy associated with creating this one print text the fact that a team of engineers and geologists had to work together to create this text may be neglected. Their work together, leading up to this text, required sophisticated literacies associated with the creation and negotiation of many other texts—geological studies, climate studies, discussions between engineers, preliminary designs for mine-waste management, and so forth. These literacies may not be categorized neatly as either descriptive or persuasive in nature, but they are central to the work of the engineers and scientists who worked to create this final, summative text. The description of content-area literacy included in the CCSS does not take into account the complexity of the coordinated use of texts and literacies in content-area classrooms. My fear is that if literacy instruction in technical subjects is reduced to the writing of the summative report, many important literacies may be neglected, making the summative report even more difficult to create. Thus, the narrow focus on descriptive and argumentative literacies on the part of the CCSS, ignores the fact that at any given moment disciplinary activities require the complex coordination of multiple literacies as individuals move from reading and writing several complex texts.

CONCLUSIONS

The likelihood that literacy educators will be called upon by schools and districts to help teachers develop curriculum and instructional practices that promote students' achievement of these standards is high. In their desire to be helpful, literacy educators must take care not to become so elated by the inclusion of the disciplines in the CCSS that they make recommendations for content-area classrooms that inhibit students' acquisition of disciplinary literacies (see Siebert & Draper, 2008). It would be a shame, for instance, for literacy instruction in mathematics classrooms to focus on helping students translate solutions to equations to prose at the expense of helping students learn to justify solutions to equations based on sound mathematical principles or for literacy instruction in science classrooms to focus on summarizing books and articles at the expense of helping students create and carry out inquiries to investigate the natural world.

Elsewhere I have pointed out that these are good times to be a literacy educator (see Draper, 2008). Literacy educators can bemoan educational reform efforts like the No Child Left Behind Act (NCLB), high-stakes testing, and now the adoption of the new CCSS, but the reality is that literacy remains at the forefront of much of these reforms. More than ever, literacy educators are being consulted to help translate the reforms into practice in both English Language Arts classrooms and content-area classrooms. However, it is precisely because of this position that literacy educators must work with resolve to maintain the disciplines in the foreground of content-area curriculum and instruction (Moje, 2008). Doing so will promote the possibility that individuals will have opportunities to build deep conceptual understandings of the world, and, ultimately, develop the powerful literacies needed, not only for career and college readiness, but for the full range of human knowledge and practices for effective participation in the world.

With this ambiguity in the CCSS as to whether the goal is to promote disciplinary learning and participation or literacy learning, educators may be unclear as to what is expected for content-area classrooms. Ultimately the responsibility for literacy instruction falls not to what is written in the CCSS, but how the CCSS are read and understood by educators. This will necessarily require multiple and varied readings. And while it is up to educators to translate these standards into classroom practices, subsequent assessment requirements may serve as the last word in what is actually being promoted by the CCSS. Rather than perpetuate a dichotomy between literacy and content learning and doing (see Draper, Hall, Smith, & Siebert, 2005), literacy educators ought to work with teachers to help them create content-area classrooms that promote literacy as abled participation in disciplinary communities of practice. This view of literacy requires both essential knowledge and skills—knowledge and skills that are developed in use in content-area classrooms that strive to resemble the disciplines. The caveat is that in order to support this kind of literacy acquisition, educators must give attention to *all* the texts and *all* the literacies necessary for participation in those disciplines. To do this, educators must take the CCSS at their word and realize that "the Standards focus on what is most essential, they do not describe all that can or should be taught" (p. 6).

AUTHOR'S NOTE

I would like to acknowledge the members of the Brigham Young University Literacy Study Group who have shaped my thinking around disciplinary literacy.

REFERENCES

Airey, J., & Linder, C. (2008). A disciplinary discourse perspective on university science learning: Achieving fluency in a critical constellation of modes. *Journal of Research in Science Teaching, 46*, 1-32.

Blumer, H. (1969). *Symbolic interactionism: Perspective and method*. Berkley, CA: University of California Press.

Common Core State Standards. (2010). Common core state standards. Retrieved February 19, 2011, from http://www.corestandards.org/

Douglass, J. H., & Roberts, R. H. (1967). *Projects in wood furniture*. Bloomington, IL: McKnight and McKnight.

Draper, R. J. (2008). Redefining content-area teacher education: Finding my voice through collaboration. *Harvard Educational Review, 78*, 60-83.

Draper, R. J., & Adair, M. (2010). (Re)imagining literacy for science classrooms. In R. J. Draper, P. Broomhead, A. P. Jensen, J. Nokes & D. Siebert (Eds.), *(Re)imagining content-area literacy instruction* (pp. 127-143). New York, NY: Teachers College Press.

Draper, R. J., Adair, M., Broomhead, P., Gray, S., Grierson, S., & Hendrickson, S., et al. (2011). Seeking renewal, finding community: Participatory action research in teacher education. *Teacher Development, 15*(1), 1-18.

Draper, R. J., Broomhead, P., Jensen, A. P., Nokes, J. D., & Siebert, D. (Eds.), (2010). *(Re)Imagining content-area literacy instruction*. New York, NY: Teachers College Press.

Draper, R. J., Hall, K. M., Smith, L. K., & Siebert, D. (2005). What's more important—literacy or content? Confronting the literacy-content dualism. *Action in Teacher Education, 27*(2), 12-21.

Draper, R. J., & Siebert, D. (2010). Rethinking texts, literacies, and literacy across the curriculum. In R. J. Draper, P. Broomhead, A. P. Jensen, J. Nokes, & D. Siebert (Eds.), *(Re)imagining literacies for content-area classrooms* (pp. 20-39). New York, NY: Teachers College Press.

Euclid. (2005/300 BC). *Elements* (R. Fitzpatrick, Trans.): Lulu.com.

Gee, J. P. (2001). Reading as situated language: A sociocognitive perspective. *Journal of Adolescent and Adult Literacy, 44*, 714-725.

Kress, G. (2000). Multimodality. In B. Cope & M. Kalantizis (Eds.), *Multiliteracies: Literacy learning and the design of social futures* (pp. 182-202). London, England: Routledge.

Langer, J. A. (2011). *Envisioning knowlege: Building literacy in the academic disciplines*. New York: NY: Teachers College Press.

Lemke, J. L. (2004). The literacies of science. In E. W. Saul (Ed.), *Crossing borders in literacy and science instruction: Perspectives on theory and practice* (pp. 33-47). Newark, DE: International Reading Association and National Science Teachers Association.

Luke, A. (1995). When basic skills and information processing just aren't enough: Rethinking reading in New Times. *Teachers College Record, 97*, 95-115.

Minard, T. E. (2011). *Tailings storage facility: Trade-off study to consider the use of flocculation of the tailings*. Unpublished technical memorandum.

Moje, E. B. (2008). Foregrounding the disciplines in secondary literacy teaching and learning: A call for change. *Journal of Adolescent and Adult Literacy, 52*, 96-107.

Moore, D. W., Readence, J. E., & Rickelman, R. J. (1983). An historical exploration of content area reading instruction. *Reading Research Quarterly, 18*, 419-438.

Nokes, J. D., & Nielson, J. (2011). *Review and critique of the Common Core State Standards: A view from science and history.* Jacksonville, FL: A paper presented at the annual meeting of the Literacy Research Association.

Paulos, J. A. (1988). *Innumeracy: Mathematical illiteracy and its consequences.* New York, NY: Hill and Wang.

Popkewitz, T. S. (2004). Educational standards: Mapping who we are and are to become. *The Journal of the Learning Sciences, 13,* 243-256.

Sebeok, T. A. (2001). *Signs: An introduction to semiotics* (2nd ed.). Toronto, Candada: University of Toronto Press.

Shumway, S., & Wright, G. (2010). (Re)Imagining literacies for technology classrooms. In R. J. Draper, P. Broomhead, A. P. Jensen, J. D. Nokes, & D. Siebert (Eds.), *(Re)Imagining content-area literacy instruction* (pp. 82-96). New York, NY: Teachers College Press.

Siebert, D., & Draper, R. J. (2008). Why content-area literacy messages do not speak to mathematics teachers: A critical content analysis. *Literacy Research and Instruction, 47,* 229-245.

Siebert, D., & Draper, R. J. (2012). Reconceptualizing literacy and instruction for mathematics classrooms. In T. L. Jetton & C. Hynd-Shanahan (Eds.), *Adolescent literacy in the academic disciplines: General principles and practical strategies* (pp. 172-198). New York: NY: Guilford Press.

Sfard, A. (2000). Symbolizing mathematical reality into being—Or how mathematical discourse and mathematical objects create each other. In P. Cobb, E. Yackel, & K. McClain (Eds.), *Symbolizing and communicating in mathematics classrooms: Perspectives on discourse, tools, and instructional design* (pp. 37-98). Mahwah, NJ: Lawrence Erlbaum.

Wenger, I. (1998). *Communities of practice: Learning, meaning, and identity.* Cambridge, UK: Cambridge University Press.

Wineburg, S. S. (1991). On the reading of historical texts: Notes on the breach between school and academy. *American Educational Research Journal, 28,* 495-519.

Jamie Myers
Professor of Education
Penn State University

Section III: Researching How and Why We Use Technologies in Literacy Practices

The definition of literacy has broadened beyond the skills of reading, writing, speaking, and listening, to include how and why we use print, images, media, and all symbols in cultural practices to negotiate our identities, community memberships, and inter-subjective understandings of the world. Our technologies for this symbolic interaction have rapidly changed. In some cases new technologies and new literacy practices have arisen together in mutually shaping ways, such as the ubiquitous social relationships enabled through texting and Twitter. In other cases, long-standing social practices adapt new technologies to accomplish traditional valued ends; a quiz in Moodle positions a learner in the same relationship to knowledge as paper and pencil. While decades of new technologies have promised to transform classroom learning, educational practices exist today much as they did a century ago because the cultural practices of knowledge and power bend and break technologies to their own purposes.

To examine the complex ways in which technologies and cultural practices mutually shape literacy activities, researchers must first establish the valued consequences of the cultural practice enacted. New digital technologies evidence generative ways to represent oneself and to interact with others. These new digital literacy practices facilitate participation in a ubiquitous symbolic interaction based on rapidly evolving activities of invention, collaboration, negotiation, reflection, critique, and convention. These practices are driven by cultural values, both pre-digital and pre-Gutenburg, for a creative and aesthetic experience of being alive, and the succinct and novel expression of life's essential meanings. These digital literacy practices afford a greater ability to transcend the isolating subjectivity of one's own mind, and participate more fully in the construction of inter-subjectivity in both action and reflection. The consequence is a greater sense of power and control in wielding symbols to create identity, friendship, love, family, community, and the knowledge within specialized hobbies and disciplines.

Each contribution is this section on technology illustrates the goal of research to describe how the characteristics of a technology enable the forms of symbolic interaction valued by the participants, and how this literacy practice affords particular potentials for creating and sharing meaning. All three studies explore digital practices in a non-classroom setting, and make comparisons to less engaging classroom literacy practices. The results emphasize how particular features of digital literacy practices support collaborative and creative thinking that deepens narrative understanding and furthers content knowledge, but unfortunately, reinforces the divide in our values for the consequences of literacy in and out of school.

Kinzer, et. al. describe substantially different narrative practices in a comparison of video game and comic book versions of the same story. Based on the measurement of eye movements and comprehension tests results, the research team explicated particular technological features of the two genres to account for the different literacy practices. With the digital comic book, readers had a more passive role, reading a fixed text with a pre-determined fixed meaning. In the video game version, readers/players made decisions within a virtual world, assuming the main character's point of view to construct embodied cognition through active problem solving. Even though the same narrative information was available in both genres, those readers who participated in a video game genre experienced greater symbolic control and collaboration within the story world, and achieved higher measures on traditional literacy measurements.

Foley and Guzzetti qualitatively describe the participatory and collaborative aspects of the social practices enacted by four elementary grade students as they authored digital media in an after-school program. The students evidenced high levels of purposeful inquiry and expression. They initiated inquiries, strategic thinking, peer response and review, and produced digital videos and music that evidenced traditional academic achievement in content knowledge and rhetorical principles of expository writing. When their literacy work was brought into the classroom, their digital video inquiries received extensive praise from the classroom teacher and fellow students. The digital literacy practices provided them with generative tools and purposes for knowledge production and communication.

Lynch highlights the characteristics of video gaming literacy practices in an individual case study of an African-American teen boy. Social cognition, embodied engagement, shifts in world view, distributed expertise, effortful persistence, self-knowledge, and avid reading of game-related paratexts were all benefits described as consequences of the video game literacy practice. But, the boy and his mother viewed the practice as play and of little use to reading/writing the valid texts of school. This contribution especially highlights how literacy practices are embedded in systems of power and authority. While the consequences of symbol use developed in the video game literacy practice are also highly valued in school, the outward form of the technology and the literacy activity is dismissed as irrelevant. In an interesting way, this study circles back to Kinzer, et. al., who in transforming the content/activity of school literacy into a video game, found high levels of school-valued engagement and comprehension as consequences in that digital literacy practice.

Technologies may support forms of symbolic interaction that more fully realize our cultural values for collaboration and power in the construction of inter-subjectivity and disciplinary knowledge. However, we must avoid oversimplified causal claims about the effects of technology. Research should provide rich descriptions of how the characteristics of technologies and the valued purposes of activity mutually shape each other, within and across multiple literacy practices. This will undoubtedly include explanations of how different cultural practices appropriate, affirm, and contest each other in literacy, as well as how valued purposes of literacy adapt, invent, and even subvert the characteristics of representation and communication afforded by technologies.

An understanding of literacy as cultural practice also means that texts in any technological mode are never decontextualized. A decontextualized text is one for which a reader either does not understand how the text gives power within a literacy practice, or chooses not to participate in the social purposes embedded in that social practice. Critical research into literacy and technology will articulate these power dynamics.

As the contributions in this section evidence, teens use digital technologies of representation and communication to construct vibrant literacy practices in which they negotiate interpretations about experience in ways of thinking that educators have long desired for the schooled practices of print technologies. It is not a simple matter of importing digital technologies, or transferring the skills from non-academic practices into classrooms. It is a matter of how power is maintained and knowledge is repackaged within the traditional practices of school. On occasion new digital literacy practices usurp traditional classroom practices, and whether instigated by teacher or students, change the nature of representation, knowledge, identity, and community in school activities. Research on technology and literacy should illuminate these classroom-based cases where the modes of technology, and the activities of inquiry and representation, engage the generative and collaborative identity and knowledge practices found within the digital forms of life outside of school, and inside genuine communities of scholarship.

Examining the Effects of Text and Images on Story Comprehension: An Eye-Tracking Study of Reading in a Video Game and Comic Book

Charles K. Kinzer
Selen Turkay
Daniel L. Hoffman
Nilgun Gunbas
Pantiphar Chantes
Apichai Chaiwinij
Tatyana Dvorkin
Teachers College Columbia University

Understanding how students comprehend information in multimodal text can offer valuable insights into the relative importance of text and images in comprehension. To this end, this study investigates the effects of text and images on sixth graders' comprehension of narratives presented in two different formats: a comic book and a video game. Both formats are popular with today's adolescents and have been suggested as vehicles potentially useful for instructional purposes. Yet, despite their popularity, there is little research available on narrative comprehension as related to playing video games or reading comics, although researchers (e.g., Mayer, 2011, p. 298) emphasizes the usefulness of knowing whether people can learn as well from a computer game as from a more conventional medium.

Previous work found differences in students' comprehension of narrative when presented in a book, video game, and comic (Kinzer, Hoffman, Turkay, Gunbas, & Chantes, 2011); results showed that students who read the story in book form achieved higher literal comprehension scores than the other two groups, though there was no difference in inferential comprehension scores. Although this finding was consistent with early studies investigating text and images in reading comprehension (e.g., Miller, 1938), it was still surprising considering today's "massively visual society" (Emmison & Smith, 2000, p. viii) in which children are presented with multimodal information in almost every aspect of their lives. Given our image-laden culture, why did the more visual formats studied fare worse as measured by comprehension?

A possible explanation is that although today's children are saturated with images, they do not necessarily use these images to aid their reading comprehension. Kinzer et al.'s (2011) findings suggested that the images in the game format might distract readers from the story, or that the images, while containing information relevant to comprehending the narrative, were ignored in favor of the text. Another possibility is that schools focus on text-based reading and comprehension, with relatively little focus on understanding and interpreting images, which may have influenced the previous findings (L. Vasudevan, personal communication, March 8, 2011).

To address these issues, four research questions were proposed: (a) Do sixth graders differ in their comprehension of a narrative presented within a comic book versus an adventure video game?, (b) Do sixth graders differ in their comprehension of information that appears in text or graphics, when presented in a comic book or video game narrative format?, (c) Do sixth graders focus differently on text and images within a narrative that is presented as a comic book and a video game?, and (d) What can eye tracking tell us about how sixth graders focus on text and images within a narrative presented in a comic book or an adventure video game?

BACKGROUND

Early work on the impact of text and graphics on student learning provided mixed results. Work that aimed to determine the effect of illustrations on elementary-aged children's comprehension of stories found either no effect (e.g., Miller, 1938; Vernon, 1953; Weintraub, 1966) or a negative effect (Rose, 1986; Samuels, 1967; Watkins, Miller, & Brubaker, 2004). However, many of these studies were conducted in times when children were not exposed to interactive text and embedded images, audio, and video, to the degree common today.

More recent work has been influenced by Paivio's (1991) dual coding theory, which suggests that graphics and text are coded into memory differently. Paivio's theory implies that comprehension is enhanced when text and images are related and research following this line of reasoning has argued for a type of multimedia principle, positing that students learn better from text and pictures than from text alone (Anglin, Vaez, & Cunningham, 2004; Mayer, 2009). Variations in the effectiveness of the multimedia principle may be related to the domain being taught. Kress & van Leeuwen (2006) argue that in technical fields images have become the major means of curricular content, whereas in the more humanistic subjects images vary in their function between illustration, decoration, and information (p. 16).

For younger children, the presence of images alongside text seems to benefit comprehension and Peeck (1993) recommends teaching visual literacy in the context of teaching reading comprehension. Gambrell and Jawitz (1993) found that fourth graders' reading comprehension increased significantly when they read text with illustrations, and Fang (1996) argues that pictures contribute to children's development of literate behavior. Sipe (1998) suggests that children construct meaning through the interplay of text and image, while Levin, Anglin, and Carney (1987) argue that easy-to-follow texts are unlikely to yield any cognitive benefits from the inclusion of pictures as they are already concrete and engaging. In contrast, Jewitt and Oyama (2001) maintain that graphics in text are needed to enhance understanding.

Of course, the mere presence of images does not mean that students access them or know how to use the information they contain, and Carney and Levin (2002) raise an important question about the ability of today's students to process pictures and text when reading, asking if the "cyberstudents" of today will differ from the book-learned "liberstudents" of the past in their ability "to process picture and text information comprehensively, and with comprehension" (Wang & Newlin, 2000, p. 23).

Use of Comics for Literacy

Comics are multimodal stories told by using an almost seamless blend of text and image (Kuechenmeister, 2009). McCloud (1993) defines comics as "juxtaposed pictorial and other images in deliberate sequence, intended to convey information" (p. 9). Although comic books are sometimes criticized as being light reading, they are often part of children's pleasure reading, which has attracted the attention of educators who view comics as a way to help students engage in text (Eikmeier, 2008; Krashen, 2004; Tiemensma, 2009). Comics have been effectively used in language classrooms (Wright & Sherman, 1994; 1999) and in teaching foreign languages (Chun, 2009; Ranker, 2007; Liu, 2004). Sherman and Wright (1996) showed that newspaper comic strips can be used to promote higher-level thinking, and Liu (2004) found that students with low-level English proficiency benefited from comics significantly more than students with high-level English proficiency. In a study of young readers of Archie comics, Norton (2003) concluded that the pleasure children derive from comics is due largely to a sense of text ownership, which in turn provides confidence to engage "energetically and critically" (p. 145). Even in middle school, where boys sometimes "don't like to read, and often don't read very well" (Blair & Sanford, 2004, p. 453), research has found those who read comics read more in general and enjoy reading more compared with boys who do not read comics (Ujiie & Krashen, 1996).

Reading and Video Games

Video games can be considered an important medium for literacy learning, as they can provide authentic purposes to read text (Commeyras, 2009). The authentic use of text can increase students' interest in reading (Watson, 1989). Interest, in turn, can result in increased persistence leading to higher overall achievement (Moje, Overby, Tysvaer, & Morris, 2008). In addition to motivating students, video game text can help with decoding and word recognition practice.

A national survey found that school-age children devote about seven hours per week to playing video games (Woodard & Gridina, 2000), and reports show an increase in the time youth spend playing video games, with boys averaging 13 hours and girls averaging five hours weekly (Gentile, Lynch, Linder, & Walsh, 2004; Rideout, Foehr, & Roberts, 2010). Given the popularity of video games among adolescents, educators might consider them as texts to promote reading.

Gee (2003) notes that adolescent game players engage in multiple literacy practices. These practices have the potential to meet state and national standards in reading, writing and technology (Steinkuehler, 2007). Studies have shown that students engage in advanced reading comprehension when playing games (Martin & Steinkuehler, 2011) and also in game-related activities outside actual play by participating in forums and affinity groups (Steinkuehler, Compton-Lilly, & King, 2009; Turkay, Kinzer, Hoffman, Gunbas, & Nagle, 2010). Steinkuehler (2011) argues that videogames "support a complex textual ecology" that can spark "expansive reading practices" (p. 13).

Taken together, the mixed modal nature of comic books and video games and their potential as instructional tools highlight the need to better understand how students process text and images in rich narrative settings. Does format alone influence how the text and images are processed? Have students developed varied strategies to decipher multimodal texts depending on form or do they treat all text and images the same? To address such questions, it is important to think about a research design that can couple measures of comprehension with measures of eye movement in response to the visual stimuli of text and images. Together, such data can help educators tease apart the relationship between what students attend to in multimodal texts, and what they subsequently comprehend about the narrative.

Eye-Tracking

Due to advances in technology, the use of eye-tracking equipment has become a more feasible way to investigate people's visual actions and attention in various contexts. Eye-tracking has been used by researchers in many areas to examine aspects of learning, skill level, cognitive processing, and emotion (Rayner, 1998; Goldberg & Kotval, 1999; Coan & Allen, 2007). This technology produces a number of objective metrics that can be used to better understand what readers look at in a stimulus, how long they look, and the visual path they take while viewing it.

The main measurement in eye-tracking research is a "fixation," a brief moment when the eye is paused—e.g., on or around a letter, word, or word group. By tracking fixations, a number of useful metrics can be derived, including: (a) *fixation duration*, the cumulative duration and average spatial location of a series of consecutive fixations within an *area of interest* (AOI), the area of a display or visual environment that is of interest to the research team; (b) *mean fixation duration*, an indicator of information complexity and task difficulty (Rayner, 1998); and (c) *number of fixations*. Such metrics have been "highly reliable and useful in inferring the moment-to-moment processing of individual words and larger segments of text" (Starr & Rayner, 2001, p. 156).

Researchers have argued that fixation duration and cognitive effort are related, with greater fixation durations linked to greater cognitive effort (Goldberg & Kotval, 1999). Work examining the processing of text and images together reveals that people favor text over pictures when reading material that includes both (e.g., Beymer, Orton, & Russell, 2007; Hegarty & Just, 1993; Rayner, Rotello, Steward, Keir, & Duffy, 2001; Schmidt-Weigand, Kohert, & Glowalla, 2010). In examining how people look at cartoons consisting of a single picture with a relevant caption, Carroll, Young, and Guertin (1992) found that processing of the two seemed to be relatively isolated events; the picture frequently was not given full inspection until the text had been read. Rayner et al. (2001) found similar results with text and pictures presented in print ads.

Eye-tracking has been also used to examine how people read non-traditional texts. Omori, Igaki, Ishii, Kurata, & Masuda (2004) showed that both page layout and balloon placement influence how easily comics are read. Studies using eye-tracking reveal that inexperienced comic readers tend to focus more on text than on visuals and tend to wander around the page (Nakazawa, 2004; Allen & Ingulsrud, 2007).

The dynamic nature of video game play complicates the analysis of eye-tracking data as compared with non-dynamic interfaces such as still images (Jennett, Cox, Cairns, Dhoparee, Epps, Tijs, & Walton, 2008). This challenge has not stopped researchers from investigating usability issues (Mat Zain, Abdul Razak, Jaafar, & Zulkipli, 2011), learning processes (Knoepfle, Wang, & Camerer, 2009), and learning in video games (Kiili & Ketamo, 2010; Law, Mattheiss, Kickmeier-Rust, & Albert, 2010). Kiili & Ketamo (2010) found that players' perception patterns varied greatly when playing an educational game, and that extraneous elements on the interface caused confusion. Similarly, Law et al. (2010) found the existence of textual feedback did not have a significant effect on attention, reporting a negative correlation between number of fixations and the understandability of the game.

Thus far, the case has been made that text and graphics play a major role in society today through "new" media such as comic books and video games, and that these media are potential vehicles for literacy exploration and instruction. The present study aims to contribute to the dialogue about the importance of understanding how text and images affect comprehension by presenting students with a single narrative in two formats and using a combination of paper-based comprehension measures and eye-tracking metrics.

PARTICIPANTS, INSTRUMENTS, PROCEDURES

Twenty (10 female and 10 male) sixth-grade public school students in New York City, all native English speakers with normal vision, participated in this study. Participants were randomly assigned to either a Game Group (GG, *n* = 10) or Comic-book Group (CG, *n* = 10).

The Narrative

The narrative used in this study was from *Trace Memory* (released outside of North America as *Another Code: Two Memories*), an adventure video game developed by CiNG (2005) and published by Nintendo for the Nintendo DS. In adventure games, players assume the role of a protagonist in an interactive story driven by exploration and puzzle-solving instead of physical challenge (Adams, 2006).

Trace Memory was chosen for its story-driven game play, and the unlikeliness of sixth-grade students in 2011 having played a game released in 2005. It was described as a "touchable mystery novel" with "lengthy conversations" (Staff Reviewer, 2005; Hruschak, 2006) and reviewers claimed it was "well written" with a "good amount of suspense" (Harris, 2005; Parish, 2005). Also, the protagonist, Ashley Mizuki Robbins, who is searching for her father on Blood Edward Island, is a 13-year-old girl—a similar age to the target audience of the study.

A 10-minute, logically complete section of the game was selected for use in the study based on its representativeness of the game's mechanics and story. Using the selected portion, a 20-page comic book was created (see Figure 1), using procedures described previously by Kinzer et al. (2011, p. 268). All images and text came directly from the game; participants in all groups thus saw and

Figure 1. Sample Comic Book Page (Left) and Nintendo DS Emulator "Pages" (Right)

read the same content. Figure 1 shows a sample comic book page and "pages" from *Trace Memory* running on the Nintendo DS game emulator.

Because the portion of the story used occurred after the beginning of the story, to ensure consistency in the "lead up" to the section to be played/read, a 2.5-minute video was created to familiarize participants with *Trace Memory*'s characters and plot to that point in the story.

Participants played *Trace Memory* on a computer using DeSmuME (DeSmuME, 2009), an open source, Nintendo DS emulator. Using the emulator ensured that eye-tracking could be done in a consistent manner, that is, both the game and the comic could be read on screen, eliminating confounds in the presentation of the narrative. This also improved accuracy in the analysis, which is most successful when eye-tracking on a fixed screen as opposed to a mobile, handheld device.

Eye-Tracking Apparatus

A Tobii X60 eye-tracking system and Tobii Studio software were used to collect real-time eye movement data, using a computer to present the materials to be read/played. The Tobii X60 eye-tracking cameras track viewers' eye-movements, capturing fixations, fixation durations, and saccades as they view information on the computer screen. The eye-tracker uses a small camera bar that sits under the screen, and the reader simply sits in front of it and views what is presented, while remaining able to use the computer's mouse and keyboard.

Three different measures were derived from the eye-tracking recordings: task duration, fixation duration, and fixation count. Fixation count is a tally of the number of fixations in a given AOI. It is generally accepted that higher numbers on these measures indicate greater difficulty or more cognitive resources being used to process information in the AOI. However, while eye-tracking shows how long one attends to a given area, it does not tell us about the success of comprehending what is being looked at (De Koning, Tabbers, Rikers, & Paas, 2010), and thus must be complemented with other performance measures.

Comprehension Measures

A comprehension test was designed by the authors to measure both literal (15 multiple-choice, three open-ended questions) and inferential comprehension of the story (seven short-answer questions). The questions were developed by experts in reading/literacy education, and vetted by three graduate assistants with knowledge about literal and inferential comprehension, including two who previously taught reading/language arts in public schools. Among the literal questions, nine could be answered only by reading the text, while four could be answered only by using information in the images. The remaining questions could be answered using information that occurred in both the text and the images. All inferential questions asked participants to explain their answers. Participants were encouraged to answer as many questions as possible and were told that they could guess if they were not sure. There was no time limit; participants completed all questions.

Visual Recall Task

In one part of the narrative, the main character searches a small hexagonal cottage filled with items that were clues about her father's whereabouts. To capture information about participants' retention of the items and information found, after reading/playing the narrative, they were asked

Figure 2. Room Image from the Game and Comic (Top) and Corresponding Mapping Task Question

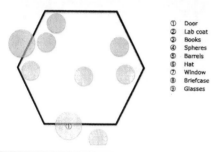

① Door
② Lab coat
③ Books
④ Spheres
⑤ Barrels
⑥ Hat
⑦ Window
⑧ Briefcase
⑨ Glasses

to indicate the items' position in the cottage on a hexagonal drawing/representation of the room (see Figure 2).

Procedure

Data collection took place in the school's computer lab. On arrival, participants were placed in front of a computer and positioned at an appropriate distance from the screen and eye-tracking camera. A research assistant introduced the eye-tracking camera and the participants practiced reading with a similar, sample narrative (either a comic book or a game). After the practice activity, participants put on headphones and watched the introductory video about the narrative they were about to read/play, and were able to ask questions about the information presented. Then participants either read the comic book or played the video game. There was no time limit. After completing the activity, they were given the comprehension measures and the visual recall task described above.

RESULTS

Measures of Pre-Task Group Equivalence

After participants were randomly assigned to one of the two groups (Game Group, GG; Comic Group, CG), their scores from the *Iowa Tests of Basic Skills* (ITBS; Hoover, Dunbar, & Frisbie, 2005) and eye-tracking data sampling rates were used to check for equivalence between groups. An independent samples *t*-test found the two groups to be equivalent on ITBS Reading Total and Language Total scores, with no statistically significant difference: Reading Total score, CG *M* = 61.40, *SD* = 23.39; GG *M* = 60.30, *SD* = 30.21; Language Total score, CG *M* = 64.20, *SD* = 26.1; GG *M* = 62.90, *SD* = 30.97. The two groups were also considered to be equivalent on eye-tracking sampling rate. Sampling rates above 80% are acceptable in terms of accuracy. An independent samples *t*-test found the two groups did not differ significantly on sampling rate: CG *M* = 91.10, GG *M* = 91.10.

To determine if knowledge related to prior use of the Nintendo DS or familiarity with comic books differed across groups and might therefore affect results, participants were asked about Nintendo DS ownership and use, and comic book reading. There was no statistical significance on number of participants who owned and used the Nintendo DS across groups (CG = 9, GG = 8) or who reported reading comics (CG = 9, GG = 9).

Comprehension Findings

The first research question investigated the impact of the presentation format of a narrative on middle school students' comprehension of the story. This was explored by using comprehension tests presented to participants after they had read the comic or played the game. Two types of comprehension questions were analyzed: literal and higher-order. Means and standard deviations for all measures discussed below appear in Table 1.

Table 1. Means and Standard Deviations for the Measures Used in Each Condition

	CONDITION			
	Comic Group (CG) *n* = 10		Game Group (GG) *n* = 10	
MEASURES				
COMPREHENSION MEASURES	Mean	*SD*	Mean	*SD*
Overall Literal Comprehension (*n*=18 items)	12.60	3.02	15.10	1.10
Text Only Literal Comprehension (*n* = 9 items)	7.30	1.49	8.50	0.53
Visual Only Literal Comprehension (*n* = 4 items)	2.50	1.08	3.40	0.52
Text + Visual Literal Questions (*n* = 5 items)	2.80	1.03	3.20	0.63
Higher-Order Comprehension (*n* = 7 items) accuracy	4.90	0.74	5.10	1.45
number of details	4.80	2.52	7.30	3.30
word count	86.10	25.55	97.30	26.16
Visual Recall Test	3.40	1.89	6.60	2.27
EYE-TRACKING MEASURES (seconds)	Mean	*SD*	Mean	*SD*
Fixation Duration Sum (Text Only Literal)	82.63	35.74	112.23	25.86
Fixation Duration Mean (Text Only Literal)	0.59	0.10	0.45	0.11
Fixation Count Mean (Text Only Literal)	15.90	5.64	28.57	3.04
Fixation Duration Sum (Image Only Literal)	5.43	1.87	22.94	9.52
Fixation Duration Mean (Image Only Literal)	0.33	0.06	0.35	0.04
Fixation Count Mean (Image Only Literal)	4.67	1.30	15.92	6.08

Literal Questions

An independent-samples *t*-test was conducted to examine the possible differences between the CG and the GG on the number of correct responses given to the literal questions. There is a statistically significant difference between the GG's and CG's overall literal question accuracy scores on the 18 questions ($t = 2.455$, $p < 0.05$), with the GG answering more questions accurately than the CG.

Higher-Order Questions

Higher-order questions were analyzed based on accuracy, level of detail, and word count (see Kinzer et al., 2011 for detailed procedures on this scoring system). A correct answer received one point. An independent samples t-test indicated no statistically significant difference between the CG and the GG. Level of detail was scored by giving one point for an accurate and relevant descriptor, or an appropriate reason. An independent samples t-test indicated no significant difference between the CG and the GG on level of detail scores, or for overall word count, which was examined within the inferential comprehension analysis because the provision of more details would be confirmed by a higher number of words used.

The second research question explored whether or not the groups differed in their comprehension of information that appeared only in the narrative's text and only in the narrative's images. Independent sample t-tests found a statistically significant difference between the number of accurate responses to literal questions that could be answered only by reading the text ($t = 2.395$, $p < 0.05$) and questions that could be answered only by attending to the images ($t = 2.377$, $p < 0.05$). For the questions that could be answered using information in either the text or image, there was no statistically significant difference between groups.

Visual Recall Task

To complement the multiple-choice and short-answer comprehension questions, we investigated differences between the two groups on visual recall of information. This required remembering story-relevant items appearing in a room within the narrative, and their locations. The room contained nine objects, all clues to solving the mystery in the narrative. The GG remembered significantly more object locations than did the CG ($t = -3.420$, $p < 0.05$).

Eye-Tracking Findings

The third research question explored the participants' attention to text and images in the narrative. Eye-tracking captured fixation points and duration to address this question and allows discussion of the possible effect of participants' attention on their comprehension of the narrative. Using such data is consistent with the majority of multimedia learning studies (e.g., see van Gog & Scheiter, 2010). Using total fixation time as a measure of time on task, it was found that the GG spent more time in the game *(M = 665.0 seconds, SD = 130.30)* than the CC group spent reading the comic *(M = 437.4 seconds, SD = 51.95)*.

Fixation Duration on Text

Using total fixation duration as a measure of how long participants looked at the text and images reveals that the GG spent more time looking at the text in the narrative *(M = 271.52, SD = 78.32)* than did the CG *(M = 225.38, SD = 112.17)*. This difference was not statistically different ($t = 1.067$; $p > 0.05$). However, as the total time within the game and comic differed, a percentage of overall time is a more appropriate unit of analysis. The CG fixated on the text 51.50% *(SD = 24.46)* of their total time, while the GG fixated on text 41.16% *(SD = 6.97)* of the time; there was no statistically significant difference between groups ($t = 1.286$; $p > 0.05$).

Text-Only Questions

There were nine questions that could be answered only by using information contained in the text. Results presented earlier showed that there was a statistically significant difference between the CG and GG in the number of these questions answered correctly, favoring the GG.

An analysis of fixation duration on the text containing information needed to answer those questions showed that there was a statistically significant difference between the GG and CG on total fixation durations ($t = 2.122$; $p < 0.05$), mean fixation durations ($t = 2.844$; $p < 0.05$), and mean fixation count ($t = 6.27$; $p < 0.05$). Thus, the participants in the GG looked at the text containing information allowing them to answer these questions longer than did the CG.

Visual-Only Questions

There were four questions that could be answered only by using information contained in the images. Results presented earlier showed that there was a statistically significant difference between the CG and GG in the number of these questions answered correctly, in favor of the GG. An analysis of fixation duration on the images containing information needed to answer those questions shows that although mean fixation duration did not differ significantly, there was a statistically significant difference in total fixation duration between the GG and CG ($t = 5.708$; $p < 0.001$). The GG also had statistically significantly more attention points (fixation count) on those images than did the CG ($t = 5.721$; $p < 0.001$).

Comprehension and Fixations

Next, we wanted to investigate the differences in eye-tracking metrics for participants who answered questions correctly versus incorrectly. To do so, we divided students into two groups, high accuracy (HA, above the mean score) and low accuracy (LA, below the mean score), for both text-only and visual-only literal questions. For questions that could be answered only by reading the text, we found no statistically significant difference on fixation durations (mean and sum) and fixation count between the HA ($n = 10$) and the LA ($n = 10$) groups. However, when the two groups were created based on the number of visual-only questions they answered correctly, five people were in the LA group and 15 people in the HA group. Because of the small visual-only LA group size, inferential statistics are problematic, though we report them here for informational purposes: Although there was no statistically significant difference on fixation duration means, there were statistically significant differences on the total fixation duration ($t = 3.48$; $p < 0.05$) and mean fixation count ($t = 3.46$; $p < 0.05$). A focus on perhaps more relevant, descriptive statistics illustrates that students with high accuracy scores spent nearly three times as long looking at the relevant area of interest (see Table 2). They also tended to fixate more often, as measured by fixation count, on the relevant part of the image.

Table 2. Descriptive Statistics on Eye-Tracking Measures for High Accuracy and Low Accuracy Groups

	Condition							
	Text-Only Questions				Image-Only Questions			
	High Accuracy Scores ($n = 10$)		Low Accuracy Scores ($n = 10$)		High Accuracy Scores ($n = 15$)		Low Accuracy Scores ($n = 5$)	
Measures	M	SD	M	SD	M	SD	M	SD
Fixation Duration Total (seconds)	104.13	37.37	90.73	30.61	16.94	11.67	5.92	2.16
Mean Fixation Duration (seconds)	0.49	0.11	0.55	0.14	0.35	0.05	0.32	0.07
Mean Fixation Count	24.72	8.37	19.74	6.80	12.06	7.49	5.02	1.43

DISCUSSION

This study examined readers' attention to and comprehension of a narrative presented in a comic book and an adventure video game. When understanding multimodal texts such as games or comics, information is available from various combinations of sources including printed text only, images only, or both text and images. Thus, when a reader does not understand information that is presented, it is often difficult to know: (a) whether or not the reader has looked at the text or image containing the information, or (b) has looked at it but did not process it in a way that leads to understanding. This study addressed the former possibility, using eye-tracking measures to determine whether or not comprehension differences might be due to the sixth-grade participants not looking at the area containing the information tested. Of course, if participants looked at the appropriate locus of information and did not provide correct answers, there are clear implications for future research that examines the processing of the information.

Additionally, different modes of texts, in this case a comic and a video game, have distinct requirements for interaction and use, and present information in different ways. We noted earlier that comics have been advocated in reading instruction for some time, and that more recently video games' use in instruction has been suggested. Yet, before implementing video games in instructional settings, we must know more about how students interact with them, whether or not they provide a means for understanding narrative elements, and in what way(s). Questions that must be considered include whether or not players attend to text in video games or ignore text in favor of the images in the game. In summary, this aspect of the study explored the potential relationship between attention to information-bearing units of text and graphics, as measured by eye fixation duration, in a narrative presented in a comic book and a video game.

What do the results reveal about whether or not sixth-grade readers are looking at the text and images within narratives? To begin with, the cumulative eye fixation totals show that the GG spent more time playing the game than did the CG in reading the comic largely because of the game's interactive features and ability to explore regions of the game world. For example, when the GG's avatars were in the hexagonal room (see Figure 2) they were able to move around, touch objects that were also described in text boxes, return to objects previously observed, and so on, while the CG saw images of the room and the objects and read about them, but did not directly interact with them. The time spent in the video game as opposed to the comic was approximately 11.1, as opposed to 7.3 minutes. Clearly, a difference in time on task was found, but how did this impact narrative comprehension? Did the increased time on task for the GG group arise from a tension between narrative and interactivity? Did the game play distract players' focus, resulting in decreased understanding of the narrative?

Our results indicate this was not the case, as the GG answered significantly more literal post-test comprehension questions correctly than did participants in the CG. The GG also answered more post-test questions that targeted information located only in the game's text. Furthermore, the GG answered more post-test questions correctly that targeted information located only in the video game's images. Overall, for the literal portion of the comprehension results, the GG performed better on the questions regardless of how the salient information was presented. Regarding the higher-order comprehension questions, the results reveal a similar trend but the difference was not statistically significant. Overall, the post-test comprehension measures indicate that the video game format did not detract from understanding the narrative.

Given these results, an obvious follow-up question is why students' comprehension scores were different between the two groups. Were the text and graphics attended to differently at the visual level? The eye-tracking results help explore this. The results clearly show that the GG spent more time "playing" than the comic group spent "reading." But when the fixation duration on images is considered as a percentage of total time, there is no statistical difference between the two groups. Despite the lack of statistical significance, the results do show that the GG spent a lower percentage (41.5%) of their time fixated on text than the CG group (51.5%). To be clear, the students in the comic book group spent a greater amount of their total fixation time on text related to the text-only questions, but scored significantly lower on the comprehension questions related to this text. When it came to fixating on images in the narrative, the students in the GG looked at the images for a significantly longer time and subsequently answered more image-related questions correctly.

These results suggest that by almost all measures, the GG performed differently than the CG in their respective narrative format. The GG also outscored the CG in the comprehension measure. Are these results due to some inherent difference in the narrative formats? Recall that the two groups had no statistical difference in their reading ability as measured by standardized test scores. What properties of the two narrative formats might lead to these differences?

Possibly, the more exploratory, open mind-set promoted by adventure games helps students comprehend narrative elements. Players can roam around the environment exploring and investigating the world and the objects in it. This openness is limited only by "boundary components" (Björk & Holopainen, 2005, p. 14), such as rules and goals, which limit what players are allowed to do in the game. It does not take long for an adventure game player to realize that trying to race through the game may be counter-productive, and that a more investigative, slower play style may prove more fruitful. From this perspective, the comic book and the adventure game begin to look different, despite being deliberately designed to be as close as possible in terms of text and graphics. Comic book readers are more limited in action possibilities: They can move from panel to panel, turn the page back and forth, look at the pictures repeatedly, or reread. Beyond this, there is not much "to do" in the narrative space of the comic.

A second possibility relates to the difference in the point of view used in comic books and adventure games. In both formats, the reader/player follows the main character, Ashley, as the story unfolds through text and images. However, in the game the reader/player often must complete or initiate an action that results in the appearance of an image or text, whereas the comic book reader encounters panels as they appear, without overt action. Thus, even though the actual image and text read in each format is the same, interactivity and "distance" from the narrative may vary perceptually and cognitively. For example, throughout the game there are periods when players watch Ashley do things such as talk to other characters. At other times, however, players take on the role of Ashley more directly, and must decide what they, operating as Ashley, do by making choices about what actions to take.

Examples of these choices include whether to try to unlock a door, pick up a stone, or examine an old book. In the comic, readers see the same images and read the same text, but without accompanying physical interactivity. The difference might result in a kind of "narrative distance" (see Booth, 1983) between the reader/player and the events of the story. Said another way, in the comic book format the reader is "once removed" from the action, whereas in the adventure game, the player may need to decide and take action before a particular event occurs. Could these processes help players better comprehend the narrative in the game? Previous work in social psychology shows that actors who perform behaviors, compared to observers who watch, often come to different causal analyses of the same situations (Gerrig & Jacovina, 2009, p. 229).

Results from the visual mapping task, where participants were compared on their ability to recall the location of specific objects found inside a room, are informative when considering possible answers to the above question. The CG read about the objects and saw their location in repeated images when reading the comic. The GG was able to move Ashley around the room, have her touch the objects, walk back and revisit objects, and generally consider the room as an active space within which they could control Ashley's exploration. On the post-test that asked participants to place objects in a representation of the room (see Figure 2), the GG remembered significantly more objects' locations. Taken together with the results discussed above, the impact of decision processes and aspects that relate to theories of embodied cognition (see Glenberg & Kaschak, 2002) may be fruitful areas for further research. We note also that eye-tracking, while labor intensive, provides a method of answering important questions related to the above discussion, especially in multimodal, digital environments such as encountered in video games.

CONCLUSION

Today's teachers must be flexible and adapt their lessons and instructional materials to capitalize on students' needs and interests as a means of inspiring them towards literacy. Popular culture materials, such as comic books and video games, may be underrepresented vehicles for doing so. Materials popular with children in free-reading time have been used for many years as motivating tools to encourage comprehension, critical thinking, characterization, plot, vocabulary and other aspects of literacy (e.g., see Fader & McNeil, 1968, for a discussion on the positive effects of using high-interest books and comics to enhance literacy instruction). Similarly, Krashen (2005) notes the potential beneficial effects of comic books used in reading instruction, especially for children who do not read well, and notes, "There is evidence suggesting that comic book reading can be a conduit to 'heavier' reading."

We feel that appropriate, adventure video games may also provide a means of using popular culture materials in reading instruction, although additional research in this area is needed to provide evidence about literacy practices within games. The work reported here shows that comprehension of narrative is part of adventure video game play and may be greater in game players than in comic book readers, and provides evidence that game play may have beneficial educational uses in literacy development.

ENDNOTE

This work was funded in part by Microsoft Research through the Games for Learning Institute. The content and opinions herein are the authors' and may not reflect the views of Microsoft Research, nor does mention of trade names, products, or organizations imply endorsement.

REFERENCES

Adams, E. (2006). *Fundamentals of game design* (2nd ed.). Indianapolis, IN: New Riders Publishing.

Allen, K., & Ingulsrud, J. E. (2007). *Strategies used by children when reading manga.* Paper presented at the Annual Congress of the Applied Linguistics Association of Australia, New South Wales, Australia.

Anglin, G. J., Vaez, H., & Cunningham, K. L. (2004). Visual representation and learning: The roles of static and animated graphics. In D. Jonassen (Ed.), *Handbook of research on educational communications and technology,* (2nd ed., pp. 865-916). Mahwah, NJ: Lawrence Erlbaum Associates.

Beymer, D., Orton, P. Z., & Russell, D. M. (2007). An eye tracking study of how pictures influence online reading. In C. Baranauskas, P. Palanque, J. Abascal, & S. Barbosa (Eds.), *Human-computer interaction – INTERACT 2007* (pp. 456-460). Heidelberg, Germany: Springer.

Blair, H. A., & Sanford, K. (2004). Morphing literacy: Boys reshaping their school-based literacy practices. *Language Arts, 81*(6), 452-460.

Björk, S., & Holopainen, J. (2005). *Patterns in game design.* Hingham, MA: Charles River Media, Inc.

Booth, W. C. (1983). *The rhetoric of fiction* (2nd ed.). Chicago, IL: University of Chicago Press.

Carney, R. N., & Levin, J. R. (2002). Pictorial illustrations still improve students' learning from text. *Educational Psychology Review, 14*(1), 5–26.

Carroll, P. J., Young, J. R., & Guertin, M. S. (1992). Visual analysis of cartoons: A view from the far side. In K. Rayner (Ed.), *Eye movements and visual cognition: Scene perception and reading* (pp. 444-461). New York, NY: Springer-Verlag.

Chun, C. W. (2009). Critical literacies and graphic novels for English-language learners: Teaching Maus. *Journal of Adolescent & Adult Literacy, 53*(2), 144–153.

CiNG. (2005). *Trace Memory* [Nintendo DS game]. Fukoko, Japan.

Coan, J. A., & Allen, J. J. B. (2007). Organizing the tools and methods of affective science. In J. A. Coan & J. J. B. Allen (Eds.), *Handbook of emotion elicitation and assessment* (pp. 3-6). New York, NY: Oxford University Press.

Commeyras, M. (2009). Drax's reading in Neverwinter Nights: With a tutor as henchman. *eLearning, 6*(1), 43-53.

DeSmuME (2009). DeSmuME Team (Version 0.9.8) [Software]. Available from http://desmume.org/download/

De Koning, B. B., Tabbers, H. K., Rikers, R. M. J. P., & Paas, F. (2010). Attention guidance in learning from a complex animation: Seeing is understanding? *Learning and Instruction, 20*(2), 111-122.

Eikmeier, G. M. (2008). D'oh! Using the Simpsons to improve student response to literature. *English Journal, 97*(4), 77-80.

Emmison, M., & Smith, P. (2000). *Researching the visual: Images, objects, contexts and interactions in social and cultural inquiry.* New York, NY: SAGE.

Fader, D. N., & McNeil, E. B. (1968). *Hooked on books: Program and proof.* New York, NY: Berkeley Publishing Corp.

Fang, Z. (1996). Illustrations, text, and the child reader: What are pictures in children's storybooks for? *Reading Horizons, 37*(2), 137–142.

Gambrell, L. B., & Jawitz, P. B. (1993). Mental imagery, text illustrations, and children's story comprehension and recall. *Reading Research Quarterly, 28*(3), 265-273.

Gee, J. P. (2003). *What video games have to teach us about learning and literacy.* New York, NY: Palgrave Macmillan.

Gentile, D. A., Lynch, P. J., Linder, J. R., & Walsh, D. A. (2004). The effects of violent video game habits on adolescent hostility, aggressive behaviors, and school performance. *Journal of Adolescence, 27*(1), 5-22.

Gerrig, R. J., & Jacovina, M. E. (2009). Reader participation in the experience of narrative. In B. H. Ross (Ed.), *The psychology of learning and motivation, 51*, (pp. 223-254). New York, NY: Academic Press.

Glenberg, A. M., & Kaschak, M. P. (2002). Grounding language in action. *Psychonomic Bulletin & Review, 9*(3), 558–565.

Goldberg, H. J., & Kotval, X. P. (1999). Computer interface evaluation using eye movements: Methods and constructs. *International Journal of Industrial Ergonomics, 24*(6), 631-645.

Harris, C. (2005). Trace Memory: The DS interactive mystery finally hits the US. Was it worth the wait? *IGN.* Retrieved from http://ds.ign.com/articles/652/652873p1.html

Hegarty, M., & Just, M. A. (1993). Constructing mental models of machines from text and diagrams. *Journal of Memory and Language, 32*(6), 717-742.

Hoover, H. D., Dunbar, S. B., & Frisbie, D. A. (2005). *Iowa tests of basic skills.* Chicago, IL: Riverside Publishing Company.

Hruschak, P. (2006). Player 1: A DS double whammy. *CiN Weekly.* Retrieved from http://web.archive.org/web/20060603141054/http://www.cinweekly.com/apps/pbcs.dll/article?AID=/20060111/ENT09/601110350/1063

Jennett, C., Cox, A. L., Cairns, P., Dhoparee, S., Epps, A., Tijs, T., & Walton, A. (2008). Measuring and defining the experience of immersion in games. *International Journal of Human Computer Studies, 66*(9), 641-661.

Jewitt, C., & Oyama, R. (2001). Visual meaning: A social semiotic approach. In T. van Leeuwen & C. Jewitt (Eds.), *Handbook of visual analysis* (pp. 134-156). London, England: Sage.

Kiili, K., & Ketamo, H. (2010, October 22). Eye-tracking in educational game design. In Meyer, B. (Ed.). *Proceedings of the 4th European conference on game based learning* (pp. 160-167). Copenhagen, Denmark: The Danish School of Education, Aarhus University.

Kinzer, C. K., Hoffman, D. L., Turkay, S., Gunbas, N., & Chantes, P. (2011). Exploring motivation and comprehension of a narrative in a video game, book, and comic book format. In P. J. Dunston, L. B. Gambrell, K. Headley, S. King Fullerton, P. M. Stecker, V. Gillis, & C. C. Bates (Eds.), *60th Yearbook of the Literacy Research Association* (pp. 263-278). Oak Creek, WI: Literacy Research Association.

Krashen, S. (2004). *The power of reading: Insights from the research* (2nd ed.). Portsmouth, NH: Libraries Unlimited.

Krashen, S. (2005). The "decline" of reading in America, poverty and access to books, and the use of comics in encouraging reading. *Teachers College Record.* Retrieved from http://www.sdkrashen.com/articles/decline_of_reading/all.html

Kress, G., & van Leeuwen, L. (2006). *Reading images: The grammar of visual design.* New York, NY: Routledge.

Knoepfle, D. T., Wang, J. T., & Camerer, C. F. (2009). Studying learning in games using eye-tracking. *Journal of the European Economic Association, 7*(2-3), 388-398.

Kuechenmeister, B. (2009). Reading comics rhetorically: Orality, literacy, and hybridity in comic narratives, *Scan, 6*(1). Retrieved from http://scan.net.au/scan/journal/display.php?journal_id=132

Law, E. L. C., Mattheiss, E., Kickmeier-Rust, M. D., & Albert, D. (2010). Vicarious learning with a digital educational game: Eye-tracking and survey-based evaluation approaches. In G. Leitner, M. Hitz, & A. Holzinger (Eds.), *Lecture notes in computer science - HCI in work and learning, life and leisure, 6389* (pp. 471-488). Berlin: Springer.

Levin, J. R., Anglin, G. J., & Carney, R. N. (1987). On empirically validating functions of pictures in prose. In D. M. Willows & H. A. Houghton (Eds.), *The Psychology of Illustration: Basic Research* (pp. 51–85). New York, NY: Springer-Verlag.

Liu, J. (2004). Effects of comic strips on L2 learners' reading comprehension. *TESOL Quarterly, 38*(2), 225-243.

Martin, C., & Steinkuehler, C. (2011, June). *Information literacy and online reading comprehension: Two interconnected practices.* Paper presented at the Games+Learning+Society Conference, Madison, WI.

Mat Zain, N., Abdul Razak, F., Jaafar, A., & Zulkipli, M. (2011). Eye-tracking in educational games environment: Evaluating user interface design through eye tracking patterns. In H. Zaman, P. Robinson, M. Petrou, P. Olivier, T. Shih, S. Velastin & I. Nyström (Eds.) *Proceedings of the Second International Conference on Visual Informatics: Sustaining research and innovations - Volume Part II* (pp.64-73). Berlin/ Heidelberg: Springer.

Mayer, R. E. (2009). *Multimedia learning.* (2nd ed.). New York, NY: Cambridge University Press.

Mayer, R. E. (2011). Multimedia learning and games. In S. Tobias & J. D. Fletcher (Eds.), *Computer games and instruction* (p. 281-305). Charlotte, NC: Information Age Publishing.

McCloud, S. (1993). *Understanding comics: The invisible art.* Northampton, MA: Kitchen Sink Press.

Miller, W. A. (1938). Reading with and without pictures. *The Elementary School Journal, 38*(9), 676-682.

Moje, E. B., Overby, M., Tysvaer, N., & Morris, K. (2008). The complex world of adolescent literacy: Myths, motivations, and mysteries. *Harvard Educational Researcher, 71*(1), 107-154.

Nakazawa, J. (2004). Manga (comic) literacy skills as determinant factors of manga story comprehension. *Manga Studies, 5,* 7-25.

Norton, B. (2003). The motivating power of comic books: Insights from Archie comic readers. *The Reading Teacher, 57*(2), 140-147.

Omori, T., Igaki, T., Ishii, T., Kurata, K., & Masuda, N. (2004). *Eye catchers in comics: Controlling eye movements in reading pictorial and textual media.* Paper presented at the 28th International Congress of Psychology. Beijing, China.

Paivio, A. (1991). Dual coding theory: Retrospect and current status. *Canadian Journal of Psychology, 45*(3), 255-287.

Parish, J. (2005). *Nintendo presents: My first adventure game.* Retrieved from http://www.1up.com/do/ reviewPage?cId=3144099&did=1

Peeck, J. (1993). Increasing picture effects in learning from illustrated text. *Learning and Instruction, 3*(3), 227–238.

Ranker, J. (2007). Using comic books as read-alouds: Insights on reading instruction from an English as a second language classroom. *The Reading Teacher, 61*(4), 296-305.

Rayner, K. (1998). Eye movements and information processing: 20 years of research. *Psychological Bulletin, 124*(3), 372-343.

Rayner, K., Rotello, C. M., Stewart, A. J., Keir, J., & Duffy, S. A. (2001). Integrating text and pictorial information: Eye movements when looking at print advertisement. *Journal of Experimental Psychology: Applied, 7*(3), 219-226.

Rideout, V. J., Foehr, U. G., & Roberts, D. F. (2010). *GENERATION M2: Media in the lives of 8- to 18-year-olds.* Menlo Park, CA: Henry J. Kaiser Family Foundation. Retrieved from http://www.kff.org/entmedia/ upload/8010.pdf

Rose, T. L. (1986). Effects of illustrations on reading comprehension of learning disabled students. *Journal of Learning Disabilities, 19*(9), 542–544.

Samuels, S. J. (1967). Attentional process in reading: The effect of pictures on the acquisition of reading responses. *Journal of Educational Psychology, 58*(6), 337-342.

Schmidt-Weigand, F., Kohert, A., & Glowalla, U. (2010). A closer look at split visual attention in system- and self-paced instruction in multimedia learning. *Learning and Instruction, 20*(2), 100-110.

Sherman, R., & Wright, G. (1996). Orchestra. *Reading Improvement, 33*(2), 124-128.

Sipe, L. R. (1998). How picture books work: A semiotically framed theory of text-picture relationships. *Children's Literacy Education, 29*(2), 97-108.

Staff Reviewer. (2005). GamesMaster deciphers the latest fiendish puzzler for DS. *Gamesradar.com.* Retrieved from http://tinyurl.com/tracememory

Starr, M. S., & Rayner, K. (2001). Eye movements during reading: Some current controversies. *Trends in Cognitive Sciences, 4*(4), 156-163.

Steinkuehler, C. (2007). Massively multiplayer online gaming as a constellation of literacy practices. *eLearning,* *4*(3), 297-318.

Steinkuehler, C., Compton-Lilly, C., & King, E. (2009, April). *Literacy practice & reading performance in* *the context of MMO games.* Presented at the Annual Meeting of the American Educational Research Association, Denver, CO.

Steinkuehler, C. (2011). *The mismeasure of boys: Reading and online videogames* (WCER Working Paper No. 2011-3). Retrieved from http://www.wcer.wisc.edu/publications/workingPapers/papers.php

Tiemensma, L. (2009). *Visual literacy: To comics or not to comics? Promoting literacy using comics.* Paper presented at the World Library and Information Congress: 75th IFLA General Conference and Council, Milan, Italy.

Turkay, S., Kinzer, C., Hoffman, D., Gunbas, N., & Nagle, C. (2010). A snapshot on youths' activities on online gaming forums: Internet and informal learning. In *Proceedings of the World Conference on Educational* *Multimedia, Hypermedia and Telecommunications 2010* (pp. 3987-3992). Chesapeake, VA: AACE.

Ujiie, J., & Krashen, S. D. (1996). Comic book reading, reading enjoyment, and pleasure reading among middle class and chapter 1 middle school students. *Reading Improvement, 33*(1), 51-54.

van Gog, T., & Scheiter, K. (2010). Eye tracking as a tool to study and enhance multimedia learning. *Learning* *and Instruction, 20*(2), 95-99.

Vernon, M. D. (1953). The value of pictorial illustrations. *British Journal of Educational Psychology, 23*(3), 180-187.

Wang, A. Y., & Newlin, M. H. (2000). Characteristics of students who enroll and succeed in psychology web-based classes. *Journal of Educational Psychology, 92*(1), 137–143.

Watkins, J. K., Miller, E., & Brubaker, D. (2004). The role of visual image: What are students really learning from pictorial representations? *Journal of Visual Literacy, 24*(1), 23–40.

Watson, D. J. (1989) Defining and describing whole language. *The Elementary School Journal, 90*(2), 129-141.

Weintraub, S. A. (1966). Illustrations for the beginning reader. *Reading Teacher, 20*(1), 61-67.

Woodard, E. H. & Gridina, N. (2000). *Media in the Home 2000: The Fifth Annual Survey of Parents and* *Children.* The Annenberg Public Policy Center of the University of Pennsylvania.

Wright, G., & Sherman, R. (1994). What is black and white and read all over? The funnies! *Reading* *Improvement, 31*(1), 37-48.

Wright, G., & Sherman, R. (1999). Let's create a comic strip. *Reading Improvement, 36*(2), 66-71.

Using Do-It-Yourself Media for Content Teaching with At-Risk Elementary Students

Leslie M. Foley
Barbara J. Guzzetti
Arizona State University

Today's youth are engaging in digital participatory media practices that barely existed less than a decade ago. These new literacies (Gee, 2003) involve producing visual and digital products and technologies representing a range of new literate skills and abilities. These do-it-yourself (DIY) or participatory media practices include: (a) creating online comics (Bitz, 2007); (b) modding or creating video games (Peppler & Kafai, 2007); (c) writing FanFiction (Black, 2005); (d) composing blogs (Witte, 2007); (e) editing and authoring self publications of zines online (Guzzetti & Gamboa, 2004); (f) writing online journals (Guzzetti & Gamboa, 2005); (g) participating and creating in online social networks of virtual worlds (Boellstorff, 2007); and (h) appropriating and renovating characters presented in movies and television in writing (Skinner, 2007). These practices permeate young people's lives and create a new image of youth culture today (Ito, Horst, Bittanti, Boyd, Herr-Stephenson, Lange, Pascole, & Robinson, 2008). With an increasing number of online tools, youth are enabled to create with new digital forms and in new digital forums for communication, learning, and self-expression.

Little empirical research has been conducted, however, on young peoples' practices with participatory media for learning subject-matter content (Guzzetti, Elliot & Welsch, 2010). Most researchers (e.g., Kist, 2003; Luce-Kapler, 2007; Steinkuehler, 2007) have described how these new literate practices engage and motivate students in their learning, but have not yet explored their impact on students' subject-matter learning. Studies that have explored the impact of these DIY practices on students' academic performance typically have been conducted with adolescents and have usually focused on students' creating video games for learning content concepts in areas like social studies or mathematics (e.g., Moshirnia, 2007; Papanastasiou & Ferdig, 2006). Hence, investigations are needed that explore the influence of digital participatory media practices on elementary and pre-adolescent students' literacy engagement and performance in content areas. With the increasing popularity of DIY media, relevant questions remain about how these new literacies practices impact students' motivation for literacy (both new literacies and traditional literacy practices) and their academic performance when integrated into content teaching.

PURPOSE

This study was designed to respond to the call to investigate the impact of incorporating new digital media on students' motivation and engagement in literacy and their performance in content areas (Lankshear & Knobel, 2003; Guzzetti, Elliot & Welsch, 2010). This study addressed two central and related questions. First, how do the new literacies of podcasting and online video-making enhance students' understanding of content in social studies and impact their writing engagement and performance in language arts? Second, how do students react to incorporating new digital participatory media into content area instruction?

This study was inspired by the first author's interest in new digital media for instruction after taking graduate classes at a local university in using DIY or participatory media for content teaching from the second author. Together with another teacher, she developed an after-school club, Husky Productions, that met twice a week and continued from October 2010 to May 2011 at the elementary school where she teaches. This program was designed to give students access to technology and opportunities to work with participatory digital media while enhancing their content area instruction in social studies and language arts. This after-school program was funded by a federal grant awarded to the state to establish 21st Century Community Learning Centers that provide at-risk students with opportunities for standards-based academic and personal enrichment designed to complement the academic program.

To systematically examine how students reacted to these new media for learning content concepts, the first author enlisted the assistance of the second author, forming a teacher/university-researcher partnership. Together, we hoped to discover ways to use DIY media practices in content teaching in this informal atmosphere and determine if and how these practices could transfer to classroom instruction. We wondered how students would react to using participatory digital media for content learning. Since most research with participatory media in content areas has been done with middle-school and high-school students (Guzzetti, Elliott & Welsch, 2010), we wondered how these new digital participatory literacies could impact these elementary students' academic motivation, engagement, and achievement. We also wondered how a teacher's own teaching practices could be enhanced by teaching with digital DIY media.

THEORETICAL FRAMEWORK

This study was informed by the theoretical positions of the New Literacies Studies (New London Group, 1996; Gee, 2003). This perspective reconceptualizes literacy as a broad range of practices representing students' interactions with print, visual, aural, or digital texts. Students apply their literacy knowledge and skills in various social settings to "read" a text (Street, 1995). New literacies include not only technical tools, but also a different mindset that emphasizes cultural and social relations that result from valuing participation, collaboration, dispersion, and distribute expertise of literacy practices (Lankshear & Knobel, 2006).

METHODS

This study was conducted as teacher research (Cochran-Smith & Lytle, 1992) or research by a teacher on her own practice and her students' responses to those practices. Teacher research is systematic and reflective inquiry into one's own teaching and students' learning (Cochran-Smith & Lytle, 1992). The methodological approach of teacher research allows teachers to observe their students in a mixture of settings and situations while constructing knowledge about their students and is often done in partnership with a university researcher or within a community of fellow practitioners. Labeled as "a quiet form of research" (Britton, 1987), teacher research allows teachers to take seriously the ordinary business of their lives as educators (Britton, 1987). Teachers can add to the public's body of knowledge by sharing information generated through their research

and contribute to the larger reform agenda through knowledge gained from this inquiry process (Cochran-Smith & Lytle, 1992).

Sample

Husky Productions was composed of eight boys and four girls from four fifth- and sixth-grade classrooms, all of whom were Hispanic. The school was located in a predominantly Hispanic community and received Title 1 funding. This suburban school in the Southwestern United States was the oldest school in the district located near the historic downtown. Key informants for this study were three Hispanic boys—Jacob, Fabian, Hugo, and one Hispanic girl, Selena (all names are pseudonyms). We focused on these four students because of their regular attendance and their high level of involvement in the after-school program. These students were considered at-risk due to their inability to meet the state standards for writing and because of their high poverty status, known risk factors for dropping out of school (U.S. Department of Commerce, 1997). The after-school program they participated in required their at-risk status.

The After-School Program

During the after-school program, students were engaged in several activities involving digital participatory media. Students used digital cameras, created podcasts and digital movies, and learned how to create multimedia presentations. The first of these activities students participated in was podcasting. The word *podcast* is derived from two words: iPod and broadcast. The EDUCAUSE Initiative (2005) describes podcasting as a "software and hardware combination that permits automatic downloading of audio files (most commonly in MP3 format) for listening at the user's convenience" (p. 9). Podcasting is a method of publishing both audio and video by using the Internet (Clyde, 2005), and is increasing in popularity among young people (Pew Internet and American Life Project, 2005).

Students created remix versions of the tune *Jingle Bells* by using the Garage Band software (http://www.apple.com/ilife/garageband/) in the school's Mac lab. Each student created a remix of the melody to include on the Holiday CD. Students added beats, sound effects, and music clips to a recording of *Jingle Bells* that they played on the xylophones. The melodies were compiled onto a holiday CD for the school. The students then created podcast commercials persuading teachers to purchase their CDs. This writing assignment addressed the fifth-grade writing performance objectives related to persuasive writing, including: (a) determining the intended audience for a writing piece, (b) selecting appropriate word choice, and (c) adding details.

Students also created digital videos by using the iMovie software on the Mac computers. Digital video-making has been described as a process of connection where teachers "work with their students to help them harness the power of voice and imagery to connect people to their community by using technology that is relevant to the way we live today" (Robin, 2008, p. 429). Digital videos allow students to construct expository texts through combining multiple media, including images, titles, voice, video, music, and transitions. Students used the iMovie program to create a video presentation of their state reports or book reports. In their classrooms, students were given an assignment to select a state, gather information, and write and present a report on that state or write a book report. Students came to the program needing help with their reports and presentations. Students gathered facts on their state by using graphic organizers (Ausubel, 1963; Barron, 1979) provided by their classroom teacher. These were: (a) tree maps to help students organize main ideas with supporting details about their state; (b) paragraph organizers to help students write a cohesive paragraph, including a topic sentence, three supporting details, and a concluding sentence; and (c) a bibliography map to help students gather citation information for the bibliography, such as author, title, and year of publication. Students transferred the information from the graphic organizers onto note cards attached to a metal ring.

We assisted students in finding information about their state on the Internet and organizing the information into a logical sequence. Students created a storyboard to help them outline their information in a sequential order by including a few sentences on a state fact and a quick sketch of a picture that would relate to the fact. These sketches helped students focus their attention when searching for images on the Internet. The storyboards also helped students present facts about their state in a logical sequence. For example, students organized their facts into categories, such as information on the official state symbols, the history of the state, and famous people from the state. Students rearranged sections in a logical order for the audience.

Students also wrote a script providing facts and exciting information about their state while addressing the state standards related to writing applications. These standards included expository writing and researching and addressed the state standard related to the writing process, including publishing. Individuals read through their scripts, making corrections where they were needed. Students then selected relevant graphics, such as pictures and images of their state from the Internet to include in their iMovie. Finally, students created an iMovie as a way to present their state report to their class by integrating graphics, text, voice, and music to inform and entertain their audience. In these ways, activities in the after-school program coordinated with content teaching by addressing relevant state standards in the classroom.

Data Collection

Data collection began in the fall of 2010 and continued through the spring of 2011 over the course of one academic year. We conducted direct observations of students captured in field notes for each day of the two-day-a-week after-school program. Observations focused on students' interactions with and production of digital media. These observations were captured in both in-the-midst field notes (Hubbard & Power, 1999) taken during class sessions and after-the-fact field notes (Hubbard & Power, 1999) following instruction. These observations focused on students' interactions with each other and their interactions with the three adults assisting in the program (the teacher researcher, the university researcher/co-author, and another teacher). These observations occurred each day and were recorded in field notes (by the second and first authors) that separated anecdotal records from comments and questions.

We also conducted in-situ interviews with individuals as they were using DIY media and recorded these in our field notes. These informal interviews were conducted to correct students' misconceptions or help to assist students in obtaining proficiency with digital media. For example, Jacob wanted to include a photo of a city in Columbia, South America in his book report presentation. When questioning him about this, he stated that Columbia City was a city in Columbia, South America. When asked where he found that information, he stated that Columbia City should be a city in Columbia. He was then directed to look up Columbia City through a Google search and check his facts. Through responding to these kinds of open-ended, leading questions, Jacob was able to clarify that Columbia City was in fact a city in Indiana, not South America. In another in-situ interview, the first author questioned Fabian on his progress with his iMovie presentation. During this interview, she discovered that Fabian was having trouble inserting an image into his presentation and demonstrated how to take a screen shot of an image and insert it into his video.

In addition to these two sources, we triangulated the data by collecting documents. We archived the first author's lesson plans that were used to guide instruction and ensure digital media were being used to address relevant state standards. These data also included copies of the students' writing, CDs, podcasts, and DVDs. We also took photographs of the students working with the digital media during the course of the program.

A fourth form of qualitative data included the first author's teacher journal. She kept records of her emotional reactions, questions, and notes about students' abilities and progress. She also recorded her reflections on the research, humorous quotes from the students, and reflections for future teaching.

In addition to these qualitative data, two pretest/posttest quantitative measures were administered. The first of these was the Estes Attitude Scale (Estes, 1971). This is a well-known attitude toward reading measure that is widely used with elementary students. The validity and reliability of the Estes Scale were reported for students in grades 3-12; the reported reliability coefficient was .94 (Estes, 1971). The attitude scale has 20 statements; eight are positive and twelve are negative. There were 100 total points possible on the Estes scale. Students' attitudes were assessed with the Estes two weeks before implementation of the program to avoid the threat of pretest sensitization (Campbell & Stanley, 1966). The Estes was given again following the last week of the 7-month program.

The second quantitative measure administered as a pretest and posttest was a district-developed measure consisting of six short-answer problem-solving or vocabulary questions. These questions tapped students' knowledge of social studies concepts through vocabulary and students' sequencing skills for language arts. An additional four questions assessed students' confidence in creating Word documents, spreadsheets, graphics, and multimedia. A final question asked students to describe what they wanted to learn or did learn in the program.

Data Analysis

Qualitative data were analyzed by thematic analysis (Patton, 1990). Data were read and reread several times. Data were annotated by writing keywords in margins of field notes or transcripts, signifying topics. These annotations often became the basis for codes and subcodes. Copies of the coded data set were used for manipulation, organization, and ease of comparisons across codes, forming larger categories from codes and identification of themes.

Member checks were conducted with key informants. Interview notes and analysis of the data were provided to the informants for affirmation, clarification, or modification. Informants supplied clarification of missing interview data or data that were unclear.

Quantitative data from the Estes Attitude Measure (Estes, 1971) were analyzed by calculating frequencies and percentage tallies. Mean scores for the group were compared from pre to posttesting. In doing so, we focused on the four students who had regular attendance throughout the program.

FINDINGS

Students' Engagement in and Attitudes Toward Literacy

Over the course of the year, the students improved in their attitudes toward and engagement in literacy. This improvement was documented quantitatively by students' scores on the *Estes Attitudes Assessment*. Students' scores increased from 66 out of 100 points in the beginning of the program to 88 out of 100 points at the end of the program. All of the students strongly agreed to statements like, "Reading is rewarding to me," and, "Books make good presents," and strongly disagreed with statements like, "Reading becomes boring after about a hour," and "Reading is something I can do without."

These positive attitudes were also evidenced in our observations. At the beginning of the program, students were reluctant to write and often asked to play online games. As we began introducing participatory media into the assignments, students expressed their desires to read and write on screen and explore their topics of interest. Students frequently stated the time went by fast because they were working so hard and having fun. For example, Fabian exclaimed, "It's over already? Today was short!" Other times, students would appear at the computer lab before the teachers did to get started on their projects. In an informal interview talking about the program, Selena stated, "It made learning become more to me. For example, finding pictures and writing was fun. I also liked how we used our time wisely when we got to work with technology." Hugo shared similar feelings, stating, "I liked when we used technology to do our schoolwork. It made the assignments fun. It helped me learn about computers. I got to do things the other kids didn't get to do." Fabian stated, "I feel happy to be in Husky Productions because I get to be with my friends while we are having fun, and we get to learn something. We are learning how to do stuff on the computer like iMovie. When we do iMovie we get to pick pictures for our state report." By the end of the program, no students asked to play online games or engaged in off-task behaviors.

Students' Performance in the Writing Process

Students showed continual engagement in the writing process, including their ability to generate ideas in the prewriting stage. By engaging in a process approach to writing (Day, 1947), students had opportunities to brainstorm ideas with their fellow classmates. Students began each assignment with a brainstorming session. Students generated topics, outlined ideas for the assignment, and listed potential digital media practices available to them. Then, students determined their purpose for writing and their intended audience. For example, Selena stated her purpose for creating a podcast commercial was to persuade teachers to purchase the Holiday CD. She declared after working so hard she wanted to make money for the school and teachers were the perfect audience to target because they had more money than the students. Students met three of the six performance objectives for the fifth-grade state writing standards for prewriting by: (a) brainstorming, (b) determining the purpose for writing, and (c) determining the intended audience.

Students' sequencing skills developed as a result of their engagement with digital media. Initially, students struggled with flow of ideas and creating clear transitions between paragraphs. All of the students jumped from fact to fact without connecting their ideas. For example, in the beginning of writing her state report, Selena simply stated random facts about Pennsylvania. There was no cohesion among the ideas she was presenting to the audience. Therefore, students were encouraged to use iMovie as a storyboard to develop and organize their ideas. Individuals added images of various facts, such as the state symbols or state capitol to their iMovies. Then, students used these images to write scripts for their voiceovers. These scripts included a topic sentence and three supporting details about each image. These voiceover scripts then became students' paragraphs in their state reports.

Creating the digital videos helped students see a clear sequence of their ideas and where the breaks in flow occurred. Students were able to correct errors in their presentations and transfer their corrections to their writing to maintain a clear progression of ideas. iMovie offered students a unique presentation of their state reports, and assisted students in improving their sequencing skills. The students showed improvement in sequencing on the district assessment, as well. Average scores improved from 46% to 92% on the short-answer problem-solving questions. Students read passages and applied inference and problem-solving skills to work out responses to questions related to sequencing and production.

Students also revised their writing for clarity and word choice. Students read and reread their work in an effort to ensure their writing was clear and free from errors. Students added details to accomplish their purpose, rearranged sentences to clarify meaning, and used resources and online reference materials, such as an online dictionary and thesaurus, to select precise vocabulary. In one instance, Selena realized she had only listed the names for the state bird, flower, and animal. She decided it would be more interesting if she added descriptive details about each state symbol instead of just listing them. Selena was able to revise her writing by adding details taken from Internet sources. In another instance, Hugo was reading his paragraphs with facts about famous cities in Texas. He realized he added a sentence with details about Austin in a paragraph about Houston. He was able to rearrange the sentences to clarify meaning. Fabian also showed evidence of revising his writing. While he was reviewing his state report, he realized he was missing information on the state flower. He was able to locate an online resource, www.statesymbolsusa.org/Oklahoma/stateWildflower, a website designated to information on the state symbols to gather details about the Indian Blanket, Oklahoma's state wildflower. He then returned to his writing and added details about the Indian Blanket.

Students also reported increased confidence levels in creating Word documents, integrating graphics and multimedia, and writing in hybrid forms. Prior to the start of the program, all of the students reported needing help with these skills. On the post assessment, all of the students reported being able to create these on their own or with minimal support.

Students' proficiency with the writing process also addressed the state standards for persuasive writing. Students reread and edited their commercials persuading teachers to purchase their CD. Fabian included persuasive words, such as "new," "in heaven," "one dollar each," "limited," and "download it":

> We, Husky Productions, have something to say. We have something NEW!!! It's the newest CD of 2011. It's the Best of them all. Don't you hate those old CDs made in 2010? Well, that's old school, yo. Plus you can use it for Christmas. We just added some remix and hip hop and it sounds like you were in heaven! If you want to hear it, it is only for one dollar each. But don't wait, it's limited. You could even download it. This CD will make your butt move. Trust me you will LOVE this CD. -Fabian

Selena included powerful persuasive words as well. She used the words "secret," "remix," "creative," and "limited-time offer":

> Do you want to know a secret? My friends and I made some music. Our family and friends loved it. They asked us to make them one too. Now we're not like any ordinary CD store. If you want some remixed or creative music, then come on down to our classroom. Limited Time Offer! -Selena

After revising the content, students edited their reports for spelling, punctuation, and grammatical errors. Individuals used various resources, such as a dictionary, the spelling and grammar check option in Microsoft Word, and word lists of commonly misspelled words to correct errors in their writing. For example, when Hugo was editing his state report, he realized he misspelled some cities in Texas and needed to add commas to a series of three when listing famous actors from Texas. He was able to use the spell-check option in Word to correct his spelling errors and use the grammar check option in Word to determine where to add commas.

Students also engaged in collaborative peer review. Partners peer reviewed their reports and presentations and offered feedback and suggestions to each other. During a peer editing session, Hugo shared his images of different cities in Texas. Jacob suggested to Hugo to "…give interesting facts about the cities." In another instance, Hugo recommended that Jacob add more details about the setting of the story since it took place in a different country. In another peer review session, Selena told Hugo to speak up during his audio recording so his voice sounded more convincing. Fabian helped Selena edit her report, making suggestions to fix spelling errors and correcting minor errors, such as capitalizing the names of cities. Feedback and suggestions were welcomed and incorporated by the students to improve their writing and presentations.

Students' Engagement in Social Studies

Students' attitudes toward and engagement in learning social studies were also evidenced as they generated numerous questions of interest. For example, Selena chose Pennsylvania for her state because her mother once lived there, but she did not know much about the state. Her mother had mentioned something to her about the Liberty Bell, but Selena did not know what it was. Selena began searching for information online. Through her searches of various websites, including www. ushistory.org/libertybell, www.50states.com/flower/pennsylvania, www.pacivilwar150.com, and www.classbrain.com, Selena found information on the Liberty Bell, the state flower, the Civil War, and famous people from Pennsylvania. Selena illustrated a new-found enthusiasm while working on her state report. She stated, "At first I only had one question, but then one thing led to another and I had a lot of questions!"

The other students shared similar experiences. Fabian started the project knowing "nothing about Oklahoma." He gathered information from various Internet resources, including Google, www.classbrain.com, www.50states.com, www.theoceancountylibrary.org, and www.ok.gov/kids. During one of his searches, Fabian found information on museums in Oklahoma. He exclaimed, "I didn't know there were pop music museums!" Fabian spent the next 20 minutes reading about museums in Oklahoma. Students spent about 35 minutes each session searching various websites for information and visited an average of eight websites for their state reports. Individuals included information regarding their state's history, state capital, famous people from the state, and state symbols.

All of the students in the program reported being excited about their state reports and presentations. For example, after learning about the tools in iMovie, Selena showed us the transitions and music she added to her video and asked, "Isn't it so cool?" When asked about how her final presentation went, Selena said, "It was so great. The other kids were jealous. They thought my presentation was cool! My teacher was clapping and smiling during my presentation. Last year, she never smiled." Her comments like these indicated that she was engaged in her learning and excited by the content.

Students' acquisition of conceptual knowledge in social studies. Students also acquired new conceptual knowledge through learning social studies vocabulary. Alvermann, Phelps, and Gillis (2010) explain that in academic disciplines, concepts are represented by content vocabulary. Therefore, mastery of academic vocabulary is crucial to comprehending content area texts (Pearson, Hiebert, & Kamil, 2007). When students are exposed to wide reading and multiple exposures to words, students can expand their vocabulary (Blachowicz, Fisher, Ogle & Watts-Taffe, 2006). Students who master academic vocabulary are enabled to talk and write like members of a discipline (Nagy & Scott, 2000). This was evident in the students' podcasting project. Students expanded their social studies vocabulary by learning new words such as, "entrepreneur, "finance," and "profit." For example, students had to develop a finance plan outlining the time needed to produce the CD, production and material costs, and how much they would need to sell the CDs for to make a profit. Because the computers already had the software to create the podcasts, the students decided it would cost about 20 dollars to create 20 CDs. They then determined if they sold each CD for five dollars, and sold all 20 CDs, they would make 100 dollars. The students were reminded that they needed to subtract the cost for the materials to determine the total profit. The students recalculated and determined they would make eighty dollars in profit which they decided to donate to the school improvement fund.

Students also showed evidence of expanding and applying these content terms or concepts when they classified themselves as entrepreneurs because they wanted to create and sell CDs to earn money for their school. Jacob demonstrated his extended vocabulary when he said his older cousin was an entrepreneur because he ran his own mechanics shop. Selena demonstrated her new vocabulary when she stated she wanted to be an entrepreneur when she grew up because she wanted to own a business as a wedding planner.

Individuals also showed other evidence of expanding their vocabulary, including the word "profit." For example, one day of the week the group shared the computer lab with students in the Gardening Club who took care of the school garden. The students in the Gardening Club also held a Farmer's Market on the last Friday of every month to sell vegetables and herbs grown in the garden. In a conversation with students in the Gardening Club, Jacob explained that profit was the amount of money you earn after paying for any necessary equipment. He also explained that if they took the money they made from the Farmer's Market and subtracted the total costs, the amount left would be their profit. In another instance, the students discussed appropriate pricing for the CD. Fabian suggested selling the CDs for more money to earn a greater profit. Hugo reminded Fabian that while earning a larger profit would be nice, they needed to keep the CDs affordable.

Students' Strategic Thinking and Problem Solving

There are claims that digital media promotes new ways of thinking and higher-order thinking skills (Kajder, 2007; Rice, 2007). This theory was illustrated in new ways by these students in their interactions with digital media. Video-making required a diversity of new digital skills, including the ability to upload photographs, search for images, and add text, transitions, music, and voice recordings. By deciding when and how to use these skills, students showed evidence of becoming strategic thinkers. For example, when working with iMovie, Selena was having trouble recording her voiceover to fit the length of her image. Through self-exploration, she discovered how to adjust the slide length. She changed the slide length from five to eight seconds to allow more time to share facts about Pennsylvania's state bird. In another instance, Selena was reviewing the music options to locate music online that would fit with her presentation. Once she found some appropriate songs, she dragged and dropped them onto the corresponding slide. Hugo explored the iMovie tools and discovered how to change a photo from color to black and white to make the picture look, "like it fit better with the time period during the civil war." Hugo also tested his script to see how long to make each slide and modified the time on each slide to fit his script.

There was evidence of students becoming problem solvers, as well. As a student encountered a problem, he or she found a way to solve it. Their strategies included looking at the Mac manuals, using the Finder search function, and searching online. For example, Hugo needed to split his music clip to add (in his words) "more peaceful music" to his presentation. After unsuccessfully searching online for directions, he decided to mute a section of the song he did not want to include. In another instance, Fabian stated he wanted to include Oklahoma's state song. We asked him if he had the state song and he replied, "No, but I could look it up online."

Students worked together to collaboratively solve problems and resolve dilemmas. When one student was struggling with a particular task, another student was quick to offer assistance and support. For example, Selena could not locate a video she had saved on her computer so Fabian helped her perform an online search to find the presentation. In another instance, Hugo asked Fabian to help him with the audio on his presentation. Together, the boys discovered how to fade the music and turn up the voice recording so Hugo's voice could be heard. Through collaborations like these, students worked together to solve problems.

DISCUSSION

This study demonstrates that elementary students have the inclination and ability to use participatory media in learning content concepts and skills that address academic state standards. Since current research has focused primarily on adolescents' engagement with new literacies practices (e.g., Guzzetti & Gamboa, 2004; Hayes, Johnson, King, & Lammers, 2008), this study demonstrates that participatory media can be appropriate for young students in the teaching-learning process, as well. Elementary students' engagement, attitudes, motivation, and achievement were impacted by incorporating podcasting and digital video-making. Students were able to stimulate and enhance their writing by using hybrid textual forms and digital images and learn new content vocabulary and concepts through engagement with DIY media.

This study also demonstrates that rather than detracting from addressing state standards and simply being an "add-on" in the curriculum, participatory media can be used to meet state standards for content areas. Students learned to use podcasts and digital videos to meet the language arts and social studies state standards for fifth and sixth grade. Podcasting and video-making enhanced students' literacy skills, including their abilities to use new information, write for a specific audience, reflect on their thinking, edit their work, and transpose written to oral text. Individuals learned aspects of the writing process, clarified and determined significance of information read online, selected information with a particular audience in mind, and navigated new technologies. Participatory media presented opportunities for students to engage in sophisticated multimodal literacies, thinking strategies, and skills of collaboration and multitasking, reflective of the abilities they will increasingly need to be empowered citizens in the 21st century. These are new skills and abilities that minority, low-income, and at-risk students often lack (Cummins, Brown & Sayers, 2007) that teachers can foster by providing practice with new digital participatory media.

Teachers can also incorporate the ethos of participatory media by allowing students freedom in their literacy practices. Freedom can include genre choice, topic choice, and the option to display their knowledge by using various participatory media. This ethic agrees with Lankshear and Knobel's (2007) idea that a new literacies approach includes both the use of technology and the view that literacy is participatory, collaborative, and distributed.

Efforts to integrate new literacies practices can prepare youth to participate in the rapidly changing technological environment of the 21st century. This endeavor requires fostering students' abilities to locate and solve problems, engage in complex situations, convert those situations into problems that can be solved, and learn how to learn (Bruce, 2002). Further investigations of participatory media among students of varying age levels, socioeconomic status, and achievement levels will assist in understanding and appreciating the benefits these new literacies practices have for a range of students. Through learning from young people, insights into the teaching-learning process can be gained that draw on relevant and motivating practices for today's students in a digital world.

REFERENCES

Alvermann, D. E., Phelps, S. F., & Gillis, V. R. (2010). *Content area reading and literacy: Succeeding in Today's Diverse Classrooms.* New York, NY: Allyn & Bacon.

Ausubel, D. P. (1963). *The psychology of meaningful verbal learning.* New York, NY: Grune & Stratton.

Barron, R. R. (1979). Research for the classroom teacher: Recent developments on the structured overview as an advance organizer. In H. L. Herber & J. D. Riley (Eds.), *Research in reading in the content areas: The fourth report.* Syracuse, NY: Syracuse University Reading and Language Arts Center.

Bitz, M. (2007). The comic book project: Literacy outside and inside the box. In J. Flood, S. Brice-Heath, & D. Lapp (Eds.), *Handbook of research on teaching literacy though the communicative and visual arts* (Vol. II) (pp. 229-237). New York, NY: Routledge.

Black, R.W. (2005). Access and affiliation: The literacy and composition practices of English-language learners in an online fan fiction community. *Journal of Adolescent & Adult Literacy, 49,* 118-128.

Blachowitz, C. L. Z., Fisher, P. J., Ogle, D., & Watts-Taffe, S. (2006). Vocabulary: Questions from the classroom. *Reading Research Quarterly, 41,* 524-539.

Boellstorff, T. (2007). *Coming of age in Second Life.* Princeton, NJ: Princeton Unviersity Press.

Britton, J. (1987). A quiet form of research. In D. Goswami & P. Stillman (Eds.), *Reclaiming the classroom: Teacher research as an agency for change.* Upper Montclair, NJ: Boynton Cook.

Bruce, B. C. (2002). Diversity and critical social engagement: How changing technologies enable new modes of literacy in changing circumstances. In D. E. Alvermann (Ed.), *Adolescents and literacies in a digital world* (pp. 1-18). New York, NY: Peter Lang.

Campbell, D. T., & Stanley, J. (1966). *Experimental and quasi-experimental designs for research.* Chicago, IL: Rand MacNally.

Clyde, L. A. (2005). Some new Internet applications coming now to a computer near you. *Teacher Librarian. 33,* 54.

Cochran-Smith, M., & Lytle, S. (1992). Communities for teacher research: Fringe or forefront? *American Journal of Education, 100,* 298-325.

Cummins, J., Brown, K., & Sayers, D. (2007). *Literacy, technology and diversity: Teaching for success in changing times.* Boston, MA: Pearson.

Day, A. G. (1947). Writer's magic. *American Association of University Professors Bulletin, 33,* 269-278.

EDUCAUSE Learning Initiative. (2005). Seven things you should know about...podcasting. Boulder, CO: EDUCAUSE. Available at: http://net.educause.edu/ir/library/pdf/ELI7003.pdf

Estes, T. H. (1971). A scale to measure attitudes toward reading. *Journal of Reading, 15,* 135-38.

Gee, J. P. (2003). *What video games have to teach us about learning and literacy.* New York, NY: Pallgrave/ MacMillan.

Guzzetti, B. J., Elliott, K., & Welsch. D. (2010). *DIY media in the classroom: New literacies across content areas.* New York, NY: Teachers College Press.

Guzzetti, B. J., & Gamboa, M. (2004). Zines for social justice: Adolescent girls writing on their own. *Reading Research Quarterly, 39,* 408-435.

Guzzetti, B. J., & Gamboa, M. (2005). Online journaling: The informal writings of two adolescent girls. *Research in the Teaching of English, 40,* 168-206.

Hayes, E., Johnson, B., King, E., & Lammers, J. (2008). *The SIMS 2 and Teen Second Life: Insights from Tech Savvy Girls, Year 2*; Retrieved from http://www.glsconference.org/2008/session.html?id=76

Hubbard, R. S., & Power, B. M. (1999). *Living the questions: A guide for teacher researchers.* New York, NY: Stenhouse Publishers.

Ito, M., Horst, H. A., Bittanti, M., Boyd, D., Herr-Stephenson, B., Lange, P. B., Pascole, C. J., & Robinson, L. (2008). *Living and learning with new media: Summary of findings from the Digital Youth Project.* Chicago, IL: The Macarthur Foundation.

Kajder, S. B. (2007). Bringing new literacies into the content area literacy methods course. *Contemporary Issues in Technology and Teacher Education, 7,* 92-99.

Kist, W. (2003). Student achievement in new literacies for the 21st century. *Middle School Journal, 36,* 6-13.

Lankshear, C., & Knobel, M. (2003). New technologies in early childhood literacy research: A review of research. *Journal of Early Childhood Literacy, 3,* 59-82.

Lankshear, C., & Knobel, M. (2006). *New literacies: Everyday practices and classroom learning* (2nd ed.). New York, NY: Peter Lang.

Lankshear, C. & Knobel, M. (2007). Sampling the "new" in new literacies. In M. Knobel & C. Lankshear (Eds.), *A new literacies sampler* (pp. 1-24). New York, NY: Peter Lang.

Luce-Kapler, R. (2007). Radical change and wikis: Teaching new literacies. *Journal of Adolescent and Adult Literacy, 51,* 214-223.

Moshirnia, A. (2007). The educational potential of modified video games. *Issues in Informing Science and Information Technology, 4,* 511-521.

Nagy, W., & Scott, J. (2000). Vocabulary processes. In M. Kamil, P. Mosenthal, P. D. Pearson, & R. Barr (Eds.), *Handbook of Reading Research* (Vol. III), (pp. 269-284). Mahwah, NJ: Erlbaum.

New London Group. (1996). A pedagogoy of mulitliteracices: Designing social futures. *Harvard Educational Review, 66,* 60-93. Retrieved from http://wwwstatic.kern.org/filer/blogWrite44ManilaWebsite/paul/articles/A_Pedagogy_of_Multiliteracies_Designing_Social_Futures.htm

Papanastasiou, F. C., & Ferdig, R. E. (2006). Computer use and mathematical literacy: An analysis of existing and potential relationships. *Journal of Computers in Mathematics and Science Teaching, 25,* 361-371.

Patton, M. Q. (1990). *Qualitative evaluation and research methods* (2nd ed.). Newbury Park, CA: Sage Publications.

Pearson. P. D., Heibert, E. H., & Kamil, M. L. (2007). Vocabulary assessment: What we know, what we need to learn. *Reading Research Quarterly, 42,* 282-296.

Peppler, K., & Kafai, Y. (2007). What video game making can teach us about literacy and learning: Alernative pathways into participatory culture. In A. Baba (Ed.), *Situated play: Proceedings of the Third Internatinoanl Conference of the Digital Games Research Association* (pp. 369-376). Tokyo, Japan.

Pew Internet and American Life Project. (2005). *Podcasting catches on.* Retrieved from http://www.pewinternet. org/Reports/2005/Podcasting-catches-on/Data-Memo.aspx.

Rice, J. (2007). Assessing higher order thinking in video games. *Journal of Technology and Teacher Education, 15,* 87-100.

Robin, B. R. (2008). The effective uses of digital storytelling as a teaching and learning tool. In J. Flood, S. B. Heath, & D. Lapp (Eds.), *Handbook of research on teaching literacy through the communicative and visual arts* (Vol. II), (pp. 429-440). New York, NY: Lawrence Erlbaum.

Skinner, E. N. (2007). "Teenage Addition": Adolescent girls drawing upon popular culture texts as mentors for writing in an after-school writing club. In E. Rowe, R. Jiménez, D. Compton, D. Dickinson, Y. Kim, K. Leander, & V. Risco (Eds.), *National Reading Conference Yearbook, 55,* (p. 275-291). Chicago, IL: National Reading Conference.

Steinkuehler, C. (2007). Massively multiplayer online gaming as a constellation of literacy practices. *E-Learning, 4,* 297-318.

Street, B. V. (1995). *Social literacies: Critical approaches to literacy in development ethnography and education.* London, England: Longmont.

U.S. Department of Commerce (1997, September). *America's children at risk.* Washington, DC: U.S. Department of Commerce. Retrieved from http://www.census.gov/prod/3/97pubs/cb-9702.pdf

Witte, S. (2007). "That's online writing, not boring school writing": Writing with blogs and the talkback project. *Journal of Adolescent & Adult Literacy, 51,* 92-96.

Subversive Literacies: Considering What Counts as Reading in a Gaming Household

Heather L. Lynch
Georgia State University

"That this revolution should not affect education in some other than a formal and superficial fashion is inconceivable."—John Dewey (1915; regarding the Industrial Revolution)

"I'm just not that into reading, Mrs. L. Don't take it personally." I tried not to show the disappointment on my face.

"But you love to read, Harris. You read all night on *World of Warcraft* (Blizzard Entertainment, 2004)," I reasoned.

"Yeah, but that's real reading. This stuff is crap… No offense." Well, at least he was trying to be nice about it.

The truth is, I agreed with Harris. I looked around the school library and, while I knew I could find something that he could pick up, enjoy, and connect to, there was a very real possibility that none of it would be as personally and critically engaging as Harris's online gaming with his international circle of friends. As an English teacher, I felt frustrated—frustrated for him and for me. What I had to offer in my classroom just couldn't compete. I had standards to teach to, outdated literature to teach with, and an old-world administration under which to teach.

Current research suggests what Harris implies: looking at video games to better and more meaningfully engage adolescent readers holds great promise in the 21st century classroom (Gee, 2007, 2008, 2010; Selfe, Mareck, & Gardiner, 2007). Teacher-researchers, such as West (2008) and Dezuanni (2010) are finding exciting ways in which to bridge the gap between the sophisticated and powerful literacy practices of adolescents in their "real" lives and the goals, standards, and possibilities in their academic lives. However, classrooms across America look remarkably the same as they did before the Internet, video games, Facebook, the blogosphere, or YouTube (National Council of Teachers of English, 2007), and their constituents seem quite content with those similarities.

The purpose of this study is to understand the perceived affordances and limitations of video games and their relationship to the literacy engagements of one avid, adolescent gamer and his mother in an African American family. Interestingly, there is little discussion in the field of literacy research that considers the rich and complex relationships among specifically African American families and digital literacies (Lewis, 2011). While researchers are just beginning to consider what video games do for and to us (Williams, 2007), few discuss the importance of parents' dispositions towards video games as they pertain to their children's educational and literacy development. Within the present study, I focus on the following questions: (a) In what ways does one family value video games in relation to purposes, goals, and futures related to literacy writ large?, (b) To what extent do these framings diverge across generations within this family?, and (c) What role does or might video games play within the life of one child in this particular family?

REVIEW OF RELEVANT LITERATURE

Digital Literacies Defined

Internet technologies, including countless and ever-developing modes of digital sources of information and communication continue to revise what literacy is and what it does for us (Lankshear & Knobel, 2006). Such technologies have brought forth the need for digital literacies, which differ dramatically from traditional static, print-based modes of reading and writing. While print is linear, digital texts, which include websites, wikis, social media, e-mail, instant messages, YouTube, video games, smart phone applications, and the like, are not. While print relies typically on visual stimulation, digital texts present multiple modes of stimuli (i.e., gestural, musical, visual, artistic, and print), each often competing for attention (Prenski, 2001). The interactive nature of digital texts allows readers to become participants in text construction as they negotiate how best to navigate multiple modalities as they are presented (Johnson, 2008; Kress, 2003).

Csikzentmihalyi (1990) rightly predicted at the onset of wide-scale digital literacies that for each new form of literacy that emerges, so does a new form of illiteracy. Warschauer, Knobel, and Stone (2004) found this to be precisely the case in their study of 64 classrooms in 8 public schools in California. From their qualitative surveys, observations, and interviews, the researchers found that students in schools containing primarily families with lower incomes had less frequent access to high-quality digital literacy practices than students in more affluent school districts. Specifically, schools in low-income districts used computer technologies to search for specific information on the Internet (i.e., looking up definitions or facts) and to create PowerPoint presentations, while their more affluent neighbors participated in virtual labs and class blogs, as well as other more sophisticated forms of researching and publishing undertakings.

Not surprisingly, this leaves students from lower-income households to explore digital literacies in their own out-of-school context, leading to a new form of social stratification: that of the digital divide (King & O'Brien, 2007). Families in which parents have the means and understandings to provide their children with sophisticated digital experiences (e.g., e-mail accounts, blogs, video games, media editing software, etc.) will inevitably better support their children's digital literacy development when compared to families who are limited in such experiences. As a result, schools leave an important realm of academic preparation to the mercy of children's out-of-school access to new technologies, falling short of the educational ideal of a social equalizer. This is especially true with the ever-increasing importance of such competencies in both social and professional realms of 21st century life (Braga, 2007).

Digital Literacy in the Home

It is important to note that relatively affluent parents are not necessarily fully aware of the implications and significance of digital literacies in their homes simply because they purchase the latest laptop or console game (Collins & Halverson, 2009). Many parents are frequently unaware of how their children use and participate in digital domains and are often and rightfully concerned about potential harms therefrom. In addition, while some parents are less facile than their children with digital technologies, other parents embrace such opportunities to learn how to harness their benefits for the betterment of their household, personal and professional interests, and children's education. As a result, the digital divide represents not only a financial chasm, but a dispositional one as well.

In her work with one family to understand the role of digital literacies in their household, Lewis (2011) found that within the family, digital literacies became "mediating tools to make sense of themselves" (p. 443), allowing them to oscillate between the roles of apprentice and expert across generations. At times, the mother was able to guide and support her children, yet at many other times, her sons introduced her to new Internet technologies and supported her learning. This is a common theme; it is often adults in the household that are least prepared to guide children as they engage with digital literacies (Gee, 2007; Hawisher & Selfe, 2004). This is especially the case with video games, which are typically viewed as "wastes of time" by parents, especially those who themselves have never played (Selfe, Mareck, & Gardiner, 2007).

Gerber (2009) conducted a multiple case study of four teenage boys and their literacy practices across school and home. From her time with the participants, Gerber found that the boys spent an average of 10 minutes a day reading in school, most of which was tightly monitored and primarily efferent (Rosenblatt, 1979). By comparison, the boys reported reading an average of 70 minutes a day in their homes, most of which centered around video games and was aesthetic in nature (Rosenblatt, 1979), and included high levels of collaboration with friends and other players. Gerber suggests that classroom teachers would do well to come to understand and build upon the sophisticated literacy practices their students often find in their gaming to reinvigorate a languishing English Language Arts (ELA) curriculum.

In Defense of Video Games

Central to Gerber's study is the understanding of video games as a legitimate mode of literacy. Indeed, researchers are flocking to the defense of video games as literacy. In her autoethnographic study of her own entrée into video games, Journet (2008) considered the role of narrative within her experiences of role-playing games (RPGs). She found that video games provide spaces for a variety of literacies, both print and multi-modal, largely in response to the powerful intersection of narrative and co-authorship found as players make decisions within the context of a structured story.

Johnson (2008) agreed that one of the most powerful aspects of many video games (especially RPGs) is in the reader's ability to impact the outcomes, relationships, narrative threads, and even out-of-game experiences. He discussed the interesting relationship between game designers and players who work together: Designers construct the narrative potentials in the games, which players then fulfill as they play the game. The narrative is transitory and idiosyncratic in response to both the player's ability and choices and is often unable to be reproduced.

Having been introduced to the world of video games by his son, Gee (2007) developed 36 learning principles based on his personal experiences with playing a wide range of "good video" games. To begin with, Gee (2008) clearly differentiates *good* video games from *poor* video games, arguing that, as with all texts, there are the high-brow choices and the beach-reading variety. While playing good games, however, Gee (2007) has outlined powerful types of learning that occur. "The Regime of Competence" principle states, for example, "The learner gets ample opportunity to operate within, but at the outer edge of, his or her resources, so that at those points things are felt as challenging but not 'Undoable'" (Gee, 2007, p. 68) . "The Active, Critical Learning" principle states, "All aspects of the learning environment…are set up to encourage active and critical, not passive, learning" (Gee, 2007, p. 41). Gee (2007) frames several critical arguments in justifying the power of video games to teach and delight young and adolescent players.

The earlier discussion highlights interesting and under-explored intersections of literacy, video games, and families. While there is a growing body of literature considering the possibilities, affordances, and limitations within gaming practices and in relation to literacy, few studies have been conducted to consider lived understandings, implications, and potentials of such a relationship. This study adds to the conversation by considering the perspectives and experiences regarding video games and literacy within one family.

THEORETICAL LENS

New Literacy Studies

The field of New Literacy Studies (NLS) concerns itself with the role of power (Schultz & Hull, 2002) and an excitement about the possibilities of new technologies and digital literacies in the classroom (Leu, 2010). Specifically, NLS "view literacy practices as inextricably linked to cultural and power structures in society, and recognize the variety of cultural practices associated with reading in different contexts" (Street, 1993, p. 7). From this perspective, literacy is less concerned with discreet skills and more interested in multiple forms and functions of reading and writing and the ways in which individuals situate and privilege them in a society. Such a lens emphasizes the cultural, social, and ideological significance of literacy, as opposed to focusing on primarily mechanical or professional skills (Bartlett, 2008; Street, 1993).

King and O'Brien (2007) provide a powerful example of the NLS position, by pointing out the unrealized potential of digital literacies in the classroom. Digital literacies represent a unique form of literacy that is quite different from traditional print-based reading tasks. While print is linear, digital texts are not; while print relies typically on visual stimulation, digital texts present multiple modes of stimuli, each often competing for attention (Kress, 2003; Prenski, 2001). The interactive nature of many digital texts, such as video games, allows readers to also become participants in text construction. NLS have concluded that digital literacies require different skills and strategies for use than do more traditional forms. Regardless, King and O'Brien (2007), as well as the National Council of Teachers of English (2007), lament the fact that little instruction informed by NLS occurs within the English/Language Arts classroom.

Social Cognition

Gee (2001, 2010) argues that true learning is social, embodied, and purpose-driven. Gee (2010) refers to this stance as *social cognition*, which argues that "thinking is tied to *peoples' experiences of goal-oriented action in the material and social world*" (p. 163, italics in the original). Learners build knowledge from lived experiences, making increasingly complex connections as they engage more fully in the world. These experiences and connections are stored not as abstract facts and pieces of knowledge, but as dynamic images tied to perceptions of the world and ourselves (Gee, 1992).

Social cognition theory suggests that learning is an active, social, and identity-forming process (Gee, 2007, 2010). It incorporates embodied engagement, affinity groups, and shifts in world views as one makes connections among experiences and knowledge throughout their life histories. Such a stance seems promising for students who attempt to resist passive, decontextualized learning disseminated in the form of lectures, text books, and multiple-choice exams. Social cognition theory is not the dominant view in traditional classrooms, and nowhere is it more obvious than in the ELA classroom.

METHODOLOGY

This case study investigates understandings, framings, and roles of video gaming within the bounded unit (Stake, 2000) of an African American family residing in a metropolis in the southeastern United States. The participants were a mother of six, Camilla, and her then 13-year-old son, Jaden. (Names are pseudonyms.) They were selected from among participants in a literacy clinic sponsored by a local university. Clinic participants attended free literacy support sessions, which were facilitated by graduate students from the university's College of Education and who provided tutoring as a part of a lab component for their course work. Participation in this study was entirely optional from members of the clinic. The participating family attended clinic activities for several years before generously deciding to be a part of this study.

Jaden was attending a local charter school designed to provide students with opportunities to engage in technology and the arts to a greater degree than typical, metro-area schools. He was generally mild-mannered and charming during each of our interviews and conversations, talking at length about his family, church, music, and video games. Jaden's father was a doctor, while his mother ran the household of eight. Camilla clearly enjoys the time she spends with her children and has high expectations for each of them.

As for myself, I am a White, middle-class woman. At the time of this study, I was 29 years old and a doctoral student. This study represents my first research project. Jaden and I met in my office, where I worked as a graduate teaching assistant at the university. I am currently a budding gamer myself, having taught enough students and known enough loved ones who were passionate and dedicated to games to convince me this is a domain worth learning more about as an educator and researcher.

DATA COLLECTION AND ANALYSIS

Both Camilla and Jaden engaged in several semi-structured interviews (Rubin & Rubin, 2005), meaning that I entered into each discussion with a list of questions in hand, yet flexibly adjusted or added questions in response to the participant's responses. Questions centered on Jaden and Camilla's literacy practices at home, their views of what is valuable about literacy, and the role and perceptions of video games in their home, especially pertaining to literacy goals. I interviewed Camilla twice and Jaden three times. All interviews occurred at the literacy clinic, with some occurring during instructional sessions and others on alternative days.

Additionally, Jaden used a camera to document the texts within his world that mattered to him. Upon returning to the clinic, he and I conducted a photo-elicitation interview (Harper, 2002) in which Jaden talked through the chosen texts, his processes for selecting them, and in what ways they matter to him. Such an approach shed light on the ways in which Jaden assigns value to text and the importance he assigns to them.

Data analysis was primarily inductive (LeCompte & Schensul, 1999). As I read through the data repeatedly, I highlighted quotes that seemed to comment on similar types of ideas and events, presented examples of common experiences, or generally seemed to be a part of a pattern. As I did so, I created a coding scheme that included using the comment feature in my word processor, which I was able to then compile and condense into specific themes. Several themes became apparent quite quickly, while others were the result of additional readings and efforts to condense, collapse, and reconfigure patterns and negotiate tensions across the data. I created a table in which I listed each of my guiding questions, pertinent quotes and observations, and lists of terms (and eventually codes) to help me unify ideas. By the time themes began to crystallize in my mind, there were approximately six over-arching categories. I condensed these into three primary findings, each of which appeared to me as striking ironies within Jaden and Camilla's family.

FINDINGS AND INTERPRETATIONS

The questions guiding this inquiry included: (a) In what ways does one family value video games in relation to purposes, goals, and futures related to literacy writ large?, (b) To what extent do these framings diverge across generations within this family?, and (c) What roles do video games play in the life of one avid gamer in this family? Throughout Jaden and Camilla's interviews, their words led me to understand that both mother and son viewed video games as a point of tension in their home, for Camilla because she perceived them as limiting her son's opportunities to develop valuable skills for his future and Jaden because his gaming was persistently limited by his mother. Despite the dispositions, skills, and interests Jaden developed through his gaming practices, both he and his mother valued static, printed texts, such as novels, textbooks, and magazines, over digital texts, such as websites, video games, and blogs. This was largely in responses to reoccurring dichotomy drawn by both between *play* and *learning*. Both expressed frustration as Camilla struggled to prepare Jaden for a successful career and future with little expertise in the very technologies that she acknowledged would support his efforts; video games were not one of those acknowledged technologies.

Video Games Are Treated As Subversive Texts, Despite Affordances

In Camilla's household, video games were limited to weekends only. During the week, her children focused on their studies, helped with family chores, and played together in the back yard or with friends. Weekends were packed with church, a Young Media Minds of America camp for Jaden, and family gatherings. For Jaden, however, his favorite times of the week arrived when he was able to steal away to play video games. He played games on his Xbox, Play Station, personal computer, and cell phone. During the week, when his mother encouraged him to spend time reading, much of his reading was centered on paratexts (Gutierrez & Beavis, 2010), or those texts that are written around video games. For Jaden, these include message boards, gaming magazines, and websites, each of which might devote themselves to specific games or gaming in general. I found it interesting, however, that, upon being asked about the types of reading he enjoys outside of school, he began listing novels (all of which are a part of the academic canon), and only hesitantly mentioned these paratexts at all, until he seemed to understand that these texts were of interest to me as well.

In discussing what he loves most about playing video games, Jaden explained, "It's like a story technically, like you're playing the story. That's what I love about video games." Through the games he played, he was able to "play the story" of a cybernetically enhanced super soldier caught in the midst of a war between humanity and a theocratic alliance of aliens in the game *Halo* (Bungie, 2001). He has saved the world from an evil genius, as he played *Sonic the Hedgehog* (Sega, 2006), and rebuilt the time/space continuum in *Time Shift* (Saber Interactive, 2007). Regardless of all the many "stories" Jaden participated in, nowhere in our body of data did he talk about video games as something connected with reading. Instead, he spoke about the paratexts and game manuals. Even when asked to take pictures of important texts in his world, Jaden brought in only one that depicted video games, which included an array of video game boxes (all others' photos were school or family-centered documents) and he proceeded to talk about the information printed on the covers and backs of the games.

Once he became more comfortable in our interviews, he began to reveal that, regardless of the rich literacy he enjoys relevant to his gaming life, he struggled to engage in literature in school. He explained,

> "And I can never just pay attention to the book that I have to read for school or something. Sometimes I pick up a book, and I might read half of it. Then put it down for, like, two weeks or something, then I'll start reading again. I just keep on dozing off and going back and forth."

Jaden's struggle to remain engaged in academic texts, as he understood it, was largely due to unfamiliar language, time periods, and genres. Alternately, when describing the ways in which engaged with gaming related paratexts, "it seems like I'm reading a little bit faster sometimes. Cause I want to get through and look at the game or something. So I might read faster sometimes, and then the books I usually read a little bit slower." One's strategies and pacing while reading are often dictated by his or her purposes for reading a text (Tovani, 2000). For Jaden, reading the self-selected paratexts serves immediate and pragmatic purposes, which likely are less present in his readings of Shakespearean dramas and Early American poetry.

The reading Jaden engaged in related to video games was akin to Worthy's (1998) construct of renegade readers, or those readers who might otherwise resist reading in academic settings. While his engagement was challenged and limited with school-related texts, when given printed texts relevant to his own purposes and interests, he was actually quite a lively and avid reader. It is also literacy that he and Camilla both view as subversive, in the sense that neither recognized any academic or future benefit to reading either the paratexts or the video games they enhance. Indeed, they viewed time spent reading them as time that could have been spent "really reading."

Despite the shared de-valuing of video games and paratexts, they clearly provided Jaden with opportunities to foster dispositions and social abilities that have been identified as critical for the 21st century society, work place, and democracy. Such dispositional affordances appeared throughout the data.

Heroic role playing. Jaden talked about the importance of being a positive leader in his school, community, and household. For example, he saw himself as responsible for supporting friends in any way that he could. "I have a friend name Craige, and I always help him out with work, cause I don't want him to mess up or anything. Because I'm a leader and I have to set an example for school. And, I always help him out." Interestingly, when he talked about playing games, he often talked about the heroic nature of the protagonist and the enjoyment he found in taking on the identity of someone fighting to protect the weak. Games seem to provide a safe place for Jaden to practice a heroic identity, something Gee (2007) discusses as the projective identity, which is present in the midst of powerful learning. The projective identity is located at the intersection of those identities which Jaden brings from his lived experiences and the ideals presented within a game (or even as a gamer); it is that which allows him to consider that he might become the type of person who makes the moral, just, and brave choices of the characters that he plays within games, even within his day-to-day life.

Flexibility in leading and following. There were many times when Jaden talked about leading others as an expert gamer, often by contributing to wikis, message boards, or YouTube tutorials. Just as frequently, however, Jaden followed the lead of more capable players, some of whom were personal friends and others who lived on the other side of the globe. Oscillating between a knowledgeable mentor and an accommodating mentee seemed incredibly comfortable for Jaden. Friedman (2005) cites such adaptability as a critical skill for success in a 21st century work place, democracy, and society, especially in light of the pace of technological development and specialization of knowledge within fields of expertise. We live in a time in which we can safely assume we are in regular contact with others who are more or less knowledgeable than ourselves about a given digital domain (Partnership for 21st Century Skills, 2011), and Jaden comfortably navigates the fluctuation in leadership through his gaming experiences.

Effortful persistence. Jaden described the extent of his research and playing of games in terms of dozens of hours. Once he had a specific task, be it to finish a game, replay it with a perfect score, compete with higher-level opponents, or simply master a specific move, he was willing to dedicate an indefinite number of hours to accomplishing that task. For example, when talking about one of his favorite video games, he shared that "I've beaten it already, like twice now. And I like play against people, against good people." Clearly, the accomplishment of just playing the game through was not enough for Jaden; he wanted the additional challenge of trying again against others who he judged as competent and worthy of the time and effort. Interestingly, he expected academic tasks to be completed with a specific timeframe, and expressed annoyance when he found such tasks to take longer than planned. There was a marked difference in the level of persistence Jaden described between his academic and gaming literacy practices. The level of enjoyment and purposefulness between the two seemed to impact Jaden's ability to persist (Csikzentmihalyi, 1990). While school-related engagements often seemed boring and laborious, he often lost track of time due to a deep level of emersion within researching and playing games.

Self-knowledge. In describing the type of student and reader Jaden perceived himself to be, he was able to characterize himself quite specifically as someone who benefits from learning by exploring and testing ideas. He saw himself as a hands-on learner, who loved a challenge and became hooked on an idea when it piqued his interest. In each instance that he talked about himself as a learner, his comments were either in the context of what he disliked about school or of what worked about a specific video game he enjoyed. High-quality video games often present learning and reading opportunities in "such a way that learners learn not only about the domain but also about themselves and their current and potential capacities" (Gee, 2007, p. 64). Jaden described just that. Through his gaming, Jaden has learned valuable lessons about himself as a player, a learner, a reader, and a writer, as well as about the type of person he hoped to become.

Clearly, Camilla values education, literacy, and future career possibilities for her son. She does not see video games as a means for fostering these possibilities, and neither does Jaden. It is critical to note that all of the above lessons, while expressed across interviews, particularly in our most animated conversations together, are based on my own interpretation of the data, rather than on Jaden's understandings and articulations of what video games are doing for him. This only more clearly punctuates his devaluing of gaming, a sentiment echoed by his mother, who clearly has his best interest at heart.

Static Print is Privileged over Digital Text Despite Interests

Based on our conversations and the photos elicited throughout the data, Jaden and Camilla define text as print. Upon asking Jaden whether he saw video games as having anything to do with reading, he paused for a moment. "Yes, on the inside of games, there's a little manual that tell you how to play the game. I usually just read through that." In discussing the photo he took of several of his current favorite games, he told me about the synopsis on the back of the box, rather than the games themselves. The ways in which he chose to talk about games and text indicate that Jaden did not view the print within games (i.e., dialogue, maps, inventories, etc.) nor the games themselves as holding legitimacy, but rather only print on paper counts as text, and therefore the potential for reading and writing. Despite the central role games play in Jaden's reading life, upon considering the possibility of video games containing opportunities to read, it seemed utterly absent to him. As texts, they were illegitimate and did not count.

Camilla shares this view, stating that she wished that he read more. When asked what she wished he read more of, she replied that she would love to see him reading more of "the classics" and Greek mythology. Later in that particular interview, she confided that in her own childhood, "I know I didn't like Shakespeare or Greek mythology. I just didn't really enjoy that, because it was just like you're reading it and then answering questions." She immediately seemed to notice that she was expecting her son to enjoy the very books that she found so lifeless in her experiences.

In a subsequent interview, Camilla talked quite proudly of the fact that Jaden had recently come to enjoy reading Greek mythology that had been a part of a unit of study in his English class. She continued by saying:

> "Oh, he loves it, so it would be great if on his <u>own</u>, which is on weekends, just pick up a book on Greek mythology or say, 'Hey, can you take me to the book store to buy me a book?' You know, but he doesn't do those things, but if, when he's in school, he has to do it, he really immerses himself in it, and just enjoys it....But on the weekends, on his down time, for him, it's like 'I just wanna play my Xbox 360.'" [laughing]

Camilla did not know that Jaden was, at that time, playing the video game *God of War* (SCE Santa Monica Studio, 2005), in which he played as the character Krato. Within the game, Krato plays a role in historical wars between Greece and the Persian Empire, becomes a part of a war among the gods and goddesses of Olympus, and explores the Underworld. Along the way, he saves Helios, frees the steeds that drive the sun from Atlas, and must appease Persephone. While neither mother nor son realized it, Jaden was reading Greek mythology in his spare time. In fact, I posit that by taking on the fictional role of a pawn in a war among the Olympians, he was positioned to better understand concepts of Greek humanism, the relationships between gods and mortals, and ancient explanations of the universe in ways that reading Homer may not have done for him with the same immediacy. Denying video games as a form of legitimate reading limited Camilla and Jaden's ability to capitalize on connections between in-school and out-of-school literacies.

Camilla Leads Jaden Into Lesser-known Territory For Her

Camilla is a dedicated mother. She understood that literacy and technology will play an important role in Jaden's future opportunities for success. She has enrolled him in the literacy clinic, which was the context of this study, as well as enrolling him in a multimedia communications program for teenagers, where Jaden participated in a video production class. She has spoken out in Jaden's school for the use of more technology in course instruction. When she explicated what such instruction might look like, she indicated that more use of PowerPoint, Word, and Internet-based research projects would make a big difference for Jaden and his peers.

It became apparent to me, however, that Camilla was in quite uncharted territory when she spoke about the use of technology, both in and out of her home. She joked about her children helping her program her cell phone and shared that her primary use of her home computer centered on sending e-mails and checking a few favorite websites. Meanwhile, down the hall, Jaden played sophisticated video games, and participated in MySpace, Facebook, e-mail, blogs, YouTube, message boards, Pandora, and chat rooms. While Camilla certainly had a measure of digital savvy, Jaden and his siblings were generally more of the expert in the family regarding technology and the uses and possibilities thereof. Indeed, Camilla is proud of the fact that her children are capable of tasks that she herself struggles with. For example, she described one of her daughter's ability with a new cell phone, saying, "The things she can do on her cell phone, the things she's figured out <u>how</u> to do [laughing], I'm just amazed and please. I mean I talk and I text, but I mean a lot of times they'll take it to the next level." Her children, in many ways, blaze the digital trail within the household.

Here we have a case of the novice mother leading the expert son. Mead (1970) describes such a phenomenon as characteristic of the *pre-figurative* world in which "the past, the culture that had shaped [young adults'] understanding—their thoughts, their feelings, and their conceptions of the world—was no sure guide to the present. And the elders among them, bound to the past, provide no models for the future" (p. 70). Camilla's understandings of literacy and technology are fit to prepare Jaden for the world in which those understandings came from: one that existed before the Internet, before notions of text became questioned, and before the break-neck speed of technological developments began.

CONCLUSION

Within Jaden and Camilla's family, video games are a source of tension. They are positioned counter to the purposes and goals that Camilla views as critical to Jaden's future ability to succeed in school and in later professional pursuits. Because of this, Jaden's parents limit the times at which he can play by allotting time only on weekends and in specific timeframes.

Entering into this study, I was interested in looking at the differences across this mother and her son regarding their attitudes towards games. While Jaden clearly enjoys playing video games and spends a great deal of time researching them and participating in gaming communities, there was surprisingly little difference between the values he places on his gaming experiences and his mother's views thereof. Both believed video games to be devoid of legitimate literacy and neither acknowledged any tangible or educative value to playing them, regardless of the sophisticated and critical modes of reading, learning, and understanding of self that Jaden has gained from being a gamer.

I feel compelled to point out that I believe Camilla to be an extraordinary mother. Throughout our time together, I was impressed with the dedication and joy she expressed when she spoke about her children. It is not my intent to criticize Camilla's understandings of literacy and its relationship to video games; rather, I feel that she is doing all that any mother can do to advocate for her children's success in the future. She is active in Jaden's education, supports a variety of out-of-school endeavors, and hopes to foster a love of reading, learning, and family.

I fear, however, that this not an uncommon case. In working with students in my own classroom, I have seen the struggle back and forth between parents who believe that video games are a frivolous waste of time and adolescents who have a hunch that play games matter somehow. Like Camilla, many of my students' parents were tethered to 20th century notions of what counts as literacy and learning. They, like Camilla, trusted that within their children's classrooms, the hard work of preparing teenagers to face and succeed in a world that does not yet exist will take place. The fact of the matter is that many schools have not made the strides one would expect at this point in the digital age (Bigum, Knobel, Lankshear, & Rowan, 2003; Lankshear & Knobel, 2010; Vasquez, Harste, & Albers, 2010).

Our schools are social institutions, created to support the children of our nation's families for a host of varied purposes. They answer most immediately to those who pick up the tab and elect board members: parents. From this perspective, parents' understandings of what their children need in order to be considered literate becomes critically important to how schools intend to meet the needs of their constituents as they interpret state-mandated curricula. This becomes all the more complex when we consider the fact that parents rarely read the very research that challenges notions of what counts as literacy in the 21st century. Indeed, education seems to be a field in which, because everyone has been taught in schools, everyone assumes they understand what makes them tick! As a result, parents are likely to expect school (more specifically reading and writing) to look much like it did in their own past experiences. Since those experiences, however, the world has seen the rise of the Internet, a technology arguably deemed second only to that of the printing press (Gates, 2000) in importance.

It is not enough that the research community is reaching out to curriculum designers, policy makers, teachers, and administrators. Parents, our students' first teachers, must also become a part of the conversation. In Camilla's case, she went so far as to bring her son to a university campus for weekly literacy support, yet she spent most of her time waiting for Jaden checking e-mail or chatting with other mothers and fathers about how to get their kids to play fewer video games and read more books. Colleges of education must think creatively how to bridge the chasm between what we are learning about the nature of literacy, text, and video games and the parents whose children fill the public classrooms around us. They must subvert the current myths surrounding the worth and legitimacy of those gamers who love to "play" a good story.

REFERENCES

Bartlett, L. (2008). Literacy's verb: Exploring what literacy is and what literacy does. *International Journal of Educational Development*, 737-753.

Bigum, C., Knobel, M., Lankshear, C., & Rowan, L. (2003). Literacy, technology and the economics of attention. *L1- Educational Studies in Language and Literature, 3*, 95-122.

Blizzard Entertainment (2004). *World of Warcraft* [PC game]. Irvine, CA: Blizzard Entertainment.

Braga, D. B. (2007). Developing critical social awareness through digital literacy practices within the context of higher education in Brazil. *Language and Education*, 180-196.

Bungie (2001). *Halo* [XBox 360 game]. Bellevue, WA: Microsoft.

Collins, A. & Halverson, R. (2009). *Rethinking education in the age of technology.* New York, NY: Teachers College Press.

Csikzentmihalyi, M. (1990). Literacy and intrinsic motivation. *Daedalus, 119*, 115-140.

Dewey, J. (1915). *The school and society.* Chicago, IL: University of Chicago Press.

Dezuanni, M. (2010). Digital media literacy: Connecting young peoples' identities, creative production, and learning about video games. In D. E. Alvermann (Ed.), *Adolescents' online literacies: Connecting classrooms, digital media, and popular culture* (125-143). New York, NY: Peter Lang.

Friedman, T. L. (2005). *The world is flat: A brief history of the twenty-first century.* New York, NY: Farrar, Straus, and Giroux.

Gates, B. (2000). Shaping the Internet Age. Retrieved from http://www.microsoft.com/presspass/exec/billg/writing/shapingtheinternet.mspx

Gee, J. P. (1992). *The social mind: Language, ideology, and social practice.* New York, NY: Bergin and Garvey.

Gee, J. P. (2001). Reading as situated language: A sociocognitive perspective. *Journal of Adolescent and Adult Literacy, 44*, 714-725.

Gee, J. P. (2007). *What video games have to teach us about learning and language.* (2nd ed.). New York, NY: Palgrave.

Gee, J. P. (2008). *Good video games + good learning: Collected essays on video games, learning, and literacy.* New York, NY: Peter Lang.

Gee, J. P. (2010). A situated-sociocultural approach to literacy and technology. In E. A. Baker (Ed.), *The new literacies: Multiple perspectives on research and practice* (165-193). New York, NY: Guildford Press.

Gerber, H. R. (2009, October). *Integrating literacy through video games.* Presented at the International Council of Educational Media: Conseil International des Medias Educatifs. Dubai.

Gutierrez, A. & Beavis, C. (2010). "Experts on the field": Redefining literacy boundaries. In D. E. Alvermann (Ed.), *Adolescents' online literacies: Connecting classrooms, digital media, and popular culture* (145-161). New York, NY: Peter Lang.

Harper, D. (2002). Talking about pictures: A case for photo elicitation. *Visual Studies, 17* (1), 13-26.

Hawisher, G. E. & Selfe, C. L. (2004). Becoming literate in the information age: Cultural ecologies and literacies of technology. *College Composition and Communication, 55*, 642-692.

Johnson, M. S. (2008). Public writing in gaming spaces. *Computer and Composition, 25*, 270-283.

Journet, D. (2008). Narrative, action, and learning: The stories of *Myst*. In C. L. Selfe & G .E. Hawisher (Eds.), *Gaming lives in the twenty-first century: Literate connections* (94-120). New York, NY: Palgrave.

King, J. R., & O'Brien, D. G. (2007). Adolescent's multiliteracies and their teachers' needs to know: Toward a digital detente. In D. E. Alvermann (Ed.), *Adolescents and literacies in a digital world* (4th Edition ed., Vol. VII, pp. 40-50). New York, NY: Peter Lang Publishing.

Kress, G. (2003). *Literacy in the new media age.* London, England: Routledge.

Lankshear, C. & Knobel, M. (2006). *New literacies* (2nd ed.). Maidenhead, UK: Open University Press.

Lankshear C. & Knobel, M. (2010). DIY media: A contextual background and some contemporary themes. In M. Knobel & C. Lankshear (Eds.), *DIY media: Creating, sharing, and learning with new technologies* (pp. 1-26). New York, NY: Peter Lang Publishing.

LeCompte, M. D. & Schensul, J. J. (1999). *Analyzing and interpreting ethnographic data.* New York, NY: Alta Mira Press.

Leu, D. J. (2010). Forward. In E. A. Baker (Ed.), *The new literacies: Multiple perspectives on research and practice* (pp. viii-xi). New York, NY: Guilford Press.

Lewis, T. Y. (2011) Family digital literacies: A case of awareness, agency, and apprenticeship of one African American family. In P. J. Dunston & L. B. Gambrell (Eds.), *60th Yearbook of the Literacy Research Association*. Oak Creek, WI: Literacy Research Association, Inc.

Mead, M. (1970). *Culture and commitment: A study of the generation gap.* Garden City, NY: Natural History Press/Doubleday.

National Council of Teachers of English. (2007). *21st century literacies: A policy research brief.* Urbana: IL.

Partnership for 21st Century Skills. (2011). P21 common core toolkit: A guide to aligning the common core state standards with the framework for 21st century skills. Retrieved from http://p21.org/images/p21_toolkit_final.pdf

Prenski, M. (2001). Digital natives, digital immigrants. *On the Horizon, 9*(5).

Rosenblatt, L. (1979). *The reader, the text, the poem: The transactional theory of the literary work.* Carbondale. IL: Southern Illinois Press.

Rubin, H. J. & Rubin, I. S. (2005). *Qualitative interviewing: The art of hearing data.* Thousand Oaks, NJ, SAGE Press.

Saber Interactive (2007). *TimeShift* [XBox 360 game]. Millburn, NJ: Sierra Entertainment.

SCE Santa Monica Studio (2005). *God of War* [Play Station game]. Santa Monica, CA: Sony Computer.

Schultz, K., & Hull, G. (2002). Locating literacy theory in out-of-school contexts. In G. Hull, & K. Schultz (Eds.), *School's Out!: Bridging out-of-school literacies with classroom practice* (pp. 11-31). New York, NY: Teachers College Press.

Sega (1991). *Sonic the Hedgehog* [Play Station game]. Tokyo, Japan: Sega.

Selfe, C. L., Mareck, A. F., & Gardiner, J. (2007). Computer gaming as literacy. In C. L. Selfe & G. E. Hawisher (Eds.), *Gaming lives in the twenty-first century: Literate connections* (22-35). New York, NY: Palgrave.

Stake, R. E. (2000). Case studies. In N. K. Denzin & Y. S. Lincoln (Eds.) *Handbook of qualitative research* (435-454). Thousand Oaks, CA: Sage Publishing.

Street, B. (Ed.). (1993). *Cross-cultural approaches to literacy.* New York, NY: Cambridge University Press.

Tovani, C. (2000). *I read it, but I don't get it: Comprehension strategies for Adolescent Readers.* Portland, ME: Stenhouse Publishers.

Vasquez, V., Harste, J., & Albers, P. (2010). From the personal to the world wide web: Moving teachers into positions of critical interrogation. In E. A. Baker (Ed.), *The new literacies: Multiple perspectives on research and practice* (pp. 265-284). New York, NY: Guilford Press.

Warschauer, M., Knobel, M. & Stone, L. (2004). Technology and equity in schooling: Deconstructing the digital divide. *Educational Policy, 18,* 562-588.

West, K. (2008). Weblogs and literary responses: Socially situated identities and hybrid social languages in English class blogs. *Journal of Adolescent and Adult Literacy, 51,* 588-598.

Williams, D. (2007). Afterward: The return of the player. In C. L. Selfe & G. E. Hawisher (Eds.), *Gaming lives in the twenty-first century: Literate connections* (253-259). New York, NY: Palgrave.

Worthy, J. (1998). 'On every page someone gets killed!': Book conversations you don't hear in school. *Journal of Adolescent and Adult Literacy, 41,* 508-518.

Shirley Brice Heath
Professor Emerita
Stanford University

Section IV: Discourse, Identity, and Social Practice

We are surrounded by the trio of operations that provide the headline of this section. Humans have an internal drive to engage with one another through multiple symbol systems that include language, gesture, images, and other representational forms. We take pride in our roles as conversationalists, readers and writers, and performers and spectators who convey our identity in every move we make, word we speak, and facial response as we listen. Our habituated patterns of everyday social practices bring us into the company of one another. There we learn to listen, question, and contribute in exchanges of information, emotion, and opinion.

Only occasionally do we stop to think about how we first learn and keep on learning through the structured symbol systems into which we are socialized. As infants and young children, we watch, imitate and create, vocalize, gesture, and engage with others, somehow sensing all the while that our emotions hold us together. Later, we add to our first intimate communicators others who provide new ways of talking and acting, and we explore new objects, situations, locations, and ideas. Throughout our lives, we work and play in situations that socialize us into ways to use words and to embellish these endlessly, in both oral and written forms. Increasingly, we choose to supplement our words with images and, whenever possible, with performance that is highly social in nature. Like the children we meet in the paper by Maloch and Zapata, we want others to have a "wow" response to what we say, show, and know.

Instructional settings and materials give us steps on the ladder by which we move upward in our later language development—covering informational topics and interpersonal relationships. If we can hold in our heads catch phrases or memorable terms, we then have short-cuts of access. Teachers such as those described by Maloch and Zapata give the young these strategies when they suggest that research benefits when we immerse ourselves in a "flood" of books, and within this flood, we begin by "steeping" ourselves in as much information as possible before "guided exploration" and concentrated "searching."

Studies on the nature of learning have for more than two decades tended to focus on discourse, identity, and social practice as these play out in formal education sites. Three chapters of this section (Maloch and Zapata; Wickstrom, Patterson, and Isgitt; and Noguerón-Liu) locate their research within classrooms, while two (Smith and Valenzuela, and Hoffman) move away from formal sites of learning into communities and "border colonias."

Future research will continue to slant in this latter direction—toward the nature of structured symbol systems within those circumstances in which individuals and groups learn on their own without direct instruction. When children learn double-dutch jump rope skills and book-reading for pleasure, they observe, try out their skills, and then immerse themselves in the challenge. Engineers told to undertake management of new technologies take up the same kinds of practices: observation, immersion, experimentation, and consultation. Becoming an expert at new tasks that no one is around to teach may be one of the primary aspects of living in the modern world. Yet we know very little about how such learning works, who is most successful in this kind of learning, and whether or not outside influence can noticeably improve learning outcomes for individuals or groups.

Common sense, while often lamented as "not common enough," tells us that rapid technological change dictates that those who live in modern economies will need to learn more and more on their own and outside formal instructional settings. Individuals and groups working in collaboration toward common ends characterize communities, families, and workplaces. When these learners go after goals they set for their own learning, they look into the future and see themselves playing particular roles. They take positions or stances toward the roles they look forward to playing. By doing so, they selectively choose not only what they will learn, but how they will recall and put into action new skills and information. Memory outweighs memos. When technologies change too rapidly to be covered in formal instruction, informal learning provides the only way to keep pace with these changes.

Where and how does literacy fit into learning that sweeps in knowledge gained through formal education but goes much deeper in those instances of special interest and further afield to embrace topics that can never be covered in classroom instruction? In modern economies, written materials will increasingly be highly selective. These printed texts will consist primarily of official records, substantive information related to special purposes, and informational and entertainment artifacts of print (e.g., magazines, newspapers, books, advertisements, and programs from concert and dramatic performances). Within all of these, however, print will appear alongside illustrative representations (e.g., photographs, pictures, graphs, charts, timelines, sketches, and schematic drawings).

On the Internet, a similar pattern prevails, though the extent of print shrinks in appearances within digital media, particularly in cases of interactivity, such as games and maps. Though in the 21st century we may read bits of information with greater frequency than was the case in earlier decades, we consult text-only materials of substantial length and verifiable origin far less frequently. Tweets, blogs, and website informational bits bear a brevity that takes into account the fact that as readers and writers, we often produce and consult information while we are on the move. We are in a hurry to get somewhere or to do something. Of critical importance in the readIT, writeIT, performIT that the digital media make possible is the consistent readiness we have both to produce and to consume information. Wikipedia tapped into this readiness, and the explosion of websites (a majority of which consist of only a page or two, while others appear as a catalogue on screen) attest to the overwhelming desire of individuals to put information, opinions, and features "out there."

It is only fair to ask what may be lost in the inevitable turn of modern economies to transmission and production of information via the Internet and other electronically mediated means. Any response to this question starts with the phrase "It all depends." For those oriented to the kinds of reading and writing generally associated with academics, the first loss that comes to mind is a trio: conceptual depth, history, and analytic memory, all of which insist on length and range of written textual materials. Moreover, to gain this trio, a reader must have a mindset that pushes one to compare, challenge, contrast, and question. Fluency and comfort with this trio comes only through intensive and repetitive practice in reading, processing, and questioning a wide range of extended texts. Specific types of writing, such as notes, responses, and sketches, reinforce memory, as does visualization of concepts, scenes, and ideas.

The truth is that learners growing up in most modern economies tend to avoid having to delve deeply into philosophical questions, historical accounts, and complex conceptual understandings. Tackling this kind of knowledge requires deep experience with extended stretches of texts that mingle fact, argument, counter-argument, and chains of reasoning. These texts reflect the range of genres that philosophers, literary figures, historians, and political and religious leaders write. Some of these texts are sacred, while others carry strong association with particular periods of political, military, or narrative history. Many mingle science and art, doubt and belief, dogma and denial, and the objective as well as subjective.

Digital media and the cultural norms that have come with it push individuals living in modern economies to view learning as a route to fulfilling expectations of financial gain for the purposes of consumption, material accumulation, and conspicuous display. Such goals stimulate a sense that doing matters more than thinking, production trumps pensiveness, and status comes from ownership.

The chapters of this section show us where a range of learners now living and learning under a variety of circumstances engage with social practices that involve discourse and reflect different senses of identity, whether as author (Noguerón-Liu) or as community member aspiring to middle-class status (Smith and Valenzuela). Several remind us that "culturally relevant" is likely to shift increasingly toward "interest relevant." All chapters challenge us to look beyond the habits and sites they have described to consider what contexts of literacy uses and productions will be in the decades ahead and how cognitive and linguistic habits will need to shift and evolve in ways we have only begun to imagine.

The Social and Textual Practices of Third Graders with Informational Texts

Beth Maloch
Angie Zapata
The University of Texas at Austin

Given the documented scarcity of informational texts in primary classrooms (Duke, 2000; Jeong, Gaffney, & Choi, 2010), along with the research that shows the value and benefits of increasing access to and knowledge about informational texts (Pappas, 1991; Purcell-Gates, Duke, & Martineau, 2007), it is clear that integrating informational texts into primary classrooms is an important area for research and practice. Although research is growing concerning how young children acquire understandings of informational texts, particularly through interventions (e.g., Purcell-Gates et al., 2007; Williams, Hall, Lauer, Stafford, DeCisto, & deCani, 2005), investigations examining the real-life work of young children with informational texts is still limited. This article seeks to address this need through the examination of the social and textual practices of third graders from three different classrooms as they engaged with informational texts in the context of classroom inquiry units.

Our broader analysis of this 8-week unit (contextualized within year-long observation/analysis) generated two themes—the social nature of informational text use and varying approaches to informational texts taken up by students (Maloch & Zapata, 2011). Clear in our earlier analysis were the ways in which students' practices, and teachers' interventions/supports, varied both within and across classrooms; we examine those differences in this article. To do so, we use case study and discourse analytic methods to closely examine nine focal students in order to generate a more nuanced accounting of the diversity of children's approaches to and interactions with informational texts. This study addresses the following research questions: How do third graders from three different classrooms, participating in similar classroom inquiry units, engage with informational texts? In what ways are students' practices with informational texts situated within and shaped by their instructional settings?

LITERATURE REVIEW

This study is situated within the growing literature around young children and informational texts. Duke's (2000) study reported a startling scarcity of informational texts in first grade classrooms. She defined informational texts, as we do, as those texts written with "the primary purpose of conveying information about the natural and social world . . . and having particular text features to accomplish this purpose" (Duke, 2003, p. 14). In fact, there are good reasons for coming to better understandings about how young children make use of informational texts. Informational texts can be motivating to young children, offering a way to invite children into literacy and "spur" overall literacy development (Caswell & Duke, 1998). Informational texts are also like those texts children are more likely to see outside of classroom walls (Smith, 2000). One reason informational texts is more scarce in primary classrooms could be that, for years, researchers and educators saw narrative as "primary" for young children—that is, a belief existed that young children were more capable of learning this type of text structure, and thus educators filled their classrooms with literature of this kind. Pappas (1991), along with other researchers (Purcell-Gates et al., 2007; Williams et al., 2005; Wollman-Bonilla, 2000), conducted research that challenged this notion, showing in her work that young children were just as capable of acquiring and understanding the text structures prominent in informational texts. Finally, it seems important that young children have the opportunity to learn about informational texts given the growing emphasis on these kinds of texts in testing and later schooling contexts, and the ways that texts such as these have important implications for children in school.

Although there is some indication that primary classrooms are integrating more informational texts (e.g., in basal readers, Moss, 2008), research as recent as 2010 found that their inclusion is still limited (Jeong et al., 2010). Despite this limited increase in informational text use, research about these texts has grown. For example, Williams et al. (2005) showed that young children's comprehension could be improved through attention to and instruction around informational text structures. Moreover, some researchers have begun to document teachers' and students' work with informational texts in primary classrooms (Maloch, 2008; Palmer & Stewart, 2003; Purcell-Gates et al., 2007; Smolkin & Donovan, 2000). These studies, overall, suggest the importance of providing students multiple opportunities for engagement with informational text within literature-rich and instructionally supportive environments. In fact, Purcell-Gates et al. (2007) found that students' authentic opportunities to engage with informational texts were even more important to students' growth than explicit teaching of text features. These findings suggest the importance of a better understanding of how young children engage with informational texts during these authentic encounters. However, few researchers have examined the ways in which young children engage with informational texts in the context of a classroom. The study reported here provides detailed portraits of young children and their work with informational texts from three different third grade classrooms. Case study portraits like this are needed because of the insights they afford of the ways young children interact, learn from, and navigate informational texts within real classrooms. In turn, these insights may be used to better understand how children learn from texts, what potential challenges they may encounter, and in what ways instruction might be aimed.

Theoretically, sociocultural and social practice perspectives on learning guided our analysis of these classrooms (Gee, 1990; Street, 2003; Vygotsky, 1978; Wertsch, 1991). Consequently, we viewed students' engagement with texts as social and textual practices, and we understood these practices as deeply rooted in classroom constructions of knowledge, task, and identity—embedded in and influenced by the classroom and school contexts in which they were a part. Further, our thinking about these classrooms was influenced by Haneda and Wells' (2000) theories about collaboration, inquiry, and learning in knowledge-building communities. They argue that learning is "an inherent aspect of engaging with others in purposeful actions that have significance beyond themselves for all the participants" and typically occurs "not on a single occasion but incrementally over time" (p. 440). As such, we were interested in understanding young children's interactions with informational texts and each other over time. Our analytic attention was drawn to not just the individual student but to the activity itself, which included the students (often more than one), the various written texts, and the dialogue that mediated the activities. Specifically, we were interested in the kinds of social and textual practices performed by young children as they engaged in activity of reading and learning from informational texts.

METHOD

This interpretive study, drawn from a year-long study, examines data collected over a period of eight weeks during three third-grade classroom inquiry units on the solar system. Our focus on this unit emerged from ongoing analysis of the larger data set suggesting the importance of classroom inquiry units as contexts for informational text reading in these classrooms. Participants included three teachers and nine focal students representing a range of academic performance within and across the classrooms. The teachers—Karen, Jane, and Jessica—had three to four years of experience, and all taught on the same third grade team at one elementary school. We selected these teachers because our previous interactions with them suggested their enthusiastic integration of informational texts. Their principal and our faculty colleagues (who had placed interns in their classrooms) also recommended them to us as exemplary. The participating classrooms (ranging in size from 18-22) included students who were ethnically and socioeconomically diverse. The ethnicity of the focal students—one African American, five Latinos, and three White—was reflective of the diversity of their classrooms and of the school. Of these nine focal students, four are highlighted in the findings of this paper: Manuel, Sonny, Ethel, and Ingrid.

In all three classrooms, teachers spent the first 2 weeks of the classroom inquiry study conducting teacher read-alouds and discussions, as they worked to establish shared knowledge about the solar system and demonstrate note-taking and research techniques. Next, students were invited to become experts on planets in order to publish travel brochures for their assigned planets. These brochures were published and shared during an end-of-unit celebration for families, school administrators, other school community members, and their fellow third graders. The students researched their planets drawing from different data sources and kept their findings in a note-taking guide provided by the teachers. The guide was structured by questions such as, "What are the physical characteristics of your planet?" and "Explain the myths and legends associated with your planet."

Data Collection

Data collection included observations in each of the classrooms two to four days a week on average, documenting (through video/audio records and photos) students' work with informational trade books, Internet articles, and web-based video (i.e., United Streaming) centered on their focus planet. Data sources used for this analysis included: (a) videotaped interactions with and around informational texts, (b) observational field notes, (c) students' note-taking packets, (d) the texts/ sources used by students, (e) the students' travel brochures, and (f) teachers' interviews. In these classrooms, we acted primarily as observers and in most cases did not participate in the classroom practices.

Data Analysis

Data analysis for the larger study was inductive (Strauss & Corbin, 1990), occurred across multiple phases, and culminated in the generation of the themes presented earlier. Coding all of the observational data in this way afforded us a more comprehensive view of these classrooms but limited our view of how individual children were situated within these overarching themes. Therefore, to conduct analysis of our focal students, we first transcribed all instances from our data for each student in which they were engaged in research. For each classroom, the focal students were working in close proximity to one another so they interacted with one another as they worked with informational texts. We compiled data relevant to each child according to the framework presented in Table 1. The categories included in this table came from our earlier analyses of the data—these were components identified as potentially important in understanding how the children interacted

Table 1. Excerpt of Focal Student Analysis (Manuel)

Book	Approach	Social	Teacher support	Note-taking guide & Brochure
Our Solar System: *Venus* (Rau, 2002)	Searching: His approach seems influenced by the teacher's initial instructions, "Read like a detective" and reinforced by the ST's questions about the note-taking guide.	Social Support Sharing books; Manuel gets this book from a peer, and shares facts with table-mates.	Student teacher's comments suggest a searching stance (e.g., Are you getting some good stuff?; Make sure you look through the book to find all of this information).	Samuel positions his pencil in the far right column as if he's about to write down this fact about the phases, but then Mary walks over and hands him another book. He immediately opens it. Examination of his note-taking guide suggests that he did not record the fact he had just read about.
Eleven Planets (Aguilar, 2008).	Searching ("I just need to find. . .")	Social Support Mary brings Manuel the book; Social Response Spontaneously shares interesting fact from book with Bella.	Manuel shares information with the teacher; teacher validates information and encourages him to record in his note-taking guide.	Has recorded under first column, "Venus is made of deadly gas called carbon dioxide 40 miles thick." Then, he adds in information from *Eleven Planets*, and moves to the next column, reading, "What are the physical features of your planet?" from the note-taking guide.
Our Solar System: Venus (Rau, 2002)	Steeping and Guided Exploration (moving in and out of these two approaches)	Social Response Manuel shares multiple facts and photos with his table-mates; Not all of this attempts are taken up by his peers.	Manuel shares two facts with the teacher (i.e., volcanos on Venus; Rotation time for Venus). She validates his finding, and helps him see where to place the information in the note-taking guide.	He has facts written for each question on the Source #1 page (book), prior to re-visiting this book (this is his second time to visit this book). During his time with the book this time, he records one more fact—under column 2 (physical features), Samuel records "Volcanoes are found on the surface of Venus". In his final brochure appears the sentence –"Did you know that Venus has volcanoes on its surface?"

with the texts. Table 1 includes an abbreviated excerpt of the data we compiled in our analytic tables as a means of illustrating our analysis.

This compilation of the data allowed us to analyze the focal students' interactions with texts by examining them *across* data sources. That is, we analyzed the students' interactions with text in relation to: (a) the actual text they consulted, (b) the videotape footage of their interaction, (c) the notes they recorded for that interaction, and (d) the ways the recorded information showed up in the final product. By examining focal students in this way, we were able to examine more systematically the diversity of approaches and practices evident among the third grade classrooms. Finally, we selected one rich episode from each classroom that included the focal students and submitted these episodes to a finer-grained analysis to further explore themes, particularly along the social dimension. From these analyses, we examined how students' approaches and practices were situated within each of these classrooms, and shaped (in part) by the instructional practices therein.

FINDINGS

Across the nine focal students—or three sets of students—analysis generated several themes relevant to students' interactions around and with informational texts. First, our focal analysis highlighted the nature and complexity of the students' social interactions around the informational texts. In fact, our attempts to study *individual* focal students were unsuccessful as none of the students worked in isolation. Instead they interacted enthusiastically and in varied ways with nearby peers. Second, we examined the ways in which these individual children moved in and out of various approaches towards text. A full description of these approaches is included in Maloch and Zapata (2011), although we include a brief definition here as context for the findings in this paper. A *steeping* approach to text featured students' free exploration of text. In the *guided exploration* approach, students' reading of texts was guided by teacher-assigned questions. In the third approach, *searching*, students intentionally searched for particular information. Our analysis exposed how students' textual and social practices with informational texts were situated within and shaped by their instructional contexts. In this way, we came to see students' work with informational texts as situated social practices, shaped by the contexts in which they occurred and the materials present in the activity.

We organize our findings around three representative and illustrative sets of transcript examples. These transcripts spotlight Manuel in Karen's classroom, Sonny in Jane's classroom, and Ethel and Ingrid in Jessica's classroom. After detailing contextual information about the classroom and focal students, we present and analyze each set of transcripts with attention to our overarching themes.

Manuel. Manuel, whom we take as our focus in these next few transcripts, sat at a table with Bella and Amber in Karen's room. Manuel, a bilingual learner, was described by Karen as an "average reader," although we observed Manuel to interact quite proficiently with text. Our first set of transcript excerpts begins with another student walking across the room to hand Manuel a much-sought-after book, *Eleven Planets* (Aguilar, 2008). Manuel immediately discarded the book he was holding, turned to this new book, and said quietly to himself, "I just need to see what the. . ." and started flipping through the book, reading aloud to himself, "Venus was. . . Friday. . . day

Figure 1. Excerpts from Manuel's Informational Text Reading and Note-Taking

Venus was the Roman
goddess of love, beauty,
and springtime. The
symbol for her bright
shining planet is the
hand mirror. Friday is
her day of the week.
The word for Friday in
many languages means
"Venus's day."

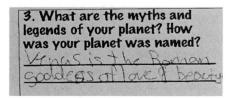

3. What are the myths and
legends of your planet? How
was your planet was named?

Venus is the Roman
goddess of love & beauty

of week." Finding the information he needed right away, Manuel stopped briefly to record notes in his note-taking packet (see Figure 1).

Then, he moved on to his next question, also related to the one he just recorded.

Manuel: (seemingly to himself) *What is Venus' legend name?* (Then looks back in book and reads quietly to himself).

In these few instances, Manuel was engaging in what we came to call a *searching* approach to the text (Maloch & Zapata, 2011). That is, he searched for the answers to questions laid out for him by his teachers in his note-taking packet. Across our three consecutive days of observation devoted to Manuel and his table of peers, Manuel primarily approached texts with this searching approach.

Examining the overarching frame and structure of this inquiry unit as well as the teacher/student interactions that accompanied Manuel's work with informational texts help illustrate how his practices were shaped by these contexts. In Karen's classroom, students' research opportunities within this inquiry unit began with several days of read-alouds and discussions led by Karen with the intent of building students' content knowledge and providing demonstrations of navigational and note-taking strategies. Karen also introduced what some call a "book flood" (Elley, 2000) in which she brought in a range of texts related to their inquiry. After giving students one day of "reading just for fun" to explore the wide range of books, the next several days and weeks were spent reading and exploring multiple texts about their planets as they gathered information and recorded notes about their planet. As students began their research, Karen encouraged them to "read like detectives," as they searched for information to fill their note-taking guides.

The provision of the note-taking guide, the requirements for its completion, and Karen's instructions to the students—to "read like a detective"—were all intended to support and scaffold students' work with informational texts. At the same time, we argue here that each of these materials/actions suggested for students a particular frame or way of viewing their work as researchers. Although intended to support the students' inquiry, these structures and instructions may have limited inquiry to an act of finding information to fit certain predefined categories. This framing was also evident in the ways the teachers (the classroom teacher and the student teacher) interacted with students during their research time. The next several transcript excerpts occurred *before* the episodes provided earlier in this section and may provide insight into Manuel's preference for a searching approach to informational texts and his dedication to the task of taking notes.

Manuel sits at his table looking through a book about Venus. The student teacher stops by and asks, "Are you getting some good stuff, Manuel?"

As we see her do here, the student teacher (and the classroom teacher) regularly checked in with Manuel. Here, her question to Manuel—"Are you getting some good stuff?"—positioned Manuel as a reading "detective," just as the teacher's charge ("read like detectives") had, and positioned his task as one of "getting" or taking from books, what Rosenblatt (1978) calls an "efferent stance." As the interaction continued, it became evident that Manuel did not believe he was "getting good stuff."

Manuel: No

Student Teacher: Why not?

Manuel: I don't even know what type of facts. I know who discovered Venus.

Student Teacher: [pointing to his note-taking packet which is open on the table] …the answer to all these questions. That could be under 'Oh WOW facts.'

Manuel interpreted the task, and the teacher's question (correctly, it seemed), as one of gaining facts from the text and expressed confusion about the "type of facts." His statement to this effect was accompanied by his physical reference (i.e., eye gaze; pointing) to his notes packet, suggesting that what he may have meant was that he was unable to find *these* facts—the ones asked for in the notes packet. This interpretation was further supported when Manuel followed his "I don't know" positioning, with one of knowing. He *did* know who discovered Venus. The juxtaposition of these statements indicated that Manuel's statement of "not knowing" may have had more to do with the school task of completing his notes packet than with growing expertise on Venus. In response, the teacher directed Manuel to his note-taking packet and suggested a possible place to store this new information he had learned, again reinforcing the school task.

In our view, Manuel's textual practices were influenced by an instructional context that emphasized task completion and a stance toward collecting information from text. As Manuel continued in his research, we saw evidences of this shaping as he approached the texts almost exclusively with a searching approach, as illustrated in the opening excerpts. Yet, his work with informational texts was not defined only by the instructional context. His devotion to the task was sometimes overridden by the allure of a "cool" book or opportunities for social engagement with his peers. For example, in the following excerpt, Manuel found information related to what Venus is made of, and he sought Bella's response.

Manuel: (After a slight intake of breath [indicating awe], he looks up towards Bella) Oh my god, hey Bella, I know what what the gasses [are made of] (reading) "in deadly clouds of carbon dioxis, 40 miles, carbon dioxis."

As we see here, Manuel's practices with informational texts, as with all of the students in our study, involved a social dimension. Manuel was often eager to share what he was learning—seemingly motivated both by the content of what we was seeing/reading and by the desire to build social connections with other students.

Another conversation was prompted when another student in the class, Ben, walked over to ask Bella a question.

Ben: Do you know who discovered Nept-, Venus?

Bella: (looking up) Yes, I do…Galileo Galilei.

Manuel: (looking at Isabella; Ben walked off as soon as he got his answer). He was like the first. He was like the first person. He was like. He was like the first person to study all the planets (talking really quickly as if to try and hold the floor).

Bella: Yeah . . . He thought that Neptune was a star.

Manuel: He thought Pluto was a planet. It used to be a planet, but then they figured out it was a dwarf planet.

Here, Manuel took advantage of the opening provided by Ben's question to share his own knowing to make social inroads with Bella.

The next day, Manuel opened his note-taking guide to find that he had notes for each category. Also in his note-taking guide was the same set of categories to complete for Internet articles and for United Streaming videos. Manuel turned to this empty page, and apparently unsure of what to do, leaned over to ask Bella about it.

Isabella: That's what you find from the computer, but we can't do that right now.

Manuel: So we skip it? [He turns the page and reads] Next, title video?

Isabella: That's for United Streaming videos.

Manuel: Okay, we have to skip that, too, don't we?

Isabella: We're doing Internet tomorrow, I think.

Manuel: So, I'm done with this right now. [Puts notes packet away] I'm just going to read my book.

Following his determination that he was "done," we observed Manuel alternate between a steeping approach and a guided exploration approach as he continued to note new and interesting information that might be relevant to his inquiry and note-taking. We found this shift quite telling in two ways. First, his announcement that he was "done" suggested his alignment with the teacher's framing of this task of note-taking and information gathering. That he continued reading and talking about Venus suggested that he was not, in fact, "done" with learning or inquiry. He was done with the task assigned by the teacher. Second, once finished with the school task, Manuel engaged more often in a steeping approach. Co-occurring with this shift in approaches was an increase in Manuel's social responses to the text and with his peers. We speculate that a steeping approach to informational text might actually afford

Figure 2. Manuel and Amber

the time and space for children to respond socially to the informational text and with their peers. These steeping and guided exploration practices, accompanied by more social interaction, can be seen in Sonny's case, as well.

Sonny. Across the hall in Jane's classroom, Sonny sat at a table with Angela, Naomi, and Denny as they all researched different planets. Jane described Sonny as an enthusiastic, but struggling, reader. Jane began her classroom inquiry unit with several read-aloud sessions in which she worked to build up enthusiasm and background knowledge for the topic of solar system, followed by a week-long set of demonstrations focused on the sun. Each day featured a different type of text (e.g., tradebook, textbook, Internet article, United Streaming video) that she and the students read together. With each of these texts, she modeled taking notes and placing them into particular categories (the same categories that later appeared in students' note-taking guides). Her instructional emphases were on the importance of reading across multiple data sources, cross-checking for accuracy, making notes in phrases rather than complete sentences, and some attention to text features (such as diagrams or captions). Also during this time, Jane flooded the room with books—books that varied by level and topic (within the solar system)—and provided students opportunities to explore them. On the day the students were to begin their individual research, Jane's instruction centered again on the importance of finding the most current sources.

Jane's introduction into the research process seemed to focus students on how they might navigate the texts to learn more about their planet. The goal she communicated was more about learning and finding/recording the most up-to-date information than on task completion, as we saw in Karen's classroom. Sonny's practices around informational texts reflected this emphasis. During our observations over several days, we observed Sonny move in and out of all three approaches to informational texts—*steeping, guided exploration,* and *searching.* The following example shows him engaged in the searching approach, not unlike Manuel, utilizing appropriate text features to navigate the text.

> Sonny is reading *Mercury and Venus* (Kerrod, 2000). Sonny looks at the Table of Contents and then flips to a page. Then, he goes back to the Table of Contents, using this pencil to track his reading of the titles, then flips to another page.

But, we also observed Sonny engaged in approaches that looked more like steeping in the text. In the following excerpt Sonny reads about Mercury, sometimes to himself, sometimes out loud.

> Sonny continues reading. When he finishes that page, he begins flipping through the rest of the pages. Interestingly, he recorded no facts from that page about Mercury, which had lots of relevant information that he could have recorded. . . .stops on the page about Uranus (p. 49), and says "Uranus!" "It says right here that Uranus was discovered by William Herschel." Continues flipping. On page 53, he says, "Neptune . . . Discovered by the Roman God" (the paragraph actually says, "Later the planet was named Neptune, after the Roman god of the sea."). Angela says, "Your planet was discovered by a Roman god?" Sonny says, "No he didn't"…and continues reading.

In this excerpt, Sonny was doing what he often did when he first picked up a new book; he was spending time getting to know the book—not just the information about Mercury, but finding information about all planets. It is not coincidental, we think, that he verbalized the information about Neptune, Angela's planet (sitting directly across from him). Also evident in this excerpt is the way that students' close proximity to one another led to more spontaneous interaction around the text. When Sonny misread part of the book, Angela questioned what he read, prompting him to go back to the text and clarify. Although in the above instance Sonny did not seem very interested in carrying on a conversation with Angela, he regularly conversed with her about what she was reading and learning or what he was learning. For example, in the following excerpt, Angela initiated.

Angela: (taps on Sonny's book and shows him something in her book) Neptune . . .

Sonny: Let me see? (Leaning in to see her book – Angela is sitting across from him; Sonny says something else to Angela, pointing at something inside the book, then they laugh together (see Figure 3).

Figure 3. Sonny and Angela

Graphic or visual displays in the texts or surprising information often prompted students to share with each other. These texts, and the features within them, served as social vehicles in this classroom (Dyson, 1993).

Sonny and Angela's interactions were situated within an instructional context focused on learning and one that provided ample demonstrations of how to navigate through informational texts. Jane's initial instructions to the students set them on a path towards finding information to inform their own learning about their planets. And, her subsequent interactions with them during their research time reinforced this path. See, for example, the following exchange.

Sonny: Geez (he puts his hand on the book, looks around, and then sees Jane walking toward him. As she approaches and sits down at the table, he lays the book down flat on the table and starts to tell her about it; he is commenting on a picture of the crater in a section called "The Sun's Little Neighbor").

Jane: Wow, you have a lot of information. Oh, you got the symbol for it?

Sonny: Uh-huh!

Jane: Cool!

Sonny: (Sonny reads to her from the page in *Scholastic Atlas of Planets*). There's a biggest crater... hold up, wait a second, it's called.... the largest Crater? (Pauses and searches through book. He points to the word on the text and then look up at Jessica).

Jessica: It's a crater... Caloris? That's cool! You have a crater on your planet!

Steve:	It's right there! (Holding up the book and pointing to the illustration).
Jane:	Did you put that under the physical characteristics?
Jane:	You need to put that, add that in there, that you have a crater (pointing to research packet of Physical Characteristics). Right here. Since you're a rocky planet you get to have cool landforms on it.
Sonny:	I like this planet!

Here, Sonny made a bid for the teacher's attention. As Jane walked over to him, he laid his book down on the table, opening it up as an invitation to Jane into this book sharing. In this exchange, she responded very differently from the teacher who worked with Manuel. Jane's first response was one of receiving Sonny's enthusiasm and learning. She noted what he had recorded in his notes packet and commented on it. Then, with no request from the teacher, Sonny began reading to her to show what he was learning. As he read, he invited her support, and she gave it by saying the correct name of the crater and then responding, "That's cool! You have a crater on your planet!" Again, Jane's utterances worked first to receive the child's knowing and enthusiasm for the book. The emphasis of her response leaned towards curiosity and learning, rather than task completion.

Ingrid and Ethel. Jessica structured the classroom inquiry on the solar system in ways that were both similar to and different from the other two teachers. In her room, the classroom inquiry unit was also launched with a book flood; and, her students relied on a note-taking guide. Like Jane did with the sun, Jessica read a series of picture books about the moon, demonstrating across these read-alouds ways of taking notes from various data sources. As she set students off to do their research, Jessica encouraged the students to read first for enjoyment before searching for information. Jessica integrated a RAN (Reading and Analyzing Nonfiction; Stead, 2001) chart into their learning, which afforded students room to hypothesize and confirm facts about the solar system as they conducted their research.

The emphasis in Jessica's class seemed to be on understanding. She spent much time modeling and reinforcing a strategy she called, "read, cover, retell." That is, as students moved through their texts, she encouraged them to read through a page or section, look away from the text, and then tell someone else (or repeat to oneself) what they had just read. Then, they thought about what they had read and if any of the new information fit into categories in their note-taking packet. This approach was more in line with what we called "guided exploration" in which students read texts, keeping in mind the questions from the note-taking packet, and recording information accordingly.

A final variation in her classroom was that she asked the students to work together on their planets. As a result, the data from this classroom includes groups of two and three students researching together around a single planet. Also, during the students' research time, unlike Jane and Karen, Jessica spent most of her time working with three students, all of whom she perceived to be struggling with informational texts, at a small round table in the middle of the room. She very carefully guided these students' navigation of texts and their note-taking. This decision translated into less moment-to-moment teacher intervention in other children's research, although children often came to her to ask questions.

Our focal student analysis in Jessica's class focused on Ingrid and Ethel, whom we present together because they worked as a team. They collaborated quietly in a corner of the room to work on

their research. Diagnosed as a selective
mute, Ingrid read silently through the
literature, often putting books in Ethel's
hands, pointing excitedly to a feature
on a spread in a book or whispering
some finding into Ethel's ear. The pair
quickly developed a unique way of
working together with Ethel taking the
lead on recording and Ingrid taking the
lead on navigating the literature. Their
social ways of being together relied on
these understood roles and proved to
be both enjoyable and productive. The
excerpts below portray a representative
episode as the girls worked to learn
about their selected planet, Venus. As
the episode began below, Ingrid had just
gone to retrieve a book, *Updated Venus*
(Chrismer, 2008). As she sat down, she
opened to the very last page.

Figure 4. Excerpt from Ingrid's Reading

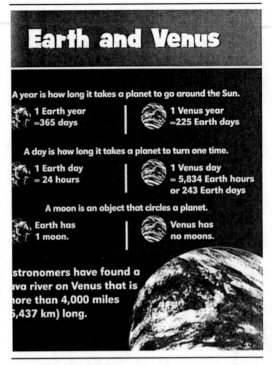

Ingrid:	(Who has the book on her lap, points and seems to be reading these same facts about revolution.)
Ethel:	Seems like faster, because a year is, wait. It goes around the sun (uses a gesture indicating revolution) faster (pointing into the text with her pencil, towards the rotating facts). It rotates (back to rotating gesture with her pencil) slower. Ah. Cool. (Ethel starts to record this information).
Ingrid:	Points to a fact about a lava river on Venus that is more than 4,000 miles long.
Ethel:	Wow!"

Ingrid's and Ethel's practices, as illustrated in the above excerpt, were situated within an instructional context in which inquiry and collaboration were valued. By asking students to work together in their research, Jessica set up a particular kind of activity for these two students that was different from the research activity of the other two classrooms. These two were *asked* to collaborate. They sat side-by-side, leaning in toward one another. Ethel had a notes packet; Ingrid held the book. Ethel thought aloud about what she was reading, using gesture to interpret the meaning of the text. These gestures—first to represent rotation, then another gesture to represent revolution when she realized her confusion—were ones the teacher used in earlier lessons to discuss these concepts. While it is impossible to know for sure, we suspect that Ethel's "talk-through" of this content also positively mediated Ingrid's meaning-making.

Although Ethel seemed ready to record information they had found, these two students did not seem to be engaged in a searching approach or focused exclusively on task completion. Ethel seemed to be engaged in something between a guided exploration and a steeping approach. Ingrid was firmly planted in a steeping approach to informational texts and did not even hold her note-taking guide in her hands or have it anywhere close to her. Before the above episode, we saw Ingrid sit, surrounded by books, selecting one at a time and looking through each text. After this episode, we observed Ingrid sit with two books in front of her, comparing the unlabeled diagram on the cover of one book with the labeled, but slightly different, diagram on the other. Clearly, she was steeping in the visuals and text of these books. Ethel's approach was angled more towards a guided exploration. She was concerned with taking notes and "staying on track" to their assigned task, but she also seemed open to following Ingrid's lead.

Figure 5. Ingrid and Ethel

In these excerpts, Ingrid and Ethel appeared engaged in exploring this text with interesting facts and making sense of them. In the interaction, we see the echoes of Jessica's instructions of read, cover, retell, and focus on making meaning from informational texts. We see the girls reading, then retelling as a way of making sense, borrowing the gestural supports provided by their teacher in earlier sessions.

In this classroom, and particularly for Ingrid and Ethel, the teacher's invitation to collaborate as researchers shaped their work with and around with informational texts. Ethel and Ingrid worked together to grow knowledge and understanding in ways that extended beyond what they might have accomplished individually.

DISCUSSION

Previous research makes clear that primary-grade children are capable of acquiring understandings about informational texts (Duke, 2003; Pappas, 1991; Purcell-Gates et al., 2007), yet few studies examine how young children navigate informational texts when engaged in day-to-day classroom activity. Case studies, such as the ones examined here, are especially useful in providing a more detailed understanding of the particulars of classroom processes. Dyson and Genishi (2005) propose that by attending closely to cases researchers can "gain insight into some of the factors that shape, and the processes through which people interpret or make meaningful" their experiences and learning (p. 3).

In this analysis, as Dyson and Genishi (2005) suggest, we set out to understand the factors and processes that shape young children's work around informational texts. Although the original intent of our study was to examine how teachers and their young students navigated and made meaning from informational texts, our analyses have pointed us to the ways students' meaning-making is embedded in socially-rich contexts of learning and how these contexts, particularly the instructional context, shape students' approaches to informational texts. Our analytic eye was drawn to the ways the teachers set up their classroom inquiries and to the teachers' moment-to-moment interventions in students' research and how their instructional practices influenced each of these students. Our findings afford insights in two areas.

First, this analysis highlights the affordances and limitations of varied instructional approaches to inquiry. Manuel's searching approach to informational texts and tight allegiance to completing the task were clearly shaped by his teacher's instructions and direction as well as the teachers' discursive interventions as he researched. The teachers' directions and interventions worked, in Manuel's case, to position his research as a task to complete. In contrast, Jane's interventions with Sonny, while ultimately also directing him to the task of note-taking, first positioned him as a learner and herself as a responder and co-inquirer. And, in Ethel and Ingrid's cases, we see students engaged in inquiring together, perhaps influenced by the symbolic "freedom" assigned to them by their teacher—freedom to explore, read first for fun, and research in ways that were meaningful to them.

Although it is clear that all of these students learned about and from informational texts, we argue here that these kinds of situated practices may set children on different trajectories in their learning. An overemphasis on school-defined tasks focused on task completion could result in trajectories that may work in school but not beyond. On the other hand, inquiry that is focused on the learning, in which searching for and locating information occurs in the service of that learning, is more likely to set students on trajectories that are more enduring as students move into contexts outside of school—trajectories in which students engage in meaningful ways with informational texts to inform themselves about things they need to know. Within the cases, it was clear to us that, move-by-move, the teachers' discursive responses to students mattered, becoming visible to us only upon our closer analysis and suggesting that teachers should consider carefully how they position informational texts and inquiry as well as the ways they support students through individual conferences and the materials they provide.

Second, across all of the cases, and regardless of the approaches taken by students or teachers, it was the social nature of their work that gave momentum and energy to the activities around informational texts. Specifically, the social spaces in the classrooms capitalized on the ways students and their teachers served as audiences for one another in their inquiry and research. In classrooms, these spaces become places to share and celebrate newly learned information, places to check or cross-check information just discovered, and places for support in the meaning-making process. As Kucan and Beck (1997) argued, when students collaborate in constructing meaning from text, they have "multiple resources at the reading construction site" (p. 289). Providing these kinds of collaborative opportunities for research may be one way to support students' engagement, exploration, and meaning-making of informational texts.

REFERENCES

Aguilar, D. (2008). *Eleven planets*. Des Moines, IA: National Geographic Children's Books.

Caswell, L., & Duke, N. K. (1998). Non-narrative as catalyst for literacy development. *Language Arts, 75*, 108-117.

Chrismer, M. (2008). *Updated Venus*. New York, NY: Children's Press.

Duke, N. K. (2000). 3.6 minutes per day: The scarcity of informational texts in first grade. *Reading Research Quarterly, 35(2)*, 202-224.

Duke, N. K. (2003). Reading to learn from the very beginning: Information books literacy in early childhood. *Young Children, 58*(2), 14–20.

Dyson, A. H. (1993). *Social worlds of children learning to write in an urban primary school*. New York, NY: Teachers College Press.

Dyson, A. H., & Genishi, C. (2005). *On the case: Approaches to language and literacy research*. New York, NY: Teachers College Press.

Elley, W. (2000). The potential of book floods for raising literacy levels. *International Review of Education, 46*(3-4), 233-255.

Gee, J. (1990). *Social linguistics and literacies: Ideology in discourses, critical perspectives on literacy and education*. London, England: Taylor and Francis.

Haneda, M., & Wells, G. (2000). Writing in knowledge-building communities. *Research in the Teaching of English, 34*(3), 430-457.

Harvey, S. (2002). Nonfiction inquiry: Using real reading and writing to explore the world. *Language Arts, 80*, 12–22.

Jeong, J., Gaffney, J., & Choi, H. (2010). Availability and use of informational texts in second, third, and fourth-grade classrooms. *Research in the Teaching of English, 44*(4), 435-456.

Kerrod, R. (2000). *Mercury and Venus*. Minneapolis, MN: Lerner Publishing Group.

Kucan, L., & Beck, I. L. (1997). Thinking aloud and reading comprehension research: Inquiry, instruction, and social interaction. *Review of Educational Research, 67*, 271-299.

Maloch, B. (2008). Beyond exposure: The uses of informational text in a second grade classroom. *Research in the Teaching of English, 42*, 315-362.

Maloch, B., & Zapata, A. (2011). "Dude, it's the Milky Way!": An exploration of students' approaches to informational text. In P. Dunston, L. B. Gambrell, S. K. Fullerton, V. R. Gillis, K. Headley, & P. M. Stecker (Eds.), *60th Yearbook of the Literacy Research Association* (pp. 332-335). Oak Creek: WI.

Moss, B. (2008). The information text gap: The mismatch between non-narrative text types in basal readers and 2009 NAEP recommended guidelines. *Journal of Literacy Research, 40*, 201-219.

Palmer, R. G., & Stewart, R. (2003). Nonfiction trade book use in primary grades. *Reading Teacher, 57*, 38–48.

Pappas, C. (1991). Fostering full access to literacy by including information books. *Language Arts, 68*, 449-462.

Purcell-Gates, V., Duke, N., & Martineau, J. (2007). Learning to read and write genre specific text: Roles of authentic experience and explicit teaching. *Reading Research Quarterly, 42*(1), 8-45.

Rau, D. M. (2002). *Venus*. Mankato, MN: Compass Point Books**.**

Rosenblatt, L. M. (1978). *The reader, the text, the poem: The transactional theory of the literary work*. Carbondale, IL: Southern Illinois University Press.

Smith, M. C. (2000). The real-world reading practices of adults. *Journal of Literacy Research, 32* 25-52.

Smolkin, L. B., & Donovan, C. A. (2000). *The contexts of comprehension: Information book read alouds and comprehension acquisition*. Center for the Improvement of Early Reading Achievement Report #2-009. Ann Arbor, MI: University of Michigan.

Stead, T. (2001). *Is that a fact?: Teaching nonfiction writing K-3*. Portland, ME: Stenhouse.

Strauss, A., & Corbin, J. (1990). *Basics of qualitative research: Grounded theory and procedures and techniques*. Newbury Park, CA: Sage.

Street, B. (2003). What's "new" in new literacy studies? Critical approaches to literacy in theory and practice. *Current Issues in Comparative Education, 5*(2), 77-91.

Vygotsky, L. S. (1978). *Mind and society: The development of higher mental processes*. Cambridge, MA: Harvard University Press.

Wertsch J. (1991). *Voices of the mind: A sociocultural approach to mediated action*. Cambridge, MA: Harvard University Press.

Williams, J., Hall, K., Lauer, K., Stafford, K., DeCisto, L., & deCani, J. (2005). Expository text comprehension in the primary grade classroom. *Journal of Educational Psychology, 97*, 538-550.

Wollman-Bonilla, J. E. (2000). Teaching science writing to first graders: Genre learning and recontextualization, *Research in the Teaching of English, 35*, 35-65.

One Teacher's Implementation of Culturally Mediated Writing Instruction

Carol Wickstrom
Leslie Patterson
University of North Texas

with Jennifer Isgitt
Keller Independent School District

According to Vygotsky (1978), we learn through interactions with others, and our thinking is shaped through the conversations in which we participate. Consequently, if students sit in classrooms in which there is little talk or collaboration, then it is likely that students are not learning as deeply as they need to be learning. Participation is doubly important for English Language Learners because they are trying to learn the content and the language at the same time. The purpose of this paper is to focus on the discourse patterns of one high school English teacher, Jennifer, who enacted the research-based principles and practices of Culturally Mediated Writing Instruction (CMWI) (Patterson, Wickstrom, Roberts, Araujo, & Hoki, 2010; Wickstrom, Araujo, Patterson, with Hoki, & Roberts, 2011). We specifically wanted to know in what ways her discourse patterns during writing instruction influenced student interaction and learning and how the students responded to the academic tasks.

BACKGROUND OF THE LARGER STUDY

In a three-year project funded by the National Writing Project (2007-2010), we investigated how middle and high school teachers who participated in a professional development workshop entitled, "Culturally Mediated Writing Instruction" (CMWI), enacted the principles and practices of CMWI in their classrooms. Rather than a fixed program with specific procedures, CMWI is a research-based approach that combines a culturally responsive stance, guided inquiry, and reading/writing workshop practices (Patterson et al., 2010; Wickstrom et al., 2011). The larger study focuses on shifts in the students' writing and also on the teacher's adoption and adaptation of the instructional practices. For that research, we documented the participants' usage of the CMWI inquiry cycle (Figure 1), and, subsequently, identified five instructional patterns used during lessons: empathy and caring, meaningful connections, inquiry stance, authentic work, and appropriate mediation (Patterson, Wickstrom, & Araujo, 2010). These patterns were clearly represented in all the classrooms, but we also noticed interesting differences across the classrooms. One of the most interesting differences we noted was each teacher's instructional discourse as she worked with the students. Our continuing analysis has focused on the classroom discourse of the teachers, particularly as it related to the fifth pattern, appropriate mediation of student learning. We were interested in how each teacher identified student strengths and needs and how he then made instructional decisions to mediate student learning in those areas. This paper responds to that question in Jennifer's classroom and is based on further analysis of the 2007-2008 data.

Conceptual Orientation of Culturally Mediated Writing Instruction

Like other instructional approaches targeting English learners, Culturally Mediated Writing Instruction is compatible with culturally responsive instruction (Gay, 2000; Ladson-Billings, 1992), critical pedagogy (Freire, 1970; Shor, 1992), and "anti-bias education" (Rebollo-Gil & Moras, 2006). Heath's (1983) seminal work argues that the teacher must consider the culture of the students that are being taught. Further, cultural lenses cannot be limited to ethnicity, socioeconomic level, or age. But, rather, one must consider a multitude of lenses that include, but are not limited to, neighborhood, family, sports, media, clubs, lunch groups, language, gangs, etc. Since that time, researchers (Lee, 2007; Moll, Amanti, Neff, & Gonzalez, 1992) added to our awareness of the wealth of knowledge that diverse populations bring to the classroom.

Initially, we framed our instructional recommendations within a socio-literate perspective (Johns, 1997). Using this perspective, we assumed that teachers would emphasize the social nature of learning and that students would gain content understandings through reading and writing to one another and to audiences beyond the classroom. However, after observing in these classrooms and exploring the literature further, we adopted a broader socio-cultural framework (John-Steiner & Mahn, 1996; Lantolf & Thorne, 2006; Vygotsky, 1978), which gave us insight into how language and literacy practices (texts and the talk) in the classroom actually mediated both language learning and content learning for the students.

This socio-cultural framework for instruction for adolescent English learners is clearly consistent with the five patterns we documented in these classrooms from 2007 through 2010. First, in order to build on the knowledge and experiences of their students, teachers need to develop *empathetic, caring, and responsive relationships* with and among students (e.g., Freire, 1970; Noddings, 2005). Second, contrary to the isolated instructional methods often proposed for use with English learners, teachers should invite, demonstrate, and facilitate *meaningful connections between and among ideas, texts, and social/cultural practices* (e.g., Moll, Amanti, Neff & Gonzalez, 1992; Wells, 2007). Third, students need to perceive *tasks and audiences as authentic* (e. g., Burke, 2003; Jago, 2008). Fourth, teachers and students should take *an inquiry stance* toward all learning in school, including social issues, curricular content, and literacy tasks (e.g., Burke, 2010; Short, Harste, & Burke, 1996; Wilhelm, 2007). Finally, students need *appropriate support or mediation* as they become more proficient, confident, and independent readers and writers of English (e.g., Ball, 2006; Fu, 2009).

Conversations of Teaching that Reveal Mediation

During the first year of the study, the research associates were puzzled as they visited the teacher researchers' classrooms. Clearly, the teachers had adopted reading and writing workshop routines (Atwell, 1998), but when the whole class worked together, the research associates noted that the lessons were conducted differently from lessons in other classrooms. There were no lectures or long teacher explanations, nor was there teacher-led turn-taking. Instead, the students and teacher were engaged in reading and writing and in loosely structured conversations about the work they were completing together. Although these actions were clearly purposeful from each teacher's perspective, we had difficulty naming and describing the relevant structures. Initially, we attempted to understand how these teachers were enacting culturally mediated writing instruction by identifying and examining small units of analysis (teaching moves)—single comments, actions, or brief exchanges between teacher and student(s). By decontextualizing the data and coding these smaller units of analysis, we were able to identify the five instructional patterns explained earlier. However, we were still intrigued by how these instructional patterns played out in the classroom instruction, so we revisited Jennifer's original transcripts. To do this analysis, we recontextualized the smaller teaching "moves" into "episodes." A teaching episode combines multiple concurrent and sequential teaching moves (actions, comments, questions) around a particular instructional focus. By recontextualizing the data in this way, we were able to determine how Jennifer's instructional moves simultaneously built on students' resources, responded to students' needs, and addressed curricular objectives. As a result, these teaching episodes provided us with a way to further investigate how Jennifer's classroom conversations mediated student learning.

THEORETICAL SUPPORT FOR CLASSROOM CONVERSATIONS OF TEACHING

Researchers (Cazden, 1988; Mehan, 1978, 1979) have documented the persistent use of the Initiation-Response-Evaluation (IRE) pattern during classroom instruction. Typically, the teacher initiates a question, the student responds, and the teacher evaluates the response. This type of turn-taking during discussion may aid the teacher in determining whether, and how deeply, students have read the material, but theorists, researchers, and educators (e. g., Cazden, 1988; Tharp & Gallimore, 1988) argue that this pattern of talk does not invite students to explore new meanings. In addition, because literacy tasks are mostly in-the-head processes that cannot be observed, it is essential, as students are apprenticed (Rogoff, 1990) into these meaning-making practices, that teachers understand what students know and what they need to know in order to make connections to the lesson. Instructional conversations can make this apprenticeship process transparent and accessible. According to Wells and Chang-Wells (1992):

> "it is crucial that the adult not only assist the learner to participate in the task, but that he or she also engage with the learner in talk about the text that externalizes in speech the internal mental processes involved in reading or writing (p. 31).

Conversations of teaching initially occur with the teacher modeling the conversational patterns needed to work through an authentic task. Then, there are opportunities for discussions to occur in multiple ways: (a) between the teacher and the whole class; (b) between the teacher and a small group; (c) between the teacher and an individual student; (d) small groups of students; or (e) pairs of students.

In classrooms that promote this approach to teaching and learning as conversation, students are encouraged to use all of their resources. The students' abilities to participate are not limited by the knowledge that was contained in a text or in a particular context, but, rather, the students are expected to make connections with any of their experiences or other resources. These conversations help students connect unfamiliar or abstract concepts through more familiar concepts. A key to these conversations is that the students are able to experience the ideas through their unique perspectives. Although the teacher can supply examples, it is essential that each student makes personally meaningful connections. As teachers invite students to participate in these conversations, they offer the opportunity to be more engaged in the learning, as well as enhancing the potential that the students will make long-lasting and meaningful connections between existing knowledge and new knowledge.

To help teachers use classroom conversations to promote learning, researchers (e.g., Cazden 1979; Daniels 2001; Eeds & Peterson, 1999; Palinscar and Brown 1984; Rogoff & Wertsch, 1984; Wells & Chang-Wells, 1992) recommend various conversational patterns that invite students to take on different roles as inquirers and problem-solvers during classroom conversations.

Tharp and Gallimore (1988) found, in a variety of classroom settings, that instructional conversations could address the needs of the students with regard to differing abilities, cultural backgrounds, and interests. Other researchers (Wells, 1986; Wells & Chang-Wells, 1992) also noted the differences in the student learning when classroom discussion resembles conversation. Through these conversations, students and teachers appear to work through ideas and understandings. The term used by Wells & Chang-Wells (1992) was "collaborative talk" (p. 54), which promotes the use of inquiry. Other studies of dialogue in a variety of settings (Applebee & Langer, 1983; Pearson & Gallagher, 1983) determined that these open-ended, problem-solving classroom discussions promote student performance. When teachers tap into the student knowledge during the lesson, they invite students to be more engaged in their learning.

Applebee and Langer (1983) used the term instructional scaffolding to describe the classroom discourse. The teacher's role is to facilitate the conversations, but the participants all share equal status so that another student might provide some facilitation as well. The goal of these discussions is to develop students' abilities to problem-solve, connect ideas across texts and situations, and promote critical thinking.

In *Curriculum as Conversation* (1996) Applebee used the terms "knowledge-out-of-context" and "knowledge-in-action." The former term resembles the same kind of knowledge that is promoted in the IRE pattern. This knowledge is static knowledge that has meaning only within the text or the context. "Knowledge-in-action" is dynamic in nature because this knowledge is constructed through various means. According to Applebee (1996),

> Such knowledge arises out of participation in ongoing conversations about things that matter, conversations that are themselves embedded within larger traditions of discourse that we have come to value (science, the arts, history, literature, and mathematics, among many others). When we take this metaphor seriously, the development of culturally significant domains for conversation and instruction becomes a matter of helping students learn to participate in conversations with those domains. (p. 3)

Our initial analysis of the data suggested that Jennifer used ongoing conversations in her classroom to support student learning, so we revisited the data that focuses specifically on and instructional episodes related to writing instruction.

A LOOK INSIDE JENNIFER'S CLASSROOM

Jennifer and Her Students

At the time of the data collection, Jennifer, who holds a master's degree, had been teaching for eight years but had only taught senior English for two years. All of her teaching was at the same high school where she now served as the department chair. The class that we studied (Jennifer chose the class) consisted of 29 students from a wide range of cultural backgrounds and languages similar to the school's population. A number of students spoke different languages and were from other cultures; however, only one Hispanic student identified herself as having limited English proficiency such that Jennifer needed to make significant modifications.

Data Collection and Analysis

Jennifer's classroom was observed five times throughout the school year. The first visit provided an overview of the classroom and school environment. During subsequent visits, a research associate took field notes, recorded classroom lessons, collected any papers distributed to students, and conducted a follow-up interview after the observation. Completed student work was collected when possible. Field notes of classroom visits were transferred to data-collection protocols developed prior to the study. Other data included teacher researcher letters posted three times throughout the year. Research associates added memos about CMWI principles and practices as they worked through the data.

In the larger study, the qualitative data were analyzed inductively (Corbin & Strauss, 2007) to identify patterns in teachers' implementation of CMWI principles and practices. Debriefing sessions with the teachers were instrumental in affirming and refining these codes. Using NVivo, one team member then analyzed the qualitative data. Two additional codes were added as a result of this analysis. Further discussion refined and confirmed those codes, helping us identify patterns within and across teachers' instructional practices.

For the purpose of this paper, the coded "teaching moves" were recontextualized so that they might be considered in the context of the lesson—as a purposeful teaching episode. The teaching episode was read and reread to determine how teacher mediation occurred throughout the lesson. The following teaching episode occurred during the second visit to Jennifer's classroom at the end of October during the second six weeks of the school year. It was Jennifer's first attempt to apply the principles and practices of CMWI to a lesson in her classroom.

The Assignment: Writing an Extended Definition

A "Definition Essay" is an extended definition about an object or concept that holds particular significance for the student writer. Jennifer indicated that this assignment was intended to fulfill at least four instructional objectives from the state curriculum standards: (a) use of multiple modes of writing; (b) use of analogies; (c) use of thesis statements in Definition Essays; and (d) use of sufficient distinguishing characteristics and details.

In terms of the CMWI principles, Jennifer saw this assignment as an opportunity for students to take an inquiry stance as they explored significant meanings attached to a particular object or concept that was important to them. Further, they would need to use their cultural capital (personal knowledge and experience) as a resource for writing.

From the beginning of the year, Jennifer had been laying the groundwork for students to use their cultural capital. For example, one of her first writing assignments was informal writing about "Where I Stand" in response to prompts about their beliefs and needs, likes and dislikes, *etc.* Their responses to these and similar invitations to write and think about their individual knowledge and experiences were recorded in their writer's notebooks. Jennifer read the student responses in order to learn more about her students. This knowledge helped Jennifer make strong student connections.

To encourage an inquiry stance as she began the "Definition Essay" assignment, she gave the students a "survey" that asked them to think specifically about what particular concepts mean. Examples included:

- How many inches of snow would have to fall before a storm is considered a blizzard?
- How many people in this room have brown hair?
- An island is described as having a tropical climate. What would the temperature be on an average summer day?

For each of these questions, students merely called out responses. Jennifer recorded responses, and then encouraged students to defend their claims. Through this inquiry, Jennifer and the students agreed that some terms needed to be explained or defined more explicitly in order to understand their meanings.

Jennifer then introduced the students to a mentor text Definition Essay entitled "I Remember Masa" by Antonio Burciaga (1988). They read, enjoyed, and discussed the piece, a memoir focusing on the definition of "tortilla." In small groups, the students analyzed the various modes of writing (narrative, expository, classification, and explanation of a process) used to define the term and shared their analyses with the class. This mentor text reinforced Jennifer's invitation to students to think about concepts from their home cultures, an essential component of CMWI.

At that point, Jennifer had the students brainstorm, in their writer's notebook, a list of terms or phrases they might define. Then she called the students' attention to their classroom "word wall" where they record interesting and important words. Jennifer led them in a conversation about how they might do an extended definition about one of those words. During the discussion, students added topics, such as: "Hanukkah," "tattoo artist," "Vietnamese Baptist daughter," "Korean New Year," "Salsa (music/dancing)," "strong black woman," "truck driver," and "nerd." At the end of the discussion, Jennifer instructed them to choose a word for their essay from these sources or from their own experiences.

Once they settled on a topic, Jennifer led them through a series of prewriting experiences to help them explore what they might say. For example, "Begin by writing down a few simple statements about your word: "A Tortilla is. . . A Guy is. . . Happiness is. . ."; "Look up and record the word's dictionary definition (if it is in the dictionary); and "Classify your word (what category or categories does it belong to?). These prewriting prompts helped the students compose drafts of what might become paragraphs in their Definition Essay. Jennifer was able to watch them work with their chosen topics, respond to their questions, and initiate conversations to help them think of details to add. Once each student had worked through all these writing activities, Jennifer reminded them of the patterns of writing development—ways authors develop their ideas: (narration, description, exemplification, explanation, comparison/contrast, classification, cause/effect, and argument).

Over a two-week period, as the students worked on their drafts, Jennifer would begin the class in whole-group conversations about a particular mode of writing, providing mentor texts, in the form of paragraphs, from published essays to demonstrate how authors had approached the extended definition task. Then, she would have the students continue working on their drafts while she walked around the room and had individual conversations to support students in their writing, speaking informally to small groups or to the whole class to call their attention to something that they seemed to need at that point, and always watching closely to see how the students were making sense of the task. This type of mediation allowed students to remain engaged in the assignment because it met their individual needs. In subsequent weeks, as she introduced the students to various texts from the British literature curriculum, she connected this exploration of familiar objects and concepts to the less familiar by examining culturally significant terms in these works. The following section draws on field notes from a writing lesson in order to describe, in detail, one teaching episode that illustrates the manner in which Jennifer used loosely structured teaching conversations to mediate student learning.

Making Sense of a Teaching Episode

Jennifer is at the front of the room as the students enter and take their seats. On the board is a brief explanation of what will happen today—writer's notebook and begin Definition Essay. Before they get started with the lesson, Jennifer checks to see how many of them were in TAKS (Texas Assessment of Knowledge and Skills, state-mandated test) testing on Thursday. Although a number of them raise their hands, she continues with the lesson.

1. Jennifer: "Today we are going to write a Definition Essay." Provides students with a handout that describes the assignment, but she does not go over it.

2. Jennifer: "What is something that you fear?—cancer, diabetes, Alzheimer's, teenage pregnancy?"

3. Gives students time to write in their writer's notebook. (Students begin to list ideas of what they fear. Jennifer scans the room.)

Jennifer begins the lesson as an invitation to think about their topics. As a way to get them engaged, she poses a question about their "fears." She provides the students with examples and encourages them to explore a topic in their writer's notebook.

> Researcher Comment: *In CMWI we see teaching as inquiry and modeling so that, rather than giving the students an explanation of what a Definition Essay is, Jennifer begins the lesson by modeling the way to explore a topic. Jennifer is intentional about the focusing of ideas because she chooses ideas that are quite common to all of us and then narrows to one that is particular to the age of the students. These suggestions help the students to explore the idea about which they will write.* See Figure 1 for Inquiry Cycle.

After a few minutes of writing, Jennifer continues:

4. Jennifer: "Love and friendship are too general."

5. Continues to give time to write in their notebooks.
   (Jennifer scans the room to see if students are writing. Students appear to be writing.)

6. Jennifer: "Value, tradition, object."

7. Jennifer: "Write down anything, even if you're thinking that it's dumb. My mother has a plate that on your birthday, you eat off of it. On the plate it says, 'You're Special.' "
   (Students are listening, but some students are also continuing to write in their notebooks. A few are chatting quietly as they write in their notebooks.)

Jennifer draws from her family culture to provide models for the students. The examples are a way for the students to search their experiences and culture to determine if there are ideas or objects about which they might write.

> *Researcher Comment: Through these examples, Jennifer is drawing from CMWI in two ways. First, she employs the inquiry cycle to continue to allow students to explore and focus their work. By doing this, she creates mini-inquiries within the larger inquiry framework. She models the way that she would find a topic to write about by drawing from her family culture. This last idea is a key aspect of CMWI because drawing on one's social and cultural capital is essential. Because CMWI is an asset-based model, we emphasize the ways that students can identify their resources.*

8. Jennifer: "My Dad is a handy man. He always wears overalls and a stocking cap. One time he made me go to a fancy store with him in his overalls. I was about 12 and was very embarrassed. (Students laugh at her explanation here and continue to write. She is laughing, as well.)

9. Jennifer: "Another time my father sent me back to college with a CB radio so that I could get on the radio and go 'Breaker, breaker.' " (These statements are said as she walks about the room while students write. She stops and talks individually with several students. Conversations are inaudible.)

> *Researcher Comment: Through these personal examples, Jennifer continues to enact the inquiry cycle as she provides more ideas for students to focus their thinking about what they might write about for this assignment. Through these examples, Jennifer helps the students search for a topic. Jennifer describes the specific details of the items as a model so the students can begin to think about the characteristics of their idea. The ease with which Jennifer shares this personal information and the manner in which it is received by the students supports the notion that this classroom is a community of practice manifesting the five CMWI instructional patterns.*

10. Jennifer: "In my other class, topics include procrastination, senioritis, garage, multiple sclerosis, shoes—specific types like flip flops." (Some students talk and show each other their writer's notebooks.)

11. Jennifer: "What is Cajun, geisha, tamales, nerd, hip hop music, quinciñera, rock music, the Yankees, etc."

12. Jennifer: "Candace, you might want to write about softball. What does it mean to be a third baseman?"

> *Researcher Comments: Within these segments of the teaching episode, the teacher turns from specific examples from her experiences to examples that might be a part of*

students' lives. In CMWI, this action fosters searching in a more specific way. First, Jennifer provides ideas from another class period. Then, she uses examples that might come from the cultural backgrounds of these students. Finally, in line 12, she connects with a specific student. Through this action, she identifies an idea that comes from the student's social and cultural resources. This action allows the student to note that she does have a topic and allows all of the students to note the specificity of the idea. The topic is not simply baseball but rather pinpoints the position that the student plays. As Jennifer works through these ideas with her students, she continues to use the inquiry cycle as a model for the students to understand how to begin their work.

13. Gives students time to write.

14. Jennifer: "Talk about your term to someone. Tell someone why you chose your term." (Students turn to one or two other people around them to discuss their writing.)

> *Researcher Comments: Jennifer again reminds the students to write and to talk. These actions occur to give the students another way to search for their topics. It gives them the opportunity to work through their ideas.*

15. Jennifer: "Talk to someone about your term. Do a draft in your writer's notebook. Brainstorm a list of everything. Remember that you are defining your term from your perspective."

> *Researcher Comment: Jennifer encourages the students to talk to one another and further delineates the way to focus their Definition Essay. This teaching conversation continues to allow the students to search for their topics. Jennifer continues to <u>model</u> ideas and give time for the students to explore their own ideas. In CMWI we see these ways of working with the students as mini-inquiry cycles. It allows the teacher to model the inquiry cycle with the whole class while focusing the students on smaller independent inquiry cycles.*

16. Most students continue to write, but Jennifer notes several students are stuck.

17. Jennifer: "Use a dictionary to help define your term. Determine what are the similarities and differences. What might confuse people?—the difference between Mexican and Puerto Rican?"

18. Female Student: "I am Puerto Rican and we are not like Mexicans."

19. Jennifer: "Everybody in my family has a stocking for Christmas." She goes to the board and writes stocking on the board. Then she lists descriptors and ideas related to the stocking.

20. (Teacher walks around the room and checks in with individual students.)

21. Jennifer: "Pick one item from your list and write 3-5 sentences of description."

22. Gives time to work. (Jennifer walks around room and talks with individual students.)

23. Jennifer: "It is time to stop but continue to work on the drafts in order to share them tomorrow."

> *Researcher Comment: Jennifer continues to give specific guidance for the assignment. The students are reminded of how to use the dictionary to provide information for their topics. Jennifer uses a personal example to demonstrate a way for the students to organize their ideas about their topics. She encourages the students to clarify the difference between ideas, like clarifying the difference between Mexican and Puerto*

Rican. This idea provided a model of explaining what the topic is and what it is not. At the end of class when Jennifer asks students to continue their work, she frames the task as an ongoing conversation rather than as a school assignment. Through this comment, Jennifer moves the students further into the inquiry cycle so that they can continue drafting their work by noticing and naming what they see as important to their topics.

So What Happened?

We focused on this particular teaching episode because it gives a clear picture of how Jennifer mediated the inquiry process using instructional conversation. Jennifer did not expect students to instantly know their topic, but her actions and words demonstrate that she expected them to use the inquiry process to find a focus. Her efforts to help them find their topic indicated that she believed that her students had ideas about which to write. She did not need to assign topics or provide a list from which they could choose. Instead, she mediated her students by providing "just-in-time" response and support so the students had topics that they were willing to investigate. By exploring her own cultural practices, Jennifer encouraged the students to explore their cultural practices and languages to find a concept that they wanted to examine more closely. In a follow-up interview, Jennifer mentioned that her students were excited about their ideas for the essay. Further, she felt that her examples demonstrated the kind of topics that they could choose and that this teaching technique provided the differentiation that her students needed.

This teaching episode demonstrates that the students are given the time to develop their individual ideas. In true workshop fashion, Jennifer is working with the entire group while allowing each student to work at his or her own pace through their writing and thinking. She integrates time to write and time to talk. Although they have the same endpoint, a Definition Essay, the students follow their individual paths to get the end point.

Academic content knowledge is woven into the lesson by suggesting the use of the dictionary, by defining of more specific terms like "Mexican" or "Puerto Rican," and by listing and explaining the ways authors develop their ideas. Defining these differences will take specific word usage, which, in turn, will expand student vocabulary. Academic terminology is integrated into the teaching conversation rather than the focus of the lesson.

Despite the wide range of examples given during this lesson, Jennifer indicated that several of the students still needed a private conversation to be convinced that their topics were "significant." One student thought that if a topic was going to be significant, it had to be something that she was proud of or something she enjoyed. At the end of the conference, they agreed that the student's Definition Essay topic could be about being a "Vietnamese Baptist daughter." The student does not like this identity, so it was hard for her to think about writing on it, but after a conversation with Jennifer, the student recognized that this identity was significant and worth writing about.

Although only one student comment could be clearly heard during this teaching episode, we want to emphasize the idea that the students were engaged in the instructional conversation during the lesson, either speaking quietly to one another, individually to Jennifer, or writing in their writer's notebooks. Thus, each student had multiple opportunities for personal responses to Jennifer's questions and comments. Because this is an English class that focuses on the reading of British literature and developing the students' abilities to write, it is appropriate that the students were engaging in the instructional conversations through their writing.

We recognized that the conversations of teaching that were promoted in Jennifer's classroom invited students to be active participants in their learning and that each of the students was able to think deeply about the chosen topic. For Jennifer, writing instruction is about mediating student

Figure 1. Culturally Mediated Writing Instruction Inquiry Cycle. This figure illustrates the recursive phases in the instructional inquiry cycle described here.

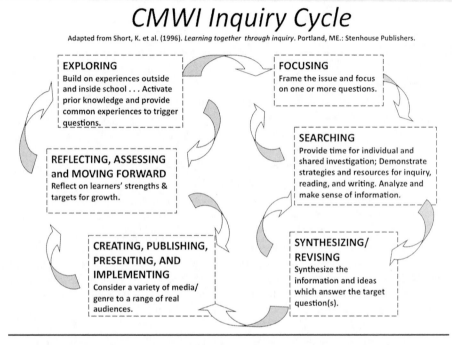

CMWI Inquiry Cycle

Adapted from Short, K. et al. (1996). *Learning together through inquiry*. Portland, ME.: Stenhouse Publishers.

EXPLORING
Build on experiences outside and inside school . . . Activate prior knowledge and provide common experiences to trigger questions.

FOCUSING
Frame the issue and focus on one or more questions.

SEARCHING
Provide time for individual and shared investigation; Demonstrate strategies and resources for inquiry, reading, and writing. Analyze and make sense of information.

REFLECTING, ASSESSING and MOVING FORWARD
Reflect on learners' strengths & targets for growth.

CREATING, PUBLISHING, PRESENTING, AND IMPLEMENTING
Consider a variety of media/ genre to a range of real audiences.

SYNTHESIZING/ REVISING
Synthesize the information and ideas which answer the target question(s).

learning through overlapping and layering instructional conversations. Jennifer's conversations of teaching provide the assistance that her students need while they demonstrate Vygotsky's (1978) theories related to the development of higher cognitive functions through interpersonal interaction.

IMPLICATIONS FOR CLASSROOM INSTRUCTION OF WRITING INSTRUCTION

In many classrooms, even in classrooms using a writing workshop (e.g., Atwell, 1998) approach, teachers teach students the "steps" of the writing process and then expect the students to follow those "steps" as they develop their writing assignments. For some students, this teaching practice is enough. But many students need more guidance. If we want students to be active participants in their learning, then we need instruction that encourages student participation and allows for various ways to participate. Teachers need to mediate the process by leading students through the process using multiple layers of assistance or "mini-inquiries" as the teacher models different kinds of support. If we want students to be active participants in their learning, then we need instruction that encourages student participation and allows for various ways to participate.

When teachers use these loosely structured conversational patterns to mediate, students are encouraged to engage in the writing process as they are able. These conversations provide multiple opportunities to engage and allow the students to determine when they are ready and how they will participate. Through this modeling, students are gradually released (Pearson & Gallagher 1983) to continue the work on their own.

Because writing occurs mostly in the writer's head, teacher conversations that model the process may support students' understandings of how to provide this writing experience for themselves. In this way, their intermental processes can move to intramental processes (Vygotsky, 1978) so that students move towards independence. Using teacher conversations in this way assumes an apprenticeship (Rogoff, 1990) approach to writing instruction that can make a difference in the way that students respond.

IMPLICATIONS FOR PROFESSIONAL DEVELOPMENT RELATED TO WRITING INSTRUCTION

Professional development for writing instruction must be more than a set of procedures, steps, or methods. Writing instruction is about inquiry. It is about the questions that teachers ask regarding their students' learning and about the instructional decisions informed by the inquiry. By leading the students through the inquiry cycle using personal and culturally relevant ideas, writing instruction can be made more engaging for the learner. Multiple opportunities to engage in a variety of experiences is essential.

However, individuals cannot teach what they do not know. They cannot set conditions for patterns that they have never experienced. Therefore, if we want teachers to adopt these practices, then we need to ensure that every teacher has participated in authentic writing/reading/learning conversations. Teachers must have professional development in which they learn by doing and by having conversations about the doing. Teachers must inquire, write, explore, confer, revise, and share. And teachers must have a Jennifer to mediate their learning through multiple overlapping and layered conversations.

REFERENCES

Applebee, A. (1996). *Curriculum as conversation: Transforming traditions of teaching and learning.* Chicago, IL: The University of Chicago Press.

Applebee, A., & Langer, J. (1983). Instructional scaffolding: Reading and writing as natural language activities. *Language Arts, 60,* 168–175.

Atwell, N. (1998). *In the middle: New understandings about writing, reading, learning* (2nd ed.). Portsmouth, NH: Boynton/Cook.

Ball, A. R. (2006). Teaching writing in culturally diverse classrooms. In C. A. MacArthur, C. A., Graham, S., & Fitzgerald, J. (Eds.) *Handbook of writing research.* New York, NY: The Guilford Press.

Burciaga, J. A. (1988). *Weedee peepo: A collection of essays.* Edinburg, TX: Pan American University Press.

Burke, J. (2003). *Writing reminders: Tools, tips, and techniques.* Portsmouth, NH: Heinemann.

Burke, J. (2010). *What's the big idea? Question-driven units to motivate reading, writing, and thinking.* Portsmouth, NH: Heinemann.

Cazden, C. B. (1979). Peekaboo as an instructional model: Discourse development at home and at school. *Papers and reports on child language development, 17,* 1-19.

Cazden, C. B. (1988). *Classroom discourse: The language of teaching and learning.* Portsmouth, NH: Heinemann.

Corbin, J., & Strauss. A. (2007). *Basics of qualitative research: Techniques and procedures for developing grounded theory.* Thousand Oaks, CA: Sage.

Daniels, H. (2001*). Literature circles: Voice and choice in book clubs and reading groups.* Portland, ME: Stenhouse.

Eeds, R., & Peterson, M. (1999). *Grand conversations: Literature groups in action.* New York, NY: Scholastic.

Freire, P. (1970). *Pedagogy of the oppressed.* New York, NY: Continuum.

Fu, D. (2009). *Writing between languages: How English language learners make the transition to fluency, grades 4-12.* Portsmouth, NH: Heinemann.

Gay, G. (2000). *Culturally responsive teaching: Theory, research, and practice.* New York, NY: Teachers College Press.

Heath, S. B. (1983). *Ways with words.* New York, NY: Cambridge University Press.

Jago, C. (2008). *Come to class: Lessons for high school writers*. Portsmouth, NH: Heinemann.

Johns, A. M. (1997). *Text, role, and context: Developing academic literacies*. Cambridge, NY: Cambridge University Press.

John-Steiner, V., & Mahn, H. (1996). Sociocultural approaches to learning and development: A Vygotskian framework. *Educational Psychologist, 31*(3/4), 191-206.

Ladson-Billings, B. (1992). Reading between the lines and beyond the pages: A culturally relevant approach to literacy teaching. *Theory into Practice, 31*, 312-320.

Lantolf, J. P., & Thorne, S. L. (2006.) *Sociocultural theory and the genesis of second language development*. Oxford, England: Oxford University Press.

Lee, C. (2007). *The role of culture in academic literacies: Conducting our blooming in the midst of the whirlwind*. New York, NY: Teachers College Press.

Mehan, H. (1978). Structuring school structure. *Harvard Educational Review, 48*, 32-64.

Mehan, H. (1979). *Learning lessons*. Cambridge, MA: Harvard University Press.

Moll, L. C., Amanti, C., Neff, D., & Gonzalez, N. (1992*).* Funds of knowledge for teaching: Using a qualitative approach to connect homes and classrooms. *Theory into Practice, 31*, 132-141.

Noddings, N. (2005). *The challenge to care in schools: An alternative approach to education*. New York, NY: Teachers College Press.

Palinscar, A., & Brown, A. (1984). Reciprocal teaching of comprehension-fostering and comprehension-monitoring activities. *Cognition and Instruction, 1*, 117-175.

Patterson, L., Wickstrom, C., & Araujo, J. (June, 2010). *Culturally Mediated Writing Instruction* (Final Report). Berkeley, CA: National Writing Project.

Patterson, L., Wickstrom, C., Roberts, J., Araujo, J., & Hoki, C. (2010). Deciding when to step in and when to back off: Culturally mediated writing instruction for adolescent English learners. *The Tapestry Journal, 2*(1), 1-18.

Pearson, P. D., & Gallagher, M. C. (1983). The instruction of reading comprehension. *Comtemporary Educational Psychology, 8*, 317-344.

Rebollo-Gil, G., & Moras, A. (2006). Defining an "anti" stance: Key pedagogical questions about engaging anti-racism in college classrooms. *Race, Ethnicity & Education, 9*, 381-394.

Rogoff, B. (1990). *Apprenticeship in thinking: Cognitive development in social contexts*. New York, NY: Oxford University Press.

Rogoff, B., & Wertsch, J. V. (1984). *Children's learning in the "zone of proximal development."* San Francisco, CA: Jossey-Bass.

Shor, I. (1992). *Empowering education: Critical teaching for social change*. Chicago, IL: University of Chicago Press.

Short, K. G., & Harste, J. C., & Burke, C. (1996). *Creating classrooms for authors and inquirers* (2nd ed.). Portsmouth, NH: Heinemann.

Tharp, R., & Gallimore, R. (1988). *Rousing minds to life*. Cambridge, NY: Cambridge University Press.

Vygotsky, L. S. (1978). *Mind in society: The development of higher psychological processes*. Cambridge, MA: Harvard University Press.

Wells, G. (1986). *The meaning makers: Children learning and using the language to learn*. Portsmouth, NH: Heinemann.

Wells, G. (2007). Semiotic mediation, dialogue and the construction of knowledge. *Human Development, 50*, 244-274.

Wells, G., & Chang-Wells, G. L. (1992). *Constructing knowledge together: Classrooms as centers of inquiry and literacy*. Portsmouth, NH: Heinemann.

Wickstrom, C., Araujo, J., Patterson, L., Hoki, C., & Roberts, J. (2011). Teachers prepare students for careers and college: "I see you", therefore I can teach you. In P. Dunston, K. H. Gambrell, P. Stecker, S. Fullerton, V. Gillis, & C. C. Bates (Eds.), *60ᵗʰ Literacy Research Association Yearbook*, (pp. 113-126), Oak Creek, WI: Literacy Research Association.

Wilhelm, J. D. (2007). *Engaging readers & writers with inquiry: promoting deep understandings in language arts and the content areas with guiding questions*. New York, NY: Scholastic.

Literacies on the Margins: Border Colonias as Sites for the Study of Language and Literacy

Patrick H. Smith
Amabilia V. Valenzuela
The University of Texas at El Paso

Border colonias—unplanned communities along the U.S.-Mexico border—are among the fastest growing and poorest communities in the U.S. (Martínez, 2010). Although in the public imagination colonias are densely populated by immigrants from Mexico, poverty, and disease (Hill, 2003), residents regard them as zones of economic opportunity and transformation where poor people can "make a middle-class kind of place" (Campbell & Heyman, 2007, p. 16). Colonias are among the most bilingual communities in the country. Many residents describe themselves as bilingual speakers of Spanish and English (de la Puente & Stemper, 2003), and even a quick walk or drive through a border colonia will attest that residents produce diverse texts, many of them bilingual and multimodal, in the form of advertisements and other publicly displayed texts. Thus, although English literacy rates for children and adults living in colonias are historically low (Ellis, 1995; Rodriguez, 2007), residents are surrounded by texts they navigate in their daily lives.

Our objectives in this paper are to introduce border colonias as sites for literacy research and to propose an agenda for research that focuses on the literacies of border colonias. To do this, we summarize colonia research conducted over the past decade and identify conceptual issues for future literacy research and practice. First, we provide an overview of border colonias and explain why they are compelling sites for studies of language and literacy. Next, we review the growing scholarly literature and documentary record on Texas border colonias, including local press, government archives, and census records. Using Quantitative Content Analysis (QCA), we summarize recent research in order to gauge the present state of knowledge about colonia literacies and related areas such as education. Informed by this analysis, we conclude with a discussion of how literacy research can contribute to more complete understandings of border colonias and, potentially, to increased agency and quality of life for colonia residents.

LOCATING BORDER COLONIAS

Although border colonias are also found in Arizona, New Mexico, and California, Texas is home to more colonia residents than any other state. Approximately 500,000 Texans live in some 2,300 colonia communities along the 1,248-mile stretch from Brownsville on the Gulf of Mexico to El Paso in the west (Texas State Energy Conservation Office, 2010). Figure 1 shows the distribution of colonias along the Texas-Mexico border.

The greatest concentrations of colonias are found in the Lower Rio Grande Valley counties of Hidalgo and Cameron counties in east Texas; El Paso County in far west Texas; and Webb County (Laredo) in between. Holz and Davies (1993, pp. 10-11) list common features of border colonias: (a) located in rural areas but often close to town; (b) developed on land units of 10 to 20 acres; (c) well-developed street pattern with mostly unpaved streets; (d) divided into small lots, typically

Figure 1. Colonias in Texas Within 100 Miles of the U.S.-Mexico Border. Adapted from Parcher and Humberson, 2007, p. 2.

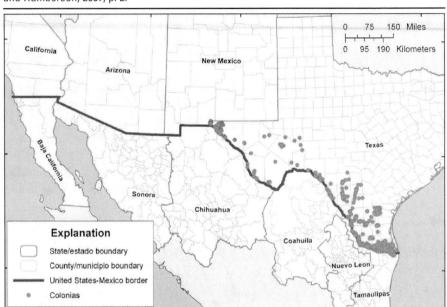

about 60 by 100 feet; (e) contain mostly small, substandard houses; (f) high frequency of litter (due to no public waste service; (g) impacted by agricultural activities on surrounding cultivated land; and (h) lack essential services.

Although they share many characteristics, each colonia experiences unique local conditions. For example, access to drinking water and waste water facilities are challenges that face colonia communities all along the border, but they are not the same in El Paso (where water scarcity is a fact of desert life) as in the lower Rio Grande Valley (where sea-level elevations experience flooding during hurricanes and tropical storms). Individuals and families in colonias have distinct personal, immigration, and labor histories, as well as dispositions for agency that allow them to react differently to environmental, structural, and economic conditions. Thus, we stress the need to avoid essentializing border colonias as sites for research.

Origins and Demographics

Colonia-like communities have existed on both sides of the U.S.-Mexico border since at least the 1950s (Richardson, 1996). In the 1980s, rapid growth in the number of colonias and in the number of colonia residents in the U.S. was spurred by increased demand for cheap labor and inexpensive housing. Weak zoning laws permitted real estate developers to create new subdivisions and sell housing lots without first installing water, drainage, and other services (Ward, 1999). In 1990 the Gonzalez National Affordable Housing Act (NAHA) defined a colonia as an "identifiable community in Arizona, California, New Mexico or Texas within 150 miles of the U.S.-Mexico border, lacking decent water and sewage systems" (cited in Núñez & Klammenger, 2010). Passage of the North American Free Trade Agreement (NAFTA) in 1994 and consequent demand for low-pay, low-skill labor at the border, is another factor in the rapid growth of colonia populations.

Research in colonias presents unique challenges. Colonias are typically unincorporated territories "at the margins" of binational cities (Núñez & Klammenger, 2010), and the county governments nominally responsible for maintaining local population records often lack the funding and perhaps the political will to carefully document populations in colonia settlements (Smith, 2010). Efforts to document colonia populations through the U.S. Census face difficulties, including: (a) identifying residences without street names or numbers; (b) hiring and training bilingual census takers; and (c) providing adequate translation of instructions (Campbell, 2003). Additionally, accurate counts of colonia residents are undermined by the effects of intimidating immigration policies that may discourage them from participating in the Census. Finally, there is the perplexing problem of definitions, as state, federal, and local agencies count colonia communities and residents using various criteria, with estimates of colonias ranging between 1,400 and 2,400 communities in Texas (Guisti, 2010).

Despite these challenges, demographic research consistently reports that colonia residents are, on average, younger, poorer, and have completed fewer years of formal schooling than other Latinas/os in Texas (Donelson & Esparza, 2010; Ellis, 1995). Although seldom reported, positive findings include a greater proportion of two-parent households; a high percentage of families owning or buying their own homes; and households in which adults and children share the same language(s) (Díaz, 2011).

A growing number of ethnographic studies seek to describe colonias from the perspective of residents. Ethnographic work thus contextualizes, and in some cases counters, the portraits of colonias as described by demographers, sociologists, and public health researchers, whose research relies primarily on surveys (Campbell, 2003). For example, Dolhinow's (2010) study of women's shifting roles in three colonias near El Paso describes transnational and community aspects of life in colonias not considered in other types of research:

> For all intents and purposes, [colonias] are Mexican communities. Yet these are in the United States, and many of these Mexican immigrants are U.S. citizens, and others are fully documented residents with social security numbers and all the other symbols of "American-ness." At the same time, you often feel as if you have stepped across the border when you walk into a colonia: the houses are often surrounded by brightly painted flowerbeds, and there is loud Mexican music playing on a Saturday morning. It always smells like strong chile is cooking, and there are other trappings of Mexican culture on display. Colonias come to exist out of transnational flows of labor and capital that converge in isolated pieces of unused farmland. They are communities with significant ties to Mexico that are reproduced in the United States (Dolhinow, 2010, p. 26).

Typically, close to 100% of colonia residents in Texas are of Mexican origin. Thus, colonias differ from immigrant beachheads in urban centers and nonborder communities in that they are not very ethnically or linguistically diverse. While this ethnic concentration may limit opportunities for immigrant integration, residents choose to live in colonias, in part, because they feel safe "being Mexican" there. A mother from a colonia in Hidalgo County expressed this feeling of security:

> In the colonias people live peacefully because if someone needs something you

can just ask your neighbor and borrow it. Here you live like a family and the children play together in the afternoon, they all play in someone's yard or in the street (Villarreal, 2008, p. 53).

Metaphors

Reinking (2011) notes the power of metaphors to "set agendas, to shape perceptions, and to inspire action" in literacy research and policy (p. 5). The following list, based on Núñez and Klammenger's (2010) work, includes metaphors commonly used to describe border colonias:

- the "Third World inside the U.S." (Galán, 2000);
- economic and political margins on the borders of globalizing cities;
- environmental hazards; "sites of failed hygiene" and pathology (Hill, 2003);
- corridors for international and internal migration, through which residents pass en route to seasonal jobs in other states;
- buffers, safety nets, and safety valves that provide affordable housing and economic opportunities, including in the informal economy, that are not easily found elsewhere;
- traps where those with poor credit or no credit are lured into monthly payments they cannot sustain; and where marginality is magnified (access to health care, basic services, and transportation);
- havens where it is easier to be Mexican and safer to live with family members whose immigration status may put others in jeopardy (Núñez & Heyman, 2007).

By examining the metaphors used to describe colonias and colonia residents, we can gain insight into the ways the literacies of border colonias are conceived and portrayed.

Why Colonias are Important Sites for Literacy Research

In keeping with our objective of proposing a research agenda that focuses on colonia literacies, we believe there are three primary reasons why colonias are important sites for literacy research. First and foremost, colonia literacies matter because of the large numbers of children and adults who live in border colonias. As the initial U.S. residence for immigrant families maintaining close ties to Mexico, colonias are ideal contexts for investigating literacies crossing borders (Smith & Murillo, forthcoming). Currently, middle-class families, including professionals with high levels of formal education, are moving to U.S. border cities to escape drug-related violence in Ciudad Juárez, Matamoros, and other cities in northern Mexico (Martínez, Alvarado, & Chávez, 2011). The integration of these newest immigrants into the local schools that serve colonia populations is a major development in education at the border (Valdés, 2011). Research in colonias can help us understand how literacy is understood and practiced by those who have been educated in two distinct education systems (Miller, 2003; Smith, Murillo, & Jiménez, 2009).

Second, border colonias are intriguing contexts for broadening current theories about the use and development of biliteracy (Reyes, 2011). As overwhelmingly bilingual communities, colonias embody discourses of place (at the border, on the margins of cities) as well as the movements and flows of people, ideas, services, and products taking place in two languages (de la Piedra & Araujo, forthcoming). Because colonia residents "incorporate daily activities, routines, and institutions located both in a destination country and transnationally" (Levitt & Glick-Schiller, 2007, p. 182), research on the forms and practices of Spanish and English literacy they generate can inform the study of biliteracy in transnational contexts.

Third, given the historic lack of access to services and the individual and collective actions of colonia residents to secure them (Donelson & Esparza, 2010), colonias are rich sites for investigating the literate consequences of immigrant agency. Border anthropologists Howard Campbell and Joseph Heyman (2007) propose the term "slantwise" to describe the moves that colonia residents make in order to secure housing, water, employment, healthcare, and education. These authors critique conventional binary models of agency that, they claim, assume that people's decisions and actions can be categorized as examples of either compliance with or resistance to government regulations. Based on participant observation in colonia households in West Texas, they argue that a more nuanced view of agency is needed to account for actions that may be instances of transgression (such as the practice of registering children at school under a U.S. address while the family's legal address remains in Mexico), but which are undertaken to realize socially accepted goals (such as attempting to provide safety or the best education possible for one's children).

CONTENT ANALYSIS

In preparation for a comparative study on literacy practices in colonias in the El Paso and lower Rio Grande Valley regions, we read everything we could find about border colonias. We soon realized that research on colonias is reported in many distinct formats and from multiple disciplinary perspectives. To make sense of these diverse sources, we created a corpus of research publications and reports about Texas border colonias. We initially searched for combinations of the keywords "colonia," "literacy," and "education," but found few examples. For this reason, we expanded our search to include publications that addressed factors commonly associated with literacy, education, and schools (for example, parents' years of education, child poverty, and school funding). Our final corpus consisted of 160 texts published between 2000 and 2011.

We used QCA to identify, categorize, and count the main themes found in our corpus. Content analysis involves a "systematic and replicable" analysis of messages (Riffe, Lacy, & Fico, 2005, p. 23) and is useful as a prelude to empirical research in underexplored domains such as border colonias (Berg, 1995). The corpus was analyzed in two phases. The first round of analysis consisted of classifying the 160 texts by literature source, resulting in the following 10 categories: journals (n = 43, 27%); books (n = 22, 14%); newspapers (n = 36, 23%); electronic media (n = 18, 11%); reports from state (n = 10, 6%), county (n = 2, 1%), and federal (n = 7, 4%) levels of government; reports from independent school districts (n = 3, 2%); university websites (n = 9, 6%); and dissertations (n = 10, 6%). The highest number of published texts was found in journals while the lowest number was found in the category of county reports.

In the second phase of analysis, we classified the texts in our corpus according to dominant theme. This classification resulted in six main themes: (a) Education/Literacy; (b) Socio-Political; (c) Economy; (d) Health/Environment; (e) Housing; and (f) Public services/Transportation.

The analysis of thematic frequencies is represented in Figure 2. The highest number (73) of published works fell under the socio-political theme, or 46% of the total number of texts.

Figure 2. Number and Percentage of Texts in a Colonia Corpus, by Theme

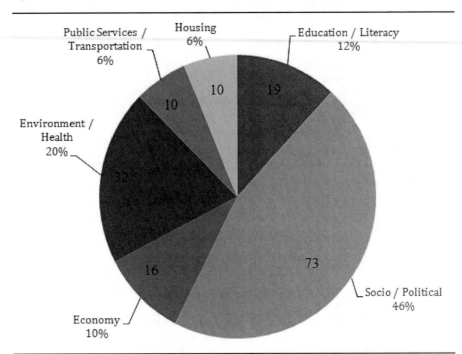

Conversely, the theme of education/literacy was represented in only 19 publications, or 12% of the texts in our corpus.

LITERACIES ON THE MARGINS

Content analysis demonstrates that research on border colonias has largely ignored issues of education, language, and literacy. This finding is consistent with previous research (Donelson & Esparza, 2010; Ward, 1999), and reflects the predominance of what Guisti (2010) calls "place-based" rather than "people-centered approaches" to colonia research and policy. These findings are relevant to our purposes of introducing colonias as research sites and proposing a research agenda focusing on the literacies of border colonias. The theme of education was addressed to different degrees. Few studies focused specifically on language or literacy. Instead, we found numerous passing or superficial mentions of literacy within general discussions of educational attainment by colonia residents and the educational issues they face. For example, an article about service learning in an after-school program in a colonia community center described a student-organized drive to raise money to buy school uniforms (Castillo & Winchester, 2001) for students living in the colonia. The authors listed activities that must have involved multiple uses of literacy (identifying and contacting local businesses for donations, record-keeping, thank-you letters), but provided few details about students' writing and reading during the project.

Across disciplinary orientations, texts in the corpus presented education as lacking or incomplete in colonia communities and, by extension, their residents. For example, Coronado

(2003) noted that parents in colonias have limited formal schooling, often leaving school in order to work. Public health research portrayed the Spanish dominance of colonia residents as limiting the effectiveness of public outreach (Peña & Rosenthal, 2010), including the nonstandard Spanish literacies of the *promotoras* (community outreach workers) who conduct surveys and disseminate information about health services. Public policy research examining access to potable water and wastewater treatment services cited residents' limited formal education and English literacy as barriers to equitable distribution of resources and services (Lopez & Reich, 1997).

Likewise, ethnographic accounts tell us little about the literacy practices of people living in border colonias. For example, Dolhinow's (2010) study of women's roles in community development found that mothers were more likely than fathers to read written communication sent home from school with children, but did not consider parents' responses to these notes. Similarly, ethnographic studies of the work of *promotoras* show that these community workers disseminate, interpret, and coproduce written texts as they conduct door-to-door surveys; schedule appointments for home visits; share information about education and health services; and translate legal and medical notices (Contreras, 2005; Villarreal, 2008), but not how *promotoras* learn to develop these specific literacy practices, or how these practices may impact families and other community residents. Thus, although ethnographic studies have reinforced the importance of multiple forms of literacy in the lives of colonia residents, overall, they provide few details about the actual uses and production of colonia literacies.

As this review has noted, border colonias are portrayed in the literature as communities "on the margins" (Núñez & Klammenger, 2010). It is not surprising then, to find that the literacies of colonia residents, like those of other marginalized communities, have received little scholarly attention. As "colonia studies" emerges as a "field of study worthy of its own identity" (Smith, 2010, p. 245), this identity is only beginning to consider literacy as an object of study or to include findings from literacy research. The paucity of literacy research in the context of border colonias, in turn, reinforces unfounded notions that literacy is unimportant in the lives of colonia residents and that colonia literacies are, therefore, unworthy of study. In the following sections, we discuss ways that literacy research can challenge these assumptions and how a research agenda focusing on the literacies of colonias might contribute to the demarginalization of colonia residents.

DE-MARGINALIZING COLONIA LITERACIES

Our review of research in border colonias identified recent studies that challenge common deficit assumptions about colonia literacies by providing details of specific literacy practices of colonia residents. Díaz (2011) examined family support for Spanish language maintenance in a colonia in Cameron County. She found strong support for children's development of oral Spanish, but less explicit support for children's literacy in Spanish. She attributed this difference to English-only discourses and practices in local schools, which were further reinforced in the after-school tutoring program that served as the focal point of her study. Díaz (2011) also noted residents' resistance when similar language policies were enacted in the local Catholic church, suggesting that family support for Spanish literacy in colonia communities is domain-specific rather than absolute.

The digital literacy practices of immigrant youth in the same Cameron County colonia were explored by Bussert-Webb (2011), who found that elementary school children's peer-to-peer, out-of-school digital literacy practices, such as text messaging, were more likely to be authored in Spanish than in English. Children attributed the choice of Spanish to their preference of that language for expressions of friendship and intimacy. This pattern was noted even among students unable to afford their own cellphone or other digital devices, which participants explained as a matter of sharing technologies and ideas for how to use them with wealthier peers.

In a pair of studies involving residents of Hidalgo County colonias, Murillo (forthcoming) worked with bilingual reading teachers to explore bilingual families' literacy practices and found that household and workplace literacies were conducted primarily in Spanish, particularly in families in which adults were self-employed. Murillo (2010) also described the use of case studies in the preparation of reading teachers at a border university. By collecting and analyzing digital photographs of publicly displayed texts in border colonias, preservice teachers came to understand the diverse forms and functions of literacies in colonia communities. They documented a range of family and work-related literacies used in colonia households, and observed that although Spanish and bilingual writing were accepted as legitimate in some domains (advertising, business, and religion), they were less welcome in local schools. In both studies, teachers expressed surprise that students in colonia families were immersed in so much reading and writing at home, and also that so much of it was taking place in Spanish.

Collectively, these studies underscore the importance of literacy in the lives of colonia residents. They show that, in contrast to uninformed and deficit views of colonia residents' literacies, children and adults in colonias are engaging in the creation and interpretation of texts in traditional print and multimodal forms. Furthermore, they suggest that teachers who may hold such deficit views about colonia literacies can learn to see them more positively when provided with explicit guidance. Finally, they provide insight into the views and practices of bilingual parents with respect to the use of Spanish literacy in school and non-school domains.

LITERACY RESEARCH AND AGENCY

Research on the literacies of border colonias could also contribute to the development of agency among colonia residents. As we have seen, Campbell and Heyman (2007) found that residents improve their lives by engaging in "slantwise" practices that defy easy categorization as either compliance or resistance. In our own work, we think that some of the ways colonia residents use written Spanish (providing religious instruction in Spanish while supporting English literacy development in school, and the production of bilingual advertisements to attract bilingual and biliterate consumers) are slantwise ways of developing biliteracy (Smith & Murillo, forthcoming). Another example comes from 8th- and 9th-grade students in colonias in the Lower Rio Grande Valley and in El Paso County, who published a book of captioned photographs depicting daily life in their communities (Chahin, 2000). Although the purpose of this collection was to show how people live in colonias, in doing so, these young photographers documented the use of literacy tools such as computers, typewriters, calendars, and televisions, as well as the presence of texts including books, birthday cards, notebooks, food and product packaging, and religious literacies. This project suggests that agency among colonia youth could be supported by research that examined the artifactual literacies (Pahl & Rowsell, 2010) of colonia life, and by writing that connects expressions of youth identity with the meanings of texts and objects found in colonias.

We also see potential for the development of agency through projects that develop youth literacies using digital tools and with the expectation of an audience beyond the level of classroom or school. Bussert-Webb's (2011) observation that colonia youth are finding ways to author digital texts although they themselves are not (yet) owners of the hardware needed to produce them is one example of slantwise agency around digital literacies that might be unnecessary or invisible among youth with easier access to computers and smartphones.

Finally, we see some evidence that the relationship between agency and literacy in colonias is highly gendered. While border colonias were often created by Mexican families that moved to the U.S. seeking employment for male family members, the demographics and local economies of colonias are contributing to a shift away from idealized notions of males as paid workers outside the home and females as unpaid workers at home (Vaccaro & Lessem, 1999). Recent research suggests that women's income generation in the informal economy (making and selling food, and engaging in the care of young children and elderly adults) is critical to the economic viability of at least some colonia households (Smith & Murillo, forthcoming). Other studies show that women are also emerging as civic leaders in colonia communities, particularly in association with religious and nongovernmental organizations (Dohlinow, 2010). Given the role women play in many colonia households as managers of calendars and other record-keeping systems that help manage family activities and obligations (e.g., doctors' appointments, bill payments, school events, and religious and civic responsibilities), literacy researchers might ask how women's leadership in family domains and in community work shapes the production and interpretation of texts and literacy practices in colonias. Conversely, what kinds of additional literacy training and knowledge are women receiving in their roles as *promotoras*? How do they learn to successfully handle the literacy demands needed in order to be able to conduct door-to-door surveys; schedule appointments for home visits; translate legal and medical documents; and interpret for non-English fluent residents? (Villarreal, 2008). Does this training and/or the literacies practiced by *promotoras* lead women to pursue additional formal education, including university degrees? We believe that research on such questions would shed light on and perhaps celebrate the role of literacy in helping women and families in colonias move away from the margins.

CONCLUSION

This study focused on border colonias, a particular type of unplanned and under-researched transnational community on the U.S.-Mexico border. In Texas, colonias are home to a growing number of Spanish-speaking and bilingual children and families of Mexican origin. Given their unique characteristics as physically bounded, ethnically and linguistically homogenous, and economically and politically marginalized communities, border colonias are promising and potentially illuminating sites for literacy research. We conducted a quantitative content analysis of a corpus of 160 scholarly texts, government reports, and examples of local journalism that addressed aspects of life in Texas border colonias. The most numerous sources in our corpus were journals, followed by newspaper articles and books. In terms of content, texts that featured socio-political and environmental/health themes were most common.

Despite the emergence of "colonias studies" as a distinct field of research, our analysis showed that very few studies have looked closely at education in border colonias. To date, even fewer examine how residents perceive, produce, and practice literacy. We argue that the lack of literacy research in border colonias reflects and reinforces the belief that literacy is unimportant in the lives of colonia residents, and that scholars are unaware of the unique forms and practices of literacy in colonias or do not consider them to be worthy of study. To counter unfounded and deficit assumptions about colonia literacies, we reviewed recent studies that focused more directly on aspects of language and literacy in border colonias. These included: (a) family support for biliteracy; (b) preservice teachers' attitudes toward colonias and the forms of language and literacy practiced in colonia households; and (c) the digital literacy practices of colonia youth. We proposed a research agenda to focus on colonia literacies, and suggested ways that such research might contribute to the de-marginalization of colonia literacies and the development of agency among residents of border colonias.

AUTHORS' NOTE

Patrick H. Smith, Department of Teacher Education, University of Texas at El Paso; Amabilia V. Valenzuela, PhD Program in Teaching, Learning & Culture, University of Texas at El Paso. This research was supported by the Office of Sponsored Projects at The University of Texas at El Paso. Correspondence concerning this article should be addressed to Patrick H. Smith, Department of Teacher Education, University of Texas at El Paso, 500 W. University Avenue, El Paso, TX 79968. E-mail: phsmith@utep.edu

REFERENCES

Berg, B. L. (1995). *Qualitative research methods for the social sciences* (2nd ed.). Boston, MA: Allyn & Bacon.

Bussert-Webb, K. (2011). Becoming socially just disciplinary teachers through a community service learning project. *Journal of Language and Literacy Education* [Online], *7*(2), 44-66. Retrieved from http://www.coe.uga.edu/jolle/2011_2/bussert_webb.pdf

Campbell, H. (2003). The U.S. Census 2000 and "colonias" along the U.S.-Mexico border: An anthropological approach. In C. T. Brenner, I. Coronado, & D. L. Soden (Eds.), *Dígame!: Policy and politics on the Texas border* (pp. 275-293). Dubuque, IA: Kendall/Hunt Publications.

Campbell, H., & Heyman, J. (2007). Slantwise: Beyond domination and resistance on the border. *Journal of Contemporary Ethnography, 36*(1), 3-30. doi: 10.1177/0891241606287000.

Castillo, Y., & Winchester, M. (2001). After school in a colonia. *Educational Leadership, 58*(7), 67-70.

Chahin, J. (2000). *Children of the Colonias Project: Through our own lenses.* Southwest San Marcos, TX: Texas State University.

Contreras, R. (2005). *Promotoras of the U.S.-Mexico border: An ethnographic study of cultural brokerage, agency, and community development.* (Unpublished doctoral dissertation). University of Florida.

Coronado, I. (2003). La vida en las colonias de la frontera/Life in colonias on the border. *Latino Studies, 1*, 193-197.

de la Piedra, M. T., & Araujo, B. (forthcoming). Transfronterizo literacies and content in a dual language classroom. *International Journal of Bilingual Education and Bilingualism.* Manuscript submitted for publication.

de la Puente, M., & Stemper, D. (2003). *The enumeration of colonias in Census 2000: Perspectives of ethnographers and census enumerators.* Washington, DC: Statistical Research Division, U.S. Census Bureau.

Díaz, M. E. (2011). *A case study of Spanish language use in a Texas border colonia*. Unpublished doctoral dissertation. The University of Texas at Brownsville.

Dolhinow, R. (2010). *A jumble of needs: Women's activism and neoliberalism in the colonias of the Southwest*. Minneapolis, MN: University of Minnesota Press.

Donelson, A. J., & Esparza, A. X. (Eds.), (2010). *The colonias reader: Economy, housing, and public health in U.S.-Mexico border colonias*. Tucson, AZ: The University of Arizona Press.

Ellis, D. R. (1995). *Socioeconomic differentials among selected colonia and non-colonia population on the Texas-Mexico border*. Unpublished doctoral dissertation, Department of Urban and Regional Science, Texas A&M University. (UMI Number 9539198).

Galán, H. (2000). *The forgotten Americans*. Austin, TX: Southwest Texas State University.

Guisti, C. (2010). Microbusiness in Texas colonias. In A. J. Donelson, & A. X. Esparza (Eds.), *The colonias reader: Economy, housing, and public health in U.S.-Mexico border colonias* (pp. 30-43). Tucson, AZ: The University of Arizona Press.

Hill, S. (2003). Metaphoric enrichment and material poverty: The making of "colonias." In P. Vila (Ed.), *Ethnography at the border* (pp. 141-165). Minneapolis, MN: University of Minnesota Press.

Holz, R. K., & Davies, C. S. (1993). *Third World Colonias: Lower Rio Grande Valley*. Working Paper No. 72. Lyndon B. Johnson School of Public Affairs. Austin, TX: University of Texas at Austin.

Levitt, P., & Glick-Schiller, N. (2007). Conceptualizing simultaneity: A transnational social field perspective on society. In A. Portes & J. DeWind (Eds.), *Rethinking migration: New theoretical and empirical perspectives* (pp. 181-218). New York, NY: Berghahn Books.

Lopez, C. M., & Reich, M. R. (1997). Agenda denial and water access in Texas colonias. In R. W. Cobb & M. H. Ross (Eds.), *Cultural strategies of agenda denial: Avoidance, attack, and redefinition* (pp. 159-179). Lawrence, KS: The University of Kansas Press.

Martínez, O. J. (2010). The U.S.-Mexico border economy. In A. J. Donelson, & A. X. Esparza (Eds.), *The colonias reader: Economy, housing, and public health in U.S.-Mexico border colonias* (pp. 15-29). Tucson, AZ: The University of Arizona Press.

Martínez, J. C., Alvarado, R., & Chávez, N. (2011, June 30). Exploring business, immigration, schools. *Mexodus Project*: University of Texas at El Paso. Retrieved from http://mexodus.borderzine.com/business/mexodus.

Miller, R. (2003). *Literacy instruction in Mexico*. Bloomington, IN: Phi Delta Kappa International Studies in Education.

Murillo, L. A. (2010). Local literacies as counter-hegemonic practices: Deconstructing anti-Spanish ideologies in the Rio Grande Valley. In V. J. Risko, R. T. Jiménez, & D. W. Rowe (Eds.), *59ʰ Yearbook of the National Reading Conference*. Oak Creek, WI: Literacy Research Association.

Murillo, L. A. (forthcoming). Learning from bilingual family literacies in the Rio Grande Valley. *Language Arts*.

Núñez, G. G., & Heyman, J. (2007). Entrapment processes and immigrant communities in a time of heightened border vigilance. *Human Organization, 66*(4), 354-365. Retrieved from http://sfaa.metapress.com/app/home/main.asp

Núñez, G. G., & Klammenger, G. M. (2010). Centering the margins: The transformation of community in colonias on the U.S.-Mexico border. In K. Staudt, C. M. Fuentes, & J. E. F. Monárrez, (Eds.), *Cities and citizenship at the U.S.-Mexico border* (pp. 147-172). New York, NY: Palgrave-Macmillan.

Pahl, K., & Rowsell, J. (2010). *Artifactual literacies: Every object tells a story*. New York, NY: Teachers College Press.

Parcher, J. W., & Humberson, D. G. (2007). *CHIPS: A new way to monitor colonias along the United States-Mexico border*. U.S. Department of Interior, U.S. Geological Survey. Retrieved from http://pubs.usgs.gov/of/2007/1230/pdf/OFR2007-1230.pdf

Peña, S., & Rosenthal, E. L. (2010). Colonias health issues in Texas. In A. J. Donelson, & A. X. Esparza. (Eds.), *The colonias reader: Economy, housing, and public health in U.S.-Mexico border colonias* (pp. 176-189). Tucson, AZ: The University of Arizona Press.

Reinking, D. (2011). Beyond the laboratory and lens: New metaphors for literacy research. In P. J. Dunston, L. B. Gambrell, K. Headley, S. K. Fullerton, P. M. Stecker, V. R. Gillis, & C. C. Bates (Eds.), *60ʰ Yearbook of the Literacy Research Association* (pp. 1-17). Oak Creek, WI: Literacy Research Association.

Reyes, M. de la Luz. (Ed.). (2011). *Words were all we had: Becoming biliterate against the odds*. New York, NY: Teachers College Press.

Richardson, C. (1996). Building strength from within: Colonias of the Rio Grande Valley. *Journal of Borderlands Studies, 11*(2), 51-68.

Riffe, D., Lacy, S., & Fico, F. G. (2005). *Analyzing media messages: Using quantitative content analysis in research.* Mahwah, NJ: Lawrence Erlbaum Associates.

Rodriguez, C. G. (2007). *A case study of the perceptions of current and former school board members of a recently annexed, rural, impoverished, South Texas, Latino school district in a high stakes accountability system.* (Unpublished doctoral dissertation). Texas A & M University.

Smith, P. H., & Murillo, L. A. (forthcoming). Researching transfronterizo literacies in Texas border colonias. *International Journal of Bilingual Education and Bilingualism,* Special themed issue on "Literacies Crossing Borders."

Smith, P. H., Murillo, L. A., & Jiménez, R. T. (2009). The social construction of literacy in a Mexican community: Coming soon to your school? In J. Scott, D. Straker, & L. Katz (Eds.). *Affirming students' rights to their own language: Bridging language policies to teaching practices.* (pp. 303-318). New York, NY: Routledge/National Council of Teachers of English.

Smith, W. D. (2010). A sustainability praxis for the future of colonias development and colonias studies. In A. J. Donelson, & A. X. Esparza. (Eds.), *The colonias reader: Economy, housing, and public health in U.S.-Mexico border colonias* (pp. 235-245). Tucson, AZ: The University of Arizona Press.

Texas State Energy Conservation Office. (2010). *Colonias projects.* Retrieved from http://www.seco.cpa.state.tx.us/colonias.htm

Vaccaro, G., & Lessem, A. (1999). Mexican women confront mainstream policy: Voices from the colonias address family self-sufficiency. *Advancing Women in Leadership Journal, 4.* Retrieved from http://www.advancingwomen.com/awl/awl_journal_archive.html

Valdés, G. (2011, June). *Teaching, learning, and leadership in times of violence.* Conference for International Research on Cross-cultural Learning in Education, University of Texas at El Paso.

Villarreal, A. C. (2008). *Language and culture in health promotion: Promotoras de salud in two colonias in the Lower Rio Grande Valley.* (Unpublished master's thesis). Department of Spanish, University of Texas Pan American.

Ward, P. M. (1999). *Colonias and public policy in Texas and in Mexico: Urbanization by stealth.* Austin, TX: The University of Texas Press.

Becoming Authors Online: Immigrant Students' Identity Work in Blog Composition

Silvia Noguerón-Liu
University of Georgia

> The affordances of the new technologies of representation and communication enable those who have access to them to be 'authors,' even if authors of a new kind—that is, to produce texts, to alter texts, to write and to 'write back.' Where before the author was publicly legitimated and endorsed figure, now there is no such gatekeeping.
> (Kress, 2003, p. 173)

> *Hacemos una página, pero una página ¿para quién o qué?... Tienes que ser experto en algo... tener un doctorado por ejemplo, para escribir sobre un tema.*
> We create a [web]page, but a page, for whom or for what?…You have to be an expert in something… having a doctorate, for example, to write about a topic.
> (Rafael, field notes, 2-1-10)

What does it mean to be an author in online spaces? This question was discussed in a web-design class for adult immigrant learners, where I participated as an instructor and researcher. As Kress (2003) states in the quote above, new technologies facilitate paths for writers to craft and publish texts. However, it takes more than new platforms to make online publishing accessible to all, as Rafael's concerns in the above quote show. This article analyzes the experiences of two students in the course and the ways they positioned themselves during the composition process and in their blogs, as well as the various resources that informed their writing efforts.

Researchers in the field of New Literacies Studies (Coiro, Knobel, Lankshear, & Leu, 2008; New London Group, 1996) have explored the potential of digital media production for historically marginalized groups to exercise agency (Hull & Katz, 2006; Hull, Zacher, & Hibbert, 2009). Studies of alternative programs highlight the ways adolescents engage in digital literacies to author counternarratives about themselves and their communities (Sandoval & Latorre, 2008; Vasudevan, 2006). Similarly, case studies of first-generation immigrant adolescents explore how they construct identities as competent multilingual writers through web design, fanfiction writing or online-based communication (Black, 2006; Lam, 2000, 2006; McGinnis, Goostein-Stolzenberg & Costa Saliani, 2007). However, the need to examine the digital literacies of adult, foreign-born, Spanish-speaking immigrants is critical. According to survey data, there is a gap in Internet use between foreign-born Latinos (51%) and Latinos born in the U. S. (85%). Furthermore, only 35% of Spanish-dominant Latinos go online, compared with 77% of bilingual Latinos and 87% of English-dominant Latinos (Livingston, 2010).

As the field of New Literacy Studies moves towards theorizing practices beyond the "local" (Brandt & Clinton, 2002), translocal inquiries raise questions about how texts and practices travel, how they are produced and consumed in various contexts, and how they are transformed and transform their readers. Considering the current shifting demographics, increasing migration and changing nature of new technologies, empirical work in literacy studies should account for the dynamic flows across sites and modalities (Baynham & Prinsloo, 2009). Building on this body of work, this article documents the experiences of novice writers of digital texts, whose lives and practices traverse spatial, textual, and digital borderlands.

THEORETICAL FRAMEWORK

This study draws from perspectives that account for the relationship between identity, transnationalism, and multimodal composition in digital platforms. A social semiotics perspective (Kress, 2009, 2011) allows me to theorize how semiotic resources are mobilized, remade, and regulated by individuals—for instance, integrating and repurposing images and videos in blog entries. However, I also consider the ways in which digital writing takes place in particular contexts, shaped by social and cultural practices (Street, 2009). Pahl and Rowsell (2011) pay close attention to local contexts in their framing of literacy as artifactual, noting the situated meanings and materiality of texts and objects, and the emic perspectives they can elicit from participants. The analysis of semiotic resources, in conjunction with the relationships, interactions, and local practices in classrooms where texts are produced, can better illustrate the nuances of multimodal composition to enact authorial agency (Hull & Katz, 2006) and adopt authorial stances, "taking on literate identities and claiming a presence as an author and narrator of one's own experiences" (Vasudevan, Schultz, & Bateman, 2010, p. 461).

To explore the flows of resources and ideas across localities, I also draw from the concept of transnational literacies, the "written language practices of people who are involved in activities that span national boundaries" (Jiménez, Smith, & Teague, 2009, p. 17). In immigrant communities, literacy practices shape and are also transformed by the circulation of information connecting individuals with their sending and receiving nations (Levitt & Glick Schiller, 2004). Previous research with Latino students documents the value of transnational knowledge, artifacts, photographs, or media during their writing process (Hurtig, 2005; McGinnis & García, 2012; Sánchez, 2007). They also point to ways students redefine themselves throughout the process, and display transnational ties in their writing.

Lastly, this analysis is informed by definitions of identity as constructed in social interaction (Bucholtz & Hall, 2005), and by the relationship between positioning and the display of agentive selves in the story-world of narratives (Schiffrin, 1996). Wortham (2000) utilized interactional positioning to analyze autobiographical narratives, noting how individuals construct present selves in relation to other characters in the story-world, to their interlocutors, or to their past selves. Positioning is also a helpful meso-analytic tool to link interactional processes and larger categories, as individuals may resist, select, or take up certain positions (De Fina & Georgakopoulou, 2012). In the study of immigrants' narratives, this mutual agent-world and world-agent directionality (Bamberg, 2004) is visible as individuals' identities shift, but also carry on dispositions from their past life narratives. Such sedimented identities have the potential of change through practice, where the authoring of texts can play a crucial role in this transformation (Pahl & Rowsell, 2011). The analysis of interactions during the composition process and of the finished products (blogs) is guided by the following questions:

- How do adult immigrant students position themselves during their composition process?
- How do they position themselves in autobiographical narratives in their blog entries?

- What transnational and semiotic resources do they draw from in the process? What resources are displayed in their texts/products?

METHODOLOGY

Data documenting the experiences of focal students come from a 9-month qualitative study of the digital literacies of adult immigrants in a community technology center in Arizona. This article explores the second phase of the study (January-June, 2010). After conducting participant observation and interviews with focal students in a Basic Computers Skills course during the first phase (August-December, 2009), my positionality shifted to that of a researcher-practitioner, because a bilingual tutor for a web-design course was needed at the time. I documented the intersections and tensions between my multiple roles in reflective field notes. These roles included being an insider/ outsider to the community; in spite of sharing a cultural and linguistic background with students, I was affiliated with a higher education institution and had a different migration trajectory (Villenas, 1996). It is also worth noting that during fieldwork, Senate Bill 1070 (SB 1070) was signed into law. One provision of this state legislation would have allowed law enforcement officers to request proof of legal residence in the country to any individual considered to be "reasonably suspicious" of undocumented status. Although a federal judge blocked the most controversial parts of the law in July 2010, the uncertainty about its impact for the Hispanic community was a concern for students at the research site.

Data Collection and Analysis

To illustrate the particular lived experiences of two focal students, I constructed case study narratives that fulfill the analytic purpose of displaying the tensions, decision-making, and critical interactions that shaped the production of their blog texts. Data included: (a) one formal individual interview with each participant, focusing on their experiences in class and educational/migration trajectories; (b) 120 hours of written reflective field notes and audiorecording of classroom interaction; (c) print and digital artifacts, including entries and comments from a group blog, and (d) text and images of their individual blogs.

Field notes, audiorecordings, interviews, and texts were coded thematically (Strauss & Corbin, 1998) and chronologically, in order to construct the sequence of events in participants' processes. Like Hull and Katz (2006, drawing on Bruner, 1994), I identified "turning points" or critical tensions and moments that shaped their self-representation as authors, and that also helped create a narrative structure in the cases. I also identified the resources mobilized in the resolution of these tensions. *Semiotic* resources referred to media in addition to text—images, videos, artifacts—and *transnational* resources referred to ideas, networks, or experiences connecting participants to their home countries.

In the identification of autobiographical narratives in students' blogs, I drew from Labov's and Waletzky's (1967) definition of narrative as a minimal unit of two clauses temporally ordered with respect to each other. Sections in the narrative structure include: (a) an orientation; (b) a series of events or cycles of a complicating action; (c) an evaluation; (d) a resolution of the complicating action, and (e) a coda or closing of the story, making a transition to the present. I paid attention to the ways in which narrators displayed self-representations through stating beliefs or emotions (epistemic selves) or by reporting actions (agentive selves) (Schiffrin, 1996).

Although blog writing does not occur in face-to-face interaction, bloggers who write using a "daily-journal" genre tend to enact an authorial voice and utilize self-presentation practices (Hevem, 2004; Warschauer & Grimes, 2007). Hence, in the analysis of positioning, I explored how participants used personal pronouns to locate themselves in relation to: (a) other persons, within reported events, (b) their audience or interlocutors; and (c) to themselves in terms of past/ present selves and social categories beyond the interaction (Bamberg, 1997; Wortham, 2000). It is relevant to note Spanish is a "pro-drop" language, where personal pronouns can be omitted (e.g., *pensé*, instead of *yo pensé*). Linguistic or pragmatic factors may shape the decision to use the subject pronouns for emphasis or contrast (Davidson, 1996; Flores-Ferrán, 2004). For the analysis, both explicit and omitted instances are considered. In the presented excerpts (translated to English by the author), any omitted personal pronoun is noted by the use of brackets around it (e.g., [I] felt for *sentí*).

Focal Participants

I purposefully selected Joselyn and Rafael as focal subjects for this inquiry because they negotiated tensions in their composition process in different ways. While they shared similar cultural and migration backgrounds—they both had lived in the U. S. for 10 years and were born and educated in Mexico—their work and family circumstances differed and shaped their stances towards the blog project. Joselyn was a 30-year-old, stay-at-home mother, who had completed a year of college in Mexico before migrating, and was expecting her third child during the study. Rafael, in his mid-40s, was employed in a labor-intensive job, in spite of receiving a Bachelor in Sciences in Mexico. He migrated to Arizona after struggling to find a job in his field, and was primarily responsible for supporting his family financially. Both participants had strong transnational ties to their home countries; however, their particular trajectories are not meant to represent the practices of their entire cultural group.

FINDINGS

Focus on the Process: Finding an Authorial Voice

In this section, I describe participants' development of their blog texts. Table 1 outlines the different key events presented in their case narratives, including the critical "turning points" or tensions reported in the following section. I argue that through the negotiation of these tensions, they resisted and took up positionalities as knowledgeable authors. I also describe the transnational and semiotic resources they deployed to develop their topics, and how the content and circulation of these resources shaped their decision-making process.

Joselyn's struggle: The emotional toll of advocacy. One of the reasons the web design course was offered was the interest voiced by Joselyn and other students who wanted to learn more about online publishing. Her enthusiasm is displayed in a comment she posted in response to a video showed in class, embedded in the group blog:

1   *Y en el segundo video es muy interesante saber que no todo el mundo sabe que es un*

2   *blog. yo misma no lo sabia sino hasta hace poco y me siento muy content [sic] de*

3   *empezar mi blog.*

1   And the second video is very interesting to know that not everybody knows what a blog

2   is. I did not know that myself until recently and [I] feel very happy to start my blog

(Group blog comment, 2-1-10)

In the video (available at http://youtu.be/5lEfbtcdbVE, *¿Qué es un blog?*), random individuals passing by a public square were asked to define a blog, and several of them could not answer. In her comment, Joselyn aligned herself with these interviewees (line 2), acknowledging her own newcomer status to blogging, but voicing her positive feelings about starting her own. In the second class, Joselyn decided to write a blog about immigration. She had a transnational audience in mind, including both "Hispanics in the U. S. and in Mexico" (handout, 2-22-10). In an outline of the themes of her blog (Figure 1), Joselyn planned to utilize a variety of semiotic resources in addition to text (images and videos) and different sources of information about news, events, and individual immigration stories.

Table 1. Key Activities and Interactions in Participants' Composition Process

Stage in the process	Date	Joselyn's activities and key interactions	Rafael's activities and key interactions
Exploring mentor texts	1-23-2010	Selects blog topic: Immigration	
	1-27-2010	Searches for other immigration blogs	
	2-1-2010	Reports coming across YouTube videos depicting discrimination towards immigrants Added response to video about blog definitions	Voices concerns about authoring legitimacy: only those with credentials or expertise can publish Added response to video about blog definitions
	2-8-2010		Voices concerns about access to technology and time to write
Brainstorming topics	2-22-2010	Identifies potential blog audience and resources	
"Try-outs" crafting entries in group blog	2-24-2010		Writes unsolicited blog post reflecting on his learning
Outlining	2-24-2010	Outlines blog sections	Selects topic: autobiography in relation to the evolution of computers
Developing first draft	3-1-2010	Considers including racism as one of her blog subsections	
	3-18-2010	Switches topic and starts new blog on child care advice.	

Figure 1. Joselyn's Outline of Immigration Blog

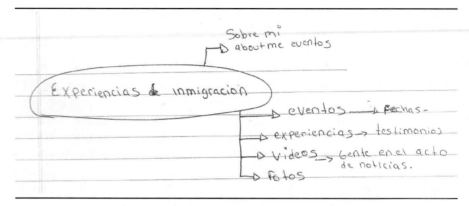

However, her online searches led her to a video depicting day laborers being filmed and chased by someone threatening to deport them. She also reported coming across videos of non-Hispanics trying to help immigrants reach their families. In the light of these findings, Joselyn intended to provide a balanced view of both positive and negative immigration experiences. However, she later considered adding a section specifically addressing issues of racism:

5   *La discriminación, lo que esta pasando ahorita. Que, simplemente porque eres morena,*

6   *o porque te ven hispano, la gente te cataloga como que tú no eres legal en este país…*

7   *Yo no tengo mucha experiencia de esto, pero tengo personas que yo conozco, que puedo*

8   *sacar información de ellos.*

5   Discrimination, what is happening now. That, simply because your skin is tanned, or

6   because they see [you] as Hispanic, people categorize you as not being legal in this country

7   … I don't have a lot of experience with this, but [I] have people I know, that [I] can

8   get information from them.

(classroom interaction, 3-1-10)

In this interaction with me, Joselyn established a cause-and-effect relation to define discrimination in the community, referring specifically to racial profiling. She used the second person singular to construct the scenario of being "categorized" as undocumented by "people," who would judge others based on skin color or perceived ethnic identity (line 6). While she distanced herself from the direct experience of being discriminated against (line 7), she reported having acquaintances who were. By doing so, Joselyn positioned her social network of immigrant acquaintances as resources for this project. Overall, by choosing this topic, Joselyn situated herself as a potential advocate for her community, whose blog could be useful to circulate news, events, and testimonies locally and beyond national borders.

However, by the time Joselyn customized a blog template, she decided to switch her topic. She started a new blog to give childcare advice to new parents. When I inquired about the reason for this change, Joselyn shared the following:

15 *Yo había escogido un tema que también me llamaba mucho la atención, está muy*

16 *popular en este, Estados Unidos, la migración, ah, pero también…. sentí yo que estaba*

17 *leyendo muchas cosas que no me gustaban, me hacían sentir como deprimente. Entonces*

18 *eso de Bebés en Apuros se me ocurrió un día que, yo dije, bueno pues, eso es un tema*

19 *que también es muy concurrido. Todos los niños, hay muchos niños en el mundo, y todo*

20 *el tiempo va a haber niños y yo tengo mis dos niñas y eso me ayudó a decir, porque no*

21 *escribo algo así, que estoy ahorita en esta etapa de mi vida teniendo mis niñas, entonces,*

22 *va a ser un poquito más fácil para mí, dejar salir algo que tienes dentro.*

15 I had picked a topic that also got my attention, it is very popular in uh, the United States,

16 immigration, but uhm, but then…. I felt that [I] was reading a lot of things that I did not

17 like, that made me feel like, depressed. Then this *Babies in Trouble* idea came up one day

18 that, I said, well, this is a very popular topic too. All children, there are many children in

19 the world, and there will be children all the time, and I have my two daughters now and

20 that helped me say, why don't [I] write something like this, now that [I] am in this stage

21 of my life having my daughters, then, it will be easier for me, to release something within

22 me.

(Joselyn, interview, 4-15-10)

In a short narrative describing this turning point, Joselyn shared the rationale in a sequence of events: (a) the moment she chose to write an immigration blog, (b) the moment she felt discomfort as a result of pursuing that topic, and (c) the moment she decided to switch topics. The complicating event that shaped her direction was feeling saddened (line 17) by texts she came across online—an instance of display of an epistemic self (Schiffrin, 1996), stating feelings and emotions. In the report of her inner dialogue (lines 17-22), she stated her decision-making—an instance of display of an agentive self, by taking action. Joselyn resolved the tension by moving away from a position vulnerable to victimization, to a more empowering role, or at least a more comfortable one.

Rafael's struggle: Connecting to academic identities. On the other hand, while students explored blogs in Spanish, Rafael resisted to the idea of creating a blog of his own. For instance, one of the mentor texts he read was "*El Blog de Lula,*" written by a Mexican self-identified housewife, who posted daily reflections and wonderings. In the following excerpt, Rafael contrasted her life with his own, positioning himself as a "tired employee," having no time or energy to write after a long day at work (line 25). He later compared his job conditions with that of a local friend who used a computer at work. He positioned himself at a disadvantage for lacking the same technology access, using the impersonal first-person reference "*uno*" in line 28:

25 *Pues escriben, "lo que me pasó cada día." Yo llego a mi casa muy cansado, ¿qué voy a*

26 *escribir?[…] Esto es para personas que tienen computadora en su trabajo. Mi amigo*

27 *trabaja en un* dealer, *y a cada rato me habla y me dice, '¿no viste esto en el YouTube?'*

28 *porque está en la computadora, y pues uno no.*

25 Well they write, "stuff that happens to me every day." I get to my home very tired, what

26 am I going to write? [...] This is for people who have computers at work. My friend

27 works at a *dealer,* and he calls me every now and then and tells me 'did you see this in

28 YouTube?' because he is in the computer, and one is not.

(Field notes, 2-8-10)

In these two utterances, Rafael distanced himself from Internet users locally and transnationally (his friend and Lula), who had the time and material resources to engage in frequent online media consumption and production. He constructed an in-group, "people who have computers at work" and excluded himself from it. In spite of his professional and academic training in Mexico—his sedimented identity and past experience, with certain dispositions and skills—Rafael's current job was labor-intensive, and denied him opportunities to use a computer. And as presented in the introductory quote to this piece, he also had concerns about his lack of credentials to become a legitimate author.

In spite of these issues, Rafael still brainstormed a few blog topics in a handout, listing his interests in extreme sports and music. However, a turning point took place when he wrote an unsolicited short entry in the blog page, in between sessions:

30 *Hola a todos*

31 *Esto es una practica fuera de clases, espero que este curso de HTLM [sic] les este*

32 *gustando tanto como a mi aunque no siempre le entiendo a la primera, ni a la segunda,*

33 *pero el secreto de todo esto y todo lo relacionado con las computadoras es la practica*

34 *(yo creo) practicar y practicar, y asi nos familiarisamos [sic] con los terminos y el*

35 *lenguaje utilizado en la informotica [sic] (totalmente nuevo para mi), recuerden, LA*

36 *PRACTICA HACE AL MAESTRO.*

30 Hello everybody

31 This is practice outside of class, [I] hope that you are all enjoying this HTLM [sic]

32 course as much as I am even if [I] don't get things the first time, nor the second time,

33 but the secret to all of this and everything related to computers is practice (I think)

34 to practice more and more, and that way [we] become familiar with the terms and language

35 utilized in informatics (totally new to me), remember, PRACTICE MAKES PERFECT.

[unsolicited blog entry, 2-23-10]

In this comment addressed to his peers, Rafael's awareness of his own progress is demonstrated in his self-presentation as a persistent learner. He displayed his enjoyment of the course, in spite of his reported struggle (not getting things the first time). He established his informal theories about learning (line 33: "I think") through constant practice and repetition, and used the second person plural (line 34) to generalize the assertion about how specialized language is learned. He concluded his statement with a popular saying in Spanish encouraging perseverance (line 35). Rafael displayed an agentive self by reporting his actions, and simultaneously, performed perseverance by completing this blog entry at home without being prompted.

A day later, in class, Rafael said he wanted to write an autobiographical account of the evolution of technology during his lifetime. He remembered computers being "as big as a room" when he was a college student in Mexico. This memory prompted his systematic online searches for videos and images about the evolution of technology. That led him to an image that matched his recollection (see image of IBM 701 at http://www-03.ibm.com/ibm/history/exhibits/701/701_141511.html). Even when this artifact was not present in the classroom, it embodied a life event associated with Rafael's academic identity prior to migration. In spite of his initial self-positioning in disadvantage, Rafael mobilized knowledge from his transnational experience that allowed him to adopt an authorial stance.

Focus on the product: agentive selves in autobiographical narratives

In this section, I analyze narrative excerpts of the blogs that Joselyn and Rafael created. I argue that the positionalities they took in relation to their audience and to their past selves allowed them to display agentive selves. I also illustrate the transnational and semiotic resources that supported these empowered positions.

Joselyn's blog: A guide to parenting. In her blog *Babies in Trouble,* Joselyn included links to resources in Spanish and English, images of babies and parents, and advice on child safety. In the following narrative excerpt in the section "About me," she shared her experiences throughout her different pregnancies:

40 *en mi experiencia ha sido un poco difícil especialmente con mi primera hija ya que* **no**

41 *sabía cómo empezar con sus primeros cuidados a pesar de que en el hospital tome las*

42 *clases no es lo mismo ya teniendo la bebe en tus brazos y peor aun si llora mucho las*

43 *primeras noches. gracias a mi suegra que viajo desde México y me ayudo en los*

44 *primeros días con mi bebe ya que a mí se me hacia tan frágil y pequeñita que ella me*

45 *ayudo a darle su primer baño y me enseno como hacerlo y créanlo es mucha ayuda tener*

46 *alguien en esos momentos*

47 *ya con mi segunda bebe todo fue totalmente diferente con la experiencia que ya tenía y la*

48 *ayuda de mi preciosa madre fue todo mas fácil. ahora que espero mi tercera bebe me*

49 *siento muy segura…*

50 *Espero disfrutes y te ayude un poco de lo que aquí encontraras y ya que gracias a estas*

51 *clases de HTML que estoy tomando me dio mucha alegría saber que puedo trasmitir*

52 *estas experiencias con todos ustedes.*

40 In my experience it has been a little difficult especially with my first daughter because [I]

41 did not know how to start taking care of her at first, even when in the hospital [I] took

42 classes it is not the same having the baby in your arms and worse if she cries a lot during

43 the first nights. Thanks to my mother-in-law who travelled from Mexico and helped me

44 the first days with my baby because [I] thought she was so fragile and tiny that she

45 helped me giving her the first bath and taught me how to do it believe it, it is great help

46 to have somebody with you in that moment…

47 with my second baby everything was totally different with the experience [I] had and the

48 help of my precious mother everything was easier. Now that I am expecting my third

49 baby [I] feel more confident …

50 I hope [you] enjoy and [you] get some help from what you will find here and that

51 thanks to these HTML classes that [I] am taking [I] was really happy to know [I] can

52 transmit these experiences to all of you.

In this narrative, Joselyn makes visible her struggle and concerns after the birth of her first daughter. In line 43, she describes her transnational ties, pointing to the trip of her mother-in-law to support her, and positioning her as a mentor who showed her how to take care of her new baby. She displayed her increase in experience in her second pregnancy, still receiving some support from her mother, and culminating in a confident position at the present time, expecting her third child (lines 48-49). By using her lived experience as evidence for the validity of her advice—in contrast with the "hospital classes" that did not prepare her enough—Joselyn reconstructed what it meant to be a mother. These narratives of struggle are a common feature in the genre of "mommy blogging" (Lopez, 2009), where women provide honest accounts that demystify idealized visions of motherhood in the mainstream media.

Joselyn addressed her audience in the informal second person in singular and plural (e.g., line 50: *espero disfrutes*), establishing a friendly tone, as opposed to addressing them in the formal second person "*usted.*" In lines 51-52 she positioned herself as an expert in relation to her audience, framing her blog content and her narrative as having a pedagogical purpose. Finally, she acknowledged the affordances of the medium, situating herself as knowledgeable in HTML, which made it possible for her to reach her readers.

Rafael's blog: An autobiography of technology evolution. On the homepage, Rafael summarized the scope of his blog, establishing an authorial voice and personal perspective through his use of the first person singular: "*En esta página hablare de mi experiencia en la evolución de las computadoras y algunos aspectos generales de los cambios tecnológicos que me ha tocado vivir.*" [In this page [I] will talk about my experience in the evolution of computers and some general aspects of the technological changes [I] have had the chance to experience].

In the first segment of this narrative, Rafael talked about his memories as a university student in Mexico, focusing on the early computer model he mentioned in class: "*La primera computadora que conocí fue cuando yo era un estudiante, la computadora era de un gran tamaño un poco mas grande que yo*" [The first computer that I knew was when I was a student, the computer was really large, a little larger than me]. Although he switched between keeping and omitting personal pronouns, it is worth noting he made them explicit when he referred to himself as a student *("yo era un estudiante")*, a possible source of emphasis in displaying an academic identity.

The complicating action was voicing the reasons for his past self to distance himself from technology. He mitigated this event by using hedges ("for some reason," "perhaps"), and referred to economic circumstances as possible obstacles. He then repositioned himself as an athlete, displaying gratifying and successful experiences with sports.

60 *Por alguna razón yo me aparte de ellas totalmente. Tal vez porque en aquellos tiempos*

61 *eran realmente caras, o porque mi tiempo libre siempre lo dedique al deporte en el cual*

62 *tuve muchas y muy bonitas experiencias a nivel nacional e internacional (U. S. A.).*

60 For some reason I distanced myself of them totally. Perhaps because in that time they

61 were really expensive, or because [I] always spent my free time in sports, in which [I]

62 had very nice and beautiful experiences at the national and international level (U.S.A).

Towards the end of the narrative, Rafael resolved this complicating event by describing a shift in his daily digital literacy practices and situating them in his household context. He contrasted his present appropriation of technology with his years of "apathy" towards computers.

65 *Ahora, después de muchos años de apatía a las computadoras comienzo a conocerlas un*

66 *poco y encuentro una herramienta muy útil para la vida diaria, pago todos mis servicios*

67 *públicos a través de ella, también puedo elaborar algunas cosas que me gustan mucho*

68 *en fotografía y música... Puedo comunicarme con casi toda mi familia que viven en*

69 *diferentes estados de Mexico y U.S.A. Todo de lo que tengo duda lo consulto en internet*

70 *y por si fuera poco mi esposa cocina platillos internacionales deliciosos, mi niña*

71 *encuentra un sinfín de juegos educativos de lectura, ciencias, etc. Y aquí estoy*

72 *aprendiendo por medio de tutórales, tratando de seguir y seguir estudiando.*

65 Now, after so many years of apathy towards computers, [I] am starting to get to know

66 them a little, and [I] find them a very useful tool for daily life, [I] pay all my bills

67 through it, [I] am also able to create things [I] like with photos and music... [I] can

68 communicate with all of my family who lives in different states in Mexico and the U.S.

69 Everything [I] have a doubt about [I] consult it in the Internet and even my wife cooks

70 delicious international dishes, my daughter finds plenty of educational games in reading,

71 science, etc. And here [I] am, learning through tutorials, trying to keep on and keep on

72 studying.

By listing the repertoire of his family digital literacy practices, he positioned himself, his wife, and daughter as frequent technology users, connected with information, people, and institutions in local and remote locations (line 68). This statement made visible the transnational aspects of their everyday routines, and the role technology had in mediating these connections. This list of actions, as opposed to emotions or intentions, also provided a display of an agentive self as a lifelong, self-directed learner (line 71).

TEACHING AND RESEARCHING DIGITAL WRITING: COMPLEXITIES AND POSSIBILITIES

In this article, I presented the experiences of Rafael and Joselyn as newcomers to digital writing. I explored the different positionalities they took up in their composition process and in the texts of the blogs they authored, as well as the resources that shaped and supported these efforts. In relation to their process, I argue that their paths to adopting authorial stances was not linear nor easy, and that their authorial stances were shaped by their taking up positions in relation to other bloggers, to their acquaintances, and to larger social categories in master narratives (e.g., as victimized immigrants or labor-intensive workers). In relation to their blog entries, Joselyn and Rafael redefined parenting and technology expertise in the story worlds of narratives of past experiences, building positive self-images in relation to their readers. These findings point to the relevance of examining both the practices and texts in the study of the intersection between writing, identity, and agency. Their interactional representations of self and others display the convergence of macro-level imposed categories, locally emergent cultural positions, and interactional stances (Bucholtz & Hall, 2005).

In relation to the role of transnational and semiotic resources, Joselyn's and Rafael's choices demonstrate how both resources were valuable, but deployed differently in their efforts to distance themselves from vulnerable positionalities. Rafael drew from memories associated with past academic identities prior to migration. He constructed a trajectory of expertise using text and images displaying devices in his home country, and technologies he was getting to know in the United States. On the other hand, the same multimedia exploration led Joselyn to user-generated videos that prompted her to change her topic. Cultural artifacts—like digital and multimodal media—bring connections to social worlds where individuals are positioned and position themselves in certain ways (Pahl & Rowsell, 2011). Hence, multimodal meaning-making is also shaped by individuals' complex histories, identities, and circumstances. In Joselyn's case, the impact of ideological forces in the region at that time shaped her stances towards her digital media consumption and her own blog-writing efforts.

These findings raise questions about the complexities of implementing digital writing projects addressing issues of social justice. While research with minority students emphasizes the affordances of digital media to examine community issues critically (Nixon, 2009) or reconstruct and reflect on the immigrant experience (Alexandra, 2008), the emotional toll of this work is not often mentioned. The authoring of counter stories can challenge deficit belief systems and open windows to understand experiences of those being marginalized (Solórzano & Yosso, 2002); however, I argue that Joselyn's choice also displayed an agentive move towards the self-representation of her expertise from an empowered position as a mother. As a practitioner, I shared Joselyn's concerns and emotions, and noticed that conversations about SB 1070 increased towards the end of the semester, when the bill was signed into law in late April. These events were discussed in the group and led to related web searches and other media production projects, where various students contributed. Reflecting and discussing immigration policy became a collective effort, not just Joselyn's interest.

Finally, this project has implications for the teaching of digital writing to culturally diverse learners. Technology-focused programs should not only focus on making computers and Internet accessible, or giving step-by-step directions in the navigation of interfaces. They should focus first on the writer, then on the writing, and lastly, on the technology (Hicks, 2009). In this research site, students benefitted from: (a) interactions with members of a learning community who shared their transnational and linguistic background, (b) access to reliable computer equipment, and (c) access to online spaces that they could visit beyond class time (e.g., Rafael's use of the group blog for "extra" practice). Family literacy programs for immigrant parents like Joselyn and Rafael should foster their authoring and academic practices, so they can think of themselves as both parents and writers (Hurtig, 2005). Furthermore, the use of new communication technologies in adult education can also support promising practices for second language and literacy development (Warschauer & Liaw, 2009).

Towards the end of the study, Rafael was aware of the possibilities for future writing. It was not only about having access to a blog platform, but also about his emergent identity as a writer. In his reflection, he displayed a new stance about the potential of writing his "anecdotes" to continue his efforts in autobiographical narratives (interview, 5-13-10): "*Me está interesando hacer una parte de mi historia, del tiempo que llevo aquí... así como hice esa [página] de las computadoras, está interesante.*" (I am getting interested in writing a part of my own story, of the time I have spent here…Just like I made this [page] about computers, it is interesting.) He claimed his authoring identity—in his language, his terms, and responding to his needs to document his lived experiences.

REFERENCES

Alexandra, D. (2008). Digital storytelling as transformative practice: Critical analysis and creative expression in the representation of migration in Ireland. *Journal of Media Practice, 9,* 101-112.

Bamberg, M. (1997). Positioning between structure and performance. *Journal of Narrative and Life History, 7,* 335-342.

Bamberg, M. (2004). Narrative discourse and identities. In J. C. Meister, T. Kindt, W. Schernus, & M. Stein (Eds.), *Narratology beyond literary criticism* (pp. 213-237). New York, NY: Walter de Gruyte.

Baynham, M., & Prinsloo, M. (2009). Introduction: The future of literacy studies. In M. Baynham & M. Prinsloo (Eds.), *The future of literacy studies* (pp. 1-20). New York, NY: Palgrave Macmillan.

Black, R. (2006). Language, culture and identity in online fanfiction. *E-learning, 3,* 170-184.

Brandt, D., & Clinton, K. (2002). Limits of the local: Expanding perspectives on literacy as a social practice. *Journal of Literacy Research, 34,* 337-356.

Bucholtz, M., & Hall, K. (2005). Identity and interaction: A sociocultural linguistic approach. *Discourse Studies, 7,* 585-614.

Coiro, J., Knobel, M., Lankshear, C., & Leu, D. (2008). Central issues in new literacies and new literacies research. In J. Coiro, M. Knobel, C. Lankshear, & D. Leu (Eds.) *Handbook of research on new literacies* (pp. 1-21). New York, NY: Erlbaum.

Davidson, B. (1996). "Pragmatic weight" and Spanish subject pronouns." The pragmatic and discourse uses of "tu" and "yo" in spoken Madrid Spanish. *Journal of Pragmatics, 26,* 543-565.

De Fina, A., & Georgakopoulou, A. (2012). *Analyzing narrative: Discourse and sociolinguistic perspectives.* New York, NY: Cambridge.

Flores-Ferrán, N. (2004). Spanish subject personal pronoun use in New York City Puerto Ricans: Can we rest the case of English contact? *Language Variation and Change, 16,* 49-73

Hevem, V. W. (2004). Threaded Identity in cyberspace : Weblogs & positioning in the dialogical self. *Identity, 4,* 321-335.

Hicks, T. (2009). *The digital writing workshop.* Portsmouth, NH: Heinemann.

Hull, G., & Katz, M. L. (2006). Crafting an agentive self: Case studies of digital storytelling. *Research on the Teaching of English, 41,* 43-81.

Hull, G., Zacher, J., & Hibbert, L. (2009). Youth, risk, and equity in a global world. *Review of Research in Education, 33*, 117-159.

Hurtig, J. (2005). Mexican mothers retelling the city: Stories from the "parents as writers" workshop. *City & Society, 17*, 235-264.

Jiménez, R., Smith, P., & Teague, B. (2009). Transnational and community literacies. *Journal of Adolescent and Adult Literacy, 53*(1), 16–26.

Kress, G. (2003). *Literacy in the new media age.* New York, NY: Routledge.

Kress, G. (2009). *Multimodality: A social semiotic approach to contemporary communication.* New York, NY: Routledge.

Kress, G. (2011). "Partnerships in research:" Multimodality and ethnography. *Qualitative Research, 11*, 239-260.

Labov, W., & Waletzky, J. (1967). Narrative analysis: Oral versions of personal experience. In J. Helm (Ed.), *Essays on the verbal and visual arts* (pp. 12-44). Seattle, WA: University of Washington Press.

Lam, W. S. E. (2000). L2 literacy and the design of the self: A case study of a teenager writing on the Internet. *TESOL Quarterly, 34*, 457-482.

Lam, W. S. E. (2006). Re-envisioning language, literacy, and the immigrant subject in new mediascapes. *Pedagogies, 1*, 171-195.

Levitt, P., & Glick Schiller, N. (2004). Conceptualizing simultaneity: A transnational social field perspective on Society. *International Migration Review, 3*, 1002-1039.

Livingston, G. (2010). *The Latino digital divide: The native born versus the foreign born.* Washington, DC: Pew Hispanic Center.

McGinnis, T., & García, A. (April, 2012). *(Re)constructing Latino identities through multimedia hybrid narratives: Young Latino men composing digital stories.* Paper presented at the American Educational Research Association Annual Conference. Vancouver, British Columbia.

McGinnis, T., Goostein-Stolzenberg, A., & Costa Saliani, E. (2007). "indnpride": Online spaces of transnational youth as sites of creative and sophisticated literacy and identity work. *Linguistics and Education, 18*, 283-304.

New London Group (1996). A pedagogy of multiliteracies: Designing social futures. *Harvard Educational Review, 66*, 60-92.

Nixon, A. S. (2009). Mediating social thought through digital storytelling. *Pedagogies, 4*, 63-76.

Pahl, K., & Rowsell, J. (2011). Artifactual critical literacy: A new perspective for literacy education. *Berkeley Review of Education, 2*, 129-151.

Sánchez, P. (2007). Cultural authenticity and transnational Latina youth: Constructing a meta-narrative across borders. *Linguistics and Education, 18*, 258-282.

Sandoval, C., & Latorre, G. (2008). Chicana/o artivism: Judy Baca's digital work with youth of color. In A. Everett (Ed.), *Learning race and ethnicity: Youth and digital media* (pp. 81-108). Cambridge, MA: MIT Press.

Schiffrin, D. (1996). Narrative as self-portrait: Sociolinguistic constructions of identity. *Language in Society, 25*, 167-203.

Solórzano, D. G., & Yosso, T. J. (2002). Critical race methodology: Counter-storytelling as an analytical framework for education research. *Qualitative Inquiry, 8*, 23-44.

Strauss, A., & Corbin, J. (1998). *Basics of qualitative research: Techniques and procedures for developing grounded theory* (2nd ed.). Thousand Oaks, CA: Sage.

Street, B. (2009). The future of 'social literacies. In M. Baynham & M. Prinsloo (Eds.), *The future of literacy studies* (pp. 21-37). New York, NY: Palgrave Macmillan.

Vasudevan, L. (2006). Making known differently: Engaging visual modalities as spaces to author new selves. *E-Learning, 3*, 207-216.

Vasudevan, L., Schultz, K., & Bateman, J. (2010). Rethinking composing in a digital age: Authoring literate identities through multimodal storytelling. *Written Communication, 27*, 442-468.

Villenas, S. (1996). The colonizer/colonized Chicana ethnographer: Identity, marginalization, and co-optation in the field. *Harvard Educational Review, 66*, 711-731.

Warschauer, M., & Grimes, D. (2007). Audience, authorship, and artifact: The emergent semiotics of Web 2.0. *Annual Review of Applied Linguistics, 27*, 1-23.

Warschauer, M., & Liaw, M. L. (2009). *Emerging technologies in adult literacy and language education.* Washington, DC: National Institute for Literacy.

Wortham, S. (2000). Interactional positioning and narrative self-construction. *Narrative Inquiry, 10*, 157-184.

Interactive and Coconstructive Discourse in Informational Text Read-Alouds

Jessica L. Hoffman
Miami University

Reading aloud is a common, even daily, instructional practice in early childhood classrooms. Reading aloud can support development of a wide array of early literacy skills: oral language and vocabulary (Blewitt, Rump, Shealy, & Cook, 2009; Hargrave & Sénéchal, 2000; Silverman, 2007; Wasik & Bond, 2001), listening comprehension (Brabham & Lynch-Brown, 2002; Morrow, 1985; Zucker, Justice, Piasta, & Kaderavek, 2010), content knowledge (Pappas & Varelas, 2004), concepts of print (Justice, Pullen, & Pence, 2008; Levy, Gong, Hessels, Evans, & Jared, 2006), and alphabet knowledge and phonological awareness (Aram, 2006; Brabham, Murray, & Bowden, 2006). In addition, decades of research (including all of the studies cited above) have demonstrated that reading aloud to children is most effective when the adult and children discuss the text while reading; however, discussion in read-alouds is not always effectively incorporated in common practice (Beck & McKeown, 2001; Dickinson, 2001; Hoffman, Roser, & Battle, 1993; Teale, 2003).

The vast majority of research on reading aloud in early childhood has studied the use of narrative children's literature, yet there is evidence that teachers use different supports for different types of texts (Smolkin & Donovan, 2001), and that students respond differently across genres (Shine & Roser, 1999). The limited amount of research on informational texts in early childhood remains largely descriptive of existing practices and/or focused on basic comprehension (e.g., Duke, 2000; Pappas, 1993; Smolkin & Donovan, 2001). Nevertheless, mounting evidence documents the changing literacy demands of our society: from the basic literacies sufficient in the previous century, to the needs for more complex processing of texts, including active analytical, critical, and interpretive meaning-construction across texts of various forms that are necessary for this age of information and communication technologies (Coiro, Knobel, Lankshear, & Leu, 2008; Kress, 2003; Lankshear & Knobel, 2008). In order for today's students to meet tomorrow's literacy demands, we must begin to emphasize active meaning-construction across all literacy instruction and with informational text specifically (Duke & Bennett-Armistead, 2003; Moss, 2005).

As a context for social interactions around texts, the classroom read-aloud has enormous potential for developing precisely the strategies that current and future literacy demands require. However, to promote active meaning-construction with young children, emphases on vocabulary, print, and basic comprehension are not enough; students must have opportunities to discuss texts that are complex enough to warrant analysis and critical thinking, while also being taught how to engage deeply with texts through interactive discussion. Other lines of research focusing on these literacies with young children have demonstrated that children are decidedly capable of constructing complex meanings with texts. Examples include studies of critical literacy (Vasquez, 2010), multiliteracies (Crafton, Brennan, & Silvers, 2007), and literary analysis and response (Hoffman, 2011; Pantaleo, 2004a, 2004b; Sipe, 2000, 2008). These lines of research are rooted in sociocultural (Vygotsky, 1978) and transactional (Rosenblatt, 1978) perspectives, for the most part remaining distinct from cognitive research on reading aloud with specific literacy skill outcome measures, and they all share a focus on active *meaning-construction* through *interactive discussion*. Active meaning-construction emphasizes the process of making meanings with texts, rather than comprehending the literal meaning presented in a text. In many ways, a focus on meaning construction demands different and more interactive forms of classroom discourse to free students to participate in more ways than are possible in a traditional three-part exchange: teacher initiation, student response, teacher feedback (Initiation-Response-Feedback [IRF]) pattern (Cazden, 2001).

Drawing on existing research, this design research study aimed to create a practical solution to the identified problem of an overemphasis on basic literacies in early childhood literacy education, with informational texts in particular. To do so, I worked collaboratively with one first grade teacher to design transformations of her classroom discourse in read alouds of informational texts to incorporate more interactive discussion that actively constructed meanings with texts.

CONCEPTIONS OF CLASSROOM DISCOURSE

Traditional Classroom Discourse: IRF

IRF (Cazden, 2001) describes a form of classroom discourse characterized by the teacher initiating (usually with a question, usually to which the answer is known), student response(s), followed by some form of teacher evaluation, feedback, or follow-up. In her classic study of classroom discourse, Cazden (2001) contrasted IRF patterns, which she described as *traditional*, with less structured, more conversational and interactive discourse, termed *nontraditional*. IRF has long been recognized as the prevailing classroom discourse format, estimated as accounting for 70% or more of all classroom talk (Wells, 1999). Although criticized for many reasons, including its value of teacher knowledge over student knowledge, teacher control over initiation of ideas for discussion, and inhibition of critical thinking and the creation of original meaning-making (Cazden, 2001; Nystrand, 1997), many researchers also discuss a place and role for IRF in teaching and learning (e.g., Cazden, 2001; Mercer, 1995; Wells, 1999). To be sure, there is no singular application of IRF in practice, and different uses can vary widely in terms of participants, contexts, and effectiveness in teaching and learning. IRF is most commonly used to describe micro-level three-part exchanges between the teacher and a student; however, IRF can also be applied at more macro-levels to understand larger structures of classroom discourse and learning activities (Wells, 1999). For example, one extended, cohesive discussion among teacher and students could be characterized by the teacher initiating with a question and concluding with some summative feedback, but also include many contributions from multiple speakers throughout, so that the macro-level IRF cycle is comprised of micro-level IRF cycles of participants' follow-up questioning and responses to each other. Examples like this demonstrate how IRF has limited utility for evaluating classroom discourse to identify forms that make differences in student learning, because many qualitatively distinct discourse patterns can be described as IRF cycles.

Dimensions of Classroom Discourse

Patterns of classroom discourse can be more meaningfully described using three interrelated dimensions. The first dimension relates to the amount of *interaction* among the teacher and students. This dimension is concerned with who talks, how, and when, but does not describe the meaning constructed in that talk. Mortimer and Scott (2003) categorized this dimension of classroom discourse as *interactive* or *non-interactive*: Interactive discourse describes talk involving back-and-forth exchanges with more than one speaker, and non-interactive discourse describes talk that is predominated by only one speaker, such as a lecture by an instructor. Other researchers have coined similar dichotomous descriptors, such as Cazden's (2001) traditional and non-traditional patterns, or Lotman's (1988) monologic or dialogic patterns; however, there is evidence to support the notion that there are varying levels of interaction, rather than merely a yes/no dichotomy. For example, qualitatively, there is an important difference between interactions in: (a) a question/ answer session between the teacher and an individual student called upon by the teacher, and (b) an open discussion among the teacher and multiple students exchanging ideas related to a topic for a length of time.

The second dimension describes the *construction of meaning* in the discourse—whose ideas are propagated in classroom talk, or the "authorship of ideas" (Adger, Hoyle, & Dickinson, 2004), not necessarily who is speaking, but whose thoughts are being expressed. Mortimer and Scott (2003) described discourse in this dimension as either dialogic (incorporating multiple perspectives) or authoritative (rooted in one authoritative source). Because the terms dialogic and authoritative can conjure up irrelevant connections for early childhood literacy professionals (i.e., the scripted program Dialogic Reading, or classroom management styles), I prefer the terms *coconstructed* and *independently constructed*. It is problematic to restrict this dimension to a dichotomy as well, because meanings can be coconstructed to varying degrees, such as a teacher posing follow-up questions to guide a student toward a particular interpretation, compared to a teacher and students truly constructing unique interpretations through the discussion itself.

The third dimension of classroom discourse is related to the focus of the discussion, or the *meaning constructed* as a product. This dimension is concerned with the difference between classroom discourse that works to build and establish basic and socially accepted knowledge, or that builds the capacity to question and explore in an effort to extend our common knowledge (Wells & Arauz, 2006). As teachers, we must strive toward both goals—the ontogenetic, to develop within individuals the knowledge society has accumulated over time, and the phylogenetic, to extend our collective knowledge with innovative ideas of individuals, and these goals are also related to the literacies we teach students. Students must acquire basic literacies (decoding, encoding, fluent reading and writing) to master the socially constructed tool as a means for communicating and acquiring existing knowledge; however, they must also develop higher-level literacies focused on actively constructing meaning with texts to push thinking in new directions. Individual segments of classroom discourse can represent either *basic literacies* or active *meaning-construction*.

Interconnectivity among the Dimensions of Classroom Discourse

In their exploration of the different instructional purposes, uses, and outcomes of different IRF exchanges in classroom discourse, Wells and Arauz (2006) explained how structurally similar IRF discourse patterns could be used to achieve different educational outcomes, and proposed ways in which certain forms of classroom discourse may better support one goal over the other—namely that more teacher control (in interaction and construction of meaning) may be better suited for developing basic, commonly accepted knowledge, and more student control (in interaction and construction of meaning) may better support creativity, innovation, and the extension of knowledge. Other researchers have described similar relationships between classroom discourse and learning (Cazden, 2001; Mercer, 1995; Nystrand, 1997) and have emphasized the cumulative quality of coconstructive classroom discourse to build knowledge over time (Alexander, 2000, 2008; Mercer, Dawes, & Staarman, 2009). In other words, interactive, coconstructive discourse works toward both goals, building students' foundational knowledge, but then working to extend current understandings to construct original meanings.

Design Goals

Design research is grounded in the understanding of education as an applied science, and therefore aims to design practical solutions for real education problems in authentic contexts by establishing goals to accomplish, rather than questions to answer (The Design-Based Research Collective, 2003; Reinking & Bradley, 2008). Based on the dimensions of classroom discourse I have identified in the existing literature, I established the following goals for read-aloud discussion, to shift the form of discourse toward: (a) more *interactive* discussion among teacher and students, and (b) more *coconstructive* discussion that integrates meaning from multiple participants' interpretations, rather than valuing an individual interpretation; and shift the focus of discourse toward (c) active construction of meaning, instead of limiting instruction to basic, literal comprehension. This paper presents data related to the first two of the three design goals.

METHODOLOGY

Research Design

In this design research study, I engaged with one first grade teacher, Ms. Engle (all names are pseudonyms) in intensive, collaborative, and contextualized (focused on the individual classroom context) professional development (PD). I also observed and video-recorded the teacher reading aloud to her class, both as part of the contextualized PD process to guide teacher reflections on practice and refine designs for classroom discourse, as well as to collect data on changes in classroom discourse.

Participants. Ms. Engle was a young, Caucasian woman with 6 years of teaching experience. She held a bachelor's degree in education and was working toward a master's degree in reading (at another university) during the study. During this study, she taught at a charter school in a large, urban Midwestern school district. Her students were 94% ($n = 15$) African American, 6% ($n = 1$) Caucasian, and 100% received free or reduced lunch.

Classroom observations. Prior to the first PD session, I observed the teacher reading first (not previously read aloud; R1) and second readings (R2) of one informational text and first readings of one narrative text in whole-group contexts (Table 1). The teacher was instructed to conduct these read-alouds in her normal manner to serve as examples of existing teacher read-aloud practice and student discussion of texts. Following the beginning of PD (Intervention Phase I), classroom observations occurred four times per month, when I observed an R1 and R2 for each of two texts. During Phase II, I observed twice a month, observing an R1 and R2 of one text. The two phases of the intervention had two purposes: (a) to front-load support from the researcher in the beginning of

Table 1. Observations and Phases of Study (White Indicates Analyzed Transcripts)

Reading No.	Baseline		Phase I		Phase II		
	Oct.		Nov.		Dec./Jan.	Feb.	Mar./Apr.
R1	Text 1 (info)	Text 2 (narr)	Text 3	Text 4	Text 5	Text 6	Text 7
R2	Text 1 (info)		Text 3	Text 4	Text 5	Text 6	Text 7

the study and decrease support over the school year, and (b) to document changes in discourse over multiple time points. Observations totaled 13 across all three phases of data collection (Table 1).

Every classroom observation was video-recorded. During the observations, I recorded discourse in field notes to identify speakers, and afterward, all video recordings were fully transcribed with field notes integrated for analysis. I then purposefully selected six observations to fully analyze to identify changes in discourse over time in first readings (Table 1, in white). The final R1 observation was removed from analysis as an outlier, because the teacher had been unable to teach the related content, which limited students' background knowledge and thus their ability to discuss the text.

Professional development. PD was based on the cycle of instruction: reflect, plan, teach, and assess. Reflection and planning occurred during PD sessions, and teaching and assessment (of the discourse) occurred during observations of read-alouds. I met with the teacher and one other teacher as part of a larger study in five 1-hour group PD sessions. Prior to each group session, we read 1-2 professional articles that I provided to establish common background knowledge of the topic. Each session followed a basic structure:

- Review—reflection on successes and challenges of previous design in implementation, through video and/or transcript analysis and/or written reflection;
- Discussion of research to inform refinements (from previously read article)—information presented by researcher with focused discussion to reconstruct meaning in the context of this classroom;
- Refinements to design—focused analysis of video and/or transcripts of read-alouds to identify opportunities for refinement and plan specific refinements to design (e.g., identifying types of questioning that resulted in active meaning construction to inform intentional use of questioning);
- Planning—teachers planned how to read and discuss the next text, with a focus on the refinement to design.

I also met with the teacher individually in five reflection meetings, 20-30 minutes each time. Reflection meetings occurred after first readings, to enable refinements to implementation between readings. These meetings also followed a basic structure. After the read-aloud observation, the teacher was given a reflection sheet to guide self-reflection prior to our meeting. We began with the teacher sharing her own reflection on the implementation of the current design, followed by guided reflection with the researcher to consider particular points not discussed in the self-reflection or expand on points the teacher did present, and culminated with collaborative planning focused on refinements to the implementation of the design.

Instructional materials. The teacher selected the texts she read for my observations from a larger sample of options I provided, which were chosen based on high quality of writing and visuals, accuracy of information, authenticity of text features and structures, extent of recognition in the field of children's literature, and alignment with the content area curriculum the class was exploring at each point in the school year (Appendix A). Books were read twice to allow meaning-making to develop over repeated readings of the text, a well documented practice (Martinez & Roser, 1985; McGee & Schickedanz, 2007; Morrow, 1988)

Data Analysis

From a design research perspective, data analysis is an ongoing, iterative process, through which the data drive iterations of refinements in the instructional design. I approached observation transcript coding from a grounded theory perspective, in which observed trends in the data determined the coding scheme (Strauss & Corbin, 1998). Codes were also constantly compared to classroom discourse data from my own previously conducted studies and the existing research literature to inform, refine, and reorganize codes. Coding and analyses of all transcripts was performed using NVivo 9 qualitative data analysis software. Classroom discourse was coded at the level of topic unit, defined as all teacher and student talk from the initiation of a subject for discussion to the initiation of a new subject for discussion, and each topic unit was coded at the two dimensions aligned with our goals: level of interaction and construction of meaning (see Appendix B for coding definitions). Percentages of talk at each code were then calculated using the number of characters at that code divided by total number of characters (NVivo 9 capabilities). Percentages of talk representing interactions between codes were calculated as number of topic units at those codes divided by total number of topic units (NVivo 9 capabilities). Using the final coding categories, a stratified selection (by observation) of 40% of the read-alouds was coded by a second rater for measures of inter-rater reliability (Cohen's Kappa = 0.50; percent agreement = 85.3).

RESULTS AND DISCUSSION

Level of Interaction

The first design goal for this project was to build *interactive* discussion among the teacher and students. Through iterative rounds of analysis in this and another related study, I identified four distinct levels of interaction within topic units: non-interaction, limited interaction (~1 micro-level IRF exchange), sustained interaction (multiple IRF exchanges), or student-student interactions. Once these levels of interaction became clearer, the teacher and I narrowed our instructional goal to supporting *sustained interaction* in particular in read-aloud discussions. Ms. Engle achieved a significant shift toward sustained interaction across the three phases of the study, evidenced by 7.8% and 25.9% decreases in non-interactive and limited interaction topic units of discourse respectively and a 37.6% increase in sustained interaction, when comparing baseline to all intervention observations (Figure 1). To illustrate, in the baseline observation, Ms. Engle frequently engaged in limited interactions with students, following traditional IRE patterns with evaluation, but provided no feedback to students, such as in Excerpt 1.

Excerpt 1. Limited interaction.

Ms. Engle: So, I'll start with Miss Lucy. What do you think you know about frogs?

Lucy: They eat flies.

Ms. Engle: Okay. So, frogs eat flies... Tony [calling on next student]...

Topic units like this characterized the discourse throughout this read-aloud, comprising over 40% of all talk.

In response to PD in which we reviewed research on interactive discussion and analyzed transcripts of classroom discourse to identify features that appeared supportive of sustained interaction, Ms. Engle intentionally changed her instructional approach to incorporate follow-up questions and invite responses from students to each other. These approaches resulted in a shift toward more sustained discussion (although topic units remained relatively short compared with the possibilities for sustained interaction documented in previous research [e.g., Hoffman, 2011; Sipe, 2008]). Excerpt 2 is an example of sustained interaction from a reading of *What Do You Do With a Tail Like This?* (Jenkins & Page, 2003). Note in particular Ms. Engle's use of follow-up questioning and invitations for student participation to drive discussion (in bold).

Excerpt 2. Sustained interaction.

Text: If you're a Horned Lizard you shoot blood out of your eyes.

Students: I knew it! Ooh!

CeCe: I knew it! They squirt, they shoot eyes, blood from their eyeball so, will go away.

Figure 1. Percent of Talk at Each Level of Interaction Across Three Phases of Observations

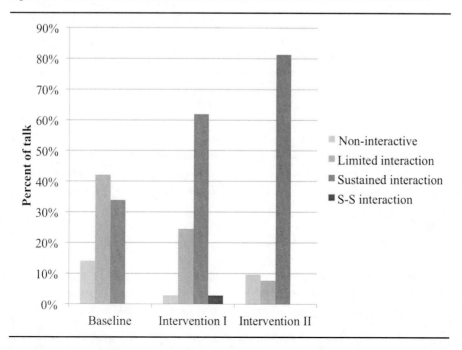

Ms. Engle: Ooh, CeCe, that's a good point! CeCe thinks that they shoot-

Tony: [unintelligible]

Ms. Engle: **What movie?** [inviting Tony to contribute]

Tony: I saw that kinda chameleon on the TV. Then he shoot, uh blood from the
              fox and he got away.

Ms. Engle: From the fox, or from- Ooh, so CeCe, [when] they do this

Student: They shoot with their eyes, and then something go away.

Ms. Engle: **Yes, then what comes out?**

Students: Blood!
              [less relevant exchange removed]

Ms. Engle: So, CeCe, so CeCe and Tony. They are squirting blood out of their eyes to
              get away. **Why do you think they squirt the blood?**

Students: So the other animals go away. So they don't eat them.

Ms. Engle: So they, so they scare the animals away. Good.

This excerpt represents a shift in the overall discourse patterns in read-aloud discussions, from mostly limited interactions at baseline to sustained interactions after invention. Sustained interactions like these provide the necessary meaning-space (McGee, 1995 [drawing on Corcoran, 1987]) for students to explore meanings with texts, but they do not in themselves equate students' active construction of meaning. Excerpt 2 demonstrates interaction among teacher and students, but the meaning constructed was rooted in pre-established knowledge in the text (and teacher) that the horned lizard squirts blood to scare predators away, and the teacher merely scaffolded students' progress toward that knowledge. Original constructions of meaning require analysis, synthesis, and critical thinking across texts and experiences, and are not limited to the comprehension of literal information seen in Excerpt 2.

Construction of Meaning

The second instructional goal was the incorporation of *coconstructed meaning* in read-aloud discussion. Co-construction of meaning is inherently interpretive, as opposed to focused on literal meanings explicitly in texts. Construction of meaning was understood as a continuum with independently (student or teacher) constructed meanings on one end and coconstructed meanings on the other, with a middle ground termed *reconstruction* in which teachers and students interactively discussed an interpretation that was still solidly characterized as pre-existing knowledge (with one "right" answer) and not necessarily open to the individual interpretations necessary for true coconstruction.

Independently constructed meaning. At baseline, the discourse was comprised mostly of meanings constructed by only one participant (either a student or the teacher) without uptake in discussion by the group. For example, Ms. Engle frequently modeled her own thinking about segments of texts she read aloud (13.6% of talk) or invited student participation but then failed to refine or extend student thinking with feedback or follow-up (28.5% of talk) (Figure 2), as seen in Excerpt 1.

Reconstructed meaning. Through PD focused on building meaning through interaction, Ms. Engle demonstrated a 19.1% decrease in percentage of talk comprised only of student interpretations, and a 21.4% increase in efforts to build from student contributions by reconstructing using her own content knowledge (Figure 2). The next excerpt was from a reading of *Rocks and Minerals* (Bingham, Parker, & Fuller, 2004) and demonstrates how Ms. Engle reconstructed student interpretations by incorporating interaction, but retaining most of the responsibility for meaning-making through the use of closed questioning, those with limited possibilities for "correct" responses and reconstructive statements of student talk that assume responsibility for the meaning-making (in bold).

Excerpt 3. Reconstruction.

Text: These form from molten rock.

Ms. Engle: What does it mean when we say molten rock, what do you think that means?

Student: Lava rock.

Ms. Engle: Yeah, lava rock. Hot rock. **Is the volcano, the stuff that comes out, is that hot or cold?**

Students: It's hot.

Figure 2. Percent of Talk at Each Level of Meaning Construction Across Three Phases of Observations

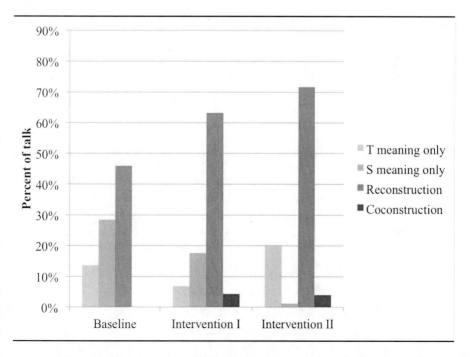

Ms. Engle: **Hot. So it forms from molten rocks so rocks are really hot-**

Student: and it melted

Ms. Engle: **. . .and then they finally cool down and harden. So they start off like this** [pointing]. . .

CeCe: What's hardens?

Ms. Engle: What do you think it means? **What does harden mean?**
              [less relevant exchange removed]

Lindsey: It means to get really hard, just like your bones.

Ms. Engle: Yes, get real hard like your bones. That's a good comparison. I like that. Lindsey said, CeCe, to answer your question: To harden means to make something real hard. **So it starts off like this (pointing), which looks almost like liquid. Remember how we talked about liquids? And what a liquid is? So they start like this and then they cool and harden and then they turn into this (pointing)**…

Examples like this demonstrate how even though discourse patterns shifted toward more interactive discussion, and students readily initiated comments and questions about the text, to the teacher and others, the actual meaning constructed remained almost exclusively in the realm of the "known." The terms molten and harden have pre-existing definitions that the teacher scaffolded students to acquire and connect to other relevant terms and concepts like heat, melting, and liquids; however, the interactions did not extend to the coconstruction of unique, interpretive, or innovative understandings.

Although we worked for several months on ways to reach true coconstruction of meaning through approaches like authentic, open-ended questioning (with the possibility for multiple interpretations) and invitations for students to respond to each other, there was only one topic unit coded as coconstructive out of the 140 total analyzed topic units. The one topic unit that was coded as coconstructive represented a spontaneous intertextual connection offered by a student and discussed among the teacher and students, which prompted a new connection for the class between two related concepts; however, even this one example was extremely limited in that it did not fully question or extend collective knowledge. A different excerpt was chosen to highlight an example ripe with potential for coconstruction, but where the teacher did not sufficiently support discussion to reach this goal. In Excerpt 4, the class was reading *What Do You Do With a Tail Like This?* (Jenkins & Page, 2003). The students' contributions touched on scientific concepts related to adaptation, reproduction, natural selection, and even genetics—all concepts complex enough to support deep, sustained, and coconstructive discussion, but the teacher never actually named these terms or pursued deeper discussion of them. The teacher's turns in bold represent what could have been the initiation of a coconstructive discussion that was instead dropped.

Excerpt 4. Potential for coconstruction.

Ms. Engle: Well what [does] the scorpion use his tail for?

Students: To STING!

Ms. Engle:	To sting people. If he stings people with his tail, **why do you think his tail looks like this?** …
Leo:	Because if somebody get all close to it, it'll sting them.
Student:	To say back off [several minutes of discussion of other animals and adaptations removed]
Wayne:	Maybe cause he was born like that?
Ms. Engle:	**Why do you think he was born like that?** Wayne. . . .had a really good comment. . . .Wayne said his tail looks like this because he was born like this and I said, "Why was he born like this?" [Students get very quiet]
Wayne:	Because he might um, his mom might have the same thing and she made him have it.
Ms. Engle:	**She made him have it? Why do you think she wanted him to have it?**
Student:	Because she's a mama scorpion.
Ms. Engle:	She's a mama scorpion.
Student:	Or a baby one.
Ms. Engle:	Let's move on, who's this last one? …

Although a typed transcript can never fully capture the feeling of the live interaction, readers who are educators likely felt their own emotional responses to this segment—the thrill of the dawning student enlightenment, and the disheartenment when it was disregarded. I chose this example to represent the potential of informational text read-aloud discussions as a context for coconstructed meanings, but also to highlight the role of the teacher in supporting coconstruction. There are many ways the teacher could have extended the discussion at those pivotal points, such as:

- Providing some preliminary background knowledge: "Animals look different because they change little bit by little bit over a long, long time based on what they need to live in their habitat."
- Asking probing follow-up questions: "So why do you think scorpions have this kind of tail now? How does it help them live in their habitat? How is that similar to or different from the way other animals use tails to survive?"
- Prompting for intertextual or personal connections: "What other ideas do you have that connect to why animals have the body parts they have? What about our trip to see the penguins at the aquarium? What special body parts do they have? Why? Are there any other books you know that talk about this?"

Any of these moves by the teacher could have catapulted this discussion into the realm of coconstruction and extended the literacies involved beyond basic understanding of the text. But without the intentional support by the teacher, the discussion fell far short of our goal.

Relationship Between Levels of Interaction and Construction of Meaning

The level of interaction and construction of meaning in topic units did not operate independently of each other; that is to say, particular levels of interaction tended to occur with particular levels of construction of meaning. Across all analyzed topic units (n = 140), units representing only teacher interpretations were most often non-interactive (e.g., teacher think-aloud), units representing only student interpretations most often involved limited interaction (e.g., Excerpt 1), and reconstructive units tended to involve sustained interaction (e.g., Excerpt 2) (Table 2). The pattern of intersecting codes indicated a relationship between the level of interaction and the construction of meaning whereby increased interaction supported higher levels of meaning construction.

Similar patterns have been observed with other teachers' interactions with students (Hoffman, 2011), but this does not mean that the pattern would represent all teachers' classroom discourse. For example, it is possible some teachers could extensively model interpretive thinking about texts, such as thinking aloud multiple perspectives and synthesis of ideas across texts, which would result in higher percentages of non-interactive coconstructed discourse. Or some teachers might encourage cooperative learning in student small groups, but not sufficiently support students to deeply engage with each other, resulting in high percentages of student-student interactions that are rooted in only one student's meaning constructions.

Other Considerations

Teacher content knowledge. First and foremost, interactive coconstructive discussion of informational texts absolutely requires extensive content knowledge from the teacher. This study focused primarily on informational science texts, for which the teacher had sufficient content knowledge for supporting basic comprehension, but may not have had the extensive knowledge necessary to support coconstruction. Speaking as an observer in the context of the scorpion discussion (Excerpt 4), the teacher appeared uneasy when trying to discuss how a scorpion inherits adaptations. When we discussed the lesson afterward in a reflection meeting, Ms. Engle explained that she recognized the complexity of the question, but simply did not know how to discuss it with young children. It is possible her difficulty discussing the concepts was due at least in part to an insufficient level of understanding of all the related scientific concepts—to support students to make such connections and explore such interpretations of informational texts, teachers must

Table 2. Percentages of Topic Units from All Transcripts at Each Intersection (n=140)

	Non-interactive	Limited interaction	Sustained interaction	S-S interaction	Total
T meaning only	**13.7%**	9.3%	3.3%	0.0%	26.2%
S meaning only	6.6%	**27.3%**	1.6%	0.0%	35.5%
Reconstruction	0.0%	13.1%	**23.5%**	0.5%	37.2%
Coconstruction	0.0%	0.0%	1.1%	0.0%	1.1%
Total	20.2%	49.7%	29.5%	0.5%	100.0%

have the academic command over knowledge to break it down into manageable explanations for a particular audience, their students. The need for extensive content knowledge has many implications and suggests many other areas for research, especially in early childhood education, where educators are typically prepared as generalists lacking the depth of content learning teachers of later grades experience.

Content instruction. For similar reasons, students must also have acquired some degree of content knowledge of the topic they are reading to be able to contribute meaningfully to interactive coconstructive discussions of informational text. Unlike narrative texts, which draw heavily on human experiences, informational texts rely almost exclusively on conceptual understanding specific to a topic. Without at least some knowledge of the topic and related concepts, students cannot begin to make connections to their own knowledge, to other texts, or to others' contributions in discussion, rendering coconstruction impossible. In an attempt to ensure a certain degree of student knowledge, the teacher and I chose texts to read aloud that were directly connected to their content instruction in the classroom. However, our attempts relied on our assumption that students would actually have extensive instruction and hands-on experiences in content area instruction, which was not always the reality. For example, in the spring of our study, the charter school officials mandated that primary grade teachers focus on teaching reading and math in order to improve testing outcomes, ignoring how significantly content knowledge affects comprehension of informational texts (Best, Floyd, & McNamara, 2008; Fox, 2009). This school decision is not an isolated case; many schools struggling to meet goals for state testing have made similar changes to instruction, with the same potential for disastrous results in the long term (Teale, Paciga, & Hoffman, 2007).

Informational texts. Another problem we encountered when searching for texts to align with the content curriculum was the limited choices of informational texts for young children for some topics. Informational text children's literature is growing; however, when searching for high-quality texts on a specific topic, we were at times faced with only one or two options, and even those were not always ideal. At times texts were too complex for first graders, or were not directly related to the students' learning in content instruction, which strained the teacher and students' abilities to make connections to their background knowledge. Students need extensive opportunities to engage with informational texts as part of content area instruction to practice the higher-level literacies required for deep processing of informational texts, including intertextuality, but currently there are limited texts available to support this need.

Limitations and Future Research

Being limited to only one teacher in one school greatly restricts generalizability to other contexts, although the selection of a classroom in an urban school serving an at-risk population supports the relevance and transferability of findings from this study to other similar contexts (Lincoln & Guba, 1985). The use of only one genre of children's literature, informational texts, also restricts conclusions to that particular genre. Because there is evidence that teachers use different supports for different types of texts (Smolkin & Donovan, 2001), and that students respond differently across genres (Shine & Roser, 1999), it was necessary to keep the genre of literature constant in this study to systematically study the changes in discourse as a result of the teacher's approach rather than text differences. Finally, this study was limited to only one part of the instructional day, albeit a significant one. Interactive and coconstructive discussion to support higher-level literacy practices must saturate students' entire educational experience in order to truly change students' approaches to texts.

Next steps in this line of research should focus on two areas of need: (a) refining professional development to better support teachers to reach goals for coconstruction (possibly including enhancing teacher content knowledge), and (b) exploring the transfer of classroom discourse designs to new contexts (different teachers and students, in other instructional areas, and/or with different genres of literature). If our goal is to initiate lasting changes to instruction that support long-term growth in student literacy achievement, we must continue to approach the problem from the perspective that all learners are capable of constructing complex meanings with texts, and thus promote teaching all students, even our youngest, interactions with text that extend beyond basic comprehension to encompass the interpretive literacies necessary to meet the demands of today and the future.

REFERENCES

Adger, C. T., Hoyle, S. M., & Dickinson, D. K. (2004). Locating learning in in-service education for preschool teachers. *American Educational Research Journal, 41*, 867-900.

Alexander, R. (2000). *Culture and pedagogy: International comparisons in primary education*. Malden, MA: Blackwell Pub.

Alexander, R. (2008). *Towards dialogic teaching: Rethinking classroom talk*. 4th ed. York, England: Dialogos.

Aram, D. (2006). Early literacy interventions: The relative roles of storybook reading, alphabetic activities, and their combination. *Reading and Writing: An Interdisciplinary Journal, 19*, 489-515.

Beck, I. L., & McKeown, M. G. (2001). Text talk: Capturing the benefits of read-aloud experiences for young children. *The Reading Teacher, 55*(1), 10–20.

Best, R. M., Floyd, R. G., & McNamara, D. S. (2008). Differential competencies contributing to children's comprehension of narrative and expository texts. *Reading Psychology, 29*, 137-164.

Bingham, C., Parker, S., & Fuller, S. (2004). *Rocks and minerals (Eye wonder)*. New York, NY: DK.

Blewitt, P., Rump, K. M., Shealy, S. E., & Cook, S. A. (2009). Shared book reading: When and how questions affect young children's word learning. *Journal of Educational Psychology, 101*, 294-304.

Brabham, E. G., & Lynch-Brown, C. (2002). Effects of teachers' reading-aloud styles on vocabulary acquisition and comprehension of students in the early elementary grades. *Journal of Educational Psychology, 94*, 465-473.

Brabham, E. G., Murray, B. A., & Bowden, S. H. (2006). Reading alphabet books in kindergarten: Effects of instructional emphasis and media practice. *Journal of Research in Childhood Education, 20*, 219.

Cazden, C. (2001). *Classroom discourse: The language of teaching and learning*. Portsmouth, NH: Heinemann.

Coiro, J., Knobel, M., Lankshear, C., & Leu, D. J. (2008). Central issues in new literacies and new literacies research. In J. Coiro, M. Knobel, C. Lankshear, & D. J. Leu (Eds.), *Handbook of research on new literacies* (pp. 1–21). Mahwah, NJ: Erlbaum.

Corcoran, B. (1987). Teachers creating readers. In B. Corcoran (Ed.), *Readers, texts, teachers* (pp. 41–74). Upper Montclair, NJ: Boynton/Cook.

Crafton, L., Brennan, M., & Silvers, P. (2007). Critical inquiry and multiliteracies in a first-grade classroom. *Language Arts, 84*, 510–518.

The Design-Based Research Collective. (2003). Design-based research: An emerging paradigm for educational inquiry. *Educational Researcher, 32*(1), 5-8.

Dickinson, D. K. (2001). Book reading in preschool classrooms: Is recommended practice common? In D.K. Dickinson & P. O. Tabors (Eds.), *Beginning literacy with language* (pp. 175–204). Baltimore: Paul H. Brookes.

Duke, N. K. (2000). 3.6 minutes per day: The scarcity of informational texts in first grade. *Reading Research Quarterly, 35*, 202-224.

Duke, N. K., & Bennett-Armistead, V. S. (2003). *Reading and writing informational texts in the primary grades: Research-based practices*. New York, NY: Scholastic.

Fox, E. (2009). The role of reader characteristics in processing and learning from informational text. *Review of Educational Research, 79*(1), 197-261.

Hargrave, A., & Sénéchal, M. (2000). A book reading intervention with preschool children who have limited vocabularies: The benefits of regular reading and dialogic reading. *Early Childhood Research Quarterly, 15*(1), 75–90.

Hoffman, J. L. (2011). Coconstructing meaning: Interactive literary discussions in kindergarten read-alouds. *The Reading Teacher, 65*, 183-194.

Hoffman, J. V., Roser, N. L., & Battle, J. (1993). Reading aloud in classrooms: From the model toward a "model." *The Reading Teacher, 46*, 496–503.

Jenkins, S., & Page, R. (2003). *What do you do with a tail like this?* Boston, MA: Houghton Mifflin Company.

Justice, L. M., Pullen, P., & Pence, K. (2008). Influence of verbal and nonverbal references to print on preschoolers' visual attention to print during storybook reading. *Developmental Psychology, 44*, 855–866.

Kress, G. (2003) Literacy in the new media age. New York, NY: Routledge.

Lankshear, C., & Knobel, M. (2008). *Digital literacies: Concepts, policies and practices.* In C. Lankshear & M. Knobel (Eds.), *Digital literacies: Concepts, policies and practices* (pp. 1-16). New York, NY: Peter Lang Publishing.

Levy, B. A., Gong, Z., Hessels, S., Evans, M., & Jared, D. (2006). Understanding print: Early reading development and the contributions of home literacy experiences. *Journal of Experimental Child Psychology, 93*(1), 63–93.

Lincoln, Y. S., & Guba, E. G. (1985). *Naturalistic inquiry.* Newbury Park, CA: Sage.

Lotman, Y. M. (1988). Text within a text. *Soviet Psychology, 26*(3), 32-51.

Martinez, M., & Roser, N. (1985). Read it again: The value of repeated readings during storytime. *Reading Teacher, 38*, 782-786.

McGee, L. M. (1995). Talking about books with young children. In N. L. Roser & M. G. Martinez (Eds.), *Book talk and beyond: Children and teachers respond to literature* (pp. 105–115). Newark, DE: International Reading Association.

McGee, L. M., & Schickedanz, J. A. (2007). Repeated interactive read-alouds in preschool and kindergarten. *Reading Teacher, 60*, 742-751.

Mercer, N. (1995). *The guided construction of knowledge talk amongst teachers and learners.* Clevedon, Avon, England: Multilingual Matters.

Mercer, N., Dawes, L., & Staarman, J. K. (2009). Dialogic teaching in the primary science classroom. *Language and Education, 23*, 353-369.

Morrow, L. M. (1985). Retelling stories: A strategy for improving children's comprehension, concepts of story structure and oral language complexity. *Elementary School Journal, 85*, 647-661.

Morrow, L. M. (1988). Young children's responses to one-to-one story reading in school settings. *Reading Research Quarterly, 23*(1), 89-107.

Mortimer, E. F., & Scott, P. (2003). *Meaning making in secondary science classrooms.* Maidenhead, Berkshire: Open University Press.

Moss, B. (2005). Making a case and a place for effective content area literacy instruction in the elementary grades. *The Reading Teacher, 59*(1), 46-55.

Nystrand, M. (1997). *Opening dialogue: Understanding the dynamics of language and learning in the English classroom.* New York, NY: Teachers College Press.

Pantaleo, S. (2004a). The long, long way: Young children explore the fabula and syuzhet of "shortcut." *Children's Literature in Education, 35*(1), 1–20.

Pantaleo, S. (2004b). Young children interpret the metafictive in Anthony Browne's "voices in the park." *Journal of Early Childhood Literacy, 4*, 211–232.

Pappas, C. C. (1993). Is narrative "primary"? Some insights from kindergarteners' pretend readings of stories and information books. *Journal of Reading Behavior, 25*(1), 97–129.

Pappas, C. C., Varelas, M., with Barry, A., & Rife, A. (2004). Promoting dialogic inquiry in information book read-alouds: Young urban children's ways of making sense in science. In W. Saul (Ed.), *Crossing borders in literacy and science instruction: Perspectives on theory and practice* (pp. 161-189). Newark, NJ: International Reading Association.

Reinking, D., & Bradley, B. A. (2008). *Formative and design experiments: Approaches to language and literacy research.* New York, NY: Teachers College Press.

Rosenblatt, L. M. (1978). *The reader, the text, the poem: The transactional theory of the literary work.* Carbondale, IL: Southern Illinois University Press.

Shine, S., & Roser, N. L. (1999). The role of genre in preschoolers' response to picture books. *Research in the Teaching of English, 34,* 197-251.

Silverman, R. (2007). A comparison of three methods of vocabulary instruction during read-alouds in kindergarten. *Elementary School Journal, 108*(2), 97-113.

Sipe, L. R. (2000). The construction of literary understanding by first and second graders in oral response to picture storybook read-alouds. *Reading Research Quarterly, 35,* 252–275.

Sipe, L. R. (2008). *Storytime: Young children's literary understanding in the classroom.* New York, NY: Teachers College Press.

Smolkin, L. B., & Donovan, C. A. (2001) The contexts of comprehension: The information book read aloud, comprehension acquisition, and comprehension instruction in a first-grade classroom. *Elementary School Journal, 102*(2), 97-122.

Strauss, A., & Corbin, J. (1998). *Basics of qualitative research: Techniques and procedures for developing grounded theory* (2nd ed.). Thousand Oaks, CA: Sage.

Teale, W. H. (2003). Reading aloud to young children as a classroom instructional activity: insights from research and practice. In A. van Kleeck, S. A. Stahl, & E. B. Bauer (Eds.), *On reading books to children: Parents and teachers* (pp. 114–139). Mahwah, NJ: Erlbaum.

Teale, W. H., Paciga, K. A., & Hoffman, J. L. (2007). Beginning reading instruction in urban schools: The curriculum gap ensures a continuing achievement gap. *The Reading Teacher 61*(4), pp. 344–348.

Vasquez, V. (2010). *Getting beyond "I like the book": Creating space for critical literacy in K–6 classrooms* (2nd ed.). Newark, DE: International Reading Association.

Vygotsky, L. (1978). *Mind in society* (M. Cole, V. John-Steiner, S. Scribner, & E. Souberman, Trans.). Cambridge, MA: Harvard University Press.

Wasik, B. A., & Bond, M. A. (2001). Beyond the pages of a book: Interactive book reading and language development in preschool classrooms. *Journal of Educational Psychology, 93*(2), 243–250.

Wells, C. G. (1999). *Dialogic inquiry: Towards a sociocultural practice and theory of education.* New York, NY: Cambridge University Press.

Wells, G., & Arauz, R. M. (2006). *Dialogue in the classroom. The Journal of the Learning Sciences, 15,* 379–428.

Zucker, T. A., Justice, L. M., Piasta, S. B., & Kaderavek, J. N. (2010). Preschool teachers' literal and inferential questions and children's responses during whole-class shared reading. *Early Childhood Research Quarterly, 25*(1), 65-83.

APPENDIX A

Texts Chosen and Read by Teacher:

Baseline:
Kasza, K. (2003). *My lucky day.* New York, NY: Putnam.
Bishop, N. (2008). *Frogs.* New York, NY: Scholastic Nonfiction.

Intervention 1:
Pringle, L. P., & Henderson, M. (2007). *Penguins! Strange and wonderful.* Honesdale, PA: Boyds Mills Press.
Page, R., & Jenkins, S. (2003). *What do you do with a tail like this?* New York, NY: Houghton Mifflin.

Intervention 2:
Bingham, C., Parker, S., & Fuller, S. (2004) *Rocks and minerals (Eye wonder).* New York, NY: DK.
Pellant, C. (2007). *The best book of fossils, rocks & minerals.* Boston, MA: Kingfisher.
Chancellor, D. (2007). *Maps and mapping.* Boston, MA: Kingfisher.

APPENDIX B

Codes and Definitions

Level of Interaction:

Non-interactive - Only one participant contributing

Limited interaction - ~ 1 IRE/IRF cycle of discourse

Sustained interaction - Several IRE/IRF cycles of discourse

S-S interaction - Students interacting among themselves in ongoing discussion

Construction of meaning:

T meaning only - T contributes meaning that is not interactively discussed with students

S meaning only - S contributes meaning that is not taken up by anyone else

Reconstruction - T builds from and extends S interpretations to represent with her own or accepted knowledge/understanding

Coconstruction - Meaning constructed integrates and builds from different perspectives or interpretations from multiple contributors

Management, other

Classroom management or other talk not relevant to meaning-making

Mark Sadoski
College of Education and Human Development
Texas A&M University

Section V: Research Methods

Innovation in literacy research methods is underappreciated and underpracticed. Many literacy researchers tend towards partisan loyalties to one research tradition or another and tow the party methodological line, seldom questioning the limitations of the methods involved. We perhaps too often assume the either-or roles of detached observers or cultural participants and follow our established methodological scripts. Despite the dictum that a research question should employ the methods most appropriate to it, we just as often forge questions to align with the methods with which we are most comfortable.

This is not a new phenomenon. Like the historical pendulum swing of literacy practices, educational research traditions have swung in and out of favor for more than a century. A wave of enthusiasm for experimentation dominated the field of education in the early 20th century, perhaps reaching its apex in the 1920s. Disillusionment with the results of educational experiments gave way to the rise of different approaches associated with narrative and psychoanalytic methods (Good & Scates, 1954). Experimental methods in educational research enjoyed a revival by mid-century (e.g., Campbell & Stanley, 1966) only to be challenged again by proponents of more ethnographic approaches (e.g., Bogdan & Bilken, 1982). Considerable debate ensued on the "paradigm wars," much of it philosophical, with calls for resolution or détente (e.g., Dillon, O'Brien, & Heilman, 2000; Kamil, 1995). How much resolution has occurred is open to question.

However, workers in the field have long been known for a healthy skepticism of scientific philosophy. Educational research involves the search for knowledge to guide practice. Keeping that goal in mind rather than adherence to fixed philosophical paradigms induces a more flexible and potentially productive mindset. New questions began to emerge. What if researchers blended methods in careful but creative ways that revealed more than could be found by employing one method or the other exclusively? What if experimentalists collaborated with their participants and found new insights to guide their designs? What if qualitative researchers categorized and quantified their observations and applied statistical analyses? Would such innovations lead to epistemological chaos or a more pragmatic approach to methods?

Researchers interested in practical theory and application forged ahead and discovered, among other productive findings, that the feedback loops inherent in qualitative methods could help define experimental questions, and conversely, that reliable but moderate statistical relationships could be found in qualitative data that would not be evident to the eye. That is, they found that methods were neither interchangeable nor mutually exclusive but they could be complementary. Another valuable result has been an increasingly critical attitude towards the claims of research studies based on the methods employed. The rigors of peer review and healthy academic debate not only keep us on our toes, but prod us to consider alternatives that might better answer our complex research questions.

By now, of course, innovative and mixed-methods research in literacy has become accepted with many chapters and volumes devoted to it (e.g., Calfee & Sperling, 2010). The papers in this section provide the flavor of this approach and some examples of it.

Bradley, Reinking, Colwell, Hall, Fisher, Frey, and Baumann provide a general introduction to formative experiments in literacy research. The formative experiment (aka design-based research, educational design research, field design research) typically involves collaboration between university-based educational researchers and their counterparts in schools in the evolution of an intervention. Three researchers summarize their studies in terms of conceptualization, rigor, resources, and challenges with a reflective final commentary. Davis, Baumann, Arner, Quintero, Wade, Walters, and Watson provide a conceptual model for formative design experiments and a summary of a study from the joint perspectives of university-based and school-based collaborators. Groenke, Bennett, and Hill report a mixed-methods study that researched the reading preferences of Black middle-school adolescents using both quantitative ratings and qualitative interviews. These studies serve as evidence that innovation in research methodology, while never beyond critical review, can be successfully conducted to produce new findings and new directions. Hopefully, both new and seasoned researchers will continue to explore innovations in research methods.

REFERENCES

Bogdan, R. C., & Bilken, S. K. (1982). *Qualitative methods for education: An introduction to theory and methods.* Boston, MA: Allyn and Bacon.

Calfee, R., & Sperling, M. (2010). *On mixed methods: Approaches to language and literacy research.* New York, NY; Teachers College Press.

Campbell, D. T., & Stanley, J. C. (1966). *Experimental and quasi-experimental designs for research.* Chicago, IL: Rand McNally.

Dillon, D. R., O'Brien, D. G., & Heilman, E. E. (2000). Literacy research in the next millennium: From paradigms to pragmatism and practicality. *Reading Research Quarterly, 35,* 10-26.

Good, C. V., & Scates, D. E. (1954). *Methods of research.* New York, NY: Appleton-Century-Crofts.

Kamil, M. L. (1995). Some alternatives to the paradigm wars in literacy research. *Journal of Literacy Research, 27,* 243-261.

Reading Contradictions: An Exploration of Reader Self-Concept, Value, and the Voluntary, Out-of-School Reading Experiences of Black Middle School Adolescents

Susan L. Groenke
Ann Bennett
Stephanie Hill
University of Tennessee, Knoxville

We hear too often about a reading "achievement gap" that exists between Black and White students in the U.S. In contrast to their White peers, Black adolescents are usually vilified in educational policy and school reform discourses as reluctant nonreaders and "at-risk" students who consistently fail to make gains in reading achievement.

However, these discourses obscure the fact that schools typically rely on narrow, limited definitions and assessments of reading and reading achievement (Groenke & Maples, 2009). Hall, Burns, and Edwards (2010) suggest that current school-based reading programs position literacy as an "autonomous set of skills" that adolescents must acquire and apply to be successful readers. When readers struggle in such programs, "it is assumed that they are either not trying hard enough or need additional skills-based instruction" (p. 8). The "achievement gap" discourse also obscures other legitimate factors that influence literacy achievement, such as the very real differences that exist among adolescents' text preferences, dispositions toward reading, and readiness levels. Reading researchers have long suggested that what adolescents like to read cannot be found in school (e.g., Worthy, Morman, & Turner, 1999). Valencia and Buly (2004) also explain adolescents do poorly on standardized reading tests for a variety of reasons that can range from poor word identification abilities and slow reading rates to fluent reading without comprehension. Reading researchers suggest that to address such range in reading preferences, abilities, and, thus, student needs, teachers should provide classroom access to books that adolescents can read with success and more multilevel, flexible, small-group reading instruction tailored to the needs of individual students (Allington, 2001; Dudley-Marling & Paugh, 2004; Groenke & Scherff, 2010).

Finally, the "achievement gap" discourse (and related "crisis" myths about a decline in adolescents' pleasure reading) obscure the fact that, although adolescents may become disengaged readers in school (or because of school), or have varying reading abilities and text preferences, they *are* reading a variety of texts outside of school for a variety of reasons (Moje, Overby, Tysvaer, & Morris, 2008). But what texts? What do urban adolescents report reading outside of school? In particular, what reading materials are interesting and personally relevant to Black middle-school-aged students? What do these texts say about about these adolescents' literacy practices?

In this paper, we share research that seeks to answer these questions. We describe early findings from an ongoing mixed-methods study to examine the reading attitudes, dispositions, and motivations of 14 Black middle-school-aged adolescents, grades 6-7, participating in the Afrocentric summer literacy enrichment program, Children's Defense Fund *Freedom Schools*® (CDFFS) (see Jackson & Boutte, 2009; Groenke, Venable, Hill, & Bennett, 2011, for more information on the program). We seek to understand how the program participants see themselves as readers, what values they place on reading, and what kinds of texts they are reading voluntarily outside of school. Findings reveal that many of the adolescents who participated in the summer program describe low self-concepts as readers or a dislike of reading, but value reading highly, and contradictorily, are reading a variety of texts outside of school (see Table 1). Adolescents' comments about in-school texts would indicate that reading materials are predominantly expository texts (e.g., content-area reading), the occasional whole-class novel read aloud by the teacher, or workbooks.

THEORETICAL FRAME: THE READING ENGAGEMENT PERSPECTIVE

We believe that motivation to read relies on engagement, or the willingness to engage with reading tasks, both in academic and nonacademic settings. Malloy, Marinak, and Gambrell (2010) explain that "engaged students choose to participate in reading tasks and persist in their attempts to make meaning [from texts]…" (p. 2). In contrast to solely cognitive measures of reading motivation, Guthrie and Wigfield (1997) describe the *engagement perspective,* which can be used as a theoretical framework for adolescent motivation-to-read research. Central to this frame are the motivational constructs of reader *self-concept* and *value.*

Reader Self-Concept

We understand reader self-concept to be comprised of how adolescents perceive themselves as readers, how they think others perceive them as readers, and how well they believe they can accomplish a given task or activity (Bandura, 1977; Eccles, 1983). In addition, we believe a relationship exists between self-concept—as determined by a reader's perceived or expected ability—and motivation to read. As other reading researchers have suggested (e.g., Morgan & Fuchs, 2007; Schunk, 1991), when readers hold negative perceptions about their academic abilities or lack skills necessary for completing academic tasks, they may also lack motivation to engage with such tasks.

Reading Value

Strongly related to reader self-concept is reader value, or the "relative attractiveness [an] individual places on a task" (Gambrell, Palmer, Codling, et al., 1996, p. 518). Whether or not adolescents see reading as a valuable pursuit is an important factor in considering adolescent motivation to read. When adolescents perceive reading as valuable and important and have personally relevant reasons for reading, they will engage with reading for multiple purposes in multiple settings. Wigfield (1997) suggests reader self-concept works recursively with reading value: When a student experiences success with a reading task, the student begins to value reading more highly, and, thus, becomes more intrinsically motivated to succeed.

Racial Identity and Reading Achievement

Tied to reader self-concept and the value a person places on reading is identity—an often unacknowledged aspect of adolescents' literacy development. Some researchers argue that racial identities position youth by shaping how they view, value, and use literacy practices. As example, while controversial, Fordham and Ogbu's (1986) "the burden of acting White" phenomenon suggests that Black adolescents resist high levels of school-based literacy achievement because they

Table 1. Text Preferences of Black Middle-School Aged Adolescent Participants

	6ᵗʰ grade	7ᵗʰ grade
Fiction	*Charlotte's Web,* E.B. White *Hoot,* Carl Hiassen *Joey Pigza Swallowed the Key,* Jack Gantos *Chasing Redbird,* Sharon Creech *Joseph,* Shelia Moses (Freedom Schools book) *Begging for Change,* Sharon Flake (Freedom Schools book) *The Hunchback of Notre Dame,* Victor Hugo *Roll of Thunder, Hear My Cry,* Mildred D. Taylor *Tale of Despereaux,* Kate DiCamillo	*Joseph,* Sheila Moses (Freedom Schools book) *The Scariest Stories You've Ever Heard,* Mark Mills *Maniac Magee,* Jerry Spinelli *Monster,* Walter Dean Myers *Winter Nights,* Hill, Ray, & Hailstock *Let That Be The Reason,* Vickie M. Stringer *Bad Boy,* Walter Dean Myers *Number the Stars,* Lois Lowry *Begging for Change,* Sharon Flake (Freedom Schools book)
Series Fiction	*Junie B. Jones* series *Lizzie McGuire* series *Hannah Montana* series *Confessions of a Teen Nanny* series, Victoria Ashton *Goosebumps* series, R.L. Stine	*Hannah Montana* series *That's So Raven* series, *Twilight* series, Stephenie Meyer
Non-Fiction	*My Life in Dog Years,* Gary Paulsen	*Michelle Obama: An American Story,* David Colbert (Freedom Schools book) *Gifted Hands,* Ben Carson Malcolm X biography (Freedom Schools book) Michael Jordan biography Grant Hill biography Shaquille O'Neal biography Randy Moss biography LeBron James biography Kobe Bryant biography Ray Allen biography Ron Ortez biography
Other	Cookbooks, recipes, menus *Time* magazine *Girl's Life* magazine *How to Draw Cats,* Barbara Soloff-Levy DJBooth.net (online site featuring new hip hop music) Disney books Joke books Bible	*Bone, Vol. 1: Out from Boneville,* Jeff Smith (graphic novel) Superman comics *Naruto* manga series, Masashi Kishimoto *Watchmen,* Alan Moore and Dave Gibbons (graphic novel) *Franken Fran,* Katsuhisa Kigitsu (comedy horror manga series) *Ultima* (role-playing video game) *Spongebob Squarepants* chapter book *Green Eggs and Ham,* Dr. Seuss Bible *Tiger Beat* magazine (fan magazine) Kidzbop.com (a video sharing and social networking site for kids and tweens) Newspaper

associate it with White identity and thus fear ridicule and rejection from Black peers. Similarly, Tatum (2008) suggests that Black adolescent males will engage with school-based texts when they resemble and help them negotiate their out-of-school contexts and identities. Work with diverse youth by Finders (1997) and Moje (2000) has also shown that young people use literacy practices to enact or develop desired identities deemed acceptable in peer communities. In addition, Marshall, Staples, and Gibson (2009) suggest that Black adolescent females look to genres like "urban lit" to negotiate their understandings of Black feminine identity, while Sutherland (2005) found the Black adolescent females in her study used literacy practices to resist teacher- and text-ascribed identity boundaries.

Social identities can also influence how adolescents are positioned at school as readers. As example, students with forms of cultural practices, experiences, and literacies that differ from "mainstream styles" typically privileged in schools are often considered "nonliterate" (Spears-Bunton & Powell, 2009). As Solórzano and Yosso (2001) suggest, when such exaggerated beliefs (e.g., "nonliterate," "low-achieving") are associated with categories or groups of people (e.g., Black students), such stereotypes function as justification for behavior toward such groups. Thus, when "nonliterate," "low-achieving" Black adolescents perform poorly on standardized tests, teachers and school administrators feel justified in their "abandonment" of them in remedial, test prep courses where academic expectations and student morale are low. Worse, as some educational researchers have found, these students drop out of school, because they feel disengaged, or they are "pushed out," so test scores will go up (Groenke, 2010).

As such, racial identity certainly matters when considering reading motivation, engagement, and achievement. Yet, while researchers have studied minority youths' academic self-efficacy and self-concept beliefs toward school work in general (Gutman & Midgley, 2000; Unrau & Schlackman, 2006), and role of racial identity in academic achievement (Chavous, Bernat, Schmeelk-Cone, et al., 2003), we know little about what motivates minority adolescent youth to read. While some research on overall academic motivation has been conducted using African American samples (cf. Long, Monoi, Harper, Knoblauch, & Murphy, 2007; Guthrie et al., 2009), little research exists that looks specifically at the reading motivations (especially voluntary reading motivations) of Black adolescents.

In addition, while important studies have reported on the reading dispositions and book preferences of predominantly White or Latino/a middle school students (e.g., Hughes-Hassell & Rodge, 2007; Ivey & Broaddus, 1995; Worthy, Morman, & Turner, 1999), Black primary and elementary students (Campbell, Griswold, & Smith, 1988; Williams, 2008; Zimer & Camp, 1974), or special needs students (Swartz & Hendricks, 2000), few studies have focused explicitly on reader self-concept, value, and reading preferences of Black adolescents in upper grades. As Williams (2008) explains, "Black participants are an extremely underrepresented sample in the literature review of book selection studies," and "a substantial research base does not appear to exist for educators to examine data patterns among children...who are Black and from economically-disadvantaged backgrounds" (p. 52). Our work seeks to address this gap in the research literature.

METHODS AND PARTICIPANTS

Research questions guiding this study were:

- How do Black middle-school-aged adolescents participating in an Afrocentric summer literacy enrichment program see themselves as readers? (self-concept)

- What value(s) do Black middle-school-aged adolescents participating in an Afrocentric summer literacy enrichment program place on reading? For what purposes do they read? (value)

- What do these Black adolescents choose to read voluntarily, for pleasure, outside of school? (book/genre preferences)

To address these research questions, we employed the Adolescent Motivation to Read Profile (AMRP) developed by Pitcher et al. (2007). Underlying this survey instrument is Guthrie and Wigfield's (1997) definition of motivation as "the beliefs, values, needs, and goals that individuals have" (p. 5). Because motivation-to-read is multidimensional, we wanted to employ a research instrument that both quantitatively and qualitatively assesses reading motivation. The AMRP is one such public-domain instrument, as it employs both a reading survey and a conversational interview. The reading survey consists of 20 items using a four-point scale assessing *self-concept* as a reader (10 items) and *value* of reading (10 items). The conversational, semistructured interview consists of 14 questions that assess what kinds of books adolescents find interesting, how adolescents find reading materials, and what adolescents read at home and school. The questions are open-ended to encourage free response. The interview provides for a more in-depth understanding and authentic insights on students' reading experiences, both in- and outside-of-school, their attitudes, and motivations.

We administered the AMRP reading survey and conversational interview in June 2010 to 14 Level III (grades 6-7) participants at a community youth center that served as the site for the CDFFS summer program. Of the 14 students who participated in this research, 88% (*n* = 12) identified themselves as African American, and 12% (*n* = 2) self-identified as "multiracial." Thirteen of the 14 participants attended the same middle school, which is classified as a Title 1 school and is located in a predominantly Black community. Data collected did not indicate whether or not participants attended the same elementary school. Also, we did not collect school-based data indicating what kinds or forms of reading instruction or curriculum the participants experienced in school.

Following the guidelines outlined by Pitcher et al. (2007), we scored the survey data and then conducted an independent group t-test on the results to determine the difference between the means of nominal variables. The small sample size (*N* = 14) rendered this approach more appropriate. The researchers conducted separate tests on each assessment of the survey, as well as the full survey score. We assumed an equal variance among the population, which a Bartlett's test confirmed. The *p*-values reported are for a two-tailed test, assuming the absolute value of *t*. The most interesting findings of these tests occurred with grade-level variables.

The researchers used Transana, an open-source transcription software program, to transcribe the 14 interviews (Woods & Fassnacht, 2010), and ATLAS.ti to code the interview data (Muhr, 1997). Researchers read and intercoded the transcripts multiple times. Because survey results revealed differences in self-concept and value by grade level, we read the sixth and seventh grade participant interview transcripts separately, looking for patterns and themes that emerged among each grade level, and then across both grade levels.

SURVEY AND INTERVIEW FINDINGS

The AMRP Survey

The average survey score was 60 (out of a possible 80 points), or 72%. Particularly interesting was that sixth grade self-concept scores were somewhat lower than value scores, indicating the adolescents placed a higher value on reading, even if they were less confident in their reading abilities. Indeed, overall, 70% ($n = 11$) of the adolescents indicated that knowing how to read well is *very important*, and 30% ($n = 3$) indicated that they think it is *important*. None of the participants indicated that knowing how to read well was unimportant.

The *t*-test focused on the grade levels of the participants. The greatest magnitude of effect was found in the value scores of the sixth and seventh graders. Beginning with the sixth graders, it was found that these participants scored, on average, 15.52 ($t(12) = 3.06$, $p < .01$) percentage points higher than the participants in seventh grade on the value aspect of the AMRP survey. On the other hand, seventh graders scored 3.69 ($t(12) = 0.52$) percentage points higher than the sixth grade participants on self-concept, but this was not found to be statistically significant at any confidence level (see Table 2).

Table 2. Results of Independent Group t-Test on Level III CDFFS Survey Data, by Grade Level

	Self-Concept	Value	Full Survey
Sixth Grade Mean	70.60	80.36	75.71
Seventh Grade Mean	74.28	64.83	69.56
Mean Difference	3.69	15.52***	6.15
Standard Error	6.99	5.06	5.31
Group Mean	72.44	72.60	72.63
Degrees of Freedom	12		
N	14		

Statistical Significance: * $p<.10$, ** $p<.05$, *** $p<.01$ (two-tailed test)
Note: All *t*-tests estimated using STATA.

The AMRP Interview

As Table 2 shows, the sixth grade participants had lower self-concepts about themselves as readers than the seventh grade participants, but placed a higher value on reading. Conversely, the seventh graders had higher self-concepts of themselves as readers, but placed a lower value on reading. Because we believe a relationship exists between reader self-concept, value, and identity, we looked to the interview data to shed light on this relationship as it pertained to the participants.

How do Black middle school-aged adolescents participating in an Afrocentric summer literacy enrichment program see themselves as readers? (self-concept)

One of the predominant themes across the sixth grade participants' interview data was the definition of reading as decoding, or the ability to apply knowledge of letter-sound relationships and letter patterns to correctly pronounce written words. Repeatedly, when asked how they defined reading, the sixth grade participants responded with a word-knowledge-based definition. One participant, Trish (all names are pseudonyms), indicated on the survey that she was an "okay" reader. When asked in the interview why she described herself this way, she responded, "…if I come across, like, a big word that I can't pronounce, like, I need help. Stuff like that." When asked what one has to learn to be a better reader, Dana—the most confident of all the sixth grade participants who mentioned wanting to read teacher-recommended *The Hunchback of Notre Dame*—responded, "…like, sound out words…" Sarah said that "reading more often" was necessary for becoming a better reader, because "like, if you don't, if I come upon a word or whatever, I, like, gain more knowledge and use my context clues and stuff."

Several sixth grade participants explicitly connected their word-based definitions of reading to feelings of frustration and low self-confidence as readers. Patricia stated that she "didn't feel confident in [herself]" as a result of her "[stumbling] over words" and her inability to "sound [words] out" on some occasions. Another participant, Donald, indicated on the survey that he thought he was a "poor" reader, and that his friends would consider him a "poor" reader, as well, because he "skipped" words he did not know. Donald went on to state that, without peer or teacher assistance and due to "skipping" words, "sometimes I never understand it [what I am reading] and I be pissed."

While we cannot be sure what kinds of domain-specific school reading tasks Donald and Patricia were referring to in their interviews, the adolescents predominantly mentioned frustrations with reading in content-area classes (e.g., social studies, science). Several participants explained that they found reading in social studies classes to be difficult because, as Trish explained, "It's like having to use big words and stuff." Deanna echoed this sentiment, "It's just…pretty hard… 'cause it's like really big words. So I can read big words but not like really, really big ones, so it's a lot harder for me to read in social studies."

Unlike the sixth grade participants who defined reading predominantly as decoding, the seventh grade participants defined reading as something more utilitarian. Similar to the sixth grade participants, when the seventh graders talked about reading, they seemed to associate it with predominantly nonfiction and expository texts in specific content-area classes. Scott described reading "…for applications and for, like directions…like directions for your work, directions to do for your work, uh, directions to do, like when your boss writes something for you, like, to take over and stuff." James complained that reading did not seem to involve stories, or fiction, at school: "Even in English…they just talk about language. They don't even tell no stories." James went on to say that he liked to read in history class, because:

> …when I look at science, it ain't really, I mean, I really don't like to read history other than boxing [history]. But it's just that it just tells you more about what

happened. It gives you a whole story, a whole passage in, other than science, 'cause science, only thing you hear about is 'mix this with flowers,' or 'put water in this to make it grow' or something like that.

Like the sixth graders, the seventh graders also complained of the "big words" in their content-area classes, and some described strategies they used to learn the definitions of words. Like sixth grade Donald, who would ask the teacher for help when he did not know a word, seventh grader Scott would also ask a teacher, but he listed other strategies, including consulting a dictionary, looking in a glossary, or using context clues.

What value(s) do Black middle-school-aged adolescents participating in an Afrocentric summer literacy enrichment program place on reading? For what purposes do they read? (value)

Despite understanding reading to be (at least in school) largely comprised of "sounding out words," the sixth grade adolescents placed a high value on reading. However, as we looked at the interview data, we noticed that various *kinds* of values emerged. Wigfield (1997) and Eccles (1983) have defined "subjective task values" that can include *interest value,* or how much an individual likes or is interested in the activity, *attainment value,* or the importance of the activity, and *utility value,* or the usefulness of the activity. Dana seemed to place an *interest* value on reading, as she often read a variety of texts (e.g., novels, magazines, Internet sites on rabbit care) both in and out-of-school, could name a favorite author (Sharon Creech) and genre (historical fiction), and talked about the "whole thrill of reading," explaining "it [reading] can take you to another place...like you can imagine going there." However, Dana also described a *utility* value for reading and seemed discouraged that her peers did not share this value. She stated:

> My friends don't really like to read...I try to tell them about good books to read so they can um get like AR points...but they don't like to read, so it doesn't really help...Um it's kind of sad because they don't like to read, because I always tell them that reading will help you later in life but they say you don't need reading so...Like um one of my friends Brittney and Jason. They don't like to read... and I try to tell them that it'll help them, but they say they don't need it. Jason wants to be an athlete and then Brittney wants to be an um architect. I think that somewhere along the line it will help.

Dana furthered that she would like to be an actress and realized the importance of reading for the purposes of knowing a script.

Another sixth grade participant, Trish, seemed to express an *interest* and *utility* value in reading, as well, as she liked to read cookbooks because she loved to cook and aspired to be a cook when she grew up. Trish revealed:

> I like cook books and stuff...cause I love to cook...I want to be...a cook when I grow older and stuff, and I want to, um, do my own show on Food Network, but me and my mom have to like get the video and everything. We're gonna call it Teen Cuisine and stuff.

Unlike the sixth graders, however, who placed a high value on reading, the seventh graders' value scores were low, even though the seventh graders predominantly answered that knowing how to read well was "very important" or "important" on the survey. This contradiction continued in the interview data, as we found that many of the seventh graders were reading voraciously outside of school, including the four seventh graders who had the lowest survey scores of all program participants and said that they read a book "never" or "not very often" on the survey. Predominantly, it seemed that all the seventh graders placed an *interest* value on out-of-school reading, and this interest seemed to be tied to texts inscribed with race and ethnicity, which we describe in more detail below.

What do these Black adolescents choose to read voluntarily, for pleasure, outside of school? (book/genre preferences)

As Table 1 exemplifies, both the sixth and seventh graders were reading a variety of texts, both in and out of school. The school texts the sixth grade participants predominantly preferred tended to be novels or biographies that teachers read aloud (e.g., *Tale of Despereaux, Charlotte's Web, My Life in Dog Years*). Out of school, the sixth graders described reading series fiction books (e.g., *Junie B. Jones, Teen Nanny*), series books related to popular TV shows (e.g., *Hannah Montana*), and a wide range of other kinds of texts including the Bible, magazines, cookbooks and recipes, online websites, and joke books. Humor seemed to be an important characteristic of the texts the sixth graders chose to read. Trish liked the *Junie B. Jones* series because "[Junie's] just so funny," and Donald liked *Joey Pigza Swallowed the Key* because the main character was "funny and crazy."

Both the sixth and seventh grade participants mentioned liking the Freedom Schools books, *Joseph* by Shelia Moses and *Begging for Change* by Sharon Flake (which were the only two of six Freedom Schools books the participants had read at the time of our interviews [see Jackson & Boutte, 2009, and Groenke et al., 2010, for more on the young adult novels Freedom Schools participants read]). Sixth grader Donald said he liked *Begging for Change* because it "taught you about life. How people do when they get frustrated." Seventh grader Brittany said she liked the novel because "it's actually, like, telling a true live story. [The characters are] having talks about, like, life."

Like the sixth graders, the seventh graders were also reading a range of genres outside of school (including manga and graphic novels, Internet websites, and newspapers), but it seemed that they were also choosing to read more texts inscribed by race and ethnicity. As example, James--who scored low on both self-concept and value on the AMRP—described himself as an athlete and described books and documentaries on Muhammad Ali, Joe Frasier, Sugar Ray Leonard, and the history of boxing that he liked to voluntarily read and view. When asked where he found such books and documentaries, he responded his church and a neighborhood African American cultural center/history museum. James explained in the interview that he lives across the street from the museum where he often goes and does research.

When asked why reading about the history of boxing was important to him, James explained, "Because it shows Black history and plus it's good to learn about what happened back in the day versus what happened in the new days, 'cause if you don't know what, if you don't know about history, then I believe you don't really have knowledge." James also explained that in the mornings, before school, he would often read books about African American athletes, such as Kobe Bryant, LeBron James, and Ray Allen. When asked why he read in the morning before school, he replied, "Because, I mean, since you are at home, and since you are getting ready to go to school, you might as well get a little knowledge in your mind."

James went on to explain that he looked up "funny knock-outs" on YouTube and said that he liked the books at Freedom Schools about Malcolm X. James also said that his mother encouraged him to read the Bible, and, because his uncle was the pastor of the church he attended, he talked a lot about the Bible with family members.

Another low-scoring seventh grade participant, Daniel, described voluntarily reading a biography on Dr. Ben Carson, a famous African American neurosurgeon. He explained that he found the book at his church. Daniel said that he was planning to read a biography on the First Lady Michelle Obama, which was part of the Freedom Schools curriculum. Daniel also stated that he had read about Malcolm X online.

Daniel also described voluntarily reading books and online articles about African American athletes, such as Randy Moss and LeBron James. Likewise, he mentioned reading about celebrities in the newspaper. He said, "Like Lil' Wayne going to jail and T.I., and all these people going to jail and stuff. And like when, when Drake broke his leg." He continued that he showed things in the newspaper to his mother, "Like, if somebody she know, or like, my friend, his mother had breast cancer and died…I showed and told my mama. I showed her."

When asked about reading at school, Daniel recalled reading *Maniac Magee* by Jerry Spinelli (1990). *Maniac Magee* is a young adult fictional novel that explores the themes of racism and homelessness. Daniel said that his teacher had the book in her classroom library and read it out loud to his class. Daniel liked the book, "Because like, he [Maniac Magee] was a White person and…it was back in the day where it was slavery and racism. And he [Maniac Magee] ends up having a Black family and he met a lot of friends." Daniel recalls that the main character got along with bullies and "he made interracial relationships back in the day."

A female seventh grader who scored low on the AMRP, Mary, mentioned several books when asked what she read voluntarily outside of school. She mentioned the book *Winter Nights* (Hill, Ray, & Hailstock, 2004). This book is published by Harlequin Kamani Arabesque, an imprint of Black Entertainment Television (BET) Books. Started in 1993, it was the first line of original African American romance novels from a major publishing house. *Winter Nights* is a multistory book for adults authored by popular Arabesque authors, all African American women. The book has been described as a "family-centered," winter holiday/romance anthology, with the stories centered around Christmas, Kwanzaa, and New Year's Eve. Mary said she found the book at the public library.

Mary also described her sister's influence on her as a reader. Mary explained that her sister was a reader and that she wanted to read the book her sister was currently reading called *Let That Be the Reason* (Stringer, 2009). This book, authored by an African American woman, is the first in a popular "urban" or "street-lit" series that describes the semiautobiographical "rags-to-riches" life-story of the author. When asked why she wanted to read this book, Mary responded that "every time [my sister] reads a book, she tells us about it and it sounds interesting." Mary went on to say that her sister got her excited about reading, "because she reads almost every day…and then she tells us about the books that she's reading." Mary also talked about reading the newspaper and doing the "fun parts" and "word searches" with her brother, and reading the Bible with her grandmother.

Finally, another low-scoring seventh grader female, Latanya, indicated on the survey that reading a book is something she "never" likes to do. Yet, her interview data suggests something altogether different. When asked if she shared reading materials outside of school, Latanya indicated the she possessed the "whole collection of *That's So Raven*." The *That's So Raven* books are series novelizations based on the popular TV sitcom by the same name, which aired on the Disney Channel between 2003 and 2007. The show and book series revolve around African American teenager Raven Baxter, her friends Eddie and Chelsea, her brother Cory, and other family members. The show blends comedy and humor with fantasy and the supernatural. Each episode and book usually depict Raven in an amusing situation that she must get out of by drawing on her ingenuity, psychic powers, and a variety of disguises.

At the time of the interview, Latanya stated that 22 books had been published as part of the series, so far. Of these 22 books, she had already read 16 of the books and had the intention of finishing the series. After indicating that each of these books contained approximately 12 chapters, she said that finishing one of the books made her feel "good," because she had "read a book," and she "pretty much get[s] something new every time I read a book."

Latanya explained in the interview that books like *That's So Raven* were given to her by her mother and that she shared these books with friends at the recreation center she attended. When asked why she liked these books, Latanya indicated that she found them "funny: That bully always be messin'."

IMPLICATIONS AND CONCLUSION

Our analyses demonstrate that—contrary to popular discourses that say Black adolescents are reluctant non-readers—they *are* reading a variety of texts, for a multitude of reasons and purposes, both in and out of school. Ultimately, the adolescents we talked to enjoy the reading they do outside of school, find it valuable, and are able to find and read texts they care about with purpose and agency—even if they do not identify as good readers in school. We think that part of this identification process as poor readers results from how they—and reading itself—might be positioned at school. If the reading instructional focus in their middle schools is decoding- and expository-text based, and they struggle with these skills and kinds of texts, then it seems like they are, to some degree, taking up and living out the literacy identity positions that are made available to them in school.

However, it would also seem the adolescents—especially the seventh graders—are doing other kinds of identity work outside of school. James reads about Black history and Black athletes. Mary and Latanya are reading texts that feature girls that look like them. We know reading motivation increases when adolescents are exposed to literature that offers them "... a view of their cultural surroundings, and provides insights into themselves..." (Heflin & Barksdale-Ladd, 2001, p. 810). Aside from the fact that the *That's So Raven* books feature a Black female protagonist and other dominant Black characters, the books in the series draw on elements of Black popular culture (Hall, 1996) such as attention to style and the body, use of humor, and expressive, vernacular language. Latanya reported liking the books because they're "funny," and she said she learned something new in each book she read. We cannot be sure what she learned, but we cannot help but wonder if she might be referring to an affirmation of her own racial identity.

The *That's So Raven* books and other books the adolescents mentioned—the Ben Carson biography, Black sports biographies—may also highlight important themes found in African American children's literature that resonate with these adolescent readers. Such themes include, but are not limited to: (a) the celebration of the strengths of the Black family; and (b) the nurturing of the souls of Black children by reflecting back to them, both visually and verbally, the beauty and competencies that we as adults see in them (Bishop, as cited in Jackson & Boutte, 2009, p. 110).

Mary seems to be interested in urban fiction or "street lit" (Gibson, 2010), a genre of African American literature that "usually features a young African American female protagonist between the ages of 16 and 23 who overcomes her austere surroundings" (p. 565). Gibson says such texts appeal to Black adolescent females, because they serve as "escape" and "guides to life" and affirm the "connections all African American women share with the characters because of their race" (p. 568).

Compton-Lilly (2012) suggests that texts themselves are cultural artifacts that have "historically constructed meanings—meanings about the types of people who read these books" (p. 40). As such, adolescents "claim or reject particular texts as they define themselves as particular types of readers" (p. 40). It would seem, then, that race, ethnicity, and Black culture(s)—inscribed as they are in the books many of these teens choose to read outside of school—cannot be ignored in considerations of them as readers. That these books are shared between these adolescents, their family members, and friends outside of school attests to their cultural and social importance in these adolescents' lives as readers, and we wonder if this ability to craft a different kind of literate identity outside of school may be one reason the seventh graders' self-concept scores remained high. We think that, in future research, teasing out the kinds of values and purposes adolescents describe for the multiple kinds of in- and out-of-school texts they encounter and choose to engage will be helpful in better understanding the relationship between reader self-concept, value, and identity.

This also points educators and literacy researchers to an important question: How do we help adolescents navigate and negotiate their reading desires and needs with school reading achievement? James misses stories, and many of the Freedom Schools participants described liking the Freedom Schools books because they are relevant and talk to their personal experiences. But these same students struggle with expository texts and "big words" in their content-area classes, and many struggle to see a value and purpose in engaging such texts.

Ultimately, we believe educators and literacy researchers need to find ways to help adolescents develop and maintain a sense of agency in literacy practice—a sense that they can assign their own purposes for literacy, but also consider more academic purposes for reading a variety of texts. Both adolescents' needs *and* their school achievement must be served by their literacy practices—these do not have to continue to be contradictory practices, but multiple *valued* practices in an always expanding literacy repertoire. Expanding the notion of what it means to be a reader is certainly one way teachers could begin to do this. Perhaps more importantly, paying attention to the multiple dimensions of literate identity (self-concept, value, identity as a reader/person), the texts we choose, and the instructional contexts we create for literacy learning can help us build upon the rich literacy practices young people bring to the classroom.

REFERENCES

Allington, R. L. (2001). *What really matters for struggling readers.* New York, NY: Longman.

Bandura, A. (1977). Self-efficacy: Toward a unifying theory of behavioral change. *Psychological Review, 84,* 191-215.

Campbell, K., Griswold, D., & Smith, F. (1988). Effects of trade back covers (hardback or paperback) on individualized reading choices by elementary-age children. *Reading Improvement, 25,* 166-178.

Chavous, T. M., Bernat, D. H., Schmeelk-Cone, K., Caldwell, C. H. et al. (2003). Racial identity and academic attainment among African American adolescents. *Child Development, 74*(4), 1076-1090.

Dudley-Marling, C., & Paugh, P. (2004). *A classroom teacher's guide to struggling readers.* Portsmouth, NH: Heinemann.

Eccles, J. S. (1983). Expectancies, values, and academic behaviors. In J. T. Spence (Ed.), *Achievement and achievement motives: Psychological and sociological approaches* (pp. 75-114). San Francisco, CA: W.H. Freeman.

Finders, M. J. (1997). *Just girls: Hidden literacies and life in junior high.* New York: Teachers College Press.

Fordham, S., & Ogbu, J. U. (1986). Black students' school success: Coping with the "burden of 'Acting White'." *Urban Review, 18,* 176-206.

Gambrell L. B., Palmer, B. M., Codling, R. M., et al. (1996). Assessing motivation to read. *The Reading Teacher, 49*(7), 519-533.

Groenke, S. L. (2010). Seeing, inquiring, witnessing: Using the equity audit in practitioner inquiry to rethink inequity in schools. *English Education, 43*(1), 83-96.

Groenke, S. L., & Maples, J. (2009). Small openings in cyberspace: Preparing preservice teachers to facilitate critical race talk. In S. L. Groenke & J. A. Hatch (Eds.), *Critical pedagogy and teacher education in the neoliberal era: Small openings* (pp. 173-190). London, UK: Springer.

Groenke, S. L. & Scherff, L. (2010). *Teaching YAL through differentiated instruction.* Urbana, IL: NCTE.

Groenke, S. L., Venable, T., Hill, S., & Bennett, A. (2011). Not your typical summer school program: Reading young adult literature in Freedom Schools. *The ALAN Review, 38*(3), 29-36.

Guthrie, J. T., Rueda, R., Gambrell, L. B., et al. (2009). Roles of engagement, valuing, and identification in reading development of students from diverse backgrounds. In L. M. Morrow, R. Rueda, & D. Lapp (Eds.), *Handbook of research on literacy and diversity* (pp. 195-215). New York, NY: The Guilford Press.

Guthrie, J. T., & Wigfield, A. (1997). Reading engagement: A rationale for theory and teaching. In J. T. Guthrie & A. Wigfield (Eds.), *Reading engagement: Motivating readers through integrated instruction* (pp. 1-12). Newark, DE: International Reading Association.

Gutman, L. L., & Midgley, C. (2000). The role of protective factors in supporting academic achievement of poor African American students during the middle school transition. *Journal of Youth and Adolescence, 29*(2), 223-248.

Hall, L. A., Burns, L. D., & Edwards, E. C. (2010). *Empowering struggling readers: Practices for the middle grades.* New York, NY: Guilford Press.

Hall, S. (1996). Introduction: Who needs "identity"? In S. Hall & P. Du Gay (Eds.), *Questions of cultural identity* (pp. 1–17). London, England: Sage.

Heflin, B. R., & Barksdale-Ladd, M. A. (2001). African American children's literature that helps students find themselves: Selection guidelines for grades K-3. *Reading Teacher, 54*(8), 810-819.

Hill, D., Ray, F., & Hailstock, S. (2004). *Winter nights.* New York, NY: Harlequin Kimani.

Hughes-Hassell, S., & Rodge, P. (2007). The leisure reading habits of urban adolescents. *Journal of Adolescent and Adult Literacy, 51*(1), 22-33.

Ivey, G., & Broaddus, K. (1995). "Just plain reading:" A survey of what makes students want to read in middle school classrooms. *Reading Research Quarterly, 36*(4), 350-377.

Jackson, T. O., & Boutte, G. S. (2009). Liberation literature: Positive cultural messages in children's and young adult literature at Freedom Schools. *Language Arts, 87*(2), 108-116.

Long, J. F., Monoi, S., Harper, B., Knoblauch, D., & Murphy, P. K. (2007). Academic motivation and achievement among urban adolescents. *Urban Education, 42*(3), 196-222.

Malloy, J. A., Marinak, B. A., & Gambrell, L. B. (2010). We hope you dance: Creating a community of literate souls [Introduction]. In J. A. Malloy, B. A. Marinak, & L. B. Gambrell (Eds.), *Essential readings on motivation.* Newark, DE: International Reading Association.

Marshall, E., Staples, J., & Gibson, S. (2010). Critical readings: African American girls and urban fiction. *Journal of Adolescent and Adult Literacy, 53*(7), 565-574.

Moje, E. B. (2000). "To be part of the story": The literacy practices of "gangsta" adolescents. *Teachers College Record, 102*, 652-690.

Moje, E. B., Overby, M., Tysvaer, N., & Morris, K. (2008). The complex world of adolescent literacy: Myths, motivations, and mysteries. *Harvard Educational Review, 78*(1), 107-154.

Morgan, P. L., & Fuchs, D. (2007). Is there a bidirectional relationship between children's reading skills and reading motivation? *Exceptional Children, 73*(2), 165-183.

Muhr, T. (1997). ATLAS.ti: The knowledge workbench (Version 6.2.27) [computer software]. Berlin: Scientific Software Development.

Pitcher, S. M., Albright, L. K., DeLaney, C. J. et al. (2007). Assessing adolescents' motivation to read. *Journal of Adolescent and Adult Literacy, 50*(5), 378-396.

Schunk, D. H. (1991). Self-efficacy and academic motivation. *Educational Psychologist, 26*, 233-262.

Solórzano, D., & Yosso, T. J. (2001). From racial stereotyping and deficit discourse toward a critical race theory in teacher education. *Multicultural Education, 9*(1), 2-8.

Spears-Bunton, L. A., & Powell, L. (Eds.). (2009). *Toward a literacy of promise: Joining the African American struggle.* New York, NY: Routledge.

Spinelli, J. (1999). *Maniac Mcgee.* New York, NY: Little, Brown and Company.

Stringer, V. (2009). *Let that be the reason.* New York, NY: Atria Books.

Sutherland, L. M. (2005). Black adolescent girls' use of literacy practices to negotiate boundaries of ascribed identity. *Journal of Literacy Research, 37*(3), 365-406.

Swartz, M. K., & Hendricks, C. G. (2000). Factors that influence the book selection process of students with special needs. *Journal of Adolescent and Adult Literacy, 43*(7), 608-618.

Tatum, A. W. (2008). Toward a more anatomically complete model of literacy instruction: A focus on African American male adolescents and texts. *Harvard Educational Review, 78*(1), 155-180.

Unrau, M., & Schlackman, J. (2006). Motivation and its relationship with reading achievement in an urban middle school. *Journal of Educational Research, 100*(2), 81-101.

Valencia, S. W., & Buly, M. R. (2004). Behind test scores: What struggling readers *really* need. *The Reading Teacher, 57*(6), 520-531.

Wigfield, A. (1997). Children's motivations for reading and reading engagement. In J. T. Guthrie & A. Wigfield (Eds.), *Reading engagement: Motivating readers through integrated instruction* (pp. 14-33). Newark, DE: International Reading Association.

Williams, L. M. (2008). Book selections of economically disadvantaged black elementary students. *Journal of Educational Research, 102*(1), 51-63.

Woods, D., & Fassnacht, C. (2010). Transana v2.42. http://www.transana.org. Madison, WI: The Board of Regents of the University of Wisconsin System.

Worthy, J., Morman, M., & Turner, M. (1999). What Johnny likes to read is hard to find in school. *Reading Research Quarterly, 34*(1), 12-27.

Zimer, S., & Camp, B. (1974). Favorite books of first graders from city and suburb. *Elementary Science Journal, 75*, 191-196.

Collaboration in Formative and Design Experiments: Where the Emic Meets the Etic

Jeni R. Davis
University of South Florida

James F. Baumann
Justin N. Arner
University of Missouri

Elizabeth Quintero
Brent Wade
Jill Walters
Heidi Watson
Columbia Public Schools

> In the beginning I did not believe that I was part of a co-research team; I thought we were guinea pigs . . . Now I feel like we have put a lot of work in [the project] and I love the changes that we have made and the tweaks we have made. I feel like it is ours now. We're part of it! (Heidi: fifth-grade teacher)

In this paper we report results from a study of the evolution of the research collaboration among three university personnel (Jeni, Jim, and Justin) and four classroom teachers (Heidi, Betsy, Jill, and Brent) as they worked together for two years on a formative design experiment (FDE) (Reinking & Bradley, 2008). The FDE explored the implementation of a multi-faceted vocabulary instruction program in the teachers' Multiphase Comprehensive Vocabulary Instruction Program (MCVIP) upper-elementary-grade classrooms.

Collaboration is considered to be an essential characteristic of effective FDEs that involve university- and school-based researchers (Barab & Squire, 2004; Shulman, 1997; Cobb, Confrey, diSessa, Lehrer, & Schauble, 2003). The literature, however, is relatively silent on the process researchers from the emic (or insider, classroom teacher) and etic (or outsider, university) perspectives underwent to form a collaboration in FDEs. The purpose of our inquiry was to understand the process that led classroom teachers and university personnel to develop and sustain a collaborative research relationship that furthered the goals of our FDE.

THEORETICAL FRAMEWORK AND RESEARCH QUESTIONS

FDEs—classroom-based educational interventions—have gained in popularity since their articulation in the early 1990s by Brown (1992) and Collins (1992), who were frustrated by the inability of conventional post-positivist, quantitative research designs to adequately address questions about pedagogical interventions. The definition of FDEs used for our research was that provided by Reinking & Bradley (2008). Specifically, FDEs are:

> grounded in developing understanding by seeking to accomplish practical and useful educational goals . . . focused on less controlled, authentic environments . . . use and develop theory in the context of trying to engineer successful instructional interventions . . . entail innovative . . . [and] seek understandings

that accommodate many complex, interacting variables in diverse contexts. (Reinking & Bradley, 2008, pp. 10-11)

Much of the research employing FDEs has been in science and mathematics education (Kelly & Lesh, 2000), but literacy researchers have employed this methodology more recently (Ivey & Broaddus, 2007; Jiménez, 1997; Reinking & Watkins, 2000). Recently there has been considerable elaboration of the methodology of design experiments (Kelly, 2003; van den Akken, Gravemeijer, McKenney, & Nieveen, 2006) and formative experiments (Reinking & Bradley, 2008), along with debate about the merits and demerits of this approach (Dede, 2004; Kelly, 2004).

Cobb et al. (2003) provided a typology of design experiments that differ by their context: (a) one-on-one teaching experiments; (b) classroom experiments; (c) preservice teacher development experiments; (d) inservice teacher development experiments; and (e) school and district restructuring experiments. Our vocabulary intervention project most closely matched Cobb et al.'s (2003) second type: "Classroom experiments in which a research team collaborates with a teacher (who might be a research team member) to assume responsibility for instruction."

Although FDEs may differ by context, there are important commonalities (Reinking & Bradley, 2008, Chapter 2), one of which is collaboration (Barab & Squire, 2004; Cobb, 2000; Cobb et al., 2003; Shulman, 1997). Collins (1990) described eight methodological criteria for design research, the first of which was "Teacher as co-investigators."

> It is critical that teachers take on the role of co-investigators . . . making refinements in the designs as the experiment progresses, evaluating the effects of the different aspects of the experiment, and reporting the results of the experiment to other teachers and researchers. (Collins, 1990, p. 2)

Our FDE, however, did not begin as a collaborative, co-researcher enterprise. Instead, we entered the study from our separate emic and etic perspectives which, over time, evolved into the kind of collaboration that Collins (1990) envisioned. In this article we present findings on the development of our collaborative pedagogical community, which involved transitioning from the distinct worlds of elementary teachers and university personnel to "a pedagogical community united by a common purpose" (Cobb, 2000, p. 331). The research questions that guided our study were:

1. Did a collaborative relationship develop between the classroom teachers and university personnel in our FDE?

2. If a relationship did develop, what was the process that led the co-researchers from their emic and etic perspectives to a collaborative pedagogical community?

METHODOLOGY

Research Site

This research took place in a Midwestern city with a population of about 100,000. The city's school district included 19 elementary schools. The elementary school for this research study served 513 students. The racial composition of the student population was 2.3% Asian, 33.5% Black, 5.8% Hispanic, 0.4% Indian, and 48.3% White. The free and reduced lunch rate was 57.0%.

Participants

The university personnel consisted of Jeni, a graduate research assistant and former elementary school teacher; Jim, a professor in literacy education and a former elementary school teacher; and Justin, the project coordinator and former elementary school teacher. Two fourth-grade (Brent and Betsy) and two fifth-grade (Jill and Heidi) teachers volunteered to participate in a two-year vocabulary instructional program. All teachers had master's degrees, and their experience ranged from five to nine years.

Data Collection

The data were collected from oral, print, and video texts. These texts came from field notes, audio recordings, video recordings, informal and formal interviews, written reflections, and instructional artifacts.

Data were gathered by university personnel and classroom teachers. The university personnel: (a) took field notes during classroom observations and research team meetings; (b) conducted formal and informal interviews with the teachers and students; (c) gathered artifacts that included lesson plans, e-mail conversations, and charts that listed ideas from all-day research meetings; and (d) gathered much of the audio and video of lessons, interviews, and research team meetings.

The classroom teachers provided written reflections on the implementation of MCVIP and the formative aspects of the study. Classroom teachers reflected in writing on the progress of this study several times each year. They also gathered video of lessons and activities that they believed to provide valuable insight into the development of MCVIP.

Date Analysis

We used content analysis in our study (Hsieh & Shannon, 2005; Lincoln & Guba, 1985), which "involves the inspection of patterns in written texts, often drawing on combination of inductive, deductive, and abductive analytical techniques" (Hoffman, Wilson, Martinez, & Sailors, 2011, p. 29). Specifically, we employed Krippendorff's (2004) approach to content analysis, which is defined as "a research technique for making replicable and valid inferences from texts . . . to the contexts of their use" (p. 18). Therefore, we made inferences from our oral, print, and video textual data about the evolutionary process that the research team experienced as they moved from disparate emic and etic perspectives to a collaborative pedagogical community.

Our analysis process involved four phases. In *Phase I: Data Identification*, we combed through our voluminous data set to extract the textual data that was germane to our research questions. For example, we did not pursue data that focused on students' vocabulary growth, but we did examine data on the negotiations required in a study involving school-based and university-based participants.

In *Phase II: Initial Categorization*, we inferred a preliminary set of categories. For example, we named one initial category "Starting Points," and another was named "Gaining Momentum." In *Phase III: Theme Construction and Category Refinement*, we inferred themes that supported or refuted our initial categories, which led to a revised set of categories with corresponding themes. For example, the initial category "Gaining Momentum" was not supported by textual data and thus was dropped. In contrast, the "Starting Points" category—which initially was inferred from teachers' concerns about the time commitment required for the study and the university personnel's worries about fulfilling their obligations to the grantor agency—morphed into a broader category named "Starting Perspectives: Struggles and Frustrations in a New Research Experience" that was supported by additional themes such as teachers' anxiety that MCVIP would displace their district curriculum and the university personnel's urgency to identify school and teacher participants.

In *Phase IV: Establishing Credibiliy*, we employed Lincoln and Guba's (1985) techniques of "prolonged engagement, persistent observation, and triangulation" (p. 301). We demonstrated *prolonged engagement* by the two years we spent with the teachers in their classrooms and in team meetings. We documented *persistent observation* by the recurrence of the categories and supporting themes in the data. Our data were *triangulated* by inferring our categories and themes from multiple data sources across multiple researchers.

RESULTS

Through content analysis we inferred four categories: (a) Starting Perspectives, (b) Establishing Trust, (c) Belief in the Project, and (d) Approaching Full Co-Researcher Status. Each of these categories was supported by several themes. Table 1 presents theses themes and categories. These findings clearly demonstrated that a collaborative relationship developed between the classroom teachers and university personnel, answering research question one affirmatively. With regard to research question two, the results revealed a clear four-step process that demonstrated our progression from our initial emic and etic perspectives to a unified co-researcher status. In the following sections, we present data that support each category.

Starting Perspectives

When the project began, our separate insider and outsider views and experiences were evident. This was especially true during the first semester of Year 1 of the study as we began to get to know one another.

Emic (Betsy, Brent, Heidi, and Jill). Initially, the classroom teachers were interested in the project and appreciated a stipend for participating. They were concerned, however, about the amount of work that would be required generating materials and preparing lessons. During a research team meeting, after the university personnel distributed copies of student handouts for a lesson, Jill inquired if they would receive student work papers for every lesson. Jill also asked if there would be lesson plans to accompany other instructional materials. Reflecting back to the beginning of the project, Brent and Heidi assumed their role would be coming up with new vocabulary lessons.

Classroom teachers also worried that the vocabulary lessons would take too much time and compete with their regular instruction. Betsy once asked, "How will all this fit in my week? High frequency words, Marazno [existing academic vocabulary program], character trait words, . . .?" Similarly Heidi stated, "I am having a hard time getting to all [vocabulary instruction] this week." She continued, "I'm not having time. We have intervention half an hour every day with a different class; then we switch for science and social studies; and [then] [vocabulary]!" On a pre-meeting reflection sheet, Jill wrote, "Time is always a factor" when asked to list factors that inhibited the effectiveness of the vocabulary program.

Etic (Jeni, Jim, and Justin). Concurrently, the university personnel felt the weight of the obligation to fulfill federal funding agency grant requirements and were pressed to identify a school and teachers to participate. Early in the study they also tried to reassure their teacher colleagues that the initial tensions and frustrations they felt would be alleviated later and that everyone would

Table 1. Categories and Themes from the Content Analysis

Category 1
Starting Perspectives: Struggles and Frustrations in a New Research Experience

Classroom teachers (emic)
- Will it consume too much time within our already packed curriculum?
- Will it be too much work?
- How will this project interfere with my regular instruction?

University Personnel (etic)
- Obligation to fulfill grant requirements
- Need for school and teacher participation
- Worry about getting a site and participants who are open to do a 2-year intervention

---

Category 2
Establishing Trust: Developing Commitment to One Another and to the Project

Classroom Teachers (emic)
- Deference to university personnel and ongoing concerns about time commitment
- Beginning to feel valued and professional
- Teachers getting to know one another more within and across grade levels

University Personnel (etic)
- Inviting and encouraging input from teachers to improve troublesome components
- Observing and working in the classrooms with the students and teachers
- Following through on promises and obligations to the teachers and study

---

Category 3
Belief in the Project: Collaborating on Curriculum and Data Gathering

Classroom Teachers (emic)
- Realizing that they have considerable say in the project and seeing significant value in the program for the students
- Believing that their input is truly invited and valued
- Beginning to view the university researchers as colleagues

University Personnel (etic)
- Conducting demonstration lessons and establishing credibility as teachers
- Listening carefully and modifying the program from teacher input
- Getting to know the teachers and students on a more personal level through multiple observations and interactions

---

Category 4
Approaching Full Co-Researcher Status: Achieving Mutual Ownership

- Teacher-led professional development within the school
- Classroom teachers and university personnel presenting papers at conferences
- Mutual decision-making about the program
- Group critique of research videos
- Integrating the vocabulary program into the broader curriculum
- Viewing the program and study as "ours"
- University and school participants establish strong professional bonds and friendships

---

work together to make the program fit more readily within the existing curriculum. In an early research meeting, Jim stated, "If that [teaching high frequency words] gets problematic, we want to hear. We want to talk about that. But we're going to modify those lessons. . . . I think maybe we can streamline them a bit, too." Jeni reassured the classroom teachers, once stating, "We want it [teaching vocabulary] to be easy and not a burden and fit with what you're already doing." Encouraging the teachers to speak openly of their frustrations with the program was significant. Jim once commented, "What we're doing is just kind of debriefing [about] what we're seeing: the good, bad, and ugly."

There were, no doubt, bumps in the road at the beginning of the study. The classroom teachers and the university personnel had a long way to go to meld their emic and etic perspectives to form a team of cohesive, collaborative research team. While implementing the program all seven researchers were faced with what seemed to be an overwhelming and complex program, as Heidi expressed in a reflection: "I was worried at first that this was going to put *another thing* on my plate. I was worried that I was going to have to create LOTS of lessons and find materials to fit each since this is what I had done in the past with vocabulary."

Establishing Trust

Building on our starting perspectives, the classroom teachers and university researchers worked to get acquainted with one another. It was important during this time for the university personnel to follow through with their promises and obligations to the study and to the teachers. Midway through Year 1 of the study, a commitment began to develop toward one another and to the project.

Emic (Betsy, Brent, Heidi, and Jill). As the study got under way, the classroom teachers shared their knowledge and understanding of vocabulary instruction. Brent shared that he didn't have a knowledge base for vocabulary instruction and Betsy followed up by saying, "We have become pretty fluid with our curriculum vocabulary instruction as far as reading and math and some writing. I don't feel like I am very good at helping kids with vocab words they would run across in their own reading."

During Year 1 of program implementation, the classroom teachers were concerned with the number of words they were introducing to the students. Jill stated, "I don't want to overwhelm them with too many words at once." The classroom teachers were torn between the quantity of words to teach each week and the quality and depth of instruction.

In addition to the number of words, classroom teachers returned to the amount of time vocabulary instruction was taking out of the already busy daily schedules. In an e-mail, Betsy wrote:

> I am going to be really honest and I hope that it doesn't offend anyone…With the HFW [High Frequency Word] lessons and the Character Trait lessons, these are already taking up about an hour three times a week. […] I don't think I will be able to fit in the Hink Pinks lessons. ☹ I'm sorry. Maybe we can fit it in a little later. Hope this is okay.

Jim responded as follows:

> Thanks for your note and candor. We're not offended at all. We WANT you to keep us informed about demands of the study, and we understand fully about having too much going on this week. Just do what is reasonable.

If the HFW and CT [character trait] lessons are consuming 3 hours a week for you and maybe others, then we need to address how to be both more efficient in the lessons and how to integrate them better into your curriculum. As we've said all along, you can expect to be spending a bit more time on vocabulary as a result of the project, but this should not come at the expense of your existing curriculum and instruction.

Please (everyone) keep us informed of issues like these. We can talk about them as necessary via email or in some individual chats at your school. Also, when we get together as a group next on Friday, November 5th, let's address this as a team.

As this exchange demonstrates, the classroom teachers and university personnel were beginning to feel comfortable exchanging ideas and opinions candidly. This would not have occurred at the beginning of the study. The gradual development of mutual respect and trust enabled team members to interact comfortably about substantive issues.

In sum, classroom teachers got to know each other more within and across grade levels and began to feel valued and professional by their participation in the research project. Near the end of Year 1, Brent asked, "Did you guys want to do a BBQ or something like that? I mean we don't want it to be one more thing you have to do to hang out with us…We just wanted to say thank you and just provide like a place to gather."

Etic (Jeni, Jim, and Justin). During this time of establishing trust and getting acquainted, the university personnel worked to develop and revise components of the vocabulary program that were troublesome for the teachers in order to be consistent with the promises and obligations that were made to the teachers and the study. The university personnel also expressed to the teachers the importance of relying on their professional knowledge, judgment, and experiences. For example, during a conversation following a modeled lesson by one of the university personnel, Jim stated, "I don't want to get us into standardizing such that you change what works for you, or if this isn't working we don't find an alternative, right? So go with it. And maybe because of you, because of your kids, this is the way to do it, then let's go for it, right? So we might have a couple little models, or a couple of scenarios for how to do it." Teachers were invited and encouraged to share input, leading the teachers to feel valued and professional.

Following an observed word learning strategy lesson, Jeni asked for Jill's input regarding the instructional materials provided for the lessons:

Jeni: Do you think the lessons are coming too quickly?

Jill: No, but I think that maybe…more examples

Jeni: More examples?

Jill: Yeah, more examples to use. Like, more pretty explicit examples. Like for the definition one. I liked the dinosaur thing that we did, but I don't feel like it was explicit enough of a definition context clue … I'd like to see them have like a passage and have to find several hard words with definition context clues because they wouldn't all pick out the same word. Like identify.

Jeni: A passage that has multiple, maybe challenging words …

Jill: Right, with definition clues. Yeah and see if they can kind of apply that.

Jeni: Would we make the hard words apparent, like bold face them, or just let them [the students]…

Jill: I would say let them see what they come up with.

Jeni: Ok

It was important for the university personnel to elicit the classroom teachers' reflections following the implementation of the lessons. Jim was adamant about the research being a formative design and that the classroom teachers were experimenters right along side of the university personnel. In an all-day meeting, Jim stated, "The lesson plan is not a script. We can make revisions if needed."

To support classroom teachers and the time taken to teach individual words, the focus became on efficiency. Jim stated, "Let's not kill high frequency words, but figure out how to instruct them more efficiently." Jeni encouraged, "You know your students, so if they are kind of glazed over, stop and say 'let's unpack this a little.' But if they're with you, then just keep moving."

Belief in the Project

Once trust was established, the research team began to develop a real commitment to the project, and teachers began to see the value in the program for their students. Over the summer between years one and two of the study, and into the fall of the second year, genuine collaboration began as the classroom teachers and university personnel worked together to improve the curriculum and to gather data.

Emic (Betsy, Brent, Heidi, Jill). Each classroom teacher devoted a 30-minute block daily to vocabulary instruction, in addition to the vocabulary they embedded in math, language arts, science, and social studies. The vocabulary instruction block was suggested by one of the classroom teachers, who argued that it would be an excellent way to implement many of the new vocabulary components. Soon everyone had a 30-minute block of vocabulary instruction. Heidi wrote, "Once I got started teaching, saw the students' excitement and their progress; I was impressed."

Prior to an all-day research team meeting, classroom teachers responded in writing to a few questions about the formative aspects of the research project (Reinking & Bradley, 2008). In response to a question about unexpected positive or negative effects of the vocabulary program, Jill wrote, "they are using the words frequently in writing and conversation. [The program] has made me more aware of words and taking a few seconds to discuss words as they come up throughout the day." Heidi wrote, "students are more aware of unknown words," and "I'm more aware of words."

Teacher interviews were conducted at the beginning and the end of each year. At the end of Year 1, teachers were asked about their opinion of the new program. Jill commented, "I would never *not* teach it…" Heidi interrupted her stating, "that was what I was just saying. Even when our grant is over, I still have kept copies of everything. I can't imagine not teaching it now. I don't know how we did without. I love it! The kids love it!"

Etic (Jeni, Jim, and Justin). University personnel taught lessons to demonstrate components of the program. Through weekly observations, the university personnel got to know the teachers and students on a more personal level, and the classroom teachers began to view the university personnel as colleagues.

The university personnel listened carefully to the classroom teachers during the bi-weekly Friday morning team meetings during which the classroom teachers reflected on the week's instruction. These conversations prompted the university personnel to significantly modify the program. Classroom teachers suggested additions, such as interactive activities during lessons and independent activities following other lessons. By making these changes, the classroom teachers realized that they had a significant say in the project and believed that their input was truly needed. Several times university personnel asked the classroom teachers for materials they may need to enhance their instruction. For instance, materials, such as dictionaries, binder dividers, picture books, and bookshelves were purchased by teacher request.

Approaching Full Co-Researcher Status

At the mid-point of Year 2 of the study, our belief in the project led the researchers to consider the project as "ours" as we took an egalitarian approach to the research process. The qualifier *approaching* is used in this category name, however, because it is unrealistic to attain complete co-researcher status given the historic power differential between public school and university positions (Reinking & Bradley, 2008). Nevertheless, a real and deep collaboration among classroom teachers and university personnel grew.

Throughout the project, university personnel encouraged classroom teachers to modify the instructional plans they provided to meet their students' needs and their own teaching styles. During an all-day meeting, the classroom teachers recorded the program changes they made since the beginning of the study that enhanced their vocabulary instruction. Brent wrote that he used "sentence fragments to help students with using the [new] word in a meaningful and correct way (sentence pattern)." Jill wrote:

> I do a lot of having them create their own examples for words and sharing those to get others [students] thinking about the words and using the context clues. I also find I'm using more advanced words in my everyday conversation and stopping to quickly define those words, just so they have quick exposure to other more difficult words.

Betsy wrote:

> I have also made the [high frequency word] . . . lessons more interactive to increase student interest and participation by asking students to stand up, sit down, put hand on head when they know the answer. We have also started highlighting answers in the text on the Smart Board when we have searched for them.

These lesson modifications were celebrated, and the classroom teachers left the meeting with new ideas to implement in their own classrooms.

One change that enhanced the relationship among the seven researchers was moving monthly all-day meetings to the family room in Jim's home. This comfortable environment eliminated the formality of the university conference room where the team had previously met and promoted friendly, candid discussion. At these meetings, classroom teachers shared video of their instruction, offered insightful critique of their own teaching and that of their colleagues, and commented on strengths and limitations of the program.

Discussions lead to negotiated but mutually-agreed-upon decisions about the program. For example, the team decided to administer a weekly posttest for newly taught high-frequency words also as a pretest, so that teachers could differentiate the lesson for students who already knew the words. The team also decided to select and teach content-critical words from the district-adopted science, math, and social studies textbooks and materials. After much discussion about nomenclature, the team decided to use *Text Words* rather than the more conventional *Academic Vocabulary* for subject-matter vocabulary, a term that better fit their existing curriculum and experiences teaching these kinds of words.

At one all-day meeting, classroom teachers and university personnel composed on a chart a detailed set of "General Principles for Text Word Instruction" to guide their selection of Text Words and the development of corresponding lessons. The team also worked through lesson pacing issues and sought the best way to integrate the vocabulary program into their broader curriculum. In a reflection on his role in the study, Brent wrote:

> I feel that I have a part in the creation of lesson plans and the sequencing of the different [research project] components. I feel that I gather data through measurable data and observations made of student work and participation in the program. I feel I am a co-researcher most when we are discussing how a component will be implemented. I also feel that my feedback is listened to, scrutinized and sometimes utilized for the betterment of the program.

In Year 2, the classroom teachers co-authored a research paper at a professional literacy meeting, and Jill and Brent joined Jeni, Jim, and Justin in conducting a three-hour workshop on the vocabulary program for teachers attending a large national literacy meeting. These conference papers and presentations provided voices for all involved in the study to express their ownership of and full participation in the project as co-researchers.

Near the end of the two-year study, the classroom teachers reflected on their role within the study. Heidi commented:

> We have been collecting data from the beginning, helping to create and tweak lessons, giving constant feedback and sharing my thoughts on how this was working for my students and myself. I feel like my opinion is valued, listened to and talked about. It has been WAY easier than what I expected.

Betsy's response represented well the four classroom teachers' sentiments about their emerging status as co-researchers:

> I am a co-researcher and truly believe that this is because of the way that Jim, Jeni and Justin have listened to us and tried to incorporate suggestions my colleagues and I made along the way to make instruction better. I also really appreciated the constant dialogue and reflection that occurred between all members of this research team.

Figure 1. Researcher Collaboration Diagram

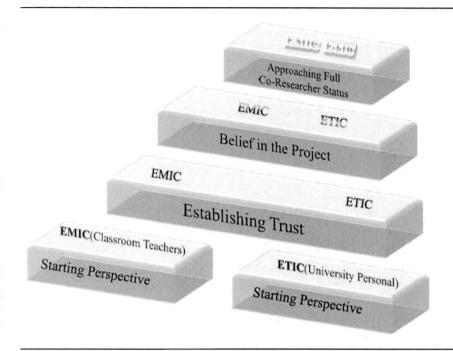

DISCUSSION

Figure 1 illustrates our process of establishing an effective collaborative pedagogical community. The separate boxes at the base of the figure signify our initially distinct emic and etic starting perspectives on educational research. The categories on the front of each step depicts our progression toward a co-researcher status. The decreasing degrees of shading of the words *emic* and *etic* demonstrate the process that we experienced as we moved from diverse perspectives to a more unified one.

Our experience demonstrates that it takes considerable time to move up the steps and through this process. For instance, it was not until near the end of our two-year collaboration that our teacher participants recognized the journey that they had completed. Jill stated that:

> Now I feel like a part of the team, not just a participant. It was, at first, surprising to me how much freedom we were given to expand on and modify the lessons we were provided with. As I've gotten further into the study, I've felt more and more like a co-researcher. This is because I am taking what was already there and trying new things. I feel like my contributions are valuable and that they affect the research findings.

We all share Jill's feelings of being part of a team and about feeling more like co-researchers than just participants.

We have learned and grown with one another, and we have discussed the possibility of a new study in which our roles might expand. Heidi, Betsy, Jill, and Brent have suggested that if Jim,

Jeni, and Justin seek another grant to examine the efficacy of the vocabulary curriculum in a more conventional experimental study, they would be in a more knowledgeable, credible position to provide the professional development to new teacher participants than those of us at the university. They are correct, and time will tell whether the collaboration continues.

As we reflect on our experience in the research project, we list below factors that enabled us to move from our originally disparate perspectives on research to co-researcher stance. We present the following, therefore, as a possible guide rather than a roadmap.

- Be secure in your knowledge and convictions of teaching, learning, and research, but likewise anticipate that they will be challenged and modified.
- Expect uneasiness—or "complicated cooperation" (Ware, Mallozzi, Edwards, & Baumann, 2008)—when beginning to establish a collaboration. It takes time to develop rapport and understanding.
- Schedule both regular short (e.g., an hour before or after school) and long (e.g., full days with substitutes) meetings to deal with the mundane and esoteric aspects of the ongoing research.
- Really listen to one another as you debate ideas and later negotiate consensus on "taken-as-shared" (Cobb, 2000) understandings about what you are learning.
- At some point you must commit to the team and the project; if you cannot, then there is no shame in excusing yourself from a research effort.
- Be wary of the "swamped with data" (Collins, Joseph, & Bielaczyc, 2004) phenomenon that can easily beset FDE researchers; collect only those data you anticipate being able to analyze and interpret.
- Do not underestimate the importance of a relaxed lunch to develop the close ties required in collaboration; and the small talk may not actually be so small.
- Exercise diplomatic candor when offering critique of one another's ideas and contributions.
- Celebrate and share your work through presentations and publications be they local, regional, or national.
- Have fun; enjoy the inquiry, the students, and one another. It's serious business, but laughs are good for the soul and the inquiry.

Recently Heidi thought about the study and commented, "When I think about my role in our [research] team, I think of myself as another piece to the puzzle." The metaphor is apt, but the picture is incomplete with even one of the pieces missing. Heidi continued, "This research team has made me look at vocabulary differently and enhanced my teaching. I will never look at words the same and have this research team to thank for that." We all believe that our vision of not only words but also literacy education research that is pragmatic and makes a difference (Dillon, O'Brien, & Heilman, 2000) is irreparably changed—both for the better.

REFERENCES

Barab, S., & Squire, K. (2004). Design-based research: Putting a stake in the ground. *The Journal of the Learning Sciences, 13,* 1-14.

Brown, A. L. (1992). Design experiments: Theoretical and methodological challenges in creating complex interventions in classroom settings. *The Journal of the Learning Sciences, 2,* 141-178.

Cobb, P., Confrey, J., diSessa, A., Lehrer, R., & Schauble, L. (2003). Design experiments in educational research. *Educational Researcher, 32,* 9-13.

Cobb, P. (2000). Conducting teaching experiments in collaboration with teachers. In A. E. Kelly & R. A. Lesh (Eds.), *Handbook of research design in mathematics and science education,* (pp. 307-333). Mahwah, NJ: Lawrence Erlbaum.

Collins, A. (1992). Toward a design science of education. In E. Scanlon & T. O'Shea (Eds.), *New directions in educational technology.* New York, NY: Springer-Verlag.

Collins, A. (1990). *Toward a design science of education.* (Technical Report No. 1). Washington, DC: Office of Educational Research and Improvement (ED).

Collins, A., Joseph, D., & Bielaczyc, K. (2004). Design research: Theoretical and methodological issues. *The Journal of the Learning Sciences, 13,* 15-42.

Dede, C. (2004). If design-based research is the answer, what is the question? *The Journal of the Learning Sciences, 13,* 105-114.

Hsieh, H. F., & Shannon, S. E. (2005). Three approaches to qualitative content analysis. *Qualitative Health Research, 15,* 1277-1288.

Hoffman, J. V., Wilson, M. B., Martinez, R. A., & Sailors, M. (2001). Content analysis. In N. K. Duke & M. H. Mallette (Eds.) *Literacy research methodologies* (2nd ed., pp. 28-49). New York, NY: Guilford.

Ivey, G., & Broaddus, K. (2007). A formative experiment investigating literacy engagement among adolescent Latina/o students just beginning to read, write, and speak English. *Reading Research Quarterly, 42,* 512-545.

Jiménez, R. T. (1997). The strategic reading abilities and potential of five low-literacy Latina/o readers in middle school. *Reading Research Quarterly, 32,* 221-243.

Kelly, A. E. (Ed.). (2003). The role of design in educational research [Special issue]. *Educational Researcher, 32*(1).

Kelly, A. E., & Lesh, R. A. (Ed.). (2000). *Handbook of research design in mathematics and science education.* Mahwah, NJ: Lawrence Erlbaum.

Kelly, A. D. (2004). Design research in education: Yes, but it is methodological? *Journal of the Learning Sciences, 13,* 115-128.

Krippendorff, K. (2004). *Content analysis: An introduction to its methodology* (2nd ed.) Thousand Oaks, CA: Sage.

Lincoln, Y. S., & Guba, E. G. (1985). *Naturalistic inquiry.* Thousand Oaks, CA: Sage Publications, Inc.

Patton, M. Q. (2002). *Qualitative research and evaluation methods* (3rd ed.). Thousand Oaks, CA: Sage.

Reinking, D., & Bradley, B. A. (2008). *Formative and design experiments: Approaches to language and literacy research.* New York, NY: Teachers College Press.

Reinking, D., & Watkins, J. (2000). A formative experiment investigating the use of multimedia book reviews to increase elementary students' independent reading. *Reading Research Quarterly, 35,* 384-419.

Shulman, L. S. (1997). Disciplines of inquiry in education: A new overview. In R. M. Jaeger (Ed.), *Methods for research in education* (2nd ed., pp. 3-29). Washington, DC: American Educational Research Association.

van den Akker, Gravemeijer, K., McKenney, S., & Nieveen, N. (Eds.). (2006). *Educational design research.* New York, NY: Routledge.

Ware, D., Mallozzi, C. A., Edwards, E. C., & Baumann, J. F. (2008). Collaboration in teacher research: Complicated cooperation. In C. A. Lassonde & S. E. Israel (Eds.), *Teachers taking action: A comprehensive guide to teacher research,* (pp. 89-100). Newark, DE: International Reading Association.

Clarifying Formative Experiments in Literacy Research

Barbara A. Bradley
University of Kansas

David Reinking
Clemson University

Jamie Colwell
Old Dominion University

Leigh A. Hall
University of North Carolina

Douglas Fisher
Nancy Frey
San Diego State University

James F. Baumann
University of Missouri

An increasing number of education researchers interested in closing the gap between research and practice are gravitating toward a methodological approach that conceptualizes and frames research much differently than conventional experimental or naturalistic approaches. That methodological approach, which is often referred to generically as *design-based research* or *education design research*, has been the topic of several themed issues of research journals: *Educational Researcher* (2003, Vol. 32. No. 1)*, Educational Psychologist* (2004, Vol. 39, No. 4)*, and *Journal of Learning Sciences* (2004, Vol. 13, No. 1); and it has been the focus of several books (e.g., McKenney & Reeves, 2012; van den Akker, Gravemeijer, McKenney, & Nieveen, 2006), including one on its use in literacy research (Reinking & Bradley, 2008).

Further, John Easton, currently the Director of the Institute of Education Sciences (IES) in the U.S. Department of Education, has called for research that involves collaboration among practitioners, researchers, and policy makers, and that focuses on relevance and usefulness. Specifically, IES invites proposals for research that designs an intervention and then tests and redesigns it through an iterative process (Viadero, 2009). Design-based research aligns well with that emphasis (Kelly, Lesh, & Baek, 2009; Reinking & Bradley, 2008; van den Akker et al, 2006), and IES has funded projects using that approach in the area of literacy (e.g., Baumann, Blachowicz, Manyak, Graves, & Olejnik, 2009; Leu, Reinking, Hutchison, McVerry, O'Byrne, & Zawilinski, 2009). In that same vein, it has been argued that design research is an approach that would allow literacy research to make a more tangible contribution toward bettering the world (Reinking, 2011).

Literacy researchers have conducted and published research using this methodological approach, often referring to their work as *formative experiments* (e.g., Ivey & Broaddus, 2007; Jiménez, 1997; Lenski, 2001; Neuman, 1999; Reinking & Watkins, 2000). Formative experiments follow the core concepts and principles of design-based research, in some cases using a framework of guiding questions (Reinking & Bradley, 2008). Yet, many literacy researchers are unfamiliar or only vaguely familiar with this approach. Thus, one purpose of this paper is to briefly introduce formative experiments to those who know little about them and to provide several examples of how they are being used among literacy researchers, ranging here from novice to more experienced. However, even among those who are using this approach in their own work, the boundaries for conceptualizing and implementing a formative experiment in their work are not always clear. Thus, another purpose of this paper is to extend the dialog about how to conceptualize and implement formative experiments. Toward that end, after a brief introduction to formative experiments, three researchers will in turn introduce their work and will then address the following questions:

- How do you conceptualize, conduct, and report a formative experiment?
- What standards of rigor should be used to determine the validity and quality of a formative experiment?
- What knowledge, skills, or resources are needed to use this approach?
- What benefits and challenges have you encountered in using this approach?

In the final section, a senior scholar in the field with considerable experience conducting formative experiments will reflect on this approach drawing on the three examples.

FORMATIVE EXPERIMENTS

Unlike conventional approaches that have been imported into education from laboratory science or sociology, design-based research emerged among diverse researchers interested in education. Ann Brown, a prominent literacy researcher and educational psychologist, was one of the first to articulate its foundational rationale, to explore its methodological application, and to give it one of its early names: *design experiments* (Brown, 1992). Her development of this approach arose from her realization that the conventional experimental methods she used in her laboratory research on metacognitive aspects of reading comprehension were inadequate when trying to translate that research into viable instruction in classrooms. Dennis Newman, one of her colleagues, shared her views and conducted research in classrooms introducing the term *formative experiment* (Newman, 1990; see also Jacob, 1992).

As that term suggests, in this approach, an instructional intervention introduced into authentic instructional settings is modified formatively based on qualitative, and occasionally quantitative, data indicating what is or is not working and why. Another fundamental characteristic of formative experiments is that they are guided predominantly by the pursuit of accomplishing a specific pedagogical goal through an intervention that can be justified as showing promise in accomplishing that goal. Although general research questions may guide data collection, the central focus is on determining how the intervention can be designed formatively to achieve a goal.

However, formative experiments, like design-based research, in general, are not only attempts to design something that works toward accomplishing a goal. Instead, they often test established pedagogical theory in the crucible of practice, and they seek to develop generalizable pedagogical theories, although those theories are what Gravemeijer and Cobb (2006) refer to as humble and local theories grounded in practice, as opposed to grand theories (e.g., theories of motivation). Ideally, formative experiments try to understand the components of an instructional intervention that are critical to success, as opposed to simply determining that one intervention works better than another or that a certain instructional move produces desirable results.

The guiding metaphors of design-based research in general, and formative experiments in particular, are engineering (designing something that works), ecology (instruction is influenced by a complex interacting web of factors), and evolution (change is slow, incremental, and established environments inherently adapt to preserve the status quo; see Reinking, 2011). Instead of asking "Which instructional intervention is best?" (the experimentalist approach) or "What is?" (the naturalistic approach), formative experiments ask "What goal do we want to achieve, and how do we get there?" A central concept is that trying to create something that works reveals deep understandings not revealed by other approaches. Formative experiments, guided by these metaphors, respond to prominent critiques of the status of literacy research and calls for other frames and approaches (e.g., Dillon, O'Brien, & Heilman, 2000; Pressley, Graham, & Harris, 2006).

In subsequent sections, several literacy researchers relate how they have used this approach and offer their responses to the four guiding questions. The order of presentation is according to level of experience as a researcher from novice to, in the case of the concluding section, a reaction from a researcher who has been active for more than 30 years.

PROMOTING DISCIPLINARY LITERACY AND CRITICAL THINKING WITH BLOGS
JAMIE COLWELL

Description of Work

I conducted a formative experiment to investigate two pedagogical goals simultaneously: (a) to improve eighth-grade social studies students' use of disciplinary literacy skills, specifically targeting critical thinking, in a state history class; and (b) to improve preservice social studies teachers' use and understanding of instructional techniques beneficial to eighth-grade students' disciplinary literacy skills. The intervention was disciplinary-literacy instruction in both settings paired with collaborative one-on-one blogging between the middle-school students and preservice teachers to extend practice using disciplinary-literacy strategies and skills. Blogging focused on discussion about primary or secondary sources that aligned with content in the middle school state history class. I collaborated with the middle school teacher and the university instructor to plan activities related to disciplinary literacy, to integrate those activities into their instruction, and to gather data to inform how this activity might be more effectively implemented to accomplish the pedagogical goals.

How Do You Conceptualize, Conduct, and Report a Formative Experiment?

Because the literature on disciplinary literacy suggests that there are challenges to integrating it into K-12 instruction as well as into teacher education (Moje, 2008, 2010/2011; Shanahan & Shanahan, 2008), I considered a formative experiment as a useful approach to confront those challenges. Specifically, I conceptualized this formative experiment as an opportunity to simultaneously address challenges in both contexts. To me, a conceptual advantage of a formative experiment is that it permits such flexibility while simultaneously investigating how to bring about desirable outcomes in literacy instruction (Reinking & Bradley, 2008). Of particular interest in this formative experiment was setting pedagogical goals to design an intervention consistent with theory, identifying factors that enhanced or inhibited achieving the pedagogical goals, modifying the intervention to achieve the pedagogical goals, and transforming the research environments. Therefore, for this study, I selected Reinking and Bradley's (2008) framework for conducting a formative experiment. That framework also allowed for extensive collaboration with a middle-school social studies teacher and university social studies professor to determine how to integrate the intervention into the two settings without compromising non-negotiable elements of the intervention (e.g., blog entries and responses to them). An important conceptual aspect of using a formative experiment was that it allowed me to focus flexibly on disciplinary literacy, while respecting the instructors' existing curricula, teaching styles, and pedagogical philosophies. A unique conceptualization in my work is addressing two distinct, yet complementary, goals simultaneously.

What Standards of Rigor Should Be Used to Determine the Validity and Quality of a Formative Experiment?

One benchmark of rigor illustrated in my study was the selection of appropriate research sites that, at least in initial work, is conducted in classrooms where neither success nor failure is not highly likely. The university site was a four-year public university with a student population that was racially and economically diverse. The methods class consisted of typical undergraduate education majors of good, but not distinguished, academic standing. The middle-school site was located in a Title I district but was not a Title I school. Most students met or exceeded state benchmark standards for content knowledge. The class also consisted of a range of student ability levels, but no student was enrolled in special education. Thus, I believe that a thoughtful selection of an appropriate site for research is an important aspect of rigor in this approach.

What Knowledge, Skills, or Resources are Needed to Use this Approach?

One challenge I faced in my project illustrates that researchers who use this approach must be sensitive to teachers' needs and perspectives, and must deal with them sensitively and carefully. A significant challenge was working collaboratively with the middle-school teacher to integrate disciplinary literacy instruction into her classroom. During initial planning meetings, our individual conceptualization of strategy instruction seemed compatible, and she was enthusiastic about using them. However, she did not integrate the strategies discussed in planning meetings. It was necessary to carefully document that inconsistency and perhaps determine why, but eventually it was necessary to share and discuss that conclusion with her and suggest ways of integrating more strategy instruction into her teaching. I did so by sharing my data and analysis that documented a lack of use, but in a way that showed I was trying to determine what factors might be relevant to increasing strategy use that were in her comfort zone of teaching. It worked. She understood and integrated the strategies into her curriculum the following day and into many lessons following that day. This example illustrates that researchers who conduct formative experiments need not only well-developed observational skills, but also highly developed pedagogical sensitivities and interpersonal skills.

Further, the need to develop good personal and professional relationships extended beyond the classroom. For example, it was necessary to work with individuals who managed the technical support in the district when it became clear that the site made available for blogging in the district did not allow for access outside of school.

What Benefits and Challenges Have You Encountered in Using this Approach?

One benefit of formative experiments is the collaboration with instructors in an authentic setting. In my case it was rewarding to be involved with research that allowed all stakeholders to work through the technological and instructional barriers to best determine how the intervention could work in specific circumstances. It was also rewarding to see the preservice teachers develop a better understanding of how a classroom teacher works through barriers in a project while staying in her comfort zone as a teacher. Further, it was gratifying that preservice teachers reported that they found the intervention informative, appealing, and approachable and that disciplinary literacy was something they were more likely to consider using in their future classrooms.

However, collaboration was also a notable challenge. The type of collaboration necessary in using this approach was time-consuming, requiring frequent meetings, extensive interviewing, and observations. There was also a constant negotiation of roles during this collaboration. I found it necessary to shift from observer to participant observer to instructor in the preservice class, and these roles had to be meticulously documented to uphold standards of rigor. Even with this challenge, the intense collaboration was rewarded by improvement in disciplinary literacy skills in both populations and instructors who indicated enthusiasm to continue using similar instruction in their future classrooms, which, to me, increased the experiment's ultimate usefulness in education.

DEVELOPING EIGHTH-GRADE STUDENTS' ENGAGEMENT AND IDENTITY AS READERS
LEIGH A. HALL

Description of Work

In a yearlong study, I investigated how an eighth-grade English teacher created reading instruction for her students that accommodated their reading identities while addressing their cognitive needs. The teacher worked to achieve three pedagogical goals with the students which were to: (a) examine and alter their involvement with classroom reading practices, (b) increase their reading comprehension, and (c) allow them to progress in who they wanted to become as readers. Twenty students participated. Five students were selected and invited to participate as focal students: three whose reading comprehension was below grade level, one who was at grade level, and one who was above grade level. These focal students were selected for closer study to gain a deeper understanding of how the intervention affected students with diverse reading comprehension abilities.

How Do You Conceptualize, Conduct, and Report a Formative Experiment?

This research project was my first attempt to use a formative experiment. I decided to use this approach because I wanted flexibility to make adjustments based on the successes or challenge the students and teacher experienced. As I began to develop the goals and instruction, I realized I needed to regularly monitor how the intervention was affecting the teacher and the students. If I was truly going to work closely with the teacher and students towards achieving specific pedagogical goals, then I needed a process that was responsive to them in ways that acknowledged the realities they faced. A formative experiment provided a framework for addressing that realization.

I have found reporting a formative experiment to be a challenge. There are many stories that can be drawn from the data, and I grapple with which ones to share. However, I have realized that trying to force my report to fit into a traditional academic model of writing may not work well. Although reporting my findings has become a source of frustration, it has challenged me as a writer and scholar to consider new forms of writing and new ways to present my data.

What Standards of Rigor Should Be Used to Determine the Validity and Quality of a Formative Experiment?

In my view, the type and amount of data collected plays a significant role in determining standards of rigor and validity of a formative experiment. What kinds and how much data are collected will vary depending on the pedagogical goals of the study. However, a critical factor of formative experiments is that they can be modified during data collection to better achieve the pedagogical goals. Therefore, a data collection plan has to create a regular assessment/feedback loop between researchers and participants around successes and challenges that are in entailed in attempting to achieve the pedagogical goals. When changes to instruction or data collection are made, a clear record must exist that shows how the decisions were reached and why.

In my study, I engaged in classroom observations two or three times each week. The observations helped me understand how students were responding to the instruction and allowed me to document what did or did not appear to be going well in the classroom. All sessions were digitally recorded and transcribed as needed. I met separately with the classroom teacher once a week for 45-60 minutes to discuss what had or had not occurred and to plan further instruction. We reviewed the pedagogical goals, examined field notes to determine the strengths and weaknesses of the instruction, and considered if and how our instructional approach needed to be modified. I also learned about difficulties the teacher was having with the instruction and was able to use that information to make suggestions to assist her.

What Knowledge, Skills, or Resources are Needed to Use this Approach?

I believe a successful formative study requires support from both the school and the university. At the school, it is important for administrators to be supportive of the time and space teachers need to meet the demands of a study. Types of support typically needed are dedicated blocks of time to plan instruction and review data. Teachers need to know this time will be respected. Any support teachers believe they need to successfully participate should be negotiated with school administrators before agreeing to participate. Researchers can help by offering to attend meetings with administrators.

At the university level, doctoral students are a beneficial resource and can play an important role in the success of a study. For my study, they assisted with transcribing some or all of the observations, conducting student and teacher interviews, and planning sessions. They also assisted with analyzing student work and classroom interactions. It would not have been possible for me alone to keep up with transcribing these documents, because the transcriptions were needed to understand how we were successful in achieving the pedagogical goals and how we might make changes to our instruction.

What Benefits and Challenges Have You Encountered in Using this Approach?

Managing, collecting, and reviewing data required a significant amount of time, even with the support of doctoral students. I also found it challenging to step back from my study and see what was or was not working. Although being in the classroom several times a week allowed me to develop an important insider view, it also made it difficult for me to pull back and clearly assess what was happening. I asked doctoral students to periodically review recent data and offer their interpretations of what was happening in the classroom in relation to the pedagogical goals. Having fresh perspectives, somewhat more removed from the project, helped me and the teacher to gain clarity about what we needed to do.

In the end, I have a good sense of what did or did not go well for the teacher, for the students, and why. Although this type of research might seem contextualized, and not generalizable, I have found that not to be entirely the case. Many teachers will relate to the overall issues the participating teacher faced. Additionally, I think this research stands to have an impact on classrooms, because the design allows for researchers to connect with teachers and students. It is an approach that acknowledges the human component of what we do as researchers.

CREATING DISTRICT-WIDE IMPROVEMENTS IN LITERACY
DOUGLAS FISHER AND NANCY FREY

Description of Work

Our project began when we became involved with Bonita (a pseudonym) school district. Achievement in the 44 elementary schools in the district had stalled and several schools were identified in need of program improvement, based on student achievement scores. The district leadership team and two researchers met to develop a plan to improve achievement that would affect the more than 27,000 students in the district. The approach selected was to conduct a formative experiment. Across the district, 65% of the students were Latino/Hispanic, 16% were Asian/Pacific Islander, 14% were White, and 5% were African American. Nearly 40% of the students were current English learners, with another 32% speaking a language in addition to English at home. The agreed-upon goal was to build student competence through teacher actions. To accomplish that goal, we worked with the district leadership team to develop in an instructional framework based on the gradual release of responsibility and to organize resources toward providing administrators and teachers with professional development experiences that would change teacher actions. Essentially, this formative experiment relied on teacher professional development focused on high-quality core instruction. We modified the professional development plans often, based on observations and feedback, resulting in significantly improved instruction, including a great deal of productive group work on the part of students who had been used to whole-class instruction.

How Do You Conceptualize, Conduct, and Report a Formative Experiment?

We conceptualize formative experiments as an approach that serves our purposes when we interact with school leaders who want to create lasting change. Unlike experimental or qualitative research in which the researcher asks a question, our experiences with formative experiments suggests that this approach is most effective when individuals inside school systems have a goal that they hope to reach. Goal-driven research allows for midcourse corrections in efforts to implement an intervention, which in our case is as broad plan for instructional improvement. As we conduct formative experiments, we keep extensive records about the initial efforts, what evidence was used to design the intervention, and every modification to the intervention. In doing so, we learn a great deal about what works, in which contexts, and with which students. We have reported our findings from formative experiments in several journal articles and conference sessions, but sometimes have found it necessary to present our data and findings as a case study with a traditional methodology section in line with that approach (Fisher & Frey, in press; Fisher, Frey, & Lapp, 2009). Reviewers and editors of our manuscripts, which typically unfold more like a story than a research report, have consistently asked us to report statically all research methods in one section, despite the fact that our methods evolved during the course of the study.

What Standards of Rigor Should Be Used to Determine the Validity and Quality of a Formative

Experiment?

In our view, documentation about each modification is critical to maintaining the credibility of a formative experiment. That documentation should include the specific reason that a modification was needed as well as the theoretical underpinnings for the next intervention. Rather than intuitive guesswork, modifications to an intervention in a formative experiment should be based on data and informed by reviews of professional literature. For example, within a formative experiment, the researcher can conduct a clinical trial, randomly assigning some participants to an intervention and others to a control condition. The data can then be used to determine the effectiveness of the intervention, modifications needed, and present an opportunity to subsequently intervene with the control group. In addition, the researcher collects information about the experiences of the individuals who have lived the experience. In other words, a phenomenological approach (Lewis & Staehler, 2010) and regular member checking (Creswell, 1997), contribute to the verisimilitude of a formative experiment. In our work, member checks have served as a way to ensure trustworthiness as we share our findings with a group of informants who discuss with us, and one another, their reflections on the findings as we present them.

What Knowledge, Skills, or Resources are Needed to Use this Approach?

For us, the most important resource is access to an authentic environment in which we can conduct a formative experiment. That environment needs to be encapsulated by trust, as the agreed-upon intervention may change as a result of data analysis and review. In terms of knowledge and skills, the research team needs to be familiar with a wide range of methodologies as the ground regularly shifts and new tools to understand phenomena are required. In addition, we have found that formative experiments require sophisticated interpersonal skills, because situations change and trust has to be maintained. Also, all the stakeholders must commit to the pedagogical goal. Without such a commitment, the modifications to the intervention may be meaningless if different stakeholders attempt to pursue different goals.

What Benefits and Challenges Have You Encountered in Using this Approach?

In our view, the most rewarding aspect of formative experiments is the impact that researchers can have in real classrooms, schools, and districts. In our work using formative experiments, we have developed strong and lasting relationships with key stakeholders who appreciate the ongoing nature of the research and our commitment to it, rather than using their schools and classrooms as "data mines." There is a level of trust and a feeling of potential impact that occurs within a formative experiment that we have not achieved with other approaches.

In terms of challenges, we have experienced two. First, the Institutional Review Board (IRB) at our institution has been cautious about this methodological approach due to the fact that interventions can change and the research may engage in new activities and directions that have not been reviewed. That ambiguity can be addressed in the proposal to the IRB as well as in regular updates to the committee members, including subsequent requests when situations dictate change.

Second, the way we have used formative experiments requires a great deal of time. There is a long-term investment required from the outset, from developing the pedagogical goal through the multiple modifications to the intervention, all of which are important in gaining deep understanding of what it takes to reach the goal. Nonetheless, we have found that the benefits significantly outweigh the challenges and formative experiments have resulted in new understandings and positive outcomes for schools and their students. Although it is difficult to unequivocally claim causation, key informants within the district attribute student achievement changes to the collective work we have done in meeting the pedagogical goal. They often point to the fact that 41 of the 44 schools met the criteria for being distinguished after our work and none of them remained in program improvement. Only 7 of the 44 schools met these criteria when we initiated our work with them. Grade-level proficiency in reading increased from 37% to 72% during the same period.

REFLECTIONS ON FORMATIVE EXPERIMENTS
JAMES F. BAUMANN

In this section I provide remarks about the three formative experiments just described. Specifically, I: (a) make observations about the contexts for the three formative experiments, (b) comment on the methods employed, and (c) offer a few musings on this emerging research methodology. Some of my remarks draw on information from the authors' more elaborated conference papers.

Contexts

Cobb, Confrey, diSessa, Lehrer, and Schauble (2003) described five different settings, or contexts, for conducting design experiments:
- one-on-one (teacher/student) experiments;
- experiments in a teacher's classroom guided by an external researcher;
- preservice teacher development experiments;
- inservice teacher development experiments; and
- school and district restructuring experiments.

I see three of the five contexts reflected in the studies discussed here.

Fisher and Frey's study is a clear example of the most ambitious setting for a design experiment: the revamping of an entire school district's elementary literacy instructional approach (Cobb et al., 2003, Setting 5). On a much smaller scale, Colwell's study involved the collaboration of one researcher and one classroom teacher to effect changes in middle school readers' engagement and identity, an instance of the Cobb et al. Setting 2. Cowell's study of disciplinary literacy is a mix of the Cobb et al. Setting 3 (pre-service teacher development) and an interesting variant of Setting 2 (an intervention involving a classroom teacher, the teachers' students, and preservice teachers). Although the majority of published formative experiments in literacy have involved the Cobb et al. (2003) second setting (e.g., Ivey & Broaddus, 2007; Reinking & Watkins, 2000), it is revealing that literacy researchers who have used formative experiments are beginning to broaden the contexts for their research.

Methods

The research methods Colwell, Hall, and Fisher and Frey employed were as varied as their research settings. Colwell used a qualitative case study design within her formative experiment. Thus, she analyzed data from field notes, interviews, videos, and journals—the qualitative data considered to be sine qua non in formative experiments (Reinking & Bradley, 2008). Hall likewise gathered and analyzed qualitative data from observation field notes, but she found that the weekly meetings between her and her teacher participant to be the most fertile for acquiring insight into the intervention implementation and revision. Fisher and Frey collected the requisite qualitative data and engaged in ambitious constant comparison analysis; however, they also collected considerable quantitative data on student achievement, and they conducted statistical analyses using that data. Thus, as formative and design experiment methods continue their evolution from obscurity to maturity across the broad educational research community (cf. Brown, 1992; Kelly, Lesh, & Baek, 2008; Sandoval & Bell, 2004; Schoenfeld, 2006; Shulman, 1997), they also are developing in our own field of literacy education (Reinking & Bradley, 2008).

Musings

In his overview of a 1997 compendium on research methods in education, Lee Shulman argued for methodological eclecticism in education research, asserting that educational researchers should "become skilled and experienced in at least two forms of research methodology" (p. 25). Shulman also argued that research questions ought to precede and guide the selection of research methodologies. As he stated,

> We must avoid becoming educational researchers slavishly committed to a particular method. . . . We must first understand our problem and decide what questions we are asking, and then we must select the mode of disciplined inquiry most appropriate to those questions. (p. 24)

In her conference presentation, Hall noted that although she had a clearly articulated research question, she could not find a research design that matched that question. After considering and dismissing several methodological approaches, she stated somewhat facetiously that "formative experiments found me and became my design of last resort." Hall reported that she is now involved in a second formative experiment. We hope that formative experiments will also "find" other researchers and that it becomes their design of first choice when it suits their pedagogical research questions.

REFERENCES

Baumann, J. F., Blachowicz, C. L. Z., Manyak, P. C., Graves, M. F., & Olejnik, S. (2009). *Development of a multifaceted comprehensive, vocabulary instructional program for the upper–elementary grades [R305A090163]*. U.S. Department of Education, Institute of Education Sciences, National Center for Education Research (Reading and Writing Program).

Brown, A. L. (1992). Design experiments: Theoretical and methodological challenges in creating complex interventions in classroom settings. *Journal of Learning Sciences, 2*(2), 141-178.

Cobb, P., Confrey, J., diSessa, A., Lehrer, R., & Schauble, L. (2003). Design experiments in educational research. *Educational Researcher, 32,* 9-13.

Creswell, J. W. (1997). *Qualitative inquiry and research design: Choosing among five traditions.* Newbury Park, CA: Sage.

Dillon, D. R., O'Brien, D. G., & Heilman, E. E. (2000). Literacy research in the next millennium: From paradigms to pragmatism and practicality. *Reading Research Quarterly, 35,* 10-26.

Fisher, D., & Frey, N. (in press). Implementing RTI in a high school: A case study. *Journal of Learning Disabilities.*

Fisher, D., Frey, N., & Lapp, D. (2009). Meeting AYP in a high-needs school: A formative experiment. *Journal of Adolescent and Adult Literacy, 52,* 386-396.

Gravemeijer, K., & Cobb, P. (2006). Design research from a learning design perspective. In J. van den Akker, K. Gravemeijer, S. McKenney, & N. Nieveen (Eds.), *Educational design research* (pp. 17-51). New York, NY: Routledge.

Ivey, G., & Broaddus, K. (2007). A formative experiment investigating literacy engagement among adolescent Latina/o students just beginning to read, write, and speak English. *Reading Research Quarterly, 42*(4), 512–545.

Jacob, E. (1992). Culture, context, and cognition. In M. D. Lecompte, W. L. Millroy, & J. Preissle (Eds.), *The handbook of qualitative research in education* (pp. 293-335). San Diego, CA: Academic Press.

Jiménez, R. T. (1997). The strategic reading abilities and potential of five low-literacy Latina/o readers in middle school. *Reading Research Quarterly, 32*, 224-243.

Kelly, A. E., Lesh, R. A., & Baek, J. Y. (Eds.). (2008). *Handbook of design research methods in education: Innovations in science, technology, engineering, and mathematics learning and teaching.* New York, NY: Routledge.

Lenski, S. D. (2001). Intertextual connections during discussions about literature. *Reading Psychology. 22*(4), 313-335.

Leu, D., Reinking, D., Hutchison, A., McVerry, G., O'Byrne, I., & Zawilinski, L. (2009, May). Internet reciprocal teaching (IRT): *A research-based model for teaching the new literacies of online reading comprehension.* Symposium presented at the annual meeting of the International Reading Association, Minneapolis, MN.

Lewis, M., & Staehler, T. (2010). *Phenomenology: An introduction.* New York, NY: Continuum International.

McKenney, S., & Reeves, T. C. (2012). *Educational design research.* New York, NY: Routledge.

Moje, E. B. (2008). Foregrounding the disciplines in secondary literacy teaching and learning: A call for change. *Journal of Adolescent & Adult Literacy, 52*(2), 96-107.

Moje, E. B. (2010/2011). Response: Heller's "In praise of amateurism: A friendly critique of Moje's 'call for change' in secondary literacy." *Journal of Adolescent & Adult Literacy, 54*(4), 275-278. doi: 10.1598/JAAL.54.4.5

Neuman, S. B. (1999). Books make a difference: A study of access to literacy. *Reading Research Quarterly, 34*, 286-311.

Newman, D. (1990). Opportunities for research on the organizational impact of school computers. *Educational Researcher, 19*, 8-13.

Pressley, M., Graham, S., & Harris, K. (2006). The state of educational intervention research as viewed through the lens of literacy intervention. *British Journal of Educational Psychology, 76*, 1-19.

Reinking, D. (2011). Beyond the laboratory and the lens: New metaphors for literacy research. *60th Yearbook of the Literacy Research Association.* Oak Creek, WI.

Reinking, D., & Bradley, B. A. (2008). *Formative and design experiments: Approaches to language and literacy research.* New York, NY: Teachers College Press.

Reinking, D., & Watkins, J. (2000). A formative experiment investigating the use of multimedia book reviews to increase elementary students independent reading. *Reading Research Quarterly, 35*(3), 384-419.

Sandoval, W. A., & Bell, P. (Eds.). (2004). Design-based research [Special issue]. *Educational Psychologist, 39*(4), 199-201.

Schoenfeld, A. H. (2006). Design experiments. In J. L. Green, G. Camilli, & P. B. Elmore (Eds.), *Handbook of complementary methods in education research* (pp. 193-205). Mahwah, NJ: Lawrence Erlbaum.

Shanahan, T., & Shanahan, C. (2008). Teaching disciplinary literacy to adolescents: Rethinking content-area literacy. *Harvard Educational Review, 78*(1), 40-61.

Shulman, L. S. (1997). Disciplines of inquiry in education: A new overview. In R. M. Jaeger (Ed.), *Methods for research in education* (2nd ed., pp. 3-29). Washington, DC: AERA.

van den Akker, J., Gravemeijer, K., McKenney, S., & Nieveen, N. M. (Eds.). (2006). *Educational design research.* New York, NY: Routledge.

Viadero, D. (2009, December). New head of U.S. research agency aims for relevance. *Education Week.* Retrieved from http://www.edweek.org/ew/articles/2009/12/02/13ies.h29html?tkn=ZPWF3L3MAyZRicsjuIeFW k8IzEH+Gargt69